Lecture Notes in Computer Science   12639

More information about this subseries at http://www.springer.com/series/7407

Xin He · En Shao · Guangming Tan (Eds.)

Network and Parallel Computing

17th IFIP WG 10.3 International Conference, NPC 2020
Zhengzhou, China, September 28–30, 2020
Revised Selected Papers

 Springer

Editors
Xin He
Institute of Computing Technology
Chinese Academy of Sciences
Beijing, China

En Shao
Institute of Computing Technology
Chinese Academy of Sciences
Beijing, China

Guangming Tan
Institute of Computing Technology
Chinese Academy of Sciences
Beijing, China

ISSN 0302-9743   ISSN 1611-3349   (electronic)
Lecture Notes in Computer Science
ISBN 978-3-030-79477-4   ISBN 978-3-030-79478-1   (eBook)
https://doi.org/10.1007/978-3-030-79478-1

LNCS Sublibrary: SL1 – Theoretical Computer Science and General Issues

This Springer imprint is published by the registered company Springer Nature Switzerland AG
The registered company address is: Gewerbestrasse 11, 6330 Cham, Switzerland

Preface

These proceedings contain the papers presented at the 17th IFIP International Conference on Network and Parallel Computing (NPC 2020), held in Zhengzhou, Henan, China, during September 28–30, 2020. The goal of the conference series is to establish an international forum for engineers and scientists to present their excellent ideas and experiences in system fields of distributed and parallel computing.

A total of 95 submissions were received in response to our call for papers. These papers originated from Asia (China and Japan), Africa, and North America (USA). Each submission was sent to at least three reviewers. Each paper was judged according to its originality, innovation, readability, and relevance to the expected audience. Based on the reviews received, 34 full papers (about 35%), comprising 12 papers published as Special Issue papers in the *International Journal of Parallel Programming* and 22 papers published as LNCS proceedings, were retained. A number of strong papers that could not be accepted to the full-paper track were considered for the short-paper track. Finally, we selected seven short papers. These papers cover traditional areas of network and parallel computing, including parallel applications, distributed algorithms, parallel architectures, software environments, and distributed tools.

We share the view that, during the past decade, the tools and cultures of high-performance computing and big data analytics are diverging to the detriment of both, and the international community should find a unified path that can best serve the needs of a broad spectrum of major application areas. Unlike other tools, which are limited to particular scientific domains, computational modeling and data analytics are applicable to all areas of science and engineering, as they breathe life into the underlying mathematics of scientific models. We sincerely appreciate the work and effort of the authors in preparing their submissions for review, and addressing the reviewer' comments before submitting the camera-ready copies of their accepted papers, and attending the conference to present and discuss their work. We also want to thank every member of the NPC 2020 Organizing Committee and Steering Committee for their help in putting together such an exciting program. Finally, we thank all the attendees.

September 2020   Xin He

Organization

General Co-chairs

Kemal Ebcioglu — Global Supercomputing Corporation, USA
Zhiwei Xu — Institute of Computing Technology, Chinese Academy of Sciences, China

Program Co-chairs

Guang R. Gao — University of Delaware, USA
Guangming Tan — Institute of Computing Technology, Chinese Academy of Sciences, China

Local Arrangements Co-chairs

Bohu Huang — Xidian University, China
Xianyu Zuo — Henan University, China

Publicity Co-chairs

Liang Yuan — Institute of Computing Technology, Chinese Academy of Sciences, China
Jiajia Li — Pacific Northwest National Laboratory, USA
Qiguang Miao — Xidian University, China
Stéphane Zuckerman — Université de Cergy-Pontoise, France

Publication Chair

Xin He — Institute of Computing Technology, Chinese Academy of Sciences, China

Web Chair

En Shao — Institute of Computing Technology, Chinese Academy of Sciences, China

Steering Committee

Kemal Ebcioglu (Chair) — Global Supercomputing, USA
Hai Jin (Vice Chair) — HUST, China
Chen Ding — University of Rochester, USA
Jack Dongarra — University of Tennessee, USA

Guangrong Gao	University of Delaware, USA
Jean-Luc Gaudiot	UCI, USA
Tony Hey	Science and Technology Facilities Council, UK
Guojie Li	Institute of Computing Technology, Chinese Academy of Sciences, China
Yoichi Muraoka	Waseda University, Japan
Viktor Prasanna	USC, USA
Daniel Reed	University of Utah, USA
Weisong Shi	Wayne State University, USA
Ninghui Sun	Institute of Computing Technology, Chinese Academy of Sciences, China
Zhiwei Xu	Institute of Computing Technology, Chinese Academy of Sciences, China

Program Committee

Quan Chen	Shanghai Jiao Tong University, China
Lizhong Chen	Oregon State University, USA
Huimin Cui	Institute of Computing Technology, Chinese Academy of Sciences, China
Dezun Dong	NUDT, China
Guang R. Gao (Co-chair)	University of Delaware, USA
Xin He	Institute of Computing Technology, Chinese Academy of Sciences, China
Bohu Huang	Xidian University, China
Weile Jia	University of California, Berkeley, USA
Keiji Kimura	Waseda University, Japan
Dong Li	University of California, Merced, USA
Jiajia Li	Pacific Northwest National Laboratory, USA
Chao Li	Shanghai Jiao Tong University, China
Weifeng Liu	China University of Petroleum, China
Minutoli Marco	Pacific Northwest National Laboratory, USA
Qiguang Miao	Xidian University, China
Israt Nisa	Ohio State University
Bin Ren	The College of William & Mary, USA
En Shao	Institute of Computing Technology, Chinese Academy of Science, China
Shaden Smith	Microsoft AI and Research, USA
Arthur Stoutchinin	ST Microelectronics, France
Guangzhong Sun	University of Science and Technology of China, China
Guangming Tan (Co-chair)	Institute of Computing Technology, Chinese Academy of Sciences, China
Dingwen Tao	WSU, USA
Parimala Thulasiram	University of Manitoba, Canada
Cornelis Vuik	Delft University of Technology, the Netherlands
Bo Wu	Colorado School of Mines, USA

Junmin Xiao	Institute of Computing Technology, Chinese Academy of Sciences, China
Xiaowen Xu	IAPCM, China
Hailong Yang	Beihang University, China
Zhibin Yu	Shenzhen Institutes of Advanced Technology, China
Jidong Zhai	Tsinghua University, China
Feng Zhang	Renmin University of China, China
Tao Zhang	Shanghai University, China
Weihua Zhang	Fudan University, China
Mingzhe Zhang	Institute of Computing Technology, Chinese Academy of Sciences, China

Contents

Algorithm

Architecture and Hardware

Big Data and Cloud

Edge Computing

Emering

Network

Storage

Accelerator

Compiler-Assisted Operator Template Library for DNN Accelerators

Jiansong Li[1,2], Wei Cao[1], Xiao Dong[1,2], Guangli Li[1,2], Xueying Wang[1,2], Lei Liu[1(✉)], and Xiaobing Feng[1,2(✉)]

[1] Institute of Computing Technology, Chinese Academy of Sciences, Beijing, China
{lijiansong,caowei,dongxiao,liguangli,wangxueying,liulei,fxb}@ict.ac.cn
[2] University of Chinese Academy of Sciences, Beijing, China

Abstract. Despite many dedicated accelerators are gaining popularity for their performance and energy efficiency in the deep neural network (DNN) domain, high-level programming support for these accelerators remains thin. In contrast to existing researches targeting the whole DNNs, we choose to dive into details and review this problem from a finer-grained level, operators. Due to performance concerns, operator programmers may have to take hand-written assembly as their first choice, which is error-prone and involves many programming chores. To alleviate this problem, we propose TOpLib, a compiler-assisted template library. By providing a unified user-view abstraction, TOpLib allows programmers to express computational kernels with high-level tensor primitives, which will be automatically lowered into low-level intrinsic primitives via expression templates. Moreover, considering memory management is performance critical and the optimization strategy of expression template is limited to enumeration based rewriting rules, we implement TOpLib with a compiler-assisted approach. We address the memory reuse challenges into the compiler, which allows TOpLib to make full use of on-chip buffers and result in better performance. Experiments over 55 typical DNN operators demonstrate that TOpLib can generate scalable code with performance faster than or on par with hand-written assembly versions.

Keywords: DNN accelerators · Template library · Address space management

1 Introduction

In recent years, many dedicated DNN accelerators are gaining popularity for their energy and performance efficiency. They have been deployed in embedded devices, servers and datacenters [1,12]. These accelerators focus on specific customization for the computations of DNNs. Typically, DNNs are usually expressed as computation graphs, where nodes represent basic operations (namely operators, e.g., convolution, pooling, activation), edges refer to data consumed or produced by these operators. These operators can be offloaded to accelerators

X. He et al. (Eds.): NPC 2020, LNCS 12639, pp. 3–16, 2021.
https://doi.org/10.1007/978-3-030-79478-1_1

to speed up computation. In this paper, we focus on the programming problems puzzling the underlying operator programmers. Due to performance concerns, they may have to take hand-written assembly as their first programming choice. Coding a highly tuned operator kernel usually requires expert knowledge to manage every hardware detail, which involves a plethora of low-level programming chores. To illustrate, we use a simple feedforward MLP kernel with the sigmoid activation function as an example. The main computations are as follows: $y = \varphi(\sum_{i=1}^{n} w_i x_i + b) = \varphi(w^T x + b)$, where $\varphi(x) = e^x/(1 + e^x)$. Figure 1a shows the implementation of feedforward MLP kernel at Cambricon-ACC [15] accelerator via hand-written assembly. For the sake of brevity, we omit the kernel explanation details. But for now it suffices to see that even this trivial MLP implementation involves many low-level programming chores. For example, the vector-vector and matrix-vector instructions, e.g., *VAV* and *MMV*, usually need special registers to store the memory address and the size of input data. Programmers have to manually allocate these registers and track the lifetime of each memory blocks, which is burdensome and error-prone. Besides, these CISC style instructions usually have special address alignment requirements, programmers have to manually check the address alignment of each memory block. This kind of low-level coding is very typical during the development of DNN operators.

To alleviate the low-level programming issues, we propose a compiler-assisted template library for operator programmers, namely TOpLib (short for **T**ensor **Op**erator **Lib**rary). TOpLib follows the philosophy of decoupling the programmers' view from the diversity of underlying hardwares. It provides an user-view abstraction for DNN accelerators. It uses C-like syntax as the surface language to represent abstract data types and operations. In terms of implementation, we can integrate the abstract data type and corresponding operations inside compiler or wrap a template library that optimizes at compile-time. The former may be straightforward and strong, but requires much engineering effort, posing a great challenge to compiler maintainers. The latter would be much more easily achieved by taking use of the meta-programming technique called expression template. But for the latter, the optimization strategy is limited to enumeration based rewriting rules. In this paper, we propose a hybrid approach to implement TOpLib. TOpLib relies on the meta-programming capability of the programming language provided by the DNN accelerators, e.g., expression template and operator overloading. Considering the memory management is performance critical, we use a compiler-assisted method to address the memory reuse challenges.

The rest of this paper proceeds as follows: Sect. 2 introduces the design principles of TOpLib. The implementation details are presented in Sect. 3. Section 4 describes experiment results. Section 5 and 6 discuss the related work and conclude respectively.

2   Design

2.1   User-View Abstraction

For most reconfigurable DNN accelerators, there are at least three levels of memory hierarchy: off-chip memory (DRAM), on-chip scratchpad memory (SPM)

```
// MLP kernel code
// $0: input size, $1: output size, $2: matrix size
// $3: input address, $4: weight address
// $5: bias address, $6: output address
// $7-$10: temp variable address

VLOAD $3, $0, #100      // load input tensor from address (100)
MLOAD $4, $2, #300      // load weight matrix from address (300)
MMV $7, $1, $4, $3, $0  // W*x
VAV $8, $1, $7, $5      // tmp=W*x+b
VEXP $9, $1, $8         // exp(tmp)
VAS $10, $1, $9, #1     // 1+exp(tmp)
VDV $6, $1, $9, $10     // y=exp(tmp)/(1+exp(tmp))
VSTORE $6, $1, #200     // store output tensor to address (200)
```

```
// MLP kernel code
// IN_SIZE: input size, OUT_SIZE: output size, MAT_SIZE: matrix size
// x: input tensor address, W: weight tensor address
// b: bias tensor address, y: output tensor address

__kernel__ void MLP(Tensor<DATA, half, IN_SIZE> x, Tensor<DATA, half, MAT_SIZE> W,
                    Tensor<DATA, half, OUT_SIZE> b, Tensor<DATA, half, OUT_SIZE> y) {
  Tensor<NEURAL, half, IN_SIZE> tx = load(x);   // load input data
  Tensor<NEURAL, half, OUT_SIZE> tb = load(b);  // load bias data
  Tensor<SYNAPSE, half, MAT_SIZE> tW = load(W); // load weight data
  Tensor<NEURAL, half, OUT_SIZE> ty = tW * tx;  // tmp = W*x
  ty += tb;                                     // tmp = W*x+b
  ty = exp(ty) / (1 + exp(ty));                 // y = exp(tmp)/(1+exp(tmp))
  store(ty, y);                                 // store result into off-chip DRAM
}
```

(a) MLP implementation via hand-written assembly at Cambricon-ACC.

(b) MLP implementation via high-level tensor algorithmic primitives of TOpLib.

Fig. 1. MLP implementation at Cambricon-ACC via hand-written assembly and TOpLib's high-level tensor algorithmic primitives. For (a), note the ISA-level description with careful on-chip buffer layout design, manual register allocation and intentional memory address alignment checking.

and registers. Unlike the caches of CPUs, which are managed by the hardware automatically and are invisible to programmers, the on-chip buffers of DNN accelerators are usually explicitly managed by programmers due to performance and power concerns. To simplify the programmability of DNN accelerators, we hide the hardware execution details and expose the performance critical parts to programmers.

Figure 2b shows View-ACC, an user-view abstraction for DNN accelerators. View-ACC consists of computation cores and on-chip SPMs, connected with wide buses to off-chip memory. Intuitively, the computation cores are responsible for the execution of DNN primitive operations, which will be thoroughly discussed in Sect. 2.3. The on-chip SPMs are abstractions for the on-chip buffers of DNN accelerators. They are fast but with size limitation, and are visible to operator programmers and compiler. They usually play the role of caching partial input data and temporary computational results. While the off-chip DRAMs are large but slow. They are used for the storage of large quantity DNN parameters and input/output data required by operators. The communications between the on-chip SPMs and the off-chip DRAMs are accomplished through explicit DMA load and store instructions.

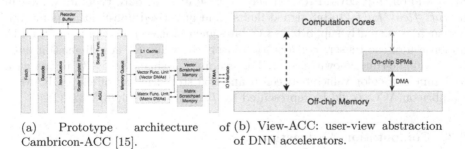

(a) Prototype architecture of Cambricon-ACC [15].

(b) View-ACC: user-view abstraction of DNN accelerators.

Fig. 2. The architectural details of Cambricon-ACC and its user-view abstraction. The dashed arrow in (b) means there is a potential data-path between computation cores and off-chip DRAM.

Let's take Cambricon-ACC (Fig. 2a) as an example. Cambricon-ACC is a prototype DNN accelerator, which is based on the Cambricon DNN ISA [15]. In Cambricon-ACC, the off-chip DRAM is used for input and output data of DNN workloads. While the on-chip SPMs for vector and matrix function units, which are used for caching of neural and synapse data, can be treated as the on-chip SPMs of View-ACC. The scalar, vector and matrix function unit in Cambricon-ACC can be treated as the computation cores of View-ACC. Other architectural components in Cambricon-ACC, e.g., reorder buffer, issue queue, fetch and decode components can be regarded as hardware implementation details, which are invisible to programmers. View-ACC hides the hardware execution details and exposes the performance critical parts to the programmers. Programmers can be released from the inner hardware execution details.

2.2 Memory Abstraction

Well-organized programs usually make frequent use of structs or classes. Array of Structures (AoS) and Structure of Arrays (SoA) describe the common techniques for organizing multiple structs/objects in memory [21]. In AoS, all fields of a struct are stored together. In SoA, all values of a fields of a struct are stored together. By our previous engineering efforts, we find that DNN operators are usually implemented in the SoA fashion. SoA benefits from the on-chip buffer utilization and is SIMD-friendly. However, in the DNN domain, the data participating in computation is usually high dimensional, not a single flat array. Therefore, we need a high-level type system with tensor as a first-class type. Tensor is a mathematical concept, which generalizes vector and matrix to higher ranks.

TOpLib represents tensor as the first-class type with *address space specifier*, an element type and shapes. Taking the memory hierarchy of DNN accelerators into consideration, TOpLib represents the hardware memory types by associating data with address spaces. All data will be expressed by aggregate type *Tensor*. Its definition will be like this, $Tensor <A, T, d_0, d_1, ..., d_{n-1}>$, where A denotes the address space of data. For Cambricon-ACC, its value can be NEURAL, SYNAPSE or DATA, which denotes the on-chip vector SPM, matrix SPM and off-chip DRAM respectively; T describes the data type, its value can be int, $float$, $half$ (16-bit signed floats) and quantized non-floating-point values such as currently supported $i8$ (8-bit signed integers); d_i represents the i-th dimension of the tensor. For a static tensor, the value of each dimension must be a compile-time known integer. For example, a single 32 by 32 image with 3 channels of color values between 0 and 255 stored in the off-chip DRAM of Cambricon-ACC, could be represented by $Tensor <DATA, i8, 3, 32, 32>$.

2.3 Computation Abstraction

Table 1 lists up the most relevant tensor primitives for typical DNN workloads. To decouple the user-view from the diversity of underlying hardwares, TOpLib

Table 1. High-level algorithmic primitives and low-level instrinsic primitives.

High-level algorithmic primitives	
$[T]_S^A = map(f, [T]_S^A)$	Apply f to each element of given tensor
$[T]_S^A = zip(f, [T]_S^A, [T]_S^A)$	Apply f to each pair of corresponding elements of given two tensors
$[T]_{S_1}^A = reduce(\oplus, [T]_{S_0}^A)$	Collapse given tensor with the associative binary operator $\oplus$
$[T]_{S_o}^{A_o} = conv([T]_{S_v}^{A_v}, \alpha_1, [T]_{S_h}^{A_h}, \alpha_2)$	Convolve input tensor v with range α_1 and a polynomial filter tensor h with range α_2
$[T]_{S_1}^A = pool([T]_{S_0}^A, \alpha, \oplus)$	Combine adjacent elements of given tensor at region α by a reduction operation $\oplus$
$[T]_{S_c}^A = matmul([T]_{S_a}^A, [T]_{S_b}^A)$	Multiply two input 2-order tensors, i.e., matrices
$[T]_{S_{dst}}^{A_{dst}} = load([T]_{S_{src}}^{A_{src}}, size)$	Load $size$ bytes of data from source tensor src
$store([T]_{S_{src}}^{A_{src}}, [T]_{S_{dst}}^{A_{dst}}, size)$	Store $size$ bytes of data from source tensor src into destination tensor dst
Low-level intrinsic primitives	
$\_map(f, p_1, p_0, n)$	Apply f to n elements starting at memory position p_0 and store results into p_1
$\_zip(f, p_2, p_0, p_1, n)$	Apply f to binary element-wise pair of n elements starting from p_0 and p_1 and store results into p_2
$\_reduce(\oplus, p_1, p_0, n)$	Collapse n elements starting from p_0 with associative binary operator $\oplus$ and store result to p_1
$\_conv(p_o, n_o, p_v, n_v, \alpha_1, p_h, n_h, \alpha_2)$	Convolution: $v_{\alpha_1} \circledast h^{\alpha_2} \to o$
$\_pool(p_1, n_1, p_0, n_0, \alpha, \oplus)$	Pooling n_0 elements starting from p_0 at region α by a reduction operation $\oplus$ and store the n_1 results to p_1
$\_matmul(p_a, n_a, p_b, n_b, p_c, n_c)$	Matrix multiplication: $a \otimes b \to c$
$\_load(p_{dst}, p_{src}, size)$	Load: $p_{dst} \xleftarrow{size} p_{src}$
$\_store(p_{src}, p_{dst}, size)$	Store: $p_{src} \xrightarrow{size} p_{dst}$

defines two-level tensor primitives. Programmers express operators with high-level tensor algorithmic primitives. And these algorithmic primitives will be lowered into low-level intrinsic primitives. The low-level intrinsic primitives are listed at the bottom of Table 1. They are abstractions for the ISAs of DNN accelerators, which present as compiler builtin functions.

High-Level Algorithmic Primitives. In Table 1, we write $[T]_S^A$ for a tensor of data type T with a shape S at the address space A. Primitives map and zip are element-wise computational patterns. In the DNN domain, typical activation

Table 2. Breakdown of execution time for each high-level algorithmic primitives in common DNN workloads. Note that primitive *load* and *store* is an abstraction for the data movement between off-chip DRAMs and on-chip SPMs, we omit them for CPUs.

Workloads	*map*	*zip*	*reduce*	*conv*	*pool*	*matmul*
AlexNet [13]	13.26%	12.07%	–	40.50%	3.39%	30.76%
GoogLeNet [22]	19.44%	17.30%	–	37.16%	25.86%	0.24%
Inception-V3 [23]	9.75%	6.65%	–	69.21%	14.08%	0.31%
MobileNetV1 [10]	21.05%	20.28%	–	58.37%	0.28%	–
ResNet50 [8]	18.06%	21.21%	–	58.55%	1.83%	0.35%
SqueezeNet [11]	11.27%	3.45%	–	63.37%	21.88%	–
VGG16 [20]	6.02%	–	–	75.77%	5.26%	12.94%
K-NN [3]	–	–	99.73%	–	–	–
SVM [9]	0.27%	0.14%	99.34%	–	–	–

and normalization operators can be expressed with *map* and *zip* primitives. For the *reduce* primitive, its operator $\oplus$ can be min, max or sum. Primitive *conv* denotes convolution operation, which can be expressed with $v_{\alpha_1} \circledast h^{\alpha_2}$. This expression convolves an input image v with range α_1 and a filter kernel h with range α_2. Primitive *pool* is a pooling operation. Its reduce operator $\oplus$ can be max, average or min. The primitive *matmul* represents for the matrix multiplication operation, which is usually used to express the inner product operations of fully connected layers in DNNs. While primitives *load* and *store* are abstractions of the data movement operations between the on-chip SPMs and off-chip DRAMs.

Low-Level Intrinsic Primitives. DNN accelerators usually provide SIMD instructions to accelerate computations. These SIMD instructions usually have the requirements of specific memory alignment and data layout. These low-level intrinsic primitives present as compiler builtin functions (see Table 1 below). Intrinsic primitives __map and __zip represent for element-wise instructions, such as the ReLU activation and vector addition. The reduce intrinsic functions consist of reduce min, max, sum. For Cambricon-ACC, the convolution, pooling and matrix multiplication intrinsic primitives have specific data layout requirements. The data layout of their input filters must follow the *NHWC* (N: batch size, H: height, W: width, C: channel) layout requirement. Primitives __load and __store denote the DMA communications between the on-chip SPMs and off-chip DRAM.

To demonstrate the representativeness of these high-level tensor primitives, we select several common DNNs running with ImageNet [5] dataset and typical ML workloads. We decompose their CPU execution time (Table 2). Obviously, these high-level algorithmic primitives characterize the DNN workloads mainly. Figure 1b shows the feedforward MLP operator kernel written by high-level algorithmic primitives of TOpLib. In this case, binary arithmetic symbols, e.g., plus and slash are syntactic sugars for element-wise addition and division *zip* primitives. Compared with hand-written assembly version in Fig. 1a, MLP operator written by high-level algorithmic primitives are more intuitive to understand.

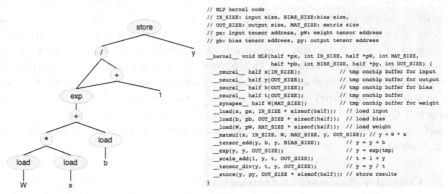

(a) Expression tree of MLP kernel. (b) Low-level instrinsic functions after lowering from high-level algorithmic primitives.

Fig. 3. Tensor expression tree of the feedforward MLP operator and the low-level instrinsic functions. In (b), _tensor_add and _tensor_div are the low-level __zip primitives; _exp and _scale_add are the low-level __map primitives.

3   Implementation

There are two ways to implement the tensor type system, i.e., integrate tensor type and the corresponding operations inside compiler or wrap a template library that optimizes at compile-time. The former is straightforward and strong, but requires much engineering effort. The latter would be much more easily achieved by taking use of the meta-programming technique called expression template. But for the latter, the optimization strategy is limited to enumeration based rewriting rules. Due to performance concerns, we implement TOpLib with a hybrid approach.

3.1   Expression Template

We use expression template to implement the mappings between high-level algorithmic primitives and low-level intrinsic primitives. Expression template is a tricky implementation technique that uses the static evaluation abilities of compilers together with templates to construct a static expression tree at compile time [19,24]. Figure 3a shows expression tree of the feedforward MLP kernel. The trick of expression template is done by letting operations and functions return abstracted operation objects that contain all necessary information to construct the expression tree, instead of calculating the result themselves. Through the use of template meta-programming, it is even possible to manipulate the expression tree at compile time to apply algebraic transformations (enumeration based rewriting rules). For example, we define fst as a notational shorthand for $map(fst, x)$, where x is a n-order tensor, marked as $[x_0, x_1, ..., x_{n-1}]$, i.e., an array of tuples. Function fst yields a tensor which is composed of the first component of each tuple in x, i.e., $fst(x) = [x_0^{(0)}, x_1^{(0)}, ..., x_{n-1}^{(0)}]$. Programmers wrote such an algorithmic expression $y = fst(reduce(+_0, x))$①, where reduce operator $+_0$ means apply a reduction summation along the *first* dimension of the input tensor x. TOpLib will transform this expression into $y = reduce(+_0, fst(x))$②. Obviously, *reduce* operation $+_0$ is more computation-intensive than the *map* operation *fst*. Compared with expression ①, the *fst* operation in ② can filter out input data of the reduce operation and maintain the original semantics. This transformation can eliminate redundant computations, and thereby reducing the overall cost.

3.2   Compiler-Assisted Optimizations

Considering the optimization strategy of expression template is limited to enumeration based rewriting rules, we conduct some compiler-assisted optimizations to guarantee performance.

Algorithm 1. Address Space Inference Optimization

Input   : $\mathcal{K}$, kernel program of current DNN operator;
Output: $\mathcal{M}$, a map of pointers in a specific address space;
for *Each kind of address space* $\mathcal{AS}_i$; **do**
 $\mathcal{GS} = \emptyset$; // Collect all pointers guaranteed in address space $\mathcal{AS}_i$
 for *Each pointer* $\mathcal{P}$ *used in kernel* $\mathcal{K}$; **do**
  if $\mathcal{P}$ *is guaranteed to point to* $\mathcal{AS}_i$; **then**
   $\mathcal{GS}.insert(\mathcal{P})$;

 $\mathcal{S} = \emptyset$; // Assume that all derived pointers point to $\mathcal{AS}_i$
 for *Each instruction* $\mathcal{I}$ *in* $\mathcal{K}$ *returning a pointer type*; **do**
  if $\mathcal{I}$ *is derived from other pointers*; **then**
   $\mathcal{S}.insert(\mathcal{I})$;

 // Iteratively prove that they are in address spaces other than $\mathcal{AS}_i$
 bool changed = true;
 while *changed* **do**
  changed = false;
  for *Each instruction* $\mathcal{I}$ *in* $\mathcal{K}$ *that is GEP, bitcast or PHINode*; **do**
   for *Each source Src of instruction* $\mathcal{I}$; **do**
    if *Src not in* $\mathcal{GS}$ *and Src not in* $\mathcal{S}$; **then**
     $\mathcal{S}.remove(\mathcal{I})$;
     changed = true;

 $\mathcal{M}[\mathcal{AS}_i] = \mathcal{S} \cup \mathcal{GS}$;
return $\mathcal{M}$;

Memory Address Space Inference. As shown in Fig. 3b, the memory address space type qualifiers only apply to variable declarations, so compiler must infer the address space of a pointer derived from a variable. Besides, knowing the address space of memory accessing allows to emit faster load and store instructions. For example, a load from on-chip SPM is usually faster than the load from

off-chip memory. We address this challenge using a compiler-assisted optimization pass (Algorithm 1). We implemente the address space inference through a
fixed-point data-flow analysis [16]. The compiler runs propagate on $\mathcal{K}$ for each
address space $\mathcal{AS}_i$. It first assumes all derived pointers (via pointer arithmetic)
point to $\mathcal{AS}_i$. Then, it iteratively reverts that assumption for pointers derived
from another one that is not guaranteed in $\mathcal{AS}_i$. finally, $\mathcal{GS}$ and $\mathcal{S}$ combined
contains all pointers in memory space $\mathcal{AS}_i$.

Algorithm 2. On-Chip Memory Reuse and Off-Chip Data Promotion

---

```
Input  : K, kernel program of current DNN operator;
Output: P, a set of memory partitions to be created;
SB = ∅;// SB is a set of tensor memory blocks in K
for Each variable V in K; do
    if GetDataType(V) is aggregate type then
        Get address space and size of V;// record meta-data of current block
        SB.insert(V);
        Get live ranges of V by data flow analysis;

for Each kind of address space ASᵢ; do
    Build interference graph IG(V, E), where:
    - V = { Bᵢ' ∈ SB | GetAddressSpace(Bᵢ')=ASᵢ};
    - E is an undirected edge connecting two memory blocks (Bₛ, Bₜ), if live ranges of Bₛ
    and Bₜ overlap;
    Coloring IG with greedy strategy;
    for vertices in IG.V with the same color; do
        Choose maximum size of colored memory blocks as current partition size;

    Reallocate partitions P for memory blocks;
    if V.size() != P.size() then
        // reuse happens
        Promote partial off-chip data into remaining on-chip memory;

return P;
```

Memory Allocator and Reuse Optimization. Consider the motivation
example in Fig. 4a, where memory blocks $B1$-$B5$ need to be allocated to a certain memory region. Assume the on-chip SPMs capacity of the DNN accelerator
is $256K$. If compiler takes a naive linear allocator for these memory blocks, i.e.,
map each block to distinct memory locations (Fig. 4b), they will exceed the total
capacity of on-chip SPMs. A careful inspection of the original operator's implementation reveals that memory block $B2, B3$ and $B5$ can in fact be shared,
leading to the allocation in Fig. 4d. We can automatically achieves this goal by
compiler static analysis without modifying the original kernel's implementation.
Our memory reuse algorithm (Algorithm 2) is partially inspired by [14]. Firstly,
the compiler collects the meta-data information (including address space and
size) of tensor variables by statically walking through $\mathcal{K}$. Then It gets the live
ranges of each tensor variable by data flow analysis. In this paper, we apply the
definition of liveness for arrays in [14] to the aggregate tensor data type. Similarly, liveness analysis for tensors is conducted on the control flow graph (CFG)
of $\mathcal{K}$. The liveness information for a tensor T can be computed on CFG of $\mathcal{K}$ by
applying the standard data-flow equations to the entry and exit of every basic
block (abbr. BB) $\mathcal{B}$:

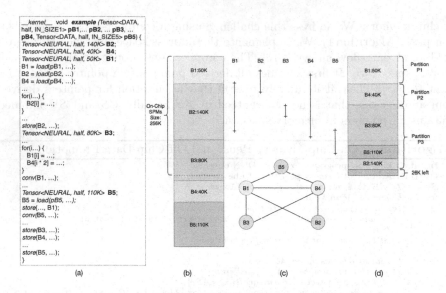

Fig. 4. A motivation example of on-chip scratch pad memory reuse.

$$IN_T(\mathcal{B}) = (OUT_T(\mathcal{B}) - DEF_T(\mathcal{B})) \cup USE_T(\mathcal{B})$$
$$OUT_T(\mathcal{B}) = \cup_{\mathcal{S} \in succ(\mathcal{B})} IN_T(\mathcal{S})$$
(1)

where $succ(\mathcal{B})$ denotes the set of all successor BBs of $\mathcal{B}$ in CFG of $\mathcal{K}$. The predicates, **DEF** and **USE**, local to a BB $\mathcal{B}$ for a tensor T are defined as follows: $USE_T(\mathcal{B})$ returns true if some elements of T are read in $\mathcal{B}$; $DEF_T(\mathcal{B})$ returns true if T is killed in $\mathcal{B}$. Figure 4c top shows the live ranges of tensor variables $B1$-$B5$. Then compiler builds interference graph (IG). However, considering the memory hierarchies of DNN accelerators, we need to build IG for different address space respectively, i.e., vertices in the same IG must have the same address space specifier. Figure 4c bottom shows the IG of tensor variables in address space NEURAL. Now compiler takes a greedy graph coloring strategy [4] by clustering the memory blocks with non-overlapping live ranges. Memory blocks with the same color will be assigned to the same memory partition. The size of each memory partition is calculated by choosing the maximum size of colored memory blocks. Figure 4d shows the memory partitions after graph coloring and there is $26K$ on-chip memory left. Compiler will try to promote some off-chip data (including but not limited to local variable or stack data) into this region. The promotion strategy can be performed by static analysis.

Table 3. Hardware specifications of experimental platform.

On-chip SPMs	Off-chip DRAM	Peak Performance	Memory Bandwidth
Neural buffer: 512 KB Synapse buffer: 1 MB	8 GB	0.5 TFLOPS	25.6 GB/s

4   Performance Evaluation

4.1   Benchmarks and Baselines

Our experiment is conducted on a prototype accelerator (Table 3). Its architecture refers to the design of Cambricon-ACC [15]. We select 55 typical operators from popular DNNs as our benchmarks. It covers some representative algorithms used in DNNs, e.g., convolution (conv), fully connection (fc), pooling (pool), scale, element-wise (ew), batch normalization (bn), local respond normalization (lrn) and ReLU activation (relu). All these benchmarks can be expressed with the high-level algorithmic primitives of TOpLib. To show the representativeness of our benchmarks, we have profiled the execution time of some popular DNNs at Cambricon-ACC and decomposed their execution time into typical layers (Fig. 5a). Finally, we extracted 55 most time-consuming operators with typical real-world data scales[1]. We choose the highly tuned hand-written assembly implementation of benchmarks as baselines. To show the quality of baselines, we have drawn the roofline of the hand-written assembly implementation versions. From the roofline in Fig. 5b, we can see that these hand-written assembly benchmarks saturate the peak performance of Cambricon-ACC in the terms of FLOPS and memory bandwidth, confirming that *our baselines are very tough to beat.*

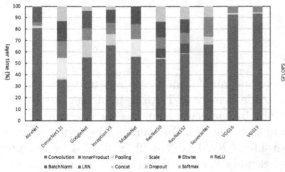

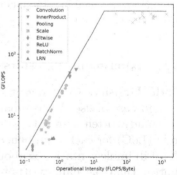

(a) Breakdown of typical layers' execution time for common DNNs at Cambricon-ACC.

(b) Roofline of the hand-written assembly implementation versions at Cambricon-ACC.

Fig. 5. Layer-wise execution time breakdown of common DNNs and roofline of hand-written assembly implementation of 55 operators at Cambricon-ACC.

---

[1] Due to space limit, the detailed data scales are clearly listed in the anonymous github repository: https://github.com/anonymous-0x00/npc20-benchmarks.

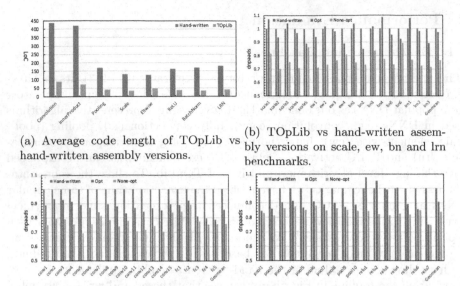

(a) Average code length of TOpLib vs hand-written assembly versions.

(b) TOpLib vs hand-written assembly versions on scale, ew, bn and lrn benchmarks.

(c) TOpLib vs hand-written assembly versions on conv and fc benchmarks.

(d) TOpLib vs hand-written assembly versions on pool and relu benchmarks.

Fig. 6. TOpLib implementation vs hand-written assembly versions on all 55 operators. For (b) (c) (d), the red bar is the normalized execution performance of TOpLib implementation enabling the memory optimization passes, the gray bar disables them. (Color figure online)

4.2   Experimental Results

Code Density. Code density is a meaningful metric to measure the simplicity and ease of use. We compare code density of TOpLib implementation with the hand-written assembly versions by manually counting the average lines of code (LoC) for each type benchmarks (Fig. 6a). On average, the code length of TOpLib implementation is about 4.9x, 5.8x, 4.3x, 3.8x, 2.7x, 4.4x, 4.8x and 4.6x shorter than the hand-written assembly versions for *conv, fc, pool, scale, ew, relu, bn* and *lrn* operators, respectively.

Execution Performance. Figure 6b, 6c and 6d shows the speedup of TOpLib implementation against hand-written assembly versions. Compared to hand-written assembly versions of all benchmarks, TOpLib achieves 91% on average if we enable the memory optimization passes. However, if we disable them, the execution performance would reduce to about 78% on average. That means memory optimization plays an important role for the producing of high-performance code. Specifically, we find that zip-heavy operators (e.g., scale, ew, bn and lrn) are compiler-friendly for the memory reuse optimization pass.

5   Related Work

This section summarizes the prior work on template library for DNN operators. CUDA [2] or OpenCL [17] is a parallel programming model for GPUs, not for the dedicated DNN accelerators. Eigen [7], Mshadow [6] and Cutlass [18] are linear algebra libraries for CPUs or GPUs. The implementation of existing libraries relies on the meta-programming capability of the C++ programming language, e.g., expression template. They overlook the compiler-assisted optimizations.

6   Conclusion

In this paper, we present TOpLib, a compiler-assisted template library to alleviate low-level programming chores of DNN accelerators. TOpLib provides a user-view abstraction of DNN accelerators, which allows programmers to express operators with high-level algorithmic primitives. We have detailed its design principles and compiler-assisted optimizations. Experimental results show that TOplib could succinctly express the typical DNN operators and produce code that is comparable to hand-written assembly versions.

Acknowledgement. This work is supported by the National Key R&D Program of China (under Grant No. 2017YFB1003103) and the Science Fund for Creative Research Groups of the National Natural Science Foundation of China (under Grant No. 61521092).

References

1. AnandTech: Cambricon, Makers of Huawei's Kirin NPU IP (2018). https://www.anandtech.com/show/12815/cambricon-makers-of-huaweis-kirin-npu-ip-build-a-big-ai-chip-and-pcie-card
2. Cook, S.: CUDA Programming: A Developer's Guide to Parallel Computing with GPUs, 1st edn. Morgan Kaufmann Publishers Inc., San Francisco (2012)
3. Cover, T., Hart, P.: Nearest neighbor pattern classification. IEEE Trans. Inf. Theor. **13**(1), 21–27 (2006)
4. Culberson, J.C.: Iterated greedy graph coloring and the difficulty landscape. Technical report (1992)
5. Deng, J., Dong, W., Socher, R., Li, L.J., Li, K., Fei-Fei, L.: ImageNet: a large-scale hierarchical image database. In: CVPR 2009 (2009)
6. DMLC teams: mshadow (2018). https://github.com/dmlc/mshadow
7. Guennebaud, G., Jacob, B., et al.: Eigen v3 (2010). http://eigen.tuxfamily.org
8. He, K., et al.: Deep residual learning for image recognition. CoRR abs/1512.03385 (2015)
9. Hearst, M.A.: Support vector machines. IEEE Intell. Syst. **13**(4), 18–28 (1998)
10. Howard, A.G., et al.: MobileNets: efficient convolutional neural networks for mobile vision applications. CoRR abs/1704.04861 (2017)
11. Iandola, F.N., et al.: SqueezeNet: AlexNet-level accuracy with 50x fewer parameters and <1 MB model size. CoRR abs/1602.07360 (2016)

12. Jouppi, N.P., et al.: In-datacenter performance analysis of a tensor processing unit. In: ISCA 2017, pp. 1–12. ACM, New York (2017)
13. Krizhevsky, A., et al.: ImageNet classification with deep convolutional neural networks. In: NIPS 2012, pp. 1097–1105. Curran Associates Inc., USA (2012)
14. Li, L., et al.: Memory coloring: a compiler approach for scratchpad memory management. In: PACT 2005, pp. 329–338, September 2005
15. Liu, S., et al.: Cambricon: an instruction set architecture for neural networks. In: ISCA 2016, pp. 393–405 (2016)
16. Muchnick, S.S.: Advanced Compiler Design and Implementation. Morgan Kaufmann Publishers Inc., San Francisco (1998)
17. Munshi, A., Gaster, B., Mattson, T.G., Fung, J., Ginsburg, D.: OpenCL Programming Guide, 1st edn. Addison-Wesley Professional, Boston (2011)
18. NVIDIA teams: Cutlass (2017). https://github.com/NVIDIA/cutlass
19. Progsch, J., et al.: A new vectorization technique for expression templates in C++. CoRR abs/1109.1264 (2011)
20. Simonyan, K., Zisserman, A.: Very deep convolutional networks for large-scale image recognition (2014). https://arxiv.org/abs/1409.1556
21. Springer, M., Sun, Y., Masuhara, H.: Inner array inlining for structure of arrays layout. In: PLDI, ARRAY 2018, pp. 50–58. ACM, New York (2018)
22. Szegedy, C., et al.: Going deeper with convolutions. In: Computer Vision and Pattern Recognition (CVPR) (2015). http://arxiv.org/abs/1409.4842
23. Szegedy, C., et al.: Rethinking the inception architecture for computer vision. CoRR abs/1512.00567 (2015)
24. Wu, J., et al.: GPUCC: an open-source GPGPU compiler. In: CGO 2016, pp. 105–116 (2016)

A Dynamic Mapping Model for General CNN Accelerator Based on FPGA

Xiaoqiang Zhao[1], Jingfei Jiang[1(✉)], Zhe Han[1], Jinwei Xu[1], and Zhiqiang Liu[2]

[1] National Laboratory for Parallel and Distributed Processing,
National University of Defense Technology, Changsha, China
{zhaoxiaoqiang18,jingfeijiang,hanzhe18,xujinwei13}@nudt.edu.cn
[2] Artificial Intelligence Research Center, National Innovation
Institute of Defense Technology, Beijing, China
liuzhiqiang@nudt.edu.cn

Abstract. As the application scenarios of convolutional neural network (CNN) become more and more complex, the general CNN accelerator based on matrix multiplication has become a new research focus. The existing mapping methods for converting convolution calculation into matrix multiplication need to be improved. This paper proposes a new dynamic mapping model to improve the flexibility and versatility of matrix multiplication. The dynamic mapping model implements two algorithms: dynamic residue processing mapping algorithm (DRPMA) and dilated convolution mapping algorithm (DCMA). The former can dynamically adjust the mapping method according to the number of output channels of the convolution layer, improve the utilization of the multiply-accumulate (MAC) array. The latter extends the efficient support for Dilated CNNs. For demonstration, we implement an accelerator with Verilog on Xilinx VC709 FPGA board and test some typical CNN models. Experimental results show that the general accelerator achieves high performance and energy efficiency.

Keywords: CNN · Matrix multiplication · Dynamic mapping model · FPGA

1 Introduction

In recent years, CNNs have become one of the most popular models in the artificial intelligence and shown excellent results in many fields including image classification [6,15], object recognition [3,13], video analysis [14,19], voice recognition [1,4]. With the widespread application of CNNs, FPGA-based CNN accelerators [2,5,7–12,16–18,20,21] have become a new research focus. However, the

Supported by National Science and Technology Major Projects on Core Electronic Devices, High-End Generic Chips and Basic Software under grant No. 2018ZX01028101 and National Natural Science Foundation of China Key Program No. 61732018.

© IFIP International Federation for Information Processing 2021
Published by Springer Nature Switzerland AG 2021
X. He et al. (Eds.): NPC 2020, LNCS 12639, pp. 17–29, 2021.
https://doi.org/10.1007/978-3-030-79478-1_2

application scenarios of CNNs have become more and more complex. Deep CNNs have appeared to improve the inference accuracy, Dilated CNNs have been used in image segmentation, semantic segmentation to enlarger the receptive field. Three-dimensional CNNs have been applied to video analysis. Researchers need to balance the versatility and performance of accelerators to adapt to complex application scenarios. The increase of CNN parameters and intermediate results will exceed the storage capacity on the FPGA chip, making the accelerator design lose the task-level and layer-level parallelism. It is necessary to improve the loop-level and operation-level parallelism to increase accelerator performance. And the application of dilated CNNs requires a more flexible accelerator architecture to support dilated convolution. In order to enable the CNN accelerator to be applied to more scenarios, we need a flexible data buffering scheme. The data buffering scheme should handle networks with different parameters, support more convolution types, and can dynamically adjust the data mapping method according network parameters to improve accelerator performance. In this work, we are motivated to present a new dynamic mapping model based on general matrix multiplication. Our contributions are shown as follows:

1. We propose a new dynamic mapping model, combining the DRPMA and DCMA, which greatly improves the flexibility and versatility of general matrix multiplication.
2. We provide a uniform general accelerator architecture for two-dimensional, three-dimensional and dilated CNNs with dynamic mapping model. The accelerator can dynamically adapt to different computing modes without reconfiguration. The convolutional layer segmentation strategy is introduced to enable the accelerator to handle CNN-base AI applications of large-scale dimensions. It achieves high performance with smaller storage and bandwidth resources and can be ASIC.
3. We implement a RISC-V+CNN heterogeneous system based on the FPGA platform, Experiments show that the utilization of the MAC array is significantly improved, the dilated convolution can be performed efficiently, and achieves an overall throughput of 329.3 GFLOP/s on VGG16 and 354.4GFLOP/s on Resnet18 respectively.

2   Related Work

At present, CNN accelerators based on FPGA are mainly divided into the following four types according to the acceleration methods. The first type is general matrix multiplication CNN accelerators [10,12,16]. [10] designed a 2D/3D general reconfigurable convolutional neural network accelerator. [12] designed a maximize resource utilization CNN accelerator. The second type is Fast Fourier Transform (FFT) CNN accelerator [8,20,21]. [21] designed a highly parallel 2D FFT CNN accelerator using FFT and Concatenate-and-Pad technique to reduce convolutional redundancy calculations. [8] designed a deep CNN accelerator using embedded FFT. The third type is Winograd CNN accelerator [7,11,17].

Winograd fast algorithm maps feature to specific domains to reduce the complexity of the algorithm. [11] designed a sparse and effective Winograd CNN Accelerator. [17] designed a Winograd CNN accelerator that adapts to large steps. The fourth type is operator customized CNN accelerator [5,9,18]. [9] designed a layer pipeline optimized CNN accelerator. [5] designed a zero weight/activation-aware CNN accelerator. To summarize, the general matrix multiplication accelerator mapping convolutions to matrix multiplications, which has a good versatility. The FFT acceleration method transforms spatial domain convolution operation into frequency domain multiplication operation, which reduces the complexity of the algorithm and is proved to be more effective for the large convolution kernel. The Winograd acceleration method uses the addition operation to replace the multiplication operation through the linear mapping, which reduces the complexity of the algorithm, and is mainly suitable for the convolution stride is 1 and the transform matrices vary with the size of convolution kernels. The customized operator accelerator is optimized according to the algorithm characteristics, which fully exploits the parallelism of algorithms and has high performance.

These four types of CNN accelerators reflect different design ideas, each has its own advantages and complements each other. To summarize, there is still a large space for exploration in the design of accelerators for CNN. Different design concepts make designers adopt different acceleration methods. Aims to quickly respond to the changes in the CNN structures and the iterative speed of artificial intelligence algorithms. We adopt general matrix multiplication method with a new dynamic mapping model, which fully explores the loop levels parallelism and support for dilated convolution.

3   CNN Basics and Matrix Multiplication

This section will introduce the operation characteristics of different convolution types, the method of mapping convolution to matrix multiplication, and analyze their common characteristics and the existing optimization space.

3.1   2D and 3D Convolution

Figure 1a illustrates the process of 2D convolution. The convolution window slides along the column and row directions of the image to extract the spatial information of the image. The input and output feature usually contains multiple channels. The convolution results of each input channel are then accumulated resulting in one channel of the output feature. And the process of calculating other output channels is similar. Figure 1b shows the process of 3D convolution. Compared with the process of 2D convolution, in addition to sliding along the row and column directions, 3D convolution also slides along the temporal direction. In the 3D CNN adds a dimension of L, which represents the convolution depth in the temporal dimension. [10] indicate that 3D convolutions can be computed in the same way as 2D convolutions by combining the accumulation of the channel loop and the temporal loop. We also adopt this method in our

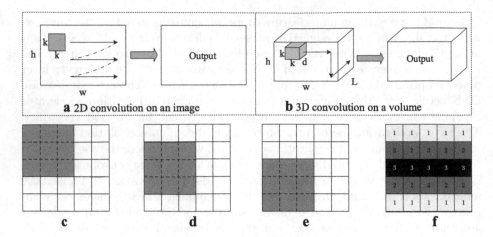

Fig. 1. 2D and 3D convolution operations.

implementation. Figure 1c–e illustrate how the convolution window slides across rows of the input feature. The pixels in gray are involved in convolutions along rows are shown as Fig. 1f. Accordingly, the first row appears in the input feature 1 time, the second row appears in the input feature 2 times, and the third row appears in the input feature 3 times. The re-usability in the row direction of the sliding window can be used to improve the parallelism of matrix multiplication.

3.2 Dilated Convolution

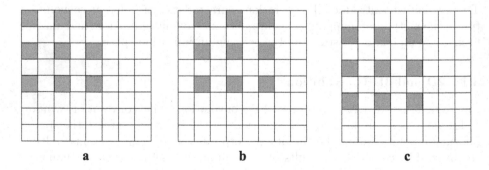

Fig. 2. Dilated convolution operations.

Figure 2 illustrates the process of the dilated convolution. The kernel size is 3×3 and the rate is 2. Figure 2a to Fig. 2b illustrate how the convolution window slides across column of the input feature. Figure 2a to Fig. 2c illustrate how the convolution window slides across row of the input feature. Compared to convolution, the dilated convolution changes the features covered by the convolution window. As shown in the shaded part of Fig. 2, the feature extraction is separated by rate-1 in both the row and column directions. We only need to load the feature according to this pattern, and then dilated convolution and 2D/3D convolution can use the same computing architecture.

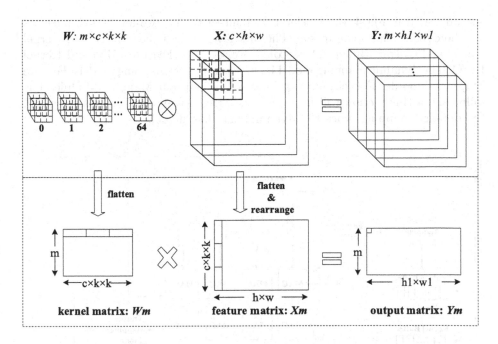

Fig. 3. Mapping convolutions to matrix multiplication operations.

3.3   Mapping Convolutions to Matrix Multiplications

Mapping convolution to matrix multiplication is an efficient implementation on FPGA. As illustrated in Fig. 3, the kernel of the convolutional layer is W with dimensions of $m \times c \times k \times k$, the input feature of X with dimensions of $c \times h \times w$, and W and X are convolved to obtain the output feature Y with dimensions of $m \times h1 \times w1$. Where m is the size of output channels, c is the size of input channels, k is the size of the convolution kernel, h is the size of input feature height, w is the size of input feature width, $h1$ is the size of output feature height, $w1$ is the size of the output feature width. The matrix multiplication method of convolution operation compresses the weight W into a weight matrix Wm, compresses and reorganizes the feature map X into a feature map matrix Xm. The result of the matrix multiplication is an output matrix Ym with dimensions of $m \times (h1 \times w1)$, which is the flattened format of the output feature. Generally, h is equal to $h1$ and w is equal to $w1$, but dilated convolution combines convolution and downsampling, thus $h1$ and $w1$ will become smaller than h and w.

In addition, Xm is almost $(k \times k)$-fold of X because of data replications during mapping. It can be avoided by reusing the overlapped data during the sliding of convolutional windows.

4   Accelerator Architecture Design

As illustrated in Fig. 4, the accelerator architecture has two-level on-chip caches for the dynamic mapping model. The first level cache is Feature Buffer, Kernel Buffer and Output Buffer. The second level cache is Feature FIFO and Kernel FIFO. The dynamic mapping model includes three sub-mapping models: Feature Mapping Module, Kernel Mapping Module, and Output Mapping Module. The following of this section will introduce the MAC Array and Buffer setting and the detailed mapping process of dynamic mapping model.

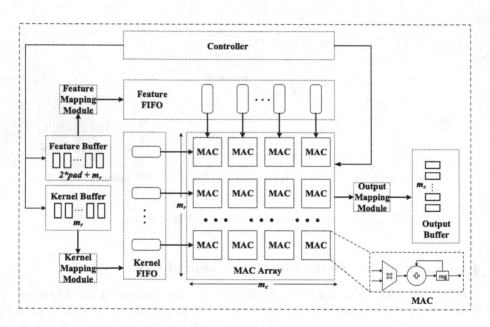

Fig. 4. Accelerator architecture with dynamic mapping model.

4.1   MAC Array and Buffer Setting

The MAC array is computing resource for matrix multiplication. As shown in Fig. 4, the MAC array includes $m_r \times m_c$ MAC units, where m_r and m_c are the size MAC array row and column respectively. The MAC unit consists of a multiplier, an adder, and a register. The register is used to store intermediate result. The MAC array taps the two loop parallelism of the output channel and the output feature column direction. Each MAC unit is responsible for calculating the matrix multiplication result of the corresponding position. Therefore, the

MAC array can calculate $m_r \times m_c$ elements in parallel. When the feature matrix and the kernel matrix is relatively large, the matrix can be divided into blocks. The kernel matrix is divided into $\lceil \frac{m}{m_r} \rceil$ blocks and the feature matrix is divided into $\lceil \frac{h1 \times w1}{m_c} \rceil$ blocks.

Limited by the chip area, the depth of the Kernel Buffer is limited. The Kernel Buffer depth required to load a complete convolutional layer is $d \times c \times k \times k$. When the input channel or the convolution kernel is large, or the temporal dimension parameter of the 3D network is large, the storage space that the layer needs will exceed the depth of the Kernel Buffer. We need to split a large convolution layer into the sum of multiple small convolution layers. Similarly, the depth of the Feature Buffer is also limited. The Feature Buffer depth required to load $k + stride$ rows feature is $d \times c \times (k + stride) \times \lceil \frac{w}{m_c} \rceil$, When the convolutional layer parameters are too large, it is also necessary to load features in blocks. Although the additional summation operation to be introduced may affect the performance of the accelerator, it ensures the versatility of the accelerator.

4.2 Dynamic Mapping Model

DRPMA. Matrix multiplication exploits the two loop level parallelism of output channel and output feature column direction. In CNN, the numbers of output channels of different convolutional layers vary greatly. For example, the output channel numbers of VGG16 are 64, 128, 256, 512. When the MAC array are designed with the dimensions of 256×32, the residue between the output channels and the MAC rows are 64, 128, 0 and 0. We cannot make full use of the MAC array with residue of 64 and 128. Through analysis, we find that the reusability in the row direction of the sliding window can be used to improve the parallelism of matrix multiplication when a residue is generated. As the residue changes dynamically with the number of output channels of the convolutional layer. We name the method of dynamic mapping based on residue as DRPMA. Assuming the residue is R, the parallelism of matrix multiplication can be improved by DRPMA is n, then the parallelism can be defined by the following formula:

$$as \quad \frac{m_r}{R} \geq 2, \quad n = \lfloor \frac{m_r}{R} \rfloor, \ 1 \leq n \leq k \tag{1}$$

$$as \quad 1 \leq \frac{m_r}{R} \leq 2, \quad n = 1 \tag{2}$$

DCMA. Dilated convolution extract the feature separated by $rate - 1$ in both the row and column directions that the reusability in row direction has lost, which means $n = 1$. The data reuse of dilated convolution in the column direction is presented every $rate - 1$, It is same as convolution when $rate = 1$. We can load the feature step by $rate - 1$ offset, the reusability of convolution and dilated convolution in the column direction can be utilized through a consistent pattern. We name the mapping method of reuse data in the column direction both for convolution and dilated convolution as DCMA. With the two algorithms of DRPMA and DCMA, We can efficiently map convolution and dilated to matrix multiplication. The following of this section will introduce the details of mapping methods.

As shown in Fig. 4, the Feature Mapping Module is connected to the Feature Buffer and Feature FIFO, and is used to map the feature in the $2 \times pad + m_c$ Block RAMs to m_c feature FIFOs. In order to save on-chip memory, the Feature Buffer only stores the $k + stride$ rows data of the input feature. When performing matrix multiplication, the Feature Buffer will prefetch the stride rows data from the external chip. The complete mapping process is as Algorithm 1.

As shown in Fig. 4, the Kernel Mapping Module is connected to the Kernel Buffer and the Kernel FIFO, and is used to map the kernel from the m_r kernel Block RAMs to the m_r kernel FIFOs. In order to save on-chip memory, the Kernel Buffer only stores the m_r rows data in the kernel matrix. The complete mapping process is as Algorithm 2.

As shown in Fig. 4, the Output Mapping Module is connected to the MAC array and Output Buffer, and is used to control the way of convolution results to Output Buffer. The Output Buffer adopts the Ping-Pong mechanism. The complete mapping process is as Algorithm 3.

Algorithm 1. Generate Feature Matrix

Input: X
Output: Xm
    for $i = 1, 2, \ldots, k + stride$
        for $j = 1, 2, \ldots, d \times c$
            for $t = 1, 2, \ldots, w$
                do store in $2 \times pad + m_c$ **feature buffer**
    for $i = 1, 2, \ldots, k \times d \times c$
        for $j = 0, rate, \ldots, (k - 1) \times rate$
            do send to m_c **feature fifo**

Algorithm 2. Generate Kernel Matrix

Input: W
Output: Wm
    for $i = 1, 2, \ldots, m_r$
        for $j = 1, 2, \ldots, k$
            for $t = 1, 2, \ldots, d \times c$
                for $q = 1, 2, \ldots, k$
                    do store in the i_{th} **kernel buffer**
    if $n == 1$
        for $i = 1, 2, \ldots, k$
        do store in the i_{th} **kernel fifo**
    else
        for $j = 1, 2, \ldots, n$
            for $t = 1, 2, \ldots, m$
                do store in the $(n \times m + t)_{th}$ **kernel fifo**

Algorithm 3. Dynamic output mapping algorithm

Input: Yi, The i_{th} results of the m_c columns
Output: Ym
  if $n == 1$
  for $i = 1, 2, \ldots, m_r$
    do store the i_{th} Yi in the m_c column output buffer
  else
    for $j = 1, 2, \ldots, n$
      for $i = 1, 2, \ldots, m$
        do store the t_{th} Yi in the m_c column output buffer
        wait $k \times d \times c$ cycles
        do store the $(n \times m + t)_{th}$ Yi in the m_c column output buffer

---

5   Evaluation

5.1   Experimental Setup

We evaluate the effectiveness of the dynamic mapping model by implementing a RISC-V+CNN heterogeneous system prototype on the Xilinx VC709 FPGA platform with 3600 DSP, 1470 BRAM, and two on-chip DDR. We assign 128 rows and 16 columns for the MAC array. Accordingly, the kernel buffer has 128 Block RAMs with depth of 1024, the feature buffer has 26 Block RAMs with depth of 4096, and the Ping-Pong output buffer has 32 Block RAMs with depth of 1024. The kernel FIFO and feature FIFO have 144 Block RAMs with depth of 512. Three typical CNNs: VGG16, C3D, and Resnet18 are tested on heterogeneous system. The CNN parameters and feature are 16-bit floating point. The software versions are implemented with Caffe on Intel Core i7-4790K CPU@ 4.0 GHz. The clock frequencies of the RISC-V CPU and CNN are 20 MHz and 100 MHz respectively.

5.2   Experimental Results

Table 1 reports the hardware resource utilization of our heterogeneous system. The RISC-V and CNN accelerator consume most of the hardware resources. RISC-V uses 290 Block RAMs to support for large-capacity data cache and instruction cache, which can adapt to complex application scenarios. The CNN accelerator consumes 382 Block RAMs for data buffering, and the heterogeneous system uses 676 Block RAMs totally. The MAC array consumes 2048 of the 2080 DSP slices for computing matrix multiplications and the other 32 DSP slices are used for building floating-point arithmetic units.

Table 1. Heterogeneous system resource utilization.

Module	DSP		BRAM		LUT	
RISC-V	32	0.8%	290	19.7%	57078	13%
CNN	2048	56.9%	382	26.0%	232752	54%
Sum	2080	57.7%	676	46.0%	307572	71%

The experiment selects VGG16 to test the effectiveness of the DRPMA. Table 2 presents the evaluation results of three layers in VGG16. The residues of conv1a, conv1b, conv2a are 64, 64, and 0 respectively. The MAC array utilization and throughput are 83.7% and 342.8GFLOP/s on conv1a and 95.3% and 390.3GFLOP/s on conv1b with DRPMA. Without the DRPMA, the MAC array utilization and throughput are 42.5% on conv1a and 48.1% and on conv1b. The MAC array utilization and throughput are the same on conv2a as the R is 0. We can conclude that the DRPMA almost increases 2× utilization of MAC array. Additionally, we can reduce MAC array column width to reduce the memory access bandwidth with DRPMA.

Table 2. DRPMA performance.

Layer	conv1a		conv1b		conv2a	
R	64		64		0	
DRPMA	83.7%	342.8	95.3%	390.3	94.2%	385.8
No	42.5%	174.1	48.1%	197.0	94.2%	385.8

The experiment also selects VGG16 to test the performance of the DCMA. We uses the Hybrid Dilated Convolution method from [1] to set rate group as 1, 2, 5. Table 3 presents the evaluation results. When the *rate* is 1, the throughput remains unchanged. When the *rate* is 2, the MAC array utilization is 89.7%, a decrease of 5%. This is caused by the load feature time increase and the idle state of the MAC array increase. When the *rate* is 5, the utilization of the MAC array is reduced by 23%. The main reason is that the feature Block RAMs we set is 26. And the Block RAMs used for padding is 10, which supports the maximum convolution kernel of the same size output is 11. The dilated convolution with a *rate* of 5 is essentially equivalent to the standard convolution with a convolution kernel of 14. This means that only the first 13 columns of the MAC array can be used. Therefore, the utilization rate of MAC array decreases sharply. In conclusion, the DCMA can efficiently support dilated convolution.

Table 3. DCMA performance.

Rate	1	2	5
Utilization (%)	94.2%	89.7%	71.6%
Throughput (GFLOP/S)	385.8	367.4	293.3

Table 4 lists the comparisons between the CPU and heterogeneous system. The heterogeneous system achieves a 5.1× and 5.3× and 24.2× and 32.6 × improvement than CPU in VGG16 and Resnet18 in terms of throughput and energy efficiency respectively. After ASIC, the energy efficiency advantage will be more obvious.

Table 4. Evaluation results on the CPU and our accelerator.

CNN model	VGG16		Resnet18	
	CPU	FPGA	CPU	FPGA
Power (W)	88	13.6	88	13.6
ThroughputGFLOP/S	63.9	329.3	66.5	354.4
Energy Efficiency (GFLOP/s/W)	0.7	24.2	0.8	26.1

Table 5 shows the comparisons with other FPGA platforms. Our heterogeneous system achieves an overall throughput of 329.3 GFLOP/s on VGG16 and 310.2GFLOP/s on Resnet18 respectively. The throughput of the heterogeneous system is better than [16] on VGG16 and lower than [10] on C3D. The usage of DSP slices determines the throughput to a certain extent. [10] high throughput is based on larger MAC array, high on-chip buffering and high bandwidth. When heterogeneous system runs C3D, the convolutional layer will be split which affects the performance. Our throughput will increase 4 × after ASIC which is the best. It needs to be emphasized that our heterogeneous system is a better choice after balancing price, versatility and performance.

Table 5. Comparisons with previous accelerator implementations.

	[16]	[10]	Ours	
FPGA	Altera StratixV	Xilinx VX690T	Xilinx VX690T	
Precision	fixed	fixed	float16	
CNN Model	VGG16	C3D	VGG16	C3D
Clock (MHz)	120	120	100	
DSPs	727	3595	2080	
Throughput (GOP/S)	118	667.7	329.3	310.2

6   Conclusions

This paper studies the mapping methods that convert convolution into matrix multiplication, and proposes a new dynamic mapping model, which improves the flexibility and versatility of matrix multiplication. The heterogeneous system prototype based on FPGA platform verifies the performance of the dynamic mapping model. And it can be applied to more complex artificial intelligence scenarios without reconfiguring the FPGA. Future work include demonstrations on dilated Resnet applications and efficient support of transposed convolution.

References

1. Abdel-Hamid, O., Mohamed, A.R., Jiang, H., Deng, L., Penn, G., Yu, D.: Convolutional neural networks for speech recognition. IEEE/ACM Trans. Audio Speech Lang. Process. **22**(10), 1533–1545 (2014)
2. Azizimazreah, A., Chen, L.: Shortcut mining: exploiting cross-layer shortcut reuse in DCNN accelerators. In: 2019 IEEE International Symposium on High Performance Computer Architecture (HPCA), pp. 94–105. IEEE (2019)
3. Girshick, R., Donahue, J., Darrell, T., Malik, J.: Rich feature hierarchies for accurate object detection and semantic segmentation. In: Proceedings of the IEEE Conference on Computer Vision and Pattern Recognition, pp. 580–587 (2014)
4. Hinton, G., et al.: Deep neural networks for acoustic modeling in speech recognition: the shared views of four research groups. IEEE Signal Process. Mag. **29**(6), 82–97 (2012)
5. Kim, D., Ahn, J., Yoo, S.: A novel zero weight/activation-aware hardware architecture of convolutional neural network. In: 2017 Design, Automation & Test in Europe Conference & Exhibition (DATE), pp. 1462–1467. IEEE (2017)
6. Krizhevsky, A., Sutskever, I., Hinton, G.E.: ImageNet classification with deep convolutional neural networks. In: Advances in Neural Information Processing Systems, pp. 1097–1105 (2012)
7. Lavin, A., Gray, S.: Fast algorithms for convolutional neural networks. In: Proceedings of the IEEE Conference on Computer Vision and Pattern Recognition, pp. 4013–4021 (2016)
8. Lin, S., et al.: FFT-based deep learning deployment in embedded systems. In: 2018 Design, Automation & Test in Europe Conference & Exhibition (DATE), pp. 1045–1050. IEEE (2018)
9. Liu, X., Kim, D.H., Wu, C., Chen, O.: Resource and data optimization for hardware implementation of deep neural networks targeting FPGA-based edge devices. In: 2018 ACM/IEEE International Workshop on System Level Interconnect Prediction (SLIP), pp. 1–8. IEEE (2018)
10. Liu, Z., Chow, P., Xu, J., Jiang, J., Dou, Y., Zhou, J.: A uniform architecture design for accelerating 2D and 3D CNNs on FPGAs. Electronics **8**(1), 65 (2019)
11. Lu, L., Liang, Y.: SPWA: an efficient sparse winograd convolutional neural networks accelerator on FPGAs. In: 2018 55th ACM/ESDA/IEEE Design Automation Conference (DAC), pp. 1–6. IEEE (2018)
12. Ma, Y., Cao, Y., Vrudhula, S., Seo, J.S.: Optimizing loop operation and dataflow in FPGA acceleration of deep convolutional neural networks. In: Proceedings of the 2017 ACM/SIGDA International Symposium on Field-Programmable Gate Arrays, pp. 45–54 (2017)

13. Nair, V., Hinton, G.E.: 3D object recognition with deep belief nets. In: Advances in Neural Information Processing Systems, pp. 1339–1347 (2009)
14. Ramanishka, V., et al.: Multimodal video description. In: Proceedings of the 24th ACM International Conference on Multimedia, pp. 1092–1096 (2016)
15. Simonyan, K., Zisserman, A.: Very deep convolutional networks for large-scale image recognition. arXiv preprint arXiv:1409.1556 (2014)
16. Suda, N., et al.: Throughput-optimized OpenCL-based FPGA accelerator for large-scale convolutional neural networks. In: Proceedings of the 2016 ACM/SIGDA International Symposium on Field-Programmable Gate Arrays, pp. 16–25 (2016)
17. Wu, D., Chen, J., Cao, W., Wang, L.: A novel low-communication energy-efficient reconfigurable CNN acceleration architecture. In: 2018 28th International Conference on Field Programmable Logic and Applications (FPL), pp. 64–643. IEEE (2018)
18. Wu, E., Zhang, X., Berman, D., Cho, I.: A high-throughput reconfigurable processing array for neural networks. In: 2017 27th International Conference on Field Programmable Logic and Applications (FPL), pp. 1–4. IEEE (2017)
19. Yang, K., Qiao, P., Li, D., Lv, S., Dou, Y.: Exploring temporal preservation networks for precise temporal action localization. arXiv preprint arXiv:1708.03280 (2017)
20. Zeng, H., Chen, R., Zhang, C., Prasanna, V.: A framework for generating high throughput CNN implementations on FPGAs. In: Proceedings of the 2018 ACM/SIGDA International Symposium on Field-Programmable Gate Arrays, pp. 117–126 (2018)
21. Zhang, C., Prasanna, V.: Frequency domain acceleration of convolutional neural networks on CPU-FPGA shared memory system. In: Proceedings of the 2017 ACM/SIGDA International Symposium on Field-Programmable Gate Arrays, pp. 35–44 (2017)

A Dynamic Protection Mechanism
for GPU Memory Overflow

Yaning Yang[1], Xiaoqi Wang[1], and Shaoliang Peng[1,2(✉)]

[1] College of Computer Science and Electronic Engineering, Hunan University,
Changsha 410082, China
{yangyn,xqw,slpeng}@hnu.edu.cn
[2] National Supercomputing Centre in Changsha, Changsha 410082, China

Abstract. Graphics Processing Units (GPU) are widely used to accelerate computation in many applications such as autonomous vehicles, artificial intelligence and healthcare. However, most existing researches just focus on the performance but ignore the security issues of GPUs. In this paper, we design an efficient mechanism to dynamically monitor GPU heap buffer overflow by using the CPU. Concretely, we first analyze the specific requirements of GPU memory allocation. Second, in order to realize the monitoring from the CPU, we map the allocated device memory to the host-side. Third, the dynamic monitoring of buffer overflow is implemented based on the mapped memory. Our results show that it is feasible to protect the GPU memory from the CPU side. Our work can improve the efficiency of GPU memory allocation and increase the security at the same time. By offloading the detection of buffer overflow to the CPU, the performance of GPU kernels will not be affected significantly.

Keywords: GPGPU · Memory allocation · Security · Memory overflow

1 Introduction

With the development of parallel computing, more and more programmers are willing to choose GPUs from vendors such as NVIDIA for high performance computing. For example, GPUs are often used to accelerate scientific compute-intensive tasks and finance operations [1]. In the field of real-time embedded systems, GPUs also show good performance advantages [2]. Further, most encryption algorithms are implemented based on GPU [3–5]. In addition, GPUs can be virtualized [6], so many cloud computing providers provide users with GPU support, enabling users to share GPUs.

Indeed, GPUs offer tremendous advantages in parallel computing, especially in some complex computing areas such as artificial intelligence [7]. However, there are certain security vulnerabilities on the GPU [8,9], such as buffer overflow. Buffer overflow is a software error caused by accessing data outside the

X. He et al. (Eds.): NPC 2020, LNCS 12639, pp. 30–40, 2021.
https://doi.org/10.1007/978-3-030-79478-1_3

buffer. It is a long-standing and common software vulnerability. Once the buffer overflows, it may cause the program to fail, system down, restart, and so on. More seriously, it can be used to execute unauthorized instructions, and even to obtain system privileges, and thus carry out various illegal operations. Infamous security attacks such as Code Red, Slammer and Morris Worm are all based on buffer overflow. If these problems occur on the GPU, it may cause the leakage of sensitive data, especially when performing computational financial operations and encryption algorithms. At present, most of the research on the vulnerability of buffer overflow targets the CPU. NVIDIA provides a tool CUDA-MEMCHECK [10] as a part of the CUDA toolkit, which can be used to detect out of bounds and misaligned memory access errors in CUDA applications, but it is clearly stated that applications would run much slower if using CUDA-MEMCHECK to detect memory errors and it may lead to failures of kernel launches such as timeout.

In response to the existence of GPU buffer overflows and the high overhead of existing tools, we design an efficient mechanism that leverages the CPU to dynamically monitor GPU heap buffer overflows. First, because of the efficiency issue of *cudaMalloc* provided by CUDA [11–13], we use *ScatterAlloc* [14] to allocate memory on the GPU. Second, we leverage the unified memory mechanism to implement our system, which has the advantage of allowing the CPU to access the memory allocated on the GPU. Third, we insert different canaries to the head and tail of dynamically allocated buffers and create a dedicated monitoring thread on the CPU to continuously detect buffer overflow. Once the canary is modified, it indicates an event of buffer overflow. The reason we use the CPU to detect buffer overflows is that if both the monitoring thread and the user threads are performed on the GPU, resource contention will inevitably occur in highly concurrent applications, which will result in high performance overhead.

The remainder of the paper is organized as follows. In Sect. 2, we introduce the background about CUDA programming model. We describe the overall design of our system and the structure of the buffer in Sect. 3 and specific implementation details in Sect. 4. Experimental evaluation is given in Sect. 5 and conclude this paper in Sect. 6.

2 Background

2.1 CUDA Programming Model

CUDA is a general-purpose parallel computing architecture introduced by NVIDIA that enables GPUs to solve complex computing problems. It includes the CUDA Instruction Set Architecture (ISA) and the parallel computing engine inside the GPU. The CUDA code is divided into two parts, one running on the host (CPU), the normal C code, and the other part running on the device (GPU), which is called kernel. In CUDA, the host and device have different memory spaces, so when executing the kernel on the device, the programmer needs to explicitly transfer the data on the host memory to the device memory. After the kernel is executed, the result needs to be transferred from the device memory back to the host memory and the device memory should be released. The CUDA runtime system provides APIs for programmers to perform these operations. A kernel is declared with the keyword _global_. A running kernel is composed of a large number of GPU threads, Threads are grouped into *blocks*, and blocks are grouped into *grids*. When the host calls a kernel, the programmer must set the dimensions of the grid and thread block with certain parameters.

2.2   Unified Memory

In the above programming model, it is necessary to separately define pointers for the host and the device and allocate memory separately on the host side and the device side, and to make an explicit copy between the CPU and GPU memory before and after the kernel is called. This procedure is tedious and error-prone. CUDA 6.0 introduces a feature called unified memory that greatly simplifies the implementation of CUDA applications [15]. The user only needs to define a pointer that can be used on both the host and the device, and the explicit memory copy is not need any more.

2.3   GPU Allocator Optimization

In terms of dynamically managing GPU memory, the current CUDA programming model supports the dynamic allocation and deallocation of device memory using APIs such as *cudaMalloc* and *cudaFree*, but the GPU needs to interrupt the CPU execution during the process of memory allocation, which has a significant impact on the performance of data-intensive applications in high-concurrency environments. In order to reduce the blocking phenomenon between threads, several approaches can be used, such as optimistic concurrency control and multi-version concurrency control. For example, we can allocate a new memory space before modifying the data and copy the new data to this space for modification, then use it to replace the old version data. The invalid data is processed by the garbage collection mechanism. This mechanism greatly increases the frequency of memory allocation requests. Most experiments show that using *cudaMalloc* and *cudaFree* provided by CUDA for memory allocation is very inefficient [11–14]. Therefore, many researchers have done a lot of work on GPU memory management and developed new allocators, such as XMalloc [11] and ScatterAlloc [14], which are optimized for dynamic memory allocation. Experiments show that ScatterAlloc is approximately 100 times faster than the CUDA toolkit allocator and up to 10 times faster than XMalloc. Therefore, we choose ScatterAlloc to manage the GPU memory in our system.

There are multiple global heaps in ScatterAlloc. The memory allocation request is directed to a different global heap by a hash operation, which reduces the probability of collisions accessing the global heap. ScatterAlloc divides memory into fixed-size pages and the pages are split into equally-sized chunks. In order to find free memory space in a page, ScatterAlloc employs a *pageusagetable* and every entry consists of three values: the chunk size, the number of allocated chunks, and a bitfield. Each bit in the bitfield represents a single chunk of memory. These fixed-size pages are gathered in super blocks, which form the largest memory unit.

3 Design Overview

3.1 Buffer Structure

For buffer overflow detection, the most common way is to add a *canary* to the buffer structure, such as StackGuard [16]. In Cruiser [17], it adds different canary words to the head and tail of the buffer. Thus, we also add canary words to the buffer in a conventional way. The specific method is to add different canaries to the head and tail of the buffer, that is, the *headcanary* and the *tailcanary* as shown in Fig. 1. In addition to canaries, we also add encryption information about the buffer size to the buffer structure. If the head canary is changed, it means that the buffer is underflowed. Similarly, the buffer is overflowed if the tail canary is corrupted. The purpose of adding the buffer size information is to locate the tail canary given a buffer address. Because we encrypt the buffer size information, it will not be leaked to attackers. The value of head canary is the result of encryption of the head canary key, the buffer size, and the buffer address. The tail canary is calculated in the same way, but with another tail canary key. In this way, the head canary and the tail canary of different buffers are different. Even if the head canary and the tail canary of one memory block are leaked, other memory blocks are safe.

Head canary	Word size	Buffer	Tail canary

Fig. 1. Buffer structure.

3.2 Overview of the System

Our design goal is to increase the efficiency of GPU parallel computing as much as possible without compromising security due to GPU buffer overflow. Therefore, we propose to leverage CPU to monitor the GPU memory by separating the monitoring thread from the user threads. The advantage of this method is that the monitoring thread does not compete with the user threads for resources, allowing the user threads to perform the corresponding calculation with maximum efficiency and the data used by the user threads is also protected. This approach ensures that applications are both efficient and secure. As shown in Fig. 2, after a buffer is allocated, we encapsulate the address of the allocated buffer into an address collection. And the user threads running on the GPU can operate the buffer normally and the monitoring thread running on the CPU will continuously monitor the corresponding buffer wrapped in the address collection. The whole process is mainly divided into three steps. First, the system allocates a buffer that is 3 words larger than what user thread requests, and the reason for adding extra 3 words is that we add two canaries and the buffer size information in the buffer structure as described in Sect. 3.1. In the second step, we encapsulate the allocated buffer and then add the buffer information to an address collection. The monitoring thread traverses the entire address collection to determine if there are buffer overflows. In the third step, when a buffer is freed, we mark the first word of the buffer as released. The monitoring thread then removes this buffer from the address collection when it checks the buffer and finds that the buffer is marked released.

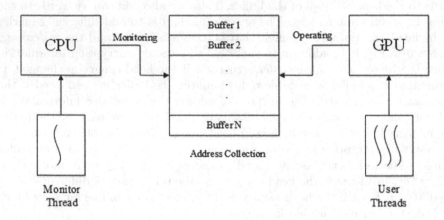

Fig. 2. System architecture.

There is a shortcoming in our system, which is that we check the canaries after the kernel is finished, because real-time detection may lead to high overhead due to frequent transmission of memory pages between the CPU and GPU. Concurrent accesses to the same memory page may lead to page swapping between the two ends. For example, a dirty page on the GPU would cause a swapping to the CPU when the monitoring thread reads the same page. In our future work, we plan to optimize this procedure by analyzing memory access patterns and make our system an online solution.

4   Implementation

4.1   Memory Allocation

In this paper, we allocate memory space by using the ScatterAlloc allocator. First, we allocate a large memory pool which is unified memory by calling the *cudaMallocManaged* function and return a void pointer, see Code 1 (from line 1 to 5). Second, we declare a pointer by adding the _managed_ keyword, which points to a block of unified memory (line 6). The actual allocation is done in a kernel (from line 7 to 9) which is called in a host function (line 13). In the original ScatterAlloc, a large memory pool was allocated by calling *cudaMalloc*, which can only be read/written on device side. To allocate memory blocks on this memory pool, it needs to read and write this memory pool. So the ScatterAlloc defined its allocation function on the device side and it was called by the kernel.

We just copied this manner of allocation. Because we encapsulate a buffer by adding two canaries and buffer size information, the actual allocation size is increased by 3 extra words.

Code 1: Memory Allocation

```
 1  static void* setMemPool(size_t memsize){
 2    void* pool = NULL;
 3    cudaMallocManaged(&pool, memsize);
 4    return pool;
 5  }
 6  __device__ __managed__ unsigned long *buffer;
 7  __global__ void alloc(size_t size, AllocHandle mMC){
 8    buffer = (unsigned long*) mMC.malloc(size);
 9  }
10  void run(){
11    ...
12    ScatterAllocator mMC(1U*1024U*1024U*1024U);
13    alloc<<<blocks,threads>>>(size + 3, mMC);
14    cudaDeviceSynchronize();
15    ...
16  }
```

4.2   Buffer Structure Construction

We have already described the structure of the buffer in Sect. 3.2, see Code 2 for the specific implementation. First, we declare a pointer p that is used to encapsulate the buffer $addr$ (line 3), then insert the head canary, tail canary, and buffer size information, which are encrypted results with encryption algorithms (from line 4 to 6). Finally, the encapsulated buffer structure is added to the thread record list by calling the $produce$ function.

Code 2: Constructing Buffer Structure

```
 1  inline void afterMalloc(void* addr, size_t word_size){
 2    ...
 3    unsigned long *p = (unsigned long *)addr;
 4    p[0] = head_canary ^ new_word_size;
 5    p[1] = new_word_size;
 6    p[2 + word_size] = tail_canary ^ new_word_size;
 7    Node node;
 8    node.userAddr = p + 2;
 9    t_threadRecord=g_threadrecordlist->getThreadRecord();
10    t_threadRecord->produce(node);
11  }
```

In some highly concurrent applications, memory allocation will occur frequently, so the $afterMalloc$ function will be called multiple times. In order to eliminate the overheads of function calls, we define it as an inline function by adding the keyword $inline$.

4.3 Buffer Overflow Detection

Once a buffer is released, the encapsulation of the buffer address information in the address collection is expired and should be removed. If a buffer is about to be released, we set the value of its first element (head canary) to zero. A buffer overflow depends on the value of the canaries we inserted before. The method *beforeFree* in Code 3 is exactly the opposite of *afterMalloc* as described in Sect. 4.2. First, we define a pointer variable p that is used to decapsulate the buffer address. The next step is to check the first two elements (the head canary and buffer size information) and the last element (tail canary) of the buffer, respectively. Because we mark the first element of the buffer that has been released as zero, it indicates a double free if the value of $p[0]$ is detected as 0 (from line 4 to 7). When the monitoring thread checks a buffer and finds the value of *head_canary_free* stored in the address collection is not the same as the precomputed value by decrypting the *head_canary*, the buffer is underflowed. Similarly, the buffer is overflowed if the *tail_canary* is corrupted. Once the buffer is overflowed, the monitoring thread will call the function *attackDetected* to abort the application (from line 8 to 16). In addition, if the buffer size information ($p[1]$) is changed, the tail canary would not be located correctly. As a result, reading the tail canary may incur segmentation fault, which essentially exposes buffer overflows.

Code 3: Buffer Overflow Detection

```
1  inline static void beforeFree(void* addr){
2    ...
3    unsigned long *p = (unsigned long*)addr - 2;
4    if(!p[0]){
5      fprintf(stderr, "Duplicate frees are detected\n");
6      return;
7    }
8    size_t word_size = p[1];
9    unsigned long head_canary_free = p[0];
10   unsigned long tail_canary_free = p[2 + word_size];
11   if(head_canary_free != head_canary ^ word_size){
12     attackDetected(addr, 2);
13   }
14   if(tail_canary_free != tail_canary ^ word_size){
15     attackDetected(addr, 1);
16   }
17   ...
18   p[0] = 0;
19 }
```

5 Evaluation

This section reports the performance of the system, including memory allocation overheads. Our experimental setup is described in Sect. 5.1. In Sect. 5.2, we show

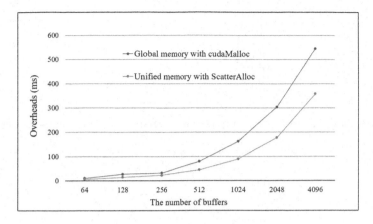

Fig. 3. Overheads about cudaMalloc and ScatterAlloc.

the feasibility of the experiment leveraging CPU to dynamically detect GPU buffer overflows and evaluate the performance overheads.

5.1 Experiment Setup

Our experiment was performed on Ubuntu 16.04.1. The CPU is Intel(R) Xeon(R) E5-2630 v3 clocked at 2.40 GHz and the host memory size is 32G. The GPU is the NVIDIA GeForce GTX 1070 (Pascal architecture) that has computing capability 6.1, 1920 CUDA Cores, 8 GB of GDDR5 memory. The CUDA runtime version is 9.0. We use *nvcc* to compile CUDA code.

5.2 Performance Analysis

Additional impact on system performance is mainly caused by memory allocation and buffer overflow detection. For memory allocation, we use *Scatter Alloc* allocator to allocate memory. As the number of threads continues to increase, the performance of the allocator almost remains essentially at a constant level. In the case of full use of the GPU, the memory allocation using ScatterAlloc is 100 times faster than the CUDA toolkit allocator, 10 times faster than using SIMD optimized XMalloc [11]. On the other hand, related studies have shown that unnecessary data copies take 16% to 537% longer to execute than the actual data movement [18], which is not acceptable in high concurrency and data-intensive applications that employ GPUs. This inefficiency is solved in our system by declaring unified memory which can be accessed by the CPU and GPU at the same time. It is not necessary to use *cudaMemcpy* to copy data between CPU and GPU.

We use *Scatter Alloc* to allocate a series of buffers on the unified memory, the buffer size is 4096B. And we use *cudaMalloc* to allocate buffers of the same size and number on the global memory and perform a simple *kernel* that calculates

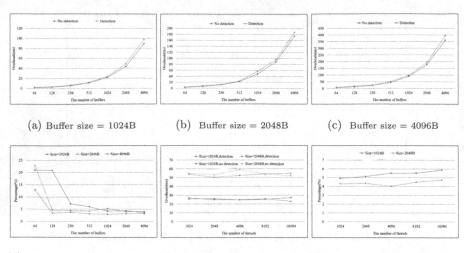

(a) Buffer size = 1024B   (b) Buffer size = 2048B   (c) Buffer size = 4096B

(d) Proportion of detection time (e) Overheads with different (f) Proportion of detection time
number of threads   with different number of threads

Fig. 4. Overheads of buffer overflow detection

the sum of two matrices with 4096 threads. Experiments show that the ratio of
the overheads of the two methods is about 60% on average. As we can see from
Fig. 3, the overhead of the first method is significantly lower than that of the
second one.

For the performance overheads of buffer overflow detection, we test the
impact of the buffer overflow detection on the overall application in the case
of different sizes and the number of allocated buffers with a fine-tuned benchmark called CUDA-quicksort [19] with 16384 threads. All results reported in this
section are average values of 10 runs. A large number of experiments have proved
that our method has little impact on system performance. As we can see from
the Fig. 4(a), 4(b), 4(c), when the buffer size is less than 512B, the overhead
when enabling the overflow detection is almost negligible. Even when the buffer
size is larger than 512B, the overhead incurred by buffer overflow detection is
only slightly higher than that when the detection is disabled. Figure 4(d) shows
how the overhead of buffer overflow detection varies with different buffer sizes.
When the buffer size is increased from 64B to 512B, the overhead caused by the
detection is gradually decreasing. As the size is larger than 512B, the overhead
remains basically unchanged at around 4%.

We also test the impact of the number of GPU threads on performance. In
Fig. 4(e), we allocate 1024 buffers of 1024B and 2048B, respectively, and measure
the performance overhead of overflow detection as compared to the case when
detection is disabled. In this experiment, the number of threads is variable. The
experimental results show that under the same conditions, when the number of

threads increases from 1024 to 16384, the overheads remain basically unchanged. The detection overhead varies between 4%–6% as shown in Fig. 4(f). This means that the number of user threads does not affect the performance of overflow detection significantly.

6 Conclusion

In this paper, we discuss the issue of GPU memory management, including the optimization of memory allocation and the use of unified memory, and we study the GPU buffer overflow problem. On this basis, we propose a new mechanism for dynamically detecting GPU memory overflow and design a prototype system that uses the CPU to detect GPU buffer. Our tests show that in high-concurrency and data-intensive applications, the performance overhead is only about 4%–6%. With this mechanism, the overflow of GPU heap memory can be effectively prevented.

Acknowledgment. This work was supported by NSFC Grants U19A2067, 61772543, U1435222, 61625202, 61272056; National Key R&D Program of China 2017YFB0202602, 2018YFC0910405, 2017YFC1311003, 2016YFC1302500, 2016YFB0200400, 2017YFB0202104; The Funds of Peng Cheng Lab, State Key Laboratory of Chemo/Biosensing and Chemometrics; the Fundamental Research Funds for the Central Universities, and Guangdong Provincial Department of Science and Technology under grant No. 2016B090918122.

References

1. Gaikwad, A., Toke, I.M.: Parallel iterative linear solvers on GPU: a financial engineering case. In: 2010 18th Euromicro Conference on Parallel, Distributed and Network-based Processing, pp. 607–614. IEEE (2010)
2. Kim, J., Rajkumar, R., Kato, S.: Towards adaptive GPU resource management for embedded real-time systems. ACM SIGBED Rev. **10**(1), 14–17 (2013)
3. Di Biagio, A., Barenghi, A., Agosta, G., Pelosi, G.: Design of a parallel AES for graphics hardware using the CUDA framework. In: 2009 IEEE International Symposium on Parallel & Distributed Processing, pp. 1–8. IEEE (2009)
4. Vasiliadis, G., Athanasopoulos, E., Polychronakis, M., Ioannidis, S.: PixelVault: using GPUs for securing cryptographic operations. In: Proceedings of the 2014 ACM SIGSAC Conference on Computer and Communications Security, pp. 1131–1142 (2014)
5. Nishikawa, N., Iwai, K., Kurokawa, T.: High-performance symmetric block ciphers on CUDA. In: 2011 Second International Conference on Networking and Computing, pp. 221–227. IEEE (2011)
6. Shi, L., Chen, H., Sun, J., Li, K.: vCUDA: GPU-accelerated high-performance computing in virtual machines. IEEE Trans. Comput. **61**(6), 804–816 (2011)
7. Le, Y., Wang, Z.J., Quan, Z., He, J., Yao, B.: ACV-tree: a new method for sentence similarity modeling. In: IJCAI, pp. 4137–4143 (2018)

8. Di, B., Sun, J., Chen, H.: A study of overflow vulnerabilities on GPUs. In: Gao, G.R., Qian, D., Gao, X., Chapman, B., Chen, W. (eds.) NPC 2016. LNCS, vol. 9966, pp. 103–115. Springer, Cham (2016). https://doi.org/10.1007/978-3-319-47099-3_9

9. Di, B., Sun, J., Li, D., Chen, H., Quan, Z.: GMOD: a dynamic GPU memory overflow detector. In: Proceedings of the 27th International Conference on Parallel Architectures and Compilation Techniques, pp. 1–13 (2018)

10. Nvidia: CUDA-MEMCHECK. https://developer.nvidia.com/cuda-memcheck. Accessed 26 Aug 2020

11. Huang, X., Rodrigues, C.I., Jones, S., Buck, I., Hwu, W.M.: XMalloc: a scalable lock-free dynamic memory allocator for many-core machines. In: 2010 10th IEEE International Conference on Computer and Information Technology, pp. 1134–1139. IEEE (2010)

12. Widmer, S., Wodniok, D., Weber, N., Goesele, M.: Fast dynamic memory allocator for massively parallel architectures. In: Proceedings of the 6th Workshop on General Purpose Processor Using Graphics Processing Units, pp. 120–126 (2013)

13. Huang, X., Rodrigues, C.I., Jones, S., Buck, I., Hwu, W.M.: Scalable SIMD-parallel memory allocation for many-core machines. J. Supercomput. **64**(3), 1008–1020 (2013)

14. Steinberger, M., Kenzel, M., Kainz, B., Schmalstieg, D.: ScatterAlloc: massively parallel dynamic memory allocation for the GPU. In: 2012 Innovative Parallel Computing (InPar), pp. 1–10. IEEE (2012)

15. Unified Memory. http://on-demand.gputechconf.com/gtc/2018/presentation/s8430-everything-you-need-to-know-about-unified-memory.pdf. Accessed 26 Aug 2020

16. Cowan, C., et al.: StackGuard: automatic adaptive detection and prevention of buffer-overflow attacks. In: USENIX Security Symposium, San Antonio, TX, vol. 98, pp. 63–78 (1998)

17. Zeng, Q., Wu, D., Liu, P.: Cruiser: concurrent heap buffer overflow monitoring using lock-free data structures. ACM SIGPLAN Not. **46**(6), 367–377 (2011)

18. Zhang, J., Donofrio, D., Shalf, J., Kandemir, M.T., Jung, M.: NVMMU: a non-volatile memory management unit for heterogeneous GPU-SSD architectures. In: 2015 International Conference on Parallel Architecture and Compilation (PACT), pp. 13–24. IEEE (2015)

19. Manca, E., Manconi, A., Orro, A., Armano, G., Milanesi, L.: CUDA-quicksort: an improved GPU-based implementation of quicksort. Concurr. Comput. Pract. Exp. **28**(1), 21–43 (2016)

AI

MTLAT: A Multi-Task Learning Framework Based on Adversarial Training for Chinese Cybersecurity NER

Yaopeng Han[1,2], Zhigang Lu[1,2], Bo Jiang[1,2], Yuling Liu[1,2], Chen Zhang[1],
Zhengwei Jiang[1,2], and Ning Li[1(✉)]

[1] Institute of Information Engineering, Chinese Academy of Sciences, Beijing, China
{hanyaopeng,luzhigang,jiangbo,liuyuling,zchen,jiangzhengwei,
lining6}@iie.ac.cn
[2] School of Cyber Security, University of Chinese Academy of Sciences,
Beijing, China

Abstract. With the continuous development of cybersecurity texts, the importance of Chinese cybersecurity named entity recognition (NER) is increasing. However, Chinese cybersecurity texts contain not only a large number of professional security domain entities but also many English person and organization entities, as well as a large number of Chinese-English mixed entities. Chinese Cybersecurity NER is a domain-specific task, current models rarely focus on the cybersecurity domain and cannot extract these entities well. To tackle these issues, we propose a **M**ulti-**T**ask **L**earning framework based on **A**dversarial **T**raining (MTLAT) to improve the performance of Chinese cybersecurity NER. Extensive experimental results show that our model, which does not use any external resources except static word embedding, outperforms state-of-the-art systems on the Chinese cybersecurity dataset. Moreover, our model outperforms the BiLSTM-CRF method on Weibo, Resume, and MSRA Chinese general NER datasets by 4.1%, 1.04%, 1.79% F1 scores, which proves the universality of our model in different domains.

Keywords: Cybersecurity · Named entity recognition · Adversarial training · Multi-task learning

1 Introduction

Named entity recognition is the task to identify entity boundaries and the recognition of categories of named entities, which is a fundamental task in the field of natural language processing (NLP).

The NER task in the general domain mainly identifies three types of entities: Person (PER), Organization (ORG), and Location (LOC).

Cybersecurity NER is a domain-specific task, which mainly extracts professional security entities from cybersecurity texts. In the domain of cybersecurity, English NER [5,18] research is much more than Chinese NER [16]. Compared

© IFIP International Federation for Information Processing 2021
Published by Springer Nature Switzerland AG 2021
X. He et al. (Eds.): NPC 2020, LNCS 12639, pp. 43–54, 2021.
https://doi.org/10.1007/978-3-030-79478-1_4

Case1: HIDDEN COBRA发动的多起攻击中，主要使用了包括DDoS僵尸网络、按键追踪及其他恶意程序工具如Destover、Wild Positron和Hangman等。
(Among the multiple attacks launched by HIDDEN COBRA, DDoS botnets, button tracking, and other malicious program tools such as Destover, Wild Positron, Hangman, etc. were mainly used.)

HIDDEN COBRA: Organization
DDos僵尸网络 (DDoS botnets), 恶意程序 (malicious program): Relevant Term
Destover, Hangman, Wild Positron: Software

Case2: 安全教育培训专家SunilYadav将会讨论一个案例，并介绍如何通过一个加密的Payload来发现并利用SQL注入漏洞。
(Security education expert SunilYadav will discuss a case and explain how to discover and exploit SQL injection vulnerabilities through an encrypted Payload.)

SunilYadav: Person
SQL注入漏洞 (SQL injection vulnerabilities), 加密 (encrypted), Payload: Relevant Term

Fig. 1. Examples of the Chinese cybersecurity NER dataset. Organization (ORG), Relevant Term (RT), Software (SW), and Person (PER) are categories of cybersecurity dataset entities.

with English NER, Chinese named entities are more challenging to identify due to their uncertain boundaries and complex composition. In this paper, we focus on Chinese cybersecurity NER. As shown in Fig. 1, compared with Chinese general NER tasks, entity extraction in the cybersecurity domain is a challenging task mainly because Chinese cybersecurity texts are often mixed with English entities, such as person, hacker organizations, and security-related entities (e.g., DDOS僵尸网络(*botnets*), SQL注入漏洞(*injection*))..

In this paper, we propose a novel framework, named multi-task learning based on adversarial training (MTLAT), to tackle the aforementioned challenges in Chinese cybersecurity NER. We design an auxiliary task to predict whether each token is an English entity, a Chinese entity or a non-entity to jointly train with NER task, which helps the model to learn semantic representations of named entities and to distinguish named entities from sequences in the Chinese cybersecurity domain. We also use Convolutional Neural Network (CNN) to enhance the ability of the model to capture local contextual information among characters sentences, which is also helpful for identifying English and security entities. Adversarial training is to enhance the security of machine learning systems [3] by making small perturbations to the input designed to significantly. In the NLP tasks, since the input text is discrete, the perturbation is added to the continuous the embedding layer as a regularization strategy [14] to improve robustness and generalization of the model.

With the above improvements, we can greatly boost the performance of the model in the extraction of name entities in the Chinese cybersecurity dataset. In summary, our main contributions are as follows:

- We propose a multi-task learning framework based on adversarial training (MTLAT) to imporve the performance of Chinese cybersecurity NER, and we use the CNN network to enhance the ability of the model to capture local contextual information. Our model can well extract cybersecurity entities and English entities from Chinese cybersecurity texts.

– Our model achieves state-of-the-art F1 score on the Chinese cybersecurity NER dataset without using any external resources like lexicon resources and pre-trained models, which make it very practical for real-world NER systems. Furthermore, compared to the BiLSTM-CRF model, our model improves F1 scores on Weibo, Resume, and MSRA datasets in the general domain for 4.1%, 1.04%, 1.79%, which proves the universality of our model.

Our code and data are publicly available[1].

2   Related Work

2.1   NER

Recently, in the NER task, compared to the traditional methods that required hand-crafted features, many NER studies mostly focus on deep learning. [4] firstly proposed the BiLSTM-CRF, which is used by most state-of-the-art models.

Chinese NER is related to word segmentation. Therefore Chinese NER models have two main methods, one based on word-level and the other based on character-level. Recently, many studies [9,10] proved that the model based on the character-level is better than the model based on the word-level. Because word-level models often suffer from data sparsity caused by overly large dictionaries, and it will also cause word segmentation errors and out-of-vocabulary (OOV) problems. Character sequence labeling has been the dominant approach [2,12] for Chinese NER. [19] proposed a lattice LSTM model, which integrates word-level information to the character-level model, but the lattice LSTM model can not batch-level training samples.

Recently, multi-task learning (MTL) gains significant attention. [15] proposed a model to train NER and word segmentation jointly. [1] proposed a NER model with two additional tasks that predict the named entity (NE) segmentation and NE categorization simultaneously in social media data. [20] proposed a novel deep neural multi-task learning framework to jointly model recognition and normalization on the medical NER task.

Recently, with the increasing number of cyberattacks, cybersecurity texts are also rapidly increasing. How to extract valuable information from cybersecurity texts has gradually become a research hotspot. [5] provided an English cybersecurity dataset that contained several categories of security entities and use CRF to solve this problem. [16] provided the Chinese cybersecurity dataset and use the CNN network to obtain the local feature of each character and use some hand-craft features into BiLSTM-CRF for entity extraction. These methods do not perform well in solving the aforementioned challenges in Chinese cybersecurity NER.

---

[1] https://github.com/xuanzebi/MTLAT.

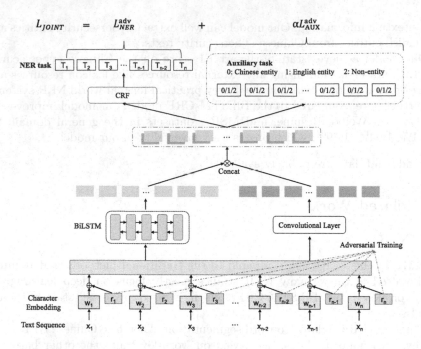

Fig. 2. The main framework of our MTLAT model.

2.2   Adversarial Training

Recently in the field of NLP, there has been a lot of researches [6,14,21] on adversarial training, mainly to obtain more accurate perturbations and add it to the embedding layer to improve the robustness and performance of the model. [14] proposed two adversarial training methods, fast gradient method (FGM) and virtual adversarial training (VAT), to enhance generalization of the model by adding perturbation on the embedding layer. To improve the robustness of neural networks against adversarial examples, many researchers pay more attention to propose more effective defense strategies and models. [13] proposed a projected gradient descent (PGD) method, which can be achieved reliably through multiple projected gradient ascent steps followed by a stochastic gradient descent step. [21] proposed a novel adversarial training algorithm Free Large-Batch (FreeLB), based on the Transformer network, which promotes higher invariance in the embedding space by adding adversarial perturbations to the embedding layer and minimizing the resultant adversarial risk inside different regions around input samples.

3   Methodology

In this paper, we propose a novel neural network framework, named multi-task learning based on adversarial training, for Chinese cybersecurity NER. The structure of the proposed model is shown in Fig. 2. In this section, we first introduce the adversarial training used in MTLAT, and we then introduce the encoding framework of the model and then introduce the decoding and training based on adversarial training and multi-task learning.

Formally, we denote a Chinese sentence as $s = \{c_1, c_2, \ldots, c_n\}$, where c_i denotes the i_{th} character, n is the number of characters in the sentence. By looking up the embedding vector from a static character embedding matrix, we obtain $\mathbf{x}_i = E\left(c_i\right)$, where $\mathbf{x}_i \in \mathbb{R}^{d_e}$ and d_e is the dimension of the input character embeddings, E is a character embedding lookup table.

3.1 Adversarial Training

In the field of NLP, since the input is discrete, the perturbations are mostly added to the embedding layer, which can enhance the robustness and performance of the model. Generally, adversarial training can be described by the following formula. Adversarial training seeks to find optimal parameters $\boldsymbol{\theta}$ to minimize the maximum risk for $\mathbf{r}_{adv}$:

$$\min_{\boldsymbol{\theta}} \mathbb{E}_{(x,y)\sim\mathcal{D}} \left[\max_{\|\mathbf{r}_{adv}\|\leq\epsilon} L\left(\mathbf{x} + \mathbf{r}_{adv}, y, \boldsymbol{\theta}\right) \right] \tag{1}$$

where $\mathbf{x} = \{\mathbf{x}_1, \mathbf{x}_2, \ldots, \mathbf{x}_n\}$, y is the sentence label sequence, $\mathcal{D}$ is data distribution, L is loss function. When get $\mathbf{r}_{adv}$ through the following methods, then add perturbations $\mathbf{r}_{adv}$ to the character embedding $\mathbf{x}$ to get new embeddings $\mathbf{x}^*$, then feed $\mathbf{x}^*$ to the model to calculate the adversarial loss:

$$L^{adv} = L\left(\mathbf{x}^*, y, \boldsymbol{\theta}\right) = L\left(\mathbf{x} + \mathbf{r}_{adv}, y, \boldsymbol{\theta}\right) \tag{2}$$

In this paper, we use the PGD [13] method to calculate the perturbation $\mathbf{r}_{adv}$. Then we introduce the most effective method of adversarial training, PGD, because it can largely avoid the obfuscated gradient problem.

PGD: [13] proposed to solve the inner maximization of Eq. 1 by using PGD (a standard method for large-scale constrained optimization) method. In particular, PGD takes the following step in each iteration:

$$\begin{aligned} \mathbf{g}\left(\mathbf{r}_t\right) &= \nabla_{\mathbf{r}} L\left(\mathbf{x} + \mathbf{r}_t, y\right) \\ \mathbf{r}_{t+1} &= \Pi_{\|\mathbf{r}\|_F\leq\epsilon}\left(\mathbf{r}_t + \alpha \mathbf{g}\left(\mathbf{r}_t\right) / \|\mathbf{g}\left(\mathbf{r}_t\right)\|_F\right) \end{aligned} \tag{3}$$

where $\mathbf{g}\left(\mathbf{r}_t\right)$ is the gradient of the loss with respect to $\mathbf{r}$, and $\Pi_{\|\mathbf{r}\|_F\leq\epsilon}$ performs a projection onto the ϵ-ball. After k-step PGD, add perturbation $\mathbf{r}_k$ to the character embedding:

$$\mathbf{x}^* = \mathbf{x} + \mathbf{r}_k \tag{4}$$

3.2 Encoding Layer

When using adversarial training methods to add perturbation $\mathbf{r}_{adv}$ to the character embedding vector $\mathbf{x}$, the embedding vector input for the current model is $\mathbf{x}^*$, and then feed it to our encoding layer.

BiLSTM: Most studies use BiLSTM to obtain text representations when processing text data, because it is a sequence model that can learn the internal connections of the text well and use context information of the text. In this paper, we use the character-level BiLSTM as the main network structure. We obtain the contextual representation $\mathbf{H} = \{\mathbf{h}_1, \mathbf{h}_2, \ldots, \mathbf{h}_n\}$, where $\mathbf{H} \in \mathbb{R}^{n \times d_h}$ and d_h is the hidden dimension of BiLSTM output:

$$\overrightarrow{\mathbf{h}}_i = \overrightarrow{LSTM^{(f)}} \left(\mathbf{x}_i^*, \overrightarrow{\mathbf{h}}_{i-1} \right)$$
$$\overleftarrow{\mathbf{h}}_i = \overleftarrow{LSTM^{(b)}} \left(\mathbf{x}_i^*, \overleftarrow{\mathbf{h}}_{i+1} \right) \tag{5}$$
$$\mathbf{h}_i = \left[\overrightarrow{\mathbf{h}}_i; \overleftarrow{\mathbf{h}}_i \right]$$

Convolutional Layer: Convolution layers are performed at every window based location to extract local features. We apply a convolutional layer to extract character representation to enhance local feature, which is helpful for extracting English entities and security entities. By the same padding, filters are applied to n possible windows in the sequence and the local contextual representation can be represented as $\mathbf{G} = \{\boldsymbol{g}_1, \boldsymbol{g}_2, \ldots, \boldsymbol{g}_n\}$, where $\mathbf{G} \in \mathbb{R}^{n \times d_c}$ and d_c is the hidden dimension of CNN output:

$$\boldsymbol{g}_i = \mathrm{Re}\,LU \left(\mathbf{W}_1 \mathbf{x}_{i-h+1:i}^* + \mathbf{b}_1 \right) \tag{6}$$

where $\mathbf{W}_1 \in \mathbb{R}^{h \times d_e \times d_c}$ and $\mathbf{b}_1 \in \mathbb{R}^{h \times d_c}$ are learnable parameters, $\mathbf{x}_{i-h+1:i}^*$ refers to the concatenation of character $\mathbf{x}_{i-h+1}^*, \mathbf{x}_{i-h+2}^*, \ldots, \mathbf{x}_i^*$ with h window size of filters are applied to the input sequence to generate character embedding representation. Finally, concat the representation obtained by BiLSTM and CNN:

$$\mathbf{R} = [\mathbf{H}; \mathbf{G}] \tag{7}$$

where $\mathbf{R} \in \mathbb{R}^{n \times (d_h + d_c)}$. Then feed $\mathbf{R}$ to CRF and multi-task network to calculate the NER loss and multi-task loss.

3.3   Training

NER Task: We use the CRF layer as the decoding layer of the NER task and calculate the probability of the ground-truth tag sequence $p(\mathbf{y}_i \mid s_i)$, and then we can calculate the NER task loss:

$$L_{NER}^{adv} = -\sum_{i=1}^{N} \log \left(p(\mathbf{y}_i \mid s_i) \right) \tag{8}$$

$$p(\mathbf{y} \mid s) = \frac{\exp \left(\sum_i \left(A_{y_{i-1}, y_i} + W_{y_i} R_i \right) \right)}{\sum_{y' \in \mathcal{Y}} \exp \left(\sum_i \left(A_{y'_{i-1}, y'_i} + W_{y'_i} R_i \right) \right)} \tag{9}$$

where $\mathcal{Y}$ denotes the set of all possible label sequences, A is the probability of transitioning from one tag to another. W_{y_i} is used for modeling emission potential for the i_{th} character in the sentence.

Table 1. Statistics of the Chinese cyber-security NER dataset.

Type	Train	Dev	Test
Sentences	38.2k	4.8k	4.8k
Chars	2210.3k	270.1k	278.4k
PER	9944	1355	1291
ORG	14557	1727	1861
LOC	18958	2290	2467
SW	5397	719	647
RT	64471	7753	8263
VUL_ID	265	25	30
Total Entities	113.5k	13.8k	14.6k

Table 2. Statistics of Chinese general NER datasets.

Dataset	Type	Train	Dev	Test
MSRA	Sentences	46.4k	–	4.4k
	Chars	2169.3k	–	172.6k
	Entities	74.8k	–	6.2k
Weibo	Sentences	1.4k	0.27k	0.27k
	Chars	73.8k	14.5k	14.8k
	Entities	1.89k	0.42k	0.39k
Resume	Sentences	3.8k	0.46k	0.48k
	Chars	124.1k	13.9k	15.1k
	Entities	1.34k	0.16k	0.15k

Auxiliary Task: Inspired by the [11], to better distinguish between Chinese and English entities, we add an auxiliary task to predict whether the pred tokens are Chinese entities, English entities, or non-entities. Additionally, the auxiliary task acts as a regular method to help the model to learn general representations of named entities. Given a set of training example $\{(s_i, \hat{\mathbf{y}}_i \in \mathbb{R}^{n\times 3})\}|_{i=1}^{N}$ for the auxiliary task, the auxiliary task loss can be defined as follows:

$$p(\hat{\mathbf{y}} \mid s) = \text{softmax}\,(\mathbf{W}_2\mathbf{R} + \mathbf{b}_2) \tag{10}$$

$$L_{\text{AUX}}^{adv} = -\frac{1}{N}\sum_{i=1}^{N} \tilde{y}_i \log\,(p\,(\hat{\mathbf{y}}_i \mid s_i)) \tag{11}$$

where $\mathbf{W}_2 \in \mathbb{R}^{(d_h+d_c)\times 3}$ and $\mathbf{b}_2 \in \mathbb{R}^3$ are trainable parameters, $\tilde{y}$ is the auxiliary task gold label of the sentence s.

Through adversarial training, we can get the NER task loss L_{NER}^{adv} and the auxiliary task loss L_{AUX}^{adv}, then we add these two losses to update parameters of the model by backpropagation algorithm for jointly training:

$$L_{\text{JOINT}} = L_{\text{NER}}^{adv} + \alpha L_{\text{AUX}}^{adv} \tag{12}$$

where α is the balancing parameter.

4 Experiments

4.1 Datasets

Chinese Cybersecurity NER Dataset: [16] collected and labeled the Chinese cybersecurity NER dataset from the Freebuf website and the Wooyun vulnerability database, mainly including security text data such as technology sharing, network security, vulnerability information, etc. The Chinese cybersecurity dataset

Table 3. Results with different methods on the Chinese cybersecurity NER test dataset.

Models	Precision (%)	Recall (%)	F1 (%)
Baseline	90.74	89.40	90.07
w/ FGM	91.81	90.25	91.03
w/ VAT	91.65	89.53	90.58
w/ PGD	92.37	90.25	91.30
w/ FreeLB	92.60	89.73	91.14
w/ MTL	91.55	90.10	90.82
w/ CNN	92.31	90.17	91.23
Lattice LSTM	91.07	**91.36**	91.21
MTLAT(ours)	**92.90**	90.74	**91.81**

includes six types of security entities, including names of the person (PER), location (LOC), organization (ORG), software (SW), relevant term (RT) and vulnerability (VUL_ID). In this paper, we mainly evaluate our model on a larger dataset that they open source[2]. The specific analysis is shown in Table 1.

Chinese General NER Datasets: We also evaluate the effect of our model on Chinese general domain NER datasets, Weibo NER [15], MSRA [8], and Resume NER [19]. Their statistics are listed in Table 2. Weibo NER is based on the text in Chinese social media Sina Weibo. MSRA comes mainly from news domain. Resume NER is collected from Sina Finance. These domains are the domains that the public often pays attention to, and can be unified into general domains. On the contrary, except for security personnel, the cybersecurity domain has received little public attention.

4.2 Comparison Methods

Baseline Model: In this paper, we use the character-level BiLSTM-CRF [7] model as the comparison baseline method. We also explore the four different methods of adding adversarial training (FGM, VAT, PGD, and FreeLB) based on the baseline model.

Lattice LSTM: Lattice LSTM [19] incorporates word-level information into character-level recurrent units, which can avoid segmentation errors. The Lattice LSTM achieves state-of-the-art performance on the Chinese general domain NER datasets.

4.3 Hyper-Parameter Settings

For hyperparameter configuration, we adjust them according to the performance on the development datasets for all NER datasets. For all of the datasets, we use

[2] https://github.com/xiebo123/NER.

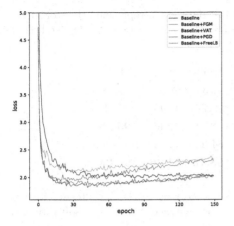
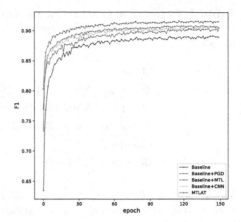

Fig. 3. Loss of the Chinese cybersecurity development dataset with four different adversarial training methods.

Fig. 4. F1 scores against training iteration number on the Chinese cybersecurity development dataset.

the Adam optimization to train our networks, and the initial learning rate was set at 0.015 for the cybersecurity NER dataset, 0.005 for other NER datasets. We set α in Eq. 12 to 1. We set the hidden sizes of BiLSTM to 256 dims. We use one layer of CNN with an output channel size of 200 and set the window size as 3. The character embedding used in our all experiments are from [17]. To avoid overfitting, we apply dropout (50% dropout rate) on the character embedding and (20% dropout rate) on the output layer. We use "BIEOS" as the decoder tag scheme for all datasets.

5 Results and Analysis

5.1 Results on the Chinese Cybersecurity NER Dataset

We first compare the impact of different adversarial training methods on the Chinese cybersecurity test dataset. As shown in Table 3, adding any kind of adversarial training method to the baseline model can improve the F1 score on the cybersecurity dataset, which proves the effectiveness of adversarial training. PGD and FreeLB use K-step iterations to obtain the optimal perturbations and obtain a higher F1 score. In addition, Fig. 3 compares the loss effect of these four methods (FGM, VAT, PGD, and FreeLB) on the development dataset. Among the four adversarial training methods, PGD can obtain better robustness and generalization on the development dataset. Therefore, the PGD method is used in our MTLAT model. We find that adding the auxiliary task (MTL) to the baseline model is helpful for recalling entities. And using the CNN network can enhance the local feature representation of the text, greatly improving the precision and recall score of entity extraction. Figure 4 shows the comparison of the effect of adding CNN, PGD and MTL to the baseline model on the development

Table 4. F1 scores on Chinese general NER test datasets. a represents the word-level LSTM model, b indicates the character-level LSTM model, and c is the lattice LSTM model.

Models	Weibo	Resume	MSRA
Zhang and Yang (2018) [19][a]	47.33	93.58	86.85
Zhang and Yang (2018) [19][b]	52.77	93.48	88.81
Zhang and Yang (2018) [19][c]	**58.79**	94.46	**93.18**
Baseline†	54.05	93.62	89.45
Baseline-CNN-PGD	**58.15**	**94.66**	91.24

Table 5. Case Study. We use red to denote the correct labels, blue to denote the wrong labels and purple to denote entities in the sentence. SW means software and LOC means location.

Case	Sentences	侵入乌克兰工控系统的罪魁祸首可能是 Win32Industroyer. (The culprit of the invasion of the Ukrainian industrial control system may be Win32Industroyer.)
	Gold label	···乌克兰(Ukrainian) (B-LOC, I-LOC, E-LOC)··· ···Win32Industroyer (B-SW, I-SW, E-SW)···
	Baseline predicted label	···乌克兰(Ukrainian) (B-LOC, I-LOC, E-LOC)··· ···Win32Industroyer (O, O, O)···
	MTLAT predicted label	···乌克兰(Ukrainian) (B-LOC, I-LOC, E-LOC)··· ···Win32Industroyer (B-SW, I-SW, E-SW)···

dataset. It shows that the MTLAT achieves the best performance by adding these three methods to the baseline model.

[19] introduce a lattice LSTM to incorporate external lexicon information into the model. Compared with the baseline model, the F1 score of the lattice model using external data is improved by 1.14%. Table 3 shows that our MTLAT model achieves 91.81% F1 score on the test dataset, which outperforms the lattice LSTM by 0.6%. Overall, our model does not require any external data on the cybersecurity dataset to achieve state-of-the-art performance, which can be more easily applied to real-world systems.

5.2 Results on Chinese General NER Datasets

Because there are few English entities in the general domain of NER datasets, we do not apply the auxiliary task on general domain datasets. We only add the adversarial training method PGD and CNN network to baseline model, namely **Baseline-CNN-PGD**. The results are reported in Table 4. It shows that our character-level baseline model outperforms the same network proposed by [19]. It can see that our model Baseline-CNN-PGD outperforms the best character-level and word-level models on all three datasets. Although the results of our model on Weibo and MSRA datasets are slightly lower than Lattice LSTM, Lattice LSTM leverages external lexicon resources and can not batch training, resulting in highly inefficient. It proves that adversarial training can improve the robustness and generalization of the model, and the CNN network enhance the ability of the model to capture local contextual information, which are of great help to improve the performance of the model, and further proves the universality of our model in different domains.

5.3 Case Study

To show visually that our model can solve the challenges of identifying English entities, a case study comparing the baseline model and our model in Table 5. In the case, there are two entities, a Chinese location entity "乌克兰(Ukrainian)" and an English software entity "Win32Industroyer". The baseline model can extract Chinese entities well, but it incorrectly recognizes English entities, while our model can extract not only Chinese entities well, but also English professional security entities.

6 Conclusion

In this paper, we propose a multi-task learning framework based on adversarial training (MTLAT) method to enhance the performance of Chinese cybersecurity NER. We incorporate adversarial training into the embedding layer to improve robustness and generalization of the model and use the CNN network to enhance feature local representations. Extensive experiments show that our model does not require any external data on the Chinese cybersecurity dataset to achieve state-of-the-art performance, which can be more easily applied to real-world systems. Moreover, compared with the BiLSTM-CRF method, our model has 4.1%, 1.04%, 1.79% F1 scores improvement on Weibo, Resume, and MSRA datasets, which proves the universality of our model in different domains.

Acknowledgments. This research is supported by National Key Research and Development Program of China (No.2019QY1303, No.2019QY1301, No.2018YFB0803602), and the Strategic Priority Research Program of the Chinese Academy of Sciences (No. XDC02040100), and National Natural Science Foundation of China (No. 61702508, No. 61802404). This work is also supported by the Program of Key Laboratory of Network Assessment Technology, the Chinese Academy of Sciences; Program of Beijing Key Laboratory of Network Security and Protection Technology.

References

1. Aguilar, G., Maharjan, S., López-Monroy, A.P., Solorio, T.: A multi-task approach for named entity recognition in social media data. CoRR abs/1906.04135 (2019)
2. Dong, C., Zhang, J., Zong, C., Hattori, M., Di, H.: Character-based LSTM-CRF with radical-level features for Chinese named entity recognition. In: Lin, C.-Y., Xue, N., Zhao, D., Huang, X., Feng, Y. (eds.) ICCPOL/NLPCC -2016. LNCS (LNAI), vol. 10102, pp. 239–250. Springer, Cham (2016). https://doi.org/10.1007/978-3-319-50496-4_20

3. Goodfellow, I.J., Shlens, J., Szegedy, C.: Explaining and harnessing adversarial examples. In: ICLR (2015)
4. Huang, Z., Xu, W., Yu, K.: Bidirectional LSTM-CRF models for sequence tagging. CoRR abs/1508.01991 (2015)
5. Joshi, A., Lal, R., Finin, T., Joshi, A.: Extracting cybersecurity related linked data from text. In: 2013 IEEE Seventh International Conference on Semantic Computing, pp. 252–259. IEEE (2013)
6. Ju, Y., Zhao, F., Chen, S., Zheng, B., Yang, X., Liu, Y.: Technical report on conversational question answering. CoRR abs/1909.10772 (2019)
7. Lample, G., Ballesteros, M., Subramanian, S., Kawakami, K., Dyer, C.: Neural architectures for named entity recognition. In: NAACL, pp. 260–270 (2016)
8. Levow, G.A.: The third international Chinese language processing bakeoff: word segmentation and named entity recognition. In: ACL, pp. 108–117. Association for Computational Linguistics (2006)
9. Li, H., Hagiwara, M., Li, Q., Ji, H.: Comparison of the impact of word segmentation on name tagging for Chinese and Japanese. In: LREC, pp. 2532–2536 (2014)
10. Li, X., Meng, Y., Sun, X., Han, Q., Yuan, A., Li, J.: Is word segmentation necessary for deep learning of Chinese representations? In: ACL, pp. 3242–3252. Association for Computational Linguistics (2019)
11. Liu, Z., Winata, G.I., Fung, P.: Zero-resource cross-domain named entity recognition. In: ACL, pp. 1–6 (2020)
12. Lu, Y., Zhang, Y., Ji, D.: Multi-prototype Chinese character embedding. In: Proceedings of the Tenth International Conference on Language Resources and Evaluation (LREC 2016), pp. 855–859 (2016)
13. Madry, A., Makelov, A., Schmidt, L., Tsipras, D., Vladu, A.: Towards deep learning models resistant to adversarial attacks. In: ICLR (2018)
14. Miyato, T., Dai, A.M., Goodfellow, I.: Adversarial training methods for semi-supervised text classification. In: ICLR (2017)
15. Peng, N., Dredze, M.: Improving named entity recognition for Chinese social media with word segmentation representation learning. In: ACL: Short Papers (2016)
16. Qin, Y., Shen, G.W., Zhao, W.B., Chen, Y.P., Yu, M., Jin, X.: A network security entity recognition method based on feature template and CNN-BILSTM-CRF. Front. Inf. Technol. Electron. Eng. **20**(6), 872–884 (2019)
17. Song, Y., Shi, S., Li, J., Zhang, H.: Directional skip-gram: explicitly distinguishing left and right context for word embeddings. In: NAACL-HLT, (Short Papers), vol. 2, pp. 175–180 (2018)
18. Weerawardhana, S., Mukherjee, S., Ray, I., Howe, A.: Automated extraction of vulnerability information for home computer security. In: Cuppens, F., Garcia-Alfaro, J., Zincir Heywood, N., Fong, P.W.L. (eds.) FPS 2014. LNCS, vol. 8930, pp. 356–366. Springer, Cham (2015). https://doi.org/10.1007/978-3-319-17040-4_24
19. Zhang, Y., Yang, J.: Chinese NER using lattice LSTM. In: ACL, pp. 1554–1564 (2018)
20. Zhao, S., Liu, T., Zhao, S., Wang, F.: A neural multi-task learning framework to jointly model medical named entity recognition and normalization. In: Proceedings of the AAAI Conference on Artificial Intelligence, vol. 33, pp. 817–824 (2019)
21. Zhu, C., Cheng, Y., Gan, Z., Sun, S., Goldstein, T., Liu, J.: FreeLB: enhanced adversarial training for language understanding. In: ICLR (2020)

Learning-Based Evaluation of Routing Protocol in Vehicular Network Using WEKA

Amal Hadrich[✉], Amel Meddeb Makhlouf[✉], and Faouzi Zarai[✉]

National School of Electronics and Telecommunications, Sfax, Tunisia
{amal.hadrich,amel.makhlouf,faouzi.zerai}@enetcom.usf.tn

Abstract. Internet of things connects any object to another and communicate with them using the most performed routing protocol. But in vehicular networks, topology and communication links frequently change due to the high mobility of vehicles. So, the key challenge of our work is to choose the best routing protocol using machine learning algorithms. When choosing routing protocol, most research focuses on the improvement of the performance of specific routing protocol using one machine learning algorithm. In this paper, we propose a solution in order to find the best routing protocol in such critical condition using machine learning algorithms in order to maximize the precision of the true positive rate. After the use of a specific algorithms such as Artificial Neural Network, Random Forest and Naive Bayes, we found that the last one is the best algorithm when it have all the true positive rate with a precision equal to 0.9987 to select the best routing protocol.

Keywords: Vehicular networks · Routing protocol · Machine learning algorithms

1 Introduction

Recent advances in networks have given rise to the emergence of vehicular networks. The research work has started from the past few years on the area of Mobile Ad-hoc Networks also called as MANETS (Mobile Adhoc NETworks). It allows the mobile nodes to communicate in one to one and one to many without any predefined infrastructure. The protocols which are required to support MANETS are more complex when compared to other non-mobile networks because of the mobility and of the non-existence predefined infrastructure or topology for MANETS. New technologies are used to provide more and more facilities including safety applications. Among these networks, Vehicular networks are a subclass of MANETs, where vehicles are simulated as mobile nodes. The vehicular network is a self organizing network to provide Intelligent Transport System (ITS). Users in vehicles connect to the Internet at any time in order to obtain the desired services. There are three types of common communication

© IFIP International Federation for Information Processing 2021
Published by Springer Nature Switzerland AG 2021
X. He et al. (Eds.): NPC 2020, LNCS 12639, pp. 55–67, 2021.
https://doi.org/10.1007/978-3-030-79478-1_5

models in vehicular networks: vehicle-to-infrastructure (V2I), vehicle-to-roadside
(V2R) and vehicle-to-vehicle (V2V) [15]. The routing protocol is an important
aspect in communication between networks. It is a set of rules that are framed
for exchanging the information in a network from one node to another node.
MANET routing protocols are divided into three categories: Proactive routing
protocol means that the routing information is maintained in the background
irrespective of communication requests like the protocol OLSR (Optimized Link
State Routing Protocol), reactive routing protocol opens the route only when it
is necessary for a node to communicate with each other such as AODV (Ad-hoc
On-demand Distance Vector), DSR (Dynamic Source Routing) and ZRP (Zone
Routing Protocol) is an example of hybrid routing protocols that is introduced
to reduce the control overhead of proactive routing protocols and decrease the
initial route discovery delay in reactive routing protocols. The main difference
between the MANET and vehicular routing is network topology, mobility patterns, demographics, density of nodes at different timings, rapid changes in node
arriving and leaving the network. Vehicular networks was divided into three
categories [1, 2]:

* Routing information: It is also divided into two categories like topology-based
  routing protocols that use link information that exists in the network and
  position-based routing protocols use GPS devices.
* Transmission strategies: It is divided into three categories, where broadcast
  routing protocols are frequently used in vehicular network, multicast such as
  cluster-based routing protocols and geocast routing protocols and unicast.
* Delay tolerant: It is useful to help balance traffic loads and reduces traveling
  time.

Figure 1 represents vehicular routing protocol chosen in our work and their categories.

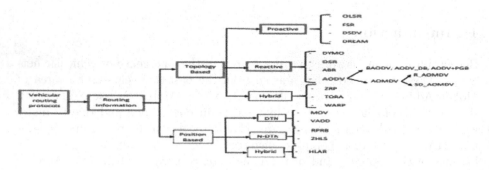

Fig. 1. Vehicular routing protocol chosen in our work.

Vehicles in their network have high mobility, which causes a changement
in the network topology and the connections unstability. Recently, the nature-
inspired intelligence algorithms have been widely used as direct search and optimization tools in many different problems where machine learning algorithms

used for the choose of the best route for the devices. For this reason, we propose a solution to choose the best routing protocol depending on the network topology using machine learning algorithms. The remainder of this paper is organized as follows. Section 2 reviews the related works. Section 3 introduces our proposed solution in order to choose the perfect routing protocol. Section 4 shows the evaluation results. Section 5 concludes this paper and gives some possible future perspectives.

2   Related Work

Researchs focus to design an efficient routing algorithms that is adaptable to the mobility characteristics of vehicular network.

Marzak *et al.* [3] proposed a new vehicular clustering algorithm based on the ANN (Artificial Neural Network) system to select cluster-head. This algorithm increases network connectivity and improves the stability of the cluster structure. Moreover, research in [4] introduced a Modified AODV routing protocol of VANET communications using fuzzy neural network algorithm to determine the best route from the source node to the destination node through several intermediate nodes. Because of the importance of stability and the security in vehicular networks, research in [6] presents a secure and stable AODV, named GSS-AODV, based on the fuzzy neural network to ensure that the calculated node stability is in accordance with the actual situation. Zaho *et al.* [5] proposed a greedy forwarding algorithm based on SVM (Support Vector Machine) to process the vehicle data and to generate routing metric. This algorithm reduces the packet loss and network delay.

The above-mentioned literatures [3–6] mainly use machine learning methods to increase the network connectivity, determine the best route, improve the performance of the network and applications, increase the stability of the protection and reduce the packet loss and network delay. But, they still do not applicated this approach only in one protocol or a cluster and use only one algorithm named ANN or SVM. However, to determine the best protocol, we have to use several machine learning algorithms according to the high value of accuracy to avoid the problem of the accidents and improve the performance and the protection. The most related work is presented by Marzak *et al.* [3] because it selects the best vehicular routing protocol using machine learning algorithm according to the feature specification, but the last mentioned autor focused on cluster routing protocol and use only ANN algorithm and in our solution, we focus in all routing protocol with the apply of machine learning algorithms.

Table 1 summarizes the studied related works and shows their limits.

3   Proposed Solution

Our proposed solution set based on the parameter of routing protocol inserted in the dataset and estimates the optimal protocol for data transmission using

Table 1. Comparison with the existing and proposed solution

Solution	Algorithm	Protocol	Limits
Clustering in vehicular ad-hoc network using artificial neural network [3]	Artificial Neural Network	Clustering routing protocols	Focus on cluster routing protocol and use only ANN algorithm
AODV Routing Protocol Modification With Dqueue (dqAODV) and Optimization With Neural Network For VANET In City Scenario [4]	Fuzzy neural network algorithm	A modified AODV routing protocol	Focus only on AODV routing protocol using fuzzy neural network
Improving Security and Stability of AODV with Fuzzy Neural Network in VANET [6]	Fuzzy neural network	GSS-AODV	Focus only on AODV routing protocol using fuzzy neural network
SVM based routing scheme in VANETs[5]	SVM neural network	Vehicular routing protocol	Use only SVM neural network
Proposed solution	All algorithms in Neural Network	All routing protocols	——

machine learning algorithms in order to minimize the cost of network maintenance. The proposed approach must ensure optimal operation of the network
by maximizing the stability, minimizing the delivery delay of information and
bandwidth.

For this research, we propose to study three vehicular routing protocols based
on three specifications, which are "AODV", "DSR" and "OLSR" with three
common parameter "TTL", "QUEUE LENGTH" and "HELLO INTERVAL".
There is more routing protocol with their categories like position based, delay
tolerant and transmissions strategies but we choose this three routing protocol
because we find that this have some common carectrestic and features based for
the select the best routing protocol.

A particular mobile node may wish to change certain of the parameters,
in particular the HELLO INTERVAL. In the latter case [10], the node should
advertise the HELLO INTERVAL in its Hello messages, by appending a Hello
Interval Extension.

The routing protocol uses minimum hop count criteria to establish routes
between sources and destinations. However [11], selecting the routing protocol

with minimum hop is not usually the best decision. A node which might not have sufficient available buffer size could be leading to have high probability of packet loss and network congestion and link breakage. Thus, the routing algorithm consider available node queue length during routing protocol selection process.

To control congestion by applying efficient local route repair method we should use the value of TTL [12]. A TTL value is only decreased by one at each node. When the TTL value declines to zero, the route request packet should be dropped even though it didn't find the destination.

To choose the best routing protocol based on the three parameters, we base our analysis on the following Machine Learning Algorithms:

* ANN, which are computational algorithms in order to simulate the behavior of biological systems composed of neurons [7],
* Random Forest, which randomly creates and merges multiple decision trees into one forest in order to create a collection of decision models to improve accuracy [9]
* Naive Bayes, which are a collection of classification algorithms based on Bayes theorem, it is not a single algorithm but a family of algorithms where all of them share a common principle, i.e. every pair of features being classified is independent of each other[8].

In Sect. 3.2 there are more description about this machine learning algorithm mentioned above. These three machine learning algorithms show interesting results to select the perfect vehicular routing protocol. Figure 2 shows the proposed algorithm of our solution in order to minimize the cost of network maintenance.

First, we choose three specific vehicular routing protocol named AODV, OLSR and DSR then we apply one machine learning algorithm like ANN, Random Forest and Naive Bayes. To test our solution, we must compare the accuracy with a threshold value beta flows the equation below 1.

$$beta = \frac{2 * precision * recal}{precision + recall} \tag{1}$$

where recall and precision show in Eqs. 2 and 3.

$$recall = \frac{TP}{TP + FN} \tag{2} \qquad precision = \frac{TP}{TP + FP} \tag{3}$$

where TP, FN and FP represent respectively True Positive, False Negative and False Positive. If the accuracy down to beta, we must change the machine learning algorithm. And if not, we compare the training time to a fixed value. If the time upper to this value, we must switch the machine learning algorithm. If not, we move to the next step in order to select the best routing protocols with the perfect feature. So, we calculate the number of features to decide. If the number of features is down to S, then we change the machine learning algorithm and if not, we test the specification of the routing protocol. If this result down

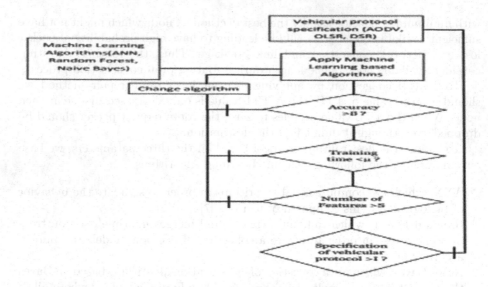

Fig. 2. Choose of the perfect vehicular routing protocol with the apply of machine learning based algorithms.

to a fixed value, representing the specification of the previous result, then we rebuild the algorithm and if not then we set this algorithm as the best vehicular routing protocol using the perfect machine learning algorithm.

The Table 2 shows the different features used in our proposed algorithm.

Table 2. Definition of the used features

Feature Name	Definition
Time To Live (TTL)	It's the number of hops that a packet is permitted to travel before being discarded by a router
QUEUE LENGTH	It is used to hold packets while the network interface is in the process of transmitting another packet
HELLO INTERVAL	A node may offer connectivity information by broadcasting local Hello messages. A node should only use hello messages if it is part of an active route

First, we need a description about the routing protocol and the algorithms chosen.

3.1 Improved Protocol Description

Security protocols are optimized for routing and routing maintenance protocol processes.

AODV Routing Protocol: The Ad hoc On-Demand Distance Vector (AODV) algorithm enables dynamic, self-starting, multihop routing between participating mobile nodes wishing to establish and maintain an ad hoc network. AODV allows mobile nodes to obtain routes quickly for new destinations, and does not require nodes to maintain routes to destinations that are not in active communication. AODV allows mobile nodes to respond to link breakages and changes in network topology in a timely manner. Route Requests (RREQs), Route Replies (RREPs), and Route Errors (RERRs) are the message types defined by AODV [11].

OLSR Routing Protocol: The Optimized Link State Routing Protocol (OLSR) operates as a table driven, proactive protocol, i.e., ex-changes topology information with other nodes of the network regularly [13]. Each node selects a set of its neighbor nodes as MultiPoint Relays (MPR). In OLSR, only nodes, selected as such MPRs, are responsible for forwarding control traffic, intended for diffusion into the entire network. MPRs provide an efficient mechanism for flooding control traffic by reducing the number of required transmissions [13].

DSR Routing Protocol: The Dynamic Source Routing protocol (DSR) is a simple and efficient routing protocol designed specifically for use in multi-hop wireless ad hoc networks of mobile nodes [14]. Using DSR, the network is completely self-organizing and self-configuring, requiring no existing network infrastructure or administration. Network nodes cooperate to forward packets for each other to allow communication over multiple hops between nodes not directly within wireless transmission range of one another.

3.2   Machine Learning Algorithms Description

Machine learning is a method of data analysis that automates analytical model building. It is a branch of technology that allows systems to learn from data, identify patterns and make decisions with minimal human intervention. It has revolutionized the world of computer science by allowing learning with large datasets, which enables machines to change, restructure and optimize algorithms by themselves [16]. After analysis, we choose to use three machine learning based algorithms, namely, Artificial Neural Network (ANN), Naive Bayes and Random Forest, because they have the most interesting results compared to other machine learning algorithms.

Naive Bayes: Classification is a fundamental issue in machine learning and data mining. Naive Bayes is the simplest form of Bayesian network, in which all attributes are independent given the value of the class variable [8].

Figure 3 shows Naive Bayes of our solution where QL and HI represent respectively QUEUE LENGTH and Hello interval. In naive Bayes, each attribute node has no parent except the class node.

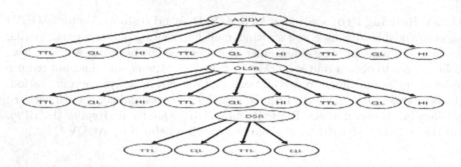

Fig. 3. Naive Bayes algorithm of our solution.

Random Forest: Random Forests in machine learning is an ensemble learning technique about classification, regression and other operations that depend on a multitude of decision trees at the training time. They are fast, flexible, represent a robust approach to mining high-dimensional data [9]. Figure 4 shows Random Forest algorithm of our solution.

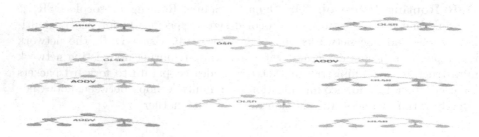

Fig. 4. Random Forest algorithm of our solution.

Artificial Neural Network: Artificial neural network (ANN) is a computational model that consists of several processing elements that receive inputs and deliver outputs based on their predefined activation functions. The ANN consists of a set of processing elements, also known as neurons or nodes, which are interconnected [7]. Figure 5 represents the ANN algorithm to our solution.

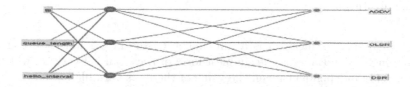

Fig. 5. ANN algorithm for our solution

4   Evaluation Results

For the evaluation procedure, we propose to use WEKA, which is a machine learning workbench that supports many activities of machine learning practitioners. The main features of WEKA are [17]:

* Data preprocessing: As well as a native file format (ARFF), WEKA supports various other formats (for instance CSV, Matlab ASCII files), and database connectivity through JDBC.
* Classification: One of WEKA's drawing cards is the more than 100 classification methods it contains.
* Clustering: Unsupervised learning is supported by several clustering schemes.
* Attribute selection: The set of attributes used is essential for classification performance.
* Data visualization: Data can be inspected visually by plotting attribute values against the class, or against other attribute values.

To test our solution, we choose k-folds cross-Validation model. It's a re-sampling procedure used to evaluate machine learning models on a limited data sample. The procedure has a single parameter called k that refers to the number of groups that a given data sample is to be split into. The general procedure is as follows:

1- Shuffle the dataset randomly.
2- Split the dataset into k groups
3- For each unique group:
    A- Take the group as a hold out or test data set.
    B- Take the remaining groups as a training data set.
    C- Fit a model on the training set and evaluate it on the test set.
    D- Retain the evaluation score and discard the model.
4- Summarize the skill of the model using the sample of model evaluation scores.

Importantly, each observation in the data sample is assigned to an individual group and stays in that group for the duration of the procedure. This means that each sample is given the opportunity to be used in the hold out set 1 time and used to train the model k-1 times.

The main objective of our work is to choose the best routing protocol based on the calculation of the performance for each protocol and algorithm in order to minimize the cost of network maintenance. First, we set k value to 10. The retrieved value of the accuracy follows the matrix below 2.

$$Accuracy = \begin{pmatrix} RandomForest & NaiveBayes & ANN \\ 82.22\% & 88.88\% & 80\% \end{pmatrix} \quad (2)$$

The simulation results show that the Random Forest Algorithm takes a delay time equal to 0.15 s, ANN algorithm takes about a 0.29 s and Naive Bayes algorithm takes a delay time equal to 0.1 s to build their model. Figures 6a, 6b and

6c show the results of our machine learning algorithms, where the abscissa axis is the protocol name and y-axis is the predicted protocol name. Figure 6a shows the result of the Random Forest Algorithm. We notice that the random forest presents errors in DSR and OLSR routing protocol, because the two protocols represent some commun interval of the value of TTL and queue length. Figure 6b shows the result of the application of the ANN Algorithm. We notice that ANN presents errors in DSR routing protocol predicted as OLSR protocol and OLSR protocol predicted as AODV and DSR protocols. Figure 6c shows the result of Naive Bayes Algorithm. We notice in this case that Naive Bayes presents errors in DSR routing protocol predicted as OLSR protocol.

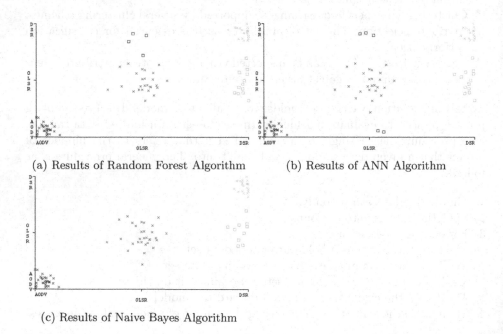

(a) Results of Random Forest Algorithm   (b) Results of ANN Algorithm

(c) Results of Naive Bayes Algorithm

Fig. 6. Results of the chosen machine learning algorithms.

To evaluate the performance of our solution, we should choose the algorithm with the accuracy ≥0.8. Thus, the best three algorithms are Naive Bayes, ANN and Random Forest. Then, we move to fix the training time, where we choose to eliminate the algorithm with training time >6 s. For the algorithm Random Forest, the training time is 3s, naive Bayes is 1s and ANN algorithm is 7s. Thus, the best two algorithms, according to the time metric, are Random Forest and Naive Bayes. Finally, we should have one feature to chose the best routing protocol. For the Naive Bayes the OLSR and AODV have a predicted margin between 0.93 and 1 for the three features TTL, HELLO INTERVAL and QUEUE LENGTH. The OLSR routing protocol has the lowest predicted margin than AODV routing protocol for the two features TTL and QUEUE LENGTH. Thus, the best routing protocol for the naive bayse is AODV. For Random Forest, the routing protocol AODV has a predicted margin between 0.91 and 1 for the three features TTL, HELLO INTERVAL and QUEUE LENGTH. Then we should compare the margin prediction between AODV routing protocol for the two algorithms. The predicted margin in Naive Bayes is 0.99 and in Random Forest equal to 0.91 for the two features for TTL and QUEUE LENGTH. Than, we can conclude, using these conditions, that best routing protocol is AODV the algorithm Naive Bayes. Table 3 resumes the results about the best algorithm.

Table 3. Summarize of the choose the best algorithm

Algorithms / Steps	Accuracy	Training time	Number of Features
ANN	AODV,OLSR	✗	NaN
Random Forest	AODV,OLSR	AODV	✗
Naive Bayes	AODV,OLSR	AODV,OLSR	AODV

To verify our resolution, Fig. 7 shows the threshold curve of the OLSR routing protocol using the Naive Bayes algorithm where the abscissa axis is the True Positive Rate and y-axis is the precision. We notice that the true positive rate is less than 0.7, which is an interesting result of our simulations.

Fig. 7. The threshold curve for OLSR routing protocol with Naive Bayes algorithm

Figure 8a shows the threshold curve of AODV routing protocol for the Random Forest algorithm, to show the variation of the precision with respect to the True Positive Rate. We notice that the true positive rate values are between 0.7 and 1. Finally, Fig. 8b shows the threshold curve of AODV routing protocol for the Naive Bayes algorithm. We notice that all the true positive rates are evaluated with a precision equal to 0.9987.

In conclusion, under specific conditions, the best routing protocol chosen is AODV using Naive Bayes Algorithm with precision of the true positive rate equal to 0.9987. Naive Bayes is the most suitable algorithm of our proposed solution since it has the most greater precision, where the AODV routing protocol is simple to be determined.

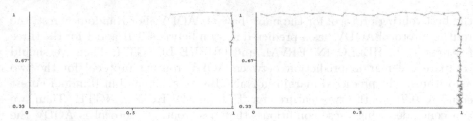

(a) Threshold curve using Random Forest (b) Threshold curve using Naive Bayes algorithm   gorithm

Fig. 8. Threshold curve of AODV routing protocol.

5 Conclusion

As the population is becoming more and more larger in the world, so vehicles are increasing per day and simultaneously accidents are rising. There is no protection for human life and the vehicles. Vehicular network is the mostly utilized connection that communicates among the vehicles. It is not only utilized for the communication purpose but also could be structured for navigation and traffic control. In this manuscript, a routing based solution has been lightened that would help in the reduction of accidents based on the choose of the best routing protocol using specific machine learning algorithms. The performance parameters are computed to depict the effectiveness of the proposed work. The threshold curve indicates that the AODV routing protocol when using Naive Bayes algorithm is the best vehicular routing protocol, based on simulation hypothesis.

In our future work, we plan to use more features to choose the best routing protocol. These features can be based on security and network characteristics, which increase the efficiency of our solution.

References

1. Suthaputchakun, C., Sun, Z.: Routing protocol in intervehicle communication systems: a survey. IEEE Commun. Mag. **49**(12), 150–156 (2011)
2. Lin, Y.-W., Chen, Y.-S., Lee, S.-L.: Routing protocols in vehicular ad hoc networks: a survey and future perspectives. J. Inf. Sci. Eng. **26**(3), 913–932 (2010)
3. Marzak, B., et al.: Clustering in vehicular ad-hoc network using artificial neural network. Int. Rev. Comput. Softw. (IRECOS) **11**(6), 548–556 (2016)
4. Saha, S., Roy, U., Sinha, D.D.: AODV routing protocol modification with Dqueue (dqAODV) and optimization with neural network for VANET in City Scenario. In: MATEC Web of Conferences, vol. 57, p. 02001. EDP Sciences (2016)
5. Zhao, L., Li, Y., Meng, C., Gong, C., Tang, X.: A SVM based routing scheme in VANETs. In: 2016 16th International Symposium on Communications and Information Technologies (ISCIT), pp. 380–383. IEEE (2016)
6. Huang, B., Mo, J., Cheng, X.: Improving security and stability of AODV with fuzzy neural network in VANET. In: Chellappan, S., Cheng, W., Li, W. (eds.) WASA 2018. LNCS, vol. 10874, pp. 177–188. Springer, Cham (2018). https://doi.org/10.1007/978-3-319-94268-1_15

7. Prieto, A., et al.: Neural networks: an overview of early research, current frameworks and new challenges. Neurocomputing **214**, 242–268 (2016)
8. Zhang, H.: The optimality of Naive Bayes. AA **1**(2), 3 (2004)
9. Segal, M.R.: Machine learning benchmarks and random forest regression (2004)
10. Park, N.-U., Nam, J.-C., Cho, Y.-Z.: Impact of node speed and transmission range on the hello interval of MANET routing protocols. In: 2016 International Conference on Information and Communication Technology Convergence (ICTC), pp. 634–636. IEEE (2016)
11. Ahmed, B., Mohamed, R., Mohamed, O.: Queue length and mobility aware routing protocol for mobile ad hoc network. Int. J. Commun. Netw. Inf. Secur. **4**(3), 207 (2012)
12. Bindra, P., Kaur, J., Singh, G.: Effect of TTL parameter variation on performance of AODV route discovery process. Int. J. Comput. Appl. **70**(4) (2013)
13. Clausen, T., Jacquet, P.: RFC3626: Optimized Link State Routing Protocol (OLSR). RFC Editor (2003)
14. Johnson, D.B., Maltz, D.A., Broch, J., et al.: DSR: the dynamic source routing protocol for multi-hop wireless ad hoc networks. Ad hoc Netw. **5**(1), 139–172 (2001)
15. Ksouri, C., Jemili, I., Mosbah, M., Belghith, A.: VANETs routing protocols survey: classifications, optimization methods and new trends. In: Jemili, I., Mosbah, M. (eds.) DiCES-N 2019. CCIS, vol. 1130, pp. 3–22. Springer, Cham (2020). https://doi.org/10.1007/978-3-030-40131-3_1
16. Ayodele, T.O.: Machine learning overview. New Adv. Mach. Learn. 9–19 (2010)
17. Bouckaert, R.R., et al.: WEKA-experiences with a Java open-source project. J. Mach. Learn. Res. **11**, 2533–2541 (2010)

Accelerating Large-Scale Deep Convolutional Neural Networks on Multi-core Vector Accelerators

Zhong Liu$^{(\boxtimes)}$, Sheng Ma$^{(\boxtimes)}$, Cheng Li, and Haiyan Chen

College of Computer, National University of Defense Technology, Changsha, China
{zhongliu,masheng}@nudt.edu.cn

Abstract. This paper proposes an efficient algorithm mapping method for accelerating deep convolutional neural networks, which includes: (1) Proposing an efficient transformation method, which converts CNN's convolutional layer and fully connected layer computations into efficient large-scale matrix multiplication computations, and converts pooling layer computations into efficient matrix row computations; (2) Designing a set of general and efficient vectorization method for convolutional layer, fully connected layer and pooling layer on the vector accelerator. The experimental results on the accelerator show that the average computing efficiency of convolution layer and full connected layer of AlexNet, VGG-19, GoogleNet and ResNet-50 are 93.3% and 93.4% respectively, and the average data access efficiency of pooling layer is 70%.

Keywords: Multi-core vector accelerators · Convolutional neural network · Vectorization · AlexNet · VGG · GoogleNet · ResNet

1 Introduction

Currently, more and more deep learning applications are being deployed to take advantage of the powerful computing power of supercomputers. For example, scientists from Princeton Plasma Physics Laboratory are leading an Aurora ESP project [1] that will leverage AI and exascale computing power to advance fusion energy research. Patton demonstrated a software framework that utilizes high performance computing to automate the design of deep learning networks to analyze cancer pathology images [2]. The award-winning project [3] developed an exascale deep learning application on the Summit supercomputer.

We design an efficient scientific computing accelerator for building a prototype supercomputer system. It leverages a multi-core vector architecture for

This work is supported by the National Natural Science Foundation of China (No. 61572025).

high-density computing. The accelerator achieves high computational efficiency in large-scale scientific computing applications, such as solving dense linear equations [4,5]. Since deep learning is currently more and more widely used, and CNN is one of the representative algorithms of deep learning, it is very necessary to study how to improve the accelerator's performance in processing deep CNNs.

2 Background and Related Work

2.1 The Architecture of Vector Accelerator

Our proposed scientific computing accelerator is a high performance floating-point multi-core vector accelerator developed for high-density computing. The accelerator integrates 24 vector accelerator cores, and achieves a peak single-precision floating-point performance of 9.2TFLOPS with a 2 GHz frequency.

The architecture of our proposed accelerator is shown in Fig. 1. The accelerator core consists of a Scalar Processing Unit (SPU) and a Vector Processing Unit (VPU). The SPU is responsible for scalar computing and flow control and provides a broadcast instruction to broadcast the data from the scalar register to the vector register of the VPU. The VPU integrates 16 Vector Processing Elements (VPEs), and provides the main computation capability.

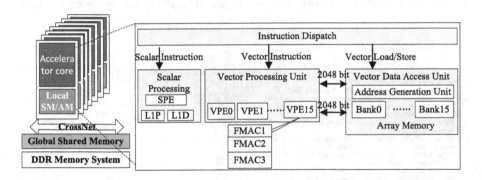

Fig. 1. The architecture of vector accelerator.

2.2 Related Work

To accelerate and optimize the computation of CNN, Maji et al. [6] propose a fast CNN optimization method, which takes advantage of the inherent redundancy in the convolutional layer to reduce the computational complexity of deep networks. Lin et al. [7] propose a novel global and dynamic pruning method to accelerate the CNN by pruning the redundant filter in the global range. Abtahi et al. [8] study the method of using FFT to accelerate CNN on embedded hardware. Dominik et al. [9] study the method of accelerating large-scale CNN with parallel graphics multiprocessor. Lee et al. [10] study how to accelerate the training of deep CNNs by overlapping computation and communication.

To solve the problem that the CPU cannot meet the computational performance requirements of deep CNNs, a large number of researchers have studied how to accelerate the computation of CNNs on emerging processor platforms, such as TPU [11], GPU [12], FPGA [13,14], NPU [15], embedded devices [16], ASIC [17], etc.

The vector accelerator is a novel architecture that has powerful computing performance while maintaining low power consumption. Some researches show that the vector accelerator has high computational efficiency in dealing with FFT [18] and matrix multiplication [5], and is suitable for accelerating large-scale CNN. Researchers also propose some vectorization methods of convolution computation on vector accelerators [19,20]. They use the method of loading weight into vector array memory and loading input image feature data into scalar storage to complete the convolution computation. The common disadvantages are: (1) The weight cannot be effectively shared, the memory bandwidth is wasted, and the computing efficiency of the vector accelerator cannot be fully utilized; (2) Because the size of the channel dimension is uncertain, and it does not match the number of processing units of the vector accelerator; 3) Different CNN models have different channel dimensional sizes for different convolutional layers, which greatly affects the efficiency of loading data, and it is not universal; (4) It needs hardware support of reduce or shuffle and the hardware cost is high.

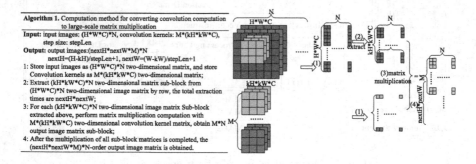

Fig. 2. Computation method for converting convolution computation to large-scale matrix multiplication.

3 Algorithm Mapping of CNN on Vector Accelerator

3.1 Computation Method for Converting Convolution Operations to Large-Scale Matrix Multiplication

As shown in Fig. 2, we propose a computation method for converting convolution computation to large-scale matrix multiplication. It converts a large number of inefficient small-scale convolution products into a large-scale matrix-matrix multiplications, which is very suitable for vectorization computations and can significantly improve the computational efficiency.

Suppose convolution computations are performed on N input images of size H*W*C with M convolution kernels of size kH*kW*C. First, store input images as a (H*W*C)*N two-dimensional matrix, and store convolution kernels as a M*(kH*kW*C) two-dimensional matrix. Second, extract (kH*kW*C) rows from input images matrix according to the convolution window, which form a new (kH*kW*C)*N matrix. Finally, the M*(kH*kW*C) convolution kernel matrix and the new (kH*kW*C)*N input image matrix are used to perform a large-scale matrix-matrix multiplication, and the computed result is M*N output images matrix. Therefore, the original M*N small convolution operations each with the size of kH*kW*C are transformed into a large-scale matrix-matrix multiplication with a M*(kH*kW*C) convolution kernel matrix and a (kH*kW*C)*N input image matrix.

3.2 Vectorization Method of Valid Convolution Layer

Based on the proposed conversion method, the computation of convolution layer is converted into matrix multiplication, which is defined as follows:

$$O[m, n] = \sum_{v=0}^{V-1} F[m, v] * I[v, n] + b[n] \tag{1}$$

The above formula can be regarded as the matrix multiplication of an M*V matrix and an V*N matrix, and the result is then added to the bias vector, where $n \in [0, N)$ and $m \in [0, M)$.

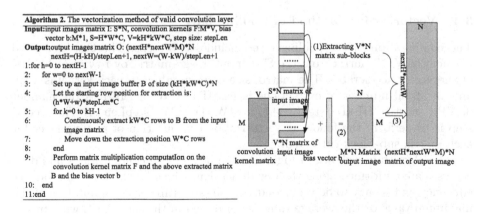

Fig. 3. The vectorization method of valid convolution layer.

As shown in Fig. 3, we can get the vectorization method of the valid convolution layer based on matrix multiplication. The M*V matrix is a convolution kernel matrix, it is stored in a kernel-dimension-last manner, and is continuously stored in the vector accelerator's off-chip memory as a two-dimensional matrix. Each row of the above M*V matrix stores a single convolution kernel, and the storage order in this row is the channel dimension first, followed by the convolution kernel width dimension, and finally the convolution kernel height dimension. The V*N matrix is a matrix sub-block consisting of V rows extracted from the S*N two-dimensional matrix of input image by row. Each column of the above S*N matrix stores a single input image, and the storage order in this column is the channel dimension first, then the image width dimension, and finally the image height dimension.

3.3   Vectorization Method of Same Convolution Layer

Usually, the same convolution always applies a new memory area in advance according to the new image size, fills the 0 element area with 0, and copies the element value of the previous image in other areas. Then, the same method as valid convolution is used to perform convolution computation on the new image. The disadvantages of this method are: (1) At least double the memory overhead; (2) The memory location of the 0 element is discontinuous, resulting in a large operation overhead of padding; (3) It takes a lot of time for copying the original image data.

As shown in Fig. 4, we propose a vectorization method for the same convolution layer, which logically has a "padding 0" operation in the computation process, but does not physically require a "padding 0" operation. The same convolution computation determines whether the input image matrix row corresponding to the convolution kernel data is a 0-element row according to the element value of the vector Z.

3.4   Vectorization Method of Pooling Layer

The computation of the pooling layer includes two steps. The first step is to extract the V*N matrix from the S*N input image matrix by row into the AM of the vector accelerator. The matrix size corresponding to each kernel is V*p, and the total number of extractions is nextH*nextW, where p is the number of VPE, nextH=(H-kH)/stepLen+1, nextW=(W-kW)/stepLen+1. The second step is to perform the following vectorization computation of pooling layer for each matrix sub-block extracted.

The algorithm is shown in Fig. 5. As can be seen, all computations and data accesses are performed along the row dimension, which has high memory access efficiency and is easy to be vectorized. At the same time, the computation of the maximum value or the average value is performed in the same VPE without the need for shuffling operations, which is convenient for software pipeline and high computation efficiency.

Algorithm 3. The vectorization method of same convolution layer

Input: input images matrix I: S*N, convolution kernels F:M*V, bias
vector b:M*1, S=H*W*C, V=kH*kW*C, step size: stepLen
padding:pad=((stepLen-1)H-stepLen+kH)/2.

Output: output images matrix O:(H*W*M)*N

1: for h=0 to H-1
2:   for w=0 to W-1
3:     Construct a vector Z of length V to record whether the
       image row corresponding to the convolution kernel element
       is a 0 element row.
4:     Set up an input image buffer B of size (kH*kW*C)*N
5:     for k=0 to kH-1
6:       Determine whether (h>(pad-1) && (w+k)>(pad-1) &&
         h<(H+pad) && (w+k)<(W+pad)) is true;
7:       If yes, continuously extract the C rows from the ((h-pad)
         *W+w-pad+k)*C-th row of input image to B; at the
         same time, set the continuous C elements starting at the
         (h-pad)*W+w-pad+k position of the vector Z to 1;
8:       If not, do not extract rows from the input image; at the
         same time, set the continuous C elements at the
         (h-pad)*W+w-pad+k position of the vector Z to 0;
9:     end
10:    Perform matrix multiplication computation on the
       convolution kernel matrix F, the above extracted matrix B
       and the bias vector b
11: end
12: end

Fig. 4. The vectorization method of same convolution layer.

3.5 Vectorization Method of Fully Connected Layer

The computation of the fully connected layer can be regarded as the product of an M*U matrix and a U*N matrix, and the result of the product is then added to the bias vector. Where the size of the weight matrix of the fully connected layer is M*U, and it is continuously stored in the off-chip memory of the vector accelerator in the input-feature-dimension-first-manner. The size of input image matrix is U*N, and it is continuously stored in the off-chip memory of the vector accelerator in the image-dimension-first-manner. Therefore, the original N matrix-vector multiplications of M*U matrix and a U vector are transformed into a large-scale matrix-matrix multiplication with M*U weight matrix and U*N input image matrix.

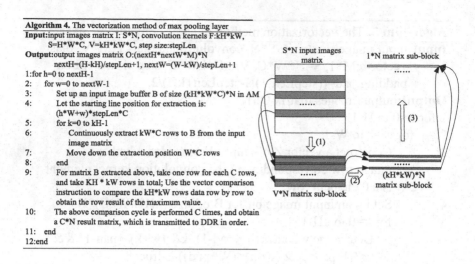

Algorithm 4. The vectorization method of max pooling layer

Input: input images matrix I: S*N, convolution kernels F:kH*kW,
S=H*W*C, V=kH*kW*C, step size:stepLen

Output: output images matrix O:(nextH*nextW*M)*N
nextH=(H-kH)/stepLen+1, nextW=(W-kW)/stepLen+1

1: for h=0 to nextH-1
2:    for w=0 to nextW-1
3:        Set up an input image buffer B of size (kH*kW*C)*N in AM
4:        Let the starting line position for extraction is:
          (h*W+w)*stepLen*C
5:        for k=0 to kH-1
6:            Continuously extract kW*C rows to B from the input
              image matrix
7:            Move down the extraction position W*C rows
8:        end
9:        For matrix B extracted above, take one row for each C rows,
          and take KH * kW rows in total; Use the vector comparison
          instruction to compare the kH*kW rows data row by row to
          obtain the row result of the maximum value.
10:       The above comparison cycle is performed C times, and obtain
          a C*N result matrix, which is transmitted to DDR in order.
11:    end
12: end

Fig. 5. The vectorization method of pooling layer.

4   Experimental Results and Performance Analysis

We conduct the experiments on a 24-core vector accelerator. Its peak single-precision floating-point performance is 9.2TFLOPS at a 2 GHz frequency, and its the peak memory bandwidth is 307 GB/s. Because the VPE length of accelerator is 16, the batch size is set to an integer multiple of 16, which is suitable for vectorization calculation. In our experiments, the value of batch size is 96.

4.1   Performance of Convolution Layers

We evaluate the performance of our proposed design with several typical modern CNN workloads, including the AlexNet, VGG-19, GoogleNet, and ResNet-50 network models.

Figure 6(a) shows the computational efficiency of 6 different types of convolution layer of GoogleNet's Inception (4e) module. The lowest efficiency is seen for the #5 × 5 reduce convolution layer, which is 62.8%. Yet, the computation operation of this type of layer accounts for only 2% of the total operations. Thus, it only has minor effect on the overall efficiency. The computational efficiency of the other 5 types of convolution layers exceeds 90%, which makes the weighted computational efficiency of the Inception (4e) module reach 93.2%.

Figure 6(b) shows the computational efficiency of the 5 different types of convolution layers of ResNet-50's block-2 module. The lowest efficiency is seen for the conv2 convolution layer as 84.1%, and the highest one is seen for the conv4 convolution layer as 93.7%. The weighted computational efficiency of block-2 modules reaches 88%.

Figure 7(a) shows the computational efficiency of all types of convolution layers for AlexNet, VGG-19, GoogleNet, and ResNet-50. The computational

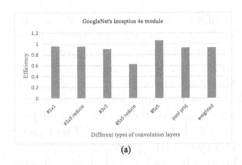
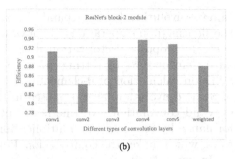

Fig. 6. The computational efficiency of GoogleNet's Inception(4e) and ResNet's block2.

efficiency of the 5 convolution layers of AlexNet is generally high, and its total weighted computational efficiency is as high as 103.9%. The first convolution layer of VGG-19 has the lowest efficiency. It is due to that the convolution kernel of this layer is the smallest one as $3 \times 3 \times 3$, making the computational efficiency of this layer to be only 37.6%. However, the computation operations of this layer accounts for only 0.44% of the total operations, which does not affect the overall computational efficiency of VGG-19, and the total weighted computational efficiency reaches 93.5%. Similarly, the computational efficiency of the first convolution layer of ResNet-50 is 63.3%. Thus, the computation operations of this layer accounts only for 3.1% of the total operations, and its weighted computational efficiency reaches 87.9%. The computational efficiency of the first two layers of GoogleNet is 63.3% and 59.6% respectively, and the proportion of computation operands of the two layers is 5.1% and 0.5% respectively, and the total weighted computational efficiency reaches 88.2%.

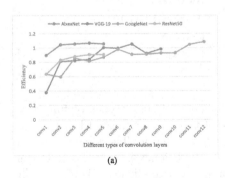
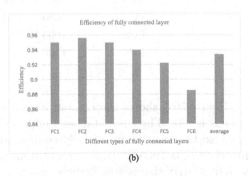

Fig. 7. The computational efficiency of all types of convolution layers and fully connected layer for AlexNet, VGG-19, GoogleNet, and ResNet-50.

Parts of the convolution layers achieve more than 100% computational efficiency because these convolution layers are Same convolution layers. These same convolution layers expand the scale of calculation matrix and increase the floating-point operations of convolution layer by padding 0 elements. However, the proposed vectorization algorithm of the Same convolution layer records all 0-element rows by setting up a Z vector, and omits the multiplication and addition calculation of 0-element rows. Therefore, the vectorization algorithm of Same convolution layer proposed in this paper not only gains the advantages of Valid convolution layer method, but also improves the computational performance by reducing the multiplication and addition calculation of 0-element rows, which makes the computational efficiency exceeding 100%.

In general, all convolution layers of the four network models have achieved high computational efficiency. A few convolution layers with small convolution kernels have lower computational efficiency, but the proportion of the computation operands of the layers is relatively small, which makes the weighted computational efficiency of the four network models very high.

4.2   Performance of Fully Connected Layers

The AlexNet, VGG-19, GoogleNet, and ResNet-50 all contain fully connected layers. AlexNet and VGG-19 have 3 fully connected layers, while GoogleNet and ResNet-50 only have one fully connected layer. As shown in Table 1, it is divided into 6 types according to the size of weight matrix.

Table 1. The six different types of fully connected layers.

Classification	Weight matrix	Network model
FC1	4096×9216	AlexNet
FC2	4096×25088	VGG-19
FC3	4096×4096	AlexNet,VGG-19
FC4	1000×4096	AlexNet,VGG-19
FC5	1000×2048	GoogleNet
FC6	1000×1024	ResNet-50

Figure 7(b) shows the computational efficiency of the 6 types of fully connected layers. The computational efficiency of the fully connected layer is high because the matrix size of fully connected layers is large. The smallest weight matrix size is 1000*1024, and its computational efficiency is 88.5%. The largest weight matrix size is 4096*25088 and its computational efficiency is 95.6%. The average computational efficiency is 93.4%.

4.3   Performance of Pooling Layers

The AlexNet, VGG-19, GoogleNet, and ResNet-50 contain 16 different types of pooling layers. Figure 8(a) shows the computational efficiency and data access efficiency of 16 different types of pooling layers, where the left ordinate is used to identify the data access efficiency, and the right ordinate is used to identify the computational efficiency. It can be seen from the figure that the computational efficiency of the pooling layer is low, about 0.22% on average, because the computation density of the pooling layer is very low. However, the data access efficiency of the pooling layer is very good, about 70% on average. This is because all data access of the pooling layer is performed in matrix rows according to the method proposed in this paper, and the data access efficiency is high.

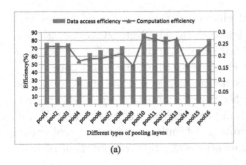 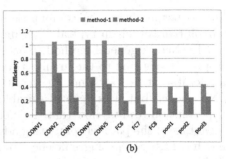

(a)   (b)

Fig. 8. (a) The computational efficiency of pooling layer for AlexNet, VGG-19, GoogleNet and ResNet-50. (b) Performance comparison of different vectorization method of AlexNet.

4.4 Performance Comparison

As shown in Fig. 8(b), we take AlexNet as an example to compare the computational performance of the convolution layer, fully connected layer and pooling layer of different vectorization methods, where the performance data of pooling layer is data access efficiency. The method-1 is the vectorization method proposed in this paper, in which input images are stored in the image-dimension-first manner; and the method-2 is the vectorization method in which input images are stored in the channel-dimension-first manner. As can be seen from the figure, the method-1 significantly improves the computational efficiency of convolution layer and fully connected layer, and the data access efficiency of pooling layer of AlexNet.

Table 2 compares the CNN inference performance of our accelerator with the other three high-performance GPUs [21]. As can be seen from the table, NVIDIA V100 achieves the best performance by images/s, followed by our accelerator. However, NVIDIA V100 has the best performance only on the AlexNet by images/TFLOPS, our accelerator achieved the best performance on the GoogleNet and ResNet-50 by images/TFLOPS.

Table 2. Comparison of CNN inference performance.

Classification	AlexNet		VGG-19		GoogleNet		ResNet-50	
	Images/s	Images/TFLOPS	Images/s	Images/TFLOPS	Images/s	Images/TFLOPS	Images/s	Images/TFLOPS
Our accelerator	3777	410	279	31	2679	291	1183	129
NVIDIA V100	8700	621	500	36	4000	286	1700	121
NVIDIA T4	2600	321	100	12	1100	136	500	62
NVIDIA P4	2600	473	100	18	1100	200	500	91

5   Conclusion

This paper analyzes the computational characteristics of feature images and convolution kernels in typical CNN models such as AlexNet, VGG, GoogleNet, and ResNet. A general method to accelerate the computation of deep CNNs is proposed according to the architectural characteristics of the multi-core vector accelerator. It is worth noting that this method does not optimize a specific CNN model, but it is general suitable for various typical deep CNN models. Experimental results show that the method proposed in this paper can take full advantage of the parallel computing advantages of multi-core vector accelerators and has high computing efficiency. It can accelerate the computation of deep CNNs.

References

1. Aurora ESP Projects. https://www.alcf.anl.gov/science/projects/AuroraESP/all. Accessed 24 Aug 2020
2. Patton, R.M., et al.: Exascale deep learning to accelerate cancer research (2019)
3. Kurth, T., et al.: Exascale deep learning for climate analytics. In: Proceedings of the International Conference for High Performance Computing, Networking, Storage, and Analysis, pp. 1–12, November 2018
4. Ma, S., et al.: Coordinated DMA: improving the DRAM access efficiency for matrix multiplication. IEEE Trans. Parallel Distrib. Syst. **30**(10), 2148–2164 (2019)
5. Liu, Z., Tian, X., Ma, S.: The implementation and optimization of parallel linpack on multi-core vector accelerator. In: 2019 IEEE 21st International Conference on High Performance Computing and Communications, pp. 2261–2269. IEEE (2019)
6. Maji, P., Mullins, R.: 1D-FALCON: accelerating deep convolutional neural network inference by co-optimization of models and underlying arithmetic implementation. In: Lintas, A., Rovetta, S., Verschure, P.F.M.J., Villa, A.E.P. (eds.) ICANN 2017. LNCS, vol. 10614, pp. 21–29. Springer, Cham (2017). https://doi.org/10.1007/978-3-319-68612-7_3
7. Lin, S., Ji, R., Li, Y., Wu, Y., Huang, F., Zhang, B.: Accelerating convolutional networks via global & dynamic filter pruning. In: Proceedings of the Twenty-Seventh International Joint Conference on Artificial Intelligence, pp. 2425–2432 (2018)
8. Abtahi, T., Shea, C., Kulkarni, A., Mohsenin, T.: Accelerating convolutional neural network with FFT on embedded hardware. IEEE Trans. Very Large Scale Integr. (VLSI) Syst. **26**(9), 1737–1749 (2018)

9. Scherer, D., Schulz, H., Behnke, S.: Accelerating large-scale convolutional neural networks with parallel graphics multiprocessors. In: Diamantaras, K., Duch, W., Iliadis, L.S. (eds.) ICANN 2010. LNCS, vol. 6354, pp. 82–91. Springer, Heidelberg (2010). https://doi.org/10.1007/978-3-642-15825-4_9
10. Lee, S., Jha, D., Agrawal, A., Choudhary, A., Liao, W.: Parallel deep convolutional neural network training by exploiting the overlapping of computation and communication. In: 2017 IEEE 24th International Conference on High Performance Computing (2017)
11. Jouppi, N.P., et al.: In-data center performance analysis of a tensor processing unit. In: Proceedings of the IEEE/ACM International Symposium on Computer Architecture (ISCA), pp. 1–12 (2017)
12. Imani, M., Peroni, D., Kim, Y., Rahimi, A., Rosing, T.: Efficient neural network acceleration on GPGPU using content addressable memory. In: Proceedings of the IEEE/ACM Proceedings Design, Automation and Test in Eurpoe (DATE), pp. 1026–1031 (2017)
13. Zhang, C., Li, P., Sun, G., Guan, Y., Xiao, B., Cong, J.: Optimizing FPGA-based accelerator design for deep convolutional neural networks. In: Proceedings of the ACM Symposium on FPGAs, pp. 161–170 (2015)
14. Rahman, A., Lee, J., Choi, K.: Efficient FPGA acceleration of convolutional neural networks using logical-3D compute array. In: Proceedings of the IEEE/ACM Proceedings Design, Automation and Test in Eurpoe (DATE), pp. 1393–1398 (2016)
15. Intel Neural Network Processor. https://www.intel.ai/intel-nervana-neural-network-processor-architecture-update. Accessed 24 Aug 2020
16. Wang, Y., Li, H., Li, X.: Re-architecting the on-chip memory sub-system of machine-learning accelerator for embedded devices. In: Proceedings of the IEEE/ACM International Conference on Computer-Aided Design (ICCAD), p. 13 (2016)
17. Hu, M., et al.: Dot-product engine for neuromorphic computing: programming 1T1M crossbar to accelerate matrix-vector multiplication. In: Proceedings of the ACM/IEEE Design Automation Conference (DAC), p. 19 (2016)
18. Liu, Z., Tian, X., Chen, X., Lei, Y., Liao, M.: Efficient large-scale 1D FFT vectorization on multi-core vector accelerator. In: 2019 IEEE 21st International Conference on High Performance Computing and Communications, pp. 484–491. IEEE (2019)
19. Zhang, J.Y., Guo, Y., Hu, X.: Design and implementation of deep neural network for edge computing. IEICE Trans. InfSyst. **101**, 1982–1996 (2018)
20. Yang, C., Chen, S., Wang, Y., Zhang, J.: The evaluation of DCNN on vector-SIMD DSP. IEEE Access **7**, 22301–22309 (2019)
21. INFERENCE using the NVIDIA T4. https://www.dell.com/support/article/zh-cn/sln316556/inference-using-the-nvidia-t4?lang=en. Accessed 24 Aug 2020

M-DRL: Deep Reinforcement Learning Based Coflow Traffic Scheduler with MLFQ Threshold Adaption

Tianba Chen, Wei Li[✉], YuKang Sun, and Yunchun Li

Beijing Key Lab of Network Technology, School of Computer Science
and Engineering, Beihang University, Beijing, China
{chentb,liw,sunyk2115,lych}@buaa.edu.cn

Abstract. The coflow scheduling in data-parallel clusters can improve application-level communication performance. The existing coflow scheduling method without prior knowledge usually uses Multi-Level Feedback Queue (MLFQ) with fixed threshold parameters, which is insensitive to coflow traffic characteristics. Manual adjustment of the threshold parameters for different application scenarios often has long optimization period and is coarse in optimization granularity. We propose M-DRL, a deep reinforcement learning based coflow traffic scheduler by dynamically setting thresholds of MLFQ to adapt to the coflow traffic characteristics, and reduces the average coflow completion time. Trace-driven simulations on the public dataset show that coflow communication stages using M-DRL complete $2.08\times(6.48\times)$ and $1.36\times(1.25\times)$ faster on average coflow completion time (95-th percentile) in comparison to per-flow fairness and Aalo, and is comparable to SEBF with prior knowledge.

Keywords: Coflow · Datacenter network · Deep reinforcement learning

1 Introduction

With the rapid development of big data analytics application, the parallel flows abstracted as coflow [3,6,13,14], appear in the datacenter network, which means that a communication stage completes only when all the flows are completed. A typical scenario is the shuffle in MapReduce and Spark. The optimization of traditional datacenter network is mostly based on packet-level and flow-level, and the datacenter network cannot perceive the communication requirement in parallel computing [3,13,14]. In recent years, some work such as Varys [6], Aalo [4] and CODA [15] have studied how to optimize the datacenter network based on coflow. The coflow scheduling without prior knowledge, Aalo [4] and CODA [15] overcome the shortcomings of Varys [6] requiring prior knowledge of coflow and use discretized Coflow-Aware Least-Attained Service (CLAS) [4] based on MLFQ [4,15] to centrally schedule coflows. In these methods, MLFQ is

X. He et al. (Eds.): NPC 2020, LNCS 12639, pp. 80–91, 2021.
https://doi.org/10.1007/978-3-030-79478-1_7

used to divide coflows into different queues according to the coflow size. CLAS sensitive to coflow size is adopted to scheduling between different queues, First-In First-Out (FIFO) sensitive to the arrival time of coflow is used within the same queue, and queue thresholds of MLFQ balance the overall performance of coflow scheduling. The fixed threshold of MLFQ queue is not sensitive to the change of traffic characteristics. Dynamics in complicated network environment make discretized CLAS scheduler based on MLFQ unable to achieve maximum scheduling performance. However, manual parameter optimization has a long cycle and is coarse in optimization granularity [2].

In order to deal with this problem, we introduce deep reinforcement learning (DRL) to automatically adjust MLFQ thresholds. DRL is a method for processing sequence decision-making in machine learning [7]. Some recent studies have applied DRL to network scheduling [2,10,12]. DRL uses neural networks with strong generalization ability to process raw and noisy inputs and optimizes the target through reward signals indirectly, suitable for dealing with network scheduling problems [2,10,12].

Therefore, we propose M-DRL, a deep reinforcement learning based coflow traffic scheduler to dynamically setting thresholds of MLFQ, which is driven by network traffic. Trace-driven simulations on the public dataset show that communication stages using M-DRL complete $2.08\times$ and $1.36\times$ faster on average coflow completion time in comparison to per-flow fairness and Aalo, and M-DRL's performance is comparable to that of SEBF using prior knowledge.

In summary, the main contribution of this paper include:

- It is the first time to model MLFQ-based coflow scheduling problem with DRL, and design state, action and reward function of DRL.
- We propose a data-driven method, M-DRL, adopting DDPG to adaptively adjust MLFQ queue thresholds to reduce the average coflow completion time.
- We conduct extensive simulations to evaluate the performance of M-DRL. The results of the experiments show that M-DRL outperforms per-flow fairness and Aalo, and is comparable to SEBF (the state-of-the-art method with prior knowledge) .

This paper is organized as follows: Sect. 2 describes the existing problem in the discretized CLAS of coflow scheduling. Modeling the coflow scheduling problem with DRL and algorithm design of M-DRL are described in Sect. 3. Section 4 evaluate our solutions. Section 5 reviews related works. Finally, the conclusion and future prospects of this paper is presented in Sect. 6.

2 Coflow Scheduling Model Without Prior Knowledge

2.1 Background

Coflow is a collection of flows between different nodes in the cluster of datacenter network. A coflow completes only when all flows are completed. If a coflow completes faster, then corresponding job completes faster. So optimization for coflow scheduling can improve the communication performance of the application [3,13,14]. To simplify our analysis, the entire datacenter fabric structure is abstracted as one non-blocking switch, which performs well in practice [4,6,15].

In some scenarios, the information about coflow size is difficult to obtain [4,15] and we need to assume that some characteristics of coflow are unknown, such as endpoints, the size of each flow, their arrival times. This kind of coflow scheduling when the characteristics of coflow is unknown is called coflow scheduling without prior knowledge [14]. Generally, only real-time information of coflow can be used, including sent size, width, arrival time and duration of coflow.

2.2   Coflow Scheduling Based on MLFQ

Coflow scheduling methods such as Aalo [4] and CODA [15], use discrete Coflow-Aware Least-Attained Service based on MLFQ [4]. MLFQ consists of K queues $(Q_1, Q_2, \ldots, Q_K)$, with queue priority decreasing from the first queue Q_1 to the last queue Q_K. There are $K - 1$ thresholds $(th_1, th_2, \ldots, th_{K-1})$ between K queues and the i-th queue contains coflows of size within $[th_{i-1}, th_i)$. Note that $th_0 = 0$, and $th_K = \infty$. Actions taken during three lifecycle events determine the priority of a coflow.

1) New coflows enter the highest priority queue Q_1 when they start.
2) A coflow is demoted from Q_i to Q_{i+1}, when its size exceeds threshold th_i.
3) Coflows are removed from their current queues upon completion.

Preemptive priority scheduling is used between different queues. High priority queues are prioritized and different coflows in the same queue use FIFO method. The discretized CLAS uses MLFQ to divide coflows into different queues and assigns coflow priority in terms of coflow size and arrival time.

CLAS is appropriate for traffic with heavy-tailed distribution [6], and FIFO is appropriate for traffic with light-tailed distribution [5]. The discretized CLAS based on MLFQ combines the CLAS with FIFO to better communication performance. The arrival time of coflow has a greater impact on scheduling performance for the FIFO scheduling within the same queue. Coarse-grained setting of queue threshold will reduce the performance of FIFO.

For example [4], the number of MLFQ queues is set to 10, and the formal queue threshold is defined as $th_{i+1} = E \times th_i$, where $E = 10$ and $th_1 = 10\,MB$. Coflow can be assigned to different queues according to the magnitude of coflow size, where

$$th_{i+1} - th_i = E \times (th_i - th_{i-1}) \tag{1}$$

The range of coflow size in queue Q_{i+1} is E times that in queue Q_i.

The experiments shows that during the scheduling process, more than 95% of coflows utilize only three priorities in MLFQ and the rest queues are empty. It's obvious that the granularity of threshold setting is too coarse, and the discretized CLAS degenerates into FIFO to some extent. Therefore, it is necessary to provide data-driven MLFQ threshold setting for different communication scenarios.

3   Data-Driven MLFQ Threshold Setting Using DRL

Manual MLFQ threshold setting often requires traffic statistics collection, offline model analysis, parameter optimization and so on, which has a long design cycle [2] and can only be optimized from the global distribution characteristics. Therefore, a data-driven threshold setting method can greatly reduce overhead of parameter optimization, and can improve coflow scheduling performance in a finer granularity.

We use deep reinforcement learning to model the coflow scheduling problem and design an M-DRL scheduler to make decisions based on the network status automatically. The algorithm DDPG [9] is used in M-DRL to optimize the MLFQ threshold setting.

3.1   DRL Formulation

We construct the coflow scheduling problem as an MDP of continuous state and continuous action in discrete time. By training historical scheduling information, we learn the optimal scheduling policy π, which defines state $s_t \in S$, action $a_t \in A$ and reward function r_t.

In the process of coflow scheduling, M-DRL controls the setting of MLFQ threshold through coflow status in the network environment. By continuously sampling and training, agent learns the appropriate MLFQ threshold setting policy, which reduces the average coflow completion time. M-DRL regards the coflow scheduling process with one hour as an episode. When an episode ends, the initial state is reset. An episode is divided into many time steps and each time step Δt is set to ten seconds. The agent obtains the state s_t from the environment every time Δt, generates an action control a_t according to the learned policy, and gets the immediate reward r_t.

State Space. The status in network scheduling is taken as state in units of coflow, including the identifier id (unique ID in cluster), coflow width $width$ (the number of flows included in the coflow), sent size of coflow $sent$ (current transmission volume of the coflow) and duration of coflow $duration$ (spent time from the arrival time of the coflow). These attributes are related to the size distribution of coflow. At the time t, the number of scheduled coflows is not fixed. We limit the maximum number of coflows represented in the state to N. The coflow in state is sorted increasingly according to the sent size. When the number of coflows is greater than N, the first N coflows represent state. We use zero padding when the number of coflow is less than N. Thus, the state at time t is represented as

$$s_t = [id_1, width_1, sent_1, duration_1, \ldots, id_N, width_N, sent_N, duration_N] \quad (2)$$

where N is set to 10, and the dimension of state is $4 \times N = 40$ because every coflow has four different attributes.

Action Space. Action is represented by MLFQ threshold. K queues have $K-1$ thresholds $(th_1, th_2, \ldots, th_{K-1})$, and action a_t should be represented by $K-1$ components

$$a_t = [th_1, th_2, \ldots, th_{K-1}] \tag{3}$$

In the experiment, K is 10 and the dimension of a_t is 9. Different MLFQ threshold settings can make the average coflow completion time different.

Reward. Since the optimization goal of M-DRL is to reduce the average completion time of coflows in an episode, we define finished coflow set and active coflow set at time t as CS_t^f and CS_t^a, then the average coflow completion time until the time t is

$$acct_t = \frac{1}{N_t^f} \sum_{c \in CS_t^f} cct^c \tag{4}$$

where N_t^f represents the number of coflows in finished coflow set and cct^c represents the completion time of coflow c. The average coflow duration time is defined as

$$acdt_t = \frac{1}{N_t^f + N_t^a} \left(\sum_{c \in CS_t^f} cct^c + \sum_{c \in CS_t^a} cdt^c \right) \tag{5}$$

where N_t^a represents the number of coflows in active coflow set, and cdt^c represents the duration of coflow c.

$acct_t$ estimates average coflow completion time of the entire episode until state s_t, and $acdt_t$ estimates the effect of coflow scheduling. Therefore, the deviation $|acdt_t - acct_{t-1}|$ represents the contribution degree of current action at time t to the goal. Thus reward function can be defined as

$$r_t = -(acdt_t - acct_{t-1}) \tag{6}$$

3.2   Algorithm Design

We use DDPG [9] with Actor-Critic structure to optimize MLFQ threshold setting, and the algorithm is implemented using popular machine learning framework TensorFlow.

The algorithm uses the Actor-Critic network structure to deal with continuous actions efficiently. Actor is a policy network that generates actions in a given state s, including actor $\mu(s|\theta^\mu)$ and target actor $\mu'(s|\theta^{\mu'})$. Critic is the Q network including critic $Q(s, a|\theta^Q)$ and target critic $Q'(s, a|\theta^{Q'})$, evaluating the value of state-action pair. The role of target network $\mu'(s|\theta^{\mu'})$ and $Q'(s, a|\theta^{Q'})$ is to eliminate the deviation caused by overestimation and stabilize the policy and Q network, thereby improving the stability of training. Soft update in Eq. 7 and 8 is used to update the target networks periodically

$$\theta^{\mu'} \leftarrow \tau\theta^\mu + (1 - \tau)\theta^{\mu'} \tag{7}$$

$$\theta^{Q'} \leftarrow \tau\theta^Q + (1-\tau)\theta^{Q'} \tag{8}$$

and the coefficient τ is 0.001. Both actor and critic network use a two fully-connected hidden layers with 600 and 600 neurons [2] respectively to fit the scheduling strategy fully. The whole algorithm consists of two parts, online inter-action and offline training.

Online Interaction. During the online interaction with the environment as shown in Fig. 1, actor $\mu(s|\theta^\mu)$ generates current action a_t according to state s_t, acting on the environment to generate the next state s_{t+1} and immediate reward r_t. This process is repeated until the end state is reached and transition $\{s_t, a_t, r_t, s_{t+1}\}$ is stored in experience replay buffer during each iteration. Here the OU noise $\mathcal{N}$ is added to the action a_t to increase the early random exploration for environment, as shown in Eq. 9

$$a_t = \mu(s|\theta^\mu) + \mathcal{N}_t \tag{9}$$

With the advance of training, the influence of noise will gradually decrease.

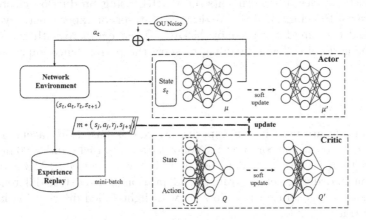

Fig. 1. Algorithm architecture based on DDPG

Offline Training. In the offline training, sample m transitions $\{s_j, a_j, r_j, s_{j+1}\}, j = 1, 2, \ldots, m$ from experience replay buffer where batch size of sampling is 32 and size of experience replay buffer is 10000. Then calculate the target Q value to estimate state s_j according to Eq. 10

$$y_j = r_j + \gamma Q'(s_{j+1}, \mu'(s_{j+1}|\theta^{\mu'})|\theta^{Q'}) \tag{10}$$

The discount factor γ is 0.99. Next, mean squared loss function in Eq. 11 is minimized to update parameters of critic network

$$\frac{1}{m}\sum_{j=1}^{m}(y_j - Q(s_j, a_j|\theta^Q))^2 \tag{11}$$

And the sampled gradients are calculated to update parameters of actor network in Eq. 12

$$\nabla_{\theta^\mu} J \approx \frac{1}{m} \sum_{j=1}^{m} \nabla_a Q(s,a|\theta^Q)|_{s=s_j, a=\mu(s_j)} \nabla_{\theta^\mu} \mu(s|\theta^\mu)|_{s_j} \qquad (12)$$

During the update, Adam optimizer is used for the gradient descent and the learning rate of actor and critic are 0.0001 and 0.001, respectively.

The setup of the coefficient, discount factor and learning rate in the algorithm refers to the paper [9]. M-DRL uses algorithm DDPG to obtain coflow status from the environment, apply MLFQ threshold actions, and repeatedly try to learn optimized MLFQ threshold setting policy, which reduces the average coflow completion time.

4   Evaluation

We conduct a series of experiments on M-DRL using production cluster trace and industrial Benchmark [4,6]. We describe dataset for experiments, evaluation metrics and the simulator used by M-DRL. Then compare with the state-of-the-art methods of coflow scheduling to show the performance improvement of M-DRL.

4.1   Workload

Two workloads are used in our experiment. One is based on Facebook's open source trace [4,6], which contains 526 coflows from 150 racks and 3000 machines, with more than 70,000 flows. And size of each flow is between 1 MB and 10 TB. In addition, in order to demonstrate the adaptation of M-DRL to different coflow distributions, we generate the coflow set with light-tailed distribution based on Facebook trace.

We categorize coflows based on their lengths (size of the longest flow in the coflow) and widths. We consider a coflow to be short if its length is less than 5 MB and narrow if its width is less than 50. Otherwise, it is long and wide. Table 1 shows four categories Short&Narrow (SN), Long&Narrow (LN), Short&Wide (SW) and Long&Wide (LW).

Table 1. Coflows binned by their length (**S**hort and **L**ong) and their width (**N**arrow and **W**ide)

Workload	Coflow Bin	1(SN)	2(LN)	3(SW)	4(LW)
Facebook	% of Coflows	60%	16%	12%	12%
	% of Bytes	0.01%	0.11%	0.88%	99.0%
LightTail	% of Coflows	0%	76%	5%	19%
	% of Bytes	0%	44.21%	0.07%	55.72%

In the Facebook workload, 12% of coflows contributes 99% of the total bytes (LW) and 60% of coflows belongs to SN and its load is only 0.01%. It shows this workload follows heavy-tail distribution and the heavy-tail characteristic are obvious. In the LightTail workload, 95% of coflows is long, accounting for 99% of total bytes. This workload has a light-tailed distribution and 80% of coflow size is between 1 GB to 1 TB. Compared with the Facebook workload, the LightTail workload has a smaller distribution range in coflow size and its coflow size is larger.

4.2   Evaluation Metrics

Varys [6] and Aalo [4] use a flow-level simulator in their evaluation. For fair comparison, we use the same simulator as Varys for trace replay and implement the common interface of RL provided by OpenAI Gym [1] which is used for scheduling and training of M-DRL.

The main evaluation metric is the improvement of average coflow completion time (CCT) in the workload. Normalized CCT is used to evaluate for fairness:

$$Normalized\ Comp.\ Time = \frac{Compared\ Duration}{M - DRL's\ Duration} \qquad (13)$$

If normalized CCT is larger (smaller), then M-DRL is faster (slower). Obviously, if normalized CCT is greater than 1, it means that M-DRL has better communication performance than the compared algorithm, otherwise M-DRL performance is worse.

4.3   Simulation Result

To verify the improvement of M-DRL, we conduct contrast experiments on the Facebook and LightTail workload and compare M-DRL against SEBF [6] (the state-of-the-art coflow scheduling method with prior knowledge), per-flow fairness and Aalo.

Comparison of CCT. Some experiments are performed on Facebook dataset to verify the effectiveness of M-DRL, per-flow fairness, Aalo and SEBF and the results are shown in Fig. 2.

As shown in Fig. 2(a), M-DRL reduces the average and 95th percentile completion times of the overall coflows by up to 2.08× and 6.48×, respectively, in comparison to TCP-based per-flow fairness. From the performance of per-flow fairness on SN, LN, SW, LW (as shown in Table 1), M-DRL ignores characteristics of coflow length and width and has better performance. It can also be further proved in Fig. 2(b) that M-DRL is better than per-flow fairness in every CCT range. In general, per-flow fairness does not consider the characteristics of coflow, only performs flow-level scheduling and treats all flows fairly, performing the worst among the four methods.

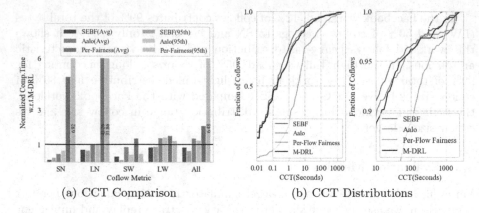

(a) CCT Comparison   (b) CCT Distributions

Fig. 2. [Facebook] Improvements of M-DRL: (a) Average and 95th percentile improvements in communication completion times using M-DRL over SEBF, Aalo and per-flow fairness. The black line represents M-DRL. (b) CCT distributions for SEBF, Aalo, per-flow fairness and M-DRL mechanism. The X-axis is in log scale.

As expected, M-DRL performs better in the overall coflows with the average completion times improved by 1.36× and 95th percentile completion times improved by 1.25× than Aalo. In detail, M-DRL outperforms Aalo on more than 99% of long coflows, LN and LW, and performs worse on SN and SW (Fig. 2(a)). In fact, coflow size is not evenly distributed on the exponent and long coflows appear more frequently in MLFQ. And M-DRL uses MLFQ thresholds sensitive to coflow size through learning in the scheduling to make coflows more evenly distributed in the queues, which means that more queues are allocated for long coflows. Therefore, M-DRL sacrifices the performance of short coflows to schedule the long coflows better and improves the overall communication performance. In Fig. 2(b), M-DRL is better than Aalo in the range of CCT 300–2500 s (red ellipse). This is because the allocation of more queues for long coflows in M-DRL has a greater impact on the scheduling of long coflows.

Compared to SEBF, M-DRL reduces the average and 95th percentile completion times of the overall coflows by up to 0.84× and 0.66×, respectively, as shown in Fig. 2(a). Although M-DRL is not as good as SEBF on short coflows and narrow coflows, M-DRL achieves improvements of 0.86× and 0.90× respectively on the long and wide coflow, LW, which is 99% of bytes. SEBF can calculate the remaining processing time of each coflow through prior knowledge that is difficult to obtain in some scenarios. And M-DRL divides a certain range of coflows into the same queue which are scheduled by FIFO, and reduces the CCT of short coflows.

Adaptation of M-DRL. We conduct experiments and retrain M-DRL on the LightTail dataset to verify its adaptation and results are shown in Fig. 3. Figure 3(a) shows that M-DRL reduces the average and 95th percentile completion times of the overall coflows by up to 1.15× and 1.15×, respectively, in

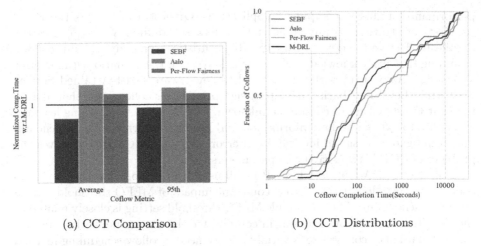

(a) CCT Comparison   (b) CCT Distributions

Fig. 3. [LightTail] (a) Average and 95th percentile improvements in communication completion times using M-DRL over SEBF, Aalo and per-flow fairness. (b) CCT distributions for SEBF, Aalo, per-flow fairness and M-DRL mechanism. The X-axis is in log scale.

comparison to per-flow fairness. M-DRL is superior when CCT is greater than 20 s (Fig. 3(b)). Per-flow fairness treats each coflows fairly and increases the CCT of shorter coflows. However, M-DRL decreases the CCT of shorter coflows though priority scheduling in M-DRL. For coflows with CCT less than 20 s (Fig. 3(b)), M-DRL uses MLFQ to make both short and long coflows in the same queue and performs worse by FIFO scheduling.

Compared to Aalo, M-DRL reduces the average and 95th percentile completion times of the overall coflows by up to 1.26× and 1.23×, respectively (Fig. 3(a)). As can be seen in Fig. 3(b), M-DRL has better performance than Aalo in the range of CCT greater than 100 s, which shows that the fine-grained division of MLFQ thresholds by M-DRL still has an advantage in large coflows of the dataset. Figure 3(a) shows that M-DRL has comparable performance to SEBF with average and 95th percentile improvements being 0.83× and 0.97×. Especially, M-DRL has comparable performance to SEBF in the range of CCT greater than 3000 s (Fig. 3(b)).

In general, M-DRL uses finer granularity to prioritize coflows by learning, showing superior performance than per-flow fairness and Aalo. This demonstrates that M-DRL has a strong adaptation.

5   Related Work

Chowdhury [3] proposed an abstraction of coflow which represents a collection of semantic-related flows to convey requirements of job-specific communications. Later, many coflow-based scheduling methods were proposed to improve the performance of cluster computing applications. Orchestra [5] adopts the First-In First-out strategy to implement inter-coflow scheduling. Varys [6] uses the Smallest-Effective-Bottleneck-First (SEBF) heuristic to greedily schedule coflows assuming that prior knowledge of coflow is known. In the scenario without prior knowledge, Aalo [4] uses the discretized Coflow-Aware Least-Attained Service with Multi-Level Feedback Queue to assign priority for coflows. Further assuming that the structure of coflows is unknown, CODA [15] uses machine learning algorithm to extract coflow information and propose an error-tolerant scheduling to mitigate occasional identification errors. Moreover, CS-DP [8] solves the problem of CODA's sensitivity to parameters.

Aalo [4], CODA [15], and CS-DP [8] all use MLFQ to provide the service to coflow, but they do not take into account the impact of MLFQ threshold setting on coflow scheduling. The reasonable MLFQ threshold setting is closely related to the distribution of coflow size, but in complicated datacenter network scenarios, the distribution of coflow size is variable, so we need a coflow scheduling method that is sensitive to the coflow size distribution.

In recent years, deep reinforcement learning [7] has been applied to architecture design [11], flow control [2] and network scheduling [10,12]. In traffic scheduling, AuTO [2] uses DDPG to make flow scheduler to adapt to the different pattern of traffic, which directly inspired us to apply DRL to optimize the coflow scheduling problem. In congestion control, MVFST-RL [12] proposes a DRL-based congestion control framework to adapt to changes in network congestion scenarios, dynamically control the transmission rate of each node to maximize the overall throughout and minimize delay and packet loss rate. In job scheduling, Decima [10] uses a graph neural network structure to process job and cluster information as the state input of algorithm PG to adapt to different cluster applications of the big data computing framework.

6 Conclusion

This paper proposes a DRL-based MLFQ threshold adaption method which is driven by coflow traffic within network environment. It realizes an adaptation to dynamic network environment by automatically setting the MLFQ threshold. Experiments show that M-DRL has comparable SEBF communication performance and performs better than Aalo and per-flow fairness.

In the future, we will toward to directly optimize the priority setting for every coflow in scheduling with deep reinforcement learning, and deploying the RL agent in an operational network to validate the effectiveness. We also plan to improve the performance of M-DRL in terms of neural network structure and better DRL algorithms for continuous action control, and compare with other non-AI scheduling to verify the performance of M-DRL.

Acknowledgement. This work is supported by the National Key Research and Development Program of China (Grant No. 2016YFB1000304) and National Natural Science Foundation of China (Grant No. 1636208).

References

1. Brockman, G., et al.: Openai gym (2016). arXiv preprint arXiv:1606.01540
2. Chen, L., Lingys, J., Chen, K., Liu, F.: Scaling deep reinforcement learning for datacenter-scale automatic traffic optimization. In: Proceedings of the 2018 Conference of the ACM Special Interest Group on Data Communication, pp. 191–205 (2018)
3. Chowdhury, M., Stoica, I.: Coflow: a networking abstraction for cluster applications. In: Proceedings of the 11th ACM Workshop on Hot Topics in Networks, pp. 31–36 (2012)
4. Chowdhury, M., Stoica, I.: Efficient coflow scheduling without prior knowledge. ACM SIGCOMM Comput. Commun. Rev. **45**(4), 393–406 (2015)
5. Chowdhury, M., Zaharia, M., Ma, J., Jordan, M.I., Stoica, I.: Managing data transfers in computer clusters with orchestra. ACM SIGCOMM Comput. Commun. Rev. **41**(4), 98–109 (2011)
6. Chowdhury, M., Zhong, Y., Stoica, I.: Efficient coflow scheduling with varys. In: Proceedings of the 2014 ACM Conference on SIGCOMM, pp. 443–454 (2014)
7. François-Lavet, V., Henderson, P., Islam, R., Bellemare, M.G., Pineau, J.: An introduction to deep reinforcement learning. arXiv preprint arXiv:1811.12560 (2018)
8. Li, C., Zhang, H., Zhou, T.: Coflow scheduling algorithm based density peaks clustering. Futur. Gener. Comput. Syst. **97**, 805–813 (2019)
9. Lillicrap, T.P., et al.: Continuous control with deep reinforcement learning. arXiv preprint arXiv:1509.02971 (2015)
10. Mao, H., Schwarzkopf, M., Venkatakrishnan, S.B., Meng, Z., Alizadeh, M.: Learning scheduling algorithms for data processing clusters. In: Proceedings of the ACM Special Interest Group on Data Communication, pp. 270–288 (2019)
11. Penney, D.D., Chen, L.: A survey of machine learning applied to computer architecture design. arXiv preprint arXiv:1909.12373 (2019)
12. Sivakumar, V.: MVFST-RL: an asynchronous RL framework for congestion control with delayed actions. arXiv preprint arXiv:1910.04054 (2019)
13. Wang, K., Zhou, Q., Guo, S., Luo, J.: Cluster frameworks for efficient scheduling and resource allocation in data center networks: a survey. IEEE Commun. Surv. Tutor. **20**(4), 3560–3580 (2018)
14. Wang, S., Zhang, J., Huang, T., Liu, J., Pan, T., Liu, Y.: A survey of coflow scheduling schemes for data center networks. IEEE Commun. Mag. **56**(6), 179–185 (2018)
15. Zhang, H., Chen, L., Yi, B., Chen, K., Chowdhury, M., Geng, Y.: Coda: toward automatically identifying and scheduling coflows in the dark. In: Proceedings of the 2016 ACM SIGCOMM Conference, pp. 160–173 (2016)

A Close Look at Multi-tenant Parallel CNN Inference for Autonomous Driving

Yitong Huang[1], Yu Zhang[1(✉)], Boyuan Feng[2], Xing Guo[1], Yanyong Zhang[1], and Yufei Ding[2]

[1] University of Science and Technology of China, Hefei, China
{hyt,guoxing}@mail.ustc.edu.cn, {yuzhang,yanyongz}@ustc.edu.cn
[2] University of California, Santa Barbara, USA
{boyuan,yufeiding}@cs.ucsb.edu

Abstract. Convolutional neural networks (CNNs) are widely used in vision-based autonomous driving, i.e., detecting and localizing objects captured in live video streams. Although CNNs demonstrate the state-of-the-art detection accuracy, processing multiple video streams using such models in real-time imposes a serious challenge to the on-car computing systems. The lack of optimized system support, for example, could lead to a significant frame loss due to the high processing latency, which is unacceptable for safety-critical applications. To alleviate this problem, several optimization strategies such as batching, GPU parallelism, and data transfer modes between CPU/GPU have been proposed, in addition to a variety of deep learning frameworks and GPUs. It is, however, unclear how these techniques interact with each other, which particular combination performs better, and under what settings. In this paper, we set out to answer these questions. We design and develop a Multi-Tenant Parallel CNN Inference Framework, MPIn-fer, to carefully evaluate the performance of various parallel execution modes with different data transfer modes between CPU/GPU and GPU platforms. We find that on more powerful GPUs such as GTX 1660, it achieves the best performance when we adopt parallelism across CUDA contexts enhanced by NVIDIA Multi-Process Service (MPS), with 147.06 FPS throughput and 14.50 ms latency. Meanwhile, on embedded GPUs such as Jetson AGX Xavier, pipelining is a better choice, with 46.63 FPS throughput and 35.09 ms latency.

Keywords: Multi-Tenant · Parallel strategy · Autonomous driving · CNN

1 Introduction

Cameras are increasingly deployed on self-driving cars because they offer a much more affordable solution than LIDARs [15]. A car can install a surround-view camera system consisting of up to 12 cameras to capture the panoramic view of the surrounding, which is critical for safe driving [4,5]. For such a system, each camera continuously generates a video stream. Upon these video streams, convolutional neural networks (CNNs) such as Faster R-CNN [13] and YOLOv3 [12] are usually deployed to achieve accurate object detection. However, these computation-intensive CNN models

© IFIP International Federation for Information Processing 2021
Published by Springer Nature Switzerland AG 2021
X. He et al. (Eds.): NPC 2020, LNCS 12639, pp. 92–104, 2021.
https://doi.org/10.1007/978-3-030-79478-1_8

usually lead to long latency and low throughput (measured by the number of simultaneous camera streams that are supported) due to the limited processing power of on-car CPU/GPUs. For example, although the original implementation of YOLOv3-416 on the Darknet [11] claims to run within 29 ms on desktop GPU – Titan X (Table 1), its actual latency can go up to 108 ms on Jetson AGX Xavier, an embedded GPU. The problem deteriorates rapidly as more cameras are installed on self-driving cars for better sensing.

Table 1. Specifications and software versions of NVIDIA devices

Platform	Titan X (Desktop)	DRIVE PX2 (Embedded)	GTX 1660 (Desktop)	Jetson AGX Xavier (Embedded)
Price	$1200	$ 15000	$ 219	$ 699
CPU	–	8-core ARM	8-core Intel i7†	8-core ARM
GPU	3584 CUDA cores	1408 CUDA cores × 2	1408 CUDA cores	512 CUDA cores
Power	250 W	80 W	120 W	30 W
FP32 OP/s	11 TFLOPS	8 TFLOPS	4.3 TFLOPS	5.5 TFLOPS
INT8 OP/s	44 TOPS	20–24 TOPS	–	22 TOPS
Software	[11]	[15]	MPInfer	MPInfer
CUDA	–	9.0	10.2	10.1
TensorRT	–	-	7.0.0	6.0.1
libtorch	–	–	1.3.1	–

† This Intel CPU does not belong to the GTX 1660 GPU card

Recently, this problem has aroused the attention from both the academic and industrial community. Firstly, the wide adoption of deep learning models has accelerated the upgrade of GPUs and the development of inference frameworks. For example, TensorRT [10] is a high performance inference framework that NVIDIA has introduced and updated frequently since 2017. Meanwhile, new GPU hardware includes desktop GPUs like GTX 1660, GTX 2080 and embedded GPUs like DRIVE PX2, Jetson AGX Xavier, etc. Secondly, several aspects of parallel execution modes have been explored and applied to deep learning inference. For example, in [15], YOLOv2 is altered to enable pipelined execution, with parallel layer execution as an option, in order to improve the throughput; in [3] and [6], the authors propose to boost the throughput via cloud-based CNN inference and dynamic batching; the effect of the CUDA context parallelism mode and the NVIDIA MPS mode is studied in [6], and several data transfer modes between CPU/GPU are evaluated in [1].

With the emergence of these hardware/software techniques, it calls for a comprehensive study of the GPU system that can carefully evaluate the effect of these techniques, preferably with combinations of techniques at different levels. Such an evaluation study should bear in mind the characteristics of self-driving systems such as low latency, low power consumption and low computing resources, and should be able to answer: (1) which parallel execution mode yields the best performance, by how much; (2) how does this performance gain change with the number of concurrent video streams, the number of parallel threads and the data transfer modes; (3) how much do the inference framework and CNN models impact the multi-stream video inference performance.

In this paper, we set out to conduct such a comprehensive evaluation study to answer these questions. We develop a Multi-tenant Parallel CNN Inference framework, MPInfer, to support several proposed techniques and serve as a common platform for performance comparison. On MPInfer, we carry out detailed performance characterization that considers different parallel execution modes, data transfer modes between CPU/GPU (pageable, pinned, unified), and GPU devices. In particular, three aspects of parallel execution modes are carefully examined: 1) pipelining, 2) batching, and 3) GPU parallelism. Here, the GPU parallelism includes: 1) parallelism across CUDA streams in a single CUDA context; 2) parallelism across CUDA contexts and 3) parallelism across CUDA contexts enhanced by NVIDIA Multi-Process Service (MPS mode for short below) [9]. Targeting at optimizing CNN inference for self-driving systems, we include embedded GPUs in our study and choose TensorRT as the baseline learning framework because of its high performance. We choose one-stage YOLOv3 and two-stage Faster R-CNN for evaluation.

We conduct the performance evaluation on GTX 1660 and Jetson AGX Xavier. Table 1 lists the specifications and software versions of these two architectures as well as Titan X and PX2 which were used by [11] and [15], respectively. Our results show that, when using YOLOv3, the MPS mode achieves the best performance on GTX 1660, reaching 147.06 FPS throughput and 14.50 ms latency. While on Jetson AGX Xavier, pipelining is a better choice, reaching 46.63 FPS throughput and 35.09 ms latency. In addition to the overall trend, we also have the following detailed observations. Firstly, when the workload (*e.g.*, 5 cameras) is close to the system capacity, the latency of MPS mode does not increase with the parallel number. Instead, when the workload (*e.g.*, 6 cameras) is much higher than the capacity, the latency of MPS mode increases approximately linearly with the parallel number. Secondly, pageable/pinned memory have similar performance impact on MPS while the unified memory performs the worst. Thirdly, compared to LibTorch, TensorRT reduces the latency by 61.7% and improves throughput by 3.19×. Fourthly, both CUDA stream and pipelining modes achieve the best energy efficiency (0.147 J of GPU per frame) on Jetson AGX Xavier. Finally, using YOLOv3 can support 5 cameras while using Faster R-CNN can only support 2 cameras.

2   Background and Related Work

GPU Programming Models. The CUDA programming model provides the CUDA stream and CUDA context for GPU parallelism. A sequence of operations in a CUDA stream execute in issue-order on the GPU. Operations in different streams can execute in parallel. A CUDA context groups CUDA streams. Different CUDA contexts execute in a time slicing style. The key difference is that different CUDA streams have shared address space while CUDA contexts do not, and CUDA context also introduces overhead during GPU context switch. Moreover, NVIDIA provides MPS for transparently enabling co-operative multi-process CUDA applications. Despite these potential benefits, CUDA programming model and optimization techniques also exist non-obvious pitfalls [16], and are largely unrecognized among the deep learning community, which hurdles the exploitation of these techniques in accelerating CNN inference.

Object Detection and Autonomous Driving. Auto-driving continuously captures images of surrounding and detects objects in these images to follow the road signs and avoid collision. These targets naturally align with object detection, leading to the wide deployment of CNNs in self-driving cars for achieving the high detection accuracy and high safety. Among these CNNs, YOLOv3 has become the most prevalent CNN due to the low computation overhead and the high accuracy. However, a tension exists between the high resource consumption of CNNs and the limited budget on self-driving cars. This tension exacerbates when multiple cameras are deployed on the self-driving cars and image streams keep coming from these cameras. This tension motivates the design of MPInfer, a multi-tenant parallel CNN inference framework for auto-driving.

Efficient CNN Inference Framework. Several works have been proposed to accelerate CNN inference for autonomous driving. NVIDIA TensorRT Inference Server [3] is a containerized server to deploy models from different frameworks in data centers and it improves utilization of both GPUs and CPUs. [15] introduces the pipelined execution of CNN models for autonomous-driving applications. LibTorch is the C++ version of the popular framework PyTorch. Darknet is a C framework introduced by the author of YOLO. TensorRT [10] provides a SDK for the high-performance deep learning inference. While the inference of individual CNN is accelerated, it is unclear how these frameworks impact the multi-stream video inference performance.

3   Design of MPInfer

Below, we present the overview, design goals and issues of MPInfer, which is a common platform to conduct comprehensive evaluation of various parallel execution modes.

3.1   Overview of MPInfer

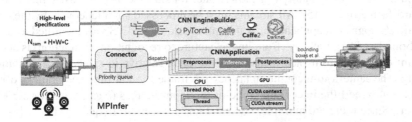

Fig. 1. Overview architecture of MPInfer

We show the overview of MPInfer design in Fig. 1. MPInfer takes a CNN model's high-level specifications and tunable parameters (*e.g.,* batch size and data type) as input.

CNNEngineBuilder then utilizes these specifications to generate a set of optimized CNN models for efficient execution. We design *CNNEngineBuilder* to be general enough for handle a large variety of CNN inference models (*e.g.,* Faster R-CNN and YOLO), considering the available resource budget and application requirements (such as inference accuracy). During the execution, MPInfer takes image streams from multiple cameras and queues these images in the connector with a *priority queue*. The *priority queue* orders the received images based on a heuristic task priority algorithm, and then dispatches them to the subsequent *CNNApplication*. *CNNApplication* holds the user-specified CNN model generated by *CNNEngineBuilder* along with the necessary pre- and post-processing, and maintains a pool of workers to execute each task and enables different parallel strategies across image streams. Finally, MPInfer outputs results such as bounding boxes to the next module (*e.g.*, planning) in the self-driving system.

3.2 Design Goals

Configurablility. Configurability is one of the key design goals because MPInfer is designed to support several proposed techniques. Our framework is equipped with the hyper-parameters on the number of cameras or the number of video streams N_c , enabling the full characterization of the workload. Upon this characterization, MPInfer maintains tunable parameters on the number of threads N_t, parallel strategies S, and interactive CPU/GPU memory management techniques M for fully unleashing the parallel computing ability in different GPU acceleration hardware. Although MPInfer is built on the high performance framework TensorRT, MPInfer is also equipped with conditional compilation to support libTorch and Darknet.

Efficiency. Our framework is also designed to choose the best parallel execution mode in a specific configuration which achieves high throughput, low latency and small frame loss rate (FLR). Throughput is measured by the number of images processed in a fixed period. A typical configuration in today's experimental auto-driving vehicle includes a surround-view camera system with up to 12 cameras. Each camera generates a stream of images at rates ranging from 10 to 40 frames per second (FPS) depending on its functionality (*e.g.*, lower rates for side-facing cameras, higher rates for forward-facing ones) [15]. All streams must be processed simultaneously by the object detection/recognition application. A minimum rate of 30 FPS was identified as a real-time boundary [14]. Latency (from image capture to recognition completion) is another relevant critical performance factor and is directly relative to safety for autonomous-driving. The camera-to-recognition latency per frame for real-time autonomous driving should not exceed the inter-frame time of the input images (*e.g.*, 33 ms for a 30 FPS camera). Since there are multiple video streams at a certain frequency, frame loss rate (FLR for short below) is considered as another important metric. FLR can be measured by $FLR = (N_{input} - N_{processed})/N_{input}$. The FLR here is used to show the impact of throughput because the input rate is usually not the same as the processing throughput.

3.3 Design Issues

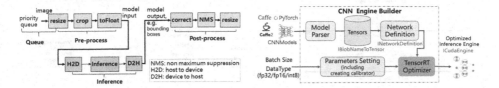

Fig. 2. Process of three-stage CNN inference   **Fig. 3.** CNN engine builder

Detailed Process of Three-Stage CNN Inference. We specify the detailed process of three stages in MPInfer, as illustrated in Fig. 2. The first stage is the *Pre-process* stage on the input images, which resizes the images and crops the input images to a target resolution, and then converts the data type of the image to be float for further processing. The second stage is the *Inference* stage, which first transports the data from the host (*e.g.,* mobile platforms or desktop servers) to the GPU device, namely H2D. The GPU device will conduct inference with CNNs on the received images and generate predictions. These predictions will be further transported to the host for the next stage, namely D2H. The third stage is *Post-process*, which corrects the generated predictions and conducts non-maximal suppression (NMS) [2] for improving the prediction accuracy. Finally, the predictions are resized to fit original image size and applied to the input images as the final results.

CNN Engine Builder. MPInfer introduces a CNN engine builder to build an optimized CNN inference model by calling TensorRT, as shown in Fig. 3. The engine builder consumes two user inputs of the CNNs and the high-level specifications. One input is the CNN model written in Caffe [7] for describing the CNN layer types, layer parameters, and the topological CNN structures. The other input is the user-defined high-level specifications on the batch size and the data type. Batch size N_b decides the trade-off between the latency and the throughput, where a larger batch size usually leads to higher throughput at the cost of higher latency. The data type of CNN weights and tensors $T_{op} \in \{\texttt{fp32}, \texttt{fp16}, \texttt{int8}\}$ guides the optimization of CNN models and shows a significant impact on the inference speed. In particular, `int8` data type consumes $4\times$ less GPU memory and shows proportional speedup compared to `fp32`, while maintaining a comparable inference accuracy [8]. The CNN engine builder feeds these two inputs to the TensorRT optimizer for optimizing individual CNN inference and generating an optimized inference engine with significantly decreased inference latency. TensorRT is chosen to be part of the infrastructure in MPInfer because it is an efficient framework that supports graph optimization, auto-tuning, and `int8` quantization. We reuse it to achieve better performance when using different parallel strategies.

Execution Strategies. One solution to support multiple camera streams is the serial execution. However, it fails to benefit from the parallel execution of heterogeneous equipments(CPU and GPU). To avoid this, we can do the *Pipelining* between CPU and GPU. As jobs on CPU and GPU can run asynchronously, the pre-process job for the current input on CPU can perform in parallel with the inference job of the previous input on

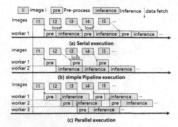 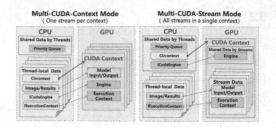

Fig. 4. Different execution strategies. The box width indicates the execution latency

Fig. 5. Memory consumption in different CUDA context/stream modes

GPU. However, due to the complex CUDA kernel design of operators in CNNs, the current operator implementations cannot fully utilize the GPU resource. To further utilize GPU, we can perform tasks in parallel on GPU. Figure 4 shows three execution strategies discussed previously. Although parallel execution in this figure only shows three workers executing in parallel, MPInfer can support more or fewer workers as needed. Longer inference latency of *Parallel* execution is due to the parallel GPU. Post-process is left with inference due to its small latency.

Resource Management of Different GPU Parallel Modes. As mentioned in Sect. 2, modern GPU programming model provides CUDA stream, CUDA context and MPS for specifying fine-grained parallelism levels. We apply these techniques in MPInfer to fully utilize GPUs and design two resource management modes to support these parallelism levels, as illustrated in Fig. 5. The first mode is *Multi-CUDA-Context*, where one CUDA context contains only one CUDA stream. In this mode, each thread maintains a CUcontext for the metadata on the CUDA context execution, an ICudaEngine for the optimized CNN model (network structure and weights), and IExecutionContext for intermediate activation values on the CNN execution. Because the resource isolation between CUDA contexts, each thread needs to instantiate the CNN model (ICudaEngine in TensorRT) alone, which causes the replica of CNN models and weights. The second mode is *Multi-CUDA-Stream*, where all CUDA streams exist in a single CUDA context and share the same engine for the optimized CNN model. This mode significantly reduces the memory overhead in repeatedly storing the same CNN model. Since MPS is a transparently server enabling co-operative multi-process CUDA applications, the resource management between MPS and CUDA context is the same. For short, CUDA context is similar to the process in the operating system, CUDA stream is similar to thread, and MPS is a server to simulate multiple processes as multiple threads.

Data Transfer Modes Between CPU/GPU. As illustrated in Fig. 2, the host input data (images, CPU side) of CNN network should be transferred to device (GPU) memory and the device output of network also needs to transfer to host side. There are three different data transfer modes between CPU/GPU for such operations. The first one is default *pageable memory allocation* of the host data (*e.g.,* memory allocated by malloc). When a data transfer of such memory occurs, GPU needs to first allocate a temporary page-locked (or pinned) memory, then transfers pageable memory to pinned memory and finally transfers pinned memory to device memory. The second one is *pinned memory allocation* of host data (*e.g.*, memory allocated by `cudaHostAlloc`). This does not need to allocate a temporary pinned memory and do the related transfer as the first one. While the allocation of pinned memory will reduce the available physical memory for OS and program, too much allocation will reduce system performance. The third one is the *unified memory allocation* of transfer data. Such memory is a single memory address space accessible from CPU and GPU, so the explicit memory transfer is not needed and the internal software/hardware will do this for the program. MPInfer separately manages the input and the output of the CNN network in each thread to support these three data transfer modes between CPU/GPU, as illustrated in Fig. 5.

Effects of Batching. Batching the input images can reduce the number of CUDA kernel launches. However, the number of cameras used for autonomous-driving is only up to 12 and the wait time to get enough batch size is unacceptable. When the batch size is smaller than 8, latency of individual image increases approximately linearly according to batch size.

4   Evaluation

4.1   Experimental Settings

The measurements are performed on a desktop server GPU (GTX 1660 + 8-core Intel i7) and an embedded GPU system (Jetson AGX Xavier), as detailed in Table 1. We conduct object detection experiments using the officially trained YOLOv3 model in Darknet format and Faster R-CNN in caffe format. Since the GTX1660 platform can support PyTorch, we use the version generated by PyTorch from Darknet as the baseline, denoted as LibTorch. For the embedded Jetson AGX Xavier, we directly use Darknet version as a baseline. The raw image size is 768×576, the input size of YOLOv3 is 416×416 and the input size of Faster R-CNN is 375×500. The length of the priority queue is set to 1, and the latest frame has the highest priority. We use int8 quantization of TensorRT to accelerate the CNN inference.

Since the common frequency of camera 30 Hz, we emulate camera inputs to the CNN at rates 30FPS or its multiples. We measure the latency, throughput and FLR over 10,000 input images in different frame rates. Latency is measured from the arrival time of the image in the priority queue to the time we get the bounding boxes, so the latency includes all three stages in the CNN inference. Throughput is measured by the number of processed images in this time period. Frame loss rate (FLR) is measured by $FLR = (N_{input} - N_{processed})/N_{input}$, where N_{input} is the total number of input images and $N_{processed}$ is the total number of processed images.

We measure the energy consumption on the embedded Xavier platform, which has two INA3221 monitors providing the current power consumption of GPU, CPU, SOC, DDR, and system 5 V. We write a program to read `/sys/bus/i2c/drivers/ina3221x` system file once per second and accumulate the current power consumption values to obtain the energy consumption. Based on practical experience, the power profile is set to 30 W to get the best performance.

Table 2. Comparison of MPInfer with advanced non-multi-tenant frameworks

(a) GTX 1660

Framework	N_c	Latency (ms) Queue	Latency (ms) Total	Throughput (FPS)	FLR (%)
LibTorch (serial)	4	4.17	35.30	31.85	73.16
	5	3.15	34.38	31.74	78.54
	6	2.73	34.00	31.68	82.10
TensorRT (serial)	4	3.71	13.52	101.62	14.06
	5	3.22	13.01	101.84	30.89
	6	2.71	12.87	97.99	44.40
MPInfer (pipelining)	4	0.08	9.56	118.65	0.02
	5	3.20	12.89	129.23	12.62
	6	2.73	12.54	127.28	28.08
MPInfer (3 CUDA Streams)	4	0.04	9.48	118.69	0.04
	5	0.06	18.83	147.78	11.17
	6	1.30	21.04	145.03	25.85
MPInfer (2 CUDA Contexts)	4	0.04	10.11	118.03	0.04
	5	2.47	17.60	130.39	11.17
	6	2.45	17.67	130.37	25.85
MPInfer (MPS+3 CUDA Contexts)	4	0.03	9.89	118.17	0.00
	5	0.04	**14.50**	**147.06**	**0.01**
	6	1.30	20.40	148.02	17.51

(b) Jetson AGX Xavier

Framework	N_c	Latency (ms) Queue	Latency (ms) Total	Throughput (FPS)	FLR (%)
Darknet (serial)	1	16.77	114.42	10.24	65.74
	2	8.43	106.16	10.23	82.79
	3	5.48	103.73	10.17	88.53
TensorRT (serial)	1	0.18	27.11	29.57	0.05
	2	8.30	35.49	36.72	36.82
	3	5.03	32.76	36.01	58.55
MPInfer (pipelining)	1	0.13	28.18	29.70	0.02
	2	8.85	**35.09**	**46.63**	**20.18**
	3	6.10	31.43	46.68	45.83
MPInfer (2 Streams)	1	0.13	27.40	29.72	0.00
	2	8.73	49.85	48.59	16.73
	3	6.01	47.15	48.57	43.94
MPInfer (2 Contexts)	1	0.70	32.26	29.52	0.49
	2	7.96	57.22	39.78	31.54
	3	3.34	56.50	36.54	57.73

Note: MPS does not work on Jetson AGX Xavier

4.2   Experimental Results

Finding the Best Parallel Execution Strategy. Table 2 (a) and (b) show the latency, the throughput, and the FLR of different strategies under different number of cameras each at 30 FPS on two GPU platforms when using YOLOv3. Columns "Queue" and "Total" indicate frame wait time in queue and the end-to-end latency including frame wait time, pre-process time, inference time of YOLOv3 and post-process time. The two tables just show the best setting of different strategies. CUDA stream mode in these two tables uses pinned memory to allocate the transfer data and all others use pageable memory. The number of threads has shown in these two tables.

On GTX 1660, MPInfer can support 5 cameras while maintaining extremely low FLR, and the best parallel mode is achieved using "MPS+3 CUDA Contexts", where the end-to-end latency is 14.5 ms, throughput is 147.06 FPS and FLR is only 0.01%. Although "3 CUDA Streams" achieves similar throughput to "MPS+3 CUDA Contexts", the latency of "MPS+3 CUDA Contexts" is 23.0% shorter than "3 CUDA Streams". This is partially because the resources of each thread in the MPS parallel mode are relatively independent, thus resulting in a lower overhead in GPU resource scheduling.

On Jetson AGX Xavier, MPInfer can fully support 1 camera and can roughly support 1.5 cameras. Because the best throughput under 2 cameras is much higher than 1 camera, we compare the performance under 2 cameras. The best parallel mode under 2 cameras is achieved using "pipelining", where the end-to-end latency is 35.09 ms, throughput is 46.63 FPS and FLR is 20.18%. Although "2 CUDA streams" achieves the highest throughput, the throughput of "pipelining" is only 4.0% worse than"2 CUDA streams", while the latency of "pipelining" is 29.6% shorter than that of "2 CUDA streams". Compared to GTX 1660, Xavier has much less computing power and therefore can't support too many parallel threads.

Finding the Best Inference Framework: TensorRT vs. LibTorch vs. Darknet. On GTX 1660 under 4 video streams, TensorRT achieves throughput of 84.50 FPS. Compared to LibTorch, TensorRT reduces latency by 61.7% and improves throughput by 3.19×. On Jetson AGX Xavier under 2 video streams, TensorRT significantly reduces latency by 66.6% and improves throughput by 3.59× compared to Darknet. Most of the benefit here comes from int8 quantization. When we conduct serial inference on GTX 1660, we can achieve 2.53× speedup with the 7.57ms inference latency, as opposed to the 19.17ms latency in the fp32 mode.

Finding the Best System Configuration: Camera Number, Frame Wait Time and FLR. The throughput of the system is limited by the aggregated camera frame rate when it is low, and increases as the number of camera increases until reaching its limit. Comparing across N_c from 4 to 6 on GTX 1660, "MPS+3 CUDA contexts" significantly increases the throughput from 118.17 FPS to 148.02 FPS and the latency also increases from 9.89 ms to 20.40 ms, due to the increased number of images in each minute.

When frames arrive faster than the process rate, frames stay in the queue until a worker is free. For serial structures like LibTorch, Darknet, and TensorRT, if the arrival time interval becomes shorter than the time required to process one image, the time that a frame stays in the queue will suddenly rise. A frame loss happens when the queue is full, the oldest frame is ejected to give way to the new frame. Note that the high FLR indicates that a large portion of images are not processed, which dramatically obstructs utilizing multiple cameras for the improving driving safety.

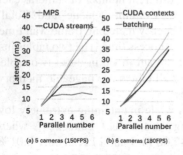

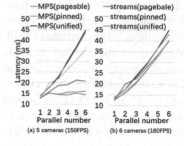

Fig. 6. Inference latency of different parallel strategies on GTX 1660

Fig. 7. Impact of different data transfer modes between CPU/GPU on GTX 1660

Impact of Different Parallel Strategies on Inference Latency. Under 6 video streams at 180 FPS, Fig. 6 shows the impact of different parallel strategies on the inference latency on GTX 1660 when using YOLOv3. Inference latency here does not include pre-process and post-process. Parallel number indicates the number of CUDA streams /contexts or the batch size of batching mode. Batching runs serially here. Figure 6 shows that latency of CUDA context and batching increases approximately linearly according to the parallel number and CUDA context is the worst one. Figure 6 (a) shows that when the workload is similar to the system capacity, the latency of MPS and CUDA stream will first increase and then become smooth as the parallel number increases. Meanwhile, MPS is the best one. Figure 6(b) shows that when the workload is much higher than the system capacity, all these strategies increase approximately linearly according to the parallel number. At such case, MPS and CUDA stream show similar performance and are better than the other two approaches. This is because the execution of MPS and CUDA stream is almost the same under a heavy workload.

Impact of Different Data Transfer Modes Between CPU/GPU. Figure 7 shows the impact of different data transfer modes between CPU/GPU on GTX 1660. From the figure, we find that the unified memory is always the worst, because it needs to maintain memory consistency between CPU and GPU. Figure 7(a) also shows that pinned memory is the best choice for CUDA stream mode and pageable/pinned memory have similar performance impact on MPS. This is because each thread in MPS has a separate memory space while each thread of CUDA stream shares the memory space of the CUDA context. Figure 7(b) shows that when the input workload is high, pageable/pinned memory have similar performance impact on both MPS and CUDA streams.

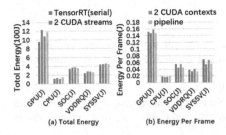

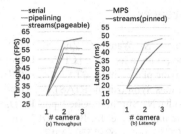

Fig. 8. Energy consumption on Jetson AGX Xavier under 2 video streams (60FPS)

Fig. 9. Throughput and latency of Faster R-CNN

Energy Consumption. Figure 8(a) gives the total energy consumption on Jetson AGX Xavier with 2 video streams sending 10000 images when using YOLOv3. Figure 8 (b) gives the average energy consumption per processed frame. Figure 8 shows that 2 CUDA streams and pipelining consume similar energy. From Fig. 8(a), we observe that 2 CUDA streams and pipelining consume the most energy. This is because the high throughput of these two versions. Indeed, if we compare the energy consumption per frame, both 2 CUDA streams and pipelining achieve the best energy efficiency, that is totally because they have lower FLR and handle more frames than others.

Faster R-CNN. Figure 9 gives the throughput and latency of Faster R-CNN under different parallel strategies and camera numbers. MPS and CUDA stream(pinned) overlap in Fig. 9 (a) and (b). Pipelining and serial overlap in Fig. 9 (b). Like YOLOv3, pageable/pinned memory have similar performance impact on MPS and pinned memory is a better choice for CUDA Stream mode. MPS and CUDA Stream(pinned) parallel modes have similar performance. When using MPS and under 2 cameras, MPInfer can achieve 59.54 FPS throughput and 35.45 ms. MPInfer can only support 2 cameras when using Faster R-CNN, but it can support 5 cameras when using YOLOv3. This is due to the greater amount of computation in Faster R-CNN.

5 Conclusion

In this paper, we design and develop a multi-tenant parallel CNN inference framework, MPInfer, to support several proposed techniques and serve as a common platform for performance comparison. Our results show that MPS mode is both the better choice for YOLOv3 and Faster R-CNN. The future work is to explore more optimization strategies to support more cameras.

Acknowledgment. This work was partially funded by the National Major Program for Technological Innovation 2030–New Generation Artificial Intelligence (No. 2018AAA0100500) and the National Natural Science Foundation of China (No. 61772487).

References

1. Bateni, S., Wang, Z., Zhu, Y., Hu, Y., Liu, C.: Co-optimizing performance and memory footprint via integrated CPU/GPU memory management, an implementation on autonomous driving platform. In: RTAS'2020 20 IEEE Real-Time and Embedded Technology and Applications Symposium (RTAS), pp. 310–323 (2020)
2. Bodla, N., Singh, B., Chellappa, R., Davis, L.S.: Soft-NMS - improving object detection with one line of code. In: ICCV 2017 2017 IEEE International Conference on Computer Vision (ICCV), pp. 5562–5570 (2017)
3. Goodwin, D.: NVIDIA TensorRT Inference Server boosts deep learning inference (2018). https://devblogs.nvidia.com/nvidia-serves-deep-learning-inference/
4. Hawkins, A.J.: Watch mobileye's self-driving car drive through Jerusalem using only cameras (2020). https://www.theverge.com/2020/1/7/21055450/mobileye-self-driving-car-watch-camera-only-intel-jerusalem
5. Heng, L., et al.: Project autovision: localization and 3D scene perception for an autonomous vehicle with a multi-camera system. In: ICRA IEEE International Conference on Robotics and Automation, pp. 4695–4702 (2019)
6. Jain, P., et al.: Dynamic space-time scheduling for GPU inference. CoRR abs/1901.00041 (2019). http://arxiv.org/abs/1901.00041
7. Jia, Y., et al.: Caffe: convolutional architecture for fast feature embedding. In: [22nd] MMACM International Conference on Multimedia, pp. 675–678. ACM, New York (2014). https://doi.org/10.1145/2647868.2654889. http://doi.acm.org/10.1145/2647868.2654889
8. Migacz, S.: 8-bit inference with TensorRT. In: GPU Technology Conference, vol. 2, p. 7 (2017)
9. NVIDIA: Multi-Process Service (vR440) (2019). https://docs.nvidia.com/deploy/pdf/CUDA_Multi_Process_Service_Overview.pdf
10. NVIDIA: TensorRT developer's guide (v7.0) (2019). https://docs.nvidia.com/deeplearning/sdk/pdf/TensorRT-Developer-Guide.pdf
11. Redmon, J.: Darknet: open source neural networks in C (2013–2016). http://pjreddie.com/darknet/
12. Redmon, J., Farhadi, A.: YOLOv3: an incremental improvement arXiv:1804.02767 (2018)
13. Ren, S., He, K., Girshick, R., Sun, J.: Faster R-CNN: towards real-time object detection with region proposal networks. In: [28th] NeurIPS Advances in Neural Information Processing Systems, pp. 91–99 (2015)
14. da Silva Carvalho, M.D., Koark, F., Rheinländer, C., Wehn, N.: Real-time image recognition system based on an embedded heterogeneous computer and deep convolutional neural networks for deployment in constrained environments. In: WCX SAE World Congress Experience. SAE International (2019). https://doi.org/10.4271/2019-01-1045
15. Yang, M., et al.: Re-thinking CNN frameworks for time-sensitive autonomous-driving applications: addressing an industrial challenge. In: RTAS 2019 IEEE Real-Time and Embedded Technology and Applications Symposium, pp. 305–317 (2019). https://doi.org/10.1109/RTAS.2019.00033
16. Yang, M., Otterness, N., Amert, T., Bakita, J., Anderson, J.H., Smith, F.D.: Avoiding pitfalls when using NVIDIA GPUs for real-time tasks in autonomous systems. In: Altmeyer, S. (ed.) [30th]ECRTSEuromicro Conference on Real-Time Systems. Leibniz International Proceedings in Informatics (LIPIcs), vol. 106, pp. 20:1–20:21. Schloss Dagstuhl-Leibniz-Zentrum fuer Informatik, Dagstuh (2018). https://doi.org/10.4230/LIPIcs.ECRTS.2018.20

A Multi-model Super-Resolution Training and Reconstruction Framework

Ninghui Yuan, Dunbo Zhang, Qiong Wang, and Li Shen[✉]

School of Computer, National University of Defense Technology Changsha,
Hunan 410073, China
lishen@nudt.edu.cn

Abstract. As a popular research field of computer vision, super-resolution is currently widely studied. In the past, the size of the training set required for super-resolution work was too large. A large training set would cause more resource requirements, and at the same time, the time overheads of data transmission would also increase. Moreover, in super-resolution work, the relationship between the complexity of the image and the model structure is usually not considered, and images are recovered in same depth. This method often cannot meet the SR-reconstruction needs of all images. This paper proposes a new training and reconstruction framework based on multiple models. The framework prunes the training set according to the complexity of the images in the training set, which significantly reduces the size of the training set. At the same time, the framework can select the specific depth according to the image features of the images to recover the images, which helps to improve the SR-reconstruction effect. After testing different models, our framework can reduce the amount of training data by 41.9% and reduce the average training time from 2935 min to 2836 min. At the same time, our framework can improve the average SR-reconstruction effect of 65.7% images, optimize the average perceptual index from 3.1607 to 3.0867, and optimize the average SR-reconstruction time from 101.7 s to 66.7 s.

Keywords: Super-resolution · Classification · Fusion · Multi-model

1 Introduction

Super-resolution (SR) is an important branch of machine vision. The main function of super-resolution is to improve the clarity of the enlarged image and reduce the image quality degradation caused by image upscaling. From the simple mathematical methods to the methods based on deep learning, the effect of SR-reconstruction is constantly improving. After the deep learning method is widely used, the optimization method of deep learning is applied to the field of SR. The optimization direction of deep learning methods is not clear, which also makes the optimization cycle of the SR models to be longer. At present, super-resolution still faces some challenges:

© IFIP International Federation for Information Processing 2021
Published by Springer Nature Switzerland AG 2021
X. He et al. (Eds.): NPC 2020, LNCS 12639, pp. 105–116, 2021.
https://doi.org/10.1007/978-3-030-79478-1_9

Firstly, the SR model becomes more and more complex, which will cause over-fitting problems. In the process of SR-reconstruction, too deep or too shallow models can reduce SR-reconstruction effect. Insufficient model depth will lead to insufficient extraction of image feature information, which can reduce the SR-reconstruction effect. However, too deep models will cause overfitting and increase resource requirements. Therefore, we hope the model depth matches the complexity of SR-reconstruction. There has been some works using multiple models for SR-reconstruction, such as MMSR (a Multi-Model Super Resolution framework) [21]. However, due to the limitation of the classification effect and the impact on the pruning of the training set, the SR-reconstruction effect of MMSR is not satisfied. In MMSR, images with simple textures are classified into lower depth models for SR-reconstruction, and a better SR-reconstruction effect is obtained in lower depth models than in deeper models. The SR-reconstruction result score is better because there are fewer artifacts and distortions in the SR-reconstruction result, but these SR-reconstruction results may lose detailed texture information. Therefore, if the images with simple textures can be recovered in models of different depths, and finally the results of the SR-reconstruction are fused, the SR-reconstruction results will get better score and lose less texture.

Secondly, in order to ensure the SR-reconstruction effect, a larger training set is generally required, which greatly increases the training time and the resource requirements. The SR training set is obtained by processing an image set composed of many images. During the processing, the images in the original image set are first cut into fragments. For training more easily, the fragments are often processed into specific data file formats. We observed the image fragments after cutting and found that there are many image fragments having almost no texture features, such as the sky, the water surface, the wall, and so on. These fragments have little impact on training, so the fragments can be pruned. The size of the training set after pruning will be greatly reduced, which can reduce time overhead and storage overhead.

Based on above analysis, we propose and implement a new SR framework based on multiple-depth models. The framework is divided into two parts: training module and reconstruction module. In the training module, the training set is reduced by pruning. In the reconstruction module, the test set is classified into models of different depths for training. The images recovered in the shallowest model need to be recovered in a medium-depth model, and finally fused as the final reconstruction result. The contributions of our framework are as follows:

- A SR framework based on multiple-depth models and an image classification strategy based on random forest are proposed. Unlike the previous single-depth model construction method, our framework can accurately assign different types of images to the appropriate models for SR-reconstruction, thereby improving SR-reconstruction effect. At the same time, multi-depth SR-reconstruction can also improve the parallelism of the SR-reconstruction process and accelerate the SR-reconstruction process. our framework can increase the average SR-reconstruction effect of 65.7% images, optimize the average perceptual index from 3.1607 to 3.0867, and reduce the average SR-reconstruction time by 34.4%.

- An image fusion algorithm is proposed. In the experiment, the fusion algorithm can significantly reduce the loss of texture information of images and improve the visual effect of the SR-reconstruction results.
- A pruning algorithm based on image texture features and edge information is proposed to prune the training set of the SR model. Through the pruning algorithm, the size of the training set is decreased by 41.9% and the average training time is reduced by 3.4%.

The rest of this paper is organized as follows. Section 2 lists some related works. Section 3 introduces our framework in detail. In Sect. 4, experimental results are given and the performance of our framework is evaluated. And in Sect. 5, some conclusions are given.

2 Related Work

2.1 Super-Resolution

Super-resolution: SR-reconstruction is an important work in the field of machine vision [3,5–7,12,13,18,22,23]. Before the deep learning methods were widely used, SR-reconstruction mainly relied on mathematical methods to calculate and predict the upscaled images information through the information in the original small images. SRCNN (Super-Resolution Convolutional Neural Network) [1,2] introduced the method of deep learning to SR-reconstruction for the first time. SRCNN achieved SR-reconstruction effect superior to the past mathematical methods through a three-layer convolution neural network. After SRCNN, deep learning based methods have gradually become the mainstream in the field of super-resolution. The optimization of deep learning based methods mainly comes from the continuous increase of the depth of the model and the optimization of the network structure. For example, VDSR (Very Deep network for Super-Resolution) [8] introduced ResNet into SR and many models are constructed with ResNet such as MSRResNet [11]. SRDenseNet [17] introduced DenseNet, and SRGAN (Super-Resolution using a generative adversarial network) [11] introduced GAN (generative adversarial network) [4]. ESRGAN [19] is based on both DenseNet and GAN. These networks have made breakthrough progress. At the same time, RED (Residual convolutional Encoder-Decoder networks) [15], DRCN (Deeply-recursive convolutional network for image super-resolution) [9], LapSRN (Deep laplacian pyramid networks for fast and accurate super-resolution) [10], SftGAN (Recovering Realistic Texture in Image Super-resolution by Deep Spatial Feature Transform) [20] and other network structures have also achieved good results. Among them, most effective models are based on ResNet, GAN, and DenseNet. In this paper, to fully verify the effect of our framework, we have also tested the models of these three structures. We put MSRResNet, SRGAN, and ESRGAN into our framework.

In addition to the model structure, how to quantitatively evaluate the SR-reconstruction results is also a problem to be considered in SR work. In the early models, traditional evaluation metrics are mainly based on mathematical calculation, such as PSNR (Peak-Signal to Noise Ratio), SSIM (Structural SIMilarity) and other methods. These evaluation metrics are traditional imagery evaluation methods, which quantify the image structure, signal-to-noise ratio, and other indicators, but these evaluation standards cannot match well with the feel of human eye. SRGAN adopts the perceptual index (PI) [14,16] to evaluate the SR-reconstruction results. The lower a perceptual index score is, the better the image quality is. Therefore, PI is also used as the evaluation metric of image quality in this paper.

2.2   Image Classification

The effect of the multi-depth framework depends greatly on the effect of the classification results. The current image classification methods are mainly divided into two types, one is the mathematical method and the other is the deep learning method.

Traditional methods mainly use mathematical methods to describe image features and classify images through some classification structures. For example, Decision Tree and random forests can be used for image classification. Due to its simple training, clear structure and strong interpretability, decision tree is used to classify images commonly. The effect of classification depends on the features provided by the user to the decision tree. Random forest is a set of decision trees. Multiple decision trees vote on the classification results, which can improve the accuracy of classification. The extraction of image features mainly depends on some mathematical methods. The characteristics of images mainly include edge characteristics, image channel value variance and so on. The edge detection operator can be used to extract the texture of the image well. Common edge detection operators include sobel operator, canny operator and so on. In MMSR, the TVAT [21] algorithm is proposed, which can well calculate the variance of the image channel value.

Non-traditional methods mainly use deep learning models for classification. At present, such methods have achieved good classification results. The deep learning based approaches extract and generate image features through convolutional neural networks and other network structures and classify images based on their features.

The advantages of traditional image classification methods is that they have strong interpretability and does not require a complicated training process. The advantage of the non-traditional classification methods is that they have a good effect on some complex cases that cannot be solved by traditional methods. In the multi-depth framework, not only the effect but also the efficiency needs to be considered, therefore our framework uses traditional methods for classification.

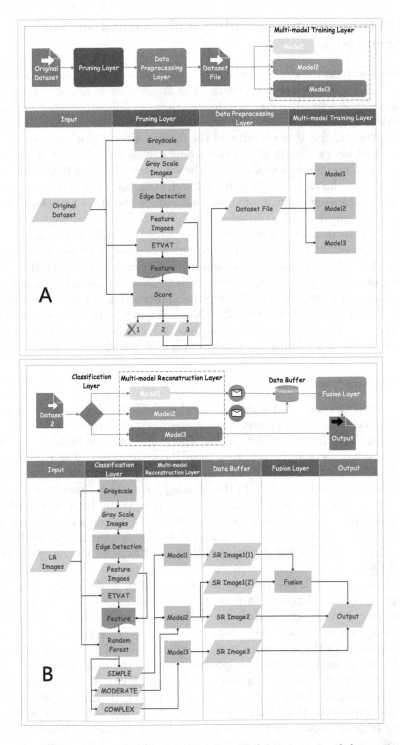

Fig. 1. The structure and data flow of the training module.

3 Multi-model SR Training and Reconstruction Framework

In order to address the issues mentioned above, we propose a multi-model training and SR-reconstruction framework. The framework is mainly divided into training module and SR-reconstruction module. In the experiment, we adjust the model depth by adjusting the number of basic blocks in the model. The basic block is the unit that constitutes the model. A basic block contains several convolutional layers. The depth of the model can be easily adjusted by setting the number of basic blocks in a model. The structure and data flow of the training module are shown in the A part of Fig. 1. The task of the training module is mainly to train the multiple models and reduce the size of the training set. The main design idea of the training module is to prune the images with less texture from the original training set. The size of the training set after pruning is significantly reduced compared to that of the original data set. The structure and data flow of the reconstruction module are shown in the part B of Fig. 1. The task of the reconstruction module is to recover low-resolution images. We input images into different models for SR-reconstruction through the classification layer, thereby improving the effect and efficiency of reconstruction. At the same time we propose fusion layer to prevent the image reconstructed in the low-depth model from losing too much texture information.

3.1 Pruning Layer

In the original training set, the data is saved in the form of images. Some images in the original training set do not have complex texture features, and even some of the images are filled by solid colors. These images have little effect on the training results, and can be removed from the training set. The pruning layer uses ETVAT (Enhanced TVAT) and the edge detection operator to determine which images should be pruned. In the pruning layer, the training image is grayscaled firstly. The purpose of grayscale is to reduce the interference of noise and illumination when performing edge detection. After grayscaling, the module uses edge detection operators to extract the features of the images and get the feature maps. The final feature maps will be used to score the images together with ETVAT.

As shown in Fig. 2, the pruning algorithm we propose is based on TVAT and edge detection operators. In part A, we use the edge detection operator to calculate score1. We first use the edge detection operator to calculate the edge feature map of the image. After that, we add the gray values of the pixels in the feature map as the first score, and this score is called Edge_score. Although this calculation method is very simple and reduces the amount of information in the edge map, it is enough for judging the complexity of the image. And we propose a voting mechanism of three channels (R, G, B) instead of calculating the mean value of the three channels to calculate score2, because we found that there are large differences in the change of different channels. Therefore, in part B we use the values of the three channels to perform TVAT operations and vote. If the change rate of more than two values exceeds the threshold, we think that this point should be calculated into the final TVAT value. We call this method ETVAT, ETVAT will help us get one score in the voting mechanism. Then in part C we use ETVAT and Edge_score to calculate the final score. The images with the final score of 1 will be pruned. In the pruning algorithm, there are several adjustable thresholds: threshold0, threshold1, threshold2, threshold3, threshold4, which are used to adjust the strength of pruning. In the experiment of this paper, we adjust the strength of pruning to about 40%.

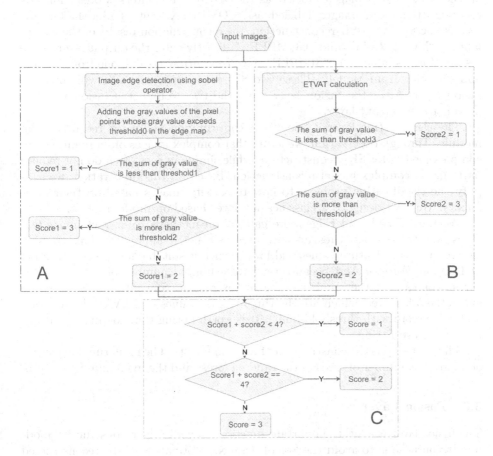

Fig. 2. The process of pruning algorithm.

3.2   Classification Layer

After the low-resolution images enters the reconstruction module, they will be classified first. We find that the training model required for images with simple textures is often shallower than that for images with complex textures. Therefore, we can also classify images based on the texture complexity of the images. The feature extraction process in the classification layer is like that in the pruning layer. After the feature extraction is completed, we use random forest to classify the images. The images are divided into three categories labeled as "SIMPLE", "MODERATE" and "COMPLEX". The three labels represent images with the simplest texture, the image with moderate texture complexity and images with the most complicated texture. In the multi-model reconstruction layer, images labeled as "SIMPLE" enters Model1 and Model2 for SR-reconstruction at the same time, images labeled as "MODERATE" enters Model2 for SR-reconstruction, and images labeled as "COMPLEX" enters Model3 for SR-reconstruction. After SR-reconstruction, the reconstruction results of the images labeled "MODERATE" and "COMPLEX" directly enter the output layer as the results. Images labeled as "SIMPLE" have two output results, one from Model1 and the other from Model2. These two SR-reconstruction results will enter the fusion layer. After the fusion layer fuses the two results, the fusion result is output to the output layer.

The classification layer is one of the core components of the reconstruction module. Through observation, we found that complex images often require more complex models for SR-reconstruction, while simple images often do not require particularly complex model reconstruction. Based on this observation, we simplify the classification problem to how to classify images based on their complexity. We have designed a classification layer based on random forest.

We use ETVAT and Edge_score calculation methods to extract image features, and the extracted features are used as a new training set. This training set contains only feature values and label, which is suitable for the construction of Random Forests. And because we have a limited number of extracted features (you can set the number of feature extraction yourself, in this paper we extracted 5 features, which are the three feature values of ETVAT, Edge_score, and Edge_score with threshold limit). It is worth noting that too many features may cause overfitting.

The next step is the construction of random forests. The main tunable parameters are the number of trees in the random forest and the maximum tree depth.

3.3 Fusion Layer

The fusion layer is another important functional layer in the reconstruction module. Its purpose is to avoid the loss of detailed information of the reconstructed images from the simple model. The fusion algorithm is shown in Algorithm 1. There is a buffer before the fusion layer because the speeds of SR-reconstruction in different models are different. We must wait for both results to be reconstructed before they can be input into the fusion layer. It has three inputs, SR image1 and SR image2 to be fused and feature map generated using the sobel operator, which identifies that pixels in SR image1 are in the texture areas or in non-texture area. For each pixel, if it locates in the texture ares, the texture information generated by model2 will be mainly added to the result SR image.

Algorithm 1. Image Fusion algorithm

Input: SR image1, SR image2, feature map
Output: the result SR image

1: **for** i in row of feature image **do**
2:   **for** j in col of feature image **do**
3:     **if** $the feature[i][j] = 1$ **then**
4:       $fusionresult[i][j] = 0.3 * SRimage1[i][j] + 0.7 * SRimage2[i][j].$
5:     **else**
6:       $fusionresult[i][j] = 0.7 * SRimage1[i][j] + 0.3 * SRimage2[i][j].$
7:     **end if**
8:   **end for**
9: **end for**

Otherwise, the non-texture information generated by the model1 will be mainly added to the result.

4 Experiments

4.1 Environment Setup

To evaluate the performance of our mechanism, we construct a small-scale cluster which consists of three heterogeneous "CPU+GPU" nodes. The main system parameters of each node are listed in Table. 1.

Table 1. System parameters of each node.

HW/SW module	Description
CPU	Intel ® Xeon® E5-2660 v3 @2.6 GHz x2
GPU	NVIDIA Tesla K80 x2
Memory	64 GB
OS	Linux CentOS 7.4
Development Environment	Anaconda 3, Pytorch 1.0

4.2 Experiment Details

We use DIV_2K dataset train models, and use PRIM dataset to test. DIV_2K is a commonly used super-resolution training set with a total of 800 images, and PRIM dataset is a standard super-resolution competition test set with a total of 100 images. To verify the effectiveness of the model, we put different types of models into the framework for testing and compare the effects with the original model. Most of the current SR models are based on ResNet, DenseNet and GAN structures. Therefore, in the experiment, we use MSRResNet to represent ResNet structures, SRGAN to represent ResNet and GAN structures, and ESRGAN to represent DenseNet and GAN structures. These three models can get good SR-reconstruction effect and they can be used as basic models to verify the effect of our framework.

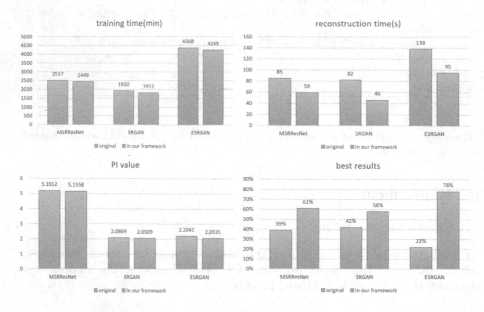

Fig. 3. Comparisons of the effects of our framework and the baseline models

In the experiment, to effectively reduce the size of the training set, we adjusted the pruning strength to about 40%. The size of the training set running in the original model was 21401.8M, and the size of the training set after the operation was reduced to 12436.6M. The experimental results are shown in Fig. 3. For MSRResNet, we can reduce the training time from 2517 min to 2449 min. The SR-reconstruction quality of 61% test images has been improved and the average perceptual index has dropped from 5.1912 to 5.155833, at the same time SR-reconstruction time has been optimized from 85 s to 59 s. For SRGAN, the training time can be reduced from 1920 min to 1812 min. SR-reconstruction quality of 58% test images have been improved and the average perceptual index has dropped from 2.0869 to 2.0509, while SR-reconstruction time has been optimized from 82 s to 46 s. For ESRGAN, the training time can be reduced from 4368 min to 4249 min. The SR-reconstruction quality of 78% test images has been improved and the average perceptual index has dropped from 2.2041 to 2.0535. The SR-reconstruction time has been optimized from 138 s to 95 s.

5   Conclusion

In the study of super-resolution, we find that a single model cannot satisfy the requirements of all input images to achieve the optimal SR-reconstruction effect. At the same time, we find that the size of the training set is usually too large, which also brings great difficulties to the research. In order to solve these problems, this paper proposes a super-resolution training and reconstruction framework based on multiple models. The framework is divided into training module and reconstruction module. In the training module, the pruning layer prunes the training set based on ETVAT and Edge_score, which effectively reduces the size of the training set and reduces the difficulty of training. The multi-model training layer trains multiple models at the same time. In the reconstruction module, the classification layer uses random forest for classification. The classification layer is based on random forests. The classification layer classifies different kinds of images into a suitable model for reconstruction and uses the fusion layer to increase the texture information of the SR-reconstruction result. In the experiment, we put MSRResNet, SRGAN and ESRGAN into the framework for optimization. After testing different models, our framework can reduce the amount of training data by 41.9% and reduce the average training time by 3.4%. For reconstruction, our framework can increase the average SR-reconstruction effect of 65.7% images, optimize the average perceptual index from 3.1607 to 3.0867, and reduce the average SR-reconstruction time by 34.4%. Our framework can improve the effect of super-resolution models while reducing the resource requirements.

Acknowledgement. This work was supported by the National Science Foundation under Grant No. 61972407 and Guangdong Province Key Laboratory of Popular High Performance Computers 2017B030314073.

References

1. Dong, C., Loy, C.C., He, K., Tang, X.: Image super-resolution using deep convolutional networks. CoRR abs/1501.00092 (2015). http://arxiv.org/abs/1501.00092
2. Dong, C., Loy, C.C., Tang, X.: Accelerating the super-resolution convolutional neural network. CoRR abs/1608.00367 (2016). http://arxiv.org/abs/1608.00367
3. Fu, Y., Zhang, T., Zheng, Y., Zhang, D., Huang, H.: Hyperspectral image super-resolution with optimized RGB guidance. In: The IEEE Conference on Computer Vision and Pattern Recognition (CVPR) (2019)
4. Goodfellow, I.J., et al.: Generative adversarial networks. ArXiv abs/1406.2661 (2014)
5. Gu, J., Lu, H., Zuo, W., Dong, C.: Blind super-resolution with iterative kernel correction. CoRR abs/1904.03377 (2019). http://arxiv.org/abs/1904.03377
6. Haris, M., Shakhnarovich, G., Ukita, N.: Recurrent back-projection network for video super-resolution. CoRR abs/1903.10128 (2019). http://arxiv.org/abs/1903.10128
7. Hu, X., Mu, H., Zhang, X., Wang, Z., Tan, T., Sun, J.: Meta-SR: a magnification-arbitrary network for super-resolution. CoRR abs/1903.00875 (2019). http://arxiv.org/abs/1903.00875

8. Kim, J., Lee, J.K., Lee, K.M.: Accurate image super-resolution using very deep convolutional networks. CoRR abs/1511.04587 (2015). http://arxiv.org/abs/1511.04587

9. Kim, J., Lee, J.K., Lee, K.M.: Deeply-recursive convolutional network for image super-resolution. CoRR abs/1511.04491 (2015). http://arxiv.org/abs/1511.04491

10. Lai, W., Huang, J., Ahuja, N., Yang, M.: Deep Laplacian pyramid networks for fast and accurate super-resolution. CoRR abs/1704.03915 (2017). http://arxiv.org/abs/1704.03915

11. Ledig, C., et al.: Photo-realistic single image super-resolution using a generative adversarial network. CoRR abs/1609.04802 (2016). http://arxiv.org/abs/1609.04802

12. Li, S., He, F., Du, B., Zhang, L., Xu, Y., Tao, D.: Fast spatio-temporal residual network for video super-resolution. CoRR abs/1904.02870 (2019). http://arxiv.org/abs/1904.02870

13. Li, Z., Yang, J., Liu, Z., Yang, X., Jeon, G., Wu, W.: Feedback network for image super-resolution. CoRR abs/1903.09814 (2019). http://arxiv.org/abs/1903.09814

14. Ma, C., Yang, C., Yang, X., Yang, M.: Learning a no-reference quality metric for single-image super-resolution. CoRR abs/1612.05890 (2016). http://arxiv.org/abs/1612.05890

15. Mao, X., Shen, C., Yang, Y.: Image restoration using convolutional auto-encoders with symmetric skip connections. CoRR abs/1606.08921 (2016). http://arxiv.org/abs/1606.08921

16. Mittal, A., Soundararajan, R., Bovik, A.: Making a "completely blind" image quality analyzer. Signal Processing Letters, **20**, 209–212 (2013). https://doi.org/10.1109/LSP.2012.2227726

17. Tong, T., Li, G., Liu, X., Gao, Q.: Image super-resolution using dense skip connections, pp. 4809–4817 (2017). https://doi.org/10.1109/ICCV.2017.514

18. Wang, L., et al.: Learning parallax attention for stereo image super-resolution. CoRR abs/1903.05784 (2019). http://arxiv.org/abs/1903.05784

19. Wang, X., et al.: ESRGAN: enhanced super-resolution generative adversarial networks. CoRR abs/1809.00219 (2018). http://arxiv.org/abs/1809.00219

20. Wang, X., Yu, K., Dong, C., Loy, C.C.: Recovering realistic texture in image super-resolution by deep spatial feature transform. In: IEEE Conference on Computer Vision and Pattern Recognition (CVPR) (2018)

21. Yuan, N., Zhu, Z., Wu, X., Shen, L.: MMSR: a multi-model super resolution framework. In: Tang, X., Chen, Q., Bose, P., Zheng, W., Gaudiot, J.-L. (eds.) NPC 2019. LNCS, vol. 11783, pp. 197–208. Springer, Cham (2019). https://doi.org/10.1007/978-3-030-30709-7_16

22. Zhang, K., Zuo, W., Zhang, L.: Deep plug-and-play super-resolution for arbitrary blur kernels. CoRR abs/1903.12529 (2019). http://arxiv.org/abs/1903.12529

23. Zhang, S., Lin, Y., Sheng, H.: Residual networks for light field image super-resolution. In: The IEEE Conference on Computer Vision and Pattern Recognition (CVPR) (2019)

Deep Visible and Thermal Image Fusion with Cross-Modality Feature Selection for Pedestrian Detection

Mingyue Li[1,2], Zhenzhou Shao[1,2]([✉]) [iD], Zhiping Shi[1,3] [iD],
and Yong Guan[1,2,3]([✉]) [iD]

[1] College of Information Engineering, Capital Normal University, Beijing, China
{2181002024,zshao,shizp,guanyong}@cnu.edu.cn
[2] Beijing Key Laboratory of Light Industrial Robot and Safety Verification,
Beijing, China
[3] Beijing Advanced Innovation Center for Imaging Technology, Beijing, China

Abstract. This paper proposes a deep RGB and thermal image fusion method for pedestrian detection. A two-branch structure is designed to learn the features of RGB and thermal images respectively, and these features are fused with a cross-modality feature selection module for detection. It includes the following stages. First, we learn features from paired RGB and thermal images through a backbone network with a residual structure, and add a feature squeeze-excitation module to the residual structure; Then we fuse the learned features from two branches, and a cross-modality feature selection module is designed to strengthen the effective information and compress the useless information during the fusion process; Finally, multi-scale features are fused for pedestrian detection. Two sets of experiments on the public KAIST pedestrian dataset are conducted, and experimental results show that our method is better than the state-of-the-art methods. The robustness of fused features is improved, and the miss rate is reduced obviously.

Keywords: Pedestrian detection · Cross-modality features · Feature fusion

1 Introduction

As a fundamental task in the field of computer vision, object detection has drawn much more attentions in several applications, such as autonomous driving, video

Supported by National Key R & D Program of China (2019YFB1309900), National Natural Science Foundation of China (61702348, 61772351), Beijing Nova Program of Science and Technology (Z191100001119075), the National Technology Innovation Special Zone (19-163-11-ZT-001-005-06) and Academy for Multidisciplinary Studies, Capital Normal University (19530012005).

© IFIP International Federation for Information Processing 2021
Published by Springer Nature Switzerland AG 2021
X. He et al. (Eds.): NPC 2020, LNCS 12639, pp. 117–127, 2021.
https://doi.org/10.1007/978-3-030-79478-1_10

surveillance, human-computer interaction, etc. Deep learning-based method [1–3] has made great progress using visible images (*e.g.*, RGB image) in recent years. However, considering the adverse environmental conditions, i.e., the visible information is partially or fully missed under the poor lighting condition at night, the accuracy of detection using only RGB image becomes relatively low. Therefore, accurate object detection under adverse environmental conditions is still a challenging problem.

Recently, thermal images have been widely used for facial recognition [4,5], human tracking [6,7] and action recognition [8,9] due to its robustness of biological characteristics. In particular, compared with the visible images, night-time thermal images provide more usable information without the need of enough illumination, so that both modalities are combined accordingly for the multi-spectral object detection [10–15]. The complementary relationship between both modalities has been proven [12], it paves an alternative way for object detection in the harsh environment, and provides new opportunities for around-the-clock applications.

In this paper, we mainly focus on the pedestrian detection using RGB and thermal images. Motivated by the complementary nature between modalities, extensive research efforts have been made. Hwang *et al.* [10] proposed an extended ACF method that uses aligned RGB and thermal images for all-weather pedestrian detection. With the latest development of deep learning, CNN-based methods [11,16–18] have significantly improved the performance of object detection based on RGB and thermal image fusion. Liu *et al.* [19] adopted the Faster R-CNN architecture and analyzed the impact of different fusion stages in CNN on the detection results. Kéonig *et al.* [20] employed Region Proposal Network (RPN) and Boosted Forest (BF) frameworks for multispectral data detection. Kihong *et al.* [13] adopted a multi-branch detection model and also introduced a cumulative probability fusion (APF) layer to combine the results from different modes at the regional proposal layer. Zhang *et al.* [15] proposed a regional feature alignment (RFA) module to capture the position offset and adaptively align the regional features of these two modalities to improve the robustness of multi-modal detection. Xu *et al.* [11] first used a deep convolutional network to learn nonlinear mapping, modeled the correlation between RGB and thermal image data, and then transferred the learned feature representation to the second deep network in this way Learned that poor lighting conditions have the characteristics of discrimination and robustness, and it also proves that RGB and thermal image fusion has the possibility of all-weather detection.

However, the aforementioned methods commonly use the channel addition or cascade as the fusion strategy, the confidence of corresponding features from RGB and thermal images is not taken into account, and it cannot guarantee the complementary characteristics between features after the fusion.

In this paper, a pedestrian detection network that can perform cross-modal fusion feature selection is designed for the above-mentioned problems. The main contributions of this work are summarized as follows:

(1) We designed a two-stream fusion network for pedestrian detection. Two branch networks with residual structure with feature squeeze-excitation (SE)[21] modules are used to learn the features of RGB and thermal image data.

(2) The fusion of two modal data will have useless redundant information. Therefore, a cross-modal fusion feature selection mechanism is proposed to extract useful information and compress useless information.

2 Proposed Method

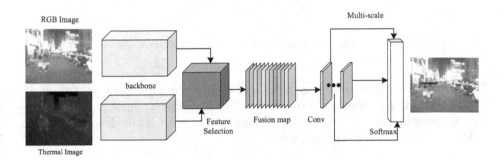

Fig. 1. Overview of the proposed method.

As shown in Fig. 1, the proposed model consists of two parts: two-branch feature extraction backbone network and cross-modal fusion feature selection module. We use the paired RGB and thermal image as the input of the two branches, and the corresponding features are extracted respectively using a two-branch backbone network. Then pass the learned features to the cross-modal feature selection module. Finally, multi-scale convolution operations are applied to fused features for further pedestrian detection.

2.1 Two-Branch Feature Extraction Backbone Network with Squeeze-Excitation Module

In order to extract the representative features of RGB and thermal images, we design a backbone network to extract features for each modality. In the backbone network, in order to improve the efficiency of feature extraction and alleviate the overfitting problem in the deep network [24], similar to yolov3 [25], we add a residual structure during feature extraction. Furthermore, to reduce the useless features for pedestrian detection, squeeze-excitation (SE) module is employed in the residual structure. It is able to improve the efficiency of feature extraction as well.

As shown in Fig. 2, the squeeze-excitation module is combined with ResNet structure. X represents the input feature, and Y represents the output feature.

120   M. Li et al.

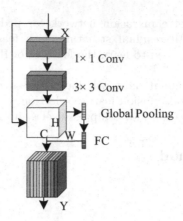

Fig. 2. ResNet structure with squeeze-excitation module.

The input layer features first go through two convolutional layer operations of 1×1 and 3×3, and then perform a global pooling operation to obtain a vector representing the importance of a single-modal data channel, which can be calculated by the following formula:

$$Z_c = \frac{1}{H * W} \sum_{i=1}^{H} \sum_{j=1}^{W} u_c(i, j),$$ (1)

where Z_c represents the calculated channel importance parameter, and W and H represent the height and width of the feature map, respectively. The formula obtains Z_c by adding up all the characteristic points in the mean value. Finally, the importance parameters calculated from all channels are fully connected to obtain the feature channel importance vector.

In order to use the vector obtained by channel squeeze, we multiply the feature output from the ResNet layer with the vector, pass to the ReLu activation function, and finally obtain the output Y through the Softmax activation function, the formula is as follows:

$$Y = s(\delta(Z * X')),$$ (2)

where Y represents the final output feature, s denotes Softmax activation function, Z represents the channel importance vector, δ is ReLu activation function, and X' represents the feature obtained after convolution operations with kernel size of 1×1 and 3×3, respectively.

2.2 Cross-Modality Feature Selection Module

After two-modality features are extracted using the backbone network, the effective fusion is carried out. Although multi-modality features have complementary

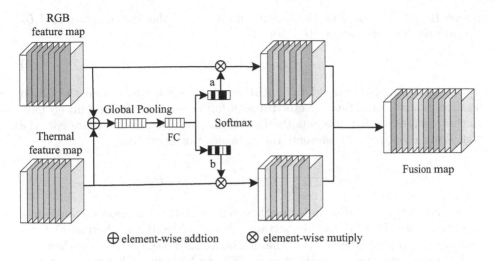

Fig. 3. Cross-modal fusion feature selection module.

information, they also have mutually redundant information. Therefore, both the complementary and redundant characteristics of RGB and thermal images are taken into account, a cross-modality feature selection module is designed to reduce the interference of redundancy or error information on subsequent detection.

As shown in Fig. 3, RGB feature map and thermal feature map respectively represent the feature maps of the two modalities output by the two backbone networks. Global Pooling represents the global pooling operation, FC represents the fully connected layer, Softmax represents the activation function, and finally Fusion map represents the final fusion feature map. The specific operations of the cross-modal fusion feature selection module are as follows: After RGB and thermal image data are extracted through the branch backbone network, the features of the two modalities are first added together to obtain the fusion feature map used to calculate the importance parameters of the two modal data. The preliminary fusion feature map obtained by reuse is subjected to global pooling, full connection, and Softmax operations. The importance parameters of RGB and thermal image features are obtained by the following formula:

$$U = U_{RGB} + U_{Thermal}, \tag{3}$$

where U represents the preliminary fusion feature obtained by adding RGB and Thermal features, and U_{RGB} and $U_{Thermal}$ represent the RGB and Thermal features output by the backbone network, respectively. The global tie pooling operation is written as

$$S_c = \frac{1}{H * W} \sum_{i=1}^{H} \sum_{j=1}^{W} U_c(i,j), \tag{4}$$

where H and W represent the height and width of the feature map, and U_c denotes the feature map at cth channel.

$$Z = F_{fc}(S) = \delta(\beta(S)). \qquad (5)$$

The parameters obtained by global pooling are used to obtain the fusion feature channel importance vector through full connection, ReLu, and normalization operations. fc represents the fully connected operation, δ represents the ReLu operation, and β represents the normalization operation.

$$a_c = \frac{e^{A_c Z}}{e^{A_c Z} + e^{B_c Z}}, b_c = \frac{e^{B_c Z}}{e^{A_c Z} + e^{B_c Z}}. \qquad (6)$$

Equation (6) indicates that a method similar to the attention mechanism is used to obtain the respective importance vectors of RGB and thermal features according to the obtained feature channel importance vectors. Among them, A_c and B_c represent the characteristics of RGB and Thermal channel count as c respectively.

$$U_{Fuse_c} = a_c * U_{RGB_c} + b_c * U_{Thermal_c}, a_c + b_c = 1, \qquad (7)$$

where represents the multiplication operation of RGB and thermal with the obtained importance vector, and then adding them to obtain features from the final fusion layer. U_{Fuse_c}, U_{RGB_c} and $U_{Thermal_c}$ respectively represent the fused features, RGB and thermal features at channel c.

2.3 Optimization

We deploy all parameter calculations to run on GPU devices. In the network model training, the stochastic gradient descent optimization algorithm is adopted. In addition, the use of gradient descent in deep learning model training is itself an approximate solution problem, and asynchronous parallel computing is more efficient than synchronous parallel computing in approximate solution problem, so we use asynchronous parallel computing mode in training model for computation on GPU.

3 Experimental Results

In order to verify the effectiveness of proposed method, we conducted several experiments on the publicly available KAIST pedestrian dataset [25] captured in various traffic scenarios with different lighting conditions. The dataset consists of 95,000 aligned RGB thermal image pairs. One pair of images are sampled every 20 frames from the whole KAIST dataset for training and testing. In our experiment, 7,472 pairs are collected as training samples and 1386 pairs for testing.

3.1 Experimental Setup

The proposed method is implemented in the Tensorflow framework, running on two NVIDIA Tesla P100 GPUs with 16G memory. Regardless of changes in day and night or lighting conditions, we put all the selected data together for training and testing. In order to ensure the adequacy of data during the experiment, data augmentation operations (rotation and zoom) are implemented. 30 epochs are set per experiment in the training stage.

The experiment is carried out in a batch format. Each small batch consists of 6 pairs of images, which are randomly selected from the training images. Stochastic gradient descent is used to optimize the model, and its weight attenuation parameter is set to 0.995. The initial learning rate is set to 1e-4, and then reduce the learning rate after the model becomes stable, so as to achieve the goal of avoiding missing the optimal solution.

3.2 Comparison with the State-of-the-Art Methods

We compare our method with advanced methods on the KAIST pedestrian dataset, including: (*i*) ACF-RGB [27], which uses ACF for RGB data; (*ii*) ACF-RGBT + THOG [25], that is, using ACF for RGB thermal data with HOG characteristics; (*iii*) CMT-CNN [11], a detection network that learns cross-modal deep representation; (*iv*) SDS-RCNN [23], which is a convolutional neural network based on simultaneous detection and segmentation. As shown in Table 1, the proposed method outperforms the state-of-the-art methods, and the miss rate is greatly reduced by 39.2%, compared with ACF-RGBT. The performance is comparable with SDS-RCNN.

Table 1. Comparison of different methods. We use miss rate as the evaluation parameter for comparison on the KAIST dataset.

Method	ACF-RGB	ACF-RGBT-HOG	CMT-CNN	SDS-RCNN	Ours
Miss rate	76.16	54.82	49.55	47.44	**46.32**

Figure 4 illustrates a part of testing results compared with the existing methods. From left to right, the detection results of ACF-RGB, ACF-RGBT-HOG, CMT-CNN, SDS-RCNN and our method are shown in sequence. It can be observed that ACF-RGB method misses some targets, wrong detections occurs. Although ACF-RGBT-HOG has a lower error rate than ACF-RGB, there are more cases of missing detection targets. The detected targets are basically correct, and a small number of targets are not detected using CMT-CNN and SDS-RCNN methods. The detection results using the proposed method is shown in the last column, where the quantities of both wrong and missing targets are reduced obviously.

Fig. 4. Comparison of the detection results of existing methods and our method. From left to right are the detection results of ACF-RGB, ACF-RGBT-HOG, CMT-CNN, SDS-RCNN and our method.

3.3 Ablation Study

In this section, a set of experiments are conducted to prove the effectiveness of the proposed single-modal feature squeeze-excitation (SE) and multi-modal fusion feature selection module. We analysis the proposed methods under 3 different settings: (1) Adjust the number of Res structures at each layer and find out the best backbone network model. (2) Add SE layer to the Res structure, add the SE layer to the Res and fusion layer, and add the SE layer to the fusion layer. (3) Experiments are performed on the fusion layer plus the cross-modal feature selection (FS) layer and the fusion layer without the cross-modal fusion feature selection layer. The detection accuracy rate AP is used as the evaluation matrix.

Table 2. Experimental results of KAIST dataset under different module settings.

	Proposed method				
Res:1,1,1,1,1	√	–	–	–	–
Res:1,2,2,2,2	–	√	√	√	√
Res+SE	–	–	√	√	√
Fusion+SE	–	–	–	√	–
Fusion+FS	–	–	–	–	√
AP(%)	46.61	51.41	52.85	52.42	53.68

Table 2 shows our comparison results. Use the detection accuracy rate AP as the evaluation parameter. We use the KAIST dataset to conduct ablation research on the model framework of this article. In the process of ablation research, we comprehensively considered the complexity of the network model and the accuracy of experimental results, and appropriately reduced the residual structure on the basis of the original yolov3 network. Reduce residual structure when considering the RGB and Thermal data feature similarities, in terms of characteristics of reuse use too much residual structural redundancy may be produced, and considering the residual structure can reuse low-level features to a certain extent, alleviate the problem of gradient vanishing. Therefore, the number of residual structures is reduced to (1, 1, 1, 1, 1) and (1, 2, 2, 2, 2) for experimental comparison. It can be seen from Table 2 that the effect of residual structure in the model is significantly better than that of (1, 1, 1, 1, 1) when the number of residual structure is (1, 2, 2, 2, 2). In addition, considering that not all features of RGB and thermal data are valid, the characteristic squeeze-excitation module (SE), which can extract effective information and compress unwanted information, is added into the method proposed in this paper. In the experiment, we compared the adding location of feature squeeze-excitation module. The experimental results show that the effect of adding feature squeeze-excitation module after the residual structure is better, because the low-level features reused by the residual structure are similar to the high-level features, the superposition features generate redundant information, and the addition of feature squeeze-excitation module produces better detection results. Finally, we use the feature selection module of cross-mode fusion proposed by us. Because the data of RGB and thermal are similar, the detection accuracy of single mode features extracted by effective feature compression is improved after the fusion selection. In this paper, we propose a two-branch detection network that adds a feature squeeze-excitation module after the residual structure and a cross-modal fusion feature selection module to the fusion layer, which improves the detection accuracy and presents better detection results.

Fig. 5. Comparison of testing results without and with cross-modality feature selection module.

As shown in Fig. 5, the first row is the detection results without cross-modality feature selection module, while the second one illustrates the results of our proposed method. It is obviously observed that pedestrian targets may not be detected or incomplete before the cross-modality feature selection module is applied. Our method can detect almost all pedestrian targets even when the light conditions are not good.

4   Conclusion

This paper proposes a cross-modal feature selection pedestrian detection method based on RGB and thermal images. The residual structure is used when extracting features from RGB and thermal image data, and the feature squeeze-excitation module is embedded after the residual structure. Finally, more practical fusion features are obtained using the cross-modal fusion feature selection module, which effectively improves the detection accuracy. In addition, we also adopted a multi-scale detection method to improve the detection effect of small targets. A set of experiments are carried out on the public KAIST pedestrian dataset. Experimental results demonstrate that the proposed method outperforms the state-of-the-art methods, even when the lighting conditions are not particularly well or there exist many small targets in the scene of detection.

References

1. Yang, B., Yan, J., Lei, Z., Li, S.Z.: Convolutional channel features. In: Proceedings of the IEEE International Conference on Computer Vision (ICCV), pp. 82–90 (2015)
2. Zhang, L., Lin, L., Liang, X., He, K.: Is faster R-CNN doing well for pedestrian detection? In: Leibe, B., Matas, J., Sebe, N., Welling, M. (eds.) ECCV 2016. LNCS, vol. 9906, pp. 443–457. Springer, Cham (2016). https://doi.org/10.1007/978-3-319-46475-6_28
3. Li, J., Liang, X., Shen, S., Xu, T., Feng, J., Yan, S.: Scale-aware fast R-CNN for pedestrian detection. IEEE Trans. Multimedia 20(4), 985–996 (2018)
4. Buddharaju, P., Pavlidis, I.T., Tsiamyrtzis, P., Bazakos, M.: Physiology-based face recognition in the thermal infrared spectrum. IEEE Trans. Pattern Anal. Mach. Intell. (PAMI) 29(4), 613–626 (2007)
5. Kong, S.G., et al.: Multiscale fusion of visible and thermal IR images for illumination-invariant face recognition. Int. J. Comput. Vis. 71(2), 215–233 (2007)
6. Leykin, A., Ran, Y., Hammoud, R.: Thermal visible video fusion for moving target tracking and pedestrian classification. In: Proceedings of the IEEE Conference on Computer Vision and Pattern Recognition (CVPR), pp. 1–8 (2007)
7. Torabi, A., Massé, G., Bilodeau, G.-A.: An iterative integrated framework for thermal-visible image registration, sensor fusion, and people tracking for video surveillance applications. Comput. Vis. Image Underst. 116(2), 210–221 (2012)
8. Zhu, Y., Guo, G.: A study on visible to infrared action recognition. IEEE Signal Process. Lett. 20(9), 897–900 (2013)
9. Gao, C., et al.: Infar dataset: infrared action recognition at different times. Neurocomputing 212, 36–47 (2016)
10. Hwang, S., Park, J., Kim, N., Choi, Y., So Kweon, I.: Multispectral pedestrian detection: benchmark dataset and baseline. In: Proceedings of the IEEE Conference on Computer Vision and Pattern Recognition (CVPR), pp. 1037–1045 (2015)

11. Xu, D., Ouyang, W., Ricci, E., Wang, X., Sebe, N.: Learning cross-modal deep representations for robust pedestrian detection. In: Proceedings of the IEEE Conference on Computer Vision and Pattern Recognition (CVPR), pp. 5363–5371 (2017)
12. González, A., et al.: Pedestrian detection at day/night time with visible and fir cameras: a comparison. Sensors 16(6), 820 (2016)
13. Park, K., Kim, S., Sohn, K.: Unfied multi-spectral pedestrian detection based on probabilistic fusion networks. Pattern Recogn. 80, 143–155 (2018)
14. Neubauer, A., Yochelis, S., Paltiel, Y.: Simple multi spectral detection using infrared nanocrystal detector. IEEE Sens. J. 19(10), 3668–3672 (2019)
15. Zhang, L., et al.: Weakly aligned cross-modal learning for multispectral pedestrian detection. In: Proceedings of the IEEE International Conference on Computer Vision, pp. 5127–5137 (2019)
16. Zhang, L., et al.: Cross-modality interactive attention network for multispectral pedestrian detection. Inf. Fusion 50, 20–29 (2019)
17. Guan, D., Cao, Y., Yang, J., Cao, Y., Tisse, C.L.: Exploiting fusion architectures for multispectral pedestrian detection and segmentation. Appl. Opt. 57(18), D108–D116 (2018)
18. Li, C., Song, D., Tong, R., Tang, M.: Illumination-aware faster R-CNN for robust multispectral pedestrian detection. Pattern Recognit. 85, 161–171 (2019)
19. Liu, J., Zhang, S., Wang, S., Metaxas, D.N.: Multispectral deep neural networks for pedestrian detection. In: British Machine Vision Conference (BMVC), arXiv:1611.02644 (2016)
20. König, D., Adam, M., Jarvers, C., Layher, G., Neumann, H., Teutsch, M.: Fully convolutional region proposal networks for multispectral person detection. In: IEEE Conference on Computer Vision and Pattern Recognition Workshops (CVPRW), pp. 243–250 (2017)
21. Hu, J., Shen, L., Albanie, S., Sun, G., Wu, E.: Squeeze-and-excitation networks. In: CVPR, pp. 7132–7141 (2018)
22. Redmon, J., Farhadi, A.: Yolov3: an incremental improvement. arXiv preprint arXiv:1804.02767 (2018)
23. Li, C., Song, D., Tong, R., et al.: Multispectral Pedestrian Detection via Simultaneous Detection and Segmentation. arXiv, Computer Vision and Pattern Recognition, arXiv:1808.04818 (2018)
24. He, K., Zhang, X., Ren, S., et al.: Deep residual learning for image recognition. In: Computer Vision and Pattern Recognition, pp. 770–778 (2016)
25. Hwang, S., Park, J., Kim, N., Choi, Y., So Kweon, I.: Multispectral pedestrian detection: benchmark dataset and baseline. In: CVPR, pp. 1037–1045 (2015)
26. Rezatofighi, H., Tsoi, N., Gwak, J., et al.: Generalized intersection over union: a metric and a loss for bounding box regression. In: Computer Vision and Pattern Recognition, pp. 658–666 (2019)
27. Dollár, P., Appel, R., Belongie, S., Perona, P.: Fast feature pyramids for object detection. TPAMI 36(8), 1532–1545 (2014)

LCache: Machine Learning-Enabled Cache Management in Near-Data Processing-Based Solid-State Disks

Hui Sun[1], Shangshang Dai[1] , Qiao Cui[1] , and Jianzhong Huang[2]([⊠])

[1] Anhui University, Hefei 230601, Anhui, China
sunhui@ahu.edu.cn, shangshangdai@stu.ahu.edu.cn
[2] Huazhong University of Science and Technology, Wuhan 430074, Hubei, China
hjzh@hust.edu.cn

Abstract. In the era of big-data, large-scale storage systems use NAND Flash-based solid-state disks (SSDs). Some upper-level applications put higher requirements on the performance of SSD-based storage systems. SSDs typically exploit a small amount of DRAM as device side cache, yet the limitation of the DRAM inside an SSD makes a better performance difficult to achieve. The wide application of the existing cache management schemes (e.g., LRU, CFLRU) provides a solution to this problem. With the popularity of near-data processing paradigm in storage systems, the near-data processing-based SSDs are designed to improve the performance of the overall system. In this work, a new cache management strategy named LCache is proposed based on NDP-enabled SSD using a machine learning algorithm. LCache determines whether I/O requests will be accessed in a period by trained machine learning model (e.g., decision tree algorithm model) based on characteristics of I/O requests. When the infrequently accessed I/Os that are not intensive are directly flushed into the flash memory, LCahe enables to update the dirty data that has not been accessed in the cache to the flash memory. Thus, LCache can generate clean data while replace cached data with priority to minimize the cost of data evicting. LCache also can effectively achieve the threefold benefits: (1) reducing the data access frequency to frequently access data pages in flash memory, (2) improving the response time by 59.8%, 60% and 14.81% compared with LRU, CFLRU, and MQSim, respectively, and (3) optimizing the performance cliff by 68.2%, 68%, and 30.2%, respectively.

Keywords: Near-data processing · Machine learning · Cache management solid state disks

This work is supported in part by the University Synergy Innovation Program of Anhui Province under Grants GXXT-2019-007, National Natural Science Foundation of China under Grants 61702004, 61572209.

X. He et al. (Eds.): NPC 2020, LNCS 12639, pp. 128–139, 2021.
https://doi.org/10.1007/978-3-030-79478-1_11

1   Introduction

NAND Flash based solid state disks (SSDs) usually use a small amount of DRAM as device-side cache, which services I/O requests in high-performance DRAM, to effectively improve the storage performance of SSDs-based systems. However, the cache size is usually minimal because of its limited space and high cost. Academia and industry have been devoted to design cache management with high space utilization, durable robustness, and high performance. When the cache space is full, the items in cache must be wiped out from the cache. The existing practice of cache management usually use statistical methods. Data pages that are rarely used recently are removed from the cache. The cache eviction is triggered when a new data is written into the cache space which is full. Thus, in this case, there are two issues affecting the overall cache performance:

1) These evicted data may enter into the cache again due to the temporal locality and spatial locality that the access patterns exhibit.
2) The data update in cache is greatly affected by I/O access pattern. When I/O access is intensive, it is easier to replace cache. However if the bandwidth of flash memory is occupied, rendering confliction for I/O access. As such, even if the cache is full, cache replacement is less likely to be triggered, and the amount of SSDs bandwidth remains idle.

Machine learning is used in computing and storage systems [1]. With the improvement of computing capability of devices, an architecture called near-data processing (i.e., NDP) [2] or in storage computing (i.e., ISC) [3] attracts attention from scholars and professionals. In NDP devices, extra computing resources are usually used to provide higher computing power. Therefore, to tackle the issues, we propose a novel cache management algorithm, named LCache, based on the NDP-enabled SSDs with adopting machine learning on the computing resources in the NDP disk. LCache predicts that the data pages marked with the tags of clean, dirty, recency, and frequency will be wrote into the cache until they are replaced according to the characteristics of applications and then proactive update method is designed for flushing the data into the flash memory, meanwhile, deleting the data page in the cache.

When user data is not accessed by the machine learning, LCache judges the status of the page in flash memory, for example if the flash chip is idle, the dirty and recency cached item is updated into the flash memory, which can balance bandwidth utilization in the cache. The clean data has the priority to be replaced to minimize the cost of replacement.

The reason that the machine learning model-based LCache is applied to the NDP devices is that the LCache needs computing resources to process prediction based on I/Os characteristics. The traditional processor inside SSDs is difficult to provide corresponding computing power. LCache can handle the problem of the computing resources during the model running in NDP device. The machine learning model of LCache is deployed into FTL through firmware.

Contributions of this paper are summarized as:

1) In this paper, we design a cache management, named LCache, for NDP-based SSDs. LCache employs the decision tree C 4.5-based model to determine whether I/Os requests will access the cache in a while.
2) In LCache, we design a proactive update mechanism, by which the machine learning model is able to judge the data pages that will not be accessed again in the future. These pages identified with dirty-recency are flushed into the flash memory when the flash chips are idle. This method can balance the bandwidth cost in flash memory. Clean data is the first replaced to improve the overall performance of cache management.
3) We evaluate the performance of LCache in real-world enterprise traces. Experimental results show that the performance of LCache in terms of response time and performance cliff. LCache reduces the response time by 59.8%, 60%, and 14.81%, respectively, compared with LRU, CFLRU and MQSim under proj_0. The performance cliff is optimized by 68.2%, 68%, and 30.2%, respectively.

2 Background and Related Work

2.1 Near-Data Processing Storage Device

Figure 1 shows the overview of NDP storage system. The host connects with the NDP device through the PCIe NVMe protocol. The NDP device side is a flash-based solid-state disk with higher computing power. The difference between the NDP device and the typical solid-state disk is that the former has a hardware acceleration computing unit. The NDP device-side mainly consists of an embedded processor, hardware acceleration processor, and DRAM. The physical structure of flash memory is primarily divided into channels, chips, dies, planes, etc. Each block contains several pages. The flash memory chip can perform write, read, and erase operations. During this operation, the flash memory chip will block other access commands, making the blocked commands wait in the corresponding chip queue.

2.2 Cache Management

There are many cache management methods proposed in the past, such as LRU [4]. However, in SSDs, the penalty of cache miss resulting in cache replacement is different. Park et al. proposed the CFLRU [5], in which the cost of cache replacement could be reduced by replacing the consistent data in the cache and flash memory. With the popularity of machine learning, Wang et al. used machine learning to predict data access patterns in the cache, which could help to improve the cache strategy of "one-time access exclusion" [1]. In Tencent QQ application, the HDDs in Tencent storage servers are used as the back-end storage and SSD is used as the cache. They use the machine learning to cache the photos that will be accessed in the cache and these image data that will not be located will not be cached, by which the cache space is able to serve more

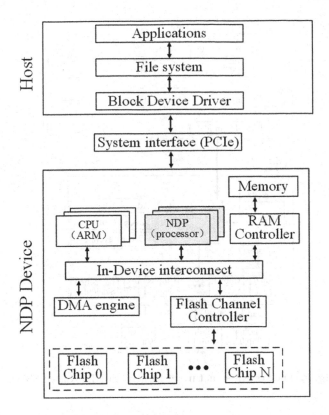

Fig. 1. Overview of near-data processing-based SSDs.

applications, thereby optimizing the SSD lifetime. MQSim [6] enclosed a new caching scheme based on the write cache inside SSD. MQSim combined hot and cold in the write-through mode, in which cold data written in the cache would be flushed to the back-end flash memory. Meanwhile, the cached data in the flash memory would be promptly deleted, thereby keeping the cache release space. The following data can be directly written into the cache instead of the eviction operation, thus, dramatically reducing the frequency of cache replacement and providing higher performance. However, there is a large amount of data written into the flash memory, resulting in a large number of erasures.

3   Overview System

LCache is an active updating cache management strategy based on machine learning with the feature of low cost, high performance and life-friendly for NDP devices. The machine learning model is trained according to different enterprise application load characteristics. By deploying the trained machine learning

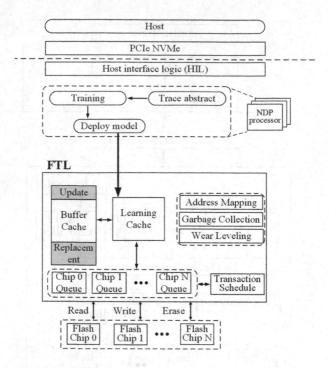

Fig. 2. The system structure of LCache in NDP-based SSDs.

model in the FTL layer of NDP devices, LCache, which adds functions to make it configurable, adequately judges whether I/O requests will re-access the cache. Simultaneously the machine learning model can decide whether the data pages will re-access the flash memory or not. When the flash memory chip is idle, these cached data pages are actively flushed into the flash memory, releasing the corresponding cache space. Even if the cache space is full, the cache will not be able to be accessed. To improve the overhead of the cache replacement, the active update mechanism is used to update recency dirty data into the flash memory when the flash memory chip is idle and then, the dirty data converts to clean one.

Figure 2 presents the system structure of LCache. The NDP device connects with the host through the PCIe NVMe protocol. The host interface logic (HIL) is responsible for splitting I/O requests from the host into several flash transactions according to the size of the flash page. Flash transaction is the basic unit of cache entries and the transaction schedule unit (TSU). We use an accelerator inside the NDP device to extract features of the machine learning trained I/O requests. The machine learning model is suitable for enterprise application.

4   System Implementation

4.1   Machine Learning Module

To predict whether the cache data will be accessed again, we use decision tree C4.5 to train the machine learning model with the real enterprise application load. The data set is selected from UMass trace [7] and Microsoft Cambridge Research [8] with a wide range of enterprise applications. The decision tree algorithm is selected for the following reasons:

1) The decision tree is one of the typical machine learning algorithms. Its computational cost is relatively low. The size of the trained model is small, about 200 bytes. The cost of the machine learning algorithm is high in storage devices with less abundant resources.
2) The model trained by the decision tree algorithm can be easily transformed into an if-else statement and implemented in C language on the device side pursuing performance.
3) The accuracy of the trained model in our test can reach 80% - 90%, which can meet our application requirements.

We describe the generation pipeline of the machine learning model with three stages, i.e., feature extraction, training set generation and model training.

Feature Extraction. A block-level I/O request contains time, device, LSN, size, operation type, etc. The feature extraction stage first splits an I/O request by the page size and then counts the frequency, distance, and size of LPN in a specific range in the past. Frequency refers to the number of times in the past to access the LPN within the cache size range. Distance is the number of separated pages of the same LPN to the current nearest access LPN in the past cache size. If there is no number found, the cache size minus 1. The revisited distance means finding the closest page that is the same as the current LPN and calculating the number of pages separated from the current page without limiting the cache size. If it exceeds the current preset range, it is set to -1.

Training Set Generation. When the features of each I/O request are extracted, the situation of entering and exiting the cache will be simulated according to the LRU. If all tags of pages in an I/O request miss, the tag of this trace is missing. Except this scenario, we consider others shall be hit.

Model Training. The training method adopted is decision tree C4.5, which is characterized by frequency, distance, and the size of a trace. The labels are 0 and 1, where "0" indicates that it will not be hit during the cache period. The notation "1" means that it will be hit. The trained model is able to classify data. According to the characteristics of the data in workload, it can be divided into (1) data will be hit in the cache (2) data will not be hit during the cache.

4.2 Proactive Update Function

The proactive update function is an essential component inside LCache. Two types of LRU linked lists (e.g., clean LRU link list and dirty LRU link list) are used to manage data in the write-buffer cache. This method can effectively search data and process the dirty or clean data to release cache space for storing the data pages that will be re-accessed in the future. Learning cache uses the update and replacement mechanism to reduce the cost of cache replacement.

Update Scheme. The cache management usually uses the write-back mechanism to ensure the data consistency between cache and flash memory. However, this mechanism is largely dependent on the I/Os access in applications, which quickly causes an imbalance of data flow from the cache to flash memory. When the I/O accesses is intensive, data updating from the cache to flash memory is frequent, which is prone to cause I/O access conflict.

As shown in Fig. 3, LCache triggers actively update judgment once new data is inserted into the cache. Then, it judges the data item that meets the requirements of active updates from the tail end of the dirty LRU list. LCache will check first if the chip is idle. When the flash memory chip corresponding to the LPA of the cache entry is idle and no flash transaction is waiting for service in the corresponding chip queue, the LPA corresponding chip will be identified as idle. If the other way around, the cache entry will not trigger an active update but proceed to check the next cache entry. LCache will execute Classifier using machine learning model. As shown in Fig. 3, Classifier outputs 0 and 1. "1" represents that the data page is likely to be accessed again in the future. "0" means that the data page is unlikely to be accessed.

When the output of Classifier is 0, the data will be actively updated and written into the flash memory. The corresponding cache entries in the write buffer cache will be deleted as the data is unlikely to be accessed again in the future, thereby freeing the space for other cache items that may be accessed.

When the output of the Classifier is 1, LCache first judges whether there is space in clean data LRU list due to it accounts for much smaller proportion in cache space than that of the dirty-data LRU linked list. If the clean data LRU list is not full, it will be separated by hot and cold via distinguishing the data from the occurrence or frequency. This method can improve SSD lifetime caused by excessive active updating. A Bloom filter is used to record the coldness and hotness of each request, similar to that in Hsieh's work [9]. According to the spatial and temporal locality, the probability of reaccessing the recency data is small. LCache actively updates the recency data into flash memory and move the cached dirty data LRU list to the clean data LRU list. If the differentiated data is frequency, then it will not be updated actively, and LCache continues to assess whether the next data item in the linked list will trigger the active update. Actively updating the recency data to flash memory and putting it into the clean data LRU list can minimize the cache replacement cost.

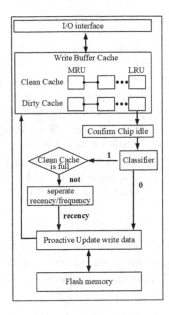

Fig. 3. The workflow in LCache.

Replacement Algorithms. When the cache space is full, the existing cached items must be moved from the cache for the newly inserted write requests. When the cache replacement occurs, LCache first replaces the clean data page from the tail of the clean data LRU list, which can minimize the cost of cache replacement. When there is no clean data page, it will continue to replace from the tail of the dirty LRU list.

4.3   Read and Write Operation

After user-level read and write requests arrive at the device, the HIL is first splitted into flash transactions. The index of the cache linked list will be queried, meanwhile, the corresponding operation will be executed with reference to hit or not.

If flash transactions belong to read requests, when cache hit occurs, if the hit data is dirty data, it will be moved to the head of the dirty LRU list. If it is clean data, it will be moved to the head of the clean LRU list. When cache miss occurs, the cache that cannot service the corresponding requests reads the corresponding data from the underlying flash memory.

If flash transactions belong to write requests, when cache hit occurs, the hit data is extracted from the corresponding LRU linked list and updated to new data. After modifying the corresponding metadata, it is inserted into the head of the dirty LRU linked list. Otherwise, the cache misses, if the cache space is not full, the new data page will be directly inserted into the head of the dirty-data LRU linked list and return the completion information. If the cache space is full,

Table 1. Details of the simulation parameters.

SSD organization	Host interface: PCIe 3.0 (NVMe 1.2) Total Capacity: 24 GB 6 channels 4 chips-per- channel
Flash microarchitecture	4KiB page, 448 B metadata-per-page, 64 pages-per-block, 1024 blocks-per-plane, 2 planes-per-die, 2 die-per-chip
Flash latencies [10]	Read latency: 75 us, Program latency: 750 us, Erase latency: 3.8 ms
Flash translation layer (FTL)	GC Policy: Greedy GC Threshold: 0.05 Address Mapping: DFTL TSU Policy: Sprinkler [11] Overprovisioning Ratio: 0.07

the cache should be triggered to replace the new data page to free up the cache space and the new data page are inserted into the dirty data LRU linked list head. Please refer to Sect. 4.2 for cache replacement algorithm.

5   Experimental Setup and Evaluation

5.1   Experimental Setup

We use an open-source simulator, MQSim [6], to simulate, evaluate and compare our proposed LCache LRU write cache strategy, CFLRU, and MQSim. MQSim, released by the cmu-safari research group, can accurately simulate the latest NVMe protocol solid-state disk prototype and the main front-end and back-end components of multi-queue solid-state disk (MQ-SSD). The default cache size in the experiment is 32 MB. The simulation parameters are shown in Table 1.

We use real enterprise-scale workload to study the performance of the cache scheme. We select several typical block-level workloads from UMass trace and Microsoft Cambridge Research.

5.2   Performance Evaluation

Response Time. Response time refers to the time from the time when I/O request enters the SQ queue to the time when the host receives the return information from SSD. It is commonly used to evaluate the performance of storage devices. Figure 4 shows the response time of LCache under different workloads compared with LRU, CFLRU and MQSim under four-type traces. In proj_0, LCache achieves an improvement of 59.8%, 60%, and 14.81%, compared with LRU, CFLRU, and MQSim respectively. It enhances about 84%, 83.3%, and 26% under prxy_0 configured with the three cache managements. In stg_0, the response time of LCache is 1.1% higher than that of MQSim, but the erase count is 47.2% lower than that of MQSim.

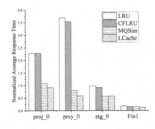

Fig. 4. Response time of LCache, LRU, CFLRU, MQSim under traces.

Standard Deviation of Response Time. The standard deviation of response time is used to evaluate the optimization of storage system performance cliff caused by different cache strategies, illustrated as Fig. 5. Compared with LRU, CFLRU, and MQSim under proj_0, the standard deviation of response time increases by 68.2%, 68%, and 30.2% respectively, and under prxy_0. Besides, LCache achieves 3%, 75. 1%, and 37. 2% improvement, respectively. LCache has a good performance in Fin1 and stg_0.

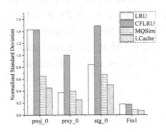

Fig. 5. Standard deviation of response time of LCache, LRU, CFLRU, MQSim under traces.

Erase Count. Erase count in flash memory intuitively reflects the SSD lifetime. Each block in flash memory has the upper limitation. Figure 6 shows that LCache has a slightly higher erase count compared with LRU and CFLRU. The reason is that LCache update mechanism can lead to much data written into flash memory compared with other strategies. However, LCache optimizes the erase count by 2.1%, 69.3%, 47.2%, and 45.4%, respectively, under proj_0, prxy_0, stg_0, and Fin1, compared with MQSim.

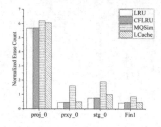

Fig. 6. Erase count of LCache, LRU, CFLRU, MQSim under traces.

6   Conclusion

With the space increment of an SSD, the cache offered inside the SSD is limited. In the paper, we propose a machine learning-based cache management, LCache, for NDP-based SSD. LCache employs decision tree C4.5 to divide I/O requests into two types, (1) data that will re-access the cache; (2) data that will not re-access the cache. The cache data is dynamically updated into flash memory in pursuant with the load status of flash memory chip through the active update mechanism. LCache effectively balances the access of I/O requests to flash memory, thereby improving the performance of the whole SSD. We simulate the performance of LCache through real-world traces and the result shows that LCache outperforms other existing caching strategies.

References

1. Wang, H., Yi, X., Huang, P., Cheng, B., Zhou, K.: Efficient SSD caching by avoiding unnecessary writes using machine learning. In: Proceedings of the 47th International Conference on Parallel Processing, pp. 1–10 (2018)
2. Balasubramonian, R., et al.: Near-data processing: insights from a micro-46 workshop. IEEE Micro **34**(4), 36–42 (2014)
3. Ki, Y.S., et al.: In-storage compute: an ultimate solution for accelerating i/o-intensive applications. Flash Memory Summit (2015)
4. Mattson, R.L., Gecsei, J., Slutz, D.R., Traiger, I.L.: Evaluation techniques for storage hierarchies. IBM Syst. J. **9**(2), 78–117 (1970)
5. Park, S., Jung, D., Kang, J., Kim, J., Lee, J.: CFLRU: a replacement algorithm for flash memory. In: Proceedings of the 2006 International Conference on Compilers, Architecture and Synthesis for Embedded Systems, pp. 234–241 (2006)
6. Tavakkol, A., Gómez-Luna, J., Sadrosadati, M., Ghose, S., Mutlu, O.: MQSim: a framework for enabling realistic studies of modern multi-queue SSD devices. In: 16th USENIX Conference on File and Storage Technologies FAST 2018, pp. 49–66 (2018)
7. Umass trace repository (2020). http://traces.cs.umass.edu/index.php/Storage/Storage
8. Snia traces (2020). http://iotta.snia.org/traces/
9. Hsieh, J.-W., Kuo, T.-W., Chang, L.-P.: Efficient identification of hot data for flash memory storage systems. ACM Trans. Storage (TOS) **2**(1), 22–40 (2006)

10. NAND flash memory MLC MT29F256G08CKCAB datasheet. Micron Technology Inc (2014)
11. Jung, M., Kandemir, M.T.: Sprinkler: maximizing resource utilization in many-chip solid state disks. In: 2014 IEEE 20th International Symposium on High Performance Computer Architecture (HPCA), pp. 524–535. IEEE (2014)

Security Situation Prediction of Network Based on Lstm Neural Network

Liqiong Chen[1(✉)], Guoqing Fan[1(✉)], Kun Guo[1], and Junyan Zhao[2]

[1] Department of Computer Science and Information Engineering,
Shanghai Institute of Technology, Shanghai 201400, China
`lqchen@sit.edu.cn`
[2] Department of Computer Science and Engineering, East China University
of Science and Technology, Shanghai 200237, China

Abstract. As an emerging technology that blocks network security threats, network security situation prediction is the key to defending against network security threats. In view of the single source of information and the lack of time attributes of the existing methods, we propose an optimal network security situation prediction model based on lstm neural network. We employ the stochastic gradient descent method as the minimum training loss to establish a network security situation prediction model, and give the model implementation algorithm pseudo code to further predict the future network security situation. The simulation experiments based on the data collected from Security Data dataset show that compared with other commonly used time series methods, the prediction accuracy of the model is higher and the overall situation of network security situation is more intuitively reflected, which provides a new solution for network security situation.

Keywords: Network security · Parallel processing · Situation awareness · Network security situation prediction model · Lstm network

1 Introduction

As network systems evolve toward sharing, complexity, and scale, network intrusions become more complex and exist in various environments. The traditional way of network security mainly uses vulnerability scanning, intrusion detection and other protection technologies which has not been able to fully meet the increasingly updated network security needs [1]. Network security situational awareness technology emerged in this context. Network Security Situation Awareness (NSSA) is an emerging technology that studies how to acquire, understand, display, and predict network entities and build network security systems [2,3].

The existing network security situation prediction methods mainly include Markov model [4], support vector machine [5] and other technologies. Although these technologies have improved the detection accuracy to a certain extent, they also have certain limitations. For example, they ignore the relevance of data in a long sequence of time. In recent years, network security situation prediction methods based on deep learning have been proposed because of their better feature learning capabilities. However, although they improved the detection accuracy, they did not consider the characteristics of the result data after prediction.

In this paper, we propose an optimal network security situation prediction (ONS^{2}P) model for large-scale cyber-attacks with associated characteristics and time dimension. The main contributions of our work are listed as follows: (i)We employ the stochastic gradient descent method as the minimum sample training loss to optimize the parameters of the ONS^{2}P model established for the target, improving the accuracy of network security situation prediction. (ii) Simulation experiments show that compared with other commonly used time series methods, the prediction accuracy of the model is higher, and the overall situation of the network security situation is more intuitively reflected.

2 ONS^{2}P Algorithm

We design the ONS^{2}P algorithm based on the sltm network and convert a one-dimensional network security situation data set into a multi-dimensional network security situation data set before prediction. The Simple code is shown in Algorithm 1.

Algorithm 1. The ONS^{2}P prediction network security situation algorithm

---
Require: History attacked data set $D = x_1, x_2, x_n$
Ensure: predicted number of future network attacks K
1. Load the historical invalid data set and convert the data to floating point type float32.
2. Convert a list of network security postures into three columns of inputs *T-2*, *T-1*, *T* and a column of output *T+1*
3. MinMaxScalar achieves standardization of data.
4. Divide the data set into training set train X and forecast set test X
5. Transform the data into *[samples, time steps, features]* to construct the lstm model.
6. Establish ONS^{2}P model
   model.add(lstm(4, $input\_shape = (3, look\_back)$))
   model.add(Dense(1))
   model.compile($loss =' mean\_absolate\_error', optimizer = sgd$)
   model.fit($trainX, trainY, epochs = 100, batch\_size = 1, verbose = 2$)
7. Use trained models to predict the number of attacks on the network K
8. Perform matrix operations on the predicted data, and output optimization.

In this paper, we also analyzed and optimized the predicted result data according to the predicted data characteristics: (1) When the hourly attack data shows an increasing trend, the predicted value is a little larger; (2) When the hourly attack data is increasing When showing a decreasing trend, the predicted value is smaller.

If the current predicted value is greater than the predicted value of the previous time, then Xi is subtracted: $p_i' = p_i + X_i(p_i - p_{i-1} >= 1)$. If the current predicted value is smaller than the predicted value of the previous time, then Xi is added: $p_i' = p_i - X_i(p_i - p_{i-1} >= 1)$. The value of Xi is calculated from the average of the absolute values of the differences between the predicted data p and the real data x of multiple experiments: $X_i = \frac{\sum_{i=1}^{n}(|x_i - pi|)}{n}$,Where xi is the real data at time i, and pi is the predicted data at time i.

3   Experiment

We conduct experiments with the malicious program attack data collected by Honeynet organization to verify the validity and rationality of our method. In order to verify the performance of ONS^{2}P model, the two methods of Moving Average (MA) and Exponential Smoothing (ES) were used as reference models to do the same experiment.

We use the Root Mean Square Error (RMSE) and Mean Absolute Error (MAE) evaluation indicators to measure the accuracy of our method predictions, and the test results are shown in Table 1. The prediction results of the simulation experiment are shown in Fig. 1.

Table 1. Comparison of experimental prediction results.

Model	ES	MA	LSTM	ONS^{2}P
Fitting RMSE	0.05	1.87	0.11	#
Prediction RMSE	0.13	0.63	0.10	0.10
Fitting MAE	0.08	0.14	0.09	#
Prediction MAE	0.12	0.13	0.08	0.06

From the comparison data of Table 1 and Fig. 1, the conclusion of this experiment can be drawn: from the overall prediction results, the ONS^{2}P model is more common than the commonly used time series prediction method. And the moving average method and the exponential smoothing method predict better. From the comparison results of the fitting error and prediction error provided in Table 1, it can be found that the commonly used time series prediction method moving average method and exponential smoothing method have large prediction errors, and the quantitative comparison results show that the ONS^{2}P model more accurately.

From the comparison data of Table 1, Fig. 2 and Fig. 3, the conclusion of this experiment can be drawn: the prediction value of the algorithm proposed in this

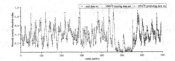

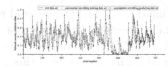

(a) Prediction results of ONS^{2}P simulation experiment

(b) Forecast results of exponential smoothing simulation experiment

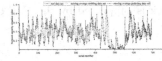

(c) Prediction results of the moving average simulation experiment

Fig. 1. Results of prediction with different methods

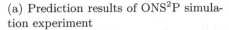

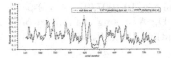

Fig. 2. Comparison of predictions before and after ONS^{2}P data optimization

Fig. 3. Comparison of error deviation before and after ONS^{2}P model data optimization

paper is closer to the actual value than the prediction value of the lstm network. Therefore, it can be seen from the experimental results that the proposed optimization algorithm predicts the network situation better than the lstm neural network, and is more in line with the actual value.

4   Related Works

Network security assessment is an important part of ensuring network security. Zhao, et al. [6] propose a grey Verhulst model or its inverse function to predict future risk values of the network system, and then correct the prediction accuracy based on multi-level residuals. In [7], authors proposed a quantitative evaluation method based on improved BP neural network to solve the problem of low efficiency and poor reliability of the existing network security situation assessment method. Lu [8] established a network security prediction model based on Grey Wolf Optimization (GWO) algorithm to optimize the support vector machine (SVM) parameters and solve the problem of SVM parameter optimization to improve the SVM prediction effect.

5   Conclusion

In this paper, we propose and establish a training model for the ONS^{2}P model. At the same time, we verify the accuracy of the model through experimental prediction data. The experimental results show that the ONS^{2}P model with the potential of learning long observation sequence is more accurate for network security situational awareness prediction, in order to further improve its prediction results. The accuracy of this paper is optimized for the prediction results. According to the experimental results, the error deviation after optimization is smaller, so a good optimization effect is obtained.

Acknowledgment. This work is supported by the NSF of China under grants No. 61702334.

References

1. Caulfield, T., Ioannidis, C., Pym, D.: The U.S. vulnerabilities equities process: an economic perspective. In: Rass, S., An, B., Kiekintveld, C., Fang F., Schauer, S. (eds.) Decision and Game Theory for Security. GameSec 2017. LNCS, vol. 10575, pp. 131–150. Springer, Heidelberg (2017). https://doi.org/10.1007/978-3-319-68711-7_8
2. Panteli, M., Crossley, P., Kirschen, D., Sobajic, D.: Assessing the impact of insufficient situation awareness on power system operation. IEEE Trans. Power Syst. **28**, 2967–2977 (2013)
3. Tianfield, H.: Cyber security situational awareness. In: Proceedings of 2016 IEEE International Conference on Internet of Things (iThings) and IEEE Green Computing and Communications (GreenCom) and IEEE Cyber, Physical and Social Computing (CPSCom) and IEEE Smart Data (SmartData), pp. 782–787 (2016)
4. Andrysiak, T., Saganowski, Ł., Maszewski, M., Marchewka, A.: Detection of network attacks using hybrid ARIMA-GARCH model. In: Zamojski, W., Mazurkiewicz, J., Sugier, J., Walkowiak, T., Kacprzyk, J. (eds.) DepCoS-RELCOMEX 2017. AISC, vol. 582, pp. 1–12. Springer, Cham (2018). https://doi.org/10.1007/978-3-319-59415-6_1
5. Tai, K.S., Socher, R., Manning, C.D.: Improved semantic representations from tree-structured long short-term memory networks. Comput. Sci. **5**(1), 36 (2015)
6. Zhao, G., Wang, H., Wang, J., Shen, L.: A novel situation awareness model for network systems' security. In: Shi, Y., van Albada, G.D., Dongarra, J., Sloot, P.M.A. (eds.) ICCS 2007. LNCS, vol. 4489, pp. 1077–1084. Springer, Heidelberg (2007). https://doi.org/10.1007/978-3-540-72588-6_172
7. Dong, G., Li, W., Wang, S., Zhang, X., Lu, J.Z., Li, X.: The assessment method of network security situation based on improved BP neural network. In: Liu, Q., Mısır, M., Wang, X., Liu, W. (eds.) CENet2018 2018. AISC, vol. 905, pp. 67–76. Springer, Cham (2020). https://doi.org/10.1007/978-3-030-14680-1_9
8. Lu, H., Zhang, G., Shen, Y.: Cyber security situation prediction model based on GWO-SVM. In: Barolli, L., Xhafa, F., Hussain, O.K. (eds.) IMIS 2019. AISC, vol. 994, pp. 162–171. Springer, Cham (2020). https://doi.org/10.1007/978-3-030-22263-5_16

Algorithm

Dynamic GMMU Bypass for Address Translation in Multi-GPU Systems

Jinhui Wei, Jianzhuang Lu, Qi Yu, Chen Li$^{(\boxtimes)}$, and Yunping Zhao

College of Computer Science, National University of Defense Technology,
Changsha 410073, China
{jinhui_wei,lichen,zhaoyunping}@nudt.edu.cn,
lujz1977@163.com, fishflag@126.com

Abstract. The ever increasing application footprint raises challenges for GPUs. As Moore's Law reaches its limit, it is not easy to improve single GPU performance any further; instead, multi-GPU systems have been shown to be a promising solution due to its GPU-level parallelism. Besides, memory virtualization in recent GPUs simplifies multi-GPU programming. Memory virtualization requires support for address translation, and the overhead of address translation has an important impact on the system's performance. Currently, there are two common address translation architectures in multi-GPU systems, including distributed and centralized address translation architectures. We find that both architectures suffer from performance loss in certain cases. To address this issue, we propose GMMU Bypass, a technique that allows address translation requests to dynamically bypass GMMU in order to reduce translation overhead. Simulation results show that our technique outperforms distributed address translation architecture by 6% and centralized address translation architecture by 106% on average.

Keywords: Multi-GPU system · Memory virtualization · Address translation architecture

1 Introduction

Graphics Processing Units (GPUs) have been widely used in graph analytics [16, 17], large scale simulation [6,14], and machine learning [8,13] due to its massive thread-level parallelism. Over the years, with the development of big data, the application footprint has increased rapidly, which raises challenges for GPUs. What is worse, as Moore's Law reaches its limit [1], improving GPU performance through integrating more transistors on a single die is more difficult than ever before. Instead, multi-GPU systems [4,7,18] have been shown to be a promising solution due to its GPU-level parallelism. Nowadays, multi-GPU systems have been used in data centers to improve the performance of cloud computing [9].

Recent support for memory virtualization [5,19,20] in GPUs has simplified programming and improved programming productivity. Memory virtualization

X. He et al. (Eds.): NPC 2020, LNCS 12639, pp. 147–158, 2021.
https://doi.org/10.1007/978-3-030-79478-1_13

requires the support of address translation. Also the details of memory hierarchy from mainstream GPU manufacturers, such as NVIDIA, AMD, and Intel, have not been published, it is accepted that current GPU supports TLB-based address translation [2,4]. Recent research [2,3,11,12] has shown that the efficiency of address translation has an important impact on GPU performance.

Currently, there are two common address translation architectures in multi-GPU systems, namely, centralized address translation architecture ("centralized architecture" for short) and distributed address translation architecture ("distributed architecture" for short). The major difference between these two architectures is that distributed architecture uses a GMMU (GPU Memory Management Unit) in each GPU node (in the system) to manage address translation for that GPU. When an address translation misses L2 TLB, the request is sent to GMMU first for page table walk in distributed architecture; while, in centralized architecture, the request is directly sent to IOMMU (Input Output Memory Management Unit) on the CPU side for translation.

In this paper, we make an in-depth analysis of these two architectures. In terms of hardware overhead, centralized architecture causes less overhead due to the absence of GMMU. In terms of performance, distributed architecture outperforms centralized architecture on average, because GMMU reduces the frequency of remote translation (translation requests are sent to IOMMU) for local translation requests (translation requests find mappings in local memory). However, we find that distributed architecture suffers from performance slowdown in certain cases. For example, for those access requests that demand for shared data (residents in other GPU node), the address translation requests are sent to page table walker in GMMU if they miss L2 TLB. As the shared data does not resident in the local GPU memory, the translation requests cannot find address mappings in local memory either. These requests are then sent to IOMMU for further translation. These unnecessary page table walks consume additional power and incur performance degradation.

To address this issue, we propose GMMU Bypass in distributed architecture to reduce unnecessary page table walks and improve address translation performance. GMMU Bypass uses two fixed thresholds to predict according to the variance in access behavior. Simulation results show that GMMU Bypass is effective at reducing the overhead of handling address translation requests.

This paper makes the following major contributions:

- To our knowledge, this is the first work to provide in-depth analysis of two address translation architectures from hardware overhead and performance points of view in multi-GPU system.
- We propose GMMU Bypass, a technique that bypasses GMMU selectively to improve the performance of multi-GPU system by profiling and predicting the memory access behavior. We evaluate the performance of our design and results show that GMMU Bypass outperforms the distributed architecture by 6% and centralized architecture by 106% averagely.

2   Background

In this section, we introduce the background on multi-GPU systems, including programming models, remote data access mechanisms, and address translation architectures.

2.1   Programming Models

Currently, there exist two programming models in multi-GPU system: discrete model and unified model [15]. Discrete model dispatches kernels to each GPU node for execution, as a result, programmers have to rewrite the code developed for single GPU in order to make it executable on multi-GPU systems. While, unified model dispatches tasks at CTA (Cooperative Thread Array) granularity, which means the CTAs of a single kernel can be dispatched to different GPU nodes for execution. In this case, the code developed for single GPU can run seamlessly on multi-GPU systems without any modification. Due to the programming convenience, the research community focuses on unified model. This paper also targets unified model.

2.2   Remote Data Access Mechanisms

There exist three remote data access mechanisms in multi-GPU system: direct cache access, page migration, and first touch migration. *Direct cache access* means that a GPU directly accesses the L2 cache of a remote GPU node to retrieve the requested data through RDMA (Remote DMA) [4,10,18]. In this case, the corresponding page will not be migrated to the requested GPU. *Page migration* refers to migrating a page from the GPU which it residents in to the requested GPU in case of a page fault. *First touch migration* is a special case of page migration. It means that CPU migrates the page to the GPU that demands it first, which is used for data allocation generally.

2.3   Address Translation Architectures

There exist two address translation architectures in multi-GPU systems: centralized/distributed architecture. The major difference between the two architectures is whether the GPU node has a GMMU. The address translation process in these two architectures is shown as follows.

Centralized Architecture. The address translation process in centralized architecture is shown in Fig. 1. The request first accesses the L1 TLB to check for the address mapping. On an L1 TLB miss, the request accesses L2 TLB (①). If the request also misses L2 TLB, the request is sent to IOMMU (on the CPU side) for further translation (②). IOMMU performs page table walk and sends the required address mapping to the GPU (③). The GPU completes the data access using the translated address. If the data residents in local memory, the data is retrieved from its memory hierarchy; otherwise, the data is retrieved from remote GPU through RDMA (④).

Distributed Architecture. The address translation process in distributed architecture is shown in Fig. 2. The request accesses L1 TLB first for address translation. On an L1 TLB miss, the request accesses L2 TLB (①). If it also misses L2 TLB, the request is sent to page table walker in GMMU for page walk (②). If the request finds the desired page table entry during page walk, the address translation is finished; otherwise, the request is sent to IOMMU for further translation (③). IOMMU performs page table walk and sends back the required address translation mapping (④). The GPU retrieves the data from its local memory or remote GPU via RDMA (⑤).

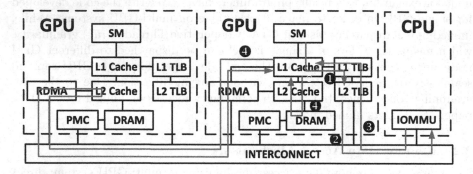

Fig. 1. Centralized address translation architecture

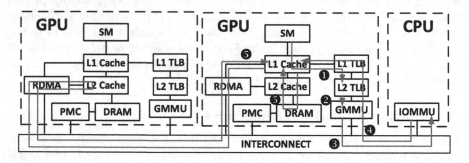

Fig. 2. Distributed address translation architecture

3   Motivation

The major difference between centralized architecture and distributed architecture is whether address translation requests are sent to GMMU for page table walk. For centralized architecture, when translation requests miss L2 TLB, the requests are directly sent to IOMMU for further translation; while, for distributed architecture, the requests are sent to GMMU for page table walk.

Despite the fact that distributed architecture incurs higher hardware overhead due to GMMU, it usually outperforms centralized architecture in terms of performance. Through further analysis, we find that the address translation requests that miss L2 TLB touch either a local page (residents in local memory) or a remote page (residents in a remote GPU node). If it touches a local page, for distributed architecture, the address translation completes after page table walk, and thus, there is no need to access the IOMMU. However, for centralized architecture, no matter where the page residents, the request is always sent to IOMMU for translation. As the communication between CPU and GPU via PCIe incurs significant overhead (refers to latency), the remote translation (accesses IOMMU) causes much longer latency than page table walk. Therefore, for address translation requests that touch local pages, distributed architecture can reduce translation overhead and improves performance.

However, if the address translation request touches a remote page, distributed architecture may cause slight performance slowdown. This is because GMMU does not store the page table entry of remote pages, therefore, the address translation request cannot find the desired address mapping in local memory after page table walk. In other words, the page table walk is unnecessary for these requests. These unnecessary page table walks waste power and may cause performance degradation.

To quantitatively show the discrepancy of two architectures, we evaluate the performance of these two architectures and an ideal scheme, which is shown in Fig. 3. The ideal scheme can predict the exact destination for each translation request, and thus, it achieves the best performance. The experimental methodology can be found in Section 5. We have two observations from Fig. 3. First, we can see that though distributed architecture significantly outperforms centralized architecture for MT, FFT, KM, and ST, it does worse than centralized architecture for RL, FIR, and MP. This result corroborates our analysis that unnecessary page table walks may harm the performance of distributed architecture. Second, we discover that the performance of the ideal scheme is better than distributed architecture, which means that there are a great number of unnecessary page table walks existing in distributed architecture. So we can propose a mechanism that selects better destinations to reduce unnecessary page table walks for improving performance.

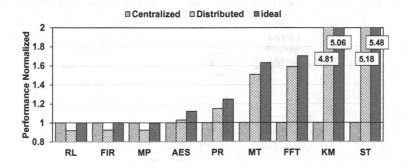

Fig. 3. Comparison of different address translation architecture

4 GMMU Bypass

To reduce unnecessary page table walks and maintain the advantages of GMMU for distributed architecture, we propose GMMU Bypass, a GMMU-side mechanism that 1) allows address translation requests to directly access IOMMU without walking the GPU page table, or 2) simultaneously sends translation requests to GMMU and IOMMU. Its architecture is shown in Fig. 4.

GMMU Bypass is a simple mechanism, it counts the number of address translation requests that touch local pages and remote pages, and calculates the ratio periodically (L/T ratio in the figure, L is the number of local pages, T is the number of all pages). If the ratio is larger than a threshold ($T1$), which means more requests touch local pages in the current epoch, then the control logic predicts more requests touching local pages in the next epoch and disables GMMU bypass. If the ratio is smaller than a threshold ($T2$), which means more requests touche remote pages in the current epoch, then it predicts that this is also the case in the next epoch and enables GMMU bypass.

However, we find that when the ratio locates between $T1$ and $T2$, the prediction accuracy is low as a result of random accesses to local pages and remote pages. The random accesses do not show a domination trend and accesses to local/remote pages account for a certain percentage. In this case, it is not appropriate to send all requests to GMMU only or IOMMU only. Instead, our mechanism sends all requests to GMMU and IOMMU simultaneously. If the request can find the desired address mapping after page table walk, then the response from IOMMU will be discarded; while, if the request cannot find the address translation, it will be discarded, since there has been a request sent to IOMMU for further translation.

By simultaneously sending requests to GMMU and IOMMU, the requests can be handled without unnecessary page table walks. Therefore, the latency caused by awaiting page table walks for remote translation in distributed architecture is eliminated. However, the performance gain comes at a cost. Sending requests to both MMUs simultaneously generates unnecessary page table walks in GMMU or IOMMU, which may cause congestion in GMMU and IOMMU. According to our evaluation, setting proper thresholds (empirically set T1 to 0.85 and T2 to 0.15) can both achieve high performance and limit the congestion effectively.

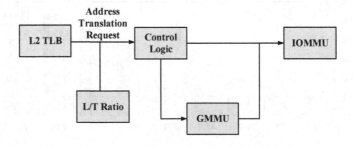

Fig. 4. GMMU bypass

5   Methodology

We evaluate Bypass GMMU with MGPUSim [15], a multi-GPU simulator that supports multi-GPU system simulation. This simulator has been validated against AMD multi-GPU systems.

5.1   Experimental Setup

We evaluate a multi-GPU system with 4 AMD GPUs. The configuration is shown in Table 1. Each GPU consists of 4 SEs (Shader Engine) and each SE consists of 9 CUs (Compute Unit). Therefore, each GPU has 36 CUs. Each CU has a private L1 vector TLB and all CUs in a GPU share an L2 TLB. Each Shader Engine is equipped with an L1 instruction TLB and an L1 scalar TLB. The 4 GPUs in the system are connected via PCIe-v3 link with bandwidth of 16GB/s in each direction. CPU and 4 GPUs are also connected via the PCIe-v3 link. The IOMMU on CPU side supports 8 concurrent page table walks and the GMMU in GPU supports 64 concurrent page table walks. The page size is 4KB, which is the default size in current GPUs.

5.2   Workloads

We use workloads from AMD APPSDK, Hetero-Mark, DNN, and SHOC benchmark suites for evaluation. These workloads cover a wide range of domains, including machine learning, graph analytics, numerical computation, etc. The average dataset size of these workloads is 64 MB. Long simulation time prevents us from evaluating workloads with larger footprint. Selected workloads are shown in Table 2.

6   Evaluation

We first compare the performance of GMMU Bypass with centralized architecture, distributed architecture, and an ideal scheme. We also make an in-depth analysis behind the performance result. Finally, we estimate the overhead of our mechanism.

Table 1. Multi-GPU system configuration

Component	Configuration	Number per GPU
CU	1.0 GHz	36
DRAM	512 MB HBM	8
L1 TLB	1 set, 32-ways	44
L2 TLB	8 set, 32-ways	1
IOMMU	8 page table walkers	–
Intra-GPU network	Single-stage XBar	1
Intra-device network	16 GB/s PCIe-v3	–
GMMU	Page table walkers	64

Table 2. Workloads characteristics

Abbv.	Application	Benchmark suite	Mem.Footprint
RL	Relu	DNN	64M
FIR	Finite impulse resp	Hetero-Mark	64M
MP	Maxpooling	DNN	64M
AES	AES-256 encryption	Hetero-Mark	64M
PR	PageRank algorithm	Hetero-Mark	64M
MT	Matrix transpose	AMDAPPSDK	64M
FFT	Fast fourier transform	SHOC	64M
KM	KMeans clustering	Hetero-Mark	64M
ST	Stencil 2D	SHOC	64M

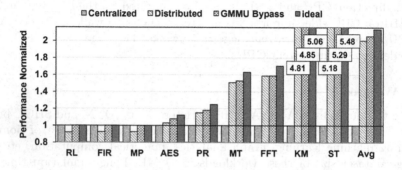

Fig. 5. Performance normalized to each address translation architecture

6.1 Performance

GMMU Bypass exposes several design parameters, including *sampling epoch*, *T1* and *T2*, We set sampling epoch to 10µs, T1 to 0.85 and T2 to 0.15 as we empirically find that these values yields best trade-off between performance and overhead. The performance comparison is shown in Fig. 5. We make three observations. First, our scheme outperforms distributed architecture for RL, FIR, and MP, which distributed architecture suffers. Second, our scheme achieves similar or slightly higher performance with distributed architecture for the rest of applications, which distributed architecture performs well. Third, the ideal scheme performs best for all applications. On average, our scheme achieves 6% performance improvement over distributed architecture and is within 96% of the ideal scheme.

6.2 Analysis

We provide an in-depth analysis of our proposed technique.

Prediction Accuracy. When the L/T ratio is larger than *T1* or smaller than *T2*, our technique disables GMMU bypass or enables GMMU bypass

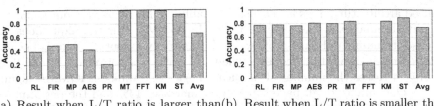

(a) Result when L/T ratio is larger than 0.85

(b) Result when L/T ratio is smaller than 0.15

Fig. 6. Prediction accuracy of our technique when L/T ratio is larger than 0.85 and smaller than 0.15

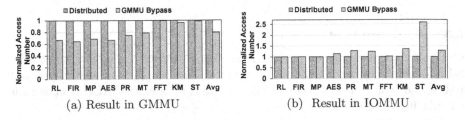

(a) Result in GMMU

(b) Result in IOMMU

Fig. 7. The number of reduplicate page table walks in GMMU and IOMMU

correspondingly. Although in this case, L/T ratio shows a domination trend, the prediction is not always accurate. We check this by calculating the prediction accuracy of our scheme. The result is shown in Fig. 6.

It shows that when L/T ratio is larger than 0.85 (*T1*), our technique achieves high prediction accuracy for MT, FFT, KM, and ST, but achieves relative low accuracy for RL, FIR, MP, AES, and PR. Through further analysis, we find that for these latter five applications, our technique only collects a few translation requests in the sampling epochs. The limited number of translation requests does not provide enough information for prediction, thereby lowers prediction accuracy. When L/T ratio is smaller than 0.15 (*T2*), our technique achieves relative high prediction accuracy except FFT. We find that FFT also suffers from limited number of translation requests in sampling epochs. The average prediction accuracy is 66% and 75% in these two cases, respectively.

Reduplicate Page Table Walks As it is not easy to predict the accurate access behavior (translation requests access local pages or remote pages)) when L/T ratio lies between 0.15 and 0.85, our techniques chooses to send the request to GMMU and IOMMU simultaneously. This generates reduplicate page table walks in GMMU and IOMMU since there is only one effective page table walk. To quantitatively show the number of reduplicate page table walks, we record the number of page table walks in GMMU and IOMMU respectively. The result is shown in Fig. 7.

Although our technique increases the number of duplicate page table walks in GMMU, the total number of page table walks is still smaller than that in distributed architecture. This is because by enabling GMMU bypass, our technique can reduce unnecessary page table walks. In IOMMU, our technique does not increase the number of page table walks dramatically except ST. This is because ST sends more translation requests when L/T ratio lies between 0.15 and 0.85, thereby increases the number of duplicate page table walks in IOMMU significantly. The number of all page table walks increases 14% and the performance improves 11% in ST specificly. On average, our technique reduces the number of page table walks by 21% in GMMU, and increases the number of page table walks by 29% in IOMMU compared to distributed architecture. Therefore, our technique does not incur a significant number of reduplicate page table walks in both GMMU and IOMMU.

6.3   Hardware Cost

Our technique is simple and incurs negligible hardware costs. It only needs two 8-bit counters to record the number of translation requests that touch local pages and remote pages respectively. In addition, a simple ALU is enough for calculating the L/T ratio.

7   Related Work

As far as we know, this paper is the first to optimize the address translation workflow for multi-GPU systems. In this section, we introduce previous research focusing on address translation designs on GPUs and performance optimization for multi-GPU systems.

7.1   Address Translation on GPU

Since the introduction of unified memory, there have been several works that target address translation designs on GPUs. J. Power *et al.* and B. Pichai *et al.* were among the first to explore such designs. In J. Power's design [12], per-CU private L1 TLB, a highly-threaded page table walker and page walk cache are essential components for efficient address translation on GPUs. B. Pichai's design includes per-CU private TLB and page table walker [11]. The authors showed the importance of making the warp scheduler to be aware of TLB design. R. Ausavarungnirun *et al.* showed that replacing the page walk cache with a shared L2 TLB can improve the performance of address translation [2].

7.2   Performance Optimization for Multi-GPU Systems

Despite multi-GPU systems utilize GPU-level parallelism, it suffers from inefficiency in certain cases. The research community proposes several optimization techniques to improve multi-GPU performance [4,7,18]. T. Baruah *et al.* proposed Griffin [4], a page allocation strategy to reduce the impact of bandwidth by making more remote accesses to be local accesses. V.Young *et al.* proposed CARVE [18], a hardware mechanism that stores recently accessed remote shared data in a dedicated region of GPU memory. G. Kim *et al.* proposes a strategy to allocate CTAs in multi-GPU system [7]. This strategy can improve the spatial locality of data access and improves the address translation efficiency for distributed architecture. Our work focuses on the address translation in distributed architecture.

8 Conclusion

The address translation efficiency has an important impact on the performance of multi-GPU systems. Although distributed architecture significantly outperforms centralized architecture for a majority of workloads, it suffers in certain cases due to unnecessary page table walks. In this paper, we propose GMMU Bypass, a technique aims at reducing the overhead of unnecessary page table walks in GMMU. The simulation result shows that our technique achieves 6% performance improvement over distributed architecture and is within 96% of an ideal scheme, which shows the effectiveness of our technique.

Acknowledgement. This work is partially supported by Research Project of NUDT ZK20-04, PDL Foundation 6142110180102, Science and Technology Innovation Project of Hunan Province 2018XK2102 and Advanced Research Program 31513010602-1.

References

1. Arunkumar, A., et al.: MCM-GPU: Multi-chip-module GPUs for continued performance scalability. ACM SIGARCH Comput. Archit. News **45**(2), 320–332 (2017)
2. Ausavarungnirun, R., et al.: Mosaic: a GPU memory manager with application-transparent support for multiple page sizes. In: Proceedings of the 50th Annual IEEE/ACM International Symposium on Microarchitecture, pp. 136–150 (2017)
3. Ausavarungnirun, R., et al.: MASK: redesigning the GPU memory hierarchy to support multi-application concurrency. ACM SIGPLAN Not. **53**(2), 503–518 (2018)
4. Baruah, T., et al.: Griffin: hardware-software support for efficient page migration in multi-GPU systems. In: 2020 IEEE International Symposium on High Performance Computer Architecture (HPCA), pp. 596–609, February 2020. https://doi.org/10.1109/HPCA47549.2020.00055
5. Ganguly, D., Zhang, Z., Yang, J., Melhem, R.: Interplay between hardware prefetcher and page eviction policy in CPU-GPU unified virtual memory. In: Proceedings of the 46th International Symposium on Computer Architecture, pp. 224–235 (2019)
6. Jermain, C., Rowlands, G., Buhrman, R., Ralph, D.: GPU-accelerated micromagnetic simulations using cloud computing. J. Magn. Magn. Mater. **401**, 320–322 (2016)
7. Kim, G., Lee, M., Jeong, J., Kim, J.: Multi-GPU system design with memory networks. In: 2014 47th Annual IEEE/ACM International Symposium on Microarchitecture, pp. 484–495. IEEE (2014)
8. Krizhevsky, A., Sutskever, I., Hinton, G.E.: ImageNet classification with deep convolutional neural networks. In: Advances in Neural Information Processing Systems, pp. 1097–1105 (2012)

9. Li, C., et al.: Priority-based PCIe scheduling for multi-tenant multi-GPU system. IEEE Comput. Archit. Lett. **18**, 157–160 (2019)
10. NVIDIA, T.: V100 GPU architecture. Whitepaper (2017). nvidia.com. Accessed September 2019
11. Pichai, B., Hsu, L., Bhattacharjee, A.: Architectural support for address translation on GPUs: designing memory management units for CPU/GPUs with unified address spaces. ACM SIGARCH Comput. Archit. News **42**(1), 743–758 (2014)
12. Power, J., Hill, M.D., Wood, D.A.: Supporting x86–64 address translation for 100s of GPU lanes. In: 2014 IEEE 20th International Symposium on High Performance Computer Architecture (HPCA), pp. 568–578. IEEE (2014)
13. Raina, R., Madhavan, A., Ng, A.Y.: Large-scale deep unsupervised learning using graphics processors. In: Proceedings of the 26th Annual International Conference on Machine Learning, pp. 873–880 (2009)
14. Sanaullah, A., Mojumder, S.A., Lewis, K.M., Herbordt, M.C.: GPU-accelerated charge mapping. In: 2016 IEEE High Performance Extreme Computing Conference (HPEC), pp. 1–7. IEEE (2016)
15. Sun, Y., et al.: MGPUSim: enabling multi-GPU performance modeling and optimization. In: Proceedings of the 46th International Symposium on Computer Architecture, pp. 197–209 (2019)
16. Wang, Y., Davidson, A., Pan, Y., Wu, Y., Riffel, A., Owens, J.D.: Gunrock: a high-performance graph processing library on the GPU. In: Proceedings of the 21st ACM SIGPLAN Symposium on Principles and Practice of Parallel Programming, pp. 1–12 (2016)
17. Wu, Y., Wang, Y., Pan, Y., Yang, C., Owens, J.D.: Performance characterization of high-level programming models for GPU graph analytics. In: 2015 IEEE International Symposium on Workload Characterization, pp. 66–75. IEEE (2015)
18. Young, V., Jaleel, A., Bolotin, E., Ebrahimi, E., Nellans, D., Villa, O.: Combining HW/SW mechanisms to improve NUMA performance of multi-GPU systems. In: 2018 51st Annual IEEE/ACM International Symposium on Microarchitecture (MICRO), pp. 339–351. IEEE (2018)
19. Zheng, T., Nellans, D., Zulfiqar, A., Stephenson, M., Keckler, S.W.: Towards high performance paged memory for GPUs. In: 2016 IEEE International Symposium on High Performance Computer Architecture (HPCA), pp. 345–357. IEEE (2016)
20. Ziabari, A.K., et al.: UMH: a hardware-based unified memory hierarchy for systems with multiple discrete GPUs. ACM Trans. Archit. Code Optim. (TACO) **13**(4), 1–25 (2016)

Parallel Fast DOA Estimation Algorithm Based on SML and Membrane Computing

Xiaofeng Bai[1], Huajun Song[1(✉)], and Changbo Xiang[2]

[1] College of Oceanography and Space Informatics, China University of Petroleum,
Qingdao, China
huajun.song@upc.edu.cn
[2] The 41st Research Institute of China Electronic Science and Technology Group
Corporation, Qingdao, China

Abstract. Direction of arrival (DOA) is widely used in communication, biomedicine, and other fields. Stochastic maximum likelihood (SML) algorithm is an excellent direction of arrival (DOA) estimation algorithm. However, the extremely heavy computational complexity in the process of SML analysis restricts its application in practical systems. Aiming at this problem of SML, this paper proposes a parallel accelerating algorithm of membrane computing (MC), particle swarm optimization (PSO), and artificial bee colony (ABC). Firstly, the solution space of SML algorithm is divided into basic membrane and surface membrane by using membrane computing; then particle swarm optimization algorithm is used for local parallel optimization in each basic membrane, and the locally optimal solution is transferred to the surface membrane; finally, the artificial bee colony algorithm is used to find the global optimum in the surface membrane. The results of the experiment show that the proposed algorithm greatly reduces the analytical complexity of SML, and the calculation time is decreased by more than 5 times compared with the commonly used optimization algorithms such as GA, AM, and PSO.

Keywords: Direction-of-arrival (DOA) · Stochastic maximum likelihood algorithm (SML) · Membrane computingd (MC) · Parallel computing · Intelligent optimization

1 Introduction

Since the 1960s, numerous fruitful algorithms about DOA have been proposed, and these algorithms are being developed rapidly. The mainstream algorithms in the current DOA field consist of linear prediction algorithms, subspace

This project is supported by "the Fundamental Research Funds for the Central Universities (NO.18CX02109A)"; This project is supported by "Science and Technology on Electronic Test & Measurement Labora-tory (6142001180514)".

ⓒ IFIP International Federation for Information Processing 2021
Published by Springer Nature Switzerland AG 2021
X. He et al. (Eds.): NPC 2020, LNCS 12639, pp. 159–169, 2021.
https://doi.org/10.1007/978-3-030-79478-1_14

decomposition algorithms, and subspace fitting algorithms. The linear prediction algorithm is the basic algorithm of DOA estimation [10]. It is not commonly used in modern engineering practical systems for its poor resolution. Afterwards, RO Schmit [12] proposed the multiple signal classification (MUSIC) algorithm. The algorithm launched the research of subspace decomposition algorithms. Then Paulraj, Roy, and Kailath [11] developed the estimation of signal parameters using rotational invariance techniques (ESPRIT) based on the decomposition of subspace. ESPRIT can obtain the closed-form solution directly, but accuracy is poor [3]. Since then, many DOA estimation algorithms have been proposed, including weighted subspace fitting (WSF) [5], deterministic maximum likelihood (DML) [2] and stochastic maximum likelihood (SML) [7]. This type of algorithm constructs the fitting relationship between the array manifold matrix and signal, then estimates the unknown parameters by calculate the cost function.

In theory, the SML algorithm has the best DOA estimation accuracy, but the huge amount of computation hinders its application. To solve its problems, a series of optimization algorithms have been proposed in recent years, such as alternating minimization (AM) [1] algorithm, alternating projection (AP) [4], EM algorithm [9], artificial intelligence optimization algorithm, etc. The conventional optimization algorithm works well in solving low-dimensional optimization problems, but as the increase in dimension and the number of solution space, the optimization ability of conventional optimization algorithms also decreases. Moreover, the solution to the SML cost function is a multidimensional optimization problem, and there are multiple local best solutions, the problem will be more complicated. Traditional optimization algorithms can't deal it well.

Membrane computing (MC) was proposed by Gheorghe Paun [6]. The basic idea of MC is to abstract the function and structure model of biological cells to build a similar computational model. MC combines the ideas of parallel computing and distributed computing. It is an ideal calculation mode suitable for multi-dimensional optimization problems of large spaces. Thus, this study aims to explore a new method suitable for SML cost function based on the theoretical framework of membrane computing.

The second part of the thesis introduce the basic model and SML algorithm about the DOA estimation. The third part describe the specific process of the SML algorithm based on MC. The fourth part analyze the results of experiment and algorithm performance. The fifth part draw the conclusion of the study.

2   Mathematical Model and SML

2.1   Array Signal Model

The q far-field narrow-band signals are incident on an antenna array from different angles $(\theta_1, \theta_2, L, \theta_a)$, and the center frequency of the signal is ω_0, the antenna array consists of p array elements, the wavelength of the signal is λ, the spacing between the elements is $d = \lambda/2$. Under ideal conditions, assume that each array element in the array is isotropic, there is no channel inconsistency, mutual coupling, and other factors, the noise of the signal is Gaussian white noise, and the variance is σ^2. The mathematical model of the signal received by the p array elements is as follows:

$$X(t) = AS(t) + N(t) \tag{1}$$

In the Eq. (1), $X(t)$ denotes a $p \times 1$ dimensional snapshot data vector of the array, A is a $p \times q$ dimensional array manifold matrix of the antenna, $S(t)$ is a $q \times 1$ dimensional signal data vector, and $N(t)$ is a $p \times 1$ dimensional noise data vector. Suppose that the received data is subjected to L fast sampling, and finally can be expressed as $X = [x(t_1), x(t_2), ..., x(t_L)]$. DOA estimation problem can be expressed as: given the observation data, then get the direction of arrival of the signal: $\hat{\Theta} = \{\hat{\theta}_1, \hat{\theta}_2, ...\hat{\theta}_q\}$.

2.2 Stochastic Maximum Likelihood Algorithm

The derived values of the variables were calculated according to the SML criterion [13], and the likelihood function of the single observation data is written as:

$$f_i(x) = \frac{1}{\pi^p det\{R\}} exp(x_i^H R^{-1} x_i) \tag{2}$$

The joint probability density function of q observations is as follows:

$$f_{SML}\{x_1, x_2, ..., x_q\} = \prod_{i=1}^{q} \frac{1}{\pi^p det\{R\}} exp(x_i^H R^{-1} x_i) \tag{3}$$

In Eq. (3), $det\{.\}$ is the determinant of the matrix, R is the covariance matrix of the observed data, and the negative logarithm of the joint probability density function is obtained:

$$-ln f_{SML} = L(Mln\pi + ln(det\{R\}) + tr\{R^{-1}\hat{R}\}) \tag{4}$$

To obtain the maximum likelihood estimation of the parameters, it is necessary to calculate the maximum value of the log likelihood function in the parameter space. For SML, f is a function of the variable θ so that the maximum likelihood function is expressed as:

$$L_{SML}(\theta) = \sigma^{2(p-q)} det\{A^+ \hat{R} A(\theta)\} \tag{5}$$

$$\hat{\sigma} = arg \ min \ L_{SML}(\theta) \tag{6}$$

In Eq. (3), $A^+ = (A^H(\theta)A(\theta))^{-1}A^H(\theta)$, the orientation estimate of the Stochastic Maximum Likelihood algorithm is to find $\theta = [\theta_1, \theta_2, ..., \theta_p]$ to bring the likelihood function $L_{SML}(\theta)$ to a minimum. Because it involves the solution of multi-dimensional nonlinear functions, it is more complicated to solve it with traditional optimization algorithms. Membrane computing is very suitable for solving such problems because of its distributed and parallel characteristics. Accordingly, the minimum value of $L_{SML}(\theta)$ is calculated by the membrane computing algorithm.

3   SML Based on Membrane Computing

In recent years, inspired by the biological laws of nature, a bionic optimization algorithm called membrane computing has received great attention from people and has achieved remarkable results in practical engineering applications. Since MC is easy to optimize in parallel, this study combined the advantages of MC with the SML algorithm and proposed an SML algorithm using the theoretical framework of MC. First, divide the solution space of the SML algorithm. Second, use the PSO algorithm in parallel for local optimization in each basic membrane. Finally, use the ABC algorithm in the surface membrane for global optimization, which is the final result. In the parsing process of the entire algorithm, since the local optimization algorithms in each of the basic membranes are performed independently, no communication is performed between the basic membranes.

3.1   Membrane Division of the Solution Space

The solution space of the SML is stratified into appropriate "base membranes". The solution of the SML cost function can be expressed by the following mathematical model:

$$L(\theta) = ln(\sigma^{2(p-q)} det\{A^+ \hat{R} A(\theta)\}) \tag{7}$$

The maximum likelihood estimation of the DOA is set as the objective function of the solution:

$$\min f(\theta), \theta = [\theta_1, \theta_2, ..., \theta_q] \in Q = [-90°, 90°] \tag{8}$$

In Eq. (8), q denotes the dimension of the solution space, $f(\theta)$ is the objective function of the algorithm, and Q is the solution space of the SML algorithm. The feasible solution space Q is spatially stratified into m sub-regions, that is, m basic membranes, $[s(1), t(1)], [s(2), t(2)], ..., [s(m), t(m)]$, the basic membranes is stratified as follows:

$$s(i) = -90° + \frac{180°}{m}(i-1) \tag{9}$$

$$t(i) = -90° + \frac{180°}{m}i \tag{10}$$

Each subspace $[s(i), t(i)]$ serves as a basic membrane region of the membrane system for intra-membrane local search. To verify the effect of the number of basic membranes (m) on the performance of the MC, the selection of the number of basic membranes is discussed below:

Figure 1 shows the variation of the DOA estimates that is run 100 times separately when the two sources are incident from different directions (10° and −30°), as the number of basic membranes increased from 2 to 10. Figure 1(a) shows that when the angle is 10° and the number of base membranes is 4, the DOA estimate is closest to the true value 10°; Fig. 1(b) suggests that when the angle is −30° and the number of base membranes is 4, the DOA estimate is the closest to the true value −30°. In general, though the DOA estimate shows an irregular change with the increase in the number of base membranes, when the number of base membranes is 4, even if two sources are incident from different directions, the DOA estimation error is the smallest, and it is more advantageous to obtain the optimal value. Therefore, in this experiment, the number of basic membranes is chosen to be 4.

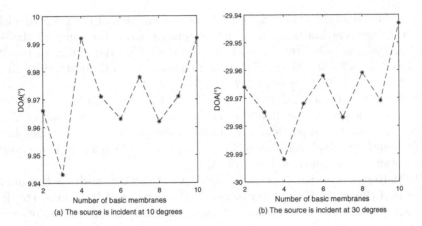

(a) The source is incident at 10 degrees   (b) The source is incident at 30 degrees

Fig. 1. Experimental results of the DOA estimate as a function of the number of basic membranes.

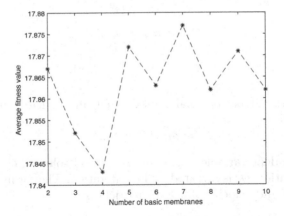

Fig. 2. Experimental results of the fitness value changing with the number of basic membranes.

The variation diagram in Fig. 2 reveals that when the number of basic membranes is 4, the average fitness value will be the smallest (SML algorithm seeks the minimum cost function value). In summary, when two sources are incident from different directions (10° and −30°), and the number of basic membranes is 4, the DOA estimation performance will be the best.

3.2   Intra-membrane Local Search Parallel Algorithm

The PSO-based intra-membrane local search algorithm based on PSO integrates the idea of parallel computing of membrane computing, and combines membrane computing with traditional PSO algorithm [8]. The following describes the specific process of local search algorithm in membrane:

(1) The cost function $L(\theta)$ of SML is the fitness function of the PSO algorithm;
(2) Since the receiving array is a uniform planar array, the range of the solution space is $[-90°, 90°]$, namely the optimized spatial extent of the PSO algorithm is $[-90°, 90°]$, and the solution space is spatially stratified into m sub-regions $[s(1), t(1)], [s(2), t(2)], ..., [s(m), t(m)]$;
(3) Construct a particle group $\Theta = \{\dot{\Theta}_1, \dot{\Theta}_2, ..., \dot{\Theta}_n\}$, the number of particles in the particle group is n, divide n particles into m parts, the number of each part is n/m, the m particles are randomly distributed in m base membranes (the surface membranes must be empty), and each particle is a potential solution to the optimization problem;
(4) Initialize various parameters in the PSO algorithm, such as the number of particles n/m, the inertia factor ω, the number of iterations, etc. Each particle continuously iterates according to the local optimal solution and the global optimal solution. Let i be the ith particle, l means the number of lth iterations, Θ_i^l is the position of the ith particle in the search space at the lth iteration, C_i^l is the local optimal solution of the ith particle after lth iteration. It is obvious that:

$$C_i^0 = \Theta_i^0 \tag{11}$$

$$C_i^{\,1} = arg \min_{\Theta_i^0, \Theta_i^1} L(\theta), ... \tag{12}$$

$$C_i^{\,l} = arg \min_{\Theta_i^0, ..., \Theta_i^l} L(\theta). \tag{13}$$

Let D^l be the global optimal solution that all particles can find after lth iterations, thus

$$D^l = min\{C_1^l, C_2^l, ... C_{n/m}^l\} \tag{14}$$

(5) The independent variable Θ_i, the local optimal solution C_i^l and the global optimal solution D^l is updated by loop iteration. The formula for updating the position and velocity of the lth particle is:

$$\theta_i^{l+1} = \theta_i^l + v_i^{l+1} \tag{15}$$

$$V_i^{l+1} = \omega V_i^l + c_1 r_1(C_i^l - \Theta_i^l) + c_2 r_2(D^l - \Theta_i^l) \tag{16}$$

L is the number of iterations, ω is the inertia factor, $\omega \in [0.4, 0.9]$, r_1, r_2 is the learning factor, and r_1, r_2 is the random number between 0 and 1;
(6) If reach the maximum number of iterations or the accuracy reaches 10^{-5}, send the global optimal solution to surface membrance; otherwise, go to step (5) and iterate again.

In the process of local search in membrane, the solution space is divided firstly, and the local optimal solution and global optimal solution are updated iteratively in different solution spaces. In the program running, the loop structure often consumes the most computing resources. Optimizing the code in the loop body or parallelizing the loop is the most common way to speed up the program running. Because the search algorithm is independent in different solution space, we can use parfor loop to accelerate the calculation, and make full use of the parallel processing ability of multi-core processor to shorten the running time of problem processing and improve the running efficiency of the algorithm.

3.3   Global Optimization Strategy

After the intra-membrane local search with PSO algorithm, the local optimal value can be easily obtained, and then send the optimal solution in each basic film to the surface film to guide the algorithm for global optimal search. Artificial bee colony (ABC) algorithm has strong global search ability. Therefore, to improve the computational efficiency of the algorithm, the ABC algorithm is used for global optimization in the surface film region.

(1) At first, initialize the population to generate initial control parameters and initial solutions. Mainly includes: the number of food sources is M (the number of solutions of optimization problem), the maximum number of iterations is P, and the maximum number of iterations of the food source whose quality has not been improved is $Limit$. The initial solution is composed of the local optimal solution transferred from the basic membrane to the surface membrane, which corresponds to the bees one by one, then records the fitness value and the optimal solution of each initial solution;

(2) According to Eq. (17), bees conduct neighborhood search to generate a new candidate solution $\dot{\theta}_{in}$, calculate the fitness value, and select the probability of $\dot{\theta}_{in}$ and θ_{in} to record the better solution;

$$\dot{\theta}_{in} = \theta_{in} + \phi_{in}(\theta_{in} - \theta_{kn}) \tag{17}$$

(3) Calculate the selection probability associated with each solution according to equation (18);

$$p_i = \frac{fit_i}{\sum_{j=1}^{M} fit_j} \tag{18}$$

(4) The observation bees according to the Roulette Wheel Selection method to select the food source with probability P_i. Then the observation bees perform a neighborhood search according to Eq. (17) to generate a new candidate solution $\dot{\theta}_{in}$, computing the fitness value and making optimal choices for $\dot{\theta}_{in}$ and θ_{in}, then record the better solutions;

(5) The scout bees judge whether there is a solution to give up according to $Limit$. If there is, a new solution will be selected from the local optimal solution to replace the abandoned solution;

(6) Record the optimal solution to date;

(7) $Cycle = Cycle + 1$, If $Cycle < P$ or the accuracy less than 10^{-5}, go to step (2); otherwise, output the optimal solution.

3.4 DOA Estimation Step Based on Membrane Computing

The above analysis reveals that the SML algorithm based on MC could be primarily stratified into three parts, and the flow chart is shown in Fig. 3.

4 Simulation and Performance Analysis

Through specific simulation experiments, the performance of the SML algorithm based on MC proposed in this paper is analyzed. And compare it with PSO, AM, and GA algorithm. The simulation environments include:

MATLAB R2016b,
i7-4770k CPU with 3.4 GHz, 4-core, and 8-thread,
12 GB DDR3 RAM.

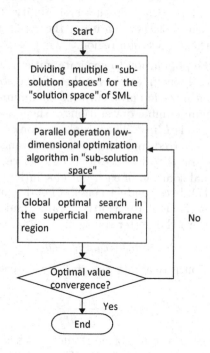

Fig. 3. Flow chart of SML algorithm based on membrane computing.

During the experiment, assuming the array is a uniform planar array, the steering vector can be simplified as:

$$a(\theta) = [1, e^{-j\phi(\theta)}, L, e^{-j(p-1)\phi(\theta)}]^T \tag{19}$$

$$\phi(\theta) = 2\pi \Delta sin\theta / \lambda \tag{20}$$

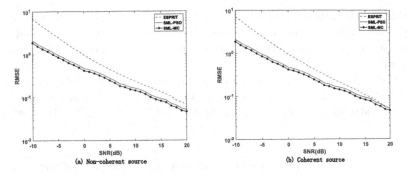

Fig. 4. RMSE relationship with signal-to-noise ratio change.

In Eq. (19), λ denotes the signal wavelength, Δ is the distance between array elements. In the experiment, $\Delta = \lambda/2$, SNR is defined as:

$$SNR_k = 10 log_{10} \frac{E[|S_k(t)|^2]}{\sigma^2} \tag{21}$$

The Root-Mean-Square-Error (RMSE) is defined as:

$$RMSE = \sqrt{\frac{1}{qN} \sum_{k=1}^{q} \sum_{m=1}^{M} |\hat{\theta}_{k,m} - \theta_k|^2} \tag{22}$$

In the Eq. (22), $\hat{\theta}_{k,m}$ denotes the derived value of θ_k in the mth experiment, and do 100 times Monte Carlo experiments for each case.

The receiving antenna adopts a 32-element uniform linear array, and four narrow-band signals are incident from the far-field. The number of snapshots of the signal is 1024, and the noise is Gaussian white noise with a mean of 0. For the SML algorithm based on MC, according to the above analysis, the solution space is divided into four basic membranes, and six particles are initialized in each basic membrane. Figure 4 describes how the RMSE of each algorithm varies with SNR. For the ESPRIT algorithm, preprocessing is required when dealing with coherent sources; for non-coherent sources, when SNR$\in [-10\,\text{dB}, 20\,\text{dB}]$, the RMSE of PSO algorithm is much better than ESPRIT algorithm, and the RMSE of SML algorithm based on MC is slightly better than PSO algorithm. For the coherent source, the RMSE of the PSO algorithm is much better than the ESPRIT algorithm when SNR$\in [-10\,\text{dB}, 15\,\text{dB}]$. When SNR$\in [15\,\text{dB}, 20\,\text{dB}]$, the performance of the PSO algorithm and ESPRIT algorithm are similar. The RMSE of the SML algorithm based on the MC is slightly better than the PSO algorithm.

Under the same experimental environment, compare the performance of SML algorithm based on MC, PSO, GA and AM algorithm.

For the AM algorithm, a search method combining long and short steps is used. First, perform a rough search with a long step size ($0.1°$) to find the range of the optimal solution, and then perform a detailed search with a short step size ($0.01°$), when the estimated accuracy meet $|G^{(l+1)} - G^l| \leq 10^{-5}$, record the result. This method reduces the computational complexity of the global search by the interactive minimization algorithm without reducing the DOA accuracy requirements.

In the artificial genetic algorithm (GA), set the number of populations as 60, set the crossover probability as 0.6, and set the mutation probability as 0.1. When the estimation accuracy of the DOA meet $|G^{(l+1)} - G^l| \leq 10^{-5}$, stop the iteration.

Table 1. Comparison of performance of different algorithms (non-coherent sources).

	MC-SML	PSO-SML	AM-SML	GA-SML
Number of particles	–	25	–	–
Average number of iterations	–	143.5	–	–
Total number of calculations	–	25 * 143.5 = 3587.5	–	46300
Spend time (seconds)	**0.88**	4.52	6.53	36.58

Table 2. Comparison of performance of different algorithms (coherent sources).

	MC-SML	PSO-SML	AM-SML	GA-SML
Number of particles	–	25	–	–
Average number of iterations	–	146	–	–
Total number of calculations	–	25 * 146 = 3650	–	46300
Spend time (seconds)	**0.95**	4.74	6.61	36.65

The results of various aspects of the SML algorithm based on the MC, the PSO, the GA, and the AM algorithm in dealing with non-coherent sources and coherent sources are listed in Table 1 and Table 2. According to Table 1, when dealing with non-coherent sources under the premise of ensuring convergence accuracy, the calculation time cost by the AM algorithm is 6.53 s, the time cost by the GA algorithm is 36.58 s, and the cost time of the conventional PSO algorithm is 4.52 s, whereas the calculation time of the proposed membrane calculation method is only 0.88 s, about 1/5 of the conventional PSO algorithm. The results suggest that the convergence speed of the proposed membrane computing algorithm is significantly improved. Table 2 shows that various algorithms spend more time processing coherent sources in the same situation than processing non-coherent sources. In brief, the results reveal that the proposed membrane computing algorithm has a significant real-time effect.

Besides, when using i5-4210M CPU with 2-core, the cost time of MC-SML is about 2.7 s, about half of the serial processing time. When using i7-860 CPU with 4-core, the cost time of MC-SML is about 2.5 s, about a quarter of the serial processing time. It can be seen that the number of CPU cores and single-core performance will affect the computational efficiency of parallel algorithms.

5   Conclusion

Based on the theoretical framework of membrane computing, this study proposed a membrane computing method suitable for SML cost function. The algorithm is capable of effectively solving the problem of DOA estimation while ensuring the estimation accuracy. According to the results of the experiment, the proposed membrane computing algorithm can perform a global search and local search simultaneously, which reduces the computational complexity of SML. Thus, it has an obvious advantage in convergence speed.

References

1. Chen, B., Xing, L., Liang, J., et al.: Steady-state mean-square error analysis for adaptive filtering under the maximum correntropy criterion. IEEE Signal Process. Lett. **21**(7), 880–884 (2014)
2. Chang, W., Ru, J., Deng, L.: Stokes parameters and DOA estimation of polarized sources with unknown number of sources. IET Radar Sonar Navig. **12**(2), 218–226 (2018)
3. Dandekar, K.R., Ling, H., Xu, G.: Smart antenna array calibration procedure including amplitude and phase mismatch and mutual coupling effects. In: IEEE International Conference on Personal Wireless communications, pp. 293–297 (2000)
4. Francois, V., Olivier, B., Eric, C.: Approximate unconditional maximum likelihood direction of arrival estimation for two closely spaced targets. IEEE Signal Process. Lett. **22**(1), 86–89 (2015)
5. Gao H, H.X.: Direction finding of signal subspace fitting based on cultural bee colony algorithm. In: IEEE Fifth International Conference on Bio-inspired Computing: Theories Applications (2010)
6. Gheorghe, P.: Computing with membranes (P systems): an introduction. In: Current Trends in Theoretical Computer Science, pp. 845–866 (2001)
7. Song, H.J., Liu, F., Chen, H.H., Zhang, H.: A stochastic maximum likelihood algorithm based on improved PSO. Acta Electron. Sinica **45**(8), 1989–1994 (2017)
8. Shao, J., Zhang, X., Liu, Y., Yang, F.: Estimation of time reversal target DOA over underwater acoustic multipath time-varying channels. In: 2014 IEEE China Summit and International Conference on Signal and Information Processing (2014)
9. Zhou, L., Zhu, W., Luo, J., Kong, H.: Direct positioning maximum likelihood estimator using TDOA and FDOA for coherent short-pulse radar. IET Radar Sonar Navig. **11**(10), 1505–1511 (2017)
10. Nguyen, A.T., Matsubara, T., Kurokawa, T.: Low-complexity and high-accuracy DOA estimation for coprime arrays using Toeplitz matrices (2017)
11. Roy R, Paulraj A, K.T.: Estimation of signal parameters via rotational invariance techniques - ESPRIT. In: Advanced Algorithms and Architectures for Signal Processing I. International Society for Optics and Photonics (1986)
12. Schmidt, R., Schmidt, R.O.: Multiple emitter location and signal parameters estimation. IEEE Trans. Antennas Propag. **34**(3), 276–280 (1986)
13. Schwartz, O., Dorfan, Y., Taseska, M., Habets, E.A.P., Gannot, S.: DOA estimation in noisy environment with unknown noise power using the EM algorithm. In: Hands-free Speech Communications and Microphone, pp. 86–90 (2017)

Segmented Merge: A New Primitive for Parallel Sparse Matrix Computations

Haonan Ji[1], Shibo Lu[1], Kaixi Hou[2], Hao Wang[3], Weifeng Liu[1(✉)],
and Brian Vinter[4]

[1] Super Scientific Software Laboratory, Department of Computer Science
and Technology, China University of Petroleum-Beijing, Beijing, China
{haonan_ji,lslslsb}@yeah.net, weifeng.liu@cup.edu.cn
[2] Department of Computer Science, Virginia Tech, Blacksburg, USA
kaixihou@vt.edu
[3] Department of Computer Science and Engineering, The Ohio State University,
Columbus, USA
wang.2721@osu.edu
[4] Faculty of Technical Sciences, Aarhus University, Aarhus, Denmark
vinter@au.dk

Abstract. Segmented operations, such as segmented sum, segmented
scan and segmented sort, are important building blocks for parallel irregular algorithms. We in this work propose a new parallel primitive called
segmented merge. Its function is in parallel merging q sub-segments to
p segments, both of nonuniform lengths. We implement the segmented
merge primitive on GPUs and demonstrate its efficiency on parallel
sparse matrix transposition (SpTRANS) and sparse matrix-matrix multiplication (SpGEMM) operations.

Keywords: Parallel computing · Segmented merge · Sparse matrix ·
GPU

1 Introduction

Since Blelloch et al. [1] reported that segmented operations can achieve better
load balancing than row-wise approaches in parallel sparse matrix-vector multiplication (SpMV), several new parallel segmented primitives, such as segmented
sum [12], segmented scan [4] and segmented sort [8] have been developed for
replacing their ordinary counterparts, i.e., sum, scan and sort, in a few irregular
sparse matrix algorithms on many-core platforms such as GPUs.

However, merge, another important fundamental routine in computer science,
has not received much attention from the view point of segmented operation.
Actually, it can be quite useful when both the input and the output matrices are
stored with indirect indices. One important higher level algorithm example is
sparse matrix-matrix multiplication (SpGEMM). It multiplies two sparse matrices A and B, and generates one resulting sparse matrix C. When the nonzeros in

each row of the input sparse matrix B are sorted in the ascending order according to their column indices, the basic operation needed is actually merge [6,10,11].

We in this paper first define a new primitive called segmented merge. It merges q sub-segments to p segments, both of nonuniform lengths. The elements in each sub-segment are ordered in advance. When all the sub-segments in one segment are merged into one sub-segment of the same length as the segment containing it, the operation is completed. In the SpGEMM scenario, the rows of B involved can be seen as the sub-segments, and the rows of C can be seen as the segments.

Although the definition and a serial code of the segmented merge can be both straightforward, designing an efficient parallel algorithm is not trivial. There are two major challenges. The first one is the load balancing problem. It happens when the lengths of the sub-segments and the segments are nonuniform, meaning that roughly evenly assigning them to tens of processing units can be difficult. The second challenge is the vectorization problem. It can be also hard to carefully determine a similar amount of elements processed by thousands of SIMD lanes on many-core processors such as GPUs.

To address the two challenges, we design an efficient parallel algorithm for the segmented merge operation on GPUs. The algorithm first preprocesses the segments and sub-segments, and records the boundaries of them for dividing the tasks. Then our method uses a binary tree for merging sub-segments in a bottom-up manner. The algorithm works in an iterative way and completes when each segment only has one sub-segment. In the procedure, each pair of sub-segments are merged independently by utilizing SIMD lanes, i.e., threads running on CUDA GPUs, and each SIMD lane merges a similar amount of elements with serial merge.

We benchmark two sparse kernels, sparse matrix transposition (SpTRANS) and SpGEMM, utilizing the segmented merge primitive on two NVIDIA Turing GPUs, an RTX 2080 and a Titan RTX. By testing 956 sparse matrices downloaded from the SuiteSparse Matrix Collection [2], the experimental results show that compared to the NVIDIA cuSPARSE library, our algorithm accelerates performance of SpTRANS and SpGEMM operation by a factor of on average 3.94 and 2.89 (and up to 13.09 and 109.15), respectively.

2   Related Work

In this section, we introduce three existing segmented primitives: segmented sum [1,12], segmented scan [4] and segmented sort [8].

2.1   Parallel Segmented Sum

When a parallel algorithm processes irregular data such as sparse matrices, it is quite common to in parallel deal with arrays of different lengths. For example, in the SpMV operation, multiplying a sparse matrix A and a dense vector x basically equals computing the dot product of every sparse row of A with x.

When the number of nonzero entries in the rows are nonuniform, it is easy to encounter the load imbalance issue on parallel processors, and thus to degrade performance [13].

To make the parallel SpMV operation more balanced, Blelloch et al. [1] proposed the segmented sum primitive. The parallel operation has five steps: (1) first gathers intermediate products into an array, (2) labels the indices and values in the same row as a segment, (3) equally assigns the entries to independent threads, (4) then sums the values belonging to the same segment up into one value and saves it , and (5) finally sums the values across multiple threads to finish the operation. Figure 1 plots an example of the parallel segmented sum. To further make the segmented sum suitable for sparse matrices with empty rows, Liu and Vinter proposed a speculative segmented sum [12].

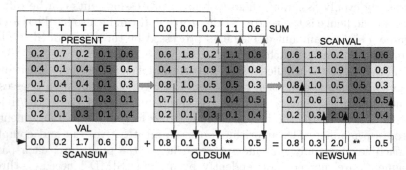

Fig. 1. An example of Blelloch's algorithm using five threads (each processes one column) to find the sum of eight segments (filled with the same color), and uses SUM and PRESENT arrays to store the intermediate results of the split segments.

2.2   Parallel Segmented Scan

The scan (also known as prefix-sum) operation sums all prefixes. For example, the row pointer array of a sparse matrix in the compressed sparse row (CSR) format is the result of scanning an array storing the number of nonzeros of the rows. Parallel segmented scan is to scan multiple segments in parallel, and the result of each segment is the same as that of a single scan. Besides the same load balancing problem as the segmented sum, segmented scan is relatively more complex because of dependencies between the prefixes.

Dotsenko et al. [4] proposed a relatively load balanced segmented scan algorithm by using a novel data structure and reduced the consumption of shared memory on GPU. This algorithm is divided into three steps: (1) stores the segments in an array and divides it into blocks of the same size, (2) each thread scan one segment and rescans when it encounters a new segment, (3) if there is a segment spanning blocks, the result of this segment is propagated. Figure 2 plots an example of the parallel segmented scan.

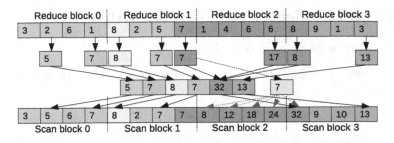

Fig. 2. An example of Dotsenko's algorithm using four threads (each for one block) to find the scan of six segments (filled with the same color) (Color figure online)

2.3 Parallel Segmented Sort

The parallel segmented sort operation simultaneously makes keys or key-value pairs in multiple segments ordered. It uses two arrays for storing a list of keys and a group of header pointers of segments. In the procedure, each processing unit obtains the information of the corresponding segment by accessing the segment pointer array, then sorts each segment in serial or in parallel. Because of the nonuniform lengths of the segments, load balancing issues often restrict the efficiency of the algorithm.

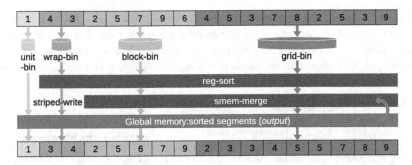

Fig. 3. An example of Hou's algorithm using four bins to store four segments (filled with the same color), and calling reg-sort and smem-merge to sort the segments. (Color figure online)

Hou et al. [8] presented an adaptive segmented sort mechanism on GPUs. It proposed a differentiated method for eliminating irregularity in data distribution and a register-based sorting method for accelerating short segments. The register-based sorting algorithm has four steps: (1) gets the amount of tasks per thread, (2) converts data into specific sequence by using shuffle functions, (3) stores data in threads into different registers to perform swap operations, and (4) swaps the data in registers to make them ordered. Figure 3 plots an example of the segmented sort.

174   H. Ji et al.

3   Segmented Merge and Its Parallel Algorithm

3.1   Definition of Segmented Merge

We first define the segmented merge primitive here. Assuming we have a key-value array

$$S = \{S_1, S_2, \ldots, S_p\}, \tag{1}$$

that includes p segments (i.e., sub–arrays[1]), and further a segment

$$S_i = \{S_{i,1}, S_{i,2}, \ldots, S_{i,q_i}\}, i \in [1, p], \tag{2}$$

contains q_i sub-segments. So we have

$$S = \{S_{1,1}, S_{1,2}, \ldots, S_{1,q_1}, S_{2,1}, S_{2,2}, \ldots S_{2,q_2}, \ldots, S_{p,1}, S_{p,2}, \ldots, S_{p,q_p}\} \tag{3}$$

Each sub-segment $S_{i,j}$ includes $n_{i,j}$ key-value pairs already sorted according to their keys. The objective of the segmented merge operation is to let $n_i = \sum_{j=1}^{q_i} n_{i,j}$ key-value pairs in each segment S_i ordered. Thus S eventually consists of p sorted segments.

3.2   Serial Algorithm for Segmented Merge

A serial segmented merge algorithm can be represented as a multi-way merge, meaning that each sub-segment of the same segment is regarded as a leaf node of a binary tree and is merged in a bottom-up manner. Figure 4 shows an example of merging eight sub-segments in to three segments using the segmented merge.

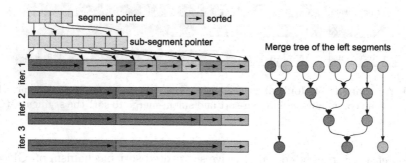

Fig. 4. An example showing the segmented merge algorithm. Here the *segment pointer* (including three segments) points to the *sub-segment pointer* pointing to eight ordered sub-segments continuously stored in the array. After the segmented merge, the eight sub-segments are merged into three ordered segments.

---

[1] We in this paper call "sub-array" "segment", since each segment further includes at least one "sub-segment". In this way, we can avoid using terms like "sub-array" and "sub-sub-array".

3.3 Simple Parallel Algorithm for Segmented Merge

Algorithm 1 shows a simple parallel pseudocode working in an iterative fashion
(lines 3–14): each segment (lines 4–12) can be processed in parallel, and each pair
of sub-segments (lines 7–11) can be also merged in parallel until each segment
has only one sub-segment.

Algorithm 1. A simple parallel segmented merge algorithm.

1: $m\_split \leftarrow$ get_split_row_num()
2: $snum \leftarrow$ get_seg_num()
3: **while** $m\_split \neq snum$ **do**
4:     **for each** segment **in parallel do**
5:         // Challenge 1: The combination of sub-segments of different
6:            lengths in different segments may bring load imbalance
7:         **for each** pair of sub-segments in segment **in parallel do**
8:             // Challenge 2: Merging sub-segments of unequal length
9:                is difficult to vectorize
10:            serial_merge(buff, segment_info, $segment\_id$)
11:        **end for**
12:    **end for**
13:    $snum \leftarrow$ get_seg_num()
14: **end while**

It can be seen that there are two **for** loops in lines 4 and 7 respectively.
Although the two loops can be parallelized straightforward, their simple implementation may bring suboptimal performance. In particular on many-core processors running a large amount of threads, this approach may bring load imbalance problem since the lengths of segments and sub-segments may be imbalanced
(see lines 5–6 and 8–9, respectively). This is the first challenge we face. Such performance degradation from irregular data distribution is actually not unusual in
sparse matrix algorithms [11,13].

3.4 Improved Parallel Algorithm for Segmented Merge on GPU

We propose a parallel algorithm for segmented merge. The main idea is to fix
the number of elements processed by a thread, and to merge the sub-segments in
the same segment in the form of binary tree until all sub-segments are merged.
The algorithm consists of three steps: (1) data preprocessing, (2) merging two
sub-sequences of each thread by using merge path, (3) merging sub-segments on
binary tree in an iterative way. Algorithm 2 shows a pseudocode of the parallel
segmented merge, and Fig. 5 gives an example.

    The first step is data preprocessing (lines 4–15 in Algorithm 2). Its objective
is to record starting and ending positions of segments and sub-segments. We
construct two arrays of size $p + 1$ and $q + 1$, respectively, as two-level pointers
(see the top left of Figs. 4 and 5). Then, we set each thread's workload to a fixed
amount $nnzpt$, and count the number of threads required in merging every pair

Algorithm 2. A parallel segmented merge algorithm

```
 1:  m_split ← get_split_row_num()
 2:  snum ← get_seg_num()
 3:  while m_split ≠ snum do
 4:      for each pair of sub-segments in segment in parallel do
 5:          tnum_local ← get_local_thread_num(segment_ptr, sub-segment_ptr)
 6:          tnum_total ← get_total_thread_num(tnum_local)
 7:      end for
 8:      malloc(thread_info, tnum_total)
 9:      for each pair of sub-segments in segment in parallel do
10:          thread_id ← get_thread_id()
11:          scatter_thread_info(thread_info, thread_id)
12:      end for
13:      for each thread in parallel do
14:          gather_thread_info(thread_info, thread_id)
15:      end for
16:      for each thread in parallel do
17:          serial_merge_using_merge_path(buff, thread_info, thread_id)
18:      end for
19:      snum ← get_seg_num()
20:      free(thread_info)
21:  end while
```

of sub-segments (line 5). As a result, each iterative step knows the total number of threads to be issued (line 6). Then each sub-segment scatters a group of information, such as global memory offset and segments size, to threads working on it (lines 9–12). After that, each thread gathers information by running the partitioning strategy of the standard merge path algorithm (lines 13–15).

The second step is merging sub-sequences of each thread by using merge path (lines 16–18 in Algorithm 2). The merge operation of sub-segments is often completed by multiple threads and these threads cooperate with each other and merge sub-sequences through the merge path algorithm [5]. The merge path algorithm is an efficient merge algorithm and has excellent parallelism. In its procedure, each thread is responsible for processing partial sub-sequences without data correlation. First, the data in the sub-sequence corresponding to the thread is compared multiple times to generate boundaries for splitting the two sub-sequences. Then based on the target matrix, the data in the two sub-sequences are placed in the output sequence according to the 'path' to complete the merge operation. In Fig. 5, two examples of merging two groups of sub-sequences is shown in the pink dotted box, and the two pairs of sub-sequences are merged with three threads.

The third step is merging sub-segments on the binary tree in an iterative way (the while loop of lines 3–21 in Algorithm 2). According to the information obtained from the above two steps, each sub-segment of the same segment can be seen as a leaf node of a binary tree to merge, and multiple iterations may be needed. When the pointers of segment and sub-segment are completely aligned, the iteration ends and the sorting is completed. If there is a single sub-segment,

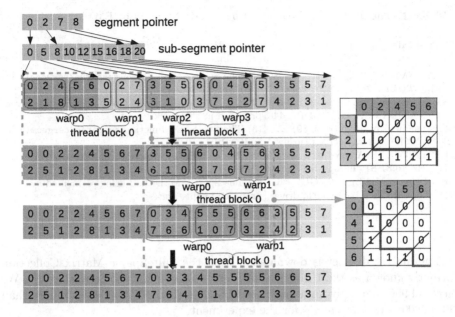

Fig. 5. An example showing the proposed segmented merge algorithm. Here the *segment pointer* (including three segments) points to the *sub-segment pointer* pointing to eight ordered sub-segments continuously stored in the array. There are two levels of arrays, with indexes on the top and values at the bottom. After the segmented merge, the eight sub-segments are merged into three ordered segments. In the computation, two thread blocks of two warps are used. (Color figure online)

it will not be processed at all in the iteration (see the segment in light pink of Fig. 5). When the sub-segments in the same segment are merged, they can be processed by the same warp of 32 threads in CUDA, but the sub segments in different segments can not cross different warps. For example, when combining the blue and light blue sub-segments in Fig. 5, although the thread elements do not reach a fixed number, they will not cross warps. So, a large amount of threads can be saved for data in a power-law fashion (i.e., several segments have much more sub-segments than the others). Moreover, because all cores can be saturated, our segmented merge method can achieve good load balancing on massively parallel GPUs.

4 Performance Evaluation

4.1 Experimental Setup

We on two NVIDIA Turing GPUs benchmark the SpTRANS and SpGEMM functions calling the segmented merge primitive proposed, and compare them with the corresponding functions in the NVIDIA cuSPARSE library v10.2. Table 1 lists the two testbeds and the participating algorithms.

Table 1. The testbeds and participating SpTRANS and SpGEMM algorithms.

The testbeds	The participating SpTRANS and SpGEMM algorithms
(1) An NVIDIA GeForce RTX 2080 (Turing TU104, 2944 CUDA cores @ 1.8 GHz, 10.59 SP TFlops, 331.2 DP GFlops, 4 MB LLC, 8 GB GDDR6, 448 GB/s bandwidth, driver v440.89) (2) An NVIDIA Titan RTX (Turing TU102, 4608 CUDA cores @ 1.77 GHz, 16.31 SP TFlops, 509.76 DP GFlops, 6 MB LLC, 24 GB GDDR6, 672 GB/s bandwidth, driver v440.89)	(1) The SpTRANS function `cusparse?csr2csc()` in cuSPARSE v10.2 (2) The SpTRANS method using segmented merge proposed in this work (3) The SpGEMM function `cusparse?csrgemm()` in cuSPARSE v10.2 (4) The SpGEMM algorithm proposed by Liu and Vinter [11] (5) The SpGEMM method using segmented merge proposed in this work

The matrix dataset is downloaded from the SuiteSparse Matrix Collection (formerly known as the University of Florida Sparse Matrix Collection [2]). We select all 956 relatively large matrices of no less than 100,000 and no more than 200,000,000 nonzero entries for the experiment.

4.2   Performance of SpTRANS Using Segmented Merge

The SpTRANS operation transpose a sparse matrix A in the CSR format to its transpose A^T also in the CSR format. From the data structure point of view, the operation is the same as converting A's CSR format to its compressed sparse column (CSC) format. Wang et al. [15] proposed two vectorized and load balanced SpTRANS algorithms for x86 processors.

To utilize higher computational power and bandwidth on GPUs, we design a new SpTRANS algorithm using segmented merge proposed in this work. Specifically, the number of nonzeros are calculated firstly, then the nonzeros are inserted into the transpose matrix in an unordered way using atomic operation. To keep the indices of the nonzeros in each row of the transpose sorted, the segmented merge primitive is called. For the long rows, they are cut into smaller pieces that can be sorted independently by utilizing on-chip shared memory. Then the long rows can be seen as segments, and the sorted pieces are processed as subsegments. Thus the segmented merge primitive can be used naturally.

Figure 6 shows the abstract performance (in GB/s) and relative speedups of SpTRANS in cuSPARSE and using our segmented merge method on NVIDIA RTX 2080 and Titan RTX GPUs. It can be seen that in most cases our method is faster than cuSPARSE. The average speedup on the two GPUs can reach 3.55× (up to 9.64×) and 3.94× (up to 13.09×), respectively. For matrices with many short rows and balanced distribution, such as *igbt3* matrix, our algorithm dynamically determines the optimal number of threads to be used in each iteration. Therefore, our algorithm has a good performance for *igbt3* matrix and achieves the speedup of 13.09× over cuSPARSE.

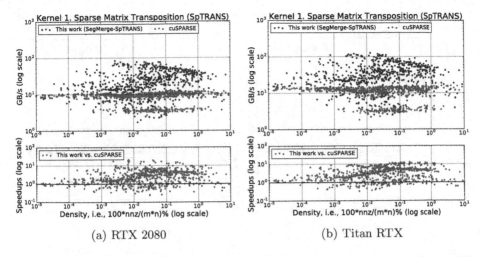

Fig. 6. Comparison of two SpTRANS methods in cuSPARSE and using the segmented merge primitive on two NVIDIA GPUs. The x-axis represents the density (the ratio of the number of nonzeros to the multiply of the number of rows and columns) of the matrices tested.

4.3 Performance of SpGEMM Using Segmented Merge

The SpGEMM operation computes $C = AB$, where the three matrices are all sparse. The most used fundamental approach for SpGEMM is the row-row method proposed by Gustavson [7]. Its parallel implementation can be straight-forward. Each thread traverses the nonzeros of a row of A, and uses the values to scale all entries of the corresponding rows of B, then merges the scaled entries into the row of C. The function for this procedure is also called sparse accumulator and has been studied by much research [3,9–11,14,16].

The SpGEMM algorithm tested is an improved version of the SpGEMM approach in bhSPARSE developed by Liu and Vinter [11]. In the original implementation, the authors assign the workload for computing the rows of C to 37 bins according to the floating point operations needed for the rows. The first 36 bins process relatively short rows, and the last bin is designed to process the rows of a large mount of nonzeros. For the rows in the last bin, the entries cannot be placed into on-chip shared memories, thus global memory has to be used. Hence the segmented merge is used for calculating the long rows, by first saving the scaled rows from B (as sub-segments) onto global memory and then merging the sub-segments belonging to the same row of C (as a segment). Note that all the rows, i.e., segments, in the last bin are involved in one segmented merge computation.

Figure 7 plots the performance of SpGEMM in cuSPARSE, bhSPARSE and bhSPARSE with segmented merge on NVIDIA RTX 2080 and Titan RTX GPUs. It can be seen that the performance of our method is significantly better than cuSPARSE and bhSPARSE. On RTX 2080, the speedups over the two methods

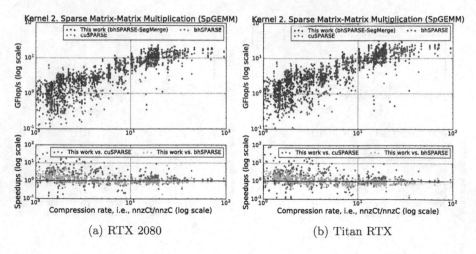

(a) RTX 2080   (b) Titan RTX

Fig. 7. Comparison of three SpGEMM methods computing A^2: cuSPARSE, bhSPARSE [11] and bhSPARSE using segmented merge. The x-axis is compression rate, i.e., the ratio of the number of intermediate nonzeros to nonzeros in C.

reach on average $2.89\times$ (up to $109.15\times$) and $1.26\times$ (up to $7.5\times$), respectively. On Titan RTX, the speedups are on average $2.53\times$ (up to $81.85\times$) and $1.22\times$ (up to $17.38\times$), respectively. Taking the *webbase-1M* matrix with many long rows as an example, cuSPARSE cannot evenly distribute the data to cores, and bhSPARSE can only use one thread block for each long row, meaning the two libraries actually underuse the GPUs. But because our algorithm avoids dealing with a long row in a thread by evenly dividing all elements to thread, our algorithm obtain $5.85\times$ and $2.31\times$ speedups over cuSPARSE and bhSPARSE, respectively.

5   Conclusion

In this paper, we have defined a new primitive called segmented merge, and presented an efficient parallel algorithm achieving good load balancing and SIMD unit utilization on GPUs. The experimental results show that two sparse matrix algorithms, SpTRANS and SpGEMM, using our parallel segmented merge are greatly faster than existing methods in cuSPARSE and bhSPARSE.

Acknowledgments. We would like to thank the invaluable comments from all the reviewers. Weifeng Liu is the corresponding author of this paper. This research was supported by the Science Challenge Project under Grant No. TZZT2016002, the National Natural Science Foundation of China under Grant No. 61972415, and the Science Foundation of China University of Petroleum, Beijing under Grant No. 2462019YJRC004, 2462020XKJS03.

References

1. Blelloch, G.E., Heroux, M.A., Zagha, M.: Segmented operations for sparse matrix computation on vector multiprocessors. Technical report, CMU (1993)
2. Davis, T.A., Hu, Y.: The university of florida sparse matrix collection. ACM Trans. Math. Softw. **38**(1), 1:1-1:25 (2011)
3. Deveci, M., Trott, C., Rajamanickam, S.: Multithreaded sparse matrix-matrix multiplication for many-core and GPU architectures. Parallel Comput. **78**, 33–46 (2018)
4. Dotsenko, Y., Govindaraju, N.K., Sloan, P.P., Boyd, C., Manferdelli, J.: Fast scan algorithms on graphics processors. In: Proceedings of the 22nd Annual International Conference on Supercomputing, ICS 2008, pp. 205–213 (2008)
5. Green, O., McColl, R., Bader, D.A.: GPU merge path: A GPU merging algorithm. In: Proceedings of the 26th ACM International Conference on Supercomputing, ICS 2012, pp. 331–340 (2012)
6. Gremse, F., Küpper, K., Naumann, U.: Memory-efficient sparse matrix-matrix multiplication by row merging on many-core architectures. SIAM J. Sci. Comput. **40**(4), C429–C449 (2018)
7. Gustavson, F.G.: Two fast algorithms for sparse matrices: multiplication and permuted transposition. ACM Trans. Math. Softw. **4**(3), 250–269 (1978)
8. Hou, K., Liu, W., Wang, H., Feng, W.c.: Fast segmented sort on GPUs. In: Proceedings of the International Conference on Supercomputing, ICS 2017 (2017)
9. Liu, J., He, X., Liu, W., Tan, G.: Register-based implementation of the sparse general matrix-matrix multiplication on GPUs. In: Proceedings of the 23rd ACM SIGPLAN Symposium on Principles and Practice of Parallel Programming, PPoPP 2018, pp. 407–408 (2018)
10. Liu, J., He, X., Liu, W., Tan, G.: Register-aware optimizations for parallel sparse matrix-matrix multiplication. Int. J. Parallel Program. **47**, 403–417 (2019)
11. Liu, W., Vinter, B.: A framework for general sparse matrix-matrix multiplication on GPUs and heterogeneous processors. J. Parallel Distrib. Comput. **85**, 47–61 (2015)
12. Liu, W., Vinter, B.: Speculative segmented sum for sparse matrix-vector multiplication on heterogeneous processors. Parallel Comput. **49**, 179–193 (2015)
13. Liu, W., Vinter, B.: CSR5: An efficient storage format for cross-platform sparse matrix-vector multiplication. In: Proceedings of the 29th ACM on International Conference on Supercomputing, ICS 2015, pp. 339–350 (2015)
14. Nagasaka, Y., Nukada, A., Matsuoka, S.: High-performance and memory-saving sparse general matrix-matrix multiplication for NVIDIA pascal GPU. In: 2017 46th International Conference on Parallel Processing (ICPP), pp. 101–110 (2017)
15. Wang, H., Liu, W., Hou, K., Feng, W.C.: Parallel transposition of sparse data structures. In: Proceedings of the 2016 International Conference on Supercomputing, ICS 2016, pp. 33:1–33:13 (2016)
16. Xie, Z., Tan, G., Liu, W., Sun, N.: IA-SpGEMM: an input-aware auto-tuning framework for parallel sparse matrix-matrix multiplication. In: Proceedings of the ACM International Conference on Supercomputing, ICS 2019, pp. 94–105 (2019)

A Hierarchical Model of Control Logic for Simplifying Complex Networks Protocol Design

Yi Yang[1], Wei Quan[1(✉)], Jinli Yan[1], Lu Tang[2], and Zhigang Sun[1]

[1] Computer College, National University of Defense Technology,
Changsha 410000, Hunan, China
{yangyi14,w.quan}@nudt.edu.cn
[2] HuNan Hua Xin Tong Networks, Changsha 410000, Hunan, China

Abstract. With the increase of network protocols complexity, the finite state machine model commonly used in hardware design is difficult to directly describe and manage complex protocol control logic. The hierarchical approach can simplify the design and implementation of complex logic. However, the control logic of the protocol is a whole, and how to divide the control logic of the protocol hierarchically is a problem that needs to be solved urgently. Therefore, by analyzing the characteristics of complex protocol control logic, this paper proposes the DoubleDeck model. This model divides the state in protocol processing into a global state perceivable by the protocol peer and a local state invisible to the outside. Next, we established a prototype system of the time synchronization protocol (AS6802) on the FPGA array based on the DoubleDeck model, which effectively verified the feasibility of the model.

Keywords: Finite state machine · Control logic · Network protocol · Hierarchical design

1 Introduction

With the development of communication technology [1,2], the complexity of the protocol has continued to increase. How to implement complex protocol control has become an important issue facing hardware implementation protocols [3]. The complexity of protocol control is mainly reflected in two aspects. One is that while the protocol entity exchanges constantly changing status information with the peer through packets, it also needs to set various types of timers to infer the network status and the behavior of the protocol peer; The second is that the protocol not only needs to monitor asynchronous trigger events, but also needs to perform various synchronous and asynchronous processing operations. In the face of complex protocol control, the finite state machine model used in traditional hardware design is not only poorly readable, but also difficult to directly describe and manage complex control behaviors [4,5].

© IFIP International Federation for Information Processing 2021
Published by Springer Nature Switzerland AG 2021
X. He et al. (Eds.): NPC 2020, LNCS 12639, pp. 182–187, 2021.
https://doi.org/10.1007/978-3-030-79478-1_16

In order to simplify the design and implementation of complex control logic, some recent studies have proposed implementation methods based on hierarchical state machines [6]. However, in the existing protocol design schemes, the control logic of the protocol is a whole, and how to set a common division standard for complex protocols and achieve feasible hierarchical division of control logic is still an urgent problem to be solved [7].

In response to the above-mentioned challenges, this paper proposes a DoubleDeck model that supports the hardware implementation of complex protocol control logic to simplify the complexity of protocol control logic design. The basic idea of DoubleDeck is to divide the state in the protocol processing process into a global state that is external to the protocol entity and a local state that is not external. Among them, the global state and the corresponding conversion logic constitute the top-level state machine to maintain the changes in the protocol processing stage. At the same time, the local state associated with the top state and the corresponding transition logic form a series of bottom state machines to control the detailed processing details of the processing stage.

2   Motivation and Related Works

2.1   Motivation

In different agents of the same protocol, the control logic executes different control state machines that are related to each other. In the process of protocol processing, the protocol entity must obtain the network status and behavior of the opposite end to correctly complete the protocol-related processing. There are two main methods for the protocol entity to obtain the network information of the opposite end. First of all, in view of the characteristics of the packet type that can reflect the processing state of the protocol, the protocol entity exchanges state information with the peer through multiple protocol-related packets. Second, the protocol entity sets up a series of timers to infer the status information of the peer.

Through the analysis of the agreement, we found that in the process of implementation of the agreement, the agreement entities showed a diverse state. Among them, some states are necessary information for the protocol peer to process events (state transitions, etc.), so the protocol peer needs to perceive such states; some states can be set to an externally invisible state because they involve the details of the event processing of the protocol peer. Regarding whether the protocol state can be perceived by the outside world, we divide the protocol state into a global state perceivable by the protocol peer and a local state that is not visible from the outside. Therefore, we can decouple the protocol control logic into global state-related conversion logic and local state-related processing logic. Therefore, in this article, we propose a two-layer state machine design model to simplify the design and implementation of complex protocol control logic by dividing complex protocol control logic into small conversion logic and processing logic.

2.2   Related Works

The finite state machine (FSM) model is widely used in hardware logic design [4]. However, when there are many protocol states and complex state transitions, the flat finite state machine model will cause problems such as poor model readability and difficulty in later debugging. Hierarchical Finite State Machine (HFSM) [6] adds elements such as state variables and state transitions on the basis of FSM to further express the dynamic behavior of the system in a fine-grained manner. HFSM uses a top-down approach to describe the system. In this method, the hardware logic is divided into multiple smaller sub-modules, which can reduce the complexity of the overall hardware design. However, the sub-modules are highly independent and need to be designed and tested separately, which increases the difficulty of later debugging to a certain extent.

3   DoubleDeck Model Overview

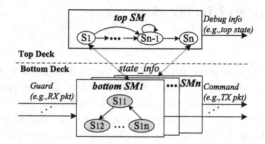

Fig. 1. The overview of DoubleDeck model.

DoubleDeck consists of top deck and bottom deck, as shown in Fig. 1. There is a top state machine on the Top deck, which is responsible for maintaining the global state of the protocol and its corresponding transition logic. The top state machine controls the conversion of the global state and sends the state information to the CPU and other external devices to facilitate later debugging and maintenance. In addition, the top state machine controls the bottom state machine to jump from the waiting state to the active state through the *state_info* signal. At the same time, the state transition of the top state depends on the feedback information of the bottom state machine. The bottom state machine that completes the processing task transfers the next stage of the protocol processing (global state) to the top state machine through the *state_info* signal. Bottom deck consists of a series of bottom state machines. The bottom state machine implements the processing logic in the global state and provides control information for the state transition of the global state. The bottom state machine array processes external trigger events based on flow rules. The bottom state machine has three states, which are waiting state, active state and end state. Among them, the active state has multiple processing states, that is, the partial state mentioned above. When the device receives protocol-related traffic, the external receiving module sends the protocol-related information to the bottom state machine array. The bottom state machine in the active state receives the information and enters the appropriate local state according to the protocol settings to generate command events. When the command event contains global state jump information, the bottom state machine enters the end state and uses the *state_info* signal to notify the top state machine to perform state transition.

4   Experiment

The AS6802 protocol describes a fault-tolerant high-precision time synchronization algorithm [8]. SM and CM are two protocol roles of AS6802. We implemented the IP core of the AS6802 protocol based on the DoubleDeck model, and implemented the prototype system of the AS6802 protocol on a network processing platform composed of multiple Arria10 SoCs (Altera FPGAs). We instantiate the IP core as three SMs and one CM, as shown in Fig. 2. In addition, the oscilloscope in Fig. 2 is used to detect the synchronization pulse signal of each node and calculate the error between the synchronization pulses in real time. The controller forms an out-of-band configuration network with all nodes through switches to realize the configuration and status monitoring of each node.

In the first experiment, we used a CM to exchange data with multiple SMs to achieve time synchronization between nodes. As shown in Fig. 3, we tested the stay time of the node in the intermediate state during the synchronization establishment process through three sub-experiments. Experimental results show that with the increase in the number of nodes, the test network can quickly synchronize the time of the entire network within 465 microseconds. In addition, the state transition conditions of the nodes are consistent with the description in the protocol.

In the second experiment, we evaluated the performance of the AS6802 IP core using 3 SMs and 1 CM. After all nodes enter the SYNC state, we obtain the maximum clock deviation of the four nodes through an oscilloscope, that is, the synchronization accuracy of the test network. We collected 50 sets of data, as shown in Fig. 4. Analyzing the experimental results, it can be found that the synchronization accuracy of the four nodes can be controlled within 25 ns, which fully meets the requirements of high-precision time synchronization.

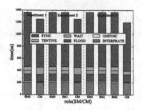
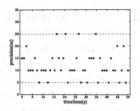

Fig. 2. An experiment environment with 4 nodes (3 *SM* and 1 *CM*).

Fig. 3. The time used by the nodes during the startup phase.

Fig. 4. Synchronization precision of the four-node network.

5 Conclusion

The traditional finite state machine model is difficult to solve the complexity problem of hardware implementation of complex protocol control logic. Although the hierarchical method has become an important means to simplify the design of complex logic, the existing work fails to provide developers with a standard for dividing complex protocol control logic. This paper decouples the control logic of the protocol into conversion logic and processing logic, and maps it to the double-layer state machine of the DoubleDeck model, which effectively simplifies the design of complex protocol control logic.

Acknowledgments. This work is supported by the Defense Industrial Technology Development Program (Grant NO. WDZC20205500110). We also thanks HuNan Hua Xin Tong Networks for their equipments to carry out our experiments.

References

1. Kotulski, Z., Nowak, T.W., Sepczuk, M., Tunia, M.A.: 5G networks: types of isolation and their parameters in RAN and CN slices. Comput. Netw. **171**, 107135 (2020)
2. Nasrallah, A., et al.: Ultra-low latency (ULL) networks: the IEEE TSN and IETF DetNet standards and related 5G ULL research. IEEE Commun. Surv. Tutor. **21**(1), 88–145 (2018)
3. Steinhammer, K., Ademaj, A.: Hardware implementation of the time-triggered ethernet controller. In: Rettberg, A., Zanella, M.C., Dömer, R., Gerstlauer, A., Rammig, F.J. (eds.) IESS 2007. ITIFIP, vol. 231, pp. 325–338. Springer, Boston, MA (2007). https://doi.org/10.1007/978-0-387-72258-0_28
4. Qi, Y., et al.: FSM-based cyber security status analysis method. In: 2019 IEEE Fourth International Conference on Data Science in Cyberspace (DSC), pp. 510–515. IEEE (2019)
5. Moshref, M., Bhargava, A., Gupta, A., Yu, M., Govindan, R.: Flow-level state transition as a new switch primitive for SDN. In: Proceedings of the Third Workshop on Hot Topics in Software Defined Networking, pp. 61–66 (2014)

6. Oliveira, A., Melo, A., Sklyarov, V.: Specification, implementation and testing of HFSMs in dynamically reconfigurable FPGAs. In: Lysaght, P., Irvine, J., Hartenstein, R. (eds.) FPL 1999. LNCS, vol. 1673, pp. 313–322. Springer, Heidelberg (1999). https://doi.org/10.1007/978-3-540-48302-1_32
7. Fragal, V.H., Simao, A., Mousavi, M.R.: Hierarchical featured state machines. Sci. Comput. Program. **171**, 67–88 (2019). And Applications, pp. 313–322. Springer (1999)
8. SAE AS6802: Time-triggered ethernet. SAE International (2011)

Architecture and Hardware

FPGA-Based Multi-precision Architecture for Accelerating Large-Scale Floating-Point Matrix Computing

Longlong Zhang[1,2], Yuanxi Peng[1(✉)], Xiao Hu[2], Ahui Huang[1,2], and Tian Tian[2]

[1] State Key Laboratory of High Performance Computing, School of Computer, National University of Defense Technology, Changsha, China
pyx@nudt.edu.cn
[2] Institute of Microelectronics, School of Computer, National University of Defense Technology, Changsha, China
xiaohu@nudt.edu.cn

Abstract. Matrix computing plays a vital role in many scientific and engineering applications, but previous work can only handle the data with specified precision based on FPGA. This study first presents algorithms, data flows, and mapping strategies to match the hardware structure for matrix computing of different precisions. Then, we propose a unified multi-precision matrix computing unit core that can handle three precisions and three matrix operation modes and can be used as a coprocessor for large-scale matrix computing which has advantages of low storage and high efficiency. Finally, we build a complete matrix computing acceleration system and deploy it on FPGA using 128 processing elements (PEs). The experimental results show that the accelerator achieves a maximum frequency of 180 MHz, and matrix computing of double-precision, single-precision, and half-precision floating-point data performs 46.1 GFLOPS, 92.1 GFLOPS, and 184.3 GFLOPS respectively, which is superior to other current designs in terms of application range and performance.

1 Introduction

Matrix computing is widely used in the fields of computing science and engineering applications, such as signal processing [1], image processing [2], and convolutional neural networks [3]. In recent years, although matrix computing has achieved good performance on many acceleration platforms such as CPU, GPU, TPU, and FPGA, its computing performance is still the bottleneck for the performance improvement of the entire system.

Compared with other platforms, field-programmable gate arrays (FPGAs) have the advantage of designing computing structures and storage schemes for specific applications. Many studies have shown that FPGAs are superior to other platforms in terms of performance and power consumption [4], and are suitable as a low-cost hardware accelerator for matrix computing.

© IFIP International Federation for Information Processing 2021
Published by Springer Nature Switzerland AG 2021
X. He et al. (Eds.): NPC 2020, LNCS 12639, pp. 191–202, 2021.
https://doi.org/10.1007/978-3-030-79478-1_17

There have been many solutions for matrix computing based on FPGAs. Some scholars have proposed algorithms and structures for fixed-point matrix multiplication [5] and matrix calculation [6]. A systolic array structure has achieved high data throughput and computing speed [7, 8]. But its demand for the number of PEs and I/O bandwidth is very high. Another linear array structure is widely used in matrix multiplication [9–11]. Some studies have carried out different types of optimization based on the structure [12], such as storage optimization [13], I/O, and storage scheduling optimization [14]. This structure has also achieved better results in the acceleration of convolutional neural networks [15, 16], multi-operation and continuous matrix computing [17].

However, matrix computing based on FPGAs still faces the following concerns. Firstly, the previous work was specifically designed for matrix computing with certain data precision. After determining the data type, the calculation structure can not handle the data with another precision. For example, the signal processing in the controller has a greater demand for matrix computing with different precisions, which requires a special hardware accelerator to speed up real-time computing capabilities. Secondly, most of the existing research was interested in matrix multiplication. In many engineering applications, such as the filtering algorithm, matrix addition and matrix subtraction are used together with matrix multiplication. Therefore, they are both important calculation models. Thirdly, consider that the matrix calculation accuracy in the deep learning model does not need to be too high. It is necessary to design a half-precision floating-point matrix calculation accelerator that satisfies performance and calculation efficiency.

This study aims to develop an efficient multi-precision matrix computing acceleration (MCA) unit core based on a unified architecture. The major contributions of this work are as follows:

- Based on the parallel block matrix computing algorithm and linear array, we present two parallel single-precision floating-point matrix computing unit. Through the splicing data and the mapping strategy from algorithm to calculation structure, each PE can complete two single-precision floating-point matrix computing in parallel, which truly improves the computing speed.
- The proposed multi-precision MCA unit core with a unified structure can handle three precisions (double-precision, single-precision, and half-precision) and three commonly used matrix operations (matrix multiplication, matrix addition and matrix subtraction) which enhances the adaptability of data types.
- We develop the MCA system based on the DSP-FPGA platform. Compare to some state-of-the-art structures, the proposed system meets engineering needs and achieves better performance.

The remainder of this paper is organized as follows. In Sect. 2, the parallel block matrix computing algorithm and linear array are introduced. The details of single-precision, half-precision floating-point matrix computing, multi-precision functional component, the MCA core and system are described in Sect. 3. The implementation results and discussion are shown in Sect. 4. Finally, Sect. 5 concludes the work.

2 The Parallel Block Matrix Computing Algorithm and Linear Array

The matrix multiplication involved in this article is shown in Eq. (1), where matrix A, matrix B, and matrix C are dense matrices of arbitrary size.

$$C_{M \times N} = A_{M \times K} \times B_{K \times N} + C_{M \times N}. \tag{1}$$

We introduce a parallel block matrix multiplication algorithm [17]. As shown in Algorithm 1, it includes three outer loops and two inner loops. The outer loops with loop variables T_p, T_{t1}, and t2 are used for the data transmission of the sub-matrix A and B, and the initialization of the sub-matrix C. The inner loops with loop variables p and t1 are used for the calculation in each PE. After the block processing, the sizes of the sub-matrix blocks A, B, and C are $S_p \times K$, $K \times S_{t1}$, and $S_p \times S_{t1}$, respectively. Parameters S_p and S_{t1} are also represent the number of PE and the depth of on-chip RAM in each PE.

Algorithm 1. Parallel block matrix multiplication.
for T_p=0 to M-1, S_p **do**
for T_{t1}=0 to N-1, S_{t1} **do**
Initialize data block $C[T_p:T_p+S_p-1,T_{t1}:T_{t1}+S_{t1}-1]$ to zero;
for t2 =0 to K-1 **do**
Load data block $A[T_p:T_p+S_p-1, t2]$;
Load data block $B[t2,T_{t1}:T_{t1}+S_{t1}-1]$;
for p=T_p to T_p+S_p-1 **do**
for t1=T_{t1} to $T_{t1}+S_{t1}$-1 **do**
C[p,t1]=C[p,t1]+A[p,t2]*B[t2,t1];
Store data block $C[T_p:T_p+S_p-1,T_{t1}:T_{t1}+S_{t1}-1]$;

As shown in Fig. 1, the structure of linear array corresponding to Algorithm 1 is usually composed of a set of PEs, a data transfer controller, and two-stage FIFOs. Each PE includes two registers for storing elements of sub-matrix A and B, a FIFO for buffering data flow a, an on-chip RAM block for storing a row of elements of sub-matrix C, and a multiply-accumulate functional component for matrix multiplication.

Before the calculation starts, all elements in the on-chip RAM block are initialized to zero in advance, and a column of elements from sub-matrix A is preloaded and distributed to the register a in each PE. When the elements from the sub-matrix B flow into the linear array by rows, the linear array starts parallel calculations. Then, each PE completes the $c^k = a \times b + c^{k-1}$ operation through the write-back mechanism and saves the intermediate result in the on-chip RAM block. After K iterations, the result of sub-matrix C is moved to the off-chip memory.

The above algorithm and structure can complete the functions of $A \times B \pm C$. When B = 1, the addition and subtraction operations can be realized. It uses the identity matrix I to realize the matrix addition (subtraction) of sub-matrix A and sub-matrix C, as shown in Eq. (2).

$$C_{M \times K} = A_{M \times K} \times I_{K \times K} \pm C_{M \times K}. \tag{2}$$

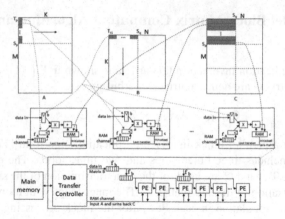

Fig. 1. Linear array architecture and computing process.

The matrix addition (subtraction) uses the same structure and similar data flow method as matrix multiplication. The sub-matrix C originally initialized to a zero matrix is loaded into the on-chip RAM block by the RAM channel in advance.

3 Multi-precision Floating-Point Matrix Computing Based on a Unified Structure

To solve the problem of multiple data types for matrix computing, we first discuss how to design algorithms, data flows, and PE structures for single-precision and half-precision floating-point matrix computing based on the aforementioned double-precision floating-point matrix computing and linear array. Then, we introduce the corresponding floating-point multiply-accumulate (subtract) functional component in each PE. Finally, we describe the multi-precision floating-point MCA unit core and take the core to build a multi-precision MCA system.

3.1 Two Parallel Single-Precision Floating-Point Matrix Computing

In this section, a PE in the proposed structure can complete two single-precision floating-point data operations in the same clock cycles.

As shown in Algorithm 2, two parallel single-precision floating-point matrix multiplication uses the same block method, loop mode, and data flow as Algorithm 1. The difference is that the size of sub-matrix A and C becomes $2S_p \times K$ and $2S_p \times S_{t1}$, respectively. In the innermost loop, the original multiply-accumulate operation becomes two parallel multiply-accumulate operations.

Algorithm 2. Two parallel single-precision floating-point matrix multiplication.

Initialize data block $C[0:2S_p-1,0:S_u-1]$ to zero;
    for t2 =0 to K-1 **do**
        Load data block $A[0:2S_p-1, t2]$;
        Load data block $B[t2,0: S_u-1]$;
           for p=0 to S_p -1 **do**
               for q=0 to S_u-1 **do**
                    $C[2p,q]=C[2p,q]+A[2p,t2]*B[t2,q]$;
                    $C[2p+1,q]=C[2p+1,q]+A[2p+1,t2]*B[t2,q]$;
Store data block $C[0: 2S_p -1,0: S_u-1]$;

Figure 2 shows the PE structure of several data types. The data sources in Fig. 2(a) and Fig. 2(b) are double-precision and single-precision floating-point data, respectively.

Generally, each PE has three source operands. In the structure of two parallel single-precision floating-point matrix multiplication, we use a data splicing mechanism when preparing the source operands. Two 32-bit single-precision floating-point data are spliced into a 64-bit source operand, that is, the two single-precision floating-point data are placed in the upper half and the lower half of the register, respectively.

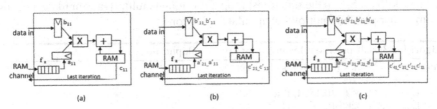

(a)   (b)   (c)

Fig. 2. The PE structure of matrix multiplication. (a) Double-precision floating-point. (b) Two parallel single-precision floating-point. (c) Four parallel half-precision floating-point.

Figure 3 describes the mapping process of single-precision floating-point matrix multiplication from algorithm to hardware structure. Firstly, the value of the sub-matrix C is initialized to zero matrix. Then, when loading a column of data ($2S_p$) from sub-matrix A, we stitch two adjacent single-precision data into a 64-bit operand and distribute it to the corresponding PE. When loading data row by row from the sub-matrix B, we also stitch two identical single-precision data into a 64-bit operand and distribute it to each PE. At the same time, the calculation of the linear array begins.

After the write-back mechanism and K iterations, the results are 64-bit operands. Each PE is responsible for calculating the two rows of sub-matrix C, where the lower 32 bits are the result of the previous row of sub-matrix C, and the upper 32 bits are the result of the subsequent row of sub-matrix C.

The single-precision floating-point matrix addition (subtraction) uses a similar algorithm and calculation structure with the single-precision floating-point matrix multiplication. The difference is that the sub-matrix B becomes an identity matrix, and the sub-matrix C participating in multiply-accumulate (subtract) operation needs to be imported into the on-chip RAM in advance.

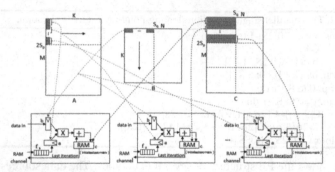

Fig. 3. The mapping process of two parallel single-precision floating-point matrix multiplication.

3.2 Four Parallel Half-Precision Floating-Point Matrix Computing

In half-precision floating-point matrix multiplication, one PE can complete four floating-point data operations in the same clock cycles. As shown in Algorithm 3, the size of sub-matrix A is $4S_p \times K$, the size of sub-matrix B is unchanged, and the size of sub-matrix C is $4S_p \times S_{t1}$. In the innermost loop, the original multiply-accumulate operation becomes four parallel multiply-accumulate operations.

Algorithm 3. Half-precision floating-point matrix multiplication.

Initialize data block $C[0:4S_p-1,0:S_{t1}-1]$ to zero;
   for t2 =0 to K-1 **do**
     Load data block $A[0:4S_p-1, t2]$;
     Load data block $B[t2,0: S_{t1}-1]$;
       for p=0 to S_p -1 **do**
         for q=0 to S_{t1}-1 **do**
           C[4p,q]=C[4p,q]+A[4p,t2]*B[t2,q];
           C[4p+1,q]=C[4p+1,q]+A[4p+1,t2]*B[t2,q];
           C[4p+2,q]=C[4p+2,q]+A[4p+2,t2]*B[t2,q];
           C[4p+3,q]=C[4p+3,q]+A[4p+3,t2]*B[t2,q];
Store data block $C[0: 4S_p -1,0: S_{t1}-1]$;

As shown in Fig. 2(c), when we prepare the source operand, four 16-bit half-precision floating-point data are spliced into a 64-bit source operand. For example, half-precision floating-point source operands $a'_{41\_}a'_{31\_}a'_{21\_}a'_{11}$ and $b'_{11\_}b'_{11\_}b'_{11\_}b'_{11}$ are operated to obtain four half-precision operation results $c'_{41\_}c'_{31\_}c'_{21\_}c'_{11}$.

Similar to the process shown in Fig. 3, when loading a column of data $(4S_p)$ from sub-matrix A, we stitch four adjacent half-precision data into a 64-bit source operand and distribute it to the corresponding PE. When loading data row by row from the sub-matrix B, we also stitch four identical half-precision data into a 64-bit source operand and distribute it to each PE. Here, each PE is responsible for calculating four rows of sub-matrix C.

Besides, the half-precision floating-point matrix addition (subtraction) has similarities with the half-precision floating-point matrix multiplication.

3.3   Multi-precision Floating-Point Multiply-Accumulate (Subtract) Functional Component

We adjust and optimize a self-designed and high-performance floating-point multiply-accumulate (subtract) functional component [18] to meet the needs of matrix calculation. Figure 4 shows the three precision floating-point data formats that comply with the IEEE 754 standard. According to the rules of data format, the multi-precision functional component can perform single-precision and half-precision floating-point operations by maximizing the logical structure of double-precision floating-point operation.

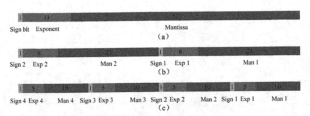

Fig. 4. Different precision floating-point formats used in the unit. (a) Double-precision format. (b) Single-precision format. (c) Half-precision format.

The multi-precision functional unit adopts a six-stage pipeline design which mainly includes the modules, such as operand preparation, mantissa multiplication, Multiply-add, normalization processing, exception judgment, and result selection.

After reading the operands, the functional unit separates the exponent and mantissa according to the format and performs corresponding operations respectively. Figure 5(a) shows that in half-precision calculation, the input 64-bit source operand is split into four half-precision floating-point format data.

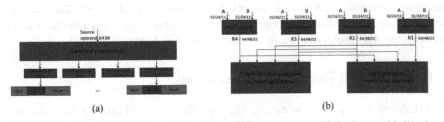

Fig. 5. (a) The process of half-precision data preparation. (b) Multiplexing multiplier in the mantissa multiplication module.

Besides, we use four single-precision multipliers to perform each group of mantissa multiplications in parallel. The hardware overhead can be saved by multiplexing the multipliers. As shown in Fig. 5(b), when performing half-precision floating-point operations, the separated 4-way multiplication operation data are respectively sent to the upper 11 bits of the four 32*32 bit multipliers.

3.4   Implementation for Multi-precision MCA Unit Core and MCA System

The MCA unit core supports matrices computing of arbitrary size. As shown in Fig. 6, the core receives the matrix operation mode signal provided externally and decides whether to load or initialize the sub-matrix C. It can also select the appropriate precision mode according to the actual needs. Then we supply the corresponding operands and process the corresponding operands according to the precision mode.

In the process of implementing the multi-precision MCA unit core, we add logic for selecting data types, data splicing, and parts that cannot be reused, but the logic delay constraints meet the design requirements.

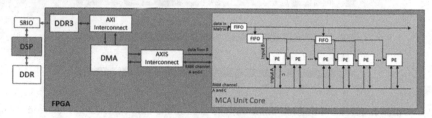

Fig. 6. The architecture of multi-precision MCA unit core and MCA system.

The overall structure of the system is shown in Fig. 6. The MCA system uses the architecture of DSP + FPGA. Firstly, the DSP sends instructions and control signals to the coprocessor and transfers the data from the memory on the host side to the DDR on the coprocessor side by starting the SRIO module. Then, the coprocessor calculates autonomously. After the overall calculation is completed, the system starts the SRIO module again and returns the calculation result. Therefore, when the coprocessor is working, the DSP can execute other instructions to achieve independent acceleration.

The coprocessor includes an MCA unit core and data transmission logic. The logic mainly includes the DMA module for selecting operation mode, controlling data flow, and transmitting data within the coprocessor. The connection between modules and the core uses the AXI protocol to facilitate communication between each other.

4   Experimental Results and Discussions

The MCA unit core is programmed in Verilog HDL, synthesized, and simulated using synthesis tools (Xilinx Vivado 2016). Then, we deployed the MCA system on the DSP + FPGA platform.

4.1   Synthesis Results

We use the 585T development board as the target device and synthesize the MCA unit using 128 PEs under typical conditions. The delay of each stage of the pipeline meets the target delay of 550 ps and the total power consumption is 5.48 W.

Different numbers of PEs directly affects the calculation efficiency and hardware overhead in the proposed structure. Table 1 shows the logical resource consumption of the MCA unit with different numbers of PEs. We can see that as the number of PEs increases, LUTs and Slice Registers increase. In addition to the number of PEs, the RAM block consumption is also related to the size of the sub-matrix block. Because the number of PEs determines the number of RAM blocks used, and the size of the sub-matrix block determines the depth of the RAM blocks.

Because the depth of the RAM block in the PE represents the number of times that the data of sub-matrix block A can be reused. To maximize the reuse of data, we can choose the depth of the RAM block according to the size of the sub-matrix B. In principle, the larger the better if the on-chip storage allows. We set the depth of the RAM block to 512 in the project.

Table 1. Resource consumption of different numbers of PEs.

PEs	LUTs	Slice registers	BRAM (18K)
32	70130	58920	41
64	139860	117700	73
128	278960	234450	140

For M × N rectangular matrices, due to the idea of block matrix, our storage requirement is only $2S_pS_{t1}$, where the parameters S_p and S_{t1} represent the number of rows and columns of the sub-matrix C, respectively. Therefore, this structure has the characteristic of low storage requirement in large-scale matrix computing.

4.2 Performance Analysis

Table 2 shows the relationship between the maximum operating frequency and peak performance of the multi-precision MCA unit with the number of PEs. When we set 128 PEs, the maximum operating frequency achieves 180 MHz. At this time, the multi-precision MCA unit can complete 128 double-precision multiplication operations and 128 addition operations in one cycle. The peak performance of double-precision floating-point matrix computing, for example, can be estimated as 180 Mhz × 128 FLOP × 2 = 46.1 GFLOPS. It can also complete two times single-precision floating-point data and

Table 2. Number of PEs, clock speed, and peak performance for double-precision/ single-precision/half-precision floating-point data.

PEs		32	64	128
Clock Speed (Mhz)		202	195	180
Peak performance (GFLOPS)	Double-precision	12.92	24.96	46.1
	Single-precision	25.85	49.92	92.1
	Half-precision	51.71	99.84	184.3

four times half-precision floating-point data at the same time. Therefore, single-precision floating-point and half-precision floating-point performance can reach 92.1 GFLOPS and 184.3 GFLOPS, respectively.

In large-scale matrix computing, we have to consider the time to initialize the system, the time to transfer data from external memory, and the calculation unit waiting for calculation data that may occur during the calculation process.

Firstly, for the time to initialize the system, the main consumption is preloading data. In multi-precision matrix multiplication and matrix addition (subtraction), the amount of preloading data are S_p and $S_p + S_p S_{t1}$, respectively. When the size of the matrix becomes larger, the ratio of data preload time to the total time will be small, and the calculation is more efficient.

Secondly, according to the characteristics of the algorithm and structure, we analyze the data transfer time in the calculation process of matrix computing. As shown in Eq. (3), we use $\vec{B}_i^r$ and $\vec{C}_i^r$ to denote elements containing the ith row of matrix B and matrix C, respectively.

$$\vec{C}_1^r = a_{1,1}\vec{B}_1^r + a_{1,2}\vec{B}_2^r + \ldots + a_{1,k}\vec{B}_k^r. \tag{3}$$

Let one PE calculates a row of elements from left to right. After k iterations, the first PE can complete the calculation of the first row of the matrix C. Then, the ith PE is responsible for the calculation of the ith row of the matrix C. More generally, the extension to all rows of the matrix C is represented by Eq. (4).

$$\vec{C}_i^r = a_{i,1}\vec{B}_1^r + a_{i,2}\vec{B}_2^r + \ldots + a_{i,k}\vec{B}_k^r. \tag{4}$$

It can be seen from this formulation that all PEs can work in parallel without affecting each other. We can reuse the data $a_{i,k}$ by reasonably setting the number of elements in a row of matrix B, and at the same time, the latency of floating-point functional component and the data moving time can be hidden into the computing time, which effectively avoids the time of waiting data and ensures the pipeline of the structure.

4.3 Discussion

As shown in Table 3, we compare the proposed multi-precision matrix calculation acceleration unit with related work.

Compared to the double-precision floating-point matrix multiplication structure [13], our calculation structure merges more precisions and more matrix calculation modes. Compared with [17], although our proposed multi-precision MCA unit places fewer PEs, it does not affect the performance of the calculation unit. We can see from Table 3 that when calculating single-precision floating-point data, the performance is close to the structure [17]. When calculating half-precision floating-point data, the performance exceeds the structure [17].

Although the proposed structure based on the circulant matrix [6] has reached a high performance, it is only for fixed-point data. This can not meet the needs of most engineering calculations, such as the nonlinear Kalman filter algorithm and the extended Kalman filter algorithm that require floating-point matrix multiplication and matrix addition. Its size of the matrices is equal to the number of PEs, and it can only handle square matrices.

Therefore, its processing capacity is limited. Besides, the computational performance of our structure on a half-precision floating-point (16bit) is better than that of the structure on fixed-point (18bit) [6]. Our preparation time for preloading data is significantly shorter than their preparation time for preloading and generating circulant matrix.

Another matrix computing system [19] with multiple accelerators attempts to set up separate computing arrays for different matrix operations. We can see that our structure is superior to the structure in both performance and energy efficiency.

Table 3. Performance and hardware overhead compared to related work.

	Ours	[17]	[13]	[19]	[6]
Supported matrix sizes	$M \times N$	$M \times N$	$M \times N$	$M \times N$	$N \times N$
No. of PEs	128	256	256	N.A	500
f (Mhz)	180	195	181	150	346
Performance (GFLOPS)	46.1/92.1/184.3	99.8	N.A	76.8	173
Power (W)	5.48	5.24	N.A	4.59	N.A
Energy efficiency (GFLOPS/W)	8.4/16.81/33.63	19.05	N.A	16.7	N.A

5   Conclusions

This paper extends the matrix calculation to a multi-precision and multi-operation environment based on the block matrix computing algorithm and linear array. Through adjusting data flow and reusing logic, the proposed multi-precision floating-point MCA unit can process half-precision, single-precision, and double-precision floating-point data at the same time. Then, we built the MCA system based on the MCA unit core. Compared with the existing matrix calculation structure, our matrix calculation unit can handle three kinds of precision and three modes of operation in a unified structure and features low storage and high efficiency. We plan to improve the arithmetic component to support more precise numerical calculations including fixed-point and extended double-precision in the future.

Acknowledgments. This work was partially supported by the National Science and Technology Major Project (2017-V-0014-0066).

References

1. Amira, A., Bouridane, A., Milligan, P.: Accelerating matrix product on reconfigurable hardware for signal processing. In: Brebner, G., Woods, R. (eds.) FPL 2001. LNCS, vol. 2147, pp. 101–111. Springer, Heidelberg (2001). https://doi.org/10.1007/3-540-44687-7_11

2. Bensaali, F., Amira, A., Bouridane, A.: Accelerating matrix product on reconfigurable hardware for image processing applications. IEE Proc. Circ. Devices Syst. **152**, 236–246 (2005)
3. Liu, Z.Q., et al.: Throughput-optimized FPGA accelerator for deep convolutional neural networks. ACM Trans. Reconfigurable Technol. Syst. **10**(3), 23 (2017)
4. Jovanovic, Z., Milutinovic, V.: FPGA accelerator for floating-point matrix multiplication. IET Comput. Digit. Tech. **6**(4), 249–256 (2012)
5. Sonawane, D., Sutaone, M.S., Malek, I.: Systolic architecture for integer point matrix multiplication using FPGA, pp. 3822–3825 (2009)
6. Abbaszadeh, A., et al.: An scalable matrix computing unit architecture for FPGA, and SCUMO user design interface. Electronics **8**(1), 20 (2019)
7. Qasim, S.M., Abbasi, S.A., Almashary, B.: A proposed FPGA-based parallel architecture for matrix multiplication. In: Proceedings of the IEEE Asia Pacific Conference on Circuits and Systems (2008)
8. Zhou, L.T., et al.: Research on Systolic multiplication technology based on FPGA. Comput. Eng. Sci. **37**, 1632–1636 (2015)
9. Jang, J.-W., Choi, S.B., Prasanna, V.K.: Energy- and time-efficient matrix multiplication on FPGAs. IEEE Trans. Very Large Scale Integr. (VLSI) Syst. **13**(11), 1305–1319 (2005). https://doi.org/10.1109/TVLSI.2005.859562
10. Zhuo, L., Prasanna, V.K.: Scalable and modular algorithms for floating-point matrix multiplication on reconfigurable computing systems. IEEE Trans. Parallel Distrib. Syst. **18**(4), 433–448 (2007)
11. Kumar, V.B.Y., et al.: FPGA based high performance double-precision matrix multiplication. Int. J. Parallel Prog. **38**(3), 322–338 (2010)
12. Dou, Y., et al.: 64-bit floating-point FPGA matrix multiplication. In: Proceedings of the 2005 ACM/SIGDA 13th International Symposium on Field-Programmable Gate Arrays, Monterey, California, USA, pp. 86–95. Association for Computing Machinery (2005)
13. Wu, G.M., Dou, Y., Wang, M.: High performance and memory efficient implementation of matrix multiplication on FPGAs. In: 2010 International Conference on Field-Programmable Technology, Beijing, pp. 134–137 (2010)
14. Jia, X., Wu, G.M., Xie, X.H.: A high-performance accelerator for floating-point matrix multiplication. In: 2017 15th IEEE International Symposium on Parallel and Distributed Processing with Applications, pp. 396–402. IEEE, New York (2017)
15. Qiao, Y.R., et al.: FPGA-accelerated deep convolutional neural networks for high throughput and energy efficiency. Concurr. Comput.-Pract. Exp. **29**(20), 20 (2017)
16. Shen, J., et al.: Towards a multi-array architecture for accelerating large-scale matrix multiplication on FPGAs (2018)
17. Zhang, L., et al.: A scalable architecture for accelerating multi-operation and continuous floating-point matrix computing on FPGAs. IEEE Access **8**, 92469–92478 (2020)
18. Tian, T.: The Research and Implementation of High Performance SIMD Floating-Point Multiplication Accumulator Unit for FT-XDSP. National University of Defense Technology (2013)
19. Wang, W.Q., et al.: A universal FPGA-based floating-point matrix processor for mobile systems. In: Proceedings of the 2014 International Conference on Field-Programmable Technology, pp. 139–146. IEEE, New York (2014)

A Configurable Hardware Architecture for Runtime Application of Network Calculus

Xiao Hu[1(✉)] and Zhonghai Lu[2]

[1] School of Computer, National University of Defense Technology,
Changsha, People's Republic of China
xiaohu@nudt.edu.cn
[2] KTH Royal Institute of Technology, Stockholm, Sweden
zhonghai@kth.se

Abstract. Network Calculus has been a foundational theory for analyzing and ensuring Quality-of-Service (QoS) in a variety of networks including Networks on Chip (NoCs). To fulfill dynamic QoS requirements of applications, runtime application of network calculus is essential. However, the primitive operations in network calculus such as arrival curve, min-plus convolution and min-plus deconvolution are very time consuming when calculated in software because of the large volume and long latency of computation. For the first time, we propose a configurable hardware architecture to enable runtime application of network calculus. It employs a unified pipeline that can be dynamically configured to efficiently calculate the arrival curve, min-plus convolution, and min-plus deconvolution at runtime. We have implemented and synthesized this hardware architecture on a Xilinx FPGA platform to quantify its performance and resource consumption. Furthermore, we have built a prototype NoC system incorporating this hardware for dynamic flow regulation to effectively achieve QoS at runtime.

Keywords: Network calculus · Hardware architecture · Hardware configuration · Network-on-chip · Quality-of-Service

1 Introduction

Network Calculus [1–4] has been an active research area and successfully applied to fulfill Quality-of-Service (QoS) requirements of various networks. Recently, it has also been successfully applied to Networks on Chip (NoCs) in Chip Many-core Processors (CMPs) and Many-Processor Systems-on-Chip (MPSoCs) [5–8].

Traditionally, network calculus is used at design time as a theoretical tool for worst-case performance derivations of packet delay upper bound, maximum buffer backlog, minimal flow throughput etc. In recent years, network calculus is also applied in dynamic network admission control to monitor the changing traffic scenario in hard real-time systems. Huang *et al.* proposed a light-weight hardware module to address the traffic conformity problem for run-time inputs of a hard realtime system [6]. The arrival curve capturing the worst-case/best-case event arrivals in the time domain can be conservatively

© IFIP International Federation for Information Processing 2021
Published by Springer Nature Switzerland AG 2021
X. He et al. (Eds.): NPC 2020, LNCS 12639, pp. 203–216, 2021.
https://doi.org/10.1007/978-3-030-79478-1_18

approximated by a set of staircase functions, each of which can be modeled by a leaky bucket. They used a dual-bucket mechanism to monitor each staircase function during run-time, one for conformity verification and the other for traffic regulation. In case too many violation events are detected, the regulator delays the input events to fulfill the arrival curve specification assumed at design time. By conducting the conformity check, the system is able to monitor and regulate the actual behavior of NoC traffic flows in order to realize dynamic QoS in time-critical applications. However, the method in [6] for the conformity check of actual traffic stream against predefined specification assumes the linear arrival curve. Since it does not compute the arrival curve, it cannot be used for general arrival curve. Also, to enable a full scale of applying network calculus for dynamic QoS assurance, a systematic approach needs to be taken. For example, to compute output arrival curve needs to realize min-plus deconvolution, because output arrival curve is the result of min-plus deconvolution between input arrival curve and service curve. Indeed, to process both arrival curve and service curve, we need to calculate basic network calculus operations, which include both min-plus convolution and min-plus deconvolution.

From the software perspective, basic network calculus operations such as arrival curve, min-plus convolution, and min-plus deconvolution can be computed at runtime but are very time-consuming due to high complexity. For example, the computation complexity of the min-plus deconvolution operation in the recursive Eq. (8) (Sect. 3.3) is $O(N)$, where N is the length of calculation window in number of data items or cycles. When $N = 128$, there are 256 (128 $\times$ 2) operations for computation. In software, it costs about 22.9 μs on an Intel Core i3-3240 3.4 GHz CPU with Windows 7 operating system (see Sect. 4.3). However, in timing-critical applications, the system requires quick verification and fast regulation of flows online in several cycles according to the computation results of network calculus. Under such circumstances, how to accelerate the calculation speed in hardware fully supporting network calculus operations becomes an open challenge. Furthermore, to be efficient, it is desirable to have the network calculus hardware architecture configurable such that different operations can be done by simple configurations on the same hardware substrate.

To address the above challenge, we propose a hardware architecture for runtime (online) computation of network calculus operations. This hardware architecture is designed by analyzing the rudimentary definitions of the arrival curve, min-plus convolution and min-plus deconvolution. Through analyzing their recursive accumulative behaviors in their mathematical representations, we are able to reckon a unified pipeline architecture to conduct these primitive operations through simple configurations via de-multiplexing and multiplexing selections. We have implemented and optimized the hardware design and synthesized it on FPGA. In a case study, the specialized hardware module is used to build a runtime flow monitor attached to regulators in the network interface of NoC so as to facilitate dynamic flow regulation. To the best of our knowledge, no previous research has touched upon this approach.

The main contributions of the paper can be summarized as follows.

1. We develop a configurable hardware architecture for runtime computation of network calculus operations including arrival curve, min-plus convolution, and min-plus

deconvolution. The hardware architecture features a unified pipeline where the three network calculus operations can be performed by runtime configurations.

2. We implement the proposed design on a Xilinx FPGA platform and evaluate its area and speed, demonstrating its efficiency and feasibility.

3. With a multi-media playback system, the architecture is prototyped and used to satisfy application QoS, showing its potential in runtime monitoring of QoS bounds.

2   Related Work

Network calculus originated from macro networks for performance guarantees in Internet and ATM [1–4]. Theoretically it transforms complex non-linear network systems into analyzable linear systems [2–4]. In real-time calculus [9], it is extended to define both upper/lower arrival curves and upper/lower service curves to compute worst-case delay bounds under various scheduling polices for real-time tasks.

In recent years, network calculus has been applied to NoCs for analyzing worst-case performance guarantees of real-time applications, for example, to determine the worst-case reorder buffer size [11], to design network congestion control strategy [13] and to develop a per-flow delay bound analysis methodology for Intel's eXtensible Micro-Architectural Specification (xMAS) [7]. Notably in industrial practices, network calculus has been employed as a theoretical foundation to build the data NoC of Kalray's MPPA-256 many-core processor to achieve guaranteed communication services in per-flow delay and bandwidth [8].

In network calculus, traffic specification (e.g. linear arrival curve) can be used not only to characterize flows but also to serve as a contract for QoS specification. Subsequently, flow regulation as a traffic shaping technique can be employed at runtime for admission control to check conformity. In [10, 12], flow regulation is used to achieve QoS communication with low buffering cost when integrating IPs to NoC architectures. Lu and Wang presented a dynamic flow regulation [12], which overcomes the rigidity of static flow regulation that pre-configures regulation parameters statically and only once. The dynamic regulation is made possible by employing a sliding window based runtime flow (σ, ρ) characterization technique, where σ bounds traffic burstiness and ρ reflects the average rate. The effectiveness of dynamic traffic regulation for system performance improvement is further demonstrated in [14].

3   Configurable Hardware Architecture

We consider network calculus in a digital system. A data packet stream, noted as *flow*, arrives cycle by cycle. The two basic operations in network calculus are *min-plus convolution* and *min-plus deconvolution* [2] in min-plus algebra, noted as $f \otimes g$ and $f \oslash g$, respectively (see definitions below). There are two input functions, f and g, in convolution and deconvolution. When the two functions are the same, they are noted as $f \otimes f$ and $f \oslash f$, respectively. The result of $f \oslash f$ is in fact the *Arrival Curve (AC)* [2], which may be separated as the third operation due to its importance.

To conduct network calculus calculations in hardware at system runtime, we propose a unified hardware architecture that can flexibly support all above three basic network calculus operations, i.e., $f \otimes g, f \oslash g$, and $f \oslash f$ (AC) by simple configurations. As such, the hardware resources consumed by these operations can be shared for efficiency so as to facilitate and justify runtime application of network calculus. In the following, we detail our flexible hardware architecture step by step.

3.1 Micro-architecture for Function $f \oslash f$ (Arrival Curve)

We start by designing a functional hardware architecture for Arrival Curve.

Definition of Arrival Curve [2]: Given a wide-sense increasing function α defined for $t \geq 0$, we say that a flow f is constrained by α if and only if for all $s \leq t$: $f(t) - f(s) \leq \alpha(t - s)$. Equivalently we say that f has α as an arrival curve.

Let d_i be the size of arrival data at cycle i, from the definition, we have:

$$(f \Phi f)(t) = \sup_{u \geq 0}\{f(t+u) - f(u)\} = \sup_{u \geq 0}\left\{\sum_{u+1 \leq i \leq t+u} d_i\right\}, \ t > 0 \quad (1)$$

Here **sup** is the supremum operator. We can define $\sum_{u+1 \leq i \leq t+u} d_i$ in Eq. (1) as an intermediate function, named $AR(t)$. Then we have

$$(f \Phi f)(t) = \sup_{u \geq 0}\{AR(t)\} \quad (2)$$

Furthermore, $AR(t)$ can be iteratively calculated by the following recursive function:

$$AR(t) = \sum_{u+1 \leq i \leq t+u} d_i = \sum_{u+1 \leq i \leq t+u-1} d_i + d_{t+u} = d_{t+u} + AR(t-1) \quad (3)$$

In particular, $AR(0) = d_0$

Compute Micro-architecture for Arrival Curve: We take advantage of the recursive equation of $AR(t)$ in Eq. (3) to define an effective hardware micro-architecture for computing arrival curve. We can observe that, by defining cascaded registers storing $AR(t)$ values, $(f \Phi f)(t)$ can be transformed into recording the maximum values in $AR(t)$ registers. In this way, we can design a pipeline circuit to efficiently calculate the arrival curve in a processing window to handle the continuous data stream.

Figure 1 draws the hardware micro-architecture for computing arrival curve. The basic logic unit is called AddShiftComp unit. There are N AddShiftComp units cascaded in a pipeline. Each unit has an adder, a comparator, a multiplexer and a shifter connected to the next unit. As a generic efficient hardware design, the arrival curve is only calculated in one sliding window with a length of N data items. The Sampling unit is used in the sampling mode, which is to be detailed in the next section. If the Sampling unit is bypassed, a new data item flows into the processing pipeline at each cycle.

In Fig. 1, $f(t)$ is the input flow and d_i is the volume of arrival data at cycle i. AR is the Accumulating Register and BR is the Bound Register. The circuit also comprises the adders, comparators and multiplexers. On each cycle, the value of every AR added with current d_i is written into the next AR. Each AR is compared with the corresponding BR, the bigger one is written into the BR again. The Samp_CTL, AR_RST and BR_RST are control signals. The Samp_CTL is designed for the sampling mode. The AR_RST and BR_RST are used to initialize the AR and BR registers. After $N + 2$ cycles, the values of the accumulating function in the window of length N are computed and stored in ARs. The maximum bound values of ARs are stored in BRs. All values in BRs represent the arrival curve. The results in BRs can be snapshotted or registered and shifted out. When clearing all ARs and BRs with related Reset (RST) signals, the process restarts. To use the results in BRs, i.e., the dynamic arrival curve, by other circuits, we design Snapshot&Shiftout registers (SFs). With Control signal, these SFs are updated with all BRs snapshoted and shifted out one by one.

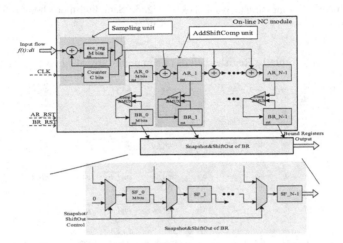

Fig. 1. Hardware micro-architecture for computing arrival curve.

Operation Details with an Example: The process of computing arrival curve is listed in Fig. 2. Taking $N = 4$ as an example, the processing details are given in Table 1. As $N = 4$, there are 4 ARs (AR_0~AR_3) and 4 BRs (BR_0~BR_3). At cycle 1, the volume of arrival data is d_0 and all ARs and BRs are cleared with AR_RSTand BR_RST. At cycle 2, the volume of arrival data is d_1 and all ARs are d_0 and all BRs are still 0. As the cycle time advances, AR_0 is equal to last data item d_{i-1}, AR_1 equal to $d_{i-2} + d_{i-1}$, AR_2 equal to $d_{i-3} + d_{i-2} + d_{i-1}$ and AR_3 equal to $d_{i-4} + d_{i-3} + d_{i-2} + d_{i-1}$. BR_0 stores the maximum value of AR_0, i.e., $\sup\limits_{0 \leq j \leq i-2} \{d_j\}$. BR_1 stores the maximum value of AR_1, i.e., $\sup\limits_{0 \leq j \leq i-3} \{d_j + d_{j+1}\}$. BR_2 stores the maximum value of AR_2, which is $\sup\limits_{0 \leq j \leq i-4} \{d_j + d_{j+1} + d_{j+2}\}$. BR_3 stores the maximum value of AR_3, which is $\sup\limits_{0 \leq j \leq i-5} \{d_j + d_{j+1} + d_{j+2} + d_{j+3}\}$. Then we get arrival curve via BR_0~BR_3.

The hardware cost can be estimated from Fig. 1 ($2 \times N \times M$ register bits for AR/BR and $2 \times N$ adders for compare/add). It is almost linear with number N of AddShiftComp units.

```
1: //Config step
2: Clear all ARs with AR_RST
3: Clear all BRs with BR_RST
4: //Work step
5: while (N)
6: { input d_i per cycle }
7: //Output step
8: Snapshot BR Registers into Snap-
shot&Shiftout registers
9: Shift out Snapshot&Shiftout registers (Arrival
Curve) to other circuits one by one
```

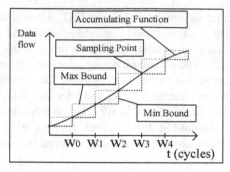

Fig. 2. Process of computing arrival curve.　**Fig. 3.** Sampling-mode bounds for Arrival Curve.

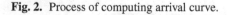

Table 1. Register details of computing arrival curve

Cycle	In	AR_0	AR_1	AR_2	AR_3	BR_0	BR_1	BR_2	BR_3
d_0	0	0	0	0	0	0	0	0	0
d_1	d_0	$0 + d_0$	$0 + 0 + d_0$	$0 + 0 + 0 + d_0$		0	0	0	0
d_2	d_1	$d_0 + d_1$	$0 + d_0 + d_1$	$0 + 0 + d_0 + d_1$		$\sup\{d_0\}$	d_0	d_0	d_0
d_3	d_2	$d_1 + d_2$	$d_0 + d_1 + d_2$	$0 + d_0 + d_1 + d_2$		$\sup\{d_0, d_1\}$	$\sup\{d_0 + d_1\}$	$d_0 + d_1$	$d_0 + d_1$
d_4	d_3	$d_2 + d_3$	$d_1 + d_2 + d_3$	$d_0 + d_1 + d_2 + d_3$		$\sup\{d_0, d_1, d_2\}$	$\sup\{d_0 + d_1, d_1 + d_2\}$	$\sup\{d_0 + d_1, d_1 + d_2\}$	$d_0 + d_1 + d_2$
d_5	d_4	$d_3 + d_4$	$d_2 + d_3 + d_4$	$d_1 + d_2 + d_3 + d_4$		$\sup\{d_0, d_1, d_2, d_3\}$	$\sup\{d_0 + d_1, d_1 + d_2, d_2 + d_3\}$	$\sup\{d_0 + d_1, d_1 + d_2, d_1 + d_2 + d_3\}$	$\sup\{d_0 + d_1 + d_2 + d_3\}$
...	...	...	...	...	...	...	...	...	...

3.2 Sampling-Based Micro-architecture for Arrival Curve

For some applications, there is a need to sample arrival curve at a larger time granularity than per cycle. For example, a system might not generate input data at each and every cycle. It is possible that the traffic generation is asynchronous and has a larger period than the arrival curve computation hardware. It might also be possible that an arrival curve at a larger time granularity is more interesting for the QoS analysis. In such cases, a larger time scale is needed to calculate arrival curve. To support this feature, we design a sampling scheme at a larger time scale as the sampling module shown in Fig. 1. It consists of a *C-bit* counter, an acc_reg register and an accumulator. Input d_i is accumulated into the acc_reg every cycle continuously. The *C-bit* counter as a controller enables the acc_reg output to the pipeline at a period of W cycles. The circuit samples the arrival curve every W cycles in the sampling mode (the ith sampling point is at $i \times W$ cycles). The max/min bound is indicated by the upper/lower stairs in Fig. 3.

Comparing with the original scheme recording all data of Full Accumulating Function (FAF) curve, the accumulating function curve recorded in the sampling mode (Sampling Accumulating Function, SAF) is composed of these sampling points. The SAF is accurate at these sampling points. Between two sampling points, the FAF may be any curve not larger than the upper sampling point and not less than the lower sampling point. Therefore, the maximum bound of FAF is the upper stairs set by sampling points and the minimum bound of FAF is the lower stairs set by sampling points.

The maximum bound of arrival curve can be expressed as:

$$\alpha_{max} = \begin{cases} \sup_{0 \leq i}\{w_i + w_{i+1}\}, 0 \leq t < T \\ \sup_{0 \leq i}\{w_i + w_{i+1} + w_{i+2}\}, T \leq t < 2T \\ \sup_{0 \leq i}\{w_i + w_{i+1} + w_{i+2} + w_{i+3}\}, 2T \leq t < 3T \\ \qquad \cdots \end{cases} \tag{4}$$

The minimum bound of arrival curve can be expressed as:

$$\alpha_{min} = \begin{cases} \sup_{0 \leq i}\{w_i\}, 0 \leq t < T \\ \sup_{0 \leq i}\{w_i + w_{i+1}\}, T \leq t < 2T \\ \sup_{0 \leq i}\{w_i + w_{i+1} + w_{i+2}\}, 2T \leq t < 3T \\ \qquad \cdots \end{cases} \tag{5}$$

3.3   Micro-architecture for Function $f \oslash g$

Definition of Min-plus Deconvolution [2]: $f \oslash g$ denotes the min-plus deconvolution. Let f and g be two functions or sequences. The min-plus deconvolution of f by g is the function:

$$(f \oslash g)(t) = \sup_{u \geq 0}\{f(t + u) - g(u)\} \tag{6}$$

Compared to common convolution, min-plus deconvolution uses the *maximum* respectively *supremum (sup)* operator to replace the *sum* operator and the *minus* operator to replace the *product* operator. Assume that $f(t)$ and $g(t)$ are two infinite data flows denoted by d_i and e_i, respectively. Time t is in clock cycle. From the definition of function $f \oslash g$, we have:

$$(f \oslash g)(t) = \sup_{u \geq 0}\left\{\sum_{0 \leq i \leq t+u} d_i - \sum_{0 \leq i \leq u} e_i\right\} \tag{7}$$

We can define $AR(t)$ in the same way as in Sect. 3.1:

$$AR(t) = \sum_{0 \leq i \leq u+t} d_i - \sum_{0 \leq i \leq u} e_i = d_{u+t} + \sum_{0 \leq i \leq u+t-1} d_i - \sum_{0 \leq i \leq u} e_i = d_{t+u} + AR(t-1) \tag{8}$$

For *AR(0)*, we have:

$$AR(0) = \sum_{0 \leq i \leq u} d_i - \sum_{0 \leq i \leq u} e_i = \sum_{0 \leq i \leq u} (d_i - e_i) \qquad (9)$$

Compute Micro-architecture for f Ø g: Since Eq. (8) is similar to Eq. (3), this means that we can reuse and enhance the hardware micro-structure for $f \, Ø \, f$ to realize the general $f \, Ø \, g$ operation. Specifically, an *SubAcc unit* is added to the input part of the hardware circuit of $f \, Ø \, f$ to calculate function $f \, Ø \, g$, as shown in Fig. 4. When $f(t) = g(t)$, the diff_reg and AR_0 register are always zero in the *SubAcc unit* so they can be omitted and the circuit turns into $f \, Ø \, f$ with *N-1* items (BR_0 is always zero).

With the function in Eq. (7), for a $f \, Ø \, g$ curve with $t = N$ cycles, the total calculation operations are $N \times (1 + 3 + 5 + \dots + (2u + 1))$. When $u = N$, the computation complexity of the deconvolution operation is $O(N^2)$.

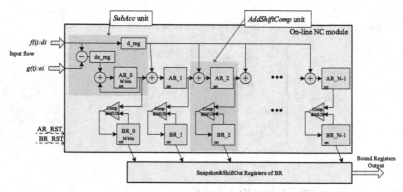

Fig. 4. Hardware micro-architecture for computing $f \, Ø \, g$

3.4   Micro-architecture for Function $f \otimes g$

Definition of Min-plus Convolution [2]: Let f and g be two functions or sequences. The min-plus convolution of f and g denoted by $f \otimes g$ is the function

$$(f \otimes g)(t) = \inf_{0 \leq s \leq t} \{f(t - s) + g(s)\} \qquad (10)$$

Compared to common convolution, min-plus convolution uses the *minimum* respectively *infimum* (*inf*) operator to replace the *sum* operator and the *sum* operator to replace the *product* operator. Suppose that $g(t)$ is an infinite data flow denoted by e_i and $f(t)$ denoted by d_i.

$$(f \otimes g)(t) = \inf_{0 \leq s \leq t} \{\sum_{0 \leq i \leq t-s} d_i + \sum_{0 \leq i \leq s} e_i\} \qquad (11)$$

Again, we can define *AR(t)* in the same way as in Sect. 3.1:

$$AR(t) = \sum_{0 \le i \le t-s} d_i + \sum_{0 \le i \le s} e_i = d_{t-s} + \sum_{0 \le i \le t-s-1} d_i + \sum_{0 \le i \le s} e_i = d_{t-s} + AR(t-1)$$

$$(12)$$

For $AR(0)$, we have:

$$AR(0) = d_0 + e_0 \tag{13}$$

Compute Micro-architecture of $f \otimes g$: Since Eq. (12) is similar to Eq. (3), we can reuse and enhance the hardware micro-structure for $f \varnothing f$ to realize the $f \otimes g$ operation. Specifically, a Mux unit is added to the hardware circuit of $f \varnothing f$ to deal with two inputs of $g(t)$ and $f(t)$, as shown in Fig. 5. There are two stages (Initial and Normal) when calculating function $f \otimes g$. The Initial Stage is to initialize the AR registers with $g(t)$ (input flow is e_{N-1}, e_{N-2}, e_1, e_0 cycle by cycle) by setting the control signal Mux_CTL. After the Initial Stage, the content of the ith AR register is $g(i)$ ($\sum_{0 \le j \le i} e_j$). The Normal Stage is to compute the function $f \otimes g$ by setting the control signal Mux_CTL to the $f(t)$ channel. The comparator is configured such that the smaller one of the two inputs is written into the BR register for the **inf** operation. The BL_CTL signals are added to enable each of the comparators to remove useless comparison results. The register content details for computing function $f \otimes g$ are similar to Table 1.

3.5 Unified Micro-architecture with Function Configuration

Combining these hardware micro-architectures by switches, we obtain a *unified configurable* hardware architecture for executing the network calculus functions as drawn in Fig. 5. The shared part is the central pipeline with AddShiftComp units, each of which contains $2M$-bit adders and 2 M-bit registers. Different network calculus operations are realized by adding switches on the Sampling unit (from the arrival curve unit in Fig. 1), SubAcc unit (from the $f \varnothing g$ unit in Fig. 4) and Mux unit (from the $f \otimes g$ unit). When configured to the arrival curve mode, d_i is switched to AddShiftComp units through the Sampling unit directly. When configured to the $f \varnothing g$ mode, d_i and e_i are switched to the SubAcc unit through each sampling unit. When configured to the $f \otimes g$ mode, d_i and e_i are switched to the Mux unit through each sampling unit.

The configurable hardware architecture generates results in one cycle because the N AddShiftComp units process data in parallel. In terms of resources, it costs only 1/3 of the non-configurable architecture which otherwise uses three individual hardware micro-architectures for the three network calculus functions. For a configurable hardware architecture with N units of AddShiftComp, the circuit only requires $2 \times N$ adders and $2 \times N$ registers with M-bit width. Thus, the hardware complexity is $O(N)$.

4   FPGA Implementation and Evaluation

We implemented the unified configurable pipeline hardware architecture on ZYNQ FPGA from Xilinx. The number of AddShiftComp units is N, the width of AR/BR register is M bits and the counter of sampling unit is C bits.

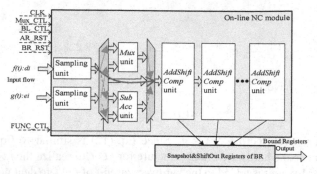

Fig. 5. Unified configurable pipeline hardware architecture for network calculus operations. The solid line is the datapath of configuration for arrival curve. (Dotted line: $f \oslash g$. Dashed line: $f \otimes g$)

We validated the three basic network calculus operations with models realized in MATLAB. When using the same sampling method and no overflows, the results of FPGA and MATLAB implementations are the same, because the configurable hardware architecture is designed accurately according to the recursive equations.

4.1 Performance Optimization

We further optimized the performance of the hardware design. Since the critical path of the circuit is the comparing and multiplexing of AR and BR, an additional register is inserted to the output of each comparator to shorten the critical path. Since the data path of input d_i to each adder has a big fan-out, an output register is added to the multiplexor.

Table 2 lists the FPGA implementation results ($N = 128, M = 16$) before and after the optimization. As can be seen, the register utilization is increased after the optimization. The total resources of LUT decrease by 25.2%. The frequency increases by 10.1%.

Table 2. Hardware implementation results. (AddShiftComp (N) = 128, AR/BR register (M) = 16)

Before Optimization		After Optimization	
Type	Value	Type	Value
LUT	6541	LUT	5222
registers	4096	registers	4112
Max Frequency	244.4 MHz	Max. Frequency	269.1 MHz

4.2 Scalability and Overhead

The required resource utilizations and the maximum frequencies of different design parameters (N AddShiftComp units and M bits width) are evaluated. As shown in Fig. 6, the required resource utilizations increase linearly and the maximum frequencies are stable around 250 MHz–280 MHz in the ZYNQ FPGA platform. These results show good scalability of the hardware architecture. When $N = 64$ & 128, the maximum frequency of $M = 16$ is a bit larger than $M = 24$ and $M = 32$. This is because the FPGA resources for logic synthesis of $M = 16$ can be limited in one hardware block region.

When using 128 AddShiftComp units and 16-bit width AR/BR registers, the FPGA resource of the configurable hardware architecture is about 6k LUTs. Compared with the area-overhead of a recent flow generator & monitor in [15], our configurable hardware architecture is acceptable. When computing the arrival curve with $N = 128$, it takes 3.7 ns on 269.1 MHz frequency to generate the result. With parallel computing in hardware, the execution time of the proposed circuit only depends on the maximum frequency. This means no matter how big N gets, it costs about the same time.

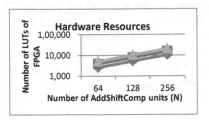 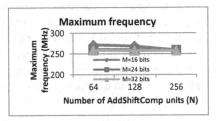

Fig. 6. Hardware resources and maximum frequencies on different design parameters

4.3 Comparison with Software Implementation

The Network Calculus such as arrival curve is computed only by software traditionlly. To obtain the speedup achieved by the specific hardware design, we realize an algorithm written in C language to do the arrival curve computation in software following the recursive function in Eqs. (2) and (3). The computer has an Intel Core i3-3240 CPU running at 3.4 GHz frequency. The operating system is Windows 7. With the same parameter as for the FPGA hardware, the length N for the arrival curve computation is set to 128. Completing the 128×2 calculation operations (comparison and addition) in Eqs. (2) and (3) takes 22.9 μs (memory accesses of CPU and the OS take most of the time). In contrast to the 3.7ns execution time in hardware, the hardware speedup is more than 6000 times.

5 System Prototype and Case Study

Researches on real-time analysis often focus on design-time (static) analysis of worst-case timing bounds. The validity of the derived bounds should however be monitored and analyzed at runtime to guarantee the system QoS. In our approach, by computing the accurate results of $f \otimes g, f \oslash g$, and $f \oslash f$ (arrival curve) at runtime, the hardware architecture can be incorporated in a runtime monitor to ensure that the input flow conforms to its specification and thus to facilitate dynamic QoS fulfillment.

Taking video data stream transfer as an example, we implemented the proposed hardware in a multimedia playback system, as shown in Fig. 7(a). The parameters ($N =$

128, M = 16, C = 12) were chosen by experience. The system is a NoC-based platform using two Xilinx Zynq FPGA evaluation boards (ZC702). Each ZC702 board contains an XC7Z020 SoC and provides peripheral ports including DDR3, HDMI port, SD card and two FMC (FPGA Mezzanine Card) connectors. The XC7Z020 SoC of Xilinx Zynq™-7000 Programmable SoC architecture integrates a dual-core ARM® Cortex™-A9 based Processing System (PS) and Xilinx Programmable Logic (PL).

The two ZC702 boards are connected by an FMC cable. With a router and other interface logic implemented in the PL, the two boards provide a hardware environment for evaluating our design for QoS. In each ZC702 board, the router has four ports and connects two ARM cores and two FMC ports, as shown in Fig. 7(b). The configurable hardware architecture is used as a runtime flow monitor attached to the arbitrator module for calculating the arrival curve so as to dynamically monitor and shape the input flow.

The prototype is constructed as a client-server system on the two Xilinx FPGA boards. The CPU Core_A in the sender board reads video frame data from the SD card and sends them to the other board (receiver board) through routers and the FMC cable. The software decoder running on the receiver CPU Core_A decodes the video frame data and sends them to the display through the HDMI port.

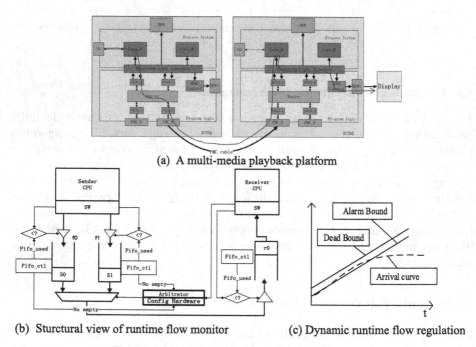

(a) A multi-media playback platform

(b) Sturctural view of runtime flow monitor   (c) Dynamic runtime flow regulation

Fig. 7. Application to a multi-media playback system

Regarding the arrival curve, we can define two experience-based bounds named Alarm Bound and Dead Bound at design time, as shown in Fig. 7(c). The alarm bound is nearer to the actual arrival curve than the dead bound. Violating the Dead Bound means that data transfers are not valid. Violating the Alarm Bound means that the system should take measures to prevent the possible violation of the dead bound. The arrival curve is calculated by the hardware implementation of our proposed architecture. The comparator of AR and BR is a violating-state indicator whenever a violation occurs.

The advantage of the proposed approach is that it can expose precise details of the behavior of the flow and service: not only if a bound is violated, but also which part violates and how much of violation. Beyond normal functionality, the approach can support finer analysis with more information. For example, when checking how tight the arrival curve bound of the input flow is, the tightest bound curve values from design-time analysis can be defined at each point and be preloaded into the BR registers. When a violation event $(AR(i) > BR(i))$ occurs, it is known that the ith time interval is violated and the volume of violation is calculated by the ith comparator. Such precise information enables the system to react to the violation for precise QoS provisioning.

6 Conclusion

To enable application of network calculus to satisfy QoS constraints at runtime, we have for the first time proposed a configurable hardware architecture to realize all essential network calculus operations for processing arrival and service curves. By configuring switches to different data paths, it can calculate arrival curve, min-plus convolution and min-plus deconvolution in a unified pipeline hardware substrate with only one cycle latency. This architecture is implemented and further optimized on an FPGA platform, showing high performance with reasonable resource cost. A case study of a multimedia playback for runtime arrival curve monitoring and QoS has been presented. By enabling to support network calculus operations at a full scale in dynamic environments, this study demonstrates the hardware implementation feasibility of bringing network calculus into action to achieve QoS at runtime beyond what is achievable at design time.

References

1. Cruz, R.L.: A calculus for network delay, part i: network elements in isolation; part ii: network analysis. IEEE Trans. Inf. Theory **37**(1), 114–131 (1991)
2. Boudec, J.-Y.L., Thiran, P.: Network Calculus: A Theory of Deterministic Queuing Systems for the Internet. LNCS, vol. 2050. Springer, Heidelberg (2004). https://doi.org/10.1007/3-540-45318-0
3. Chang, C.-S.: Performance Guarantees in Communication Networks. Springer, London (2000). https://doi.org/10.1007/978-1-4471-0459-9
4. Jiang, Y., Liu, Y.: Stochastic Network Calculus. Springer, London (2008). https://doi.org/10.1007/978-1-84800-127-5
5. Qian, Y., Zhonghai, L., Dou, W.: Analysis of worst-case delay bounds for on-chip packet-switching networks. IEEE Trans. Comput.-Aided Design Integr. Circuits Syst. **29**(5), 802–815 (2010)
6. Huang, K., Chen, G., Buckl, C., Knoll, A.: Conforming the runtime inputs for hard real-time embedded systems. In: Proceedings of the 49th Design Automation Conference (DAC) (2012)
7. Lu, Z., Zhao, X.: xMAS-based QoS analysis methodology. IEEE Trans. Comput. Aided Des. Integr. Circuits Syst. **37**(2), 364–377 (2018)

8. de Dinechin, B.D., Durand, Y., van Amstel, D., Ghiti, A.: Guaranteed services of the NoC of a manycore processor. In: Proceedings of International Workshop on Network on Chip Architecture, Cambridge, U.K., pp. 11–16 (2014)
9. Wandeler, E., Thiele, L., Verhoef, M., Lieverse, P.: System architecture evaluation using modular performance analysis: a case study. Int. J. Softw. Tools Technol. Transf. **8**(6), 649–667 (2006). https://doi.org/10.1007/s10009-006-0019-5
10. Lu, Z., Millberg, M., et al.: Flow regulation for on-chip communication. In: Proceeedings of 2009 Design, Automation and Test in Europe Conference (DATE), Nice, France, April 2009
11. Du, G., Li, M., et al.: An analytical model for worst-case reorder buffer size of multi-path minimal routing NoCs. In: Proceedings of International Symposium on Networks-on-Chip (NOCS), September 2014
12. Lu, Z., Wang, Y.: Dynamic flow regulation for IP integration on network-on-chip. In: The 6th ACM/IEEE International Symposium on Networks-on-Chip (NOCS), May 2012
13. Du, G., Ou, Y., et al.: OLITS: an Ohm's law-like traffic splitting model based on congestion prediction. In: Proceedings of 2016 Design, Automation and Test in Europe Conference, March 2016
14. Lu, Z., Yao, Y.: Dynamic traffic regulation in NoC-based systems. IEEE Trans. VLSI Syst. **25**(2), 556–569 (2017)
15. Du, G., Liu, G., et al.: SSS: self-aware system on chip using a static-dynamic hybrid method. ACM J. Emerg. Technol. Comput. Syst. **15**(3), 28 (2019)

FEB^3D: An Efficient FPGA-Accelerated Compression Framework for Microscopy Images

Wanqi Liu[1,2]($\boxtimes$), Yewen Li[1,2], Dawei Zang[1], and Guangming Tan[1,2]

[1] Institute of Computing Technology, Chinese Academy of Sciences,
Beijing 100095, China
{liuwanqi,liyewen,zangdawei,tgm}@ncic.ac.cn
[2] University of Chinese Academy of Sciences, Beijing 100049, China

Abstract. With the rapid development of fluorescence microscope technologies, high-content screening and light-sheet microscopy are producing ever-larger datasets that pose great challenges in data storing and data sharing. As a popular compression tool, B^3D introduces a noise dependent compression algorithm for microscopy images to preserve the numerical intensities of all pixel within their uncertainties by exploiting the natural variability of each pixel value. Nevertheless, the high complexity of the processing flow restricts the deployment of the tool since the throughput and power consumption cannot satisfy the increasing demand. In this paper, we propose an efficient FPGA-accelerated data compression framework based on B^3D. Following the co-design methodology, the compression processing flows are partitioned into different blocks to deploy on CPU or FPGA according to their computation characteristics. Also, we design a custom accelerator core that consists of multiple full on-chip pipelines using the channel function of the Intel OpenCL toolkit to implement data-flow driven computation. Our experiments show that the proposed framework achieves up to 32× throughput for a single pipeline compared with Intel Xeon E3-1220 v5 operating at 3.00 GHz, and 6× energy-efficiency compared with GPU implementation.

Keywords: Data compression · FPGA · Throughput

1 Introduction

Fluorescence microscope technologies such as the high-content screening, the single molecule localization microscopy, and the light-sheet microscopy provide new opportunities for biological research by increasing the speed of imaging, the number of specimens or the resolution of the observed structures [4]. Although these new technologies push biology to a new level, the production speed and volume of experimental image data at such a fast pace still pose a formidable challenge to data processing, storage, and transmission. For example, the rate

© IFIP International Federation for Information Processing 2021
Published by Springer Nature Switzerland AG 2021
X. He et al. (Eds.): NPC 2020, LNCS 12639, pp. 217–230, 2021.
https://doi.org/10.1007/978-3-030-79478-1_19

Table 1. Data sizes in microscopy devices.

	Imaging device	Image size	Frame rate	Data rate	Exp size
SPIM	2x sCMOS camera	2048 × 2048	50/s	800 MB/s	10 TB
SMLM	2x EMCCD camera	512 × 512	56/s	56 MB/s	500 GB
Screening	CCD camera	1344 × 1024	8.5/s	22 MB/s	5 TB
Confocal	Zeiss LSM 880	512 × 512	5.0/s	12.5 MB/s	50 GB
SPIM ×2	4x sCMOS camera	2048 × 2048	100/s	1600 MB/s	20 TB

of image data generated by single-plane illumination microscopy (SPIM) [5] is about 800 MB/s with 10 TB experiment size (Table 1). The real-time data handling becomes a bottleneck for new discoveries in many cases. A straightforward solution to this problem is to perform image compression.

Nonetheless, microscopy image compression generally means incompatibilities with previous tools, especially in the aspects of loss control, compression ratio, and compression speed. Unlike common photos that only need preserving those structures recognized by the human visual system, scientific images, however, are obtained through sets of quantitative measurements and therefore their compression should instead preserve the numerical values of all pixel intensities within their uncertainties [4]. Although the compression ratio (original size/compressed size) can be substantially increased with lossy compression algorithms such as JPEG2000 [13], their use is often discouraged as the loss of information depends heavily on the image content and cannot be explicitly controlled.

As a novel compression toolkit for microscopy image compression, B^3D [4,5] can compress microscopy images both in lossless mode and lossy mode with a better compression effect. In particular, its lossy mode introduces a noise dependent compression algorithm for microscopy images to preserve the numerical intensities of all pixel within their uncertainties by exploiting the natural variability of each pixel value. As a result, the user can specify the maximally tolerated pixel error in proportion to the inherent noise to control the information loss. Although B^3D can solve loss control and compression ratio problems of microscopy images compression, the high complexity of the processing flow restricts the deployment of the tool since the throughput and power consumption cannot satisfy the increasing demand, such as SPIM×2 (Table 1). For example, the throughput of single thread CPU implementation of B^3D is nearly 10 M/s, which cannot meet the requirement of data production speed for microscopy images.

In addition to CPU and GPU, Field Programmable Gate Array (FPGA) is another popular device used for algorithm acceleration because of its high parallelism, high energy efficiency, external connectivity [9], low latency, and so on. Its computation features are compatible with the characteristic of the critical blocks of B^3D. In this article, we propose an FPGA-accelerated data compression framework based on B^3D, called FEB^3D, to improve the throughput and energy efficiency of microscopy images compression tasks. Following the co-design methodology, the lossy and lossless processing flows are partitioned into different blocks to deploy on CPU or FPGA according to their computation characteristics. Also, we design a custom accelerator core that consists of multiple full on-chip pipelines using the channel function of the Intel OpenCL toolkit [1] to implement data-flow driven computation. Our contributions can be summarized as follows:

1. Following the co-design methodology, we propose an FPGA-accelerated data compression framework based on B^3D, called FEB^3D, by partitioning the compression processing flows into different blocks to deploy on CPU or FPGA according to their computation characteristics.
2. We design a custom accelerator consisting of multiple full on-chip pipelines, which use the channel function of the Intel OpenCL toolkit to implement data-flow driven computation. Each pipeline includes six-stages which correspond to six algorithm blocks.
3. We implement a prototype according to the proposed framework and methods. The results show that the prototype achieves up to 32× throughput for a single pipeline compared with Intel Xeon E3-1220 v5 operating at 3.00 GHz, and 6× energy-efficiency compared with GPU implementation.

The rest of this paper is organized as follows. In Sect. 2, we introduce various techniques used in image compression and background knowledge of CPU and FPGA co-design. In Sect. 3, we describe our hardware design, system collaboration, and further optimizations. In Sect. 4, we evaluate our design on Xeon CPU and Intel FPGA for microscopy images. In Sect. 5, we discuss the related works. In Sect. 6, we present our conclusion.

2   Background

2.1 B^3D Algorithm

Compression is a common and effective way to reduce the heavy burdens of massive data. Some commonly used compression algorithms such as deflate [7] only support the lossless mode and work well on sequence data. The image data compression algorithm like JPEG2000 supports lossy mode and works well on many kinds of images, but it comes at the cost of accuracy loss in the image transform domain (Fourier or Wavelet) so that the compression error of each pixel cannot be controlled and thus, is not suitable for scientific analysis. However, B^3D focuses on the microscopy image data compression, and adopts a strategy that compression errors can be controlled related to the standard deviation of the noise. It mainly involves five key steps: stabilizing transform, quantization [10], data prediction [15], run-length coding, and Huffman coding [11] (Fig. 1). Among them, the stabilizing transform and quantization are only used for the lossy mode. This paper mainly discusses the lossy mode. The detailed description of these steps is shown as follows.

- **Stabilizing transform.** This operation is the key to achieving B^3D error controlled lossy compression, including a nonlinear transformation, which transforms the input pixel intensity value to a new value, i.e., T (Eq. (1)) [6]. I is the intensity value, while the rest parameters are determined by imaging sensors.

- **Quantization.** To make the transformed values more similar, each value is quantified by q. For example, if q equals 1, the quantified value will only be the multiple of 1.

- **Data prediction.** After data quantization, B^3D predicts quantified T of each pixel based on its neighboring T values (the top and the left). Then the difference between the predicted value and the original value is calculated, and this difference is often small because neighboring pixel values are similar. This operation can make the values of the whole image more concentrated.

- **Run-length coding.** Run-length coding can encode a series of repeated values (difference) into the value itself and the number of consecutive occurrences (i.e., value and count). Thanks to the good local correlation of the microscopy image data, this coding operation is able to significantly reduce the data volume.

- **Huffman coding.** Finally, Huffman coding is performed to further compress the run-length coding results by encoding less frequent symbols with more bits.

$$T = 2\sqrt{(I - offset)g + \sigma^2} \tag{1}$$

The main operations used in B^3D are listed above. There are only three steps in the lossless mode, i.e., data prediction, run-length coding, and Huffman coding. Moreover, the order of the prediction and the quantization can be changed [5]. When the prediction is before the quantization, there is a serious data dependency because the neighbor values used in the prediction should be uncompressed by their own neighbor values (last cycle). Conversely, when the prediction is after the quantization, this dependency disappears. Within a certain quantization error range, the two modes above have their own advantages and disadvantages. In some cases, the former has a better compression ratio than the latter, but it is not good for the pipeline and can lead to bad performance in FPGA. We choose the latter eventually, which achieves high performance.

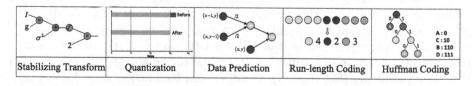

Fig. 1. Calculation steps in B^3D algorithm.

2.2 FPGA and OpenCL

Compared to CPU and GPU, FPGA provides a high level of parallelism, config-urability and high power efficiency that enables custom to implement dedicated high parallel pipelines suited to the particular needs of an application. For example, compression cores can be integrated with many specific pipelines that work parallel. In addition, various algorithmic choices can be altered depending on the characteristics of the data being processed. This flexibility may enable even higher levels of compression than a more general fixed approach, such as CPU and GPU. However, previous FPGA implementations were written in a hardware description language such as Verilog HDL or VHDL which are akin to assembly language for hardware. This makes FPGA design time-consuming and difficult to verify. Instead, OpenCL is a C-based language intended for application acceleration on heterogeneous systems. The use of OpenCL for FPGA implementation enables more productivity gains while maintaining high efficiency [3] as the generated system matches or exceeds the speed of prior work.

3 Design and Implementation

In this section, we describe the design and implementation of FEB^3D. Our main purpose is to improve the performance and energy efficiency of B^3D by mapping and optimizing the algorithm on the FPGA-accelerated platform. Therefore, we focus on the five main steps of B^3D, analyze the characteristics of the data path and each computing kernel, and then design a framework suitable for FPGA-accelerated implementation (Sect. 3.1). Moreover, we describe the optimized design of each kernel in detail (Sect. 3.2). In Sect. 3.3, we use further optimization methods to make our compressor work better. As already mentioned before, B^3D has both lossy and lossless modes. We mainly describe the design of lossy mode, and the lossless mode is the same as the lossy mode after removing two kernels (i.e., stabilizing transform and quantization).

3.1 The Co-design Framework

Modular and systematic thinking is extremely important for mapping software algorithms to FPGA-accelerated co-design frameworks. Therefore, we divide the tasks of the B^3D algorithm into several parts, and each part is processed by its own suitable computing resources (CPU or FPGA). Of course, most of the computing load is allocated to FPGA in our design because of its rich computing units, good parallelism, and flexible data path. In order to better divide and assign the computing tasks, we analyze the data path and the computing characteristics of the algorithm, respectively.

- **Data path.** According to the execution order of the B^3D algorithm, the microscopy image data requires to be loaded first. Then the original pixel values should be transformed into the floating-point data which remain the

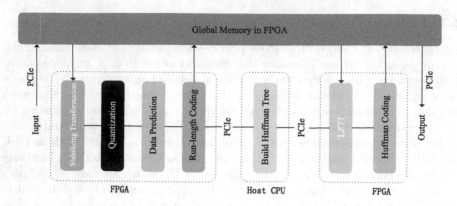

Fig. 2. Overall co-design framework of FEB^3D.

same number before and after. Next, the transformed values above are quantified by the quantization step q and the quantified values are then predicted by their neighbors, and we obtain the differences between their predicted values and themselves by simple subtraction. Furthermore, the differences are encoded to a series of data pairs, which include two values, i.e., the difference and its count. After the run-length coding, generally, the total number of data is significantly reduced. In addition, the differences and the counts are used to build a Huffman table, and then they are encoded by this Huffman table. The output data of the Huffman coding is a bitstream. At the end of the compression process, this bitstream is written to a file in a particular format. The data path from the original image to the compressed file is as described above. Obviously, the entire calculation process is streaming, which is suitable for pipeline design.

- **Computing characteristics.** One of the most critical features of B^3D is the error control, which is implemented by stabilizing transform. In order to avoid the reduction of compression ratio and compressed image quality, the transformed value should be the floating-point type. Therefore, there are a large number of floating-point calculations in this algorithm, which is a heavy computing burden for the CPU because of its relative lack of computing resources. Moreover, there are some complex operations like square root (Eq. (1)) in the step of the stabilizing transform and division operations in the quantization, which are also not the CPU friendly computing characteristics. This algorithm has a high degree of data parallelism, hence, FPGA is able to take advantage of its computing resources and get better parallel design. 90% of the computing time is spent on data loading, stabilizing transform, quantization, data prediction, run-length coding and generation of Huffman codes implemented on FPGA, and the rest 10% of time consumption is for constructing Huffman tree implemented on CPU. LAWRENCE L. LARMORE et al. [12] proposed a method to construct Huffman tree in parallel, but for us it is hard to be implemented efficiently on FPGA. This will be considered as the future work.

Based on the analysis above, we can draw the following ideas about the co-design framework of FEB^3D as Fig. 2.

1. According to the analysis of the computing characteristics, we can come up with the allocation plan for the computing tasks: The construction of the Huffman tree is assigned to the CPU, and the rest is assigned to the FPGA.
2. The pipeline design is good for implementing this algorithm. We build a six-stage pipeline, including data loading, stabilizing transform, quantization, prediction, run-length coding, and Huffman coding. The first five kernels are communicated via FIFO, and the last kernel is connected with CPU, communicated via PCIe.

3.2 Hardware Optimized Design

After the framework of the algorithm is determined, each computing kernel requires to be implemented on the hardware, i.e., FPGA. Furthermore, in order to achieve higher performance, we optimize the hardware level design based on the characteristics of each kernel, and also fully consider the connection between kernels (Fig. 3).

We notice that for the pipeline design, both the execution speed of each single computing kernel and the balance between each kernel speed are equally significant. For instance, if most of the kernels are running slow (without effective optimizations), the overall performance will undoubtedly be very tremendously low. On the other hand, if there is only one bad-performance kernel (the other kernels perform well), this bad-performance kernel will become the performance bottleneck of the entire system, which seriously reduces the overall performance. For the reasons above, we follow the two principles below when optimizing the hardware design: The first is to accelerate each computing kernel as much as we can and the second is to reduce the performance difference between the six kernels as much as possible.

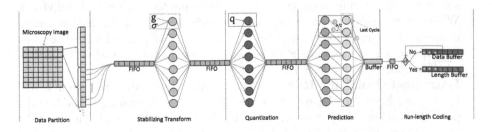

Fig. 3. Data flow and hardware optimized design.

- **Data loading.** This is the first kernel performed on FPGA. In our design, the microscopy image data (TIFF, such as Zebrafish) is read from the disk to the memory by CPU, and then we use the OpenCL function interface to write the data in the CPU memory to the global memory of the FPGA via PCIe. When the above process is completed, FPGA reads data from its global memory. Considering the advantages of the FPGA, we read a block of data in one cycle, i.e., eight unsigned short integers (Type $ushort8$ in the OpenCL), instead of a single unsigned short integer. This operation is effective for FPGA because of the increasing of the reading rate, which also reflects the flexibility of the data type and the data path on FPGA. During the same cycle, this kernel writes an $unshort8$ variable (containing eight unsigned short integers, i.e., sixteen bytes) to the FIFO, and then waits for the next cycle. This $ushort8$ variable is stored in the latch (consists of on-chip logic units, not the memory), which is the fastest way. The main operations of this kernel are the data reading (global memory) and the data writing (FIFO) rather than the complex calculation. Therefore, the speed of the data loading kernel is high.
- **Stabilizing transform.** This is the second kernel performed on FPGA, which is aimed to transform the input data to another data with Eq. (1), based on the camera parameters (such as the read noise). The input data of this kernel in a cycle is an $ushort8$ variable, received from the data loading kernel via FIFO. The data parallelism of this kernel is tremendously high, because there is nearly no dependency on the input $ushort8$ variable, i.e., eight unsigned short variables. In other words, these eight variables are calculated by themselves, using Eq. (1), and mapped to the hardware, which means that there are eight computing units performed in parallel during the same cycle. Although the computing complexity of Eq. (1) is not low, this concurrent design helps the stabilizing transform kernel achieve good performance. The output of this kernel is an $float8$ variable (i.e., eight floating-point variables), which is then written to the FIFO at the end of this cycle.
- **Data quantization.** In our design, the data quantization is the third kernel. As mentioned before (Sect. 2.1), there will be severe data dependency if the prediction is performed before the quantization. Therefore we choose the scheme that the prediction is performed after the quantization. As for a single variable, the quantization step includes multiplication and a division. When the transformed $float8$ variable is received by the quantization kernel, these eight floating-point variables are calculated in parallel with the same operations. The output of the quantization kernel is also an $float8$ variable, which is then sent to the FIFO.
- **Data prediction and Run-length coding.** The data prediction kernel is the fourth. After the quantization of eight floating-point variables, the predicted values ($float$) are calculated by their neighbors (i.e., the left and the top), and the differences ($float$) between the predicted values and the original values are obtained in parallel. In Fig. 3, the top comes from the last cycle. Unlike the previous kernels, the output of the prediction kernel is not $float8$, but $float$. The reason is that the run-length kernel will be obviously slower

than others if eight floating-point variables are processed in the run-length
kernel together. The run-length step compares the neighbors, and records
the counts one by one, limited by data dependence, thereby leading to bad
performance. We adopt a pipeline design on FPGA, so the performance of
the kernels requires to be balanced. In order to solve this problem, we adopt
a data buffering strategy, which means that during one cycle, the prediction
kernel only sends a single $float$ variable to the run-length kernel via FIFO,
and the rest seven $float$ variables are stored in the latch, waiting for the next
cycle. As for the run-length kernel, the input is a $float$ variable. At the end
of this kernel, three kinds of variables are written to the global memory, i.e.,
values, values counts, and the length of data, and after that they are sent
to the CPU via PCIe for constructing the Huffman tree and obtaining the
Huffman table.

- **LZ77 & Huffman coding.** In our design, in order to get a better compression ratio, the Huffman coding kernel is updated to the LZ77 [18] and
  Huffman kernel, based on the proposal of Mohamed S. Abdelfattah et al.
  [3]. This is the last kernel on FPGA. The inputs are the outputs of the run-
  length kernel and the Huffman table computed by CPU. The outputs are a
  bitstream and CPU reads it via PCIe. It is worth noting that this kernel is
  not the bottleneck (nearly 3GB/s), and the throughput of the whole design
  is no more than 2GB/s.

3.3 Further Optimizations

In addition to the framework design and specific hardware optimized design, we
also propose further optimizations for higher performance as follows.

1. **Further Parallelism and Data Partition.** The previous proposed six-
   stage flow design is with a single pipeline. Today, there are abundant resources
   on FPGA, making it possible to duplicate multiple pipelines (parallel execution). Moreover, the data loading, the stabilizing transform, the data quantization, the data prediction, and the run-length coding kernels are tremendously lightweight. Therefore, we duplicate five copies of the above kernels.
   This further parallelism makes use of the bandwidth of PCIe and the resources
   of FPGA, which further improves performance (nearly 6×). Correspondingly,
   in order to cope with the pipeline duplication, the data partition is necessary.
   As is shown in Fig. 3, We divide the image data by row, and each pipeline
   processes multiple rows. Moreover, it is worth noting that the number of rows
   is required to be at least two because the predicted value is calculated by its
   left value and its top value, as shown in Sect. 2.1. The data partition can
   influence the compress ratio, and the number of rows is able to be adjusted.
2. **The Strategy of Building Huffman Tree.** Building the Huffman tree is
   processed on CPU, which nearly takes up 10% of the whole time. In order
   to further improve performance, we need to reduce the time consumption of
   this step. We put together one hundred images into a single image, and build
   the Huffman tree for this single image instead of building a hundred trees.

Furthermore, inspired by Bulent Abali et al. [2], w e notice that it takes a long time to count the frequency of each symbol for building the Huffman tree because of the passing of massive input data. Therefore, We only count the frequencies of a part of the input data (10%), selected randomly.

4 Experiment and Evaluation

4.1 Experimental Setup

- **Platform.** There are three different experimental platforms, including CPU, GPU and FPGA. The CPU is an Intel Xcon E3-1220 v5 (80W) running at 3.00 GHZ. The GPU is an NVIDIA GeForce GTX 970 (165W) graphics processing unit, which is used by Bálint Balázs et al. [4]. The last platform is a Intel Arria 10 GX FPGA (42W) device. The above platforms are of similar magnitude (None of them are the latest products). Our design is implemented with Intel OpenCL SDK. Software designs are compiled using Microsoft Visual Studio 2012. Moreover, We use the Intel OpenCL IP function $write\_channel\_intel()$ for the FIFO design.
- **Datasets.** We use two kinds of fluorescence microscopy image data as our datasets. One is the images of Zebrafish, and the another is the images of the brain of Caenorhabditis elegans. There are 100 images (400 M in size) in both two datasets.
- **Baselines.** We have two baselines for comparison: our implementation of CPU-based B^3D using C++ and the B^3D library based on GPU, proposed by Bálint Balázs et al. [4,5].

4.2 Results and Analysis

In our design, a key point is to reduce the bottleneck of the pipeline, so that the data flow is executed quickly and smoothly. As is described in Sect. 3.2, the execution time of the run-length coding kernel is significantly longer than other kernels, making it a main bottleneck of the pipeline. Therefore, we design a buffer in the prediction kernel to reduce the burden of the run-length coding kernel (Fig. 3). We adjust the buffer size and measure the execution time and resource consumption of the first five pipeline stages. As is shown in Fig. 4, the larger the buffer size, the shorter the running time and the lower the resource usage. The reason for shortened running time is that the larger buffer can better balance execution time of the first five kernels (8 is enough). The resource is saved is because the larger buffer reduces the hardware complexity of the run-length coding kernel, which saves far more resources than that brought about by a larger buffer.

We compare our FPGA-accelerated design with the above baselines. We refer the single pipeline design as FPGA, and the further optimized FPGA as the design with six pipelines (excepts LZ77 and Huffman coding) and the use of the strategy of building the Huffman tree in Sect. 3.3.

Table 2. Throughput of CPU and FPGA implementation (MB/s).

	CPU	CPU×8	FPGA	FPGA(FO)
Zebrafish	9	46	285	1782
Elegans	6	31	205	1282

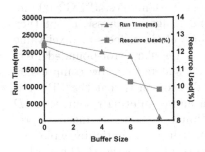

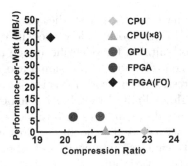

Fig. 4. Buffer sizes.   Fig. 5. Efficiency and ratios.

1. **FPGA versus CPU.** We evaluate our FPGA-accelerated design and the CPU implementation on the above two datasets. As is shown in Table 2, the throughput of FPGA design far exceeds that of single-thread CPU (32×). Even for the multi-thread CPU implementation (×8), the performance is worse than the single pipeline FPGA design. Moreover, the performance-per-watt of FPGA is also better than that of CPU (Fig. 5). The compression ratio of FPGA is lower because of the parallelism design and reducing symbols of the frequency count (Sect. 3.3).
2. **FPGA versus GPU.** GPU implementation enjoy high performance (beyond 1 GB/s). From Fig. 5 we can know that the performance-per-watt of the single pipeline FPGA-based design is close to that of GPU because of the high power consumption of GPU and the further optimized one is much better than GPU (6×).
3. **Resource utilization.** Table 3 demonstrates that the first five kernels consume far fewer resources than the last kernel (LZ77 and Huffman) so that we can duplicate multiple copies for the fist five kernels.

Table 3. Resource utilization from synthesis for single pipeline.

Kernel name	ALUTs	FFs	RAMs	DSPs
Load data	2291	2188	13	0
Photon transform	9477	6407	24	29
Prediction	2677	2964	0	8
Quantization	14801	10133	37	36
rle coding	5080	12660	82	0
lz77 huffman	315228	149105	1430	0
Total	**430317 (55%)**	**341658 (22%)**	**1873 (75%)**	**140 (10%)**

5   Related Work

There have been many studies on data compression techniques. JPEG2000 and LZW [14] are both widely used in conventional image compression, but they are not suitable for scientific image data because of the defects of pixel value error control and compression ratio. SZ [8] is a popular error-bounded lossy compression framework for scientific data, but it suffers from low compression throughput limited by CPU implementation. The reason is that the CPU has hardware disadvantages in terms of parallelism and computing resources. B^3D introduce a noise dependent compression algorithm for microscopy images to preserve the numerical intensities of all pixel within their uncertainties by exploiting the natural variability of each pixel values. However, CPU-based B^3D has a low throughput, which cannot meet the requirement of the microscopy image data production rate obviously. GPU-based lossless B^3D gets a performance improvement compared to the CPU implementation, but the power consumption is also really high. Moreover, GPU generally improves performance through SIMT (single instruction, multiple threads) [16], accompanied by a certain synchronization overhead. Field programmable gate array (FPGA) is popular in the algorithm acceleration field because of its configurability, high energy efficiency, low latency, external connection, and so on. Xiong et al. proposed GhostSZ [17], and Tian et al. proposed WaveSZ [16], both of them implemented SZ algorithm based on FPGA and got performance improvement. B^3D is more suitable for microscopy image data because the stabilizing transform step is based on camera parameters, and the run-length coding step is also suitable for this kind of image data. As we know, FEB^3D is the first FPGA-accelerated framework based on B^3D, and we improve both throughput and energy efficiency through customized hardware co-design.

6   Conclusion

In this work, we propose an efficient FPGA-accelerated data compression framework called FEB^3D, which can improve the performance and the energy efficiency of B^3D, an effective compression algorithm for fluorescence microscopy images both in lossy and lossless modes. We properly assign the computing tasks to FPGA and CPU, and design each hardware kernel according to their characteristics. Moreover, we also adopt further optimizations both in hardware and software in order to further improve performance. The throughput of this framework far exceeds the CPU implementation ($32\times$ for the single pipeline), and the performance-per-watt of the further optimized FPGA design is about $6\times$ higher than that of the GPU implementation.

Acknowledgments. This work is supported by the National Natural Science Foundation of China under grant no. 61902373, is supported by Strategic Priority Research Program B of the Chinese Academy of Sciences under grant no. XDB24050300, grant no. XDB44030300.

References

1. Intel FPGAs and Programmable Devices - Intel FPGA. https://www.intel.com/content/www/us/en/products/programmable.html. Library Catalog: www.intel.com
2. Abali, B., Blaner, B., Reilly, J., Klein, M., Mishra, A., Agricola, C.B.: Data compression accelerator on IBM POWER9 and z15 processors. In: ISCA. IEEE, Los Angeles (2020)
3. Abdelfattah, M.S., Hagiescu, A., Singh, D.: Gzip on a chip: high performance lossless data compression on FPGAs using OpenCL. In: IWOCL, pp. 1–9. ACM Press, Bristol (2014)
4. Balázs, B., Deschamps, J., Albert, M., Ries, J., Hufnagel, L.: A real-time compression library for microscopy images. bioRxiv, July 2017
5. Balázs, B., Deschamps, J., Albert, M., Ries, J., Hufnagel, L.: A real-time compression library for microscopy images - supplementary notes and figures. bioRxiv, p. 15 (2017)
6. Bernstein, G.M., Bebek, C., Rhodes, J., Stoughton, C., Vanderveld, R.A., Yeh, P.: Noise and bias in square-root compression schemes. Publ. Astron. Soc. Pac. **122**(889), 336–346 (2010)
7. Deutsch, P.: DEFLATE compressed data format specification version 1.3. Techical report RFC1951, RFC Editor, May 1996
8. Di, S., Cappello, F.: Fast error-bounded lossy HPC data compression with SZ. In: 2016 IEEE International Parallel and Distributed Processing Symposium (IPDPS), pp. 730–739. IEEE, Chicago, May 2016
9. Geng, Tet al.: O3BNN: an out-of-order architecture for high-performance binarized neural network inference with fine-grained pruning. In: Proceedings of the ACM International Conference on Supercomputing, pp. 461–472. ACM, Phoenix Arizona, June 2019
10. Gray, R., Neuhoff, D.: Quantization. IEEE Trans. Inf. Theory **44**(6), 2325–2383 (1998). Conference Name: IEEE Transactions on Information Theory
11. Huffman, D.: A method for the construction of minimum-redundancy codes. Proc. IRE **40**(9), 1098–1101 (1952)
12. Larmore, L.L., Przytycka, T.M.: Constructing Huffman trees in parallel. SIAM J. Comput. **24**(6), 1163–1169 (1995)
13. Rabbani, M., Joshi, R.: An overview of the JPEG 2000 still image compression standard. Signal Process.: Image Commun. **17**(1), 3–48 (2002)

14. Savari, S.A.: Redundancy of the Lempel-Ziv-Welch code. In: Proceedings of the Data Compression Conference, DCC 1997 (1997)
15. Tao, D., Di, S., Chen, Z., Cappello, F.: Significantly improving lossy compression for scientific data sets based on multidimensional prediction and error-controlled quantization. In: 2017 IEEE International Parallel and Distributed Processing Symposium (IPDPS), pp. 1129–1139. IEEE, Orlando, May 2017
16. Tian, J., et al.: waveSZ: a hardware-algorithm co-design of efficient lossy compression for scientific data. In: PPoPP, pp. 74–88. ACM, San Diego, February 2020
17. Xiong, Q., Patel, R., Yang, C., Geng, T., Skjellum, A., Herbordt, M.C.: GhostSZ: a transparent FPGA-accelerated lossy compression framework. In: FCCM, pp. 258–266. IEEE, San Diego, April 2019
18. Ziv, J., Lempel, A.: A universal algorithm for sequential data compression. IEEE Trans. Inform. Theory **23**(3), 337–343 (1977)

NUMA-Aware Optimization of Sparse Matrix-Vector Multiplication on ARMv8-Based Many-Core Architectures

Xiaosong Yu[1], Huihui Ma[1], Zhengyu Qu[1], Jianbin Fang[2], and Weifeng Liu[1(✉)]

[1] Super Scientific Software Laboratory, Department of Computer Science
and Technology, China University of Petroleum-Beijing, Beijing, China
{2019215847,2019211254,2019215846}@student.cup.edu.cn,
weifeng.liu@cup.edu.cn
[2] Institute for Computer Systems, College of Computer, National University
of Defense Technology, Changsha, China
j.fang@nudt.edu.cn

Abstract. As a fundamental operation, sparse matrix-vector multiplication (SpMV) plays a key role in solving a number of scientific and engineering problems. This paper presents a NUMA-Aware optimization technique for the SpMV operation on the `Phytium 2000+` ARMv8-based 64-core processor. We first provide a performance evaluation of the NUMA architecture of the `Phytium 2000+` processor, then reorder the input sparse matrix with hypergraph partitioning for better cache locality, and redesign the SpMV algorithm with NUMA tools. The experimental results on `Phytium 2000+` show that our approach utilizes the bandwidth in a much more efficient way, and improves the performance of SpMV by an average speedup of 1.76x on `Phytium 2000+`.

Keywords: Sparse matrix-vector multiplication · NUMA
architecture · Hypergraph partitioning · `Phytium 2000+`

1 Introduction

The sparse matrix-vector multiplication (SpMV) operation multiples a sparse matrix A with a dense vector x and gives a resulting dense vector y. It is one of the level 2 sparse basic linear algebra subprograms (BLAS) [13], and is one of the most frequently called kernels in the field of scientific and engineering computations. Its performance normally has a great impact on sparse iterative solvers such as conjugate gradient (CG) method and its variants [17].

To represent the sparse matrix, many storage formats and their SpMV algorithms have been proposed to save memory and execution time. Since SpMV generally implements algorithms with a very low ratio of floating-point calculations to memory accesses, and its accessing patterns can be very irregular, it is a typical memory-bound and latency-bound algorithm. Currently, many

© IFIP International Federation for Information Processing 2021
Published by Springer Nature Switzerland AG 2021
X. He et al. (Eds.): NPC 2020, LNCS 12639, pp. 231–242, 2021.
https://doi.org/10.1007/978-3-030-79478-1_20

SpMV optimization efforts have achieved performance improvements to various degrees, but lack consideration on utilizing NUMA (non-uniform memory access) characteristics of a wide range of modern processors, such as ARM CPUs.

To obtain scale-out benefits on modern multi-core and many-core processors, NUMA architectures is often an inevitable choice. Most modern x86 processors (e.g., AMD EPYC series) and ARM processors (e.g., Phytium 2000+) utilize NUMA architecture for building a processor with tens of cores. To further increase the number of cores in a single node, multiple (typically two, four or eight) such processor modules are integrated onto a single motherboard and are connected through high-speed buses. But such scalable design often brings stronger NUMA effects, i.e., giving noticeable lower bandwidth and larger latency when cross-NUMA accesses occur.

To improve the SpMV performance on modern processors, we in this work develop a NUMA-Aware SpMV approach. We first reorder the input sparse matrix with hypergraph partitioning tools, then allocate a row block of A and the corresponding part of x for different NUMA nodes, and pin threads onto hardware cores of the NUMA nodes for running parallel SpMV operation. Because the reordering technique can organize the non-zeros in A on diagonal blocks and naturally brings the affinity between the blocks and the vector x, the data locality of accessing x can be significantly improved.

We benchmark 15 sparse matrices from the SuiteSparse Matrix Collection [3] on a 64-core ARMv8-based Phytium 2000+ processor. We set the number of hypergraph partitions to 2, 4, 8, 16, 32 and 64, and set the number of threads to 8, 16, 32, and 64, then measure the performance of their combinations. The experimental results show that, compared to classical OpenMP SpMV implementation, our NUMA-Aware approach greatly improves the SpMV performance by 1.76x on average (up to 2.88x).

2   Background

2.1   Parallel Sparse Matrix-Vector Multiplication

Sparse matrices can be represented with various storage formats, and SpMV with different storage formats often has noticeable performance differences [1]. The most widely-used format is the compressed sparse row (CSR) containing three arrays for row pointers, column indices and values. The SpMV algorithm using the CSR format can be parallelized by assigning a group of rows to a thread. Algorithm 1 shows the pseudocode of an OpenMP parallel SpMV method with the CSR format.

2.2   NUMA Architecture of the Phytium 2000+ Processor

Figure 1 gives a high-level view of the Phytium 2000+ processor. It uses the Mars II architecture [16], and features 64 high-performance ARMv8 compatible xiaomi cores running at 2.2 GHz. The entire chip offers a peak performance

Algorithm 1. An OpenMP implementation of parallel SpMV.

1: #pragma omp parallel for
2: **for** $i = 0 \rightarrow A.row\_nums$ **do**
3:    $y[i] = 0$
4:    **for** $j = A.rowptr[i] \rightarrow A.rowptr[i+1]$ **do**
5:       $y[i] = y[i] + A.val[j] * x[A.col[j]]$
6:    **end for**
7: **end for**

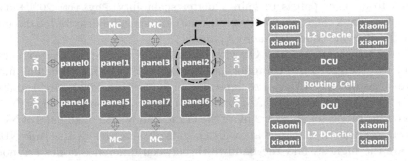

Fig. 1. A high-level view of the `Phytium 2000+` architecture. Processor cores are groups into panels (left) where each panel contains eight ARMv8 based Xiaomi cores (right).

	node0	node1	node2	node3	node4	node5	node6	node7
node0	16.83	15.88	13.88	14.89	15.14	14.58	12.20	13.15
node1	15.53	16.78	14.55	15.28	14.93	15.27	13.49	14.34
node2	14.29	14.89	16.90	15.63	12.80	13.35	15.51	14.06
node3	14.92	15.56	15.98	17.39	13.37	14.55	14.50	15.29
node4	15.40	14.01	12.59	12.64	17.78	15.76	13.94	14.62
node5	13.91	14.92	13.29	13.75	16.13	17.30	14.75	15.42
node6	11.93	12.57	14.77	14.48	13.75	14.43	16.71	16.22
node 7	13.04	13.65	14.94	15.44	14.49	15.50	15.55	16.89

Fig. 2. STREAM triad bandwidth test on `Phytium 2000+`.

of 563.2 Gflops for double-precision operations, with a maximum power consumption of 96 W. The 64 hardware cores are organized into 8 `panels`, where each panel connects a memory control unit.

The panel architecture of `Phytium 2000+` is shown in the right part of Fig. 1. It can be seen that each panel has eight `xiaomi` cores, and each core has a private L1 cache of 32KB for data and instructions, respectively. Every four cores form a `core group` and share a 2MB L2 cache. The L2 cache of `Phytium` 2000+ uses an *inclusive* policy, i.e., the cachelines in L1 are also present in L2.

Each panel contains two Directory Control Units (`DCU`) and one `routing cell`. The `DCU`s on each panel act as dictionary nodes of the entire on-chip network. With these function modules, `Mars II` conducts a hierarchical on-chip network, with a local interconnect on each panel and a global connect for the entire chip. The former couples cores and L2 cache slices as a local cluster, achieving a good data locality. The latter is implemented by a configurable cell-network to connect panels to gain a better scalability. `Phytium` 2000+ uses a home-grown `Hawk` cache coherency protocol to implement a distributed directory-based global cache coherency across panels.

We run a customized Linux OS with Linux Kernel v4.4 on the `Phytium` 2000+ system. We use gcc v8.2.0 compiler and the OpenMP/POSIX threading model.

We measure NUMA-Aware bandwidth of `Phytium` 2000+ by running a Pthread version of the STREAM bandwidth code [15] bound to eight NUMA nodes on the processor. Figure 2 plots the `triad` bandwidth of all pairs of NUMA nodes. It can be seen that the bandwidth results obtained inside the same NUMA node are the highest, and the bandwidth between difference nodes are noticeable much lower. On `Phytium` 2000+, the maximum bandwidth within the same nodes is 17.78 GB/s, while the bandwidth of cross-border access can be down to only 11.93 GB/s. The benchmark results further motivate us to design a NUMA-Aware SpMV approach for better utilizing the NUMA architectures.

2.3   Hypergraph Partitioning

Hypergraph can be seen as a general form of graph. A hypergraph is often denoted by $H = (V, E)$, where V is a vertex set, and E is a hyperedge set. A hyperedge can link more than two vertices, which is different to an edge in a graph [18]. A hypergraph can also correspond to a sparse matrix through the row-net model (columns and rows are vertices and hyperedges, respectively).

The hypergraph partitioning problem divides a hypergraph into a given number of partitions, and each partition includes roughly the same number of vertices. Its effect is that the connections between different partitions can be minimized. Thus when hypergraph partitioning is used for distributed SpMV, both load balancing (because the sizes of the partitions are almost the same) and less remote memory accesses (because connections between partitions are reduced) can be obtained for better performance [4,17,22]. In this work, we use PaToH v3.0 [19,23] as the hypergraph partitioning tool for preparing the sparse matrices for our NUMA-Aware SpMV implementation.

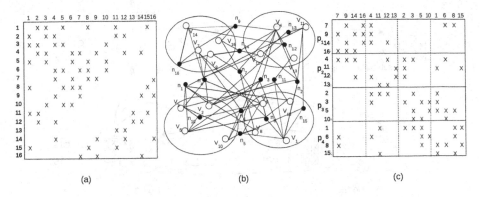

Fig. 3. (a) An original sparse matrix A of size 16×16, (b) A row-net representation of hypergraph H of matrix A, and a four-way partitioning of H, (c) The matrix A reordered according to the hypergraph partitioning. As can be seen, the non-zero entries in the reordered matrix are gathered onto the diagonal blocks, meaning that the number of connections between the four partitions are reduced.

3   NUMA-Aware SpMV Alogrithm

The conventional way of parallelizing SpMV is by assigning distinct rows to different threads. But the irregularity of accessing x through indirect indices of the non-zeros of A may degrade the overall performance a lot. To address the issue, considering the memory accessing characteristics of the NUMA architecture, storing a group of rows of A and part of the vector x most needed by the rows onto the same NUMA node should in general bring a performance improvement. In this way, the cross-node memory accesses (i.e., accessing the elements of x not stored on the local node) can be largely avoided.

To this end, we first need to partition the hypergraph form of a sparse matrix. Figure 3 plots an example showing the difference between a matrix before and after reordering according to hypergraph partitioning. It can be seen that some of the non-zero elements of the matrix move to the diagonal blocks. The number of non-zeros in the off-diagonal blocks in Fig. 3(a) is 48, but in Fig. 3(c), the number is reduced to 38.

After the reordering, the matrix is divided into sub-matrices i.e. row blocks, and the vector is also divided into sub-vectors. For example, the matrix in Fig. 3 now includes four sub-matrices of four rows. Then we use the memory allocation API in libnuma-2.0 [2] to allocate memory for the sub-matrices and sub-vectors on each NUMA node. Figure 4 demonstrates this procedure, and Algorithm 2 lists the pseudocode. As can be seen, the local memory of each NUMA node contains one sub-matrices of four rows and one sub-vector of four elements. In Algorithm 2, the *start* and *end* (line 3) represent the beginning and the end of the row positions for each thread, and the $Xpos$ and *remainder* (line 6) are used to locate the vector x needed for local calculation.

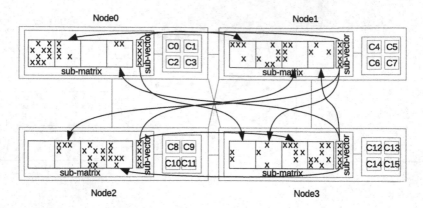

Fig. 4. The computational process of the NUMA-Aware SpMV algorithm on a 16-core four-node NUMA system. The four row blocks of the sparse matrix in Fig. 3(c) are allocated onto the four nodes, and the four sub-vectors are also evenly distributed. When computing SpMV, the cross-node memory accesses for remote x are visualized by using lines with arrows.

When the matrix and vector are allocated, our algorithm creates Pthread threads and bind them to the corresponding NUMA nodes (lines 10–12 in Algorithm 2). For the example in Fig. 4, we issue and bind four threads to each NUMA node and let each one computes a row of the sub-matrix allocated on the same NUMA node (lines 1–9). Since the memory on the node only stores a part of the full vector, the threads will access both the local sub-vector and the remote ones. In the example in Fig. 4, the threads in NUMA node 0 will also access the sub-vectors stored in nodes 1 and 4.

Algorithm 2. A NUMA-Aware Pthread implementation of parallel SpMV.

1: **function** $SpMV$
2:     $numa\_run\_on\_node(numanode)$
3:     **for** $i = start \rightarrow end$ **do**
4:         $suby[i] = 0$
5:         **for** $j = A.subrowptr[i] \rightarrow A.subrowptr[i+1]$ **do**
6:             $suby[i] = suby[i] + A.subval[j] * subx[Xpos][remainder]$
7:         **end for**
8:     **end for**
9: **end function**
10: **for** $i = 0 \rightarrow thread\_nums$ **in parallel do**
11:     $pthread\_create(\&thread[i], NULL, SpMV, (void*)parameter)$
12: **end for**
13: **for** $i = 0 \rightarrow thread\_nums$ **in parallel do**
14:     $pthread\_join(thread[i], NULL)$
15: **end for**

---

4   Performance and Analysis

4.1   Experimental Setup and Dataset

In this work, we benchmark 15 sparse matrices from the SuiteSparse Matrix Collection [3] (formerly known as the University of Florida Sparse Matrix Collection). The 15 sparse matrices include seven regular and eight irregular ones. The classification is mainly based on the distribution of non-zero elements. The non-zero elements of regular matrices are mostly located on diagonals, while those of irregular matrices are distributed in a pretty random way. We in Table 1 list the 15 original sparse matrices and their reordered forms generated by the PaToH library. Each matrix is divided into 2, 4, 8, 16, 32 and 64 partitions, and reordered according to the partitions. In terms of the sparsity structures of these matrices, as the number of partitions increases, the non-zero elements will move towards the diagonal blocks.

We measure the performance of OpenMP SpMV and NUMA-Aware SpMV on Phytium 2000+. The total number of threads is set to 8, 16, 32 and 64, and the threads are created and pinned to NUMA nodes in an interleaved way. We run each SpMV 100 times, and report the average execution time. For both algorithms, we run original matrices and their reordered forms according to hypergraph partitioning.

4.2   NUMA-Aware SpMV Performance

Figure 5 shows the performance comparison of OpenMP SpMV and NUMA-Aware SpMV running the 15 test matrices. Compared to OpenMP SpMV, our NUMA-Aware SpMV obtains an average speedup of 1.76x, and the best speedup is 2.88x (occurs in matrix $M6$). We see that both regular and irregular matrices obtain a significant speedup. The average speedup of irregular matrices is 1.91x, and that of regular matrices is 1.59x.

According to the experimental data, it can be seen that hypergraph partitioning has greatly improved our NUMA-Aware SpMV, but has little impact on OpenMP SpMV. Moreover, for the same matrix, the number of partitions brings noticeable different performance. In can also be seen that, after partitioning, the more non-zero elements the diagonal blocks have, the better the performance.

Specifically, in Fig. 6, with the increase of the number of blocks, the number of remote memory accesses has been continuously decreased. Before partitioning matrix $M6$, SpMV needs a total of 16,242,632 cross-node accesses to the vector x. But when the matrix is divided into 64 partitions, that number drops to 1,100,551, meaning that the number of cross-node accesses decreased by 93.22%. As can be seen from Table 1, the non-zero elements of the split matrix move towards the diagonal. As for the matrix $circuit5M$, the best performance is achieved when having 16 partitions, and the number of cross-node accesses has been dropped by 65%, compared to the original form.

Table 1. Sparsity structures of the original and reordered sparse matrices. The top seven are regular matrices and the bottom eight are irregular ones.

Matrix Name #rows& #non-zeros	Original	#par.=2	#par.=4	#par.=8	#par.=16	#par.=32	#par.=64
Transport 1.6M&23.4M							
af_shell6 0.5M&17.5M							
bone010 0.9M&47.8M							
x104 0.1M&8.7M							
ML_Laplace 0.3M&27.5M							
pre2 0.6M&5.8M							
Long_COUP 1.4M&84.4M							
circuit5M 5.5M&59.5M							
NLR 4.1M&24.9M							
cage15 5.1M&99.1M							
dielFilterV3 1.1M&89.3M							
germany_osm 11.5M&24.7M							
M6 3.5M&21M							
packing − 500 2.1M&34.9M							
road_central 14M&33.8M							

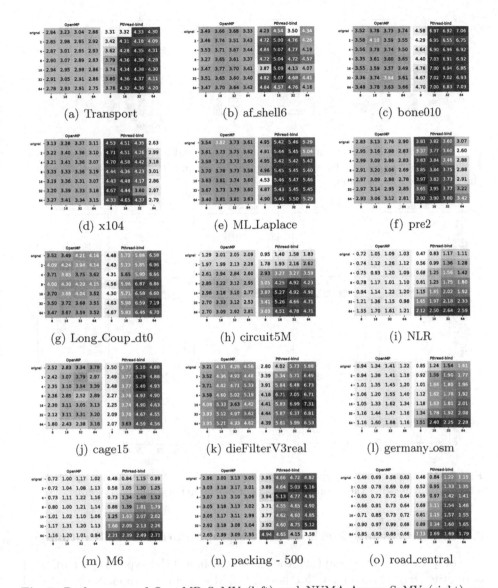

Fig. 5. Performance of OpenMP SpMV (left) and NUMA-Aware SpMV (right) on **Phytium** 2000+. In each subfigure, x-axis and y-axis refer to the number of threads and partitions, respectively. The heatmap values are in single precision GFlop/s.

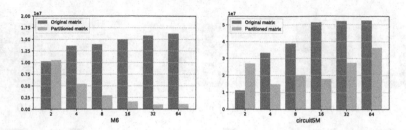

Fig. 6. Comparison of communication volume before and after partitioning under different number of blocks (the x-axis is the number of partitioned blocks, the y-axis is the communication volume).

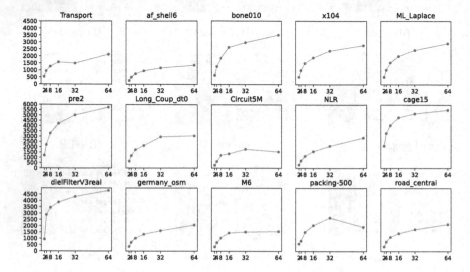

Fig. 7. The ratio of hypergraph partition time to a single NUMA-Aware SpMV time. The x-axis represents the number of blocks from the hypergraph partitioning.

4.3   Preprocessing Overhead (Hypergraph Partitioning Runtime)

The preprocessing overhead (i.e., the execution time of the hypergraph partition) is another important metric for parallel SpMV. Figure 7 reports the ratio of the running time of the hypergraph partition to a single NUMA-Aware SpMV. From the overall perspective of the 15 matrices, due to the different distribution of non-zero elements of the matrix, the best observed performance of NUMA-Aware SpMV is mainly concentrated when the numbers of partitions are 16 and 32. It can be seen that as the number of partitions increases, the ratio increases accordingly. As the number of partition blocks increases, the partition time in general increases as well. Specifically, the matrix *pre2* has a maximum ratio of 5749 times when the number of hypergraph partitions is 64. In contrast, the minimum ratio is 257, which is from the matrix *Af_shell6*.

5   Related Work

SpMV has been widely studied in the area of parallel algorithm. A number of data structures and algorithms, such as BCSR [7], CSX [12] and CSR5 [14], have been proposed for accelerating SpMV on a variety of parallel platforms. Williams et al. [20], Goumas et al. [6], Filippone et al. [5], and Zhang et al. [21] evaluated performance of parallel SpMV on shared memory processors.

Hypergraph partitioning received much attention when accelerating SpMV on distributed platforms. Over the past few decades, researchers have proposed a few partitioning approaches and models for various graph structures and algorithm scenarios [4,17,22,24,25]. A few software packages containing these algorithms have been developed and widely used. For example, Karypis et al. developed MeTiS [9,11], ParMeTiS [10] and hMeTiS [8], and Çatalyürek et al. developed PaToH [19,23], which is used in this work.

6   Conclusions

We have presented a NUMA-Aware SpMV approach and benchmarked 15 representative sparse matrices on a Phytium 2000+ processor. The experimental results showed that our approach can significantly outperform the classical OpenMP SpMV approach, and the number of generated hypergraph partitions demonstrates a dramatic impact on the SpMV performance.

Acknowledgments. We would like to thank the invaluable comments from all the reviewers. This research was supported by the Science Challenge Project under Grant No. TZZT2016002, the National Natural Science Foundation of China under Grant No. 61972415 and 61972408, and the Science Foundation of China University of Petroleum, Beijing under Grant No. 2462019YJRC004, 2462020XKJS03.

References

1. Asanovic, K., et al.: The landscape of parallel computing research: a view from berkeley. Technical report Uc Berkeley (2006)
2. Bligh, M.J., Dobson, M.: Linux on NUMA systems. In: Ottawa Linux Symposium (2004)
3. Davis, T.A., Hu, Y.: The university of Florida sparse matrix collection. ACM Trans. Math. Softw. **38**(1), 1–25 (2011)
4. Devine, K.D., Boman, E.G., Heaphy, R.T., Bisseling, R.H., Çatalyürek, Ü.V.: Parallel hypergraph partitioning for scientific computing. In: International Parallel & Distributed Processing Symposium (2006)
5. Filippone, S., Cardellini, V., Barbieri, D., Fanfarillo, A.: Sparse matrix-vector multiplication on GPGPUs. ACM Trans. Math. Softw. **43**(4), 1–49 (2017)
6. Goumas, G., Kourtis, K., Anastopoulos, N., Karakasis, V., Koziris, N.: Performance evaluation of the sparse matrix-vector multiplication on modern architectures. J. Supercomput. **50**, 36–77 (2009)
7. Im, E.J., Yelick, K., Vuduc, R.: Sparsity: optimization framework for sparse matrix kernels. Int. J. High Perform. Comput. Appl. **18**(1), 135–158 (2004)

8. Karypis, G., Aggarwal, R., Kumar, V., Shekhar, S.: Multilevel hypergraph partitioning: applications in VLSI domain. IEEE Trans. Very Large Scale Integr. (VLSI) Syst. **7**(1), 69–79 (1999)
9. Karypis, G., Kumar, V.: Analysis of multilevel graph partitioning. In: Supercomputing 1995: Proceedings of the 1995 ACM/IEEE Conference on Supercomputing, pp. 29–29 (1995)
10. Karypis, G., Kumar, V.: Parallel multilevel k-way partitioning scheme for irregular graphs. In: Proceedings of the 1996 ACM/IEEE Conference on Supercomputing, Supercomputing 1996, p. 35-es (1996)
11. Karypis, G., Kumar, V.: A fast and high quality multilevel scheme for partitioning irregular graphs. SIAM J. Sci. Comput. **20**(1), 359–392 (1998)
12. Kourtis, K., Karakasis, V., Goumas, G., Koziris, N.: CSX: an extended compression format for SPMV on shared memory systems. In: Proceedings of the 16th ACM Symposium on Principles and Practice of Parallel Programming, PPoPP 2011, pp. 247–256 (2011)
13. Liu, W.: Parallel and scalable sparse basic linear algebra subprograms. Ph.D. thesis, University of Copenhagen (2015)
14. Liu, W., Vinter, B.: CSR5: An efficient storage format for cross-platform sparse matrix-vector multiplication. In: Proceedings of the 29th ACM on International Conference on Supercomputing, ICS 2015, pp. 339–350 (2015)
15. McCalpin, J.D.: Stream: sustainable memory bandwidth in high performance computers. Technical report, University of Virginia, Charlottesville, Virginia (1991–2007). A continually updated technical report
16. Phytium: Mars ii - microarchitectures. https://en.wikichip.org/wiki/phytium/microarchitectures/mars_ii
17. Uçar, B., Aykanat, C.: Partitioning sparse matrices for parallel preconditioned iterative methods. SIAM J. Sci. Comput. **29**, 1683–1709 (2007)
18. Uçar, B., Aykanat, C.: Revisiting hypergraph models for sparse matrix partitioning. Siam Rev. **49**(4), 595–603 (2007)
19. Uçar, B., Çatalyürek, V., Aykanat, C.: A matrix partitioning interface to PaToH in MATLAB. Parallel Comput. **36**(5), 254–272 (2010)
20. Williams, S., Oliker, L., Vuduc, R., Shalf, J., Yelick, K., Demmel, J.: Optimization of sparse matrix-vector multiplication on emerging multicore platforms. Parallel Comput. **35**(3), 178–194 (2009)
21. Zhang, F., Liu, W., Feng, N., Zhai, J., Du, X.: Performance evaluation and analysis of sparse matrix and graph kernels on heterogeneous processors. CCF Trans. High Perform. Comput. **1**, 131–143 (2019)
22. Çatalyürek, V., Aykanat, C.: Hypergraph-partitioning-based decomposition for parallel sparse-matrix vector multiplication. IEEE Trans. Parallel Distrib. Syst. **10**(7), 673–693 (1999)
23. Çatalyürek, V., Aykanat, C.: Patoh (partitioning tool for hypergraphs). In: Padua, D. (ed.) Encyclopedia of Parallel Computing, pp. 1479–1487. Springer, Heidelberg (2011). https://doi.org/10.1007/978-0-387-09766-4_93
24. Çatalyürek, V., Aykanat, C., Uçar, B.: On two-dimensional sparse matrix partitioning: models, methods, and a recipe. SIAM J. Sci. Comput. **32**(2), 656–683 (2010)
25. Çatalyürek, V., Boman, E.G., Devine, K.D., Bozda, D., Heaphy, R.T., Riesen, L.A.: A repartitioning hypergraph model for dynamic load balancing. J. Parallel Distrib. Comput. **69**, 711–724 (2009)

CARAM: A Content-Aware Hybrid PCM/DRAM Main Memory System Framework

Yinjin Fu[1,2(✉)] 🆔 and Yang Wu[2]

[1] PengCheng Laboratory, Shenzhen 518055, China
[2] Army Engineering University, Nanjing 210007, China

Abstract. The emergence of Phase-Change Memory (PCM) provides opportunities for directly connecting persistent memory to main memory bus. While PCM achieves high read throughput and low standby power, the critical concerns are its poor write performance and limited durability, especially when compared to DRAM. A naturally inspired design is the hybrid memory architecture that fuses DRAM and PCM, so as to exploit the positive aspects of both types of memory. Unfortunately, existing solutions are seriously challenged by the limited main memory size, which is the primary bottleneck of in-memory computing. In this paper, we introduce a novel Content Aware hybrid PCM/ DRAM main memory system framework—*CARAM*, which exploits deduplication to improve line sharing with high memory efficiency. CARAM effectively reduces write traffic to hybrid memory by removing unnecessary duplicate line writes. It also substantially extends available free memory space by coalescing redundant lines in hybrid memory, thereby further improving the wear-leveling efficiency of PCM. To obtain high data access performance, we also design a set of acceleration techniques to minimize the overhead caused by extra computation costs. Our experiment results show that CARAM effectively reduces 15%–42% of memory usage and improves I/O bandwidth by 13%–116%, while saving 31%–38% energy consumption, compared to the state-of-the-art of hybrid systems.

Keywords: Phase change memory · Hybrid memory management · Deduplication · Content awareness · Line sharing

1 Introduction

The limited main memory capacity has always been a critical issue for multi/many-core systems to meet the needs of concurrent access to working sets. Unfortunately, conventional DRAM is not the ideal storage medium for in-memory computing due to its high power consumption, even though it achieves low access latency. Moreover, Phase change memory (PCM) is attracting an increasing attention as a promising candidate for next-generation memory [1]. However, there are some crippling limita-tions that prevent PCM from completely replacing DRAM in future systems, such as low write performance, high power cost of write access, and limited long-term endurance. These drawbacks have led designers toward the adoption of hybrid main memory architectures

© IFIP International Federation for Information Processing 2021
Published by Springer Nature Switzerland AG 2021
X. He et al. (Eds.): NPC 2020, LNCS 12639, pp. 243–248, 2021.
https://doi.org/10.1007/978-3-030-79478-1_21

[2–7], which couple the large-capacity PCM with the small-capacity DRAM, in order to combine the best of both memory media. Further-more, *deduplication* can improve space efficiency by replacing redundant data with references to a unique copy in storage systems [8], due to its excellent ability in removing redundancy with higher throughput than lossless compression techniques [9]. Hence, we can enable deduplication for a hybrid PCM/DRAM memory structure that fits the characteristic of storage class memory due to their merits in DRAM-like performance and lower power consumption than DRAM.

In this paper, we present *CARAM*, a content-aware hybrid DRAM/PCM main memory system design framework by leveraging the deduplication technique at the line level. We use DRAM buffering for unique line writes to PCM, and also exploit the available DRAM space for memory address mapping to store deduplication metadata. We also introduce a deduplication-based hybrid memory line write processing to elevate space efficiency by enabling line sharing. Finally, we evaluate the space saving, I/O performance, and power consumption with real-world traces using a simulator that we build for content-aware hybrid memory evaluation. *To the best of our knowledge, this is the first study on the architectural design of content-aware hybrid PCM/DRAM main memory system by enabling line sharing to the most extent using deduplication.*

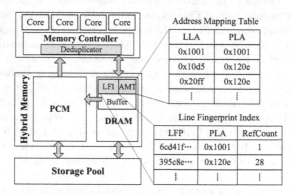

Fig. 1. The architecture of CARAM.

2 System Design of CARAM

2.1 The Overview of System Architecture

Our CARAM design aims to improve space efficiency, power efficiency, and the endurance limit of traditional DRAM/PCM main memory. Figure 1 presents our architectural design of CARAM. The on-chip memory controller replays memory requests from the core's LLCs to the DRAM controller or the PCM controller. Line-level deduplication is performed in a deduplicator module, which generates line fingerprints with light-weight hashing SuperFastHash [12]. To support the deduplication process for line fingerprint management and line address mapping in duplicate identification, we store a line fingerprint index (LFI) and an address mapping table (AMT) in a persistent battery-backed DRAM, along with a write buffer for the PCM write accesses to overcome the slow write speed of PCM. We assign all the PCM and the remaining part of DRAM to a single physical memory address space used for the unique line writes after deduplication. The hybrid main memory is used for page cache to hide the access latency in the underlying persistent storage pool, and all the unique pages in both DRAM and PCM are managed by page caching algorithms, such as LRU [6] and CLOCK [7].

In our CARAM design, the AMT is an in-memory table that consists of multiple entries, each of which is a key-value pair {logical line address (LLA), physical line address (PLA)}. Each entry requires 4B for storing the LLA and another 4B for PLA. The pair is a many-to-one mapping to support line sharing after deduplication. We need to update the AMT when there are new lines or line updates in hybrid main memory. The LFI is responsible for the fingerprint management of memory lines. Each of its entries contains a mapping between a line fingerprint (LFP) and a pair: {physical line address (PLA), RefCount}. RefCount presents the corresponding reference count in the hybrid main memory. Each fingerprint is 4B long for SuperFastHash value, while each RefCount is 2B long. Each entry is a one-to-one mapping to record the metadata information of a unique line in main memory at that time. The LFI can be updated when a memory line is renewed or swapped.

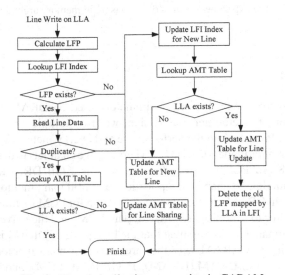

Fig. 2. Line deduplication processing in CARAM.

2.2 Line Deduplication Processing

As shown in Fig. 2, the line deduplication processing of our CARAM is performed in the deduplicator module of the memory controller. When a line write request on a LPA is issued from the LLC, the corresponding line fingerprint LFP is calculated in CPU using weak hashing SuperFastHash. Then it queries the LFI in DRAM to check whether its line fingerprint exists or not. If yes, it further reads and compares the data in PLA line with the writing line data, if it is duplicate, we can find the mapping of LLA to the same PLA in the AMT, and if it exists in the table, we can deduce that the line write is a duplicate request and drop it; otherwise, the write operation is a duplicate line write, and it updates the AMT for line sharing in hybrid memory. On the other hand, if the line fingerprint LFP does not exist in the LFI or not a duplicate, which means a new line is issued, and it needs to add the new LFP and its metadata into the LFI after the line write is finished in the hybrid main memory. Then it also queries the LLA in the AMT. If it is found, then it updates the AMT for the line update after line edition or page swapping, and deletes the old LFP mapped by LLA in the PFI; Other-wise, it means a new line write is issued, and adds the new LLA into the AMT.

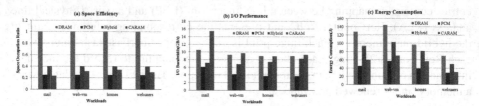

Fig. 3. The experiment results of various main memory architecture.

3   Evaluation

We build a trace-driven hybrid memory simulator based on DRAMsim2 [10] for our studies. To support the heterogeneous design, we use multiple channels to simulate DRAM and PCM. We calculate the performance and energy metrics by referring to the energy and performance models used in [2]. There are two channels in the current version: one channel for 8 GB PCM, and another channel for 2 GB DRAM. We implement the deduplicator module to enable deduplication in hybrid main memory by modifying some components in DRAMsim2 to support simulation for PCM memory. We can easily modify the simulator to support pure DRAM, pure PCM, and the naïve hybrid memory simulation for comparisons. We assume that the byte price of DRAM is four times that of PCM, and compare CARAM with the three kinds of main memory configuration with the same cost: 4 GB DRAM (DRAM), 16 GB PCM (PCM), and the hybrid 2 GB DRAM + 8 GB PCM memory (Hybrid). We feed the simulator with modified I/O traces down-stream of an active cache from four types of application systems: a mail VM server (mail), a web VM server for online course (web-vm), a file server (homes) and a web server for personal pages of users (web-users), in the CS department of FIU [11]. The four workloads were obtained by adding hash calculation time with 1 byte/cycle on each volume as a downstream of a last-level cache. It records the same line fingerprint for all 256B lines from every 4 KB block, and the fingerprint value is the first 4B value of the MD5 value of the block.

As shown in Fig. 3, we evaluate various main memory architectures in terms of space efficiency, I/O performance, and energy consumption. Limited main memory size is the primary bottleneck for in-memory computing. Here, we assume the space occupation ratio of DRAM is 1 in all four applications. As shown in Fig. 3(a), the ratio of PCM is very low, and it has only a quarter of DRAM's value due to its low unit price. The ratio of the naïve hybrid memory is more than 0.4, while CARAM can improve it to approach or even better than that of PCM, by saving 15%–42% memory space of hybrid main memory systems via deduplication.

CARAM enables deduplication in hybrid main memory, and it can significantly reduce line writes to enhance I/O performance through line sharing. Figure 3(b) shows that CARAM can achieve higher performance range from 13% to 116% than the naïve hybrid main memory system, since it performs a large number of low-overhead metadata updates only instead of duplicate line writes. Also, it performs the best under the mail workload mainly due to its lowest space occupation ratio.

We evaluate the energy consumption of the four memory architectures with the I/O traces first, but their values are almost the same under the four different workloads due to the domination of idle time. To differentiate these schemes, we stress-test their energy consumption by continuously issuing the read or write line request without the greatest common idle intervals. Results in Fig. 3(c) show that our CARAM can save 31% –38% energy consumption than that of the naïve hybrid main memory, since it can significantly reduce the number of write operations in main memory.

4   Conclusions

In this paper, we present a content aware hybrid DRAM/PCM main memory system, called CARAM, by exploiting line sharing with deduplication technique, and implement it in a trace-driven hybrid memory simulator based on DRAMsim2. Specifically, we introduce line-level deduplication processing of write access in our hybrid structure to balance space saving and system performance. Evaluation results show that CA-RAM constantly outperforms the existing hybrid memory systems in terms of space saving, I/O bandwidth, and power consumption. We will study the combination of de-duplication and memory compression running real data as a direction of future work.

Acknowledgments. This research was supported by the NSF-Jiangsu grant BK20191327. We would like to thank Prof. Patrick P.C. Lee, the Chinese University of Hong Kong for his help on the initial design of the system.

References

1. Lee, B.C., Zhou, P., Yang, J., et al.: Phase change technology and the future of main memory. IEEE Micro **30**(1), 131–141 (2010)
2. Lee, H., Baek, S., Nicopoulos, C., et al.: An energy-and performance-aware DRAM cache architecture for hybrid DRAM/PCM main memory systems. In: IEEE ICCD 2011, pp. 381–387 (2011)
3. Ham, T.J., Chelepalli, B.K., Xue, N., et al.: Disintegrated control for energy-efficient and heterogeneous memory systems. In: IEEE HPCA 2013, pp. 424–435 (2013)
4. Qureshi, M.K., Srinivasan, V., Rivers, J.A.: Scalable high performance main memory system using phase-change memory technology. IEEE ISCA **37**(3), 24–33 (2009)

5. Dhiman, G., Ayoub, R., Rosing, T.: PDRAM: a hybrid PRAM and DRAM main memory system. In: IEEE DAC, pp. 664–669 (2009)
6. Ramos, L., Gorbatov, E., Bianchini, R.: Page placement in hybrid memory systems. In: International Conference on Supercomputing, pp. 85–95 (2011)
7. Lee, S., Bahn, H., Noh, S.H.: CLOCK-DWF: a write-history-aware page replacement algorithm for hybrid PCM and DRAM memory architectures. IEEE Trans. Comput. **63**(9), 2187–2200 (2014)
8. Wang, Q., Li, J., Xia, W., et al.: Austere flash caching with deduplication and compression. In: USENIX ATC, pp. 713–726 (2020)
9. Baek, S., Lee, H.G., Nicopoulos, C., et al.: Designing hybrid DRAM/ PCM main memory systems utilizing dual-phase compression. ACM TODAES **20**(1), 1–31 (2014)
10. DRAMsim2. https://github.com/ericlove/DRAMSim2
11. FIU Traces. http://iotta.snia.org/traces/390
12. Hsieh, P.: The superfasthash function (2004). http://www.azillionmonkeys.com/qed/hash.html

Big Data and Cloud

Optimization of RDMA-Based HDFS Data Distribution Mechanism

Xiao Zhang$^{(\boxtimes)}$, Binbin Liu, Junhao Zhao, and Cong Dong

School of Computer Science, Northwestern Polytechnical University,
Xian 710129, Shaanxi, China
zhangxiao@nwpu.edu.cn

Abstract. Hadoop Distributed File System (short for HDFS) is a high availability file system designed to run on commodity hardware. It uses multiple replicas to ensure high reliability, and many data are transmitted between storage nodes. The performance of data transmission has a great impact on the latency of writing operations. Remote Direct Memory Access (short for RDMA) is a protocol with low latency and high through which is running on the Infiniband network. When HDFS runs on the Infiniband network, the default protocol IPoIB can not take advantage of the high-speed network. The latency of the writing process is similar to a TCP/IP network. In this paper, we present a new RDMA-based HDFS writing mechanism. It enables *DataNodes* to read data parallelly from the *Client* through RDMA. And by using RDMA primitive, the transmission latency is slower than the original TCP/IP protocol. The experiments show that our approach reduces the latency of the writing process by 10.11%–40.81% compared with the original HDFS.

Keywords: Distributed file system · RDMA · Data distribution mechanism · HDFS · Performance optimization

1 Introduction

HDFS provides high-throughput data access, and programs running on HDFS usually have large data sets. Typical HDFS file sizes are in GBs or TBs volume level. An HDFS cluster can support hundreds of nodes and thousands or millions of files. Through the analysis of the existing HDFS, it is found that the communication protocol used is mainly TCP/IP. Due to the excessive processing delay of the TCP/IP protocol, there are multiple memory copies, and now the memory bandwidth performance is very large with high CPU bandwidth and network bandwidth. The difference causes HDFS to have a higher write latency. With the popularity of IB equipment and the rapid progress of research on RoCE (RDMA Over Converged Ethernet), iWARP (Internet Wide Area RDMA Protocol) and other Ethernet-based analog IB equipment, RDMA has gradually

X. He et al. (Eds.): NPC 2020, LNCS 12639, pp. 251–262, 2021.
https://doi.org/10.1007/978-3-030-79478-1_22

stepped out of the field of high-performance computing and has been applied to the optimization of distributed file systems. RDMA can be used to obtain higher data transmission performance, reducing the time for replicas to be transmitted between nodes, thereby shortening the execution time of HDFS write operations and reducing write latency. In order to accelerate the data transmission speed between nodes and reduce the write latency of HDFS, this paper designs a new write data distribution mechanism for HDFS based on RDMA, so that each data node can read data in parallel. The experiment results show that the optimized HDFS write latency is reduced by 10.11%–40.81%. The main contributions of this paper are as follows:

(1) Analyze the advantages and disadvantages of the HDFS writing process and communication mechanism.
(2) Analyze the three implementation methods of IB network and the two primitives of RDMA, determine the most suitable primitive usage scheme for HDFS optimization, minimize the modification of the source code architecture, and greatly reduce the HDFS write delay.
(3) A data distribution mechanism based on RDMA technology is proposed, so that each data node can read data in parallel.
(4) Evaluate the optimizations achieved in this paper and reduce the overall time-consuming of HDFS write operations.

2   Related Work

RDMA was first used in the field of high-performance computing. With the reduction of hardware costs and the progress of Ethernet-based RDMA research (such as RoCE and iWARP), RDMA is gradually used in the field of distributed storage. The paper of Jiesheng Wu and others used RDMA to optimize the IO performance of PVFS [1]. They designed a RDMA-based transport layer to make PVFS data transmission transparent and stable in performance; designed a buffer management method for flow control, Dynamic and balanced buffer sharing; an efficient memory registration and deregistration scheme was proposed. Brent Callaghan proposed a storage protocol that supports RDMA on the WAN(Wide Area Network) [2], and use it to accelerate NFS performance [3]. The paper by Qingchao Cai et al. proposes an efficient distributed memory platform GAM, which provides directory-based cache coherence protocol through RDMA, so it can integrate the memory of each node, and ensure consistency through state transition, read through RDMA and take the data of the remote node [4]. Anuj Kalia's paper proposes FaSST [5], a high-performance, scalable, and distributed memory transaction processing system that uses RDMA message primitives and datagram transmission methods to design a new RPC (Remote Procedure Call), so it can maintain low overhead and simple system design. These studies show that RDMA can benefit traditional distributed and parallel file systems.

With the development of Hadoop, the performance of HDFS has received a lot more attention. They applied RDMA to HDFS to improve its performance.

Sayantan Sur's paper studies the impact of high-performance interconnection networks on HDFS [6]. When the underlying storage medium is HDD (Hard Disk Drive), the network equipment is replaced by Gigabit Ethernet card to IB network card (IPoIB), the performance can be improved by 11%–100%; when the underlying storage medium is replaced by SSD (Solid State Drive), the high-speed Internet can bring 48%–219% performance improvement. At present, the network becomes the IO bottleneck because of the emergence of NVMe SSD and even NVM (Non-volatile Memory) devices, and the application of RDMA can bring more obvious performance improvement effects. Since Hadoop has released many versions, and many HDFS-based optimizations are tightly coupled with the RDMA design, it cannot be easily applied to the production environment; so Adithya Bhat and others have designed a RDMA-based HDFS plug-in that can flexibly interact with Hadoop2.5, 2.6 version combination [7].

HDFS communication is mainly based on RPC, and using RDMA to modify the RPC interface to optimize communication bottlenecks is also a solution. For example, Li Liang designed and developed a set of RDMA-based network communication architecture in his paper, and implemented and provided an RPC over RDMA communication interface [8]; Yang Heng optimized RDMA-based RPC in his paper. Registered memory blocks are used repeatedly to reduce memory registration time and improve performance [9]. They eventually increased the RPC communication rate by 30%, but it was not applied to HDFS, but only provided us with an idea. After all, RPC still has serialization overhead, and if it does not cooperate with the distribution mechanism of modifying write data, it will still waste RDMA communication performance, and the reduction in HDFS write latency is not obvious. As stated in Dushyanth Narayanan's paper, although RDMA reading is not as flexible as RPC, it can bring benefits in terms of latency and throughput, and we should use reasonable design to give full play to its advantages [10].

Nusrat Sharmin Islam et al. performed a series of optimizations on HDFS based on RDMA. Firstly, they designed a set of java buffer management mechanism, and modified the data transmission protocol of HDFS using RDMA-based UCR (Unified Communication Runtime) library [11]. Next, they further optimized the RPC of HDFS to make RDMA compatible with Java's IO interface and reduce its memory copy [12]. Finally, due to the improvement of IO performance, the HDFS software stack has become a new bottleneck, and they have proposed SOR-HDFS [13], using the SEDA (Staged Event-Driven Architecture) [14] to improve HDFS write performance. SOR-HDFS divides the HDFS write process into four stages, each of which has an input queue and a thread pool associated with it. At any stage, the threads in the thread pool will use the data in the input queue, process it and provide it to the input queue in the next stage. This allows the different stages of data transmission and IO to overlap to the greatest extent, thereby accelerating the overall speed of the write process.

3 Background and Motivation

In this section, firstly, we outline the existing HDFS write data process and determine its performance bottlenecks. Then, we introduced the different implementations of RDMA, determine our usage plan and clarify the reasons.

3.1 HDFS Introduction

HDFS is an important part of the Hadoop ecosystem. As a distributed file system, it is built on a cluster of multiple servers, and each server can be responsible for one or more roles, which are *NameNode*, *DataNode*, and *Client*. As shown in the figure, the various roles are interconnected through the network, using RPC for control flow, and using Socket for data flow. As shown in Fig. 1, where *NameNode* acts as a cluster metadata server, it stores cluster metadata information, contacts the *DataNode* through a heartbeat mechanism and monitors the cluster status. The *Client* must also pass the *NameNode* to register and obtain the required file information. As a data center of the cluster, *DataNode* provides storage services, sends heartbeat information to *NameNode* through RPC, reports the status of data blocks, and transmits data with other nodes through the pipeline flow constructed by Socket. The Client provides an interactive interface between the cluster external application and HDFS. The upper layer application can interact with the *NameNode* to obtain cluster information and file metadata information through the *Client*, and interact with the *DataNode* to read or write files through the *Client*.

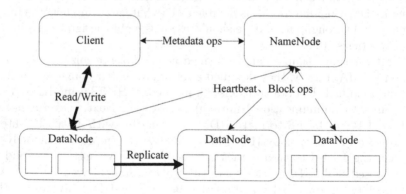

Fig. 1. HDFS architecture

HDFS saves redundant copies of data on multiple *DataNode* nodes. The default number of copies is 3, which are stored on this node, the same rack node, and adjacent rack nodes. This design not only performs data backup, but also improves security. It also makes it possible to access neighboring nodes as much as possible when reading data to improve access efficiency; but at the same time it also increases the overall data transmission amount when data is written, this phenomenon will be more serious under the poor network performance and pipe line data transmission.

3.2   The Writing Process of Original HDFS

In HDFS, the completion of a file write operation requires the cooperation of the entire cluster. The process of writing a file is shown in Fig. 2. First, the Client needs to do some preparation work. For example, contact the *NameNode* to apply for the data block information, initialize the *DataStreamer* thread; create a file lease to avoid conflicting file write operations; *NameNode* will also update the metadata information after receiving the request from the client, allocate the data block and return block information; the *client* can establish a Pipeline connection with the *DataNode* based on the returned information. Then, the *client* can perform formal data transmission operations. For example, cyclically writes data to the data queue; at the same time, the *DataStreamer* thread will also take out the data in the data queue in parallel, calculate the checksum, and encapsulate it into a packet to write into the pipeline stream; *DataNode* reads the packet from the pipeline stream and check the checksum, write it to disk, and pass the packet to the downstream node. Finally, after receiving all ACK messages, the Client performs the finishing work. For example, close the pipeline flow and contact the *NameNode* to update the file status.

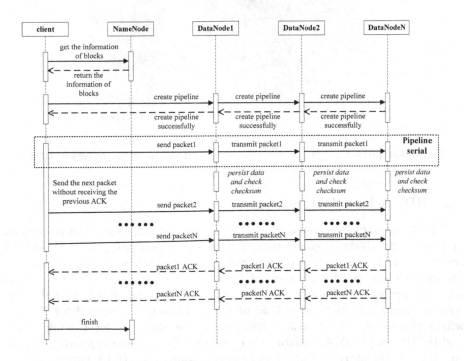

Fig. 2. The flowchart of HDFS writing process

It can be seen from the previous introduction that although the *Client* does not need to wait for the ACK information of the previous packet when passing the packet, each *DataNode* needs to wait for the packet data from the upstream node. This serial pipeline flow slows down the entire write process. On the *DataNode* side, each node can check the checksum and persist the data only after receiving the entire packet from the upstream node. We divide the HDFS writing process into four parts: communicating with *NameNode* (registering file information and obtaining data block information), establishing PipeLine, transmitting data, and completing files; and the process of transmitting data can be divided into four at each *DataNode* Stage: Receiving the packet, checking the checksum, persist the data, and transmitting the packet. As shown in Fig. 3, receiving and transmitting packets account for 66% of the data transmission stage, and then account for 43% of the entire write process, is the bottleneck of the entire writing process. Therefore, improving the data transmission environment and optimizing the data distribution mechanism can greatly reduce HDFS write latency.

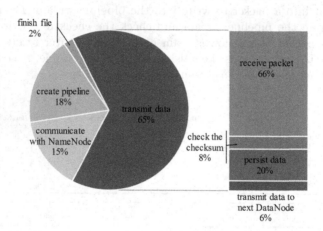

Fig. 3. The proportion of time cost in each phase of the write process of HDFS

3.3   RDMA Introduction

RDMA technology contains three major features: low CPU usage, kernel bypass, and zero copy. RDMA reduces the server-side data processing delay in network transmission. It transmits data directly from the memory of one computer to another without the intervention of both operating systems. There are three different implementations of RDMA, namely InfiniBand, RoCE and iWARP. Among them, InfiniBand is a kind of network specially designed for RDMA, which guarantees reliable transmission from the hardware level, while RoCE and iWARP are RDMA technologies based on Ethernet and support the corresponding verbs interface. InfiniBand network supports RDMA new generation network protocol, with good performance, but the price of network card and switch is also very high. With the development of technology, the emergence of RoCE and iWARP which are based on Ethernet, reduced the cost of hardware and promoted the research on RDMA. But in order to obtain the best optimization effect, this paper uses InfiniBand to build the corresponding RDMA network.

RDMA accesses remote memory using two types of primitives [15]: 1) message primitives, *send* and *recv*, similar to socket programming, before sending a message, the receiver needs to call the *recv* primitive in advance to specify the received message The stored memory address, such primitives are also called two-side RDMA; 2) memory primitives, *read* and *write*, these primitives can directly read or update remote memory without intervention from the remote CPU, They are called one-side RDMA. Obviously, the advantage of memory primitives is that they can obtain higher performance, and save CPU resources when there are computationally intensive tasks at the remote end; the disadvantage is that because there is no CPU participation, it is easy to cause consistency problems. On the contrary, the advantages of message primitives are that information can be transmitted in time, and there is feedback for reading and writing; the disadvantage is that the overhead is large and the delay is high. As shown in Figs. 4(a) and (b), due to the need to create queue pairs and maintain memory buffers in advance when establishing RDMA connections, it takes some time, and Java Socket does not need to maintain the above information; therefore, in small-scale data transmission, the performance of RDMA is not as good as Java Socket; but with the increase of data scale, after all, the preliminary preparation of RDMA only needs once, so the performance is greatly overtaken. In view of the above characteristics of RDMA, in the design of this paper, we will choose to use message or memory primitives according to whether the communication process needs feedback, and only choose to use RDMA when the network connection can be established or be used many times, so as to give full play to RDMA performance, reduce HDFS write latency.

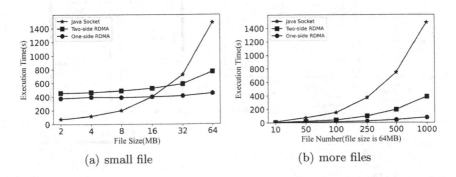

(a) small file   (b) more files

Fig. 4. The time cost of the different communication ways

4   The Design and Implementation of JUCX HDFS

According to the previous analysis, data distribution is the bottleneck of the entire writing process. The read performance of one-side RDMA is much higher than other network transmission methods, and reading data from the *Client* to the *DataNode* does not require feedback, so here is the most It is suitable to use one-side RDMA. However, one-side RDMA need to determine the corresponding memory address, data transmission also needs to know the packet size, and these two information are small, the *DataNode* and *Client* need to interact in time, so use the message primitives of RDMA. Finally, the operation of Pipeline and ACK, because it is only a simple RPC transmission control flow, and the amount of data is small, almost no impact on performance, so retain the original Java Socket communication method.

The overall write process after optimization is shown in Fig. 5(a). Since the data distribution part was mainly modified, the process of contacting the *NameNode* in the early stage and completing the file in the later stage has not changed, so it is not reflected in the figure. In the packet data transmission process, first, the client sends the memory address and packet length of the packet data to each *DataNode* through the message primitive, that is, the *send* function. Then, the *DataNode* can read the packet data directly through the memory primitive, namely the *get* function, according to the received information. Although the *send* function still serially sends RDMA information to each *DataNode*, due to the small amount of data, it can be considered that each *DataNode* starts to read data from the *Client* at almost the same time, that is, to persist data in parallel.

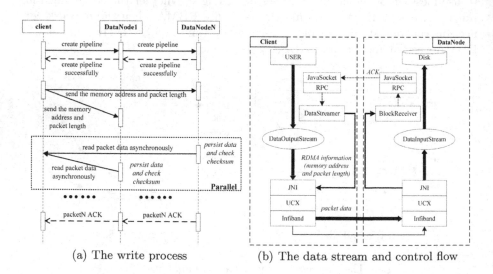

(a) The write process   (b) The data stream and control flow

Fig. 5. RDMA-based HDFS write distribution mechanism

In this paper, RDMA uses JNI (Java Native Interface) to call the underlying UCX (Unified Communication X) library. The detailed data flow after optimization is shown in Fig. 5(b). First, the client-side *DataStreamer* thread constructs a packet, temporarily stores the data in memory, and sends related information to the *DataNode* through the RDMA *send* function. Then, the *BlockReceive* thread of the *DataNode* can receive information through the *recv* function. After determining the remote address and read length, the packet data in the client memory can be directly read through RDMA and persisted to the disk. Finally, the ACK message is returned to the client via the original RPC. The experiment uses HDFS cluster built by Hadoop 2.9.0 to analyze the performance of HDFS under different storage media and different networks. This paper directly uses the put file system interface provided by HDFS to test the execution time of write operations. The put command can upload files locally to the HDFS cluster, that is, the complete HDFS write process is executed. Use the put command to upload 1-5GB files to the HDFS cluster and record the execution time of the command to analyze the reduction effect of this optimization on HDFS write latency.

DataNode can also implement a parallel data distribution mechanism using TCP/IP, but TCP/IP will perform multiple memory copies, so the transmission performance is far lower of RDMA. And the first consideration in this paper is to apply RDMA technology to HDFS more efficiently, so this paper does not implement the data distribution mechanism under TCP/IP.

5   Evaluation

5.1   Experimental Setup

The experiment used 6 machines with the same hardware configuration to build the Hadoop 2.9.0 cluster. The software and hardware configuration of the machine is shown in Table 1. Among them, one machine is used as the *NameNode* node, one is used as the Client node, and the remaining four are used as *DataNode* nodes. Commands are executed under the *Client* node to avoid the influence of *NameNode* and *DataNode*.

Table 1. The configuration of platform

Name	Describe
Model	Sugon S650
CPU	AMD Opteron(TM) 6212, 2.6 GHz, 16 cores
Memory	40 GB
HDD	1 TB SEAGATE 7200 rpm
SSD	250 GB SamSung MZ-76E2508
1GigE NetWork	Intel 82574L Gigabit Network Connection
IB NetWork	Mellanox Technologies MT26428
Operating System	Ubuntu 16.04 Linux, kernel 4.4.0-119-generic

5.2 Single Replica

First, in order to test the optimization effect of RDMA, regardless of the effect of the copy distribution mechanism, we set the cluster to single replica mode. Different back-end storage media will also affect the write performance, so we use HDD and SSD as *DataNode* storage disk for experiments. The experiment results are shown in Fig. 6(a) and (b). The optimized HDFS in this paper reduces the write latency of 22.87%–40.81%. Consistent with the previous analysis, due to the time-consuming preparations such as establishing RDMA connections, the performance improvement is not obvious when the data volume is small, and it can be greatly improved when the file size is 5 GB. When the storage medium is replaced by HDD to SSD, the data persistence time is reduced, and the two stages of data transmission and data persistence have pipeline design, so the overall write performance of HDFS is improved, and the performance optimization of data transmission is covered. It is reflected in the test results that the overall optimization rate under SSD is lower than under HDD.

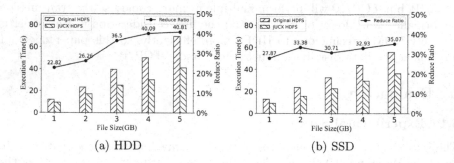

(a) HDD   (b) SSD

Fig. 6. HDFS write performance in single-replica

5.3 Multiple Replicas

Next, in order to verify our write distribution mechanism, we adjusted the number of cluster replicas to perform the same test. Observing the experimental results, we can see that due to the increase in the number of replicas, the workload of data transmission increases. Whether it is the original HDFS or our optimized HDFS, the execution time of the write operation has increased. According to Figs. 7(a) and (b), HDFS optimized in this paper reduces the write latency of 10.11%–25.32%. However, due to the pipeline mechanism in HDFS's own design, during the packet transmission, *DataNode* is also performing data persistence, so the performance improvement of the data transmission process will be covered by the data persistence process, so the performance improvement in the case of multiple replicas is not as high as in the case of single replica. In the future, we will design new solutions and optimize the data persistence process, but this is not the work of this paper. Through the new write distribution mechanism, we have retained the complete RDMA optimization to improve the write performance, so that the new HDFS we designed has a large increase in write latency under two replica configurations and two underlying storage configurations.

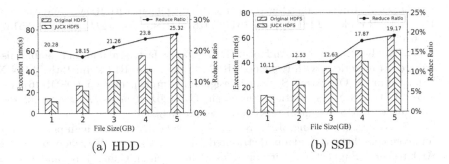

(a) HDD   (b) SSD

Fig. 7. HDFS write performance in multiple-replica

6 Conclusion

This paper proposes a RDMA-based data distribution mechanism that improves the HDFS write process and optimizes HDFS write performance. By analyzing the existing HDFS writing process, it can be found that the data transmission process has a large overhead and a high time-consuming account. This is caused by the underlying TCP/IP protocol and the serial pipe stream data transmission method. Therefore, we used the high throughput and zero copy features of RDMA to modify the HDFS write process, so that the *DataNode* can read data from the *Client* in parallel, reducing the data transmission time for writing files and improving the overall write performance. Experiments show that, compared to the existing HDFS, the optimized HDFS using the method proposed in this paper reduces the write latency by 10.11%–40.81%.

Acknowledgement. This work is supported by the National Key Research and Development Project of China (2018YFB1004400), Beijing Municipal Natural Science Foundation-Haidian original innovation joint fund(L192027).

References

1. Wu, J., Wyckoff, P., Panda, D.: PVFS over infiniband: design and performance evaluation. In: 2003 International Conference on Parallel Processing, 2003. Proceedings, pp. 125–132. IEEE (2003)
2. Yu, W., Rao, N.S.V., Vetter, J.S.: Experimental analysis of infiniband transport services on wan. In: 2008 International Conference on Networking, Architecture, and Storage, pp. 233–240 (2008)

3. Callaghan, B., Lingutla-Raj, T., Chiu, A., Staubach, P., Asad, O.: NFS over RDMA. In: Proceedings of the ACM SIGCOMM Workshop on Network-I/O Convergence: Experience, Lessons, Implications, NICELI 2003, pp. 196–208. Association for Computing Machinery, New York, NY, USA (2003). https://doi.org/10.1145/944747.944753

4. Cai, Q., et al.: Efficient distributed memory management with RDMA and caching. Proc. VLDB Endow. **11**(11), 1604–1617 (2018). https://doi.org/10.14778/3236187.3236209

5. Kalia, A., Kaminsky, M., Andersen, D.G.: Fasst: fast, scalable and simple distributed transactions with two-sided (RDMA) datagram RPCs. In: 12th USENIX Symposium on Operating Systems Design and Implementation (OSDI 16), pp. 185–201. USENIX Association, Savannah, GA (2016). https://www.usenix.org/conference/osdi16/technical-sessions/presentation/kalia

6. Sur, S., Wang, H., Huang, J., Ouyang, X., Panda, D.K.: Can high-performance interconnects benefit hadoop distributed file system. In: Workshop on Micro Architectural Support for Virtualization, Data Center Computing, and Clouds (MASVDC). Held in Conjunction with MICRO, p. 10. Citeseer (2010)

7. Bhat, A., Islam, N.S., Lu, X., Wasi-ur-Rahman, Md, Shankar, D., (DK) Panda, D.K.: A plugin-based approach to exploit RDMA benefits for apache and enterprise HDFS. In: Zhan, J., Han, R., Zicari, R.V. (eds.) BPOE 2015. LNCS, vol. 9495, pp. 119–132. Springer, Cham (2016). https://doi.org/10.1007/978-3-319-29006-5_10

8. Liang, L.: Research and implementation of communication protocol based on RDMA across user and kernel space. Master's thesis, Huazhong University of Science and Technology (2016)

9. Heng, Y.: Research and implementation of optimization of RPC over RDMA in user-space. Master's thesis, Huazhong University of Science and Technology (2016)

10. Dragojevic, A., Narayanan, D., Castro, M.: RDMA reads: To use or not to use? IEEE Data Eng. Bull. **40**(1), 3–14 (2017)

11. Islam, N.S., et al.: High performance RDMA-based design of HDFs over infiniband. In: SC 2012: Proceedings of the International Conference on High Performance Computing, Networking, Storage and Analysis, pp. 1–12. IEEE (2012)

12. Lu, X., et al.: High-performance design of hadoop RPC with RDMA over infiniband. In: 2013 42nd International Conference on Parallel Processing, pp. 641–650. IEEE (2013)

13. Islam, N.S., Wasi-ur Rahman, M., Lu, X., Panda, D.K.: High performance design for HDFs with byte-addressability of NVM and RDMA. In: Proceedings of the 2016 International Conference on Supercomputing, pp. 1–14 (2016)

14. Welsh, M., Culler, D., Brewer, E.: Seda: an architecture for well-conditioned, scalable internet services. ACM SIGOPS Oper. Syst. Rev. **35**(5), 230–243 (2001)

15. Kalia, A., Kaminsky, M., Andersen, D.G.: Design guidelines for high performance RDMA systems. In: 2016 USENIX Annual Technical Conference (USENIX ATC 16), pp. 437–450 (2016)

Reducing the Time of Live Container Migration in a Workflow

Zhanyuan Di[1,2], En Shao[1,2(✉)], and Mujun He[3]

[1] University of Chinese Academy of Sciences, Beijing, China
{dizhanyuan,shaoen}@ncic.ac.cn
[2] State Key Laboratory of Computer Architecture, Institute of Computing Technology, CAS, Beijing, China
[3] Chongqing University, Chongqing, China

Abstract. As a lightweight virtualization solution, container technology can provide resource limiting capabilities and can run multiple isolated process sets under a single kernel instance. Multi-tenant preemption leads to competition in computing, storage, and network resources, resulting in degraded computing service performance. Virtualization service migration can provide a solution to the problem of resource shortage in supercomputing systems. However, the resource overhead and delay in the migration process also reduce the efficiency of high-performance computers. To solve this problem, this dissertation proposes a method of container migration and a tool for supporting container migration. Also, this paper optimizes the startup of containers from checkpoints and proposes a multi-container migration strategy, reducing migration time by 30% compared to sequential migration. The migration method in this paper provides valuable experience for service migration in supercomputers and data centers.

Keywords: Container · Live migration · CRIU · Docker · Workflow

1 Introduction

With the popularity of Linux in the field of servers, more and more manufacturers provide users with Linux-based services. Operating system virtualization technology has also developed, which is lightweight virtualization technology. As a representative of virtualization technology at the operating system level, docker [6] has become more and more popular in recent years. Container virtualization technology is more like a lightweight alternative to the hypervisor, with higher resource usage efficiency than virtual machines. With the development of clusters, grids, and cloud computing, the application of virtualization technology is more widespread. The wide applicability of virtualization technology makes it a commonly used technology in cloud computing centers and has become the basic architecture of cloud computing technology. It has also been applied in a large number of cloud-based supercomputers.

© IFIP International Federation for Information Processing 2021
Published by Springer Nature Switzerland AG 2021
X. He et al. (Eds.): NPC 2020, LNCS 12639, pp. 263–275, 2021.
https://doi.org/10.1007/978-3-030-79478-1_23

In the field of high-performance computing, service migration [20] based on virtualization provides an effective and feasible solution to solve the resource shortage of supercomputing systems. In the field of supercomputing system structure design, high-performance computers regard computing performance as their core. The computing resource overhead of service migration, the time overhead of service interruption, and the network overhead of data migration will all seriously affect the usage efficiency of high-performance computers.

Virtualization service migration is divided into cold migration and live migration [12]. The main discussion in this paper is live migration technology. Compared with cold migration, live migration saves the entire service running state and directly transfers or dumps this information in the form of files. Finally, using the saved information, the service can be restored to the original platform or even to a different platform. Through live migration technology, it can also effectively solve problems such as load balancing, system hardware, and software maintenance and upgrade, fault recovery, and rapid service deployment.

The container live migration technology implemented by CRIU [17] can quickly copy and migrate containers by saving the container running state, and realize dynamic load balancing by migrating applications to hosts with less load and meet the needs of high-performance service migration by migrating applications from failed hosts.

However, the current research is not aimed at docker and unnecessary file operations in docker's internal implementation increase the container startup time. Also, the current multi-container migration is only a repetition of the single-container migration, which cannot meet the requirements of dependencies between multiple containers and the need for full resource utilization.

More specifically, the major contribution of this paper includes:

- We propose a method of container migration and a tool for supporting container migration. The tool runs the client of the migration tool on the node where the container or workflow to be migrated and the server on the migration destination host.
- We implement the optimization for starting docker container from checkpoint. By modifying the original code of docker, this paper optimizes the container startup process, reduces unnecessary startup overhead, and greatly improves the performance of the container startup from the checkpoint.
- Aiming at the problem of workflow dependencies and resource utilization, we propose a strategy to migrate containers through pipelines. This strategy controls the migration process in stages, greatly improving the performance of multi-container migration and reduces container migration overhead.

2   Background and Motivation

2.1   Live Migration

In general, there are two ways to migrate virtual machines, memory-based and disk-based. Unlike container live migration, the content saved by virtual machine live migration is relatively simple, and only the physical resources occupied by the virtual machine and the saved state need to be considered. In the field of virtual machines, most of the current popular virtualization solutions provide solutions for live migration [12]. Migration at the entire virtual machine level can use an efficient and easy way to transfer memory, including the state and application level of the internal storage of the kernel State.

There are currently some thermal migration solutions for containers. OpenVZ is an open-source virtualization platform that uses the Virtuozzo kernel. Due to its highly customized kernel, Virtuozzo is one of the first batches of server vendors to provide container live migration solutions. On OpenVZ, the application process checkpoint tool in the kernel is used to save and restore container processes.

A better solution is to accomplish the same thing in the mainstream Linux kernel environment, so Virtuozzo established the CRIU (Checkpoint-restore in Userspace) project team to carry out this effort. As a new solution, CRIU has two advantages over other solutions: 1. This is the only solution that does not require any special operating environment. CRIU runs on a conventional Linux kernel and does not need to recompile the application. 2. This program was originally designed to be used in conjunction with containers, and the traditional checkpoint reduction program did not take this into account [20]. However, there is currently no live migration solution for docker containers. Also, the existing methods have not considered the optimization of multi-container migration.

2.2 Motivation

At present, as an implementation of the more popular container technology, docker integrates the function of starting the container from the checkpoint. This function uses the open-source software CRIU, which is a tool running on the Linux operating system, and its function is to save and restore checkpoints in userspace. Therefore, this function can be used to freeze and restore a single container on the machine.

However, the built-in function of docker cannot meet the needs of migration between different nodes, nor can it meet the live migration needs of multiple containers. Therefore, there is a need for a feasible solution that can implement the multi-container live migration between different nodes. This solution is best based on the process saving and recovery functions provided by CRIU, combined with the docker container management method. In view of the characteristics of high-performance virtualization services, this method can complete the overall live migration of multiple interrelated containers. After the migration is completed, the docker on the destination host should continue to manage and control the container process like the source host. Finally, we need to optimize performance for application scenarios to minimize migration overhead.

This paper will focus on the feasibility and implementation of container live migration and study the efficient migration solution of multiple containers for different migration scenarios.

3 Overview of Architecture

The design principle of migration tool is driven by two critical factors: building and optimizing the migration tool. These two factors are shown in Fig. 1. The migration tool runs in C/S (client-server) mode, runs the client of the migration tool on the node where the container or workflow to be migrated, and runs the server on the migration destination host. On the destination host, the server of the migration tool is responsible for receiving and processing control messages, sending the information of environment and node status, and completing the creation and recovery of new containers from the received files. On the local machine (source host), the migration tool is responsible for checking the environment, completing container analysis and process dumping, sending files and parameter information needed for container recovery to the server, and controlling the various stages of container migration.

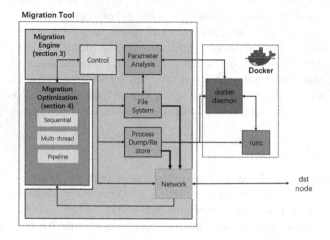

Fig. 1. Architecture of migration tool

4 Building Migration Engine

First, we designed a docker container migration engine to handle parameters, processes, and file systems. Second, we modified the source code of docker to avoid unnecessary file operations that reduce the startup time of the docker container.

4.1 Migration Engine

As shown in Fig. 1, the main module of migration tool contains four parts.

Parameter Analysis. The migration engine needs the parameters of the containers. The engine uses the python library provided by docker to obtain the parameters. As shown in Fig. 1, the migration engine will send the relevant information to the destination host. The server on the destination host receives and creates new containers based on the information to ensure that the configuration of the container has not changed before and after the migration.

Process Dump. The migration engine uses runc to dump the process. Runc is a CLI tool that generates and runs containers according to OCI (Open Container Initiative) standards. Runc can obtain all running containers managed by docker. Therefore, the migration engine directly manages the currently running container through runc. Runc calls CRIU through RPC. CRIU is a tool for process dumping and recovery on Linux. It can freeze a running application and persist its state to disk.

File System. In docker, each container is composed of multiple readable mirror layers, and a layer of readable and writable containers will be added when running the container. For the container to be migrated, the migration engine handles the container layered file system in two ways: 1. The engine completes the migration of the readable and writable container layer 2. The existing container layer is packaged into a new image layer, the packaged image is transferred to the destination node, and the container is created according to the image.

Process Restore. When restoring the container process, the migration engine calls docker to restore the container process from the checkpoint. Docker calls runc to complete the creation and start of the container. After setting the working environment for CRIU, runc will complete the recovery of the container process by calling CRIU through RPC.

4.2 Modification to Docker

At present, the implementation of docker will cause unnecessary overhead during the container startup phase. Docker applies its file reading and writing framework to the dump file. This framework is effective when dealing with small files and facilitates unified management. However, the reading and writing speed under this framework is too slow for large files with hundreds of megabytes. Docker applies a function to output the file system difference between two different directories. This function will output the content in a stream. Docker calls this function to traverse the dump directory and package the contents, and the packaged files will be output to the pipe. After that, docker outputs these contents from the pipe to temporary files in a fixed directory. Contained will read from the previously saved image file through the docker stream, and the read content will be stored by containerd in temporary directory. After completing the operation for the dump file, containerd will prepare for the next call to runc to complete the recovery of the container process, and the temporary directory will eventually be passed to runc as the new dump file path.

During the test, it was found that docker's way of reading and writing large files takes a long time. The average time of files of about 1 GB is between 20 and

30 s, which seriously affects the container startup and increases the migration overhead. Therefore, the process of starting the docker container was modified in the migration plan to bypass the process of repeatedly reading and writing files. After modifying the source code of dockerd and containerd and recompiling them, the time overhead caused by repeated file operations is saved. This part is reflected in the experiment in Sect. 4.3 and 6.2.

4.3   Case Study: Analysis of Container Migration Time Reduction

This experiment tests the migration tool to migrate a single container. Two containers in WGS (Whole Genome Sequencing), wgs indel and wgs call, were used for testing. See Sect. 6.1 for details of the containers.

Case study1: The wgs indel container starts the migration operation of the migration tool when it reaches 600 s. At this time, the memory occupied by the container is 1351143424 bytes. As shown in Fig. 2, the total migration time is 44.778 s (original) and 22.945 s (modified).

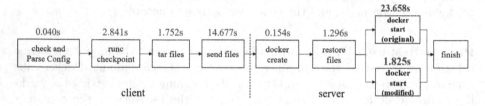

Fig. 2. Wgs indel container migration process

In the same way, the wgs call container was tested, and the test results are as follows (Fig. 3):

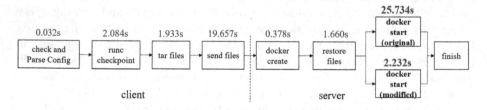

Fig. 3. Wgs call container migration process

As shown in Fig. 4, the modification of docker reduces the migration time by nearly 50% compared to the original version.

Case study2: In addition, we used httpd: 2.4.43, mongo: 4.2, mysql: 8.0.19, nginx: 1.17.9, redis: 6.0-rc3 for testing and the containers can be successfully recovered. All test containers use the official image in docker hub. Since the time required for migration is closely related to the machine platform, the specific information of the migration process is not listed here.

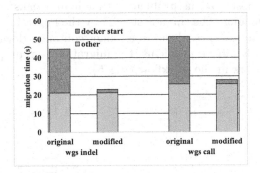

Fig. 4. Comparison of migration time between original and modified version

5 Optimizing Migration Tool

This section proposes a migration solution for scenarios where multiple containers in the workflow need to be migrated. The migration process is controlled in stages and the total migration time is reduced.

5.1 Workflow Migration

Requirements for Container Order. In a containerized microservices architecture, there are dependencies between services. After being packaged into containers, this dependency is transferred between the containers. To ensure the correctness of the service, it is necessary to carry out the container dump (stop) and the container recovery in a fixed order. Therefore, the migration tool needs to resolve the dependencies between multiple containers to ensure that the containers are stopped and restored in the correct order during the migration process.

Migration Overhead of Multiple Containers. During the container migration process, the migration time overhead generally consists of four parts: process dump, file packaging, network transmission, and process recovery. At each stage, the emphasis on resource utilization is different. When migrating multiple containers, the resource utilization efficiency of the sequential migration method is low. For example, network transmission is only one of four phases. During the execution of the other three phases, the network bandwidth is idle and cannot be fully utilized. Therefore, the migration tool needs to provide a corresponding optimization method in the case of multi-containers to reduce the total migration time of multi-container migration.

In general, users migrate containers in sequence when multiple containers need to be migrated. This approach is not suitable for multi-container migration with complex dependencies. And if the migration process is processed in stages, multiple threads are used to complete the migration, instead of completing them sequentially. The most obvious problem is that it may cause a single container downtime to be too long. The threads started by the migration tool will preempt resources from each other, resulting in a longer container downtime.

In response to the above problems, the migration tool proposes a migration solution for containers in the workflow (Fig. 5).

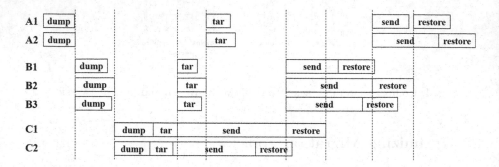

Fig. 5. Schematic diagram of pipeline migration

Pipeline Migration. Different from multi-threaded simple parallel jobs, pipeline migration migrates various stages in parallel through the pipeline. The containers of the first start level can be transmitted preferentially on the premise of ensuring the stopping sequence, which reduces the downtime of the containers. To optimize the migration performance, the migration tool adopts a mode that ranks the order of stopping and restoring. The tool does not distinguish the order of containers that are stopped or restored at the same level. This approach ensures that containers with a high startup level will be completed first while avoiding resource competition caused by multiple threads.

To test if our migration method is effective in multi-container migration, we show a comparative case study in Fig. 7 between three methods.

6   Experiment and Evaluation

6.1   Methodology

We mainly used the program in WGS (Whole Genome Sequencing) for testing. WGS sequenced the entire genome of an organic organism to obtain complete genome sequencing information. Multiple containers can be used for WGS together, and each container is responsible for performing one of the steps of gene sequencing. For some of these stages, you can also use multiple containers to complete in parallel. Wgs indel and wgs call were used in the experiment. Wgs indel is responsible for re-alignment in the process, finds the correct area, and performs re-alignment and selection of genetic information. Wgs call is a variant detection link in the WGS process, which mainly deals with genes Mutation site. These two steps are also the most time-consuming in the WGS workflow. In a WGS workflow, multiple indels and calls can be run simultaneously.

6.2 Optimization of Container Startup

This experiment tested the optimization made by the modification to docker during the container startup phase. In this section, the test container used is wgs indel. When the memory occupied by the container is small, for example, when the memory of the container process on the test platform is less than 200 MB, there is no significant difference between the original docker and the modified docker. When the memory usage increases gradually, the optimized container startup speed is significantly improved. When the memory usage of the container process reaches more than 700 MB, the optimized docker container startup time has dropped to less than one-tenth of the container startup time before optimization (Fig. 6).

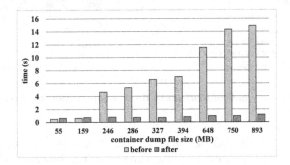

Fig. 6. Optimization of container start from checkpoint

For containers that occupy more than 200 MB of memory, using optimized dockerd and containerd programs for container startup will significantly reduce container startup time. For the migration tool, it will also significantly reduce the time taken for container migration and reduce container downtime.

6.3 Test on Workflow Migration

In this section, the three migration methods for multi-container migration in Sect. 3 will be tested. For convenience, these test containers are called A1, A2, B1, B2, C1, and C2, respectively. Among them, C1 and C2 are wgs call containers, and the rest are wgs indel containers. After checking the migration environment, the migration tool officially started. 300 s after the startup of these containers, the migration tool is started. Specify the migration order as follows: dump order: first level: A1, A2; second level: B1, B2; third level: C1, C2 startup order: first level: C1, C2; second level: B1, B2; third level: A1, A2. The migration order is not considered in sequential migration. The migration process is shown in Fig. 7.

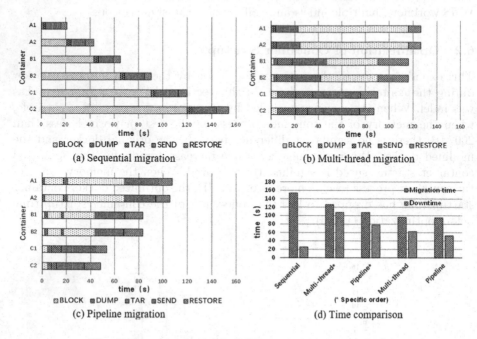

(a) Sequential migration

(b) Multi-thread migration

(c) Pipeline migration

(d) Time comparison

Fig. 7. Time comparison of different migration methods

Figures 7(a), (b), and (c) identify the time taken by each container in each stage of the migration process and the time that it is blocked by the migration tool. Among the three migration methods, the total time taken for sequential migration is the longest, reaching 153.8 s. The total time for multi-thread migration is 126.4 s, which is 18% less than the sequential migration. The total pipeline migration time is 107.7, which is 30% less than the sequential migration. The pipeline method can alleviate the problems of resource competition and insufficient resource utilization, thereby reducing the total time of multi-container migration.

7   Related Work

Container virtualization technology originally originated on UNIX. By changing the root directory of the process through chroot, it can have the isolation of disk space from the process level. In 2005, OpenVZ was released. This container solution achieved resource management and environmental isolation with the help of a customized Linux kernel. In 2007, Google proposed a common method: Cgroups, used to solve resource management problems on Linux machines [5]. During this period, containers were mainly managed in two aspects, such as resource containers [2,16] and secure containers [11,13,15].

Initially, the namespace on Linux was obtained by the kernel from a single global table for each resource to obtain information. Later, the namespace developed into Plan9-esque [18], each resource of each process can be in a specific namespace [4]. Namespace technology does not provide the function of resource management. Linux provides resource management through Cgroups technology [14].

Process migration was a hot topic in the field of systems research in the 1980s [3,7,10,19], but it was not widely used at the time. The research work on process dump and recovery is currently divided into two categories: system level and application level. Process dumping at the system level was once seen as a more likely solution. This dumping method can be implemented as a general mechanism, and checkpoint and restore operations can be integrated into the cluster resource scheduler [20]. Berkeley Lab's Checkpoint/Restart (BLCR) is a system-level solution consisting of a library and a kernel module, and the application must actively provide support for checkpoints [8,9]. Compared to projects at the system level, process dumping and recovery at the user level generally run on the Linux kernel without special modification, and the operating system does not need special support during the dumping and recovery process. DMTCP (Distributed Multi-Threaded CheckPointing) is a typical user-level application checkpoint restoration project. It implements checkpoint saving and restoration of processes at the library level [1].

Virtuozzo has always been committed to providing real-time migration solutions for virtualization technology. As the first organization to propose live migration of containers, Virtuozzo supports live migration on its containers. However, the implementation method is to integrate the main processes and functions required to perform container live migration into the Virtuozzo kernel, which is a highly customized Linux kernel by Virtuozzo.

A better solution is to accomplish the same thing in the mainstream Linux kernel environment, so Virtuozzo established the CRIU (Checkpoint-restore in Userspace) project team to carry out this effort [20].

The current research is not conducted on docker, and the multi-container migration is not optimized. Based on the current research, this paper proposes a method for docker container migration. Also, this method improves the startup speed of the container and greatly reduces the total time of multi-container migration.

8   Conclusion

This study aims to achieve the live migration of docker containers between nodes, especially the migration of workflows composed of multiple containers. The migration tool implemented in this paper can migrate containers between different nodes, providing a variety of migration options. Also, the tool optimizes the performance of docker containers starting from checkpoints and proposes a optimization solution for multi-container migration in workflow scenarios.

Acknowledgement. This work is supported in part by National Program on Key Research Project (No. 2018YFB0204400), by NSFC (No. 61702484, No. 61972380), by CASSPRP (XDB24050200). Sponsored by CCF-Baidu Open Fund.

References

1. Ansel, J., Arya, K., Cooperman, G.: DMTCP: transparent checkpointing for cluster computations and the desktop. In: 2009 IEEE International Symposium on Parallel & Distributed Processing, pp. 1–12. IEEE (2009)
2. Banga, G., Druschel, P., Mogul, J.C.: Resource containers: a new facility for resource management in server systems. In: OSDI, vol. 99, pp. 45–58 (1999)
3. Barak, A., La'adan, O.: The MOSIX multicomputer operating system for high performance cluster computing. Future Gener. Comput. Syst. **13**(4–5), 361–372 (1998)
4. Bhattiprolu, S., Biederman, E.W., Hallyn, S., et al.: Virtual servers and checkpoint/restart in mainstream Linux. ACM SIGOPS Oper. Syst. Rev. **42**(5), 104–113 (2008)
5. Clark, J.: Google: 'EVERYTHING at Google runs in a container'[OL]. https://www.theregister.co.uk/2014/05/23/google_containerization_two_billion
6. Docker[OL]. https://docs.docker.com/get-started/overview/
7. Douglis, F., Ousterhout, J.: Transparent process migration: design alternatives and the Sprite implementation. Softw. Pract. Exp. **21**(8), 757–785 (1991)
8. Duell, J.: The Design and Implementation of Berkeley Lab's Linux Checkpoint/Restart. Lawrence Berkeley National Laboratory (2005)
9. Hargrove, P.H., Duell, J.C.: Berkeley lab checkpoint/restart (BLCR) for Linux clusters. J. Phys. Conf. **46**, 494–499 (2006)
10. Jul, E., Levy, H., Hutchinson, N., et al.: Fine-grained mobility in the Emerald system. ACM Trans. Comput. Syst. (TOCS) **6**(1), 109–133 (1988)
11. Kamp, P.H., Watson, R.N.M.: Jails: confining the omnipotent root. In: Proceedings of the 2nd International SANE Conference, vol. 43, p. 116 (2000)
12. Kotikalapudi, S.V.N.: Comparing live migration between Linux containers and kernel virtual machine: investigation study in terms of parameters (2017)
13. MacCarty, B.: SELinux-NSA's open source security enhanced Linux: beating the O-day vulnerability threat (2005)
14. Menage, P.B.: Adding generic process containers to the Linux kernel. In: Proceedings of the Linux Symposium, vol. 2, pp. 45–57 (2007)
15. Morris, J., Smalley, S., Kroah-Hartman, G.: Linux security modules: general security support for the Linux kernel. In: USENIX Security Symposium, pp. 17–31. ACM, Berkeley (2002)
16. Nagar, S., Franke, H., Choi, J., et al.: Class-based prioritized resource control in Linux. In: 2003 Linux Symposium (2003)
17. Pickartz, S., Eiling, N., Lankes, S., et al.: Migrating LinuX containers using CRIU. In: IEEE International Conference on High Performance Computing, Data, and Analytics, pp. 674–684 (2016)

18. Pike, R., Presotto, D., Thompson, K., et al.: The use of name spaces in Plan 9. Oper. Syst. Rev. **27**(2), 72–76 (1993)
19. Powell, M.L., Miller, B.P.: Process migration in DEMOS/MP. ACM SIGOPS Oper. Syst. Rev. **17**(5), 110–119 (1983)
20. Vasyukov, A., Beklemysheva, K.: Using CRIU with HPC containers field experience. Int. J. Eng. Comput. Sci. **7**(07), 24106–24108 (2018)

RDMA-Based Apache Storm for High-Performance Stream Data Processing

Ziyu Zhang$^{(\boxtimes)}$, Zitan Liu, Qingcai Jiang, Zheng Wu, Junshi Chen, and Hong An$^{(\boxtimes)}$

University of Science and Technology of China, Hefei, China
{zzymm,jauntyliu,jqc,zhengwu,cjuns}@mail.ustc.edu.cn, han@ustc.edu.cn

Abstract. Apache Storm is a scalable fault-tolerant distributed real-time stream-processing framework widely used in big data applications. For distributed data-sensitive applications, low-latency, high-throughput communication modules have a critical impact on overall system performance. Apache Storm currently uses Netty as its communication component, an asynchronous server/client framework based on TCP/IP protocol stack. The TCP/IP protocol stack has inherent performance flaws due to frequent memory copying and context switching. The Netty component not only limits the performance of the Storm but also increases the CPU load in the IPoIB (IP over InfiniBand) communication mode. In this paper, we introduce two new implementations for Apache Storm communication components with the help of RDMA technology. The performance evaluation on Mellanox QDR Cards (40 Gbps) shows that our implementations can achieve speedup up to 5× compared with IPoIB and 10× with 1 Gigabit Ethernet. Our implementations also significantly reduce the CPU load and increase the throughput of the system.

Keywords: Apache Storm · RDMA · InfiniBand · Stream-processing framework · Cloud computing · Communication optimization

1 Introduction

With the increase of Internet users and the development of hardware equipment, processing massive amounts of data in real-time has posed a great challenge to system design. Real-time stream processing frameworks such as Apache Storm [1], Apache Spark [2], and Apache Flink [3] have attracted more attention than batch processing frameworks such as Apache Hadoop [4]. Streaming systems must handle high-speed data streams under strict delay constraints. To process massive data streams, modern stream processing frameworks distribute

Z. Zhang—The work is supported by the National Key Research and Development Program of China (Grants No. 2018YFB0204102).

processing over numbers of computing nodes in a cluster. These systems sacrifice single-node performance for the scalability of large clusters and rely on Java Virtual Machine (JVM) for platform independence. Although the JVM provides a high-level abstraction from the underlying hardware, the processing overhead caused by its data (deserialization) serialization, the dispersion of objects in memory, garbage collection, and frequent context switching caused by inter-process communication reduce the efficiency of data access provided by the computing framework [5,6]. Therefore, the overall performance of the scalable computing framework built on the JVM is severely limited in terms of throughput and latency.

In general, the most advanced systems focus on optimizing throughput and latency for high-speed data streams. The data stream model is implemented by utilizing a scalable system architecture based on message passing mechanism [7–9]. From the perspective of the development of modern hardware, the potential performance bottleneck of the scalable streaming computing system is that it cannot fully utilize current and emerging hardware trends, such as multi-core processors and high-speed networks [5]. Due to frequent cross-node communication, the Internet has an important impact on the performance of modern distributed data processing systems. Restricted by the traditional communication protocol, the current streaming computing system cannot fully utilize the 40 Gbps network [6]. In addition, the huge load caused by the transmission pipeline based on the data flow model severely limits the computing performance of the CPU [10]. Optimize the execution strategy to solve the problem of unbalanced CPU load in the computing system, such as reducing the size of the partition or simply adding more cores to each network connection can only obtain sub-optimal performance [11].

InfiniBand is an industry-standard switched fabric that is designed for high-speed, general-purpose I/O interconnects nodes in clusters [12]. One of the main features of InfiniBand is Remote Direct Memory Access (RDMA), which allows software to remotely read or update memory contents of another remote process without involving either one's operating system [13]. A direct way to run Apache Storm over InfiniBand is to use the IP over InfiniBand (IPoIB). IPoIB wraps Infiniband devices into regular IP based Ethernet cards, making applications transparently migrated into InfiniBand based device provides a useful feature, that is, using InfiniBand devices easily by IP address is like using Ethernet devices. Cross-node data transmission is realized based on event-driven asynchronous I/O library. Although the asynchronous method can effectively reduce the waiting time during the transmission process, the overhead of context switching cannot be ignored. On the other hand, due to the inherent defects of the TCP/IP protocol stack, the system kernel will copy data buffer multiple times during the message sending and receiving process [11], consuming a lot of CPU resources. As the amount of data and the complexity of the calculation topology increase, the IPoIB mode exacerbates the above problems.

In this paper, we experiment on the cluster of high-performance interconnected hardware devices and prove that the inherent defects of the TCP/IP protocol stack used in the communication component are the main reason for the excessive CPU load. Secondly, We use InfiniBand's remote direct Memory access (RDMA) technology to redesign the data transmission pipeline of Apache Storm.

The rest of this paper is organized as follows. In Sect. 2, we examine the overall process of Apache Storm inter-worker communication and the overhead introduced by Netty communication component and its underlying TCP/IP protocol stack. Section 3 presents our optimization on Storm's messaging layer and explains how we design and implement the RDMA-based Storm in detail. Section 4 demonstrates the evaluation result of our newly designed Storm. Finally, Sect. 5 gives our conclusion.

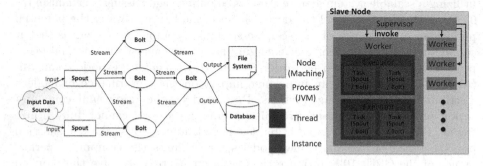

Fig. 1. Computational topology and logical structure

2   Background and Motivation

2.1   Parallel Processing of Data Streams

Parallelism is key to the fast streaming of Storm. Storm handles user-defined computational topology in parallel by creating a large number of Spouts and Bolts as shown in Fig. 1. Spouts get the data stream from the data source, convert the data stream into the smallest data structure tuple, then send them to one or more Bolts. Next, Bolts process the tuple, and then send tuple to the next Bolt or database according to the topology user have specified. By instantiating multiple Spouts and Bolts, the process can be executed in parallel [1]. Figure 1 shows that a node in the cluster runs multiple Worker processes according to the user's definition and the Worker handles user-defined computational topology. It processes tuples by executing Executor and Executor handles or emits tuples by instantiating Spout or Bolt.

2.2   Message Processing Structure

Apache Storm applies a distributed producer-consumer pattern and a buffer mechanism to handle data transmission among operators (Spout and Bolt) as shown in Fig. 2. Since different operators are distributed on different nodes in the cluster, the partitioning method requires frequent inter-process communication. A complete communication process is as follows:

1. Each Worker process has a receiver thread (listening to the specified port). When new message arrives, the receiver thread puts the tuple from the network layer into its buffer. When the amount of tuple reaches a certain threshold, the receiver thread sends tuple to the corresponding (one or more) Executors' incoming-queues specified by the task number in the tuples.
2. Each Worker process contains multiple Executors, which are the actual components that process the data. The Executor contains a worker thread with an incoming queue and a sender thread with an outgoing queue. The messages emit by receiver thread gets processed in the worker thread, and then put into the outgoing queue ready to be sent.
3. When the tuples in the outgoing queue of the Executor reaches a certain threshold, the sending thread of the executor will get the tuples in the outgoing queue in batches and send them to the transfer queue of the Worker process, which will be sent to the network by the sending thread then.

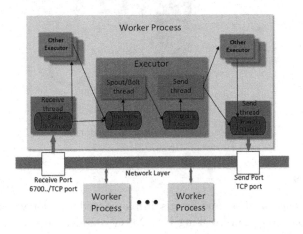

Fig. 2. Communication inside and outside worker processes

2.3 InfiniBand and RDMA

The streaming system on modern hardware must effectively use three key hardware resources to achieve high resource utilization: CPU, main memory, and network [14,15]. However, Trivedi [6] and Steffen [5] prove that the large load caused by the data transmission pipeline has become the bottleneck of the CPU, and the streaming computing system cannot currently fully utilize the high-performance interconnect. The development of network hardware technology makes the network communication speed may exceed the memory bandwidth in the future.

The commonly used Ethernet technology provides 1, 10, 40, or 100 Gbit bandwidth [5]. InfiniBand, an industry-standard switched fabric that is designed for High Performance Computing (HPC) cluster interconnection, on the other side, provides bandwidth comparable or even faster than the main memory and its main feature, Remote Direct Memory Access (RDMA) allows software to read or update the remote memory contents without any CPU involvement [12]. This important trend will lead to drastic changes in streaming system design. In particular, the traditional idea of network layer and kernel-user boundary data encapsulation is inconsistent with the future development trend of network technology. Therefore, the speed of using high-performance interconnection networks to transfer data between nodes is greater than or equal to the speed of memory access will bring new challenges to the design of future streaming computing systems [16]. Our work presents a possible solution to the above problem.

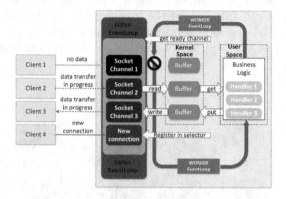

Fig. 3. Netty's NIO communication model

2.4   Analysis

The Storm communication module is implemented by Netty framework currently. Based on NIO (non-blocking IO), Netty uses Reactor as its multiplexing model. During a communication, the server uses a thread pool to receive client connections concurrently as shown in Fig. 3. When the TCP connection gets accepted, the server registers the newly created Socket-Channel (an abstraction of network operations, including basic I/O operations) to a thread in the I/O thread pool. In order to handle service requests delivered to a service handler by one or more inputs concurrently, Netty uses the Reactor multiplexing model as shown in Fig. 3. The Listen-EventLoopGroup (bossGroup) is responsible for listening sockets. When new clients arrive, it allocates corresponding Channels and routes them to the associated request handlers.

A straightforward way to run existing applications on InfiniBand is to use IP over InfiniBand (IPoIB). However the existing TCP/IP stack will cause frequent context switching, which consumes lots of CPU resources as throughput gets bigger. A typical stream processing application involves bunches of data transfer between workers, and the problem grows worse with higher parallelism or smaller message size. The excessive use of CPU could also result in a throughput decrease since workers have to wait for the context switching to finish. To sum up, stream processing applications like Apache Storm cannot fully utilize InfiniBand and its communication modules need targeted optimization.

3 Design

3.1 Messaging Transport Layer and Basic Model

The message component of the Storm source code defines several interfaces to describe the communication needs between workers. Based on these, we wrote our own components to support RDMA communication. The relevant interfaces are indicated in Fig. 4.

- TransportFactory: Used to create the communication context, which is used by WorkerState in the Worker process.
- Context: Used to provide actual context for server and client communication component for different hardware devices (Ethernet or InfiniBand) according to different configuration parameters.
- Connection Callbacks: Receive messages asynchronously and notify the receiver thread for subsequent processing

The communication is one-way for workers, that is, the clients actively connect to the server and send their message. The server is required to implement *registerRecv()* call, and call when new messages arrive, and the client is required to implement *send()* call.

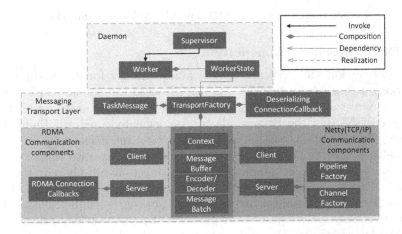

Fig. 4. Communication module components of Storm

3.2   JXIO-based Implementation

JXIO is a high-performance asynchronous reliable messaging library optimized for hardware acceleration. Figure 6 shows the communication timing logic based on JXIO. Figure 5 shows the main classes involved and their respective functionalities are as follows:

- The Server class is responsible for Initializing parameters, binding IP addresses, setting listening ports, registering memory pools, and initializing event handling queues to handle client connections and IO events.
- ServerPortal is for listening to incoming connections. It can accept/reject or forward the new session request to another portal. Two event handlers for ServerPortal are required to implement, namely onSessionNew for a new session arrival notification and onSessionEvent for events like CLOSED.
- ServerSession is for receiving Message from client and sends responses. ServerSession handles three events on his lifetime, namely onRequest for requests from the client, onSessionEvent for several types of session events, and onMsgError when error occurs.

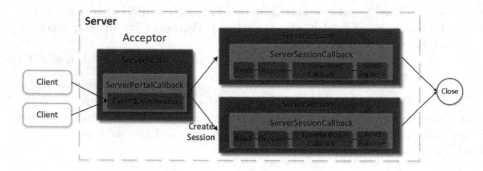

Fig. 5. Basic model for JXIO-Based RDMA communication

3.3   DiSNI-Based Implementation

DiSNI (former known as jVerbs [17]) is a Java library for direct storage and networking access from userspace. The DiSNI-based component consists of two parts: the Server and the Client. Figure 6 shows the communication timing logic based on DiSNI. On the Server side, we implemented our own Endpoint by inheriting RdmaEndpoint class and overriding *init*() and *dispatchCqEvent*() call. Since calls to *serverEndpoint.accept*() are blocked, a separate thread (Server-Main) for server logic is necessary. Once connection established, the *init*() method will set up several recv Verbs call, whose number is configured by recv-CallInitialized. Once messages arrive, *dispatchCqEvent*() will be called, and the normal TaskMessages are passed to upper layer by calling IConnectionCallback registered by *registerRecv*() call. On the Client side, Client.Endpoint is responsible for client logic. Once *send*() is issued by upper layer, messages are put into the task message queue, waiting for client thread to take.

4   Performance Evaluation

4.1   Experimental Setup

We use 8 Sugon nodes with dual Intel Xeon E5-2660 processors and 128 GB
RAM each for our evaluation cluster setup. Each node runs CentOS Linux release
7.3.161, and are connected with both 1GigE and Mellanox 40G QDR InfiniBand
via an Ethernet and an InfiniBand switch, respectively. We use our modified
Storm based on v2.0.0 and Zookeeper-3.4.5 in our experiments. The Zookeeper
is deployed on all 8 nodes of the cluster, so that the Storm nimbus and supervisor
daemon can share the state information at a minimal cost. The Storm nimbus
daemon is deployed on node1 and Storm supervisor daemon is deployed on the
remaining 7 nodes.

To find the best buffer size of Storm performance, we run Storm on 4 nodes
at first, adjusting the message size by setting configuration parameter *topol-
ogy.transfer.buffer.size*, and determine the best size with the minimal processing
delay and CPU load. Then, we use *the transferred tuple per second* to benchmark the performance of Storm under the best buffer size tested. The topology
we use is designed to maximize inter-worker communication, therefore broadcast
grouping is used. We use 4 worker processes per node for all the tests mentioned.

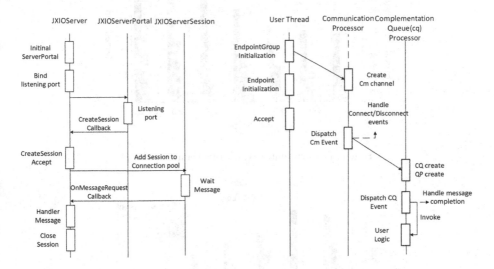

Fig. 6. RDMA communication diagram (left: JXIO, right: DiSNI) each of the horizontal timelines corresponds to a representative object with its name given above. The
rectangle marks significant events that happened during the process.

4.2   The Effect of Message Size on Performance

We run Storm on 4 nodes, and 4 Worker processes per node, a total of 16
processes running on the cluster. Each Worker process contains 5 Executors,

and each Executor chooses to be a Spout or a Bolt. We conclude our experiment
in two aspects according to the experimental data as shown in Fig. 7 and Fig. 8:

- The increase in send buffer size will result in an increase in processing delay,
  which has the most significant impact on TCP and has less impact on RDMA
  implementations. Both RDMA and IPoIB achieve significant improvements
  over TCP. Compared with TCP, RDMA can achieve an acceleration ratio of
  around 10, and compared with IPoIB, RDMA can achieve an acceleration
  ratio of around 5. The DiSNI version of Storm has a slightly lower processing
  latency than the JXIO version.
- The send buffer size will also affect the CPU load. Because IPoIB takes advantage of the hardware, it can process more packets than TCP at the same time.
  However, this exacerbates the shortcomings of TCP/IP protocol stack, that
  is, frequent context switching and memory copying, which will increase the
  CPU load. RDMA significantly reduces CPU load compared to IPoIB because
  there is no need to interrupt the operating system for memory copying.

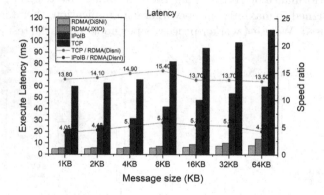

Fig. 7. Experimental result of execute latency

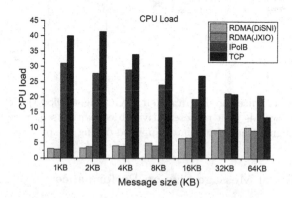

Fig. 8. Experimental result of CPU load

4.3   The Impact of Distributed Scale on Performance

We test the scalability of RDMA based Apache Storm, testing on 2, 4, 6, and 8 nodes, respectively. The result we measure is the total number of tuples in a certain length of time. This data is used to represent the network's total throughput.

As shown in Fig. 9, when the number of nodes in the cluster is 2 and the total number of working processes is 8, the number of connections between processes is 8*8. At this time, the throughput of systems based on RDMA (DiSNI), RDMA (JXIO), IPoIB, and TCP are 894 Tuples/s, 660 Tuples/s, 316 Tuples/s, and 444 Tuples/s. When the cluster size increased to 8 nodes and the number of processes increased to 32, the throughput rates of the three modes are 3482 Tuples/s, 3138 Tuples/s, 1900 Tuples/s and 1058 Tuples/s. After the scale is expanded by 4 times, the system throughput based on RDMA, IPoIB, and TCP modes has increased by 4 times, 6 times, and 2 times respectively.

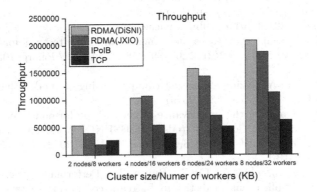

Fig. 9. Experimental result of transferred tuples

5   Conclusion

In this paper, we reconstruct the communication module of the streaming processing framework Storm with two different RDMA-based Java interfaces, JXIO and DiSNI, respectively. The experimental results show that the optimized Storm achieves significant performance improvement. When complex stream topologies are specified, the frequent memory copying of the TCP/IP protocol stack causes the CPU to perform context switching frequently, which will increase the CPU load. The accelerated transmission of IPoIB's underlying hardware exacerbates the above consequences. The experiment shows that the optimized Storm can effectively use RDMA technology to reduce CPU utilization significantly. When the message buffer size increases, the RDMA version of the Storm shows good acceleration characteristics. It can significantly reduce the processing delay and Bolt can process and send more Tuples. The throughput of the topology network increases linearly when the cluster size increases. Experimental results show that the scalability of the optimized Storm is improved compared to the TCP version.

6   Related Work

The work is inspired by Seokwoo Yang's [11], which implements JXIO acceleration on an earlier version of Storm. Our work differs from Yang's in two ways: First, we have implemented JXIO acceleration in the current version of Storm, and lots of interfaces have to be reconsidered since the messaging interface has been changing a lot. Second, JXIO is based on a high-level, request-response based communication paradigm, which limits the possibility for further optimizations. The native Verbs call and SVC design in DiSNI [17] are brought to address and solve such problems, and we achieved lower CPU load and latency with the help of the direct JNI interface the DiSNI have provided.

References

1. Apache Storm (2019). https://storm.apache.org/
2. Apache Spark (2019). http://spark.apache.org/
3. Apache Flink (2019). https://flink.apache.org/
4. Abadi, D.J., et al.: Aurora: a new model and architecture for data stream management. VLDB J. **12**(2), 120–139 (2003). https://doi.org/10.1007/s00778-003-0095-z
5. Zeuch, S., et al.: Analyzing efficient stream processing on modern hardware. Proc. VLDB Endow. **12**(5), 516–530 (2019)
6. Trivedi, A., et al.: On the [ir]relevance of network performance for data processing. In: Clements, A., Condie, T. (eds.) 8th USENIX Workshop on Hot Topics in Cloud Computing, HotCloud 2016, Denver, CO, USA, 20–21 June 2016. USENIX Association (2016)
7. Sun, D., Gao, S., Liu, X., Li, F., Buyya, R.: Performance-aware deployment of streaming applications in distributed stream computing systems. Int. J. Bio-Inspired Comput. **15**(1), 52–62 (2020)
8. Liu, X., Buyya, R.: Resource management and scheduling in distributed stream processing systems: a taxonomy, review, and future directions. ACM Comput. Surv. **53**(3), 50:1–50:41 (2020)
9. Amarasinghe, G., de Assunção, M.D., Harwood, A., Karunasekera, S.: ECSNeT++: a simulator for distributed stream processing on edge and cloud environments. Future Gener. Comput. Syst. **111**, 401–418 (2020)
10. Zhang, S., He, B., Dahlmeier, D., Zhou, A.C., Heinze, T.: Revisiting the design of data stream processing systems on multi-core processors. In: 33rd IEEE International Conference on Data Engineering, ICDE 2017, San Diego, CA, USA, 19–22 April 2017, pp. 659–670. IEEE Computer Society (2017)
11. Yang, S., Son, S., Choi, M.-J., Moon, Y.-S.: Performance improvement of Apache Storm using InfiniBand RDMA. J. Supercomput. **75**(10), 6804–6830 (2019). https://doi.org/10.1007/s11227-019-02905-7
12. MacArthur, P., Liu, Q., Russell, R.D., Mizero, F., Veeraraghavan, M., Dennis, J.M.: An integrated tutorial on InfiniBand, verbs, and MPI. IEEE Commun. Surv. Tutor. **19**(4), 2894–2926 (2017)
13. Agostini, E., Rossetti, D., Potluri, S.: GPUDirect Async: exploring GPU synchronous communication techniques for InfiniBand clusters. J. Parallel Distributed Comput. **114**, 28–45 (2018)

14. Zhang, S., He, J., Zhou, A.C., He, B.: BriskStream: scaling data stream processing on shared-memory multicore architectures. In: Boncz, P.A., Manegold, S., Ailamaki, A., Deshpande, A., Kraska, T. (eds.) Proceedings of the 2019 International Conference on Management of Data, SIGMOD Conference 2019, Amsterdam, The Netherlands, 30 June–5 July 2019, pp. 705–722. ACM (2019)

15. Corral-Plaza, D., Medina-Bulo, I., Ortiz, G., Boubeta-Puig, J.: A stream processing architecture for heterogeneous data sources in the Internet of Things. Comput. Stand. Interfaces **70**, 103426 (2020)

16. Akidau, T., et al.: The dataflow model: a practical approach to balancing correctness, latency, and cost in massive-scale, unbounded, out-of-order data processing. Proc. VLDB Endow. **8**(12), 1792–1803 (2015)

17. Stuedi, P., Metzler, B., Trivedi, A.: jVerbs: ultra-low latency for data center applications. In: Proceedings of the 4th Annual Symposium on Cloud Computing, SoCC 2013 (2013)

Payment Behavior Prediction and Statistical Analysis for Shared Parking Lots

Qingyu Xu[1], Feng Zhang[1]($\boxtimes$), Mingde Zhang[1], Jidong Zhai[2], Jiazao Lin[3], Haidi Liu[3], and Xiaoyong Du[1]

[1] Key Laboratory of Data Engineering and Knowledge Engineering (MOE), and School of Information, Renmin University of China, Beijing, China
`fengzhang@ruc.edu.cn`
[2] Department of Computer Science and Technology, Tsinghua University, Beijing, China
[3] Zhongzhi Huaching (Beijing) Technology Co., Ltd., Beijing, China

Abstract. As the sharing economy is booming in China, many intelligent shared parking lots appear. Since more and more Chinese households own cars, it is necessary to study the payment behavior of shared parking lots, which may represent the entire sharing economy. In detail, we analyze the factors that influence users' payment and predict users' payment behavior of whether and when users will deliver parking bills after parking. We use 29,733 real parking records provided by Huaching Tech, a top smart parking company in China, in our study. After a comprehensive statistical analysis, we use decision tree model to predict users' payment behavior. Experiments show that the decision tree model can reach 79% accuracy.

Keywords: Payment behavior · Payment time prediction · Shared parking lots

1 Introduction

For intelligent shared parking lots, users' untimely payment behavior has become a serious problem. Fortunately, based on users' parking and payment records, we can predict their payment time and provide timely action to reduce delayed payment behaviors. To achieve this goal, we need to analyze the parking dataset containing parking records and user data with parking and payment history.

Parking-related behavior prediction has become a hot research topic in recent days. There are many works related to parking occupancy analysis [3,5]. Alho and others [1] proposed a prediction method for urban freight parking demand using linear regression and generalized linear models. We also explored the relations between parking and weather information [4,13,14]. In terms of payment

X. He et al. (Eds.): NPC 2020, LNCS 12639, pp. 288–293, 2021.
https://doi.org/10.1007/978-3-030-79478-1_25

prediction, Wen and others [12] explored customer behavior and developed a probabilistic graphical model to predict the consumption behavior of a single user. Moreover, the existing fraud detection method is not suitable for our scenario [2].

Compared with the previous work, we predict the payment behavior with limited information, which poses large difficulties in our research. In detail, currently, most users have a small number of parking records; even worse, the users who have delay payments usually have only one or two parking records. We not only need to clean and preprocess the data, but also need to design appropriate classification criteria.

We provide an effective solution to payment behavior prediction. We first analyze the factors that may cause users' delay payment, and extract relevant features from the obtained payment records. Second, we divide the features into two categories: numerical features and category features, and then we preprocess these two types of features. Third, we use decision tree model [10] and 10-fold cross-validation [6] to predict payment behavior. Experiments show that we can predict the payment types of orders and gain good prediction results of 79.73% accuracy.

2   Background and Motivation

We introduce the delayed payment behavior and decision tree model in this section.

Delayed Payment. The purpose of delayed payment is to provide customers with a time buffer for convenience. However, by analyzing the payment records provided by Huaching Tech (http://www.huaching.com/), we find that 4.22% users prefer to pay after three days, and some users forgot to pay the parking fee, which could be a potential problem in the sharing economy. Fortunately, if we can predict the user payment behavior, the parking system can provide better services, such as payment reminders, which is also the motivation of this work.

Decision Tree. The decision tree model is a predictive model, and it is composed of a tree-like model and possible results [10]. According to the different types of target variables, the decision trees can be categorized as classification trees, regression trees, and CART (Classification And Regression Trees) [10]. In our work, we use payment records to train and generate CART for predicting the users' payment time. We choose this model due to its simplicity and effectiveness.

3   Payment Behavior Prediction and Statistical Analysis

We show our prediction method and statistical analysis in this section.

Payment Records. We randomly select a parking lot in Hangzhou, China. Our users' parking dataset spans 14 months from April 9th, 2019 to June 29th,

2020, which consists of 29,733 parking records. We divide the records into three categories: 1) arrears, whose payment durations are more than three days, 2) late payments, whose payment durations are longer than one day but less than three days, and 3) timely payments, whose payment durations are less than one hour.

To better understand the correlation between payment data and predict payment behavior, we analyze the correlations between payment time and related features. The related features can be divided into two categories: categorical features and numerical features. The categorical features include year, month, and user's identity (whether a user has a membership). The numerical features include 1) the money calculated as order amount minus deposit amount, 2) the total number of parkings, 3) the parking duration of this record, and 4) the average payment duration in days.

Categorical Features. We first explore the relationship between user late payment ratio and different category features. We show part of the relation between dates and payment behaviors in Fig. 1. We can see that the ratio of orders to be paid has an upward trend, possibly because the number of users is increasing year by year. We can also observe that there is a sharp decrease in February 2020, which is due to the coronavirus pandemic (COVID-19) [7].

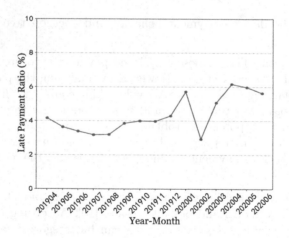

Fig. 1. Relation between dates and payment behaviors.

Numerical Features. We next analyze the numerical features and possible influence factors. We first clean up the outliers. We regard the records with the parking duration less than 5 min as noise data. From our analysis of these numerical features, we find that there is a certain linear correlation between the user's past payment time and the payment time of this order. We also observe that the users who have unpaid records have only one or two parking times.

4   Experiment

In this section, we evaluate our payment prediction method and analyze the results.

Evaluation Method. We use the decision tree model [10], as discussed in Sect. 2, to predict users' payment behavior. We train and test the model using 10-fold cross-validation [6]. The evaluation metrics we use are the average F1-macro [11] shown in Eq. 1 and accuracy [8] shown in Eq. 2. In the 10-fold cross-validation, the datasets are divided into ten equal parts. There are ten rounds, and one part is used as a test set and the rest as a training set in one round, which means that we use 26,760 records as training data and the rest as test data in one round. Our validation results(F1-macro, accuracy) are averaged over the rounds.

$$\text{Average F1} - \text{macro} = \sum_{j=0}^{10} \sum_{l=1}^{3} \frac{2 * \left(\text{precision}_{jl} * \text{recall}_{jl}\right)}{\text{precision}_{jl} + \text{recall}_{jl}}/30 \qquad (1)$$

$$\text{Average accuracy} = \sum_{j=0}^{10} \frac{\text{CR}_j}{\text{AL}_j}/10 \qquad (2)$$

In Eq. 1, l denotes the classes to be classified. In Eq. 2, CR stands for the number of correctly predicted results, and AL denotes the number of all test samples.

Decision Tree. We use the decision tree, CART [10], to predict the orders' payment type. As described in Sect. 2, decision tree is a supervised model of classification and it learns decision rules from features. We develop the model by using the *DecisionTreeClassifier* module in SKlearn [9] with python. The depth of the decision tree is automatically set by SKlearn.

Results. We use the features mentioned in Sect. 3 and use the CART model for our prediction. We demonstrate our partial results in Fig. 2; other parts of the results are similar. To distinguish between unpaid orders and paid orders, we change the payment time of unpaid orders to negative values. From Fig. 2, We have the following observations. First, our method can predict most cases; on average, it achieves 79.73% accuracy. Second, 80.26% of cases belong to timely payments, 2.96% of cases belong to late payments, and 16.79% of cases belong to arrears, which implies that the current payment situation is fine. Third, our method is good at identifying unpayable orders, which is important to shared parking scenarios.

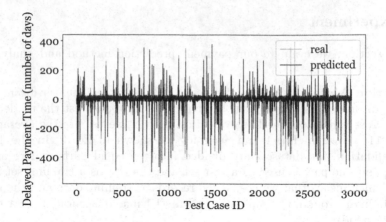

Fig. 2. Predicted payment time vs real payment time.

5   Conclusion

In this paper, we have analyzed payment behavior for a shared parking lot by leveraging related payment features. We exhibit our methods on how to perform feature analysis, and also use the CART model for parking payment prediction. Experimental results demonstrate the advantage of our method, and show that the CART model is effective in payment prediction, which achieves 79.73% accuracy.

Acknowledgments. This work is supported by the National Key Research and Development Program of China (No. 2018YFB1004401), National Natural Science Foundation of China (No. U1911203, 61802412, and 61732014), and Beijing Natural Science Foundation (No. L192027).

References

1. Alho, A.R., Silva, J.d.A.E.: Freight-trip generation model: predicting urban freight weekly parking demand from retail establishment characteristics. Transp. Res. Rec. 2411(1), 45–54 (2014)
2. Cahill, M.H., Lambert, D., Pinheiro, J.C., Sun, D.X.: Detecting fraud in the real world. In: Abello, J., Pardalos, P.M., Resende, M.G.C. (eds.) Handbook of Massive Data Sets. MC, vol. 4, pp. 911–929. Springer, Boston, MA (2002). https://doi.org/10.1007/978-1-4615-0005-6_26
3. Chen, X.: Parking occupancy prediction and pattern analysis. Dept. Comput. Sci., Stanford Univ., Stanford, CA, USA, Technical Report CS229-2014 (2014)
4. Feng, N., Zhang, F., Lin, J., Zhai, J., Du, X.: Statistical analysis and prediction of parking behavior. In: Tang, X., Chen, Q., Bose, P., Zheng, W., Gaudiot, J.-L. (eds.) NPC 2019. LNCS, vol. 11783, pp. 93–104. Springer, Cham (2019). https://doi.org/10.1007/978-3-030-30709-7_8
5. Florian, M., Los, M.: Impact of the supply of parking spaces on parking lot choice. Transp. Res. Part B: Methodol 14(1–2), 155–163 (1980)
6. Geisser, S.: Predictive Inference: An Introduction (1993)

7. Mehta, P., et al.: COVID-19: consider cytokine storm syndromes and immunosuppression. Lancet (London Engl.) **395**(10229), 1033–1034 (2020)
8. Metz, C.E.: Basic principles of roc analysis. In: Seminars in Nuclear Medicine, vol. 8, pp. 283–298. WB Saunders (1978)
9. Pedregosa, F., et al.: Scikit-learn: machine learning in python. J. Mach. Learn. Res. **12**, 2825–2830 (2011)
10. Qiu, Q., Huang, W.: Forward supervised discretization for multivariate with categorical responses. Big Data Inf. Anal. **1**(2/3), 217–225 (2016)
11. Sasaki, Y., et al.: The Truth of the F-measure 2007 (2007)
12. Wen, Y.T., Yeh, P.W., Tsai, T.H., Peng, W.C., Shuai, H.H.: Customer purchase behavior prediction from payment datasets. In: Proceedings of the Eleventh ACM International Conference on Web Search and Data Mining, pp. 628–636 (2018)
13. Zhang, F., et al.: PewLSTM: Periodic LSTM with weather-aware gating mechanism for parking behavior prediction. In: Proceedings of the Twenty-Ninth International Joint Conference on Artificial Intelligence, IJCAI-20, pp. 4424–4430. International Joint Conferences on Artificial Intelligence Organization, July 2020
14. Zhang, F., Liu, Y., Feng, N., et al.: Periodic weather-aware LSTM with event mechanism for parking behavior prediction. IEEE Trans. Knowl. Data Eng. (2021)

Edge Computing

Location-Based Service Recommendation for Cold-Start in Mobile Edge Computing

Mengshan Yu[1,2], Guisheng Fan[1(✉)], Huiqun Yu[1], and Liang Chen[1]

[1] Department of Computer Science and Engineering,
East China University of Science and Technology, Shanghai, China
{gsfan,yhq}@ecust.edu.cn
[2] Shanghai Key Laboratory of Computer Software Evaluating and Testing,
Shanghai, China

Abstract. With the rapid development of the 5G and Internet of Things (IoT), mobile edge computing has gained considerable popularity in academic and industrial field, which provides physical resources closer to end users. Service recommendation in such a distributed environment is a hot issue. However, the cold-start problem for service recommendation in mobile edge computing is still urgent to be solved. In this paper, we propose a service recommendation method based on collaborative filtering (CF) and user location, by comprehensively considering the characteristic of services at the edge and mobility of users. In detail, we first synthesize the service characteristics of each dimension through multidimensional weighting method. We further introduce the idea of Inverse_CF_Rec to the traditional CF and then predict the lost QoS value to solve the problem of sparse data. Finally, a recommendation algorithm based on predicted QoS value and user geographic location is proposed to recommend appropriate services to users. The experimental results show that our multidimensional inverse similarity recommendation algorithm based on collaborative filtering (MDICF) outperforms Inverse_CF_Rec in terms of the accuracy of recommendation.

Keywords: Mobile edge computing · QoS · Service recommendation · Multiple dimension

1 Introduction

In recent years, the edge computing paradigm has been widely adopted as a good complement to cloud computing, which brings the processing to the edge of the network [1]. And the service recommendation problem is a hot issue in edge computing. For example, when a mobile user send a service request, edge servers that have enough resources to process the information will intercept and respond to the user request [2]. And the recommendation system becomes very important if there are more than one edge server which can process user requests.

© IFIP International Federation for Information Processing 2021
Published by Springer Nature Switzerland AG 2021
X. He et al. (Eds.): NPC 2020, LNCS 12639, pp. 297–309, 2021.
https://doi.org/10.1007/978-3-030-79478-1_26

Usually, service recommendation algorithms consider quality of service (QoS) as the decision variable [3]. So, how to calculate the QoS value of the service more accurately is one of our key research points.

According to our survey, most service recommendation methods are based on massive historical data [3,4,6,9,13], such as the memory-based collaborative filtering (MCF) [3]. However, the mobility of users may lead to the fluctuation of QoS value in mobile edge computing [5]. When a mobile user moves from the wireless coverage range of one edge server to that of another edge server, the historical QoS value will become invalid and the QoS value on the new edge server is null [6]. In the field of service recommendation in edge computing, the data density is generally sparse, that is, there exists the cold start problem. And our proposed method is based on collaborative filtering. However, it is difficult to calculate the similarities between object user and other users when the object user moves to a new edge sever. To solve it, the similarities between the object user and other users who have data on the object user's historical edge server and new edge server is considered. We also calculate the similarities among users on object user's new edge server. Because of the sparse data matrix, calculating the similarities among users directly may lead to imprecise results. So authors in Ref [7] introduce the sociological theory, namely an enemy's enemy is a friend, which represents that the opposite user of a opposite user is likely to be a similar user of the object user. However, their work only consider user requirements on a single dimension. In actual decision, considers on multiple dimensions are more common.

According to aforementioned issues, we propose a multi-dimensional inverse similarity recommendation algorithm based on collaborative filtering (MDICF).

(1) Considering the multi-dimensionality of user needs and service performance at the edge, we adopt a multi-dimensional linear weighting method to take into account the needs of every dimension. For each mobile user, our weight coefficients in different dimensions are dynamically adjusted for a more comprehensive understanding of user needs.
(2) Aiming at the mobility of users and sparse data of services at the edge, we use inverse similarity to predict users QoS value based on collaborative filtering and calculate the distance between the user and the service by obtaining their latitude and longitude. A MDICF method is proposed to recommend appropriate services to users within a reasonable range.

The rest of this paper is organized as follows. Section 2 shows the related work. Section 3 details our prediction recommendation method. Section 4 introduces the design and experimental results of our experiments and Sect. 5 summarizes our methods and prospects for future work.

2   Related Work

Because of high interpretability, collaborative filtering (CF) is widely used in various recommendation systems. CF is mainly divided into two categories: Model-based and Memory-based. Memory-based CF is also called Neighborhood-based

CF, which can be divided into user-based similarity CF and content-based similarity CF. The basic idea of that method is to find similar user sets or items based on user or content similarity, and recommend to target users based on ratings of similar users or items. The similarity among users or content is mainly calculated by using Pearsons Correlation Coefficient and Cosine Similarity. In addition, hybrid recommendation algorithm contains a mixture of matrix decomposition and deep learning. This method incorporates different recommendation algorithms, so it has a powerful feature extraction ability and can automatically retrieves a deeper representation of data.

In recent years, there have been many researches on CF in the field of recommendation system. The author of [11] takes into account the number of times a user calls a service when calculating the historical QoS similarity generated when a user calls the same service. They improve authenticity and persuasion of data by using the average of all QoS. The collaborative filtering model based on matrix factorization [11,12] has also been widely used in Web service recommendation. As a potential linear model, the performance of matrix factorization is not good enough when capturing complex interactions. With the rapid development of service-oriented computing and cloud computing, many machine learning and deep learning models are applied to recommendation systems in combination with traditional collaborative filtering. The authors in [10] propose a hybrid web recommendation algorithm based on matrix factorization and deep learning which combines collaborative filtering and text content. The invocation between mashups and services and their functions are integrated into a deep neural network to describe the complex interactions between services. Article [11] proposed a model combined a compressed interaction network and DNN. On the level of vectorization, the feature interaction was generated in an explicit way. But they have serious bottlenecks in running efficiency and memory consumption. Such deep learning models can solve many problems, but there are serious bottlenecks in terms of operating efficiency and memory consumption.

In addition, the exiting recommendation algorithm in edge computing rarely take into account the location characteristics of users and services. In fact, the QoS of services in edge computing are usually closely related to the location relationship between users and services. Now that smart phones and other devices that support GPS navigation are widely used, they can collect more and more location information, which also provides reliable conditions for our location-based recommendations. There have been many researches on location-based service recommendation before. They usually introduce location information as a new dimension to recommendation algorithms. The article [14] proposed a location-aware personalized CF web service recommendation method which select similar users or services of target users in users and web services at two locations.

3 Motivation

In this section, we illustrate our method through a scenario. Vehicle-road collaboration is an important part of smart transportation. As a good complement to cloud computing, edge computing performs most of the calculations near the road at the edge. As shown in Fig. 1.

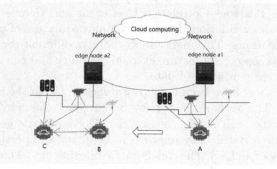

Fig. 1. Service recommendation in mobile edge computing

It integrates a local map system, traffic signal information, nearby moving targets and multiple sensor interfaces [8] at the edge node near the road. A self-driving vehicle A drives away from the coverage of edge node $a1$ and enters coverage of edge node $a2$. It needs to obtain the required services in $a2$. And we need to consider the problem of spare data when historical information of A is little at edge node $a2$. In addition, since there are many kinds of integrated at edge nodes near the road, we need to consider multidimensional feature such as response time, throughput and so on. Therefore, we propose a multi-dimensional weighted inverse similarity method to predict unknown QoS values and make recommendations based on geographic location.

4   Multidimensional Inverse Similarity Recommendation Algorithm Based on CF

According to the aforementioned analysis, we consider using collaboration filtering with reversed user similarity to predict the unknown QoS values, and the problem of multi-dimension for the QoS value is also considered. Then we recommend services to object user based on locations of user and services. Specifically, we adopt linear weighted sum method to integrate QoS in different dimensions into one comprehensive QoS. Then the problem is transformed into a linear programming problem. Our method is mainly divided into two steps:

(1) QoS prediction. This step includes the calculation of user similarity, the determination of users with similar behaviors and similar users and prediction of QoS. We predict unknown QoS through the calculation of user similarity and similar credibility.

(2) Service recommendation. We can get all services within a certain distance from the user through our calculating. We recommend services for the object user based on the predicted QoS in the previous step.

The overview of our approach is shown in Fig. 2 as follow.

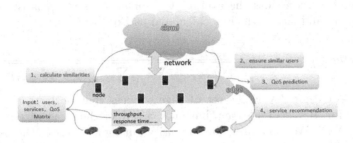

Fig. 2. Overview of MDICF

4.1 QoS Prediction

Linear Weighted Sum Method. In mobile edge computing, the focus of services at different locations may be different. Thus, we consider adopting linear weighted sum method to integrate different dimension of QoS in one service with one dimension. This is a method commonly used in the multi-objective optimization problem which keeps the original data in each dimension. The linear weighted sum method is formalized in Eq. (1):

$$\begin{cases} q = \sum_{i=1}^{S\_q}(p_i * x_i) \\ \sum_{i=1}^{S\_q} p_i = 1 \end{cases} \tag{1}$$

wherein $p_i \in [0,1]$, x_i indicates the weight coefficient and QoS value of each dimension in one service, respectively.

In this paper, we consider the response time and throughput of services at edge. So, we transform the Eq. (1) into Eq. (2):

$$\begin{cases} q_{(i,k)} = \alpha * tp_{(i,k)} + \beta * rt_{(i,k)} \\ \alpha + \beta = 1 \end{cases} \tag{2}$$

wherein α and β are weight coefficients between 0 and 1, $tp_{(i,k)}$ and $rt_{(i,k)}$ respectively represent the quality of service in terms of response time and throughput when $service_k$ is called by $user_i$, $q_{(i,k)}$ represents the weighted quality of service when $service_k$ is called by $user_i$, which is used when we calculate the similarities later. The calculation of α and β will be introduced later.

Calculate the User Similarity. Pearson correlation coefficient (PCC) is widely used in the similarity calculation because of its simplicity and efficiency. Thus, we consider using PCC to calculate the similarities of users. We use $U = \{u_1, u_2, u_3, ..., u_m\}$ to represent the user set that call for services, $E\_S = \{es_1, es_2, es_3, ..., es_n\}$ to represent the set of services at edge. In our method, $q_{(i,k)}$ represents the QoS of edge $service_k$ when $user_i$ calls for edge $service_k$ and q_i represents the average QoS of $user_i$. $sim_{(i,j)}$ is the similarity between $user_i$ and $user_j$ which is calculated as Eq. (3):

$$sim_{(i,j)} = \frac{\sum_{es_k \in IN} (q_{(i,k)} - \bar{q}_i) * (q_{(i,k)} - \bar{q}_i)}{\sqrt{\sum_{es_k \in IN}(q_{(i,k)} - \bar{q}_i)^2} * \sqrt{\sum_{es_k \in IN}(q_{(j,k)} - \bar{q}_j)^2}} \tag{3}$$

In this equation, IN is the set of edge services that both $user_i$ and $user_j$ have called for. If $user_i$ and $user_j$ have not called for the same edge service, IN is equal to $Null$. We calculated the similarity among all users in the user set. In addition, in the user similarity matrix, $sim_{(i,j)}$ is empty when IN is $Null$ (i.e. $sim_{(i,j)} = Null$ if $IN = Null$).

Calculate Similar Users. We have obtained the similarity matrix of users in previous sections. Now we define and calculate several key variables. $threshold\_P$ ($-1 \leq threshold\_P \leq 1$) denotes pre-defined similarity threshold and is adjusted in our experiment. $potential\_similar$ and $potential\_opposite$ represent potential similar user set and potential opposite user set, respectively. $rel\_matrix_{opposite}$ and $rel\_matrix_{similar}$ denote the reliability matrix of opposite users and similar users, respectively. The calculations about them will be introduced in detail later. $rel\_matrix_{opposite}$ is a user set opposite to the object user. As we can see in Eq. (4), users whose similarity with the object user is less than the threshold are defined as opposite users.

$$opposite\_users_{object\_user} = \{user_i | sim_{(object\_user,i)} \leq threshold\_P\} \tag{4}$$

We determine potential similar users based on the theory that "the enemys enemy is a possible friend" [16]. The inaccurate results will be obtained if we directly define the opposite users of $opposite\_users$ as the similar users. So we quote a reliability calculation as Eq. (5) [7]. In this equation, $user_j$ is the opposite user of object user and the $user_k$ is the opposite user of $user_j$, that is $user_j \in opposite\_user_{object\_user}$ and $user_k \in opposite\_user_j$.

$$reliability(object\_user, user_k) = sim_{(object\_user,j)} * sim_{(j,k)} \tag{5}$$

For each object user, we establish a credibility matrix for the potentially similar user set called rel_matrix_i. The similar credibility constraints between each user in the matrix and object user are as shown in Eq. (6).

$$reliability_{similar} = \{k \in potential\_similar,$$
$$reliability(object\_user, user_k) \geq -threshold\_P\} \tag{6}$$

In addition, we know that the friend of the enemy may be an enemy. Therefore, we use a opposite credibility constraint to determine the opposite user show in Eq. (7).

$$reliability_{opposite} = \{k \in potential\_opposite,$$
$$reliability(object\_user, user_l) \leq threshold\_P\} \tag{7}$$

wherein $user_j$ is the opposite user of $object\_user$ and $user_l$ is the similar user of $user_j$, that is, $user_j \in opposite\_users_{object\_user}$ and $user_l \in similar\_user_j$.

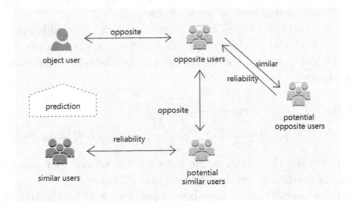

Fig. 3. QoS prediction in mobile edge computing

We then add the opposite users obtained by above constraints to the opposite user set. The relationship between users is shown in Fig. 3. We get $opposite\_users$ by calculating user similarities, and the potential similar users of opposite users can be obtained. Then, the similar users of opposite users with reliability constraint $reliability_{opposite}$ can be added into the original opposite user set. Next we get potential similar users with calculating opposite users of users in $opposite\_users$. At last, we obtain similar user set $similar\_users$ of object user through the constraint of similar reliability ($reliability_{similar}$).

QoS Prediction. We have obtained the similar users and similar reliability between all similar users and the object user. Now we regard the reliability as the probability of user similarity. So we can predict the missing QoS when the object user is calling service that has not been called before by Eq. (8) and $user_k \in similar\_users$. In this equation, $q_{(k,i)}$ and $predict\_q_{(object\_user,i)}$ denote the QoS when $user_k$ calls $service_i$ and the predicted QoS when the object user is calling $service_i$, respectively.

$$predicted\_q_{(object\_user,i)} =$$
$$\frac{\sum_{user_k \in similar\_users} reliability(object\_user, user_k) * q_{(k,i)}}{\sum_{user_k \in similar\_users} reliability(object\_user, user_k)} \tag{8}$$

4.2 Service Recommendation

It cannot be ignored in service recommendation that the wireless coverage distance of the edge server is limited. To solve this problem, we need to calculate the distance between the object user and the service to ensure that the recommended service is within the wireless coverage area. As shown in Fig. 1 in Sect. 3, we need to find a service on Edge node $a2$ that meets the needs of users.

In this paper, we use a general geographic distance calculation method, Haversine equation, to calculate the distances between users and services according to attitude and longitude. Because it uses a sine function, it can maintain enough significant figures even at small distances.

We use (lon_1, lat_1) and (lon_2, lat_2) to represent the longitude and latitude of the object user and the service, respectively. $dis(u, s_i)$ represents the distance between the object user and the i-th service. The distance calculation is shown in Eq. (9) as follow.

$$\begin{cases} dis_{(u,s_i)} = 2R \cdot arctan(\frac{\sqrt{hav(\theta)}}{\sqrt{1-hav(\theta)}}) \\ hav(\theta) = sin^2(\frac{lat_1-lat_2}{2}) + coslon_1 coslon_2 sin^2(\frac{lon_1-lon_2}{2}) \end{cases} \tag{9}$$

Wherein θ represents the center angle between the object user and the service, and R represents radius of earth. Here we take 6371 km.

Based on the calculation of the above equation, we find the recommendable service set s in the range which is shown in Eq. (10). We select the $top - K$ services from the predicted data to recommend to the object user.

$$s = \{s_1, s_2, \cdots, s_c\}, dis_{(u,s_i)} \leq \lambda \tag{10}$$

4.3 Algorithm Design

Our improved inverse user similarity collaborative filtering algorithm predicts the QoS value of the unknown service that the object user calls for. And the recommendation algorithm is based on geographic location. The implementation of our algorithms is shown as the pseudo-code of Algorithm 1.

Assuming that each QoS matrix includes m users and n service data, and all of them are in k dimensions. The analysis of our time complexity is as follow:

(1) Linear weighted sum method: The time complexity of QoS linear weighting on k dimensions is $O(k * m * n)$.
(2) Calculate the user similarity: We calculate the user similarity based on the existing user and service data offline. Here, it is $O(1)$. If he is a new user, the time complexity is $O(m)$.
(3) Calculate similar users: According to the user similarity matrix, we judge the reliability of indirect friends between users. The maximum number of opposite users is m, and the maximum number of opposite users opposite users is m. In other words, the time complexity of finding indirect similar users is $O(m^2)$ under the worst possibility.
(4) Distance calculation: The distance between object user and each service need to be calculated, so the complexity is $O(n)$.

(5) Service recommendation: We maximized the number of indirect friends as m and the number of edge services in the recommended range as n, so the worst time complexity of our QoS prediction and service recommendation is $O(m * n)$. Since indirect similar users judgment and geographical location calculation are conducted at the same time, we assume $l = Max(m^2, n)$. Based on the above analysis, the time complexity of our algorithm is $O(l + m * n)$.

Algorithm 1. MDICF

Input: U ; E_S; tp_Matrix; rt_matrix;
Output: recommendation service
Begin:
1: Initialization: $predict\_q = \phi$; $similar\_users = \phi$; $threshold\_P$
2: **for** $(q_{(i,k)}$ in QoS Matrix) **do:**
3:     $q_{(i,k)} = \alpha * tp_{(i,k)} + \beta * rt_{(i,k)}$
4: **end for**
5: **for** $(user_i$ in $U)$ **do:**
6:     **for** $(user_j$ in $U)$ **do:**
7:         calculate $sim_{(i,j)}$ by Equation(3)
8:     **end for**
9: **end for**
10: calculate $opposite\_users$ by Equation(4)
11: **for** $(user_k$ in $potential\_similar)$ **do:**
12:     calculate $reliability\_similar$ by Equation(6)
13:     update $similar\_users < - user_k$
14: **end for**
15: **for** $(user_q$ in $potential\_opposite)$ **do:**
16:     calculate $reliability\_opposite$ by Equation(7)
17:     update $opposite\_users < - user_q$
18: **end for**
19: repeat 11-18
20: **for** $(es_i$ in $E_S)$ **do:**
21:     **if** $q_{(object\_user,i)} = \phi$ **then**
22:         calculate $predicted\_q_{(object\_user,i)}$ by Equation(8)
23:     **end if**
24: **end for**
25: **for** $(es_i$ in $E_S)$ **do:**
26:     calculate $dis(object_user, i)$
27:     **if** $dis \leq \lambda$ **then:**
28:         add es_i into $potential\_service$
29:     **end if**
30: **end for**
31: **return** Top-3 services with $predicted\_q$ in $potential\_service$

---

5 Experiment

In this section, we first verify the rationality of our experiment, and then we compare our algorithm with other related algorithms. The results of experiments is calculated by running an average of 100 times.

5.1 Experiment Environment and Datasets

Datasets. In our experiment, we adopt the public dataset WSDream of the Chinese University of Hong Kong. The dataset describes real-world QoS evaluation results including both response time and throughput values, obtained from 339 users on 5825 web services as a user-service matrix. We use the real response time and throughput in the dataset to simulate the response time and throughput of the service that the user calls for at the edge. In addition, we calculate the distance between the user and service through the latitude and longitude of them in the dataset. Since we mainly consider the case where the data matrix is sparse, we randomly delete some quality items based on the original data set and obtain data matrixes with different data density d. In this paper, the data density d of the nine experimental configurations varies from 5% to 50%, namely 5%, 10%, 15%, 20%, 25%, 30%, 35%, 40% and 50%.

5.2 Experimental Design

Our algorithm is an improvement based on the traditional collaborative filtering method. Compared with traditional service recommendation, the mobility of edge users and the immediacy of demand are the important points that we need to consider. At the same time, the demand for computing power and throughput cannot be ignored. Therefore, we comprehensively consider the throughput, response time of the service and mobility of users and recommend services at the edge to end users in this paper.

Parametric Design. At the beginning of the experiment, we weight the quality of service in two dimensions. We use the linear weighting sum method in Ref. [15], where α and β are adaptive for different object users. Generally, the most important demand has the maximum weight coefficient value according to the user preferences. Since the α and β for each test user in this experiment are different, no quantitative explanation will be made here.

The threshold of similar user judgement and reliability judgement refer to the design in Ref. [7], tentatively set $threshold\_P = -0.6$. We also performed it during the experiment. After verification, we find the results of our algorithm under this threshold is relatively good.

Since this experiment is based on the WSDream dataset, the geographical distances between users and services are larger than those in our scenario, so λ should also be relatively large. Through calculation, the distance between the user and service in the data set ranges from 0 to 50000. In a real scenario at the edge, the value of λ needs to be reset according to the real coverage. Finally, we recommend the $top-3$ services to target users within this geographic range.

5.3   Experiment Results

We use Mean Absolute Error (MAE) to measure the error between our predicted value and the true value, and compare it with other methods.

In this paper, we adopt Mean Absolute Error (MAE) to measure the error between our predicted value and the true value.

$$MAE = \frac{1}{c} \cdot \sum_{i=1}^{c} |predicted\_q_i - q_i| \qquad (11)$$

In Eq. (11), c represents the number of prediction services, $predict\_q_i$ represents the predicted value, and q_i represents the true value. The smaller the MAE value, the higher the prediction accuracy.

When the data density d is 5%, the number of edge services es is 1000, and the number of different users u is varied from 100 to 300, the QoS value that predicted by our proposed method is shown in Fig. 4(a).

When the data density d is 5%, the number of users u is 100, and the number of edge services s is varied from 1000 to 3000, the QoS value that predicted by our proposed method is shown in Fig. 4(b).

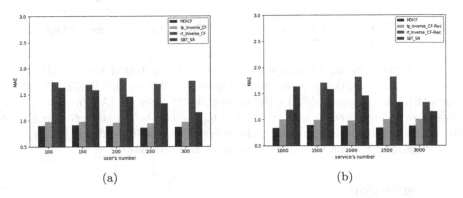

(a)   (b)

Fig. 4. Recommendation accuracy

As can be seen in the figure, compared with other methods, our method performs significantly better on the MAE evaluation index. Among them, the lowest prediction accuracy is the $Inverse\_CF\_Rec$ method when the response time is the evaluation standard. This method only considers the response time of the service as the evaluation index. However, the response time is affected by the distance besides the service application at edge. Therefore, it is difficult to make an accurate recommendation based on only one evaluation index. Followed by SBT-SR, this method only considers the theory that "the enemys enemy is a friend", but ignores "the enemys friend may be an enemy". It take less consideration about some potential similar users and potential opposite users which may lead to reduce prediction accuracy. The method our proposed has the best performing which comprehensively considers the service response time, throughput and potential similar users. At last, we consider the geographical location of users to improve the feasibility of recommendation.

In addition, we also made comparisons in different data densities. As shown in Fig. 5, when the number of edge services s is 1000, the number of users u is 100 and data density d is varied from 5% to 50%, the QoS value that predicted by our proposed method is significantly smaller than that predicted by other method in the case of data density.

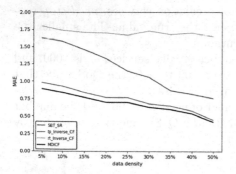
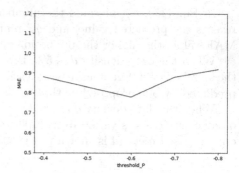

Fig. 5. MAE of different data density   **Fig. 6.** Different threshold on MAE

In this experiment, we selected object users in the test dataset, and verified the rationality of taking *threshold_P* equal to -0.6 as the similar threshold when the data density is 5% for 100 users and 1000 services. As shown in Fig. 6, we set as below: *threshold_P* $= -0.4, -0.5, -0.6, -0.7, -0.8$. Regardless of the accuracy to the decimal place, the selected threshold performs well in QoS prediction, and we can consider our value to be reasonable.

6 Conclusion

In this paper, we combine quality indicators of multiple dimensions into one comprehensive QoS value and take the geographical location of end users into consideration. These handling strategies make our method better fit the characteristics of services at edge and end users. To solve the cold start problem for the service recommendation system in edge computing, we propose a multi-dimensional inverse user similarity recommendation algorithm based on collaborative filtering (MDICF). The experimental results demonstrate the effectiveness of our algorithm for service.

In the future, we plan to improve our prediction model through deep learning when facing sparse data. In addition, how to combine the predicted QoS value with geographic location information more closely is also the focus of our future work.

Acknowledgement. This work was supported by the National Natural Science Foundation of China (No. 61702334,61772200), the Project Supported by Shanghai Natural Science Foun-dation (No.17ZR1406900, 17ZR1429700) and the Planning Project of Shanghai Insti-tute of Higher Education (No. GJEL18135)

References

1. Wang, S., Zhao, Y., Xu, J., Yuan, J., Hsu, C.H.: Edge server placement in mobile edge computing. J. Parallel Distrib. Comput **127**, 160–168 (2019)
2. Ahmed, A., Ahmed, E.: A survey on mobile edge computing. In: 2016 10th IEEE International Conference on Intelligent Systems and Control, pp. 1–8 (2016)
3. Zheng, Z., Ma, H., Lyu, M.R., King, I.: QoS-aware web service recommendation by collaborative filtering. IEEE Trans. Serv. Comput. **4**(2), 140–152 (2011)
4. Kang, G., Tang, M., Liu, J., Liu, X., Cao, B.: Diversifying web service recommendation results via exploring service usage history. IEEE Trans. Serv. Comput. **9**(4), 566–579 (2016)
5. Arshad, R., Elsawy, H., Sorour, S., Alnaffouri, T.Y., Alouini, M.S.: Handover management in dense cellular networks: a stochastic geometry approach. In: 2016 IEEE International Conference on Communications, Kuala Lumpur, pp. 1–7 (2016)
6. Wang, S., Zhao, Y., Huang, L., Xu, J., Hsu, C.H.: QoS prediction for service recommendations in mobile edge computing. J. Parallel Distrib. Comput. **127**, 134–144 (2019)
7. Zhou, Y., Tang, Z., Qi, L., Zhang, X., Dou, W., Wan, S.: Intelligent service recommendation for cold-start problems in edge computing. IEEE Access **7**, 46637–46645 (2019)
8. Ekiz, N., Salih, T., Kucukoner, S., Fidanboylu, K.: An overview of handoff techniques in cellular networks. Int. J. Inf. Technol. **2**, 132–136 (2005)
9. Herlocker, J.L.: An empirical analysis of design choices in neighborhood-based collaborative filtering algorithms. Inf. Retriev. **5**, 287–310 (2002)
10. Xiong, R., Wang, J., Zhang, N., Ma, Y.: Deep hybrid collaborative filtering for web service recommendation. Exp. Syst. Appl. **110**, 191–205 (2018)
11. Li, S., Wen, J., Luo, F., Gao, M., Zeng, J., Dong, Z.Y.: A new QoS-aware web service recommendation system based on contextual feature recognition at serverside. IEEE Trans. Netw. Serv. Manage. **14**(2), 332–342 (2017)
12. Lian, J., Zhou, X., Zhang, F., Chen, Z., Xie, X., Sun, G.: Xdeepfm: combining explicit and implicit feature interactions for recommender systems. In: 2018 24th ACM SIGKDD Conference on Knowledge Discovery and Data Mining, London, pp. 1754–1763 (2018)
13. Li, K., et al.: A personalized QoS prediction approach for cps service recommendation based on reputation and location-aware collaborative filtering. Sensors **18**(5), 1556 (2018)
14. Liu, J., Tang, M., Zheng, Z., Liu, X., Lyu, S.: Location-aware and personalized collaborative filtering for web service recommendation. IEEE Trans. Serv. Comput. **9**(5), 686–699 (2016)
15. Xie, Y., et al.: A novel directional and non-local-convergent particle swarm optimization based workflow scheduling in cloud-edge environment. Future Gener. Comput. Syst. **97**, 361–378 (2019)
16. Lianyong Q., Xuyun Z., Yiping W., Yuming Z.: A social balance theory-based service recommendation approach. In: 2015 9th Asia-Pacific Services Computing Conference, Bangkok, THAILAND, pp. 48–60 (2015)

An Adaptive Delay-Limited Offloading Scheme Based on Multi-round Auction Model for Mobile Edge Computing

Huamei Qi[1], Yiran Wang[1], Su Jiang[2], Chunmeng Yang[1(✉)], and Jia Wu[1(✉)]

[1] School of Computer Science and Engineering, Central South University,
Changsha, People's Republic of China
qhm@csu.edu.cn
[2] Information Technology Department, China Life Ecommerce Company Limited
Changsha Regional Branch, Changsha, Hunan, People's Republic of China

Abstract. Mobile edge computing (MEC) has been widely used in many
scenarios due to its advantages such as low latency, high bandwidth, and
strong real-time performance. For mobile edge computing in networks
with multiple mobile users and multiple MEC servers, this paper proposes an adaptive delay-limited offloading scheme based on a multi-round
auction model. First, a multi-round auction model is adopted. Users and
servers select each other to achieve a globally optimal match. The proposed evaluation function is based on the delay and energy consumption
that can be reduced by offloading, and weights the two parts based on
the user's optimization needs. At the same time, a mechanism for adaptive delay limitation is proposed. The threshold is dynamically updated
according to the unloading feedback, which makes the algorithm dynamically adapt to the load changes in the network. Experimental results
show that the proposed offloading scheme has obvious advantages in
reducing the total delay and the total energy consumption of the system, effectively improving the system performance.

Keywords: Mobile edge computing · Computation offloading ·
Auction model · Delay limit

1 Introduction

The dramatic increase in the number of mobile terminal devices has driven the
development of mobile cloud computing (MCC). However, due to the shortcomings of mobile cloud computing such as high latency [10], mobile edge computing (MEC) came into being [9]. Mobile edge computing has been widely used in
fields such as computationally intensive scenarios, intelligent video acceleration,
Internet of Vehicles and Internet of Things [7]. Taking a video surveillance system as an example, a mobile cloud computing network captures various video

Supported by Natural Science Foundation of China (project number: 61803387).

information through a video surveillance device, and then sends it to a cloud surveillance server for processing. This method will transmit huge video data, which not only increases the traffic load of the core network, but also has a high delay. The mobile edge computing network can directly perform data analysis on the MEC server close to the monitoring equipment. This not only reduces the pressure on the network, but also solves the bottleneck problems such as delay and energy consumption of the monitoring system [15].

Some computationally intensive applications consume a lot of resources and energy. Mobile devices have limited resources. This makes computing offloading a key technology for mobile edge computing [23]. Zhang et al. [20] propose optimization of offloading decision based on coordinate descent method in ultra-dense networking. The iterative method finally obtains the optimal offloading decision, which effectively reduces the energy consumption of the system. Wei and Zeng [14] design an edge computing offloading scheme based on Stackelberg game theory. Through the mutual influence and evolution of strategies in a Stackelberg games of "leader with multiple followers", the optimal utility of both parties is achieved. These algorithms have a good effect in a network with one MEC server, but cannot be applied in a network with multiple MEC servers.

There are also some offloading schemes applicable to networks with multiple MEC servers. The computation offloading scheme based on the improved auction model proposed in [11] considers that there are multiple users and multiple servers in the network. The evaluation function of the algorithm only considers the time delay, and does not consider the energy consumption. This is not fair enough for some computing tasks with the goal of reducing energy consumption. Lin [8] uses a multi-round auction algorithm, which is applicable to the situation of multiple users and multiple MEC servers in the network. The effect of actual offloading is not considered in the evaluation function. This standard is not objective enough.

The above solutions have achieved good results, but the following problems still exist.

1) The offloading scheme based on the auction model can realize the bidirectional selection of multiple users and multiple MEC servers in the network. But the evaluation function given in the above schemes all have deficiencies.
2) None of the existing algorithms consider the impact of delay on the network. Some algorithms give users a fixed delay tolerance, but it is difficult to meet the needs of the entire network.

Based on the above analysis, this paper proposes an adaptive delay-limited offloading scheme based on the multi-round auction model. The contributions of this paper are listed as follows.

1) The proposed evaluation function in the multi-round auction model is based on the delay and energy consumption that can be reduced by offloading, and weights the two parts based on the user's optimization needs.
2) A mechanism for adaptive delay limitation is proposed. The threshold is dynamically updated according to the offloading feedback, which makes the

algorithm dynamically adapt to the load changes in the network and improve the overall performance of the network.

The rest of this paper is organized as follows. Section 2 concludes the related work. The offloading scheme proposed in this paper is described in Sect. 3, including four parts: scenario description, calculation model, multi-round auction model, and adaptive delay-limited mechanism. Section 4 demonstrates the simulation results. Finally, Sect. 5 concludes this study.

2   Related Work

Offloading schemes with different optimization goals are suitable for different types of computing tasks [5]. Offloading schemes with the goal of reducing latency are suitable for time-sensitive tasks, while offloading schemes with the goal of reducing energy consumption are suitable for energy-constrained tasks. In order to better meet the needs of users, the scheme proposed in this paper belongs to the offloading scheme with the trade-off between latency and energy consumption, because the evaluation function proposed in this paper is related to both latency and energy consumption. According to different optimization goals, the existing offloading schemes in mobile edge computing can be divided into the following three.

2.1   Offloading Scheme with the Goal of Reducing Latency

The distributed computing offload algorithm designed in [3] quantifies the calculation delay index to achieve lower calculation time overhead. Wang et al. [12] propose a scheme that considers interference management when offloading, and allocates resources by minimizing delay. Chen et al. [2] use the idea of software-defined networking. The task offloading problem is expressed as a mixed integer nonlinear calculation process, and the problem of reducing delay is transformed into task offloading placement problem and resource allocation sub-problem. Compared with random unloading and unified unloading, this scheme can shorten the delay to a greater extent. Yu et al. [17] propose a complete polynomial time approximation scheme, which effectively shortens the calculation delay. Yuan and Cai [19] transform the optimal content offloading problem into the content maximum delivery rate problem, thereby reducing the delay. The evaluation function proposed in [11] is based on the effect of reducing latency.

2.2   Offloading Scheme with the Goal of Reducing Energy Consumption

Zhang et al. [21] use an artificial fish school algorithm, and experiments show that the algorithm has a significant reduction in energy consumption. Zhao et al. [24] propose a greedy heuristic method based on linearization and Gini coefficient to minimize system energy consumption. Geng et al. [6] use heuristic search algorithm to solve offload decision and task scheduling problems, which can significantly reduce the energy consumption of mobile devices. Zhang et al. [22] propose an energy-aware offloading scheme, which optimizes the allocation of communication and computing resources through an iterative search algorithm, thereby reducing the energy consumption of mobile devices. Xu et al. [16] propose a particle swarm optimization algorithm for energy consumption optimization, which converges stably.

2.3 Offloading Scheme with the Trade-Off Between Latency and Energy Consumption

Dai et al. [4] propose a calculation offload and resource allocation mechanism based on the multiplier method to solve the convex optimization problem of minimum energy consumption and delay weighted sum. Wang et al. [13] design a computational offload algorithm (CAMEGA) based on improved genetic algorithm with the goal of minimizing the weighted sum of delay and energy consumption. Yu et al. [18] propose a power distribution algorithm based on game theory, and uses a binary search method to optimize transmission power to reduce transmission delay and energy consumption. Zhao [25] designs a heuristic algorithm based on simulated annealing to find the optimal solution. Bozorgchenani et al. [1] model task offloading in MEC as a constrained multi-objective optimization problem (CMOP) that minimizes both the energy consumption and task processing delay of the mobile devices. Lin [8] designs an evaluation function which is the weighted sum of the user's demand for delay and energy consumption.

3 Adaptive Delay-Limited Offloading Scheme Based on Multi-round Auction Model

3.1 Scenario Description

The MEC servers are deployed on the small base stations in the network to process users offloaded tasks. They have strong real-time performance and they can provide a good user experience. Suppose that there are n mobile users in the network, forming a set $U = \{U_1, U_2, ..., U_n\}$, and m MEC servers, forming a set $S = \{S_1, S_2, ..., S_m\}$.

3.2 Calculation Model

Local Execution. Assume that the required tasks for user U_i is x bits. Each bit of computation requires the CPU to run C cycles. The user's local computing capability is F_{local} as cycle/s. Let P_{local} be the local compute power, the time and energy required for local execution can be defined as below:

$$T_{local} = \frac{xC}{F_{local}} \tag{1}$$

$$E_{local} = \frac{xC}{F_{local}} \times P_{local} \qquad (2)$$

Where T_{local} is the time required for local execution, and E_{local} is the energy consumption required for local execution.

Offloading Execution. Assume that the user U_i offloads the computing task to the MEC server S_j. The bandwidth allocated to each base station is B. The channel noise power is σ^2. The channel gain is H_n. The transmit power is P_{send}. The upload rate R_{send} can be obtained:

$$R_{send} = \frac{B}{n} \times \log_2(1 + \frac{P_{send} \times H_n}{\sigma^2}) \qquad (3)$$

Similarly, the download rate $R_{receive}$ from the MEC server to the mobile user can be obtained.

The offloading time consists of three parts: task upload time, task calculation time on the server, and calculation result download time.

$$T_{offload} = T_{calculate} + T_{send} + T_{receive} \qquad (4)$$

$$T_{calculate} = \frac{xC}{F_{server}} \qquad (5)$$

$$T_{send} = \frac{x}{R_{send}} \qquad (6)$$

$$T_{receive} = \frac{\alpha x}{R_{receive}} \qquad (7)$$

Where $T_{calculate}$ is the task compute time on the server. F_{server} is the server compute capability as cycle/s. T_{send} is the task upload time. $T_{receive}$ is the result download time. α is the data compression ratio between the calculated result and the original data.

As calculated results are compressed, the energy consumption of download is negligible. We then get:

$$T_{offload} = \frac{xC}{F_{server}} + \frac{x}{\frac{B}{n} \times \log_2(1 + \frac{P_{send} \times H_n}{\sigma^2})} + \frac{\alpha x}{\frac{B}{n} \times \log_2(1 + \frac{P_{receive} \times H_n}{\sigma^2})} \qquad (8)$$

$$E_{offload} = \frac{xP_{send}}{R_{send}} \qquad (9)$$

Where $T_{offload}$ is the offloading time. $E_{offload}$ is the offloading energy consumption.

Offloading Conditions. The computing resources required for the offloading tasks cannot exceed the total resources provided by the MEC servers. At the same time, The tasks that can be offloaded need to meet the following conditions:

$$T_{offload} \leq T_{local} \qquad (10)$$

$$E_{offload} \leq E_{local} \qquad (11)$$

3.3 Multi-round Auction Model

The multi-round auction model consists of evaluation stage and auction stage. According to formulas (8) and (9), it can be seen that due to the differences in channel conditions and the servers, the time and energy required for the same task to be offloaded to different MEC servers are various. The multi-round auction model allows users and MEC servers to perform a two-way selection, which is suitable within multiple users and MEC servers scenarios. More details of the multi-round auction model refers to [8].

Evaluation Stage. In the user's evaluation stage, each user performs a separate evaluation on all cases of offloading to different MEC servers, and the improved evaluation function proposed in this paper is:

$$price = \omega_t \times \rho_t \times (T_{local} - T_{offload}) + \omega_e \times \rho_e \times (E_{local} - E_{offload}) \qquad (12)$$

$$\omega_t + \omega_e = 1 \qquad (13)$$

Where ρ_t and ρ_e represent the bid constants of delay and energy consumption. ω_t and ω_e are the weights of delay and energy consumption. The users determine ω_t and ω_e according to the task type and different needs. For example, $\omega_t = 1$ and $\omega_e = 0$, which indicates only low delay is expected for the task offloading and not energy consumption.

After the users evaluate the resources of each MEC server, they give each element in the respective set $S = \{S_1, S_2, ..., S_m\}$ a price. $S_j.price$ represents the evaluation of the user offloading the task to the S_j server. Find the element with the biggest value of $S_j.price$ in the set S, S_j is determined to be the highest priority MEC server corresponding to the task, and $S_j.price$ is the bidding price for S_j of the task. As the larger the value of $price$, the better the MEC server fulfillment of users need.

Auction Stage. In the auction stage, each MEC server allocates resources to tasks which select this server as the highest priority server. The order of resource allocation is determined by the bidding prices of these tasks. After the first round of auction, if some tasks fail to be offloaded and there are remaining server resources, the second round of auction will be conducted. The S set will be updated, and the task will participate in the auction again with the new bid until no resources remain or the task is completely offloaded.

3.4 Adaptive Delay-Limited Mechanism

Based on the multi-round auction model, this paper proposes an Adaptive delay-limited mechanism. Since the success of the auction depends on the $price$, the time for the task to wait for the final auction is mainly related to the $price$. The smaller the value of $price$ is, the more likely the auction fails, and the longer the waiting time will be.

Algorithm 1. The Offloading Algorithm

Input: The number of MEC servers m, the number of users n, and the parameter b.
Output: The match matrix $match$.
$price \leftarrow \rho_t * \omega_t. * T_{dis} + \rho_e * \omega_e. * E_{dis}$
$P_0 \leftarrow (1 - b) * P_{max}$
// Find tasks performed locally
$[row, cell] \leftarrow find(price < P_0)$
$price(:, cell) \leftarrow 0$
$j \leftarrow length(cell)$
while $j < n$ **do**
    // Record the $price$ of tasks with big T_{wait}
    $[row, cell] \leftarrow find((T_{local} - T_{offload} < T_{wait})$
    $P(1, cell) \leftarrow price(1, cell)$
    $temp\_p \leftarrow price$
    // Match the best task for each server
    for $i \leftarrow 1$ to m **do**
        $max\_p \leftarrow max(max(price))$
        $[row, cell] \leftarrow find(temp\_p \equiv max\_p)$
        $temp\_p(:, cell) \leftarrow 0$
        $temp\_p(row, :) \leftarrow 0$
        $price(:, cell) \leftarrow 0$
        $T_s(1, cell) \leftarrow T_{calculate}(1, cell)$
        $match(row, k) \leftarrow max\_p$
        // Task offloaded successfully
        $j + +$
    end for
    $T_{wait} \leftarrow T_{wait} + max(T_s)$
    $k + +$
end while
$P_{max} \leftarrow max(P_{max}, max(P))$

If there are many tasks in the network, some of them will fail to be offloaded. Since the server computing capacity has a greater advantage than the local computing capacity, the time waiting for the next auction has little effect on tasks with not very strict latency requirements. The optimization effect brought by persistent offloading is still considerable. However, for tasks with small values of $(T_{local} - T_{offload})$ and strict latency requirements, their $price$ is relatively small. These tasks are likely to fail in multiple auctions. The delay caused by waiting for the next auction may have a great impact on them. If these tasks exit the auction early and choose to execute locally, the result can better meet their needs. At the same time, the latency of other tasks in the network will be reduced, and the burden on the entire network will be reduced.

Algorithm 1 shows the offloading algorithm proposed in this paper. The algorithm is comprising of threshold update and condition verification. A nested loop is used to match user and server resources.

The *price* of all tasks with a queue delay longer than $(T_{local} - T_{offload})$ are recorded in the set P. Find the maximum value in P and assign it to P_{max}. Set a threshold P_0, which needs to be updated according to the change of the network. After each time period, update P and P_{max} to get a new P_0:

$$P_{max} = \max\{P_{max}, \max P\} \tag{14}$$

$$P_0 = (1 - b)P_{max} \tag{15}$$

Where $b \in (0, 1)$. Its role is to provide a detection range for the estimation of P_0, allowing the threshold to change up and down.

Before each auction, an additional verification is required. The tasks to participate in the auction must meet the following conditions:

$$price \geq P_0 \tag{16}$$

It can be seen that when the network load is heavy, additional conditions will become stricter to maximize the overall benefit. When the network load is light, the probability of failure in auctions will be greatly reduced, and the value of P_0 will also adapt to changes in the network and become very small, which will allow more computing tasks to participate in the auction.

4   Simulation Results and Analysis

The experiment assumes that there are three MEC servers in the network, the number of users increases from 100 to 1000, and each user requests to offload a task. Other parameters in the experiment are shown in Table 1.

Table 1. The simulation parameters

Parameter	Value
Bandwidth allocated to each base station	20 MHz
Channel noise	-170 dBm/Hz
Channel gain	$[-50, -30]$ dBm
CPU operating capacity	1000 cycles/bit
Computing capability of local CPU	$[0.1, 1]$ GHz
Computing capability of MEC server	100 GHz
Calculation amount of each task	$[50, 200]$ kB
Local computing power	0.1 W
Local transmit power	0.1 W
Base station transmit power	1 W
Data compression rate	0.2

Figure 1 compares the delay and energy consumption of tasks executed locally and offloaded in different ways. The experiment was conducted under the condition of different number of users. The delay and energy consumption of all users were accumulated to obtain the total delay and total energy consumption. The evaluation function in [8] is only based on the needs of users, and the offloading effect of this scheme is difficult to compare with other schemes. So the offloading scheme in [11] was used for this experiment, which compensates tasks with T_{wait} through the evaluation function. It can be seen that the multi-round auction scheme with adaptive delay limitation proposed in this paper has certain advantages in reducing delay and energy consumption. The reason for the advantage is that the optimization objective of the evaluation function contains a reduction in delay and energy consumption. Another reason is that the multi-round auction ensures that each user and each MEC server can get the best global match in each auction.

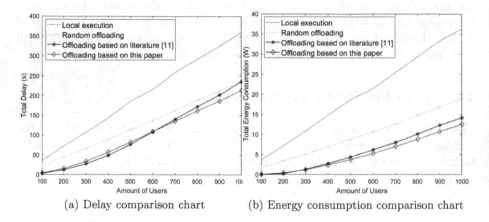

(a) Delay comparison chart   (b) Energy consumption comparison chart

Fig. 1. Comparison chart of different offloading methods

Figure 2 is a delay comparison chart of different delay limiting methods. The experiment was conducted on the basis of using the same multi-round auction model. For the offloading method with fixed delay limit, after experimental comparison, the best performance was achieved in all aspects when T_0 was 0.3 s. It can be seen that when the number of users is small, the total delay of the adaptive -delay-limited method and the non-delay-limited method is significantly lower than that of the fixed-delay-limited method. This is because some tasks can only be executed locally because they do not meet the fixed delay limit, which increases the delay. When the number of users is large, the total delay of the offloading method with fixed delay is the lowest. Because of the fixed delay limit, Some users no longer insist on offloading, which reduces the queuing delay and reduces the total delay. Although the total delay of the adaptive-delay-limited method is not the lowest, the advantages are also obvious compared with the non-delay-limited method.

Figure 3 is an energy consumption comparison chart of different delay limiting methods. It can be seen from the figure that the total energy consumption of the non-delay-limited method is always the lowest of the three. All tasks are offloaded, and users only need to consume the energy when uploading. However, in practical applications, the non-delay-limited method is hard to be accepted, because the continuous queuing delay will make the total delay increase significantly. The fixed-delay-limited method has the highest total energy consumption. This is because the fixed delay limit causes many tasks to be executed locally, which increases user energy consumption. The adaptive-delay-limited method is significantly better than the fixed-delay-limited method in terms of energy consumption.

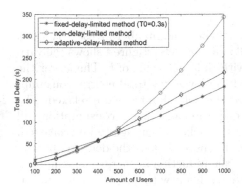 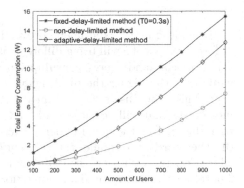

Fig. 2. Delay comparison chart of different delay limiting methods

Fig. 3. Energy consumption comparison chart of different delay limiting methods

Combining the delay result and energy consumption result of offloading, it can be known that the offloading method with adaptive delay limitation has obvious advantages. This is because the offloading effect caused by the load change will give the mechanism a feedback, so that P_0 is constantly updated. The delay limit can find the best value in a short time to adapt to the load changes in the network.

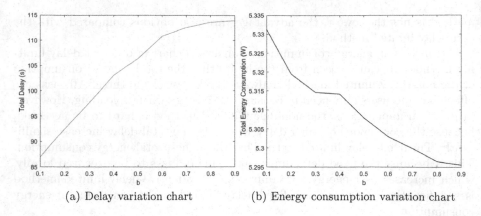

(a) Delay variation chart   (b) Energy consumption variation chart

Fig. 4. Variation chart of different b

In addition, the experiment proves that when the number of users is fixed, different values of b will bring different offloading effects. Figure 4 shows the variation of delay and energy consumption with different value of b. The larger the value of b, the higher the total delay, and the lower the total energy consumption. This is because a larger b means that the delay limit is more relaxed. The more tasks that will be successfully offloaded, the more energy consumption will be reduced. But the queuing delay causes the delay advantage to be weakened. In other words, the smaller the value of b, the more obvious the delay reduction. The larger the value of b, the more obvious the reduction in energy consumption. Therefore, the multi-round auction offloading scheme with adaptive delay limitation proposed in this paper can be applied to networks with different densities, and can also be applied to networks with different emphasis on optimization goals through the adjustment of b.

5   Conclusion

In the research of mobile edge computing offloading, in order to make the offloading scheme better applicable to the network of multiple users and multiple MEC servers, this paper adopts a multi-round auction model, in which users and MEC servers select each other to achieve the global best match. Based on the time delay and energy consumption actually reduced by offloading, and considering the optimization needs of users, a better evaluation function is proposed. This paper also designs an adaptive delay limit mechanism to continuously adapt to load changes and find the optimal delay limit to improve the overall performance of the network. Experiments show that the offloading scheme proposed in this paper can effectively reduce the total delay and total energy consumption of network devices in networks with different loads. And compared with the fixed delay limited method and non-delay limited method, it has obvious advantages.

References

1. Bozorgchenani, A., Mashhadi, F., Tarchi, D., Monroy, S.S.: Multi-objective computation sharing in energy and delay constrained mobile edge computing environments. IEEE Trans. Mob. Comput. (2020)
2. Chen, M., Hao, Y.: Task offloading for mobile edge computing in software defined ultra-dense network. IEEE J. Sel. Areas Commun. **36**(3), 587–597 (2018)
3. Chen, X., Jiao, L., Li, W., Fu, X.: Efficient multi-user computation offloading for mobile-edge cloud computing. IEEE/ACM Trans. Networking **24**(5), 2795–2808 (2015)
4. Dai, M., Liu, Z., Guo, S., Shao, S., Qiu, X.: Edge computing offload and resource allocation mechanism based on terminal energy consumption and system delay minimization. Electron. Inf. Sci. **41**(11), 2684–2690 (2019)
5. Dong, S., Li, H., Qu, Y., Zhang, Z., Hu, L.: Review of researches on computing offloading strategies in mobile edge computing. Comput. Sci. **46**(11), 32–40 (2019)
6. Geng, Y., Yang, Y., Cao, G.: Energy-efficient computation offloading for multicore-based mobile devices. In: IEEE INFOCOM 2018-IEEE Conference on Computer Communications, pp. 46–54. IEEE (2018)
7. Li, Z., Xie, R., Sun, L., Huang, T., et al.: Overview of mobile edge computing. Telecommun. Sci. **34**(1), 87–101 (2018)
8. Lin, X.: Calculation task offloading strategy based on resource joint configuration in mobile edge computing network. Master's thesis, Beijing University of Posts and Telecommunications (2017)
9. Mach, P., Becvar, Z.: Mobile edge computing: a survey on architecture and computation offloading. IEEE Commun. Surv. Tutor. **19**(3), 1628–1656 (2017)
10. Pan, J., McElhannon, J.: Future edge cloud and edge computing for internet of things applications. IEEE Internet Things J. **5**(1), 439–449 (2017)
11. Sheng, J., Teng, X., Li, W., Wang, B.: Calculation offloading strategy based on improved auction model in mobile edge computing. Computer Application Research (2019)
12. Wang, C., Yu, F.R., Liang, C., Chen, Q., Tang, L.: Joint computation offloading and interference management in wireless cellular networks with mobile edge computing. IEEE Trans. Veh. Technol. **66**(8), 7432–7445 (2017)
13. Wang, Y., Ge, H., Feng, A.: Computing offloading strategy for cloud-assisted mobile edge computing. Computer Engineering (2019)
14. Wei, Z., Zeng, L.: Edge computing offloading decision-making method based on stackelberg game theory. Math. Pract. Underst. **49**(11), 91–100 (2019)
15. Xie, R., Lian, X., Jia, Q., Huang, T., Liu, Y.: Summary of mobile edge computing offloading technology. J. Commun. **39**(11), 138–155 (2018)
16. Xu, J., Li, X., Ding, R., Liu, X.: Multi-resource calculation offloading strategy optimized for energy consumption in mobile edge computing. Comput. Integr. Manuf. Syst. **25**(4), 954–961 (2019)
17. Yu, R., Xue, G., Zhang, X.: Application provisioning in fog computing-enabled internet-of-things: A network perspective. In: IEEE INFOCOM 2018-IEEE Conference on Computer Communications, pp. 783–791. IEEE (2018)
18. Yu, X., Shi, X., Liu, Y.: Joint optimization of offloading strategy and power in mobile edge computing. Computer Engineering (2019)
19. Yuan, P., Cai, Y.: A greedy strategy for content offloading in mobile edge computing. Comput. Appl. **39**(9), 2664–2668 (2019)

20. Zhang, H., Li, H., Chen, S., He, X.: Task offloading and resource optimization based on mobile edge computing in ultra-dense networks. Electron. Inf. Sci. **41**(5), 1194–1201 (2019)

21. Zhang, H., Guo, J., Yang, L., Li, X., Ji, H.: Computation offloading considering fronthaul and backhaul in small-cell networks integrated with MEC. In: 2017 IEEE Conference on Computer Communications Workshops (INFOCOM WKSHPS), pp. 115–120. IEEE (2017)

22. Zhang, J., et al.: Energy-latency tradeoff for energy-aware offloading in mobile edge computing networks. IEEE Internet Things J. **5**(4), 2633–2645 (2017)

23. Zhang, K., Gui, X., Ren, D., Li, J., Wu, J., Ren, D.: Review of research on computing migration and content caching in mobile edge networks. J. Softw. **30**(8), 2491–2516 (2019)

24. Zhao, P., Tian, H., Qin, C., Nie, G.: Energy-saving offloading by jointly allocating radio and computational resources for mobile edge computing. IEEE Access **5**, 11255–11268 (2017)

25. Zhao, Y.: Research on computation offloading in mobile edge computing systems with limited resources. Master's thesis, Beijing University of Posts and Telecommunications (2019)

An Efficient Data Transmission Strategy for Edge-Computing-Based Opportunistic Social Networks

Jingwen Luo, Jia Wu$^{(\boxtimes)}$, and Yuzhou Wu

School of Computer Science and Engineering, Central South University,
Changsha 410083, China

Abstract. As wireless network has developed rapidly in recent years, especially with the maturity and wide application of 5G wireless system, millions of mobile users have been able to quickly exchange large amounts of data in social networks. Despite the positive impact of the recent advances in edge computing on opportunistic social networks (OSNs), classical OSN algorithms rely on only a few source nodes to forward data, which often results in data transmission delay, excessive resource consumption and even loss of source nodes. Therefore, we propose an efficient edge-computing-based data transmission strategy in OSNs. It classifies nodes into new communities according to their degree of association. Source nodes forward data through relay nodes in community, which effectively reduces the resource consumption of a single node. The experiment results of comparison with the three algorithms show that the proposed method can effectively reduce the resource consumption during data transmission as well as enhance the information transmission efficiency.

Keywords: Edge computing · Opportunistic social networks · OSNs · Data transmission · Data management

1 Introduction

The development of wireless network coupled with mobile devices has contributed to the rapid development of social networks in recent years, therefore users are able to enjoy different kinds of services and applications [1]. Especially with the rapid application of 5G (5th Generation Wireless Systems), the number of mobile terminals and devices increases significantly, reconstructing the social networks. Millions of mobile users have been able to quickly exchange large amounts of data in the social network, forming a significant network paradigm in 5G [2]. Mobile devices that are carried by users are characterized by a strong randomness and mobility, making them a social node, and the correlation between nodes can help establish communities [3].

© IFIP International Federation for Information Processing 2021
Published by Springer Nature Switzerland AG 2021
X. He et al. (Eds.): NPC 2020, LNCS 12639, pp. 323–335, 2021.
https://doi.org/10.1007/978-3-030-79478-1_28

Also, innovations keep emerging in different fields, with mobile edge computing included, which will dramatically affect social networks [4]. By incorporating edge computing into the opportunistic social networks (OSNs), the system can better evaluate users' current situation in the social network, optimize the network by calculating and evaluating, and give reasonable selection suggestions. It can significantly increase the data transmission of nodes and effectively reduce the network's data transmission delay.

In OSNs, Vahdat etc. al. proposed the Epidemic routing algorithm [5], and Lu etc. al. proposed an improved Epidemic scheme which is energy-saving n-epidemic algorithm [6]. However, those algorithms adopt flooding techniques to transmit data, which increases the network overhead significantly. Spyropoulos etc. al. brought forward the Spray and Wait routing algorithm [7], and Wang etc. al. brought forward a dynamic Spray-and-Wait algorithm [8]. The calculation and update of node quality by those algorithm can be restricted by the energy consumption. Edge computing as a new computing paradigm in recent years, which, in social networks, could be capable of solving many issues like latency, limited battery life of mobile devices, and bandwidth cost, etc. [9,10].

However, edge computing can nott completely solve the existed problems in OSNs where nodes search opportunities to exchange data in the way of "store-carry-forward" in their communities [11]. For the traditional opportunistic algorithms, a lot of communities use one or two nodes existing in the social network for information delivery. Those nodes have to transmit a large amount of data as well as calculate many tasks that will consume more energy [12,13]. In the traditional opportunistic network protocol, due to the lack of enough cache or overhead for source node, data transmission may cost a long time in the community [11]. What's worse is that for these nodes, information transmission will consume many resources by using flooding technology and data will be lost as the source node dies.

To solve above-mentioned limitations, the paper focuses on proposing an efficient data transmission scheme based on edge computing in OSNs, reconstructing the community taking into account to which degree the edge or the source node is associated with the neighbor nodes. The correlated community nodes take charge of a data transmission task, i.e., allocating some source nodes. The proposed scheme is capable of reducing source node consumption as well as prolonging the source node's life cycle. The paper mainly makes three contributions as follows.

- Regarding community reconstruction, source nodes are required to conduct reconstruction based on the degree of association between nodes, and information transmission shall be performed in proper communities;
- The proposed algorithm is characterized by an effective information delivery and is capable of reducing the energy consumption by source nodes during data transmission;
- As shown by experiments, the method can dramatically lower the energy consumption as well as enhance the delivery efficiency of data.

2   System Model

In OSNs, the scarcity of source nodes and ineffective information transmission may cause the enormous resources consumption of single source node and the death of source node, finally data carried by the source node will loss. For preventing the nodes resource from being over-consumed as well as reducing the node death rate, it is necessary to focus on searching some proper adjacent nodes for helping the source node to deliver a part of data. On that account, we define the changing theorems of communities and propose a data transmission algorithm with a high effectiveness based on edge computing in this section.

2.1   Community Definition

Suppose a user sends a data download request to the associated network. Firstly, considering the download content and the user's information, the system can check whether the associated edge or source nodes have the cache data. If yes, the system can decide who (edge user or source node) sends the requested information directly to the mobile user based on channel, correlation, and energy consumption, etc. If not, edge user or source nodes will get current data based on their computing power, channel conditions, degree of association, energy consumption, and so on, and then send the obtained data to the requested user. The process is shown in Fig. 1.

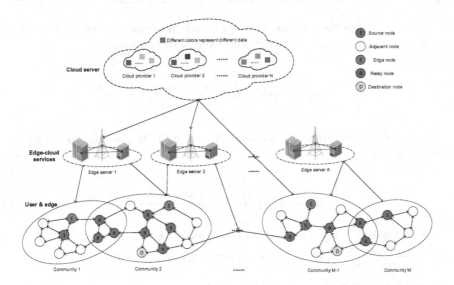

Fig. 1. The opportunistic social networks with edge computing.

However, in the process of user movement, the community of node may change. Therefore, the changing form of communities during user movement shall be proved.

Based on the weighted networks in social networks [14], the network topological structure can be expressed as G =(N, E, ω), where N represents the node number in current network, E can be expressed as $N = \{(a, b) \mid a \in N, b \in N\}$, both of a and b is nodes, ω is the weight between a and b. There are n adjacent nodes for source node N_s at t moment, and $n \subseteq N$. When source node and adjacent node meet the condition $\upsilon \omega_{ij} \geq \theta$, the source node can forward information through the adjacent node, which can be called relay node. $\upsilon \omega_{ij}$ represents the association between source node N_i and adjacent node N_j, υ stands for a coefficient, ω_{ij} means weight between N_i and N_j, and θ stands for the threshold. Here the structural degree exhibited by community is defined as S_X, which can predict the changes in the community X.

$$S_X(t) = \frac{\omega_x}{T} - \frac{\omega_s^2}{(2T)^2} = \frac{4T\omega_x - \alpha_s^2}{(2T)^2} \tag{1}$$

$S_X(t)$ denotes the structural degree exhibited by community X, T means the total weight in networks, ω_x means the total weight of community X, α_i means the total degree of N_i, $\Delta\omega$ denotes the weight variation, ω_{ij} denotes the edge weight between N_i and N_j, E_X^i denotes the total edge weight of N_i in X. The theorem and proof are as follows.

Theorem 1. *When the community X is divided into two sub-communities X_i and X_j, it should satisfy the requirements $\frac{\alpha_i \alpha_j}{2T} < \omega_{ij} < \Delta\omega + \frac{\alpha_i \alpha_j + \alpha_s \Delta\omega + \Delta\omega^2}{2(T+\Delta\omega)}$.*

Proof. Suppose the community X is split into sub-communities of X_i and X_j, and considering the increase in the total weight of community,

$$\begin{cases} \omega_i + \omega_j < T \\ \frac{S_i}{T} - \frac{\alpha_i^2}{4T^2} + \frac{S_j}{T} - \frac{\alpha_j^2}{4T^2} < \frac{\alpha_i + \alpha_j + \omega_{ij}}{T} - \frac{(\alpha_i + \alpha_j)^2}{4T^2} \\ \omega_{ij} > \frac{\alpha_i \alpha_j}{2T} \end{cases} \tag{2}$$

With the decrease in the given total weight, it is possible to rewrite the formula as follows.

$$\omega_i^* + \omega_i^* > T^* \tag{3}$$

$$\omega_{ij} < \Delta\omega + \frac{\alpha_i \alpha_j + \alpha_s \Delta\omega + \Delta\omega^2}{2(T + \Delta\omega)} \tag{4}$$

Thus, the sub-communities X_i and X_j satisfies the theorem $\frac{\alpha_i \alpha_j}{2T} < \omega_{ij} < \Delta\omega + \frac{\alpha_i \alpha_j + \alpha_s \Delta\omega + \Delta\omega^2}{2(T+\Delta\omega)}$, then the community X is separated.

Theorem 2. *During node N_i movement, the edge of the node N_i connects node N_j and becomes the only edge of node N_j. With the decline of the weight between N_i and N_j, N_j can not be separated from the community.*

Proof. Similar to theorem 1, the assumption that edge weight reduction between N_i and N_j is represented by Δw, $\Delta w < 0$. With the separation of community X, below theorem should be satisfied.

$$
\begin{cases}
\omega_i + \omega_j < \mathrm{T} \\
\frac{4T\omega_i - \alpha_i^2}{(2T)^2} + \frac{4T\omega_j - \alpha_j^2}{(2T)^2} < \frac{4T(\alpha_i + \alpha_j + \omega_{ij}) - (\alpha_i + \alpha_j)^2}{(2T)^2} \\
\omega_{ij} > \frac{\alpha_i \alpha_j}{2T}
\end{cases}
\tag{5}
$$

ω_i^* and ω_j^* is the edge weight of N_i and N_j after community X separate, T^* is the community total weight ater separate. Then,

$$
\begin{cases}
\omega_i^* + \omega_j^* > T^* \\
\omega_{ij} < \frac{\varepsilon_s \varepsilon_i + \varepsilon_s \Delta w + \Delta w^2}{2(\kappa + \Delta w)} + \Delta w
\end{cases}
\tag{6}
$$

That is

$$
\frac{\alpha_i \alpha_j}{2T} < \omega_{ij} < \frac{\alpha_i \alpha_j + \alpha_i \Delta w + \Delta w^2}{2(T + \Delta w)} + \Delta w
\tag{7}
$$

It can be explained as

$$
\frac{\alpha_i \alpha_j}{2T} < \omega_{ij} < \frac{\alpha_i \alpha_j + \alpha_i \Delta w}{2(T + \Delta w)}
\tag{8}
$$

Because

$$
\frac{\alpha_i \alpha_j + \alpha_i \Delta w}{2(T + \Delta w)} - \frac{\alpha_i \alpha_j}{2T} = \frac{\alpha_i \Delta w (T - \alpha_j)}{2T(T + \Delta w)} < 0
\tag{9}
$$

$\frac{\alpha_i \alpha_j}{2T} < \omega_{ij} < \frac{\alpha_i \alpha_j + \alpha_i \Delta w + \Delta w^2}{2(T + \Delta w)}$ is a false proposition.

Hence, the only edge of N_j connects N_i and the weight decreases. N_j can not be separated from the community.

Theorem 3. *N_i in community X, the edge weight as well as the weight of community Y increase, satisfying the equation $4(T + \Delta w)(E_Y^i - E_X^i + \Delta w) + (\alpha_i + \Delta w)(\alpha_X - \alpha_Y - \alpha_i) - \Delta w^2 > 0$, thus it is possible for N_i to join into community Y.*

Proof. Community X and Y see rising edge weight, and communities' structure degree is:

$$
S_X + S_Y = \frac{2T\omega_X - (\alpha_X + \Delta w)^2}{4(T + \Delta w)^2} + \frac{2T\omega_Y - (\alpha_Y + \Delta w)^2}{4(T + \Delta w)^2}
\tag{10}
$$

With N_i leaving community X as well as jointing into community Y, communities' structure degree is:

$$
S_{X-i} + S_{Y+i} = \frac{4T(\omega_X - E_X^i) - (\alpha_X + \Delta w)^2}{4(T + \Delta w)^2} + \frac{4T\omega_Y - (\alpha_Y + \Delta w)^2}{4(T + \Delta w)^2}
\tag{11}
$$

To proof that the the join of N_i will increase the structure degree exhibited by community Y, it is necessary to first proof $S_{X-i} + S_{Y+i} > S_X + S_Y$.

$$4(T + \Delta\omega)\left(E_Y^i - E_X^i + \Delta\omega\right) + (\alpha_i + \Delta\omega)(\alpha_X - \alpha_Y - \alpha_i) - \Delta\omega^2 > 0 \quad (12)$$

Above theorems assist in proving the changes of community in the course of node movement.

2.2   Data Transmission Model

During the data transmission of OSNs, multiple hop transmission is needed to deliver data to destination nodes. Besides, the delivery of complete data to community's node is usually conducted in an overlay way, which will greatly increase the routing overhead as well as the energy consumption. Therefore, an Edge-Computing-based Efficient Data Transmission (ECEDT) scheme is designed to reduce the routing overhead as well as the energy consumption of source nodes.

In this scheme, the source node N_s and the relay nodes communicate with each other, with the later receiving as well as storing certain data from the former. Relay nodes take charge of broad information transmission to other nodes. The movement of source node is along with searching for relay nodes from adjacent nodes, as well as reconstructing the old community into new ones. Reconstructed communities are able to relieve the pressure suffered by source node

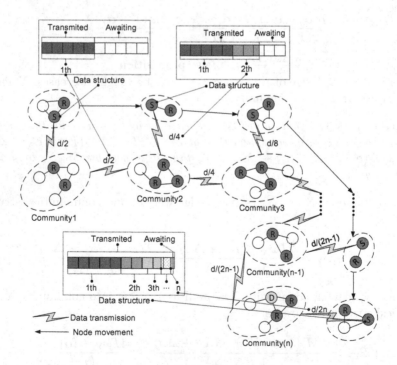

Fig. 2. The process of data transmission.

for data transmission and information spread, which enables the transmission of data on the line. For a clear description of the delivery process of information, how ECEDT scheme works is explained below:

Step 1: The total data that are carried by the source node N_s are expressed as $T_0(\vartheta) = \vartheta_0$, and N_s sends a message of "HELLO" to the adjacent nodes for searching those that can be used in a community.

Step 2: After receiving the message of "HELLO" in the community, the adjacent node will give a response, followed by establishing a connection to the source node. If adjacent node meets the condition $vw_{ij} \geq \theta$, it can be converted into a relay node.

Step 3: The source node begins to communicate with the relay node, together with transmitting 50% of data to the relay nodes of community with multiple perceptions. With the source node marking the completion of data transmission, the relay node regarding community 1 will receive information from N_s after the first data transmission (as shown in Fig. 2).

Then, the information carried by community 1 are as follows.

$$T_1(\vartheta) = \frac{1}{2}T_0(\vartheta) = \frac{1}{2}\vartheta_0 \tag{13}$$

$T_{sur1}(\vartheta)$ represents the surplus data that were unset by N_s after the first transmission.

$$T_{sur1}(\vartheta) = T_0(\vartheta) - T_1(\vartheta) = \vartheta_0 - \frac{1}{2}\vartheta_0 = \frac{1}{2}\vartheta_0 \tag{14}$$

Step 4: The source node keeps moving, together with sending the message of "HELLO" as well as searching for relay nodes.

Step 5: The source node firstly communicates with community 2, followed by sending 50% of data that are unset to the nodes in the community. Also, data are transmitted between communities, and the nodes in community 1 are capable of broadcasting 50% of the information provided by the source node (Fig. 2).

Information below are received by community 2:

$$T_2(\vartheta) = \frac{1}{2}T_{sur1}(\vartheta) + T_1(\vartheta) = \frac{1}{2^2}T_0(\vartheta) + T_1(\vartheta) = \frac{3}{4}\vartheta_0 \tag{15}$$

Below equation describes the surplus information that are unsent by N_s after the second transmission:

$$T_{sur2}(\vartheta) = T_0(\vartheta) - T_2(\vartheta) - T_1(\vartheta) \tag{16}$$

As is well known, data of community 2 covers all the data provided by community 1, i.e. $T_1(\vartheta) \subseteq T_2(\vartheta)$. Therefore, equation (16) can be rewritten into:

$$T_{sur2}(\vartheta) = T_0(\vartheta) - T_2(\vartheta) = \varphi_0 - \frac{1}{2^2}\vartheta_0 - \frac{1}{2^1}\vartheta_0 = \frac{1}{4}\vartheta_0 \tag{17}$$

The source node marks the unsent surplus information and keeps moving.

Step 6: It is assumed that communities can achieve data communication, therefore, with the source node meeting the community 3 and beginning to transmit information, community 3 is able to see the message from the previous two communities.

$$T_3(\vartheta) = \frac{1}{2}T_{sur2}(\vartheta) + T_2(\vartheta) + T_1(\vartheta) = \frac{7}{8}\vartheta_0 \qquad (18)$$

The surplus information are marked by source node, and the source node keeps moving. Equation 17 shows the surplus information unsent by N_s after the third transmission.

$$T_{sur3}(\vartheta) = T_0(\vartheta) - T_3(\vartheta) = \vartheta_0 - \frac{1}{2^3}\vartheta_0 - \frac{1}{2^2}\vartheta_0 - \frac{1}{2^1}\vartheta_0 = \frac{1}{8}\vartheta_0 \qquad (19)$$

Step 7: Repeat abovementioned procedures.

Step 8: With the source node searching for target node's community after information transmission is performed for n times, $\frac{1}{2^n}T_0$ denotes target node's community information, and $\sum_{k=1}^{n-1} T_k(\vartheta)$ denotes the communication data between different communities. Figure 2 displays the entire transmission process.

When $n \to \infty$, the ECEDT scheme transmits the same amount of information with the Epidemic and Spray and Wait algorithm. If the data are transmitted for a long time, those received by the destination node will be more complete. And ECEDT, Epidemic and Spray and Wait exhibit a time complexity of $O(2n-1)$, $O(n)$ and $O(2n)$ respectively. But the routing overhead of ECEDT, Epidemic and Spray and Wait is $\sum_{k=1}^{n}(\frac{1}{2})^k = 1 - (\frac{1}{2})^n$, n and n. ECEDT has an obviously lower routing overhead compared with Epidemic and Spray and Wait $n \to \infty$.

3   Simulation and Analysis

For evaluating the performance exhibited by ECEDT, a simulation tool named Opportunistic Network Environment (ONE) is adopted [15], and is compared with the three basic approaches, i.e. Information cache management and data transmission (ICMT) algorithm [16], Status estimation and cache management (SECM) algorithm [17], and Spray and Wait algorithm [7].

The experiment sets the simulation parameters: The simulation time lasts for 1–6 hours, and the network area is 4500m×3400m. The transmission adopts the broadcast pattern, that involves 400 nodes moving at 0.5 to 1.5m/s in a random manner. Each node has 5MB cache storage information. The social model is adopted for nodes for data transmission, and each node has the max transmission domain of $10m^2$. Data packet is sent each 25–35 at the transmission speed of 250KB/s. The initial energy of each node reaches 100 Joules, and 1J energy will be consumed for sending a data packet. Based on the simulation report data, the experimental results are shown in Fig. 3-4.

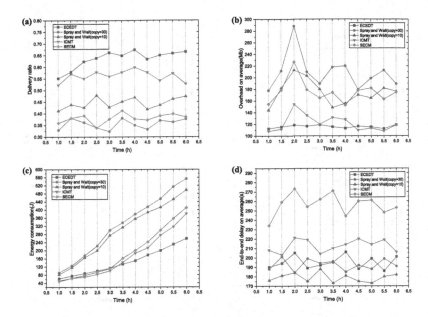

Fig. 3. Relationship between time and different parameters.

Figure 3 shows the relationship between time and four parameters. In Fig. 3(a), the transmission rates of Spray and Wait(copy = 30 and copy = 10) and SECM are lower than ECEDT. Spray-and-Wait and SECM algorithms deliver information to nodes by copying a large amount of duplicate information and using the flooding method, leading to more information loss. ICMT algorithm controls the time interval of delivery information that improves the transmission and receiving of effective information, which is its delivery ratio higher than the other two. ECEDT combining multi-sensing community and mobile node transmission base on edge-computing, the transmission rate of the algorithm is effectively improved and is the highest among all algorithms.

In Fig. 3(b), the routing overhead of the ECEDT is maintained steady, and ICMT's performance is also good. But the routing overhead of Spray and Wait routing algorithm(copy = 30) is highest. Spray and Wait(copy = 10) and SECM have a local flooding phenomenon, which overhead remains in a high range.

In Fig. 3(c), the energy consumption of Spray and Wait is highest, and each node needs energy to transmit information through spray. Several communities bear the energy consumption and extend the information transmission time of nodes in the ECEDT algorithm, thus reducing the number of information transmission times to source nodes. The energy consumption of the ECEDT is less than the other.

In Fig. 3(d), the SECM adopts a encounter delivery method that mass copied information transmit, and its average delay is highest. ECEDT's delay remained in a fairly good range. The transmission delay of Spray and Wait is lowest. It can indicate that their information diffusion capability is strong.

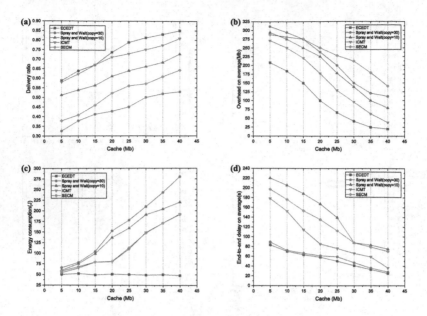

Fig. 4. Relationship between cache and different parameters.

Node ache acts as a significant indicator for social networks and can directly impact algorithms' transmission efficiency. Figure 4 displays the relationship between cache and 4 parameters. In Fig. 4(a), Spray and Wait algorithm adopts flooding method, and its delivery ratio is lowest. The raising delivery ratio of ECEDT is significant in increasing node cache due to combining community and node mobile delivery data. ICMT's delivery rate is also good.

Figure 4(b) show that a larger node cache can reduce the node overhead. The routing overhead of the ECEDT drops faster than the other three.

In Fig. 4(c), ECEDT adopts a data delivery method assisted by the community that reduces energy consumption significantly. Other algorithms' energy consumption increase as the cache enlarges, while ECEDT's energy consumption remains steady.

Figure 4(d) show that the delivery delay decline with the increasing cache, the delay of ECEDT and Spray and Wait(copy = 30) lower than the other two algorithms.

Based on the above experiment analysis, ECEDT performs better than other algorithms with regard to the transmission rate, the energy consumption and the routing overhead, however, it exhibits a higher time delay than that of the Spray and Wait routing algorithm. In practice, ECEDT performs better regarding the information transmission for a long time.

The actual environment sees different kinds of information transfer approaches. Hence, it is necessary to attach importance to various moving approaches. Three different mobile modes are chosen for confirming the performance exhibited by ECEDT, namely Shortest Path Map Based Movement

(SPMBM), random way point (RWP), and random walk (RW) [15]. The simulation results are shown in Figure 5.

In Fig. 5(a), the RWP model exhibits the best overall performance and the largest delivery rate, and the RWP model exhibits a higher delivery rate than the RW model.

In Fig. 5(b), considering the node movement process as well as the information transfer process, community can share information with abundant nodes while transferring information and reconstructing node. The routing overhead of ECEDT suffers a slight impact, and the routing overhead of the three models ranges from 110 to 120.

In Fig. 5(c), the three models present a slightly different energy consumption. As shown in the result, ECEDT exhibits a stable performance for node information transmission, and model change consume many energy.

In Fig. 5(d), for three models in the range of 185–220, RW and SPBM present the largest and smallest delay, respectively. The results demonstrate the effectiveness of SPMBM model of ECEDT regarding information transmission.

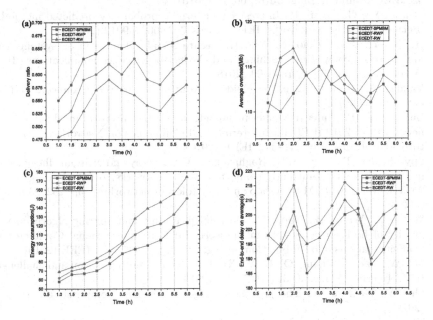

Fig. 5. Relationship between time and different parameters in three mobile models.

4   Conclusion

The paper focuses on designing a data transmission scheme with a high efficiency, i.e. (edge-computing-based efficient data transmission (ECEDT), which can assist in solving the problem that source nodes consume excessive energy. The performance exhibited by traditional opportunistic network algorithms is compared and analyzed. As indicated by the experiment, the proposed scheme can well transmit data and performs excellently in three mobile models, which demonstrates its steadiness in various environments. In edge-computing-based OSNs, the proposed scheme is capable of lowering nodes' energy consumption, prolonging the life cycle of network as well as remarkably enhancing the efficiency of data transmission. The future work is suggested to pay attention to energy consumption reduction regarding source nodes and relay nodes.

References

1. Ye, M., Yin, P., Lee, W.C.: Location recommendation for location-based social networks. In: Proceedings of the 18th SIGSPATIAL international conference on advances in geographic information systems, pp. 458–461 (2010)
2. Su, Z., Xu, Q.: Content distribution over content centric mobile social networks in 5g. IEEE Commun. Mag. **53**(6), 66–72 (2015)
3. Wu, J., Yu, G., Guan, P.: Interest characteristic probability predicted method in social opportunistic networks. IEEE Access **7**, 59002–59012 (2019)
4. He, Y., Yu, F.R., Zhao, N., Yin, H.: Secure social networks in 5g systems with mobile edge computing, caching, and device-to-device communications. IEEE Wirel. Commun. **25**(3), 103–109 (2018)
5. Vahdat, A., Becker, D., et al.: Epidemic routing for partially connected ad hoc networks (2000)
6. Lu, X., Hui, P.: An energy-efficient n-epidemic routing protocol for delay tolerant networks. In: 2010 IEEE Fifth International Conference on Networking, Architecture, and Storage, pp. 341–347. IEEE (2010)
7. Spyropoulos, T., Psounis, K., Raghavendra, C.S.: Spray and wait: an efficient routing scheme for intermittently connected mobile networks. In: Proceedings of the 2005 ACM SIGCOMM workshop on Delay-tolerant networking, pp. 252–259. ACM (2005)
8. Wang, G., Wang, B., Gao, Y.: Dynamic spray and wait routing algorithm with quality of node in delay tolerant network. In: 2010 International Conference on Communications and Mobile Computing, vol. 3, pp. 452–456. IEEE (2010)
9. Shi, W., Cao, J., Zhang, Q., Li, Y., Xu, L.: Edge computing: vision and challenges. IEEE Internet Things J. **3**(5), 637–646 (2016)
10. Shi, W., Dustdar, S.: The promise of edge computing. Computer **49**(5), 78–81 (2016)
11. Wu, J., Chen, Z., Zhao, M.: Community recombination and duplication node traverse algorithm in opportunistic social networks. Peer-to-Peer Netw. Appl. **13**(3), 940–947 (2020)
12. Liu, H., Kou, H., Yan, C., Qi, L.: Link prediction in paper citation network to construct paper correlation graph. EURASIP J. Wirel. Commun. Netw. **2019**(1), 1–12 (2019)
13. Yuan, Y., Ong, Y.S., Gupta, A., Xu, H.: Objective reduction in many-objective optimization: evolutionary multiobjective approaches and comprehensive analysis. IEEE Trans. Evol. Comput. **22**(2), 189–210 (2017)
14. Newman, M.E.: Analysis of weighted networks. Phys. Rev. E **70**(5), 056131 (2004)

15. Keranen, A.: Opportunistic network environment simulator. Special Assignment report, Helsinki University of Technology, Department of Communications and Networking (2008)
16. Wu, J., Chen, Z., Zhao, M.: Information cache management and data transmission algorithm in opportunistic social networks. Wirel. Netw. **25**(6), 2977–2988 (2019)
17. Wu, J., Chen, Z., Zhao, M.: Secm: status estimation and cache management algorithm in opportunistic networks. J. Supercomput. **75**(5), 2629–2647 (2019)

Emering

Shadow Data: A Method to Optimize Incremental Synchronization in Data Center

Changjian Zhang[1], Deyu Qi[1(✉)], and Wenhao Huang[1,2]

[1] School of Computer Science and Engineering, South China University of Technology, Guangzhou, China
csa@scut.edu.cn
[2] Guangzhou Mingsen Technology Company Ltd., Guangzhou 510000, China

Abstract. With the continuous increase of data, the data center that plays the role of backup is facing the problem of energy hunger. In practice, to reduce the bandwidth, the local data is synchronized to the data center based on incremental synchronization. In this process, the data center will generate a huge CPU load. To solve this pressure of the data center, first, we analyze the process of the Rsync algorithm, the most commonly used in incremental synchronization, and CDC algorithms, another way of chunking algorithm. Then we propose a data structure called Shadow Data, which greatly reduces the CPU load of the data center by sacrificing part of the hard disk space in the local node.

Keywords: Data synchronization · Shadow data · Data backup

1 Introduction

In case of the loss of important data caused by the PC crash, companies and individuals choose to put these data in their own or third-party data centers [1,2]. However, data centers face challenges from data synchronization and others [3,4]. As more and more data is managed in data centers, more and more requests for data synchronization will be made. In this case, data centers usually increase their processing capacity by adding servers.

Since most of the synchronization requests in the data center are incremental synchronization, to increase the parallel processing capacity of the data center, we start with the process of incremental synchronization. We analyze why incremental synchronization would cost a lot of data center resources, and remove the most CPU consuming steps from the process, store the Shadow Data of backup in the local node instead.

The main contributions of this paper are as follows:

1. We analyze the process of incremental synchronization algorithms, including the Rsync algorithm and CDC(content-defined chunking) algorithms. Then we find out the steps caused CPU load of the data center in this process.

ⓒ IFIP International Federation for Information Processing 2021
Published by Springer Nature Switzerland AG 2021
X. He et al. (Eds.): NPC 2020, LNCS 12639, pp. 339–348, 2021.
https://doi.org/10.1007/978-3-030-79478-1_29

2. We propose a data structure, Shadow Data. After finding out the cause of the CPU load in the data center, we propose to store the Shadow Data of the data center in the local hard disk, which can cut off several steps of incremental synchronization at the data center to reduce the CPU load.
3. In the experiments, we test the practicability of Shadow Data. For the same size of local data that you want to synchronize to the data center, the Shadow Data can reduce the CPU load of the data center to about 14% of the original.

2   Background and Related Work

2.1   Incremental Synchronization

With the growth of the size of one single file, the synchronization of the file always goes incremental. When incremental synchronization is implemented, it is achieved through multiple network communications between the local and data center. The simplified communication flow of incremental synchronization between local and data center is shown in Fig. 1 [5,6]. It should be noted that the synchronization process discussed in this paper is the upload process of one single file in the data center. The upload process refers to copying the local data to the data center. Corresponding to this is the download process, which copies the data in the data center to the local.

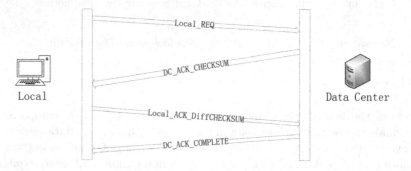

Fig. 1. The communication flow between the local and data center to complete the synchronization of one single file.

As mentioned above, the communication process shown in Fig. 1 is simplified. We remove some confirmation messages and focus on the key messages the four in Fig. 1. A detailed introduction to these messages is as follows:

1. Local_REQ: Request message. It is sent to the data center from the local node, indicating that a synchronization request about one single file is to be initiated. The message content is: $|LocalFileInfo|DCFileInfo|$. $LocalFileInfo$: information about local file in this synchronization request. $DCFileInfo$: information about target file in the data center.
2. DC_ACK_CHECKSUM: message sent by data center to local. It contains chunk abstract information for the target file stored in the data center.

The message content is: $|Over\_flag|Chunk\_abstract|$. $Over\_flag$ indicates whether it is the last message. $Chunk\_abstract$: abstract information for one chunk.

3. Local_ACK_DiffCHECKSUM: message sent by local to data center. After comparing the local file and the checksum content, local node gets the different chunk information, and sent to data center with $Local\_ACK\_DiffCHE$ $CKSUM$ message. The message content is: $|Over\_flag|Chunk\_info|$. $Over\_flag$ indicates whether it is the last message. $Chunk\_info$: chunk information. There are two kinds of chunk information: one for the same chunk and the other for the different chunk.

4. DC_ACK_COMPLETE: message sent by data center to local. This message is to tell local that the synchronization request is finished. The message content is: $|Complete\_info|$. It contains some information about result.

The actual message sent is $messagehead + messagecontent$. $messagehead$: $|Mes_head|Mes_type|$. Mes_head contains some version information. Mes_type is the type of this message.

2.2 Related Work

Academic circles have done a lot of research on incremental synchronization among files. The Rsync algorithm [5], proposed by Andrew Tridgell, claims to complete the synchronization task through multi-segment communication and propose a strong and weak hash code to improve synchronization performance. The weak hash function chosen by Rsync is the Adler-32, which is a rolling-check algorithm, and the strong one is MD5. To optimize the resource usage of Rsync, Chao Yang et al. proposed an optimized communication process to reduce the data center CPU load during downloading [6]. Besides, many scholars optimize the Rsync algorithm from the perspective of the chunking algorithm. Won Youjip et al. proposed MUCH algorithm base on Rabin to speed up the chunking process with multi-thread [7]. Jihong Ma et al. proposed UCDC algorithm, claims the definition of a chunking mark is: for a value of a string, taking the remainder from being divided by a fixed value [8]. Instead of division, some chunking algorithms using byte comparison are proposed: LMC(Local Maximum Chunking) algorithm decides to set a cut-off point when the maximum value of a window data is in the middle of the window [9]; in order to speed up the validation of the window data, AE [10] and RAM [11] algorithms are proposed. For AE, if the maximum value of bytes in the data window is located at the end of the window, the cut-off point is set at the end of the window. For RAM: if a byte value with no less than all byte values in the window is read out of the window, a cut-off point is set at this byte. To make the cut point of chunk more stable, Changjian Zhang et al. proposed MII [12] and PCI [13] algorithms, set a cut-point based on the length of a increasing interval and number of '1' in binary window Separately.

However, the focus of these studies is to improve the synchronization performance without considering the optimization of synchronization process and reducing unnecessary steps with the idea of space for time.

3   The Design of Shadow Data

3.1   What Makes the CPU Load in the Data Center

Before explaining the design of the Shadow Data, first, we discuss the reasons
for the CPU load in data centers. As shown in Fig. 1, $DC\_ACK\_CHECKSUM$
messages are sent by the data center. Before sending, the data center needs to
chunk the backup files and calculate the summary information. These processes
generate a lot of calculations, especially in the calculation of strong checksum,
such as MD5.

3.2   Why Shadow Data

For the backup system, when a local file is synchronized to the data center, at
this point, the local and data center are consistent. At the next time point, the
local data has changed and needs to do one synchronization. However, the local
does not need to ask the data center for the content of the local data at the
previous time point, because the content once existed at its own disk.

    For example, as shown in Fig. 2, the content of the backup file in the data
center at t1 time is the content of the local file at t0 time, and then after
synchronization, the content of the backup file becomes the content of the local
at t1 time. At t2 time, if the local file wants to synchronize for one time, it needs
to know its data at t1 time. In the normal communication process, it needs the
$DC\_ACK\_CHECKSUM$ messages from the data center. As shown in Fig. 2,
we can see that the data of local at t1 time can also be obtained from its previous
records.

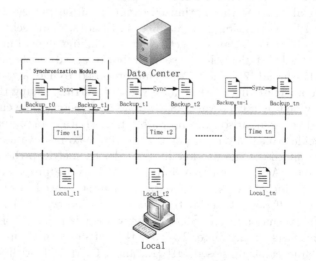

Fig. 2. The change of files in both local and the data center during synchronization of
one single file.

3.3   What Is Shadow Data

The comparison of the "synchronization module" shown in Fig. 2 before and after using Shadow Data is shown in Fig. 3. $AbstractInfo$ denotes $DC\_ACK\_CHECKSUM$ message, and $DiffInfo$ denotes $Local\_ACK\_DiffCHECKSUM$ message.

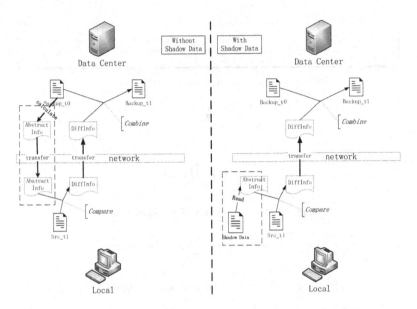

Fig. 3. The comparison of the "synchronization module" with and without using Shadow Data.

Shadow Data is proposed to replace the abstract information of backup files sent from the data center. For example, at t1 time, when the local node completes a synchronization, it stores its own summary information on its disk. Thus, when it needs to synchronize at t2 time, it will no longer need to ask data from the data center, which removes the most CPU load of the data center and, at the same time, saves one data transmission. In practice, the amount of data transmitted this time is about half of the total amount of data transmitted during synchronization. The abstract information stored on the local disk here is called Shadow Data, the shadow of the backup file.

The Shadow Data format is a chunk abstract information list, which is stored in the order of the backup file chunks. The specific format is $AbstractInfo; Abstr\ actInfo; ...AbstractInfo;$. Where $AbstractInfo$ is in the form of: $ChunkAbstract, StartIndex, ChunkLength$. $ChunkAbstract$ refers to the strong checksum of chunks, such as MD5, and the weak check if needed; $StartIndex$ indicates the starting index of the chunk in the backup file; $ChunkLength$ indicates the length of the chunk. Based on this design, in the $Local\_ACK\_DiffCHECKSUM$ message, the format of

$Chunk\_info$ is: $1, ChunkIndex, BlockLength$, if it is the same block, and $0, ChunkData$, if it is a different one. In the data center, after receiving $Local\_ACK\_DiffCHECKSUM$ message, the new backup file can be merged only by random reading without calculation.

The storage format of the Shadow Data is shown in Fig. 4, and the format of $Local\_ACK\_DiffCHECKSUM$ message is shown in Fig. 5.

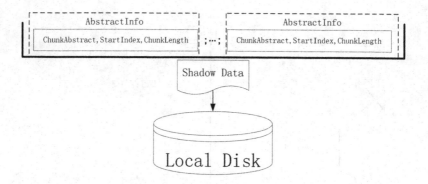

Fig. 4. Storage format of Shadow Data.

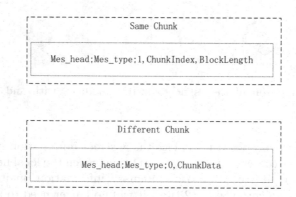

Fig. 5. Format of $Local\_ACK\_DiffCHECKSUM$ message.

It is worth noting that Shadow Data is only applicable to data centers that play a backup role, not data centers that play a sharing role. Because the latter will have multiple different clients to update the data in the data center.

4   Evaluation

4.1   Experiment Setup

The experimental environment of the data center is shown in Table 1. For the local environment, we only implement a client on another machine, connecting the port of the data center for interaction.

Table 1. Experimental environment

Operating system	CPU	Memory	IDE
Windows 10	i5-7500 3.40GHz	16g	Idea2019.3

The datasets are randomly generated data. Three files with a size of about 2.1G are generated by the Mersenne Twister Pseudo-Random Number Generator [14]. The three files are divided into three groups. These three files act as backup files. In each group, the backup file is randomly modified to generate a new file, which will act as the local file. The experimental datasets are shown in Table 2.

Table 2. The datasets

Group Id	Backup file	Local file
Group1	2.1G	about 2.1G
Group2	2.1G	about 2.1G
Group3	2.1G	about 2.1G

In the experiment, we use the CDC algorithms instead of Rsync, and the type of CDC algorithms is PCI algorithm. Since we only simulate the incremental synchronization process, using Shadow Data to reduce the steps of the data center, the choice of synchronization algorithm will not affect the final experimental results and the same to the datasets.

4.2 CPU Load of the Data Center

We have carried out the synchronization process for three groups of data respectively, and then monitored the CPU utilization of the thread responsible for synchronization in the data center with the help of the monitoring tool. The experimental results of the three groups of data are shown in Figs. 6, 7 and 8 separately.

Let's focus on one of the three groups of test data, figure (a) shows the situation when there is no Shadow Data. In this case, the data center needs to calculate the abstract information of the backup file, and the resulting CPU utilization is shown as the first irregular polygon in the figure. The second irregular polygon in the figure means the CPU utilization for generating new files, the same as the first one in figure (b). From the two irregular areas, we can see that the CPU utilization generated by calculating the abstract information of the backup file is much higher than the CPU utilization generated by generating the new file, which is more than six times. In other words, with Shadow Data, the CPU utilization of the data center with single synchronization can be reduced to about 14% of the original. The reason is obvious, since there is no need to

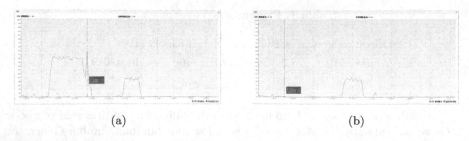

(a)   (b)

Fig. 6. CPU load in the data center without((a)) and with((b)) Shadow Data based on the group1 dataset.

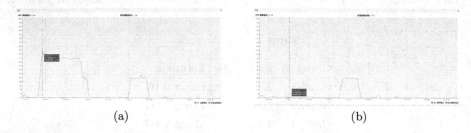

(a)   (b)

Fig. 7. CPU load in the data center without((a)) and with((b)) Shadow Data based on the group2 dataset.

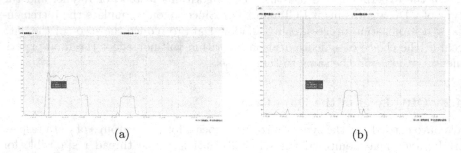

(a)   (b)

Fig. 8. CPU load in the data center without((a)) and with((b)) Shadow Data based on the group3 dataset.

calculate the abstract information of the backup file with Shadow Data. Since the actual CPU load is not easy to capture in the running of the algorithm, so in this paper, the CPU utilization is used to approximate the CPU load, which may not be rigorous, but in qualitative analysis, it makes sense.

4.3   Sacrifice of Disk on Local Node

The use of Shadow Data makes it necessary to store part of the data locally, which is put on the local disk. When the local wants to initiate one synchronization, it will be read from the local. In the experiment, we use memory mapping to read, which speeds up the reading speed. In Table 3, we show the cost of local disks corresponding to three groups of test data.

Table 3. Cost of Local Disk

Group Id	Number of chunks (piece)	Cost of disk (KB)
Group1	2508184	68583.2
Group2	2391516	65393.0
Group3	2446812	66905.0

The size of disk usage is related to the number of chunks. In this experiment, the average block size [9] is used, which is close to the average block size of Rsync. It can be seen that for about 2.1G backup files, about 65M local disk capacity needs to be consumed to store Shadow Data, aka the abstract information. However, this saves a transmission of this data from the data center. In fact, if it is sent from the data center, the data sent should be greater than 65M, because the message header should also be included. In the multi round communication proposed by Rsync algorithm, the client and the server must be dual channels, which can not be guaranteed in some applications. Using shadow data can simplify the communication process of file incremental synchronization, which only needs a single channel from client to server to complete one synchronization. The results of synchronization can be obtained by querying the server by the client.

5   Conclusion

By analyzing the process of incremental synchronization algorithm, we find out the steps, which generate the server-side CPU load. Shadow Data is proposed to remove these steps. Shadow Data is stored on the disk of the local node to replace the abstract information of backup files, which should be sent from the data center. In the experimental part, we verify the practicability of Shadow Data.

References

1. Elahi, B., Malik, A.W., Rahman, A.U., Khan, M.A.: Toward scalable cloud data center simulation using high-level architecture. Softw. Pract. Exp. **50**(6), 827-843 (2020)
2. Tang, X., Wang, F., Tong, L.I., Zhang, P.: Research and implementation of real-time exchange system in data center. Comput. Sci. **70**, 104–125 (2017)
3. Nizam, K.K., Sanja, S., Tapio, N., Nurminen, J.K., Sebastian, V.A., Olli-Pekka, L.: Analyzing the power consumption behavior of a large scale data center. Comput. Sci. Res. Dev. **34**, 61–70 (2018)

4. Zhi, C., Huang, G.: Saving energy in data center networks with traffic-aware virtual machine placement. Inf. Technol. J. **12**(19), 5064–5069 (2013)
5. Tridgell, A.: Effcient algorithms for sorting and synchronization. https://www.samba.org//tridge/phd_thesis.pdf. Accessed February 1999
6. Chao, Y., Ye, T., Di, M., Shen, S., Wei, M.: A server friendly file synchronization mechanism for cloud storage. In: IEEE International Conference on Green Computing & Communications, IEEE & Internet of Things(2013)
7. Won, Y., Lim, K., Min, J.: Much: multithreaded content-based file chunking. IEEE Trans. Comput. **64**(5), 1375–1388 (2015)
8. Ma, J., Bi, C., Bai, Y., Zhang, L.: UCDC: unlimited content-defined chunking, a file-differing method apply to file-synchronization among multiple hosts. In: 2016 12th International Conference on Semantics, Knowledge and Grids (SKG), pp. 76–82 (August 2016)
9. Bjørner, N., Blass, A., Gurevich, Y.: Content-dependent chunking for differential compression, the local maximum approach. J. Comput. Syst. Sci. **76**(3–4), 154–203 (2010)
10. Zhang, Y., Feng, D., Jiang, H., Xia, W., Fu, M., Huang, F., Zhou, Y.: A fast asymmetric extremum content defined chunking algorithm for data deduplication in backup storage systems. IEEE Trans. Comput. **66**(2), 199–211 (2017)
11. Widodo, R.N.S., Lim, H., Atiquzzaman, M.: A new content-defined chunking algorithm for data deduplication in cloud storage. Futur. Gener. Comput. Syst. **71**, 145–156 (2017)
12. Zhang, C., et al.: MII: a novel content defined chunking algorithm for finding incremental data in data synchronization. IEEE Access **7**, 86932–86945 (2019)
13. Zhang, C., Qi, D., Li, W., Guo, J.: Function of content defined chunking algorithms in incremental synchronization. IEEE Access **8**, 5316–5330 (2020)
14. Matsumoto, M., Nishimura, T.: Mersenne twister: a 623-dimensionally equidistributed uniform pseudo-random number generator. ACM Trans. Model. Comput. Simul. **8**(1), 3–30 (1998)

DROAllocator: A Dynamic Resource-Aware Operator Allocation Framework in Distributed Streaming Processing

Fan Liu[1,2], Zongze Jin[1(✉)], Weimin Mu[1], Weilin Zhu[1], Yun Zhang[1], and Weiping Wang[1]

[1] Institute of Information Engineering, Chinese Academy of Sciences, Beijing, China
{liufan,jinzongze,muweimin,zhuweilin,zhangyun,wangweiping}@iie.ac.cn
[2] School of Cyber Security, University of Chinese Academy of Sciences, Beijing, China

Abstract. With the rapid development of Internet services and the Internet of Things (IoT), many studies focus on operator allocation to enhance the DSPAs' (data stream processing applications) performance and resource utilization. However, the existing approaches ignore the dynamic changes of the node resources to allocate the operator instances to guarantee the performance, which increasing the number of migration leads to the waste of resources and the instability. To address these issues, we propose a framework named DROAllocator to select the appropriate nodes to allocate the operator instances. By capturing the change tendency of the node resources and the operator performance, our allocation mechanism decreases the number of migration to enhance the performance. The experimental results show the DROAllocator not only decrease the number of migrations to allocate the operator instances to ensure the end-to-end throughput and the latency, but also enhance the resource utilization.

Keywords: Data stream processing · Operator allocation · Resource change · Deep learning

1 Introduction

With the increasing development of Internet services and the Internet of Things (IoT), a huge amount of data has been generated from the social networks, the electronic commence, the urban intelligent transportation, and so on. The data is usually in the form of continuous streams and it should be processed by the distributed stream processing systems (DSPSs), such as Flink [1], to mine the values.

Many studies have focused on the DSPSs [2]. Especially, in the multi-user and multi-task concurrent competition environment, to adapt the fluctuating and abrupt data stream load by provisioning appropriate resources, many researchers [3–5] adopt the operator instantiation and the operator allocation to enhance the efficiency of the DSPSs. The operator instantiation determines the number of operator instances and the resource requirements for each operator instance to process the varying data in real-time. The operator allocation refers to the results of the operator instantiation to allocate the operator instances to the appropriate nodes.

The existing approaches make operator allocation decisions based on different current states of resources, including CPU, memory, networks, disk, load, and so on. Nardelli et al. [6] considers the network delays to allocate the operator instances and proposes several heuristics to achieve the best trade-off between the resolution time and the quality of the computed allocation solution. Li et al. [7] refers to the state of the nodes and the workload to decide where the operator instances are allocated and adopts a novel approach using the deep reinforcement learning to minimize the end-to-end latency. Wang et al. [8] proposes a network-aware and partition-based resource management scheme, which leverages the inter-operator traffic, the network condition and the resource capacity to arrange the operator instances, to enhance the performance of the DSPSs. Pietzuch et al. [9] uses the current state of the stream, the network, and the node resources to allocate the operator instances to improve the network utilization and reduce the stream latency.

However, the above approaches only consider the current state and ignore the change of the resources to allocate the operator instances to the nodes. Concretely, the nodes are used by multiple tasks and users, so the resources of the nodes are constantly changing. The resource changes of the nodes affect the available resources of the containers [10]. Accordingly, the performance of the operator instances in the containers is affected. It will cause the failure of the allocation scheme and requires operator migration to ensure the DSPAs' performance shortly, which is costly and unstable.

For example, the traditional approaches collect the resource metrics of the nodes at present, then analyze the appropriate allocation node for different goals, such as minimizing the end-to-end latency. Finally, the operator instances are allocated to the selected nodes by containers, such as Kubernetes [11]. With the DSPAs running, due to the change of node resources, it can not provide enough resources for the execution of the operator instances. Thus, we have to migrate the operator instances to other available nodes to ensure the system stability and low cost of adaptation.

In this paper, we propose a Dynamic Resource-aware Operator Allocation Framework (DROAllocator) to allocate the operator instances to the appropriate nodes. We consider the change tendency of the node resources and the performance of operator instances from the past to the future to select the appropriate allocation nodes and reduce unnecessary migration. The contributions of our work are summarized as follows:

- We first consider the change of the resources of nodes to address the problem which ignores the change. We present the DROAllocator which contains three core parts: the Node Resource Predictor, the Node Clusterer, and the Resource Aware Scheduler.
- To predict the resources in the next time, we adopt BiGRU to capture the feature of the change tendency of the node resources in the Node Resource Predictor.
- To measure the relationship between the resources of the node clusters and the performance of the operator instances, we first aggregate the nodes with similar resource state and change pattern into a cluster and leverage the Pearson correlation coefficient in the Node Clusterer.
- In the Resource Aware Scheduler, we propose a greedy-based merge algorithm to find the appropriate nodes for the operator instances and use a cost-based reallocation instance selection algorithm to find the best combination of the operator instances to adapt the dynamically fluctuating data input rate.
- Finally, we run the DROAllocator on DataDock, which is our data stream processing system. The experimental results demonstrate that our DROAllocator not only decrease the number of migration while ensuring the DSPAs' performance, but also enhances the resource utilization.

The rest of this paper is organized as follows. Section 2 describes the design of our DROAllocator. The experimental results are shown in Sect. 3. Finally, we conclude our work in Sect. 4.

2   Framework

2.1   Overview

In this paper, we consider the change tendency of the node resources and the performance of operator instances from the past to the future to select the appropriate allocation nodes and reduce unnecessary migration. We design the DROAllocator to allocate the operator instances to the appropriate nodes. As shown in Fig. 1, the DROAllocator contains three core modules: the Node Resource Predictor (NRP), the Node Clusterer (NC) and the Resource Aware Scheduler (RAS).

At the runtime, the Metric Collector collects the resources of each node, the performance metrics of each operator instance, and the data input rate in real-time, then stores them in MetricDatabase. The NRP analyzes the large collected data of node resources to get the change tendency of node resources. Then the NC aggregates the nodes into multiple clusters at different times based on the prediction results of the NRP. Besides, we refer to the result of the QEScalor [12], which analyzes the requirements of resources for the operator instances quantitatively based on the data input rate. Finally, the RAS allocates the operator instances to the most appropriate nodes and perform the instance reallocation, to satisfy the resource requirements of the operator instances with least migrations. As shown in Fig. 1, we use the green part to present the state before the operator instance allocation. And we use the blue part to present the operator instance allocation at time t_0. At last, we use the red part to illustrate the allocation is still valid in the future t_f.

2.2   Node Resources Predictor

In the multi-user and multi-tasking competition environment, the available resources of a node change dynamically over time. Compared with the existing methods, many studies [13,14] demonstrate the Recurrent Neural Network (RNN), which models the time series data and the process prediction tasks, can show better performance. The BiGRU networks not only consider the dependence of time series from the past to the future, but also the dependence from the future to the past, which are more efficient than the BiLSTM in the training process [15]. We use the BiGRU to learn the changing patterns of node resources and make multi-step prediction of the node resources.

The input of our NRP is $x_t = (nr_i^{t-h+1}, nr_i^{t-h+2}, ..., nr_i^t)$, which presents the sequence of the resources of node i over the past h time period. We consider the CPU utilization, the memory consumption, and the system load average to represent the node resource state, which are significant resource factors affecting the operator performance [16]. So the resources of node i at time t can be expressed as $nr_i^t = (cpu_i^t, mem_i^t, load_i^t)$. And the output is $y_t = (nr_i^{t+1}, nr_i^{t+2}, ..., nr_i^{t+f})$, which denotes the sequence of the node resources in the future f time period.

During the training process, the NRP continuously reads the sequences of the node resources over the past h time period and in the future f time period from the MetricDatabase to build the NRP, which are normalized to the range [0,1] with the Min-Max scaler [15]. During the predicting process, we get the multi-step prediction of the node resources in the future f time period.

2.3   Node Clusterer

The performance of an operator instance is related to the resource changes of the running node, as shown in Fig. 2. The performance of the compute-intensive operator instance improves with the decrease of CPU utilization. The impact of nodes with similar resources on the performance of operator instances is considered to be similar. In order to find the nodes that satisfy the operator instance in the future, we aggregate the physical nodes into multiple clusters based on the resources of the nodes, which dynamically change over time. We use the K-means clustering algorithm [17] to aggregate the nodes at every moment in the future f time period.

Our NC takes the resource state of the nodes at the current and the future moments as the input, which are multi-step prediction results of the NRP. The input is expressed as $D_{nr} = (D_{nr}^{t+1}, D_{nr}^{t+2}, ..., D_{nr}^{t+f})$, where $D_{nr}^{t+j} = (nr_1^{t+j}, nr_2^{t+j}, ...)$. Our NC aggregates the nodes into multiple clusters at the current and future moments, and we use $D_{cls} = (D_{cls}^{t+1}, D_{cls}^{t+2}, ..., D_{cls}^{t+f})$ as the output, where D_{cls}^{t+j} denotes the clusters at time $t + j$.

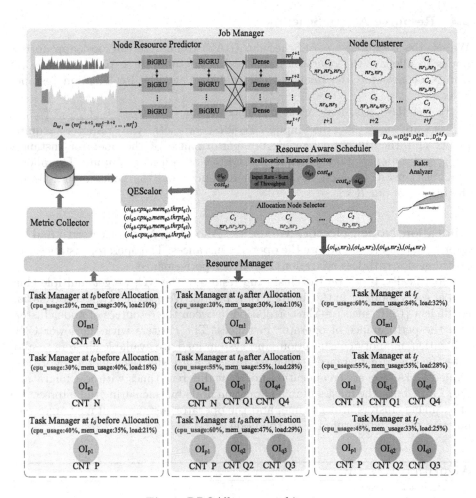

Fig. 1. DROAllocator architecture.

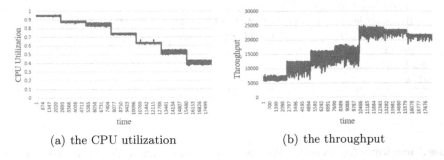

(a) the CPU utilization   (b) the throughput

Fig. 2. Correlation analysis between the CPU resource and the performance of the compute-intensive operator instance.

2.4   Resource Aware Scheduler

We use the Resource Aware Scheduler (RAS) to analyze the most appropriate nodes to allocate the operator instances. It contains three parts: the Allocation Node Selector, the Reallocation Analyzer, and the Reallocation Instance Selector.

In the RAS, the node cluster results of our NC, $D_{cls} = (D_{cls}^{t+1}, D_{cls}^{t+2}, ..., D_{cls}^{t+f})$, are used as the input. Besides, we use the resource requirements and the theoretical maximum performance of the operator instances $(oi_{qk}, cpu_{qk}, mem_{qk}, thrpt_{qk})$ from the QEScalor [12] as the input. The allocation relationship between the operator instances and the nodes (oi_{qk}, TM_i) is the output of our RAS.

Allocation Node Selector. We use the Allocation Node Selector to find the appropriate nodes to allocate the operator instances. The operator instances run on the nodes with less migration and higher performance.

Specifically, based on the clustering results of the NC, we get multiple clusters at every moment in the future f time period. We use the Pearson correlation coefficient [18] to measure the correlation between the resources of node clusters and the performance of operator instances. The clusters with the lower CPU utilization, memory consumption, and system load are available clusters to allocate the operator instances. Then we present a greedy-based merge algorithm, named GMA, to get the allocation nodes at different times with less migration. Our GMA finds the most suitable allocation node by calculating the intersection of available clusters at each time, and the operator instance will not migrate or migrate rarely when running on the node.

Algorithm 1. GMA.

$exit\_intsct$ = true
while $exit\_intsct$ **do**
    $exit\_intsct$ = false
    for $k \in [t+1, t+f)$ **do**
        $intsct$ = intersection($D_{cls}^{k}, D_{cls}^{k+1}$)
        if !$intsct$.isempty() and ($intsct$!= D_{cls}^{k} or $intsct$!= D_{cls}^{k+1}) **then**
            D_{cls}^{k} = $intsct$, D_{cls}^{k+1} = $intsct$, $exit\_intsct$ = true
        end if
    end for
end while

Reallocation Analyzer. We use the Reallocation Analyzer to measure whether some instances of an operator should be reallocated to other nodes, when the overall processing performance of the instances of an operator is less than the data input rate. Specifically, we monitor the actual performance of all instances of the operator at time t from the MetricDatabase, and calculate the sum of the actual performance of all instances, which is represented as ϑ_{actual}^t. We get the theoretical maximum performance of all instances of the operator from the QEScalor, and calculate the sum of the theoretical performance of all instances, which is represented as ϑ_{peak}. We get the data input rate at time t from the MetricDatabase, which is represented as γ^t.

Then, we compare ϑ_{actual}^t with ϑ_{peak} and compare ϑ_{peak} with γ^t. If $\vartheta_{actual}^t <$ ϑ_{peak} and $\vartheta_{peak} \geq \gamma^t$, we get that the operator instances can not process the data with the input rate because some instances do not achieve their theoretical maximum performance. Thus if we reallocate some or all of these instances to other more appropriate nodes, the operator instances may process the data with the input rate. In this case, we calculate the difference between the data input rate and the sum of actual performance, which is denoted as $\gamma^t - \vartheta_{actual}$, and is the input of the Reallocation Instance Selector.

While in other cases, such as $\vartheta_{actual}^t = \vartheta_{peak}$ or $\vartheta_{peak} < \gamma^t$, it demonstrates that the operator instantiation of the QEScalor is unreasonable and our RAS is unable to process these cases. So we feed these cases back to the QEScalor to adapt the fluctuating data input rate.

Reallocation Instance Selector. When the Reallocation Analyzer gets that it's necessary to reallocate and migrate some instances, we use the Reallocation Instance Selector to find the best combination of the operator instances that fail to achieve the maximum performance. Then these instances are reallocated by the Allocation Node Selector to the nodes with more resources to get better performance. We build a cost model to evaluate the total cost of the reallocation of the instances. The cost is defined as:

$$\min \quad C(n) = \sum_{k=1}^{n} c_{rsc}^k + c_{on} + c_{off} + c_{rrt}, \quad \text{s.t.} \quad \sum_{k=1}^{n} \Delta p_k \geq \Delta W \qquad (1)$$

where $C(n)$ is the total cost, n is the number of selected instances, c_{rsc}^k is the cost of system resources used by the kth selected instance, c_{on} is the startup cost, c_{off} is the shutdown cost, and c_{rrt} is the re-routing cost. In the constraint, we use Δp_k, which represents the performance improvement, to indicate the difference between the optimal performance and the actual performance of the kth operator instance. We use ΔW to denote the difference between the data input rate and the sum of the actual performance of all operator instances.

Then we propose a cost-based reallocation instance selection algorithm, named CRISA, to find the best combination of the operator instances that fail to achieve the theoretical optimal performance. We use the CRISA to pick the best combination, which satisfies the constraint and the least cost. Our CRISA is divided into 3 steps. Firstly, we compare the theoretical optimal performance of the operator instances with the actual runtime performance to obtain the set of candidate reallocation operator instances. Secondly, we rank the candidate set in descending order according to the theoretically improved performance of the candidate reallocation operator instances. At last, we iteratively select k operator instances from the candidate set with the minimum reallocation cost.

Algorithm 2. CRISA.

---

for $k \in [0, o_q.instance\_num)$ do
  if $oi_{qk}.actual\_thprt < oi_{qk}.peak\_thprt$ then
    $oi_{qk}.incrs\_thprt = oi_{qk}.peak\_thprt - oi_{qk}.actual\_thprt$
    $candidates.$append(oi_{qk})
  end if
end for
sort_in_desc$(candidates.incrs\_thrpt)$
for $k \in [1, candidates.num]$ do
  for $j \in [0, candidates.num)$ do
    $k_candidates = $ select_oi$(candidates[j, candidates.num), k)$
    if sum$(k\_candidates.incrs\_thrpt) \geqslant \Delta W$ and $C(k\_candidates) < min_C$ then
      $mgrt\_ois = k\_candidates, min_C = C(k\_candidates)$
    else
      break
    end if
  end for
end for

---

3 Experiments

3.1 Datasets and Settings

We collect the resources of the physical machine nodes, the performance metrics of the operator instances, and the data input rate in experiments, as shown in Table 1.

Specifically, The node resource dataset is divided into a training set and a testing set. The training set includes data from the first 20 d, which are used to train the prediction models. And the testing set contains data from the next 10 d, which are used to evaluate the effectiveness of the models. Besides, to construct the operator performance dataset, we run the compute-intensive operator instances (the keyword extraction operator) which consumes a lot of CPU resources on every node. The node resource dataset and the operator performance dataset are used to analyze the correlation between the cluster resources and the operator performance. Furthermore, we get the operator instantiation data, including the resource requirements and the theoretical maximum performance of every operator instance, from the QEScalor to construct the operator instantiation dataset.

We conduct experiments in a cluster environment which consists of eleven machines. These machines are all configured with Intel Xeon CPU E5-2620 v3

2.30 GHz 24 cores, 128 GB memory, and 599 GB disks. We use one machine to run JobManager and MetricDatabase to collect data in real-time. We use three machines with NVIDIA TESLA P4 GPUs to conduct training and testing of our prediction, clustering, and scheduling models. The remaining seven machines are used to run the operator instances which are deployed by Kubernetes.

In the node resource prediction analysis, we compare our NRP with the ARIMA, the SVR, the GRU, and the BiLSTM. Specifically, we all use ReLU as the activation function, adam as the optimizer, MSE [15] as the loss, and we set the size of hidden layer to 128 for the LSTM, the GRU, the BiLSTM and our NRP. We use rbf as the kernel, scale as the gamma, and C is set to 100.0 for the SVR. In the operator instance allocation, we collect the migration number and calculate the sum of throughput of 22 operator instances running on the 7 nodes for 24 h. We do our experiments repeatedly ten times.

Table 1. The datasets in the experiments

Dataset name	Metrics	Collection frequency	Collection duration
Node resource dataset	CPU utilization, memory consumption and system load average	1 min	30 days
Operator performance dataset	Throughput (Number of data processed per minute)	1 min	30 days
Input rate dataset	Input rate (Number of data received per minute)	1 min	30 days
Operator instantiation dataset	CPU_req, mem_req, thrpt_peak	–	30 days

3.2 Metrics

We use the Root Mean Square Error (RMSE) and the Mean Absolute Error (MAE) metrics [15] to evaluate the performance of the node resource prediction models. And we use the overall throughput and the cumulative number of migrations of the operator instances to evaluate the performance of the operator instance allocation.

3.3 Results

Operator Instance Allocation Analysis. To evaluate the performance of the operator instance allocation, we compare our RAS with the system default allocation scheme and the RES-ODP [6]. We use the overall throughput and the cumulative number of migrations of the operator instances to measure the operator instance allocation.

As shown in Fig. 3, the overall throughput of our RAS is higher than the default scheme. And there is a bit difference between our RAS with the RES-ODP. But the throughput of our RAS is more stable and the change is small, compared with other methods. More importantly, our RAS is significantly lower than other methods for the cumulative number of migrations.

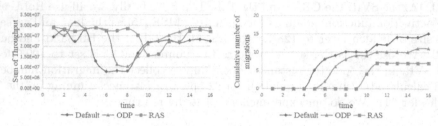

(a) the sum of end-to-end throughput   (b) the cumulative number of migrations

Fig. 3. Operator instance allocation analysis.

The system default allocation scheme which leverages round-robin only considers whether the node is available the current time. The RES-ODP, which uses the linear relaxation of the ILP formulation of ODP, considers the current network delay when allocating the operator instances. When the resources of the nodes change over time and the allocation nodes are no longer appropriate to run some instances, these methods should reallocate and migrate some or all instances to other nodes. Thus our RAS outperforms the default and the RES-ODP allocation scheme, which takes the change of the node resources into account and tries to allocate the instances to the nodes with the longest runtime and the least migration.

Node Resource Prediction Analysis. The experimental results of the five-step forward prediction are shown in Table 2. The recurrent neural networks, such as the LSTM, the GRU, the BiLSTM, and the NRP, perform significantly better than the traditional methods for the node resource prediction, such as the ARIMA and the SVR. The recurrent neural networks capture more latent information from the massive of the collected data and learn the changing trend of the node resources more accurately. Besides, our NRP outperforms the LSTM and GRU, because the NRP analyzes data of node resources in two directions to get more latent features in the time dimension. Furthermore, our NRP shows faster training and higher prediction accuracy than BiLSTM.

Correlation Analysis Between the Resources of Node Clusters and the Performance of the Operator Instances. We calculate the Pearson correlation coefficient between the node resources and the performance of the compute-intensive operator instances. We get -0.8946, -0.4554, -0.7214 for the correlation

Table 2. The five-step ahead prediction performance of node resources for different models

Model type	ARIMA	SVR	GRU	LSTM	BiLSTM	NRP
RMSE	0.0517 ± 0.0003	0.0449 ± 0.0004	0.0243 ± 0.0002	0.0289 ± 0.0002	0.0282 ± 0.0003	0.0234 ± 0.0002
MAE	0.0397 ± 0.0002	0.0341 ± 0.0003	0.0145 ± 0.0003	0.0156 ± 0.0002	0.0136 ± 0.0002	0.0116 ± 0.0003

coefficient between the CPU utilization, memory consumption, system load with the performance of the compute-intensive operator instances respectively.

The results show the resources of the node clusters and the operator performance are negatively correlated. The operator performance is higher in the node clusters with the lower CPU utilization, memory consumption, and system load.

4   Conclusion

In this paper, we propose an operator allocation framework, named DROAllocator, to address the problem which ignores the dynamic changes of the node resources to allocate the operator instances to guarantee the performance. It contains three core modules: the Node Resource Predictor (NRP), the Node Clusterer (NC) and the Resource Aware Scheduler (RAS). We use the NRP to get the precise change tendency prediction of the node resources by the BiGRU. Then we refer to the change tendency of the node resources and analyze the relationship between the resources of the node clusters and the performance of the operator instances. Finally, the RAS allocates the operator instances to the most appropriate nodes and reallocate some operator instances when the overall performance of the operator instances is less than the data input rate. Experiments demonstrate our framework not only improve the DSPAs' performance, but also enhance the resource utilization.

References

1. Carbone, P., Katsifodimos, A., Ewen, S., Markl, V., Haridi, S., Tzoumas, K.: Apache flink[TM]: stream and batch processing in a single engine. IEEE Data Eng. Bull. **38**(4), 28–38 (2015)
2. Neumeyer, L., Robbins, B., Nair, A., Kesari, A.: S4: distributed stream computing platform. In: ICDMW 2010, The 10th IEEE International Conference on Data Mining Workshops, Sydney, Australia, 13 December 2010, pp. 170–177 (2010)
3. Zhang, S., He, J., Zhou, A.C., He, B.: Briskstream: scaling data stream processing on shared-memory multicore architectures. In: Proceedings of the 2019 International Conference on Management of Data, SIGMOD Conference 2019, Amsterdam, The Netherlands, June 30 - July 5 2019, pp. 705–722 (2019)
4. Lombardi, F., Aniello, L., Bonomi, S., Querzoni, L.: Elastic symbiotic scaling of operators and resources in stream processing systems. IEEE Trans. Parallel Distrib. Syst. **29**(3), 572–585 (2018)

5. Cardellini, V., Grassi, V., Presti, F.L., Nardelli, M.: Distributed qos-aware scheduling in storm. In: Proceedings of the 9th ACM International Conference on Distributed Event-Based Systems, DEBS 2015, Oslo, Norway, June 29 - July 3 2015, pp. 344–347 (2015)
6. Nardelli, M., Cardellini, V., Grassi, V., Presti, F.L.: Efficient operator placement for distributed data stream processing applications. IEEE Trans. Parallel Distrib. Syst. **30**(8), 1753–1767 (2019)
7. Li, T., Xu, Z., Tang, J., Wang, Y.: Model-free control for distributed stream data processing using deep reinforcement learning. Proc. VLDB Endow. **11**(6), 705–718 (2018)
8. Wang, Y., Tari, Z., Huang, X., Zomaya, A.Y.: A network-aware and partition-based resource management scheme for data stream processing. In: Proceedings of the 48th International Conference on Parallel Processing, ICPP 2019, Kyoto, Japan, 05–08 August 2019, pp. 20:1–20:10 (2019)
9. Pietzuch, P.R., Ledlie, J., Shneidman, J., Roussopoulos, M., Welsh, M., Seltzer, M.I.: Network-aware operator placement for stream-processing systems. In: Proceedings of the 22nd International Conference on Data Engineering, ICDE 2006, 3–8 April 2006, Atlanta, GA, USA, p. 49 (2006)
10. Lloyd, W., Pallickara, S., David, O., Lyon, J., Arabi, M., Rojas, K.: Performance implications of multi-tier application deployments on infrastructure-as-a-service clouds: towards performance modeling. Future Gener. Comp. Syst. **29**(5), 1254–1264 (2013)
11. Bernstein, D.: Containers and cloud: from LXC to docker to kubernetes. IEEE Cloud Comput. **1**(3), 81–84 (2014)
12. Mu, W., Jin, Z., Zhu, W., Liu, F., Li, Z., Zhu, Z., Wang, W.: QEScalor: quantitative elastic scaling framework in distributed streaming processing. In: Krzhizhanovskaya, V.V., Závodszky, G., Lees, M.H., Dongarra, J.J., Sloot, P.M.A., Brissos, S., Teixeira, J. (eds.) ICCS 2020. LNCS, vol. 12137, pp. 147–160. Springer, Cham (2020). https://doi.org/10.1007/978-3-030-50371-0_11
13. Liao, D., Xu, J., Li, G., Huang, W., Liu, W., Li, J.: Popularity prediction on online articles with deep fusion of temporal process and content features. In: The Thirty-Third AAAI Conference on Artificial Intelligence, AAAI 2019, The Thirty-First Innovative Applications of Artificial Intelligence Conference, IAAI 2019, The Ninth AAAI Symposium on Educational Advances in Artificial Intelligence, EAAI 2019, Honolulu, Hawaii, USA, January 27 - February 1 2019, pp. 200–207 (2019)
14. Qin, Y., Song, D., Chen, H., Cheng, W., Jiang, G., Cottrell, G.: A dual-stage attention-based recurrent neural network for time series prediction. In: Proceedings of the Twenty-Sixth International Joint Conference on Artificial Intelligence, IJCAI 2017, Melbourne, Australia, 19–25 August 2017, pp. 2627–2633 (2017)
15. Mu, W., Jin, Z., Wang, J., Zhu, W., Wang, W.: BGElasor: elastic-scaling framework for distributed streaming processing with deep neural network. In: Tang, X., Chen, Q., Bose, P., Zheng, W., Gaudiot, J.-L. (eds.) NPC 2019. LNCS, vol. 11783, pp. 120–131. Springer, Cham (2019). https://doi.org/10.1007/978-3-030-30709-7_10
16. Zhu, J., et al.: Perphon: a ml-based agent for workload co-location via performance prediction and resource inference. In: Proceedings of the ACM Symposium on Cloud Computing, SoCC 2019, Santa Cruz, CA, USA, 20–23 November 2019, p. 478 (2019)
17. Yu, H., Wen, G., Gan, J., Zheng, W., Lei, C.: Self-paced learning for K-means clustering algorithm. Pattern Recognit. Lett. **132**, 69–75 (2020)
18. Ahmed, Z., Kumar, S.:"Pearson's correlation coefficient in the theory of networks: A comment", CoRR, vol. abs/1803.06937 (2018)

A Medical Support System for Prostate Cancer Based on Ensemble Method in Developing Countries

QingHe Zhuang[1,2], Jia Wu[1,2]($\boxtimes$) (iD), and GengHua Yu[1,2]

[1] School of Computer Science, Central South Universtiy, Changsha, China
[2] "Mobile Health" Ministry of Education-China Mobile Joint Laboratory, Changsha, China

Abstract. As a cancer with high incidence rate, Prostate cancer (PCa) endangers men's health worldwide. In developing countries, medical staff are overloaded because of the lack of medical resources. Medical support system is a good technique to ease contradiction between the large number of patients and small number of doctors. In this paper, we have collected 1,933,535 patient information items from three hospitals, constructed a medical support system for PCa. It uses six relevant tumor markers as the input features and output a quantitative indicator EM value for staging and recommending treatment method. Classical machine learning techniques, data fusion and ensemble method are employed in the system to make the results more correct. In terms of staging PCa, it reaches an accuracy of 83%. Further research based on the system and collected data are carried out. It is found that the incidence of prostate cancer has been rising in the past five years and diet habit and genetic inheritance have a great impact on it.

Keywords: Prostate cancer · Tumor marker · Medical support system · Machine learning

1 Introduction

In 2018, PCa's morbidity and mortality are 13.5% and 6.7% respectively in male patients. In 185 countries, it has the highest morbidity in 105 countries and the highest mortality in 46 countries [1]. Undoubtedly, PCa has become one of the main threats to men's health worldwide.

Even though PCa is not high-fatal, in developing countries that lack medical resources, many patients can't receive timely and effective diagnosis and therapy, which will worsen the condition of patients. Scarce medical resource, specially the lack of high-quality medical resources may lead to patients' distrust to doctors and aggregate the conflict between them [2]. Sometimes doctors even get physically injured by family members of patients because of their distrust to

© IFIP International Federation for Information Processing 2021
Published by Springer Nature Switzerland AG 2021
X. He et al. (Eds.): NPC 2020, LNCS 12639, pp. 361–372, 2021.
https://doi.org/10.1007/978-3-030-79478-1_31

doctors. Take China for example, there are only 2.59 practitioners for every 1000 people [3]. Patients need to wait hours for diagnosis or examination [4]. Things get worse in some top-class hospitals. In Beijing, a small number of medical staff in 3A grade hospitals need to serve not only over 20 million local people but also people seeking treatment from other regions. Overloaded burden increases the chance of mistakes and causes severe consequences. At the same time, inspection charge of PCa accounts for a large portion. Many high-end inspection methods including MRI and PET-CT are too expensive for poor patients to afford.

Other developing countries may face similar dilemmas:

- Due to the scarce medical resources, it is difficult for patients to get timely diagnosis and treatment.
- The long-term workload of doctors increases the chance of mistakes and aggregates the conflicts between doctors and patients.
- Many hospitals in developing countries have poor medical equipment and many patients in developing countries cannot afford expensive checking fare.

Scarce medical resources, long-term overloaded medical staff and difficult access to medical care have severely restricted the life expectancy of patients in developing countries. Fortunately, these problems may be eased by building medical support system which aims to offer help for medical staff [4]. By analyzing large amounts of data, the medical support system can extract a diagnostic model. It will serve doctors with suggestions relevant to diagnosis or treatment based on the learned model [6,7]. Combining suggestions form the system and their own knowledge, doctors will give the final decision. Contradiction between doctors and patients may be eased if the medical support system work well [8,9]. In this work, we constructed a medical support system which can diagnose if a patient has PCa, determine the pathological stage, recommend treatment method, and evaluate the effectiveness of treatment method. Given the low income in developing countries, the system is featured as inputting six tumor markers with relatively low testing price and high relevance to PCa. Classical machine learning techniques and ensemble method are adopted to extract the knowledge inside data and improve system's performance.

Compared with other works, the main innovations and contributions of our system include:

- Unlike other system based on CT or MRI, the constructed system only uses features that are cheap for people in developing countries and also reached good performance, which makes it possible to deploy the system in other developing countries.
- In addition to the diagnosis, the system can give treatment plan and evaluate its effectiveness quantificationally at the same time.
- The system is trained based on a large amount of patient information from three high-level hospitals in China and some factors affecting PCa are analyzed via the constructed system.

2   Design of Medical Support System

2.1   Overall Requirements and Framework of the System

Medical support system aims to provide some advice for doctors. Its functions contain determining PCa's benignancy or malignancy and pathological stage, recommending suitable treatment plan and judging effectiveness of treatment plan. Determining PCa's benignancy or malignancy and pathological stage can be regard as a classification task. But in order to give a cancer treatment plan and estimate its efficacy at the same time, the whole problem is considered as a regression problem. Our system will transform the discrete input feature into continuous variable which cane evaluating the malignancy of PCa, abbreviated for EM. The larger EM stands for the higher malignancy. If the value does not decrease after a certain treatment plan is executed, it means that the treatment plan has little efficacy and another a new one needs to be selected. At the same time, the medical support system needs to have good parallelism and be able to process multiple patients' simultaneous diagnosis requests. After the medical system is invested, the amount of data obtained will increase over time. The decision model will be retrained to further improve the generalization performance.

2.2   Detailed Description of the Medical Support System

In this medical support system, six tumor markers with high relevancy to PCa is used as input feature. They include Prostate-specific Antigen (PSA), Prostate-specific membrane antigen (PSMA), total Prostate-Specific Antigen (tPSA), Red Blood Cell (RBC), Hemoglobin (HB), and Prostate Acid Phosphatase (PAP). Machine learning techniques including Support Vector Machines (SVM) and Neural Networks (NN), mainly Multilayer Perceptron (MLP) and Radical Basis Function Neural Network (RBF) are ensembled to acquire good performance in classification.

Figure 1 depicts the main flow of the medical support system. First, in preprocessing module, relevant data from different hospital systems are collected. Then six important tumor markers' level are extracted from thousands of information items. After data cleaning and normalizing, input vector $x = (x_{PSA}, x_{PSMA}, x_{tPSA}, x_{RBC}, x_{HB}, x_{PAP})$ is formed. In decision module, it will firstly use a binary SVM to determine tumor's malignancy or benignancy. In clinical experience, increase of tumor marker doesn't mean a malignant tumor for sure. They don't have high specificity and there may be other reasons that lead to the increase such as lesions or inflammations. So the system cannot determine it simply by critical threshold. Sometimes one tumor marker is abnormal while others are normal. In this circumstance, doctors will find it hard to give correct results. Data mining or machine learning models are able to extract features with high specificity and make use of these features for decision. That's the motivation they are deployed in the system. If diagnosed as benign tumor, relevant therapy will be recommended according to the previously recorded similar samples in the database. If judged as malignant tumor, then an ensemble model is executed to complete pathological stage division. The pathological stage for malignant tumor includes four stages: I, II, III, and IV. That is to say, the system must complete a four-classification task. Since SVM is mainly used in binary classification, multi-classification SVM (M-SVM) which combines binary SVM and DS (Dempster/Shafer) evidence theory is constructed according to [10]. Unlike binary SVM, M-SVM can output probabilistic result and reduce the number of used binary SVMs compared with other extending method. The output result from a M-SVM is a four-dimensional vector, whose value in each dimension represents the possibility of corresponding class. In order to reduce the risk brought by choosing specific kernel function, different M-SVMs with different kernels are trained as is shown in Fig. 1. Here three commonly used kernel functions: linear kernel, polynomial kernel and Gaussian kernel are chosen simultaneously. For binary SVMs in each M-SVM, the same kernel functions are used. While in different M-SVM, different kernel functions are used.

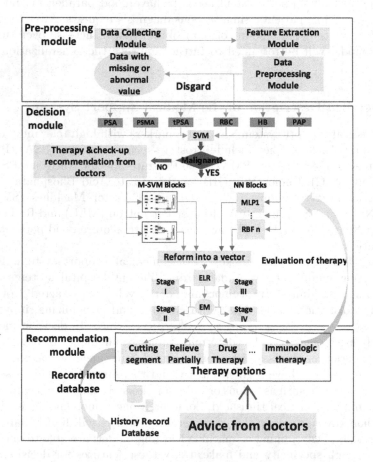

Fig. 1. Overall framework of the proposed system.

While training, hyperparameters in kernel functions and binary SVMs are tuned to reduce the generalization error below threshold ϵ. In order to reduce risk further, widely used MLP neural network and RBF neural network are added into the system. Because 6 input features are chosen and the samples are classified into four classes, the input and output layers of the MLP and RBF networks are 6 units and 4 units respectively. Three group MLP neural networks with different structures are selected. ReLU function is used as the activation function in MLP neural networks. Similarly, three RBF networks with different structure are used. The hidden unit number in three networks are set as 10, 14, 16, respectively. Use k-means clustering algorithm to determine the center c_i of each hidden unit. In RBF neural network, radical basis function is used as the activation function. As in SVMs, the hyperparameters are adjusted to reduce the generalization error below the threshold ϵ.

Ensemble algorithm

Input:
Training set: $D = \{(x_1, y_1), (x_2, y_2), \ldots, (x_m, y_m)\}, y_i \in \{I, II, III, IV\}$.
Primary classifier: $S = \{SVM_1, \ldots, RBF_3\}$
Output: Second learning algorithm $H(x) : ln(y_{EM}) = w^T x + b$
Begin:
$D' = \emptyset$
for i **in** D**do:**
  for t **in** S **do:**
    $z_{it} = S_t(x_i)$; /*z_{it} is a four-dimensional vector. */
  end for
  $y_i' = map(y_i)$; /*map function convert the class label into a numerical value.*/
  $D' = D' \cup ((z_{i1}, z_{i2} \ldots z_{it}), y_i')$
end for
use D' to train $H(x)$;
output $H(x)$;
End

Finally, outputs of each M-SVM and all MLP and RBF networks are reshaped into one vector as the input of the secondary learner. Instead of averaging the results of different classifiers, a second learner is introduced to learn the weight of each base learner. The selection of the second learner is based on the priori knowledge. By observing the tumor marker level of all samples, it is found that for benign tumors and patients in stage I, the tumor marker levels are usually close to normal range. But for patients in stage III and stage IV, the level of tumor markers deviates greatly. Therefore, we made an priori assumption that the increase of tumor markers conforms to the exponential law as PCa worsens. This hypothesis is basically true in medicine. In the early stages like stage I and stage II, symptoms are slight or not obvious. Tumors are often latent and grow slowly. However, in stage III or IV, they develop savagely and spread throughout the body, causing the tumor marker levels really high. Hence, Exponential Linear Regression (ELR) is selected as a secondary learner to ensemble the results of M-SVM, MLP and RBF models. We add supervising label 3, 4, 5, 6 manually for the input patient samples in stage I II III IV, respectively. The output value of exponential linear regression model is not set to start from 1 in order to improve the model's robustness to normal people and benign tumor cases. Finally, the evaluation of PCa's malignancy (EM) is output. Ensemble algorithm shows the procedure integrating the results of base learners by exponential linear regression. Pathological stage of malignant PCa is determined by EM value.

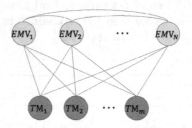

Fig. 2. Relationship between EMV and TM.

In recommendation module, a probabilistic graphical model on the basis of that treatment selection mainly depends on EM value is used. The relationship between EM value (EMV) and treatment method (TM) is shown in Fig. 2. Selection of TM is related to EMV. Meanwhile, selection of TM will also have an impact on EMV. They depend on each other. Figure 3 depicts the building and training process of the model. First, numerical EM value is divided by interval parameter e to form discrete set of EMV ($EMVS = emv_1, emv_2, \ldots, emv_N$) and treatment method set (TMS) containing commonly used tumor treatment methods such as chemotherapy, radiotherapy, excision, drug method, hospital charge is formed simultaneously. Treatment process of patient i can be characterized as a sequential data: $\left(E_i^1, T_i^1\right), \ldots, (E_i^t, T_i^t), \ldots, \left(E_i^{|t_i|}, T_i^{|t_i|}\right)$, $i = 1, 2, \ldots Tot$ where E_i^t and T_i^t represents EM value and treatment method of patient i in treatment interval t and belong to EMVS and TMS respectively. $|t_i|$ is the total treatment interval of patient i, Tot is total number of data.

Use these data, two kinds of conditional probability distribution, $P(EMV| TM, EMV)$ and $P(TM|EMV)$ can be learned. $P(TM|EMV)$ means the possibility of selecting TM in the state of EMV. Similarly, $P(EMV|TM, EMV)$ means the possibility of EM value changing into state EMV after TM is used in state EMV. Parameter can be estimated by (1) and (2).

$$P\left(TM = tm_k | EMV = emv_j\right) = \frac{1 + \sum_{i=1}^{Tot} \sum_{t=1}^{|t_i|} sgn\left(E_i^t = emv_j, T_i^t = tm_k\right)}{N + \sum_{i=1}^{Tot} \sum_{t=1}^{|t_i|} sgn\left(E_i^t = emv_j\right)}$$

$$(1)$$

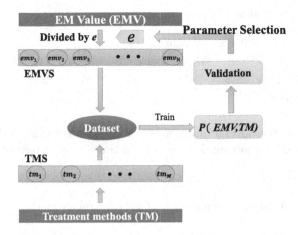

Fig. 3. Building and training process of the recommendation model.

$$P\left(EMV = emv_m | TM = tm_k, EMV = emv_j\right)$$
$$= \frac{1 + \sum_{i=1}^{Tot} \sum_{t=1}^{|t_i|-1} sgn\left(E_i^t = emv_j, T_i^t = tm_k, E_i^{t+1} = emv_m\right)}{NM + \sum_{i=1}^{Tot} \sum_{t=1}^{|t_i|} sgn\left(E_i^t = emv_j, T_i^t = tm_k\right)} \quad (2)$$

Selection of interval e follows (3):

$$e = argmax_e \prod_{i=1}^{Tot} P\left(E_i^1\right) P\left(T_i^{|t_i|} | E_i^{|t_i|}\right) \prod_{t=1}^{|t_i|-1} P(T_i^t | E_i^t) P(E_i^{t+1} | E_i^t, T_i^t) \quad (3)$$

When new patient with malignant PCa comes, the system will recommend treatment method to doctors. The recommendation procedure is rough and primary so final decision must be made by doctors. But it can relieve burden of medical staff to some extent.

3   Experiment

3.1   Dataset and Models' Training

From three top-class hospitals in China: First Xiangya Hospital, Second Xiangya Hospital and Third Xiangya Hospital, we obtained a large amount of data. Records of the tumor markers (PSA, PSMA, tPSA, RBC, HB, and PAP), diagnostic results (benign, stage I, stage II, stage III, stage IV) and treatment process are screened and preprocessed. A total of 12186 patients' data is extracted and the distribution is shown in Table 1.

Table 1. Distribution of the collected data.

	Benign	Malignant			
		Stage I	Stage II	Stage III	Stage IV
Number	3628	2864	1523	1795	2376

Table 2 shows the normal range of tumor markers relevant to PCa. Values of malignant patient's tumor marker are several times or even tens of times beyond the normal range.

Table 2. Normal range of different tumor marker.

Types of tumor marker	Normal range
Total Prostate-Specific Antigen	4–20 µg/L
Hemoglobin	120–165 µg/L
Red Blood Cell	12–15 g/100 ml
Prostate Acid phosphatase	0–9 U/L
Prostate-specific membrane antigen	0–4 ng/mL

The data set is divided into three parts: training set, validation set and test set, accounting for 70%, 20% and 10% respectively. First of all, we choose the appropriate kernel function and penalty parameter to train SVM_0. Secondly, we extract all malignant samples for the training in the next step. Because SVM and neural networks are not sensitive to data, and arbitrary division of data is likely to lead to the problem of imbalanced data which means two datasets don't have same distribution. Hence we choose the same training set to train all base learners. For M-SVM blocks' training, malignant samples are firstly divided in two ways which have been described elaborately in [10], forming two datasets $S_A = \{S_{I,II}, S_{III,IV}\}$ and $S_B = S_{I,III}, S_{II,IV}$, where $S_{i,j}$ represents the union of c_i, c_j. S_A and S_B are then used to train two binary SVMs. The output of M-SVM is the fusion result of these two binary SVMs. For neural networks, the malignant samples are directly marked as $(1,0,0,0)^T, (0,1,0,0)^T, (0,0,1,0)^T, (0,0,0,1)^T$ by their stages. Back propagation and gradient descent are performed to obtain good classification ability. Finally, the output of M-SVM blocks and neural networks are reshaped into one vector, which is used as the input of exponential linear regression model. The loss function of exponential linear regression uses mean square loss function.

3.2 Analysis of the Results of Experiments

After training, all malignant samples are input into the model, and calculate the range of their EM values, which are listed in Table 3. As Table 3 shows, EM values of all the malignant examples have a rough 0.5 deviation around the

Table 3. EM value of each stage of PCa.

Clinical stage of PCa	Range of $lnEM$
Stage I	2.7–3.6
Stage II	3.6–4.5
Stage III	4.5–5.3
Stage IV	>5.3

supervising value set in advance. The model has a good fitting ability on the malignant samples of different stages, which indirectly proves the correctness of our hypothesis that the tumor marker level increases exponentially as PCa worsens.

In order to verify the effectiveness of our medical support system, accuracy of the system on different scale data sets with that of doctors and other method are compared. As shown in Fig. 4, when the dataset is small, accuracy of medical support system is very low, no better than random guess (50%). While accuracy of doctors is high, almost 100%. However, when the size of dataset increases, accuracy of the medical support system increases and doctors' accuracy starts to decrease because of overloaded burden and cumulative errors. As the amount of data reaches 4000, accuracy of the system is roughly the same with that of doctors. This implies our medical support system can make full use of the increasing amount of data to improve generalization performance.The final result is based on 12186 patients' data. For SVM_0, it reaches 89.9%, 86.6%, 98.9% in terms of accuracy, recall and precision (take malignant samples as positive). In Fig. 4, it can also be seen that accuracy of proposed model is always higher than others' instead of being an average of other models. This demonstrates the correctness of strategy of using secondary learners to ensemble them. It may be explained as that base classifiers play a role of feature extractor and this makes it easier for secondary learner to determine the clinical stage. The confusion table of the proposed ensemble model is shown in Table 4. The final accuracy is roughly 87.4%.

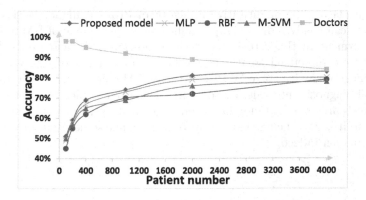

Fig. 4. Comparison of doctors and the system.

Table 4. Confusion Table of the ensemble model.

Prediction	Real label			
	Stage I	Stage II	Stage III	Stage IV
Stage I	2621	101	24	9
Stage II	204	1312	67	25
Stage III	25	66	1476	271
Stage IV	14	44	228	2071

Average EM value of different years are calculated to explore the development trend of PCa in recent years. As shown in Fig. 5, the mean EM value of patients from three hospitals has been increasing from 2014 to 2018. This implies an increase in proportion of patients with PCa which will make medical resources more precious, so it is necessary and urgent to establish a medical support system.

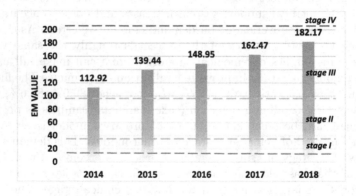

Fig. 5. Average EM value in the past five year.

By calculating the quantitative indicator of PCa's malignancy (EM value), the system can easily judge therapy's efficacy by the change of EM and recommend treatment methods to improve the condition of PCa patients. Figure 6 shows the recommended treatment methods and changes of EM value of one patient diagnosed with stage IV PCa. At first, EM value is very high. In the end of several diagnosis intervals, the patient's EM value comes to a relatively low level, which proves the tumor has been controlled by the recommended treatment plan. It is convincing that the system can make some decisions and relieve doctor's burden indeed.

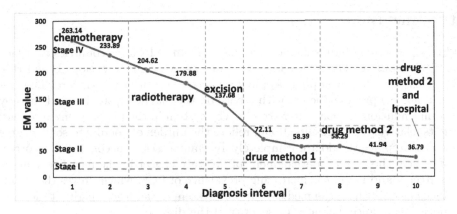

Fig. 6. A treatment process of a PCa patient.

3.3 Relevant Analysis Based on the System

By controlling different input variables, influence of a certain factor on prostate cancer are evaluated. Here, relevant information of some patients is collated to evaluate impact of patients' diet habits and genetic inheritance. Diet habits are divided into high-fat diets and none high-fat diets by description in medical record. Genetic inheritance is defined by malignant tumor incidence in the patient's family members (lineal relatives). From the data of 2014–2018, it can be inferred that high-fat diet with tends to worsen the condition of patients. EM value for patients with high-fat diet is 2.43–2.63 times of those without high-fat diet, and in terms of genetic inheritance, it's 6.26–7.98 times, as shown in Fig. 7.

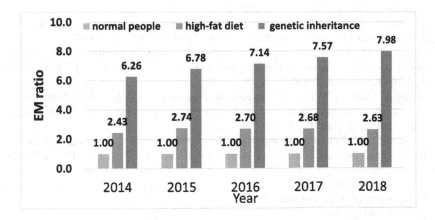

Fig. 7. Influence of diet habit and genetic inheritance.

4   Conclusion

This paper mainly builds medical support system of PCa for countries that lack medical resources. The selected features are cheap for underdeveloped countries, which ensures that even poor people have access to cancer health care. The system is able to provide doctors with advice on the diagnosis, staging and therapy recommendation of PCa. After training the system in the big data environment, it gets relatively good results. It can relieve the burden of doctors to some degree but can't replace the doctor completely. In many cases, it needs doctor's correction. Using the system, development of prostate cancer in the past five years is researched, and found the increasing prevalence of PCa, which proves the significance of establishing the medical support system. In addition, high-fat diet and genetic inheritance increase the severity of the disease.

References

1. Freddie, B., Jacques, F., Isabelle, S.: Global cancer statistics 2018:GLOBOCAN estimates of incidence and mortality worldwide for 36 cancers in 185 countries. CA Cancer J. Clin. **68**(6), 394–424 (2018)
2. Wu, J., Guan, P., Tan, Y.: Diagnosis and data probability decision based on non-small cell lung cancer in medical system. IEEE Access **7**(November), 44851–44861 (2019)
3. Department of Planning Development and Information Technology, "Statistical Communiqué on China's Health Care Development in 2018" (2019)
4. Wu, J., Tian, X., Tan, Y.: Hospital evaluation mechanism based on mobile health for IoT system in social networks. Comput. Biol. Med. **109**(April), 138–147 (2019)
5. Wu, J., Tan, Y., Chen, Z., Zhao, M.: Data decision and drug therapy based on non-small cell lung cancer in a big data medical system in developing countries. Symmetry (Basel) **10**(5), 1–16 (2018)
6. Malmir, B., Amini, M., Chang, S.I.: A medical decision support system for disease diagnosis under uncertainty. Expert Syst. Appl. **88**, 95–108 (2017)
7. Stylios, C.D., Georgopoulos, V.C., Malandraki, G.A., Chouliara, S.: Fuzzy cognitive map architectures for medical decision support systems. Appl. Soft Comput. J. **8**(3), 1243–1251 (2008)
8. Wang, P., Zhang, P., Li, Z.: A three-way decision method based on Gaussian kernel in a hybrid information system with images: an application in medical diagnosis. Appl. Soft Comput. J. **77**, 734–749 (2019)
9. Tashkandi, A., Wiese, I., Wiese, L.: Efficient in-database patient similarity analysis for personalized medical decision support systems. Big Data Res. **13**, 52–64 (2018)
10. Hao, Z., Shaohong, L., Jinping, S.: Unit model of binary SVM with DS output and its application in multi-class SVM. In: Proceedings of the 2011 4th International Symposium on Computational Intelligence and Design (ISCID 2011), vol. 1, no. 2, pp. 101–104 (2011)

The Entry-Extensible Cuckoo Filter

Shuiying Yu, Sijie Wu, Hanhua Chen$^{(\boxtimes)}$, and Hai Jin

National Engineering Research Center for Big Data Technology and System,
Services Computing Technology and System Lab, Cluster and Grid Computing Lab,
School of Computer Science and Technology, Huazhong University of Science and
Technology, Wuhan, China
{shuiying,wsj,chen,hjin}@hust.edu.cn

Abstract. The emergence of large-scale dynamic sets in real applications brings severe challenges in approximate set representation structures. A dynamic set with changing cardinality requires an elastic capacity of the approximate set representation structure, while traditional static structures, e.g., bloom filter, cuckoo filter, and their variants cannot satisfy the requirements. Existing dynamic approximate set representation structures only provide filter-level extensions, which require a single membership query to probe all discrete filters one by one. The large number of small discrete memory accesses takes up the vast majority of query time and results in unsatisfied query performance. To address the problem, in this work we propose the *entry-extensible cuckoo filter* (E2CF) to reduce memory access overhead for dynamic set representation and accelerate the membership query. E2CF utilizes adjacent buckets with continuous physical addresses in a cuckoo filter to extend bucket entries, which avoids many discrete memory accesses in a query. To further make E2CF space and time efficient, we adopt asynchronous extension and fine-grained splitting methods. Experiment results show that compared to state-of-the-art designs, E2CF reduces the query and insertion time by 82% and 28%, respectively.

Keywords: Dynamic set representation · Set membership query ·
Entry-extensible · Cuckoo filter

1 Introduction

Since the emergence of large-scale sets in big data applications [4], set representation and membership query structures have been widely used [6]. Set representation means organizing set information based on a given format, while the membership query means determining whether a given item belongs to a set. In practice, the performance of set membership query is crucial to applications. For example, in network security monitoring applications [9], the long membership query time results in late detection and failed protection. Furthermore, the performance of set membership query directly affects deletion and non-repeatable insertion, which need to search the item first.

© IFIP International Federation for Information Processing 2021
Published by Springer Nature Switzerland AG 2021
X. He et al. (Eds.): NPC 2020, LNCS 12639, pp. 373–385, 2021.
https://doi.org/10.1007/978-3-030-79478-1_32

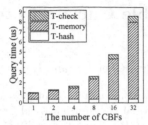 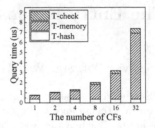

Fig. 1. The time breakdown of a query in DBF and DCF

In real-world applications, precise set storage and query cannot meet the requirements of space and time efficiency. Fortunately, approximate set representation and membership query structures can reduce storage overhead and accelerate query at the cost of a small probability of false positive on the query result, and thus have attracted much efforts in academia [2,7].

The most widely-used approximate set representation structures are *bloom filter* (BF) [2], *cuckoo filter* (CF) [7], and their variants [3,8,14]. BF [2] is a fixed-length array of bits, which are initially set to "0". When inserting an item, BF maps the item into the array by k independent hash functions and transforms the corresponding bits to "1". BF queries whether an item belongs to the set by checking if all its k bits are "1". However, BF does not support deletion. If one deletes an item by flipping its k bits to "0", other existent items that share the k bits will also be regarded as not in the set.

To support deletion, *counting bloom filter* (CBF) [8] replaces each bit of a BF with a counter of d bits. Inserting or deleting an item will increase or decrease the value of the corresponding counter. However, it requires $d\times$ more space than a BF. CF [7] is an array of m buckets and each bucket contains b entries. For an incoming item, CF stores its fingerprint in one of the entries. CF can support deletion by searching and removing the corresponding fingerprint.

The cardinality of the sets in real applications is constantly changing and unpredictable [5,10,11]. For example, the arrival of items in stream processing applications shows high dynamics [12]. Since aforementioned static structures [2,7,8] cannot adjust capacity, they fail to represent the dynamics of set cardinality, and the cost of rebuilding a larger static structure is unacceptable. Very limited work has been done to cope with frequently changing sets. The notable exceptions include *dynamic bloom filter* (DBF) [10] and *dynamic cuckoo filter* (DCF) [5]. To dynamically extend and downsize capacity, DBF [10] appends and merges multiple homogeneous CBFs. However, using multiple CBFs leads to the problem of unreliable deletion. DCF [10] further utilizes multiple CFs to store the fingerprint of an item, and thus supports reliable delete operation.

However, the query performance of existing dynamic set representation structures [5,10] is unsatisfied. Both DBF [10] and DCF [5] are filter-level extensions, which require a single membership query to probe all conjoint filters one by one until the result is found. Today's CPU reads data from memory at a coarse-grained granularity of cache lines, which are typically 64 to 128 bytes [3]. However, a query in DBF and DCF must access multiple discrete counters and buckets, which are usually much smaller than a cache line [7,8]. Therefore, a query in existing dynamic set representation structures performs a large number of small discrete memory accesses and reads a large amount of unnecessary data from memory, resulting in long membership query time.

In Fig. 1, we examine the query performance of DBF and DCF by experiments with real-world network traffic traces [1]. We deploy DBF and DCF on a server with an Intel 2.60 GHz CPU and 64 GB memory. In each experiment, we run 1×10^6 queries and record the average query time. We breakdown the query time into three parts, including hash computation time, memory access time, and item check time. The results show that with the increase of the number of static filters, the memory access time grows rapidly and contributes a significant fraction of 90% to the query time. If we can reduce the memory access time, the query performance can be greatly improved.

Based on the observation, we propose the *entry-extensible cuckoo filter* (E2CF), a dynamic set representation structure that satisfies the requirement of fast membership query. E2CF exploits the entry-level extension to store entries with the same indexes at continuous physical addresses. By adopting the asynchronous extension and fine-grained splitting, E2CF achieves both space and time efficiency. We implement E2CF and conduct comprehensive experiments with real-world traces to evaluate the design. The results show that compared to existing designs, E2CF reduces the query and insertion time by 82% and 28%, respectively.

To summarize, our contributions are threefold:

- We identify the problem of long membership query time in existing dynamic set representation structures.
- We propose a novel structure to improve membership query performance by exploiting entry-level extension of CF.
- We implement E2CF and conduct comprehensive experiments with real-world traces to evaluate our design.

The rest of the paper is organized as follows. Section 2 introduces the related work. Section 3 presents E2CF design. Section 4 analyzes the performance of E2CF. Section 5 evaluates our design. Section 6 concludes the paper.

2   Related Work

2.1   Static Structures

Bloom Filter and Counting Bloom Filter. *Bloom filter* (BF) [2] contains an array of n bits. Initially, all the n bits are set to "0". When inserting an item, BF maps the item into the array by k independent hash functions and flips the k corresponding bits to "1". When determining whether item x belongs to a set, BF checks whether the k corresponding bits of x are all "1".

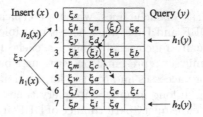

Fig. 2. The process of inserting and querying items in CF

To support deletion in BF, Fan et al. [8] propose *counting bloom filter* (CBF), which replaces each bit of BF with a counter of d bits. When inserting and deleting an item, CBF increases or decreases the value of the corresponding counter. However, it requires $d\times$ more space than a BF.

Cuckoo Filter. *Cuckoo filter* (CF) [7] consists of an array of m buckets and each bucket contains b entries. For an incoming item x, CF generates its fingerprint (denoted as ξ_x) by a hash function and inserts it in one of the entries. To alleviate collisions during insertion, CF computes two candidate buckets for x and stores its fingerprint ξ_x in one entry of the two buckets. The two candidate bucket indexes $h_1(x)$ and $h_2(x)$ are calculated by Eq. (1). With one of the two candidate bucket indexes and ξ_x stored in it, CF can compute the other index of x by using the known index to perform a XOR operation with $hash(\xi_x)$.

$$h_1(x) = hash(x)$$
$$h_2(x) = h_1(x) \oplus hash(\xi_x)$$
(1)

Figure 2 presents the examples of inserting x and querying y. For the insertion, since both the two buckets of ξ_x are full, CF randomly kicks out a fingerprint as a victim, e.g., ξ_f, and stores ξ_x in it. Then CF computes the other candidate bucket index for victim ξ_f. Since the other bucket 3 of ξ_f is also full, CF evicts a new victim ξ_i and stores ξ_f in bucket 3. The eviction repeats until all items find empty entries or the number of relocations reaches the pre-defined *maximum number of kickouts* (MNK). For the query of y, CF reads the fingerprints from its two candidate buckets and checks whether ξ_y exists in them. For an item deletion, CF finds the corresponding fingerprint and removes it.

Guo et al. [10] reveal that data sets in real applications are highly dynamic. However, existing static structures [7,8] lack the ability to extend capacity. In addition, allocating large enough capacity in advance will cause a waste of space. Therefore, it is rather important to design a set representation structure that supports dynamically extending and downsizing capacity.

2.2 Dynamic Structures

Dynamic Bloom Filter. Guo et al. [10] propose the *dynamic bloom filter* (DBF), which is an approximate set representation structure that copes with dynamically changing of set cardinality. A DBF consists of a linked list of s homogeneous CBFs. When the current CBF is full, DBF extends its capacity by appending new building blocks of CBFs. For a query, DBF checks every CBF independently to determine whether the item exists in it.

Dynamic Cuckoo Filter. Chen et al. [5] propose the *dynamic cuckoo filter* (DCF), which uses a linked list of s homogeneous CFs to dynamically adjust capacity. DCF always maintains an active CF. When a new item comes, DCF tries to insert it into the active CF. If the active CF is full, DCF appends a new empty CF and stores the item in it. Then the new CF becomes the active CF. For a query, the DCF, however, needs to probe the candidate buckets in all the CFs to check whether the fingerprint exists in it. Clearly, a query process in DCF will access discrete memory multiple times, resulting in long query time.

Consistent Cuckoo Filter. Luo et al. [11] propose the *index-independent cuckoo filter* (I2CF), which adds and removes buckets adaptively to cope with dynamic set. However, I2CF can only handle small-scale capacity extension. To deal with large-scale highly dynamic data set, Luo et al. [11] further propose the Consistent cuckoo filter, which consists of a linked list of I2CFs.

Existing dynamic structures typically adopt filter-level extension, which requires a membership query to probe all discrete homogeneous filters, resulting in unsatisfied query performance. Differently, E2CF exploits entry-level extension, reduces memory accesses, and further improves query performance.

Table 1. Notations

Notation	Explanation
ξ_x	The fingerprint of the item x
PCF_k	The k_{th} PCF in E2CF
k_1, k_2	The serial number of PCFs which an item belongs to
$h_1(x), h_2(x)$	The two candidate bucket indexes of x in primary CF_0
$h_1(x)', h_2(x)'$	The two candidate bucket indexes of x in PCF_{k_1} and PCF_{k_2}
m	The number of buckets in primary CF_0
b	The number of entries in a bucket of primary CF_0
l_h, l_l	The highest and lowest levels that PCFs exist
f	The length of fingerprint
α	The maximum permissible load factor of PCF

3   Entry-Extensible Cuckoo Filter

3.1   Overview

As aforementioned, the query performance of existing dynamic set representation structures suffers from the large number of small discrete memory accesses. The

E2CF exploits the entry-level extension to avoid many time-consuming memory accesses. An E2CF is initially a standard CF, i.e., CF_0. When E2CF needs to extend capacity, it creates a new *partial cuckoo filter* (PCF) and alternately moves half of the old buckets to the new PCF. We call the newly allocated filter PCF because it only contains partial buckets of the primary standard CF_0. Then, the empty entries of the removed buckets are merged into the adjacent remaining buckets. In this manner, the entries with the same index are stored in continuous physical addresses. For a query, E2CF determines which two candidate buckets the fingerprint resides in and reads them from memory. To improve space efficiency, E2CF allows every PCF to extend capacity independently. E2CF also leverages a fine-grained splitting method to support operations during splitting. We summarize the notations used in this paper in Table 1.

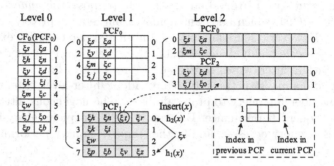

Fig. 3. An example of E2CF

3.2   Entry-Level Extension

E2CF exploits the entry-level extension to reduce the large number of small discrete memory accesses. However, if we directly allocate new memory to extend entries, the physical addresses of entries with the same indexes will be discrete. Fortunately, we find that the physical addresses of the adjacent buckets in a CF are continuous, which could be utilized in entry extension.

Initially, E2CF consists of a primary CF, denoted as CF_0, which has m buckets. Each bucket in CF_0 has b entries. When the number of items increases, E2CF extends its capacity. E2CF first allocates a new PCF_1, which has the same size as CF_0. To leverage the continuous memory addresses of adjacent buckets to extend entries, E2CF moves the buckets with odd indexes from CF_0 to PCF_1. The empty entries of these buckets in CF_0 are then merged into the adjacent buckets with smaller even indexes, which forms new PCF_0. After the extension, both PCF_0 and PCF_1 have $m/2$ buckets and each bucket contains $2 \times b$ entries. The process of moving buckets with odd index to the new PCF is called splitting.

Figure 3 illustrates an example of E2CF. For simplicity, we only plot the fingerprints in the primary CF_0 during splitting. When CF_0 in level 0 starts to split, E2CF will allocate a new PCF_1 and move the fingerprints in buckets with odd indexes, e.g., ξ_h and ξ_n in bucket 1, to PCF_1. Then the buckets with even indexes in CF_0 absorb the adjacent empty entries. Since PCF_0 and PCF_1 in level 1 are derived from the same PCF in level 0, we call them brother PCFs. However, if we split all PCFs in E2CF simultaneously, the space cost will increase exponentially, which is unacceptable for applications with expensive storage.

To solve the problem, we adopt the asynchronous extension method, which enables each PCF to extend capacity independently. A PCF performs splitting only when one of the following two conditions is met. First, the load factor of a PCF, i.e., the ratio of the used entries to the total entries, exceeds the pre-defined maximum permissible load factor α. Second, the number of relocations reaches MNK. We will split the PCF that performs the last kicking out.

Once a PCF reaches the split condition, E2CF splits it independently. For example, in Fig. 3, if PCF_0 in level 1 reaches the split condition, E2CF splits PCF_0 into PCF_0 and PCF_2 in level 2. Since PCF_1 in level 1 does not satisfy the split condition, it remains in level 1. At this moment, E2CF contains three grey PCFs, i.e., PCF_0, PCF_1, and PCF_2. The total number of buckets in E2CF remains eight. When a new item comes, E2CF finds its candidate PCFs and buckets according to our insertion method (Sect. 3.3).

To help locate the PCFs and buckets, we assign a serial number for each PCF. After the split of PCF_k in level l, the serial number of the PCF that holds even index buckets remains k. For the newly allocated PCF that receives odd index buckets from the PCF_k, its serial number is the sum of k and 2^l. For example, when the PCF_0 in level 1 splits, the serial number of PCF_0 does not change. The serial number of the newly allocated PCF is the sum of 0 and 2^1, which is two. Algorithm 1 presents the splitting process.

3.3 Operations of E2CF

Insertion. When inserting an item x, E2CF first calculates its fingerprint ξ_x. Then E2CF needs to determine which PCFs (PCF_{k_1} and PCF_{k_2}) and buckets (bucket $h_1(x)'$ and $h_2(x)'$) the fingerprint ξ_x belongs to. For an item x, E2CF computes the primary candidate bucket indexes $h_1(x)$ and $h_2(x)$ by Eq. (1). Since we do not know in which levels the candidate PCFs exist, we search from the lowest level l_l. We calculate the serial number k_1 of the first PCF by Eq. (2). If PCF_{k_1} exists in the level, then we calculate $h_1(x)'$ by Eq. (2). Otherwise, we

---

Algorithm 1: E2CF: Splitting ()

---

1 **if** PCF_k in level l reaches the split condition **then**
2   new $PCF_{k+pow(2,l)}$;
3   **for** $n = 1; n < m/pow(2,l); n+ = 2$ **do**
4      $\lfloor$ move $PCF_k.B[n]$ to $PCF_{k+pow(2,l)}.B[(n-1)/2]$;
5   increase the levels of PCF_k and $PCF_{k+pow(2,l)}$ by 1;

---

repeat the same computation from level $l_l + 1$ to l_h until PCF_{k_1} and $h_1(x)'$ are found. Similarly, we can obtain another candidate PCF_{k_2} and bucket indexes $h_2(x)'$ of item x. During the insertion, the PCF that reaches the split condition performs splitting operation.

$$k_i = h_i(x)\%2^l$$
$$h_i(x)' = \lfloor h_i(x)/2^l \rfloor \quad i \in \{1, 2\} \tag{2}$$

Figure 3 presents an example of inserting item x. When there are no empty entries in the two candidate buckets of x, E2CF randomly kicks out a fingerprint ξ_t, which is called a victim, and stores ξ_x. For ξ_t, E2CF calculates its another candidate bucket and continues the relocation. For an insertion, if both two candidate buckets have empty entries, E2CF inserts the item into the bucket in the lower level to ensure load balance. In this manner, the value of $l_h - l_l$ is usually very small in practice, resulting in little index computation overhead. Algorithm 2 presents the detailed process of the insertion in E2CF.

Membership Query. For a query of item x, E2CF computes k_1 and $h_1(x)'$ by Eq. (2). If a matched ξ_x is identified in a bucket of PCF_{k_1}, E2CF returns success. Otherwise, E2CF further calculates k_2 and $h_2(x)'$ and checks whether ξ_x exists in PCF_{k_2}. If both the two candidate buckets do not contain ξ_x, E2CF returns failure. Since E2CF only needs to read two buckets and entries in each bucket have continuous physical addresses, very little memory access overhead is introduced in a query.

Algorithm 2: E2CF: Insert (x)

---

1 $fp = \xi_x$, $h_1(x) = hash(x)$, $h_2(x) = h_1(x) \oplus hash(fp)$;
2 **for** $j = 0; j < MNK; j + +$ **do**
3   // Calculate k_1 and $h_1(x)'$
4   **for** $l = l_l; l \leq l_h; l + +$ **do**
5           $k_1 = h_1(x)\%2^l$;
6   **if** PCF_{k_1} *belong to level l* **then**
7               $h_1(x)' = \lfloor h_1(x)/2^l \rfloor$;
8   break;

9   **if** $j = 0$ **then**
10   calculate k_2 and $h_2(x)'$;
11   **if** $PCF_{k_1}.B[h_1(x)']$ *or* $PCF_{k_2}.B[h_2(x)']$ *has an empty entry* **then**
12   put fp to the empty entry;
13   **return** *success*;
14   randomly kick out a victim ξ_t from the two buckets and store fp;
15      $fp = \xi_t$;
16   let $h_1(x)$ be another primary candidate bucket index of the victim ξ_t;
17 PCF_{k_1}.Splitting () and insert fp;

Deletion. For the deletion of item x, E2CF searches the position of ξ_x by a membership query and removes it from E2CF. If the fingerprint ξ_x is not in E2CF, the delete operation returns failure.

However, deletions may result in the reduction of space utilization in E2CF. To improve space efficiency, we compress sparse PCFs to downsize the capacity of E2CF. For a PCF$_p$ in the highest level l_h, if the load factors of both PCF$_p$ and its brother PCF are less than $\alpha/2 - 0.1$, we merge them into a PCF in level $l_h - 1$. If the sparse PCF$_p$ is not in level l_h, we first try to move the fingerprints in level l_h to it. Then, we merge the sparse PCFs in the highest level l_h. With the compression method, we can restrict the maximum level difference in E2CF, i.e., $l_h - l_l \leq 2$, which improves the insertion and query performance.

3.4   Fine-Grained Splitting

The dynamic sets in real applications typically require real-time insert and query operations [9]. However, supporting real-time operations is difficult when E2CF is splitting. To solve the problem, we design a fine-grained splitting method, which allows E2CF to perform operations during splitting.

When a PCF starts to split, we mark it as in the splitting state. In E2CF, we add a 1-bit flag to each bucket. For the primary CF$_0$, we initialize the flag to "0", which represents that the bucket has not split. When a new item x is inserted into a bucket with flag "0" in the splitting CF$_0$, we check whether the bucket index $h_1(x)'$ is odd. If so, we flip the flags of old buckets $h_1(x)'$ and $h_1(x)' - 1$ to 1, move the bucket $h_1(x)'$ to the newly allocated PCF, and store ξ_x in the new PCF. Otherwise, we change the flags of old buckets $h_1(x)'$ and $h_1(x)' + 1$, move the bucket $h_1(x)' + 1$ to the new PCF, and store ξ_x in the old PCF. When moving the bucket, we move the flag together. After CF$_0$ is split into PCF$_0$ and PCF$_1$ in level 1, all the flags are converted to "1". So for PCFs in even levels, flag "0" indicates that the bucket has not split; while for PCFs in odd levels, flag "1" does. The PCF splitting process finishes when all flags of the buckets in the old PCF are flipped. Then we reset the PCF to non-splitting state.

In this manner, E2CF moves buckets during insertion. For an operation on the splitting PCF, if its candidate bucket has been moved, we perform it on the newly allocated PCF. Otherwise, we operate on the old splitting PCF.

4   Analysis of E2CF

4.1   Query Performance

According to Fig. 1, the memory access time dominates the query time. Therefore, we use the memory access time T_{mem} to represent the query performance. Today's CPU reads data from memory at cache line granularity. We denote the size of a cache line as M and use T_c to represent the time of reading a cache line size memory. For DBF and DCF, they access small discrete memories that are much smaller than M. Their memory access time is calculated by Eq. (3).

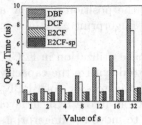

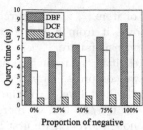

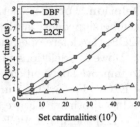

Fig. 4. Query time with different values of s

Fig. 5. Query time with different negative query rates

Fig. 6. Query time with different set cardinalities

$$T_{DBF-mem} = k \times T_c \times s, \ T_{DCF-mem} = 2 \times T_c \times s \qquad (3)$$

where k represents each CBF in DBF has k independent hash function, and s is the number of static filters in DBF and DCF. The memory access time of a query in E2CF is calculated by Eq. (4), where s is the number of PCFs in E2CF.

$$T_{E2CF-mem} = 2 \times T_c \times \lceil \frac{2^{\lceil log_2 s \rceil} \times b}{\lfloor \frac{M}{f} \rfloor} \rceil \qquad (4)$$

In practice, M is typically 64 to 128 bytes. In E2CF, we set $b = 4$ and $f = 16$ bits. Therefore, $\lfloor \frac{M}{f} \rfloor \in [32, 64]$. Also, $s \leq 2^{\lceil log_2 s \rceil} \leq 2 \times s$. Equation (5) presents the range of $T_{E2CF-mem}$, which is much smaller than that of DBF and DCF.

$$T_c \times \lceil \frac{s}{8} \rceil \leq T_{E2CF-mem} \leq T_c \times \lceil \frac{s}{2} \rceil \qquad (5)$$

4.2 False Positive Rate

According to [7], the false positive rate of CF can be computed by Eq. (6).

$$FP_{CF} = 1 - (1 - \frac{1}{2^f})^{2b} \approx \frac{2b}{2^f} \qquad (6)$$

In E2CF, PCFs may exist in multiple levels, and the number of entries in the PCFs of level l is $2^l \times b$. We use n_l to denote the number of PCFs in level l. The false positive rate of E2CF is calculated by Eq. (7). When all the PCFs exist in one level, the false positive rate of E2CF and DCF [5] is the same.

$$FP_{E2CF} = 1 - \sum_{l=l_l}^{l_h} \frac{n_l}{s} \times (1 - \frac{1}{2^f})^{2 \times 2^l \times b} \approx \frac{b}{2^f \times s} \sum_{l=l_l}^{l_h} (2^{l+1} \times n_l) \qquad (7)$$

5   Performance

5.1   Experiment Setups

We implement E2CF and make the source code publicly available[1]. We conduct the experiments on a server with an Intel 2.60 GHz Xeon E5-2670 CPU and 64 GB RAM. The CPU has 32 KB L1 data cache, 32 KB instruction cache, 256 KB L2 cache, and 20 MB L3 cache. The size of a cache line in the server is 64 bytes. We use both real-word network traffic traces [1] and synthetic data set to evaluate the performance.

We compare E2CF with DBF [10] and DCF [5], respectively. For E2CF and DCF, we set $m = 2^{22}$, $b = 4$, $\alpha = 0.9$, and $f = 16$. For DBF, the parameters are calculated based on the same false positive rate as E2CF. We run each experiment five times and record the average value.

5.2   Results

Figure 4 compares the query time with different values of s. The E2CF-sp means some PCFs are in the splitting state during the query. We perform negative queries, which mean searching for a non-existent item. The result shows that the splitting state barely affects the query performance and E2CF reduces the query time by up to 85% and 82% compared to DBF and DCF, respectively. That is because DBF and DCF need to access small discrete memory multiple times while E2CF only needs to read entries in continuous memory.

Figure 5 presents the query time with different proportions of negative queries when $s = 32$. The result shows that E2CF always greatly outperforms DBF and DCF. Figure 6 compares the query time [13] with different set cardinalities. The result shows that E2CF reduces the query time by up to 82% compared to DCF.

Figure 7 shows the instantaneous insertion time with different MNKs. We test non-repeatable insertion, which does not allow an item to be inserted twice. With the increase of the number of inserted items, E2CF reduces the instantaneous insertion time by up to 45% and 28% compared to DBF and DCF, respectively.

Figure 8 plots the cumulative insertion time with different MNKs. When we increase MNK from 10 to 40, more relocations will occur, and the insertion time of DCF and E2CF increases. The result shows that compared to DBF and DCF, E2CF reduces the cumulative insertion time by up to 41% and 22%.

Figure 9 presents the deletion time with different values of s. When s increases, the deletion time of DBF and DCF grows linearly, while the time of E2CF is essentially unchanged. Figure 10 plots the deletion time with different set cardinalities. The result shows that E2CF reduces the deletion time by up to 84% and 79% compared to DBF and DCF, respectively.

Figure 11 compares the memory cost when increasing set cardinalities. E2CF-syn denotes E2CF without asynchronous extension. As shown in the figure, E2CF

---

[1] https://github.com/CGCL-codes/E2CF.

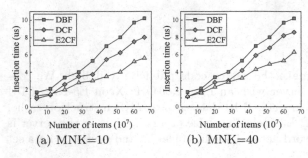

(a) MNK=10   (b) MNK=40

Fig. 7. Instantaneous insertion time

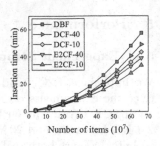

Fig. 8. Cumulative insertion time

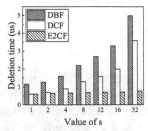

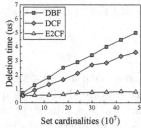

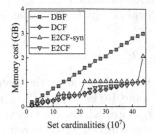

Fig. 9. Deletion time with
different values of s

Fig. 10. Deletion time with
different set cardinalities

Fig. 11. Memory cost with
different set cardinalities

reduces the memory cost by up to 66% and 50% compared to DBF and E2CF-syn and achieves comparable space efficiency with DCF. But note that E2CF greatly outperforms DCF in terms of the query, insert, and delete performance.

6 Conclusion

In this paper, we find that the query performance of existing set representation structures is subject to long memory access time. We design and implement the E2CF, a dynamic structure that supports fast membership query for large-scale dynamic data set. The E2CF exploits entry-level extension to extend and downsize capacity. We further adopt asynchronous extension and fine-grained splitting methods to achieve space and time efficiency. Theoretical analysis and experiment results show that E2CF greatly outperforms existing schemes.

Acknowledgement. This research is supported in part by the National Key Research and Development Program of China under grant No. 2016QY02D0302, and NSFC under grant No. 61972446.

References

1. WIDE project (2020). http://mawi.wide.ad.jp/mawi/
2. Bloom, B.H.: Space/time trade-offs in hash coding with allowable errors. Commun. ACM **13**(7), 442–426 (1970)
3. Breslow, A., Jayasena, N.: Morton filters: faster, space-efficient cuckoo filters via biasing, compression, and decoupled logical sparsity. Proc. VLDB Endow. **11**(9), 1041–1055 (2018)
4. Chen, H., Jin, H., Wu, S.: Minimizing inter-server communications by exploiting self-similarity in online social networks. IEEE Trans. Parallel Distrib. Syst. **27**(4), 1116–1130 (2015)
5. Chen, H., Liao, L., Jin, H., Wu, J.: The dynamic cuckoo filter. In: Proceedings of ICNP, pp. 1–10 (2017)
6. Dayan, N., Athanassoulis, M., Idreos, S.: Optimal bloom filters and adaptive merging for LSM-trees. ACM Trans. Database Syst. **43**(4), 16:1–16:48 (2018)
7. Fan, B., Andersen, D.G., Kaminsky, M., Mitzenmacher, M.: Cuckoo filter: practically better than bloom. In: Proceedings of CoNEXT, pp. 75–87 (2014)
8. Fan, L., Cao, P., Almeida, J.M., Broder, A.Z.: Summary cache: a scalable wide-area web cache sharing protocol. IEEE/ACM Trans. Networking **8**(3), 281–293 (2000)
9. Groza, B., Murvay, P.: Efficient intrusion detection with bloom filtering in controller area networks. IEEE Trans. Inf. Forensics Secur. **14**(4), 1037–1051 (2019)
10. Guo, D., Wu, J., Chen, H., Yuan, Y., Luo, X.: The dynamic bloom filters. IEEE Trans. Knowl. Data Eng. **22**(1), 120–133 (2010)
11. Luo, L., Guo, D., Rottenstreich, O., Ma, R.T.B., Luo, X., Ren, B.: The consistent cuckoo filter. In: Proceedings of INFOCOM, pp. 712–720 (2019)
12. Monte, B.D., Zeuch, S., Rabl, T., Markl, V.: Rhino: efficient management of very large distributed state for stream processing engines. In: Proceedings of SIGMOD, pp. 2471–2486 (2020)
13. Peng, B., Lü, Z., Cheng, T.C.E.: A tabu search/path relinking algorithm to solve the job shop scheduling problem. Comput. Oper. Res. **53**, 154–164 (2015)
14. Wang, M., Zhou, M., Shi, S., Qian, C.: Vacuum filters: more space-efficient and faster replacement for bloom and cuckoo filters. Proc. VLDB Endow. **13**(2), 197–210 (2019)

Monitoring Memory Behaviors and Mitigating NUMA Drawbacks on Tiered NVM Systems

Shengjie Yang[1,2], Xinyu Li[1,2], Xinglei Dou[1,2], Xiaoli Gong[3], Hao Liu[4],
Li Chen[2], and Lei Liu[1,2(✉)]

[1] Sys-Inventor Lab, Beijing, China
lei.liu@zoho.com
[2] SKLCA, ICT, CAS, Beijing, China
liulei2010@ict.ac.cn
[3] Nankai, Tianjin, China
[4] AMS, PLA & Tsinghua, Beijing, China

Abstract. Non-Volatile Memory with byte-addressability invites a new
paradigm to access persistent data directly. However, this paradigm
brings new challenges to the Non-Uniform Memory Access (NUMA)
architecture. Since data accesses cross NUMA node can incur significant
performance loss, and, traditionally, OS moves data to the NUMA node
where the process accessing it locates to reduce the access latency. However, we find challenges when migrating data on NVM, which motivates
us to migrate the process instead. We propose SysMon-N, an OS-level
sampling module, to obtain access information about NVM in low overhead. Furthermore, we propose N-Policy to utilize the data collected by
SysMon-N to guide process migration. We evaluate SysMon-N and N-
Policy on off-the-shelf NVM devices. The experimental results show that
they provide 5.9% to 3.62× bandwidth improvement in the case where
cross-node memory accesses happen.

Keywords: DRAM-NVM · NUMA · OS · Migration · Scheduling

1 Introduction

Non-Volatile Memory (NVM) attaches to the memory bus promises DRAM-like
latency, byte-addressability, and data persistence. NVM will become common-
place soon. Previous studies (e.g., [4]), focusing on kernel-bypassing, redesign the

This project is supported by the National Key Research and Development Program
of China under Grant No.2017YFB1001602 and the NSFC under grants No.61502452,
61902206, 61702286. This work originates from L. Liu's series of studies in ISCA,
PACT, TPDS, TC, etc. [5–12] on memory systems conducted in Sys-Inventor Lab.
More details refer to Sys-Inventor Lab - https://liulei-sys-inventor.github.io.

file system dedicated to NVM for reducing software overheads stemmed from kernel involvement. A critical feature of this type of file system is the "direct access" (i.e., DAX) style interface through the $mmap()$ system call, through which the user process can map the NVM-based file into its address space and access the file content directly by load/store instructions from user space [1]. Different from the on-demand paging data access, NVM possesses both byte-addressability and persistency, which allows user processes to access the persistent data directly. However, NVM is usually mounted on a specific node and forms a tiered/hybrid memory system with DRAM on NUMA servers, leading to the risk of cross-node accesses (i.e., remote access). Remote access may cause dramatic performance degradation, and there are many studies to provide shreds of evidence for this.

In terms of the performance loss due to the remote accessing on DRAM, previous work moves data from remote NUMA node to the local node where the user process is running on. However, we find some challenges in the previous studies about the NVM-based systems. (1) There is no "struct page" for persistent data in NVM that managed by the DAX-aware file systems [1], leading to the complexity of page migration on the system using both DRAM and NVM. (2) Since the data blocks to be migrated are persistent, the process of page migration needs to be guaranteed as atomic and consistent using a transaction-like mechanism, which will introduce extra overheads on the critical path. (3) The persistent data usually has a much larger size than the volatile data, and frequent migrating of them will produce significant overheads [13]. These challenges motivate us to seek a new design.

In this work, we propose an new mechanism. Instead of moving persistent data, we migrate the process to the original node where the persistent data locates. In order to achieve our goal, we propose SysMon-N and N-Policy. SysMon-N is an OS-level memory behavior sampling module that can obtain the NVM access "hotness" (i.e., access times within a sampling interval) and the access mode (i.e., remote or local) for a user process with low overheads. N-Policy is a process migration policy designed for the user processes which use MVM. For instance, N-Policy reduces the expensive remote accesses to NVM by migrating the process to the node that is close to NVM. The experimental results show that SysMon-N and N-Policy can increase the bandwidth of read-intensive applications by 5.9% and the bandwidth of write-intensive applications by 2.71× to 3.62× when the incorrect core is allocated and remote access occurs.

2   The Art of Our Design

2.1   SysMon-N - Sampling Memory Systems with NVM

To tackle the problems mentioned above, we first design a practical OS-level memory behavior sampling module to capture the NVM access information. Our prior efforts [5,6,8] propose SysMon as an OS-level memory behavior monitoring module. SysMon periodically checks the access bits in Page Table Entries (PTEs) to obtain the page hotness. However, merely checking PTEs can not distinguish whether the page is located in NVM or DRAM. So, we design SysMon-N, based on SysMon [5], to provide the physical address information of the data, it achieves two objectives. (1) Sampling pages in NVM to collect the page hotness information while avoiding sampling pages in DRAM to narrow down the sampling space; (2) Checking whether remote access occurs and collecting related data access information.

As a preprocessing step, SysMon-N collects the NUMA topology information of the platform by scanning ACPI static resource affinity table (SRAT), where the topology information of all processors and memories are stored. By checking the ACPI_SRAT_MEM_NON_VOLATILE flag of the SRAT entries, SysMon-N can get the range of physical address of all NVM devices. Usually, the physical locations of all pages in a Virtual Memory Aera (VMA) are the same. For a specific VMA, SysMon-N gets the physical address of VMA's start page and checks whether it falls in the physical address range of an NVM device. If so, it means that all pages of the VMA are on one specific NVM device, and it is necessary to traverse the VMA's memory address. Otherwise, the VMA is not in NVM and can be skipped to narrow down the sampling space.

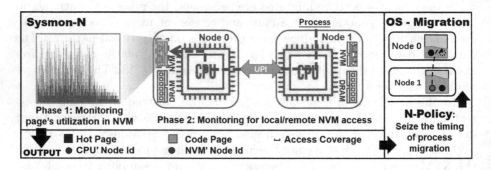

Fig. 1. Workflow of SysMon-N

Figure 1 shows the workflow of SysMon-N. It has two phases. In phase 1, SysMon-N checks each page's access_bit within the monitored process to find the hot pages in NVM and their corresponding physical address area. Besides, considering the massive pressure that NVM's large capacity puts on the limited number of TLBs, it is natural for OS to use the huge page on NVM. The detection of the huge page utilization on NVM are basically the same with the 4KiB-based pages; SysMon-N uses the PMD entries to complete the address translation since the OS omits the last level PTE for 2MiB huge pages.

In phase 2, by comparing the *node id* of CPU where the process running on and that of the NVM node where the data are stored, SysMon-N can determine whether remote accesses occur or not. SysMon-N obtains the set of CPUs on which it's eligible to run by checking process's CPU affinity mask, and then calls the *cpu_to_node*() kernel function to check the node corresponding to the CPU. Finally, SysMon-N compared the CPU node id with NVM node id for the result:

if the two node ids are the same, the process has accessed the page on remote NVM; otherwise, the process only touches the local NVM.

Finally, after sampling, SysMon-N has the number of hot and cold pages and related physical address ranges, and provides the information to N-Policy for making a decision.

2.2   N-Policy - for NVM

N-Policy leverages the formation provided by SysMon-N, and guides process migration accordingly. The key component of N-Policy is a *conditional migration model* which is depicted in Fig. 2. It has two principles. (1) Eliminating remote access whenever possible; (2) Trying to avoid unnecessary migration. The inputs of N-Policy include: (1) the number of hot/cold pages on per node; (2) access coverage for each node; (3) CPU's node id on which the process locates; (4) node id for the used NVM.

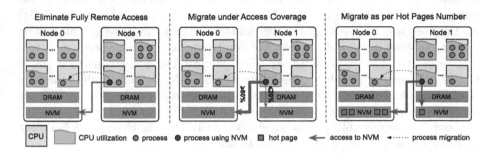

Fig. 2. Conditional Migration Model of N-Policy

After each SysMon-N sampling epoch is completed, the N-Policy immediately decides whether to migrate according to three data access conditions as shown in Fig. 2. The first case is when completely remote access occurs (no data are accessed from local NUMA node), the migration action is triggered to migrate the process to the same node of data. This situation is determined by judging whether there is intersection between the set of the node id of CPU which the process are allowed to run on and that of NVM where accessed data locates. N-Policy makes process migration in this case, easing the overhead of cross-node access by placing the process on the same node as the NVM being used.

If the two set of node ids have intersections, N-Policy compare *access coverage* on different nodes to further decide whether to execute migration. Access coverage symbolizes the amount of data accessed by the process on each NUMA node. If the access coverage of different nodes is unbalanced (i.e., in Fig. 2, N-Policy considers access coverage on remote NUMA node greater than 80% as unbalanced access). N-Policy will select the least utilized CPU on the NUMA node with the broadest access coverage as the target of process migration.

Finally, information about page hotness is also taken into account in N-Policy. Hot pages indicate frequently accessed pages and the data on them is often more important than other pages (may not be right in some cases), and should be accessed closer for reducing latency. To ensure fast access to hot pages, N-Policy compares NUMA node's hotness and migrate the process to the node with the more hot pages.

To avoid significant overheads caused by repeated and meaningless migrations, we let N-Policy receives messages from SysMon-N for every 10 s. N-Policy uses the function *sched_getaffinity()* of the Linux kernel to bind a process to the corresponding CPU nodes for migration.

3   Effectiveness of N-Policy on Bandwidth and Latency

Our experimental platform is a server with dual CPU sockets of Intel Xeon Gold 6240M CPU (each has 36 cores); it has 512 GB Intel® Optane™ DC persistent memory on per socket, i.e., 1024 GB NVM on our platform. We configure the namespace [3] for the Optane PMM, which represents a certain amount of NVM that can be formatted as logical blocks, and then deploy the ext4-DAX file system on it to support direct data access. We don't consider I/O in experiments [14].

We use the Flexible I/O Tester (Fio) [2] with libpmem engine to evaluate the effectiveness of N-policy collaborated SysMon-N. We adjust the minimum read/write block size of I/O operations to perform reads and writes to NVM in different situations, and record bandwidth under different block sizes with and without N-Policy enabled, respectively. To verify the effectiveness of N-Policy, all data accesses of Fio are set as remote access.

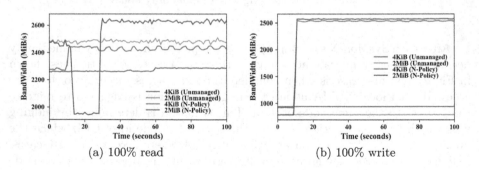

(a) 100% read   (b) 100% write

Fig. 3. Unmanaged vs. Use N-Policy to guide migration

Figure 3-(a) presents the 100% read case. As a baseline, we launch Fio [2] in two cases with a single data access size of 4KiB and 2MiB, respectively. The corresponding memory bandwidth of the two cases is stable with an average of 2273 MiB/s and 2482 MiB/s, respectively. When N-Policy is enabled, it conducts process migration to eliminate the remote access which occurs at the timing around 10s. The bandwidth changes accordingly as the process is migrated to the optimal node. N-Policy can improve the bandwidth by 6.94% and 5.90% for 4KiB and 2MiB block size, respectively. Figure 3-(b) shows the 100% write case. N-Policy achieves better results in this case. By eliminating the remote access with process migration, the bandwidth of Fio can increase by 2.71× and 3.26× in the case of 4KiB and 2MiB block sizes, respectively. This is because reading and writing bandwidth on NVM are not symmetric and NVM is more sensitive to write operations.

References

1. Direct Access for files. https://www.kernel.org/doc/Documentation/filesystems/dax.txt
2. Fio - Flexible I/O tester. https://fio.readthedocs.io/en/latest/
3. Persistent Memory Concepts. https://docs.pmem.io/ndctl-user-guide/concepts
4. Rao, D.S., et al., System software for persistent memory. In: EuroSys (2014)
5. Xie, M., et al.: Sysmon: monitoring memory behaviorsvia OS approach. In: APPT (2017)
6. L. Liu, et al.: Hierarchical hybrid memory management in OS for tiered memory systems. In: IEEE TPDS (2019)
7. X. Li, et al.: Thinking about a new mechanism for huge page management. In: APSys (2019)
8. Liu, L., et al.: Going vertical in memory management: handling multiplicity by multi-policy. In: ISCA (2014) (revised version)
9. Liu, L., et al.: BPM/BPM+: software-based dynamic memory partitioning mechanisms for mitigating DRAM Bank-/channel-level interferences in multicore systems. In: ACM TACO (2014) (revised version)
10. Liu, L., et al.: A software memory partition approach for eliminating bank-level interference in multicore systems. In: PACT (2012) (revised version)
11. Liu, L., et al.: Rethinking memory management in modern operating system: horizontal, vertical or random?. In: IEEE Trans. Comput. (TC) (2016)
12. Liu, L., et al.: Memos: a full hierarchy hybrid memory management framework. In: ICCD (2016)
13. Chen, S., et al.: Efficient GPU NVRAM persistence with helper warps. In: DAC (2019)
14. Lv, F., Cui, H.-M., Wang, L., Liu, L., Wu, C.-G., Feng, X.-B., Yew, P.-C.: Dynamic I/O-Aware scheduling for batch-mode applications on chip multiprocessor systems of cluster platforms. J. Comput. Sci. Technol. **29**(1), 21–37 (2014). https://doi.org/10.1007/s11390-013-1409-2

Network

TPL: A Novel Analysis and Optimization Model for RDMA P2P Communication

Zhen Du[1,2], Zhongqi An[2], and Jing Xing[2(✉)]

[1] University of Chinese Academy of Sciences, Beijing, China
[2] High Performance Computer Research Center, Institute of Computing Technology, CAS, Beijing, China
duzhen18z@ict.ac.cn, {anzhongqi,xingjing}@ncic.ac.cn

Abstract. With increasing demand for networks with high throughput and low latency, RDMA is widely used because of its high performance. Because optimization for RDMA can fully exploit the performance potential of RDMA, methods for RDMA optimization is very important. Existing mainstream researches design optimization methods by constructing a more complete hardware view and exploring relation between software implementation and specific hardware behavior. However, the hardware architecture of NIC (like InfiniBand) is a "black box", which limits development of this type of optimization. So existing methods leave unsolvable problems. Besides, with development of RDMA technology, new features are proposed constantly. So, analysis and optimization methods of RDMA communication performance should be advancing with the times. The contributions of this paper are as follows: 1) We propose a new RDMA point-to-point communication performance analysis and optimization model: TPL. This model provides a more comprehensive perspective on RDMA optimization. 2) Guided by TPL, we design corresponding optimization algorithms for an existing problem, like WQE cache miss and a new scenario, like DCT. 3) We implement a new RDMA communication library, named ORCL, to put our optimizations together. ORCL eliminates WQE cache miss in real-time. And we simulate the workload of the in-memory KV system. Compared with existing RDMA communication implement, ORCL increases throughput by 95% and reduces latency by 10%.

Keywords: RDMA · Performance tuning · Optimization model

1 Introduction

With the development of the in-memory key-value stores [8,12], NVM distributed filesystem [6,11], distributed deep learning systems [7,18] and distributed graph processing system [3,14,20]. RDMA is widely used because of its high throughput and low latency. A well-optimized RDMA communication is related to low-level details, like hardware architecture and RDMA software options. And good optimization can increase performance by 10 times [9]. RDMA system designers need

© IFIP International Federation for Information Processing 2021
Published by Springer Nature Switzerland AG 2021
X. He et al. (Eds.): NPC 2020, LNCS 12639, pp. 395–406, 2021.
https://doi.org/10.1007/978-3-030-79478-1_34

to face many difficulties to improve RDMA performance. Besides, P2P communication is the bottom of the mainstream RDMA communication library [1,5], which is the basis of RDMA optimization.

Many published results have analyzed and optimized RDMA P2P communication performance. They can be divided into two categories. One focus on traditional RDMA communication [4,9,15,19], to exploit hardware view and find relation between RDMA options and low-level transmission process. The other is focus on new features of RDMA, like DCT [13,16,17]. These results follow the development of RDMA technology. They do tests and propose how to use these new features appropriately.

However, previous studies ignore following aspects: 1) The analysis and optimization of RDMA communication are not systematic enough. They only focus on hardware details, including CPU, NIC and PCIe, and transmission process of a single message. But they ignored dispatches of multiple messages and cooperation of different hardware. 2) RDMA new features like DCT(dynamically connected transport) and DM(device memory), should be optimized and included in RDMA communication optimization model. As far as we know, this article is the first one for DCT optimization and application of DM.

The contributions of this paper are as follows: 1) This paper presents a better analysis and optimization model of RDMA point-to-point communication—TPL. 2) Guided by TPL, we design algorithms to solve a remaining problem (WQE cache miss) and optimize a new feature (DCT). 3) We design and implement a new RDMA communication library—ORCL. In ORCL, WQE cache miss is eliminated. And we simulate workload of the in-memory KV system in our cluster. Compared with existing RDMA communication implement, ORCL increases throughput by 95% and reduces latency by 10%.

The rest of the paper is organized as follows: In Sect. 2, we provide the background information of RDMA. In Sect. 3, we propose TPL. In Sect. 4, we introduce two optimization cases guided by TPL. In Sect. 5, we evaluate our algorithm.

2   Background

2.1   Low-Level Details Related to RDMA P2P Communication Performance

Figure 1 shows hardware topology of RDMA P2P communication. PCIe root complex is core component of PCIe. It schedules communication between CPU, memory controller, and PCIe devices.

Figure 2 shows the relation between main data structures and hardware. InfiniBand RDMA verbs is programming interface of RDMA communication. It contains several basic data structures: work queue element (WQE), queue pair (QP), completion queue (CQ), completion queue element (CQE) [2]. These data structures are stored in memory and some parts of them are cached in NIC cache [9].

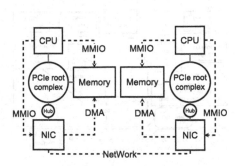

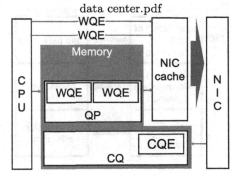

Fig. 1. Hardware topology of P2P communication

Fig. 2. Data structures and hardware

Verbs includes two main types of transport: RC (reliable connected transport), DCT (dynamically connected transport). RC promises the correctness and sequence of messages. Programmers need to establish a connection between QP before communication. DCT is a new protocol introduced by Mellanox in recent years. DCT has the same functionality as RC, but it can establish connections by hardware and connections can be changed. So DCT has much stronger scalability than RC.

2.2   Optimization Method Focusing on Hardware View and Single Message Transmission Process

Before reading this paper, we strongly recommend you to read this published guideline [9]. This guideline is basis of a series of RDMA P2P communication optimizations that have been proposed in recent years. It points out that there are a series of parameters and implementation details corresponding to different hardware behaviors that determine the performance of RDMA P2P communication, including several factors: 1) Transport flag, like *inlined* and *signaled*, 2) Transport type, like *RDMA write*, *RDMA read*, 3) Verbs type. This guideline constructs a more detailed hardware view and maps different communication implementations to different software and hardware processes for analysis and optimization.

3   TPL: Analysis and Optimization Model of RDMA P2P Communication Performance

TPL stems from some observations in our practice: 1) The opinions in existing guidelines have no way to explain all the phenomena we encounter. The factors that affect performance are more complicated. 2) The coordination between

398   Z. Du et al.

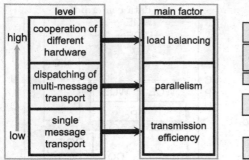

Fig. 3. Hardware topology of P2P communication

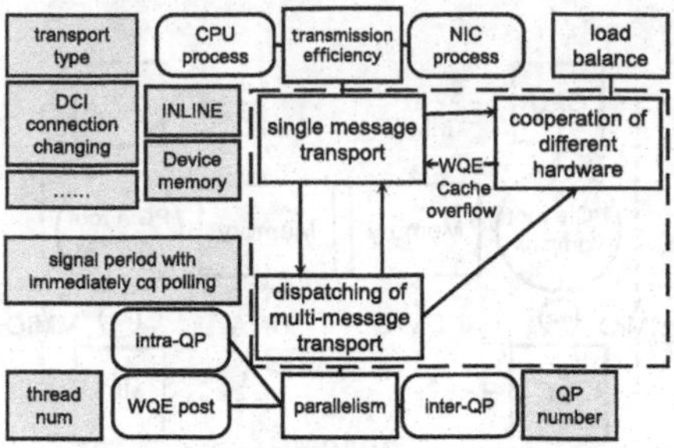

Fig. 4. Data structures and hardware

hardware also affects performance. 3) The key to solving the problem of performance degradation is sometimes irrelevant to specific transmission step that directly leads to degradation. 4) A new model is needed to face new features, like DCT.

As shown in Fig. 3, we found implementation communication will affect performance at three levels from low to high: single message transport, dispatching of multi-message transport, and coordination of different hardware. Optimization goals of different levels are different.

3.1 Transmission Efficiency of a Single Message

The transmission process of a single message includes steps of sending a message. Taking *RDMA write* as an example, the transmission process includes: 1) WQE is transferred from the CPU to the NIC, 2) payload is transferred from the memory to the NIC, 3) local NIC sends the message to remote NIC, 4) the payload is transferred from the remote NIC to remote memory.

3.2 Parallelism of WQE Submission and Handling

WQE submission and handling are respectively performed by CPU and NIC. Parallel processing can improve throughput of RDMA communication. WQE submission parallelism is determined by thread number of CPU.

There are two types of parallelism in WQE handling: intra-QP parallelism and inter-QP parallelism. The reason for intra-QP parallelism is the pipeline inside the process of WQE handling. Intra-QP parallelism is determined by signal period [9] (signaled WQE is submitted periodically, and CQ is polled to wait for the completion of the corresponding WQE). Inter-QP parallelism is determined by the number of QP and PU (QPs and PUs are bound, WQEs of different QPs can be handled by different PUs at the same time).

3.3   Load Balance Between CPU and NIC

Throughput of RDMA communication meets bucket theory. Maintaining load balance between CPU and NIC can also improve performance. Because Infini-Band NIC is a black box and only provides limited programming interfaces, the load balancing between the CPU and the NIC can only be adjusted indirectly.

3.4   Relation Between Three Dimensions

Only optimizing a certain dimension cannot maximize RDMA P2P communication performance. Adjustments to one dimension may affect other dimensions. So, three dimensions of TPL are not orthogonal and the relation between them is shown in Fig. 4.

4   Optimization Algorithm Design Based on TPL

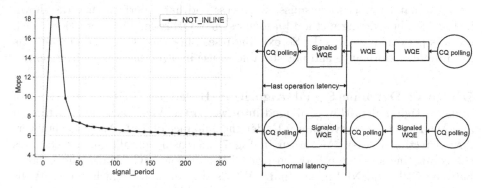

Fig. 5. WQE cache misses recurrent. The relation between signal period and throughput

Fig. 6. Definition of last operation latency and normal latency

TPL is the design principle and guideline of RDMA P2P communication performance optimization. This section will show two typical applications of TPL in the old problem (WQE cache miss) and a new scenario (DCT optimization).

4.1   TPL-Based Systematic Analysis and Single-Dimensional Optimization

WQE cache miss is a legacy problem that is difficult to solve in traditional verbs types. To increase RDMA communication performance, WQEs are cached in in-chip memory of NIC. When too many WQEs need to be cached, the WQE cache

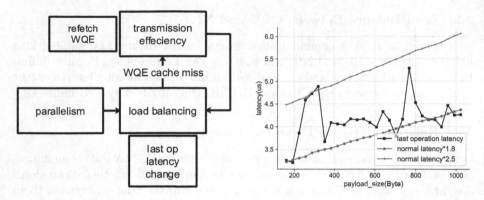

Fig. 7. Use TPL to explain the cause of WQE cache miss

Fig. 8. The relation between last operation latency and normal latency with best parameters

will be filled which causes WQE cache miss. WQE cache miss causes WQE re-fetching that lengthens transmission process and harm performance (as shown in Fig. 5). The existing method [9] focuses on WQE re-fetching detection which reduces performance directly. So existing researches use PCIe counter, but it is harmful to performance and not suitable to use in a production environment.

Design of Dynamic Signal Algorithm Based on TPL. The design of dynamic signal algorithm is divided into two parts: WQE cache miss detection and WQE cache miss avoidance. Under the guidance of TPL, WQE cache over-flow detection is easy. As shown in Fig. 7, increasing parallelism exacerbates the computing speed gap between fast CPU and slow NIC. Worse load balance between CPU and NIC makes many WQEs stay in cache, which causes WQE cache miss and reduces transmission efficiency. Lower transmission efficiency makes the situation of load balance even worse. Although the transmission process influences performance directly, load balance is the key to solve WQE cache miss. To analyze the situation of load balancing, we define two concepts (Fig. 6): 1) Last operation latency. When the signal period size is greater than 1, the interval between WQE submission at the end of the signal period and receiving the CQE corresponding to the WQE. Last operation latency is a characterization of load balance. 2) Normal latency. It is transport latency when signal period size is equal to 1. The normal latency is a reference used to determine whether last operation latency means WQE cache miss and bad load balancing.

As shown in Fig. 8, by adjusting the parameters, we can get good performance when the last operation latency is between 1.8*normal latency and 2.5*normal latency. WQE cache miss happens when last operation latency is greater than 2.5*normal latency. Last operation latency is less than 1.8*normal latency when NIC performance is not fully utilized.

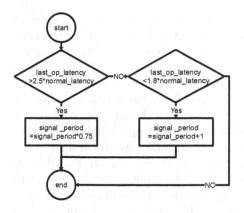

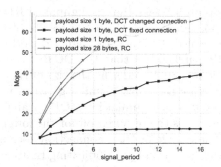

Fig. 9. The flow chart of dynamic signal period

Fig. 10.   Throughput   comparison between DCT and RC

WQE Cache Miss Avoidance. According to TPL, developers can adjust the gap of running speed between CPU and NIC in multiple ways: number of threads, number of QPs, and signal period. Adjusting the signal period is the easiest. To improve the throughput as much as possible while preventing the overflow of the WQE cache, the signal period should be increased when the last operation latency is less than 1.8*normal latency. Correspondingly, when the final operating delay is higher than the 2.5*normal latency, the signal period should be reduced. WQE cache miss will affect other PCIe devices, the signal period should be conservatively increased and radically reduced. In this way, the last operation latency can be kept within a reasonable interval. The flow chart of this algorithm is shown in Fig. 9.

4.2 TPL-Based Multi-dimensional Optimization

The technology of RDMA has been improving rapidly during the past decade. Besides, the HPC system based on RDMA is also highly customized. The designers of the RDMA system need to face new scenarios as and make optimization. This section will take new RDMA hardware and new verbs type (DCT) as an example to show how to optimize new scenarios under the guidance of TPL (Fig. 10).

Testing and Analysis of DCT and DM Guided by TPL. TPL simplifies the test design of RDMA communication. By separately fixing three of four factors, containing the transmission process, intra-QP parallelism, inter-QP parallelism as well as WQE-posting parallelism, the impact of these four factors on performance can be tested. And load balance also needs to be taken into consideration while analyzing test results.

Most test results of DCT are similar to RC. Compared with RC, the characteristics of DCT performance are mainly reflected in intra-QP parallelism. Figure 9 shows the throughput of RDMA write in different verbs types and signal period size. From the results of this test, the following conclusions can be revealed: 1) When the signal period is equal to 1, DCT throughput is less than RC, indicating that the DCT has higher latency and lower transmission efficiency. 2) Considering the size of the WQE header, the throughput of fixed connection DCT has a similar growth rate with RC. This comparison indicates that the two have similar intra-QP parallelism scalability, and lower transmission efficiency is the only reason for the lower performance of fixed connection DCT. 3) The change of DCT connection does not affect latency, but it affects the growth rate of throughput, indicating that changing the connection will reduce the scalability of intra-QP parallelism. According to TPL, there are two optimization methods: 1) Directly relieving the decline of intra-QP parallelism. 2) Increasing inter-QP parallelism to make up for the decline in intra-QP parallelism.

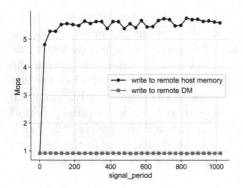

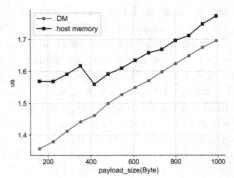

Fig. 11. Single thread read and write bandwidth to the local device memory

Fig. 12. Latency with different payload size in different buffer type

DM (device memory) is a new feature proposed in recent years. Users can explicitly copy the payload to the NIC by MMIO, which expands the way the payload is copied from memory to NIC. So, DM affects the transmission efficiency of a single message.

Figure 13 shows the local device memory read and write performance. The local read and write performance is seriously asymmetric, and the DM write bandwidth is 200 times higher than the DM read bandwidth. This result shows that DM should not be used as a receive buffer to avoid reading DM.

Improving DCT Single Message Transmission Efficiency (T). When sending small messages, MMIO takes less time to copy the payload to NIC than DMA. Therefore, using DM as a sending buffer can shorten the transmission time of a single message. The test result shown in Fig. 12 shows that setting DM as send buffer reduces the latency by 15% while transmitting small messages.

Improving Load Balancing (L). According to the previous tests, changing DCT connection frequently causes the decrease of intra-QP parallelism scalability (will be mentioned below). Using DM as send buffer transfers part of the overhead from NIC to CPU (from DMA read to MMIO write), making the load between CPU and NIC more balanced when DCT connection is changed frequently. Figure 12 shows the effect of this optimization. When the DCT connection is frequently changed, DM can improve throughput by 30%.

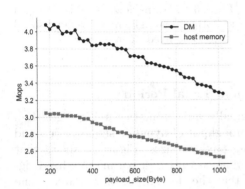
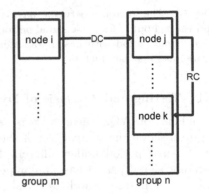

Fig. 13. Throughput of different payload size and send buffer type

Fig. 14. Messages sent from node I to node K

Improving the Parallelism of DCT (P). We improve intra-QP parallelism. To reduce the probability of changing the DCT connection, all of the nodes are grouped. The nodes in the group are connected by RC. DCT is used for sending messages between groups. Sending messages to nodes outside the group requires forwarding, Fig. 14 shows this process. Node I from group m sends the message to node K from group N, and node J forwards this transmission. Node J and node I have the same index within their group.

5   Evaluation

ORCL is the RDMA communication library that we design under the guidance of TPL. ORCL-Classic is designed for mlx4 NIC, ORCL-Advanced is designed for mlx5 NIC. To prove that the optimization guided by TPL is effective, we test the effect of the dynamic signal period in ORCL-Classic on the elimination of WQE cache miss, and the performance of ORCL-Advanced delay under the workload of small-grain KV storage. The test platform of dynamic signal is two E5 nodes equipped with ConnectX-3, each node has 4 threads. The test platform of ORCL-Advanced is two E5 nodes equipped with ConnectX-5.

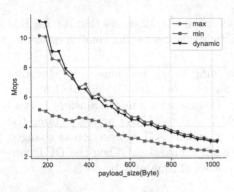

Fig. 15. The relation between payload and throughput of dynamic signal period, fixed signal period with best parameters as well as worst parameters

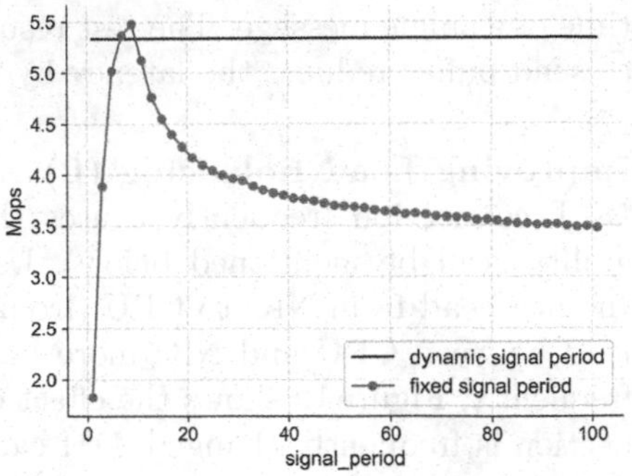

Fig. 16. The payload size is changed smoothly. Throughput of dynamic signal period and fixed signal period

5.1 Testing and Analysis of Dynamic Signal Period

Avoidance of WQE cache miss is essentially an automatic tuning algorithm. Figure 9 shows the comparison of the throughput of dynamic signal period and fixed signal period under different fixed payload sizes. Figure 15 shows that dynamic signal period has similar performance with best-parameters fixed signal period. Figure 16 and Fig. 17 shows that the throughput of dynamic signal period is not lower than 90% of the best fixed signal period's throughput.

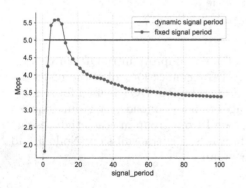

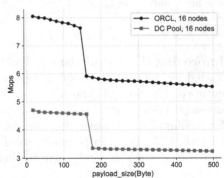

Fig. 17. Payload size is changed randomly. Throughput of dynamic signal period and fixed signal period

Fig. 18. Throughput of ORCL and tradi-tional implement in the different payload

5.2 Throughput Test of ORCL-Advanced

Because the results of the latency test are similar to the result shown in Fig. 11, this subsection only shows the throughput of ORCL. We simulated a load of distributed hash-based in-memory KV storage with traces from YCSB. We simulated the scale of 16 nodes at two physical nodes. The test result is shown in Fig. 18. ORCL throughput is 95% higher than DC Pool (traditional implement designed by Hari Subramoni [16]).

6   Related Work

Designing high-performance RDMA systems is an active area of research. Anuj published three paper [8–10]. He revealed the effects of different verbs types, transport types as well as designs on performance. And these researches propose a serious method to improve performance. ScaleRPC [4] improves the RDMA system scalability by improving CPU L3 cache hit rate. RFP [15] improves the performance when the number of clients is much higher than servers, by using different verbs in different transport direction between servers and clients.

Some works [13,16,17] for DCT test and research have been published. But these works don't include optimization of DCT. So, this paper is the first paper for DCT optimization.

7   Conclusion

In this article, we reveal the one-sidedness of existing RDMA communication optimization methods, and propose a new, more systematic analysis and optimization model: TPL. Under the guidance of this model, it is easier for us to find the key to solve the problem of performance degradation. The test results show that TPL can effectively solve the problem that existing methods are hard to solve. And TPL can has strong adaptability to new scenarios.

Acknowledgment. This work was supported by the National Key R&D Program of China (2018YFC0809300) and the National Natural Science Foundation of China (61502454).

And this work is supported in part by National Program on Key Research Project (No. 2018YFB0204400), by NSFC (No. 61702484, No. 61972380), by CASSPRP (XDB24050200).

References

1. Openucx/ucx. https://github.com/openucx/ucx
2. Barak, D.: Verbs programming tutorial. Open SHMEM (2014)
3. Chen, R., Shi, J., Chen, Y., Zang, B., Guan, H., Chen, H.: Powerlyra: differentiated graph computation and partitioning on skewed graphs. ACM Trans. Parallel Comput. (TOPC) 5(3), 1–39 (2019)
4. Chen, Y., Youyou, L., Shu, J.: Scalable RDMA RPC on reliable connection with efficient resource sharing. In: Proceedings of the Fourteenth EuroSys Conference 2019, pp. 1–14 (2019)

5. Gabriel, E., et al.: Open MPI: goals, concept, and design of a next generation MPI implementation. In: Kranzlmüller, D., Kacsuk, P., Dongarra, J. (eds.) EuroPVM/MPI 2004. LNCS, vol. 3241, pp. 97–104. Springer, Heidelberg (2004). https://doi.org/10.1007/978-3-540-30218-6_19
6. Islam, N.S., Wasi-ur-Rahman, M., Lu, X., Panda, D.K.: High performance design for HDFS with byte-addressability of NVM and RDMA. In: Proceedings of the 2016 International Conference on Supercomputing, pp. 1–14 (2016)
7. Jia, C., et al.: Improving the performance of distributed tensorflow with RDMA. Int. J. Parallel Prog. **46**(4), 674–685 (2018)
8. Kalia, A., Kaminsky, M., Andersen, D.G.: Using RDMA efficiently for key-value services. In: Proceedings of the 2014 ACM Conference on SIGCOMM, pp. 295–306 (2014)
9. Kalia, A., Kaminsky, M., Andersen, D.G.: Design guidelines for high performance {RDMA} systems. In: 2016 {USENIX} Annual Technical Conference ({USENIX}{ATC} 2016), pp. 437–450 (2016)
10. Kalia, A., Kaminsky, M., Andersen, D.G.: Fasst: fast, scalable and simple distributed transactions with two-sided ({RDMA}) datagram RPCS. In: 12th {USENIX} Symposium on Operating Systems Design and Implementation ({OSDI} 2016), pp. 185–201 (2016)
11. Lu, Y., Shu, J., Chen, Y., Li, T.: Octopus: an RDMA-enabled distributed persistent memory file system. In: 2017 {USENIX} Annual Technical Conference ({USENIX}{ATC} 2017), pp. 773–785 (2017)
12. Mitchell, C., Geng, Y., Li, J.: Using one-sided {RDMA} reads to build a fast, CPU-efficient key-value store. In: 2013 {USENIX} Annual Technical Conference ({USENIX}{ATC} 2013), pp. 103–114 (2013)
13. Park, J., Son, Y., Yeom, H.Y., Kim, Y.: SoftDC: software-based dynamically connected transport. Cluster Comput. **23**(1), 347–357 (2020)
14. Shi, J., Yao, Y., Chen, R., Chen, H., Li, F.: Fast and concurrent {RDF} queries with RDMA-based distributed graph exploration. In: 12th {USENIX} Symposium on Operating Systems Design and Implementation ({OSDI} 2016), pp. 317–332 (2016)
15. Su, M., Zhang, M., Chen, K., Guo, Z., Wu, Y.: RFP: when RPC is faster than server-bypass with RDMA. In: Proceedings of the Twelfth European Conference on Computer Systems, pp. 1–15 (2017)
16. Subramoni, H., Hamidouche, K., Venkatesh, A., Chakraborty, S., Panda, D.K.: Designing MPI library with dynamic connected transport (DCT) of infiniband: early experiences. In: Kunkel, J.M., Ludwig, T., Meuer, H.W. (eds.) ISC 2014. LNCS, vol. 8488, pp. 278–295. Springer, Cham (2014). https://doi.org/10.1007/978-3-319-07518-1_18
17. Takagi, M., Yamaguchi, N., Gerofi, B., Hori, A., Ishikawa, Y.: Adaptive transport service selection for MPI with InfiniBand network. In: Proceedings of the 3rd Workshop on Exascale MPI, pp. 1–10 (2015)
18. Xue, J., Miao, Y., Chen, C., Wu, M., Zhang, L., Zhou, L.: RPC considered harmful: fast distributed deep learning on RDMA. arXiv preprint arXiv:1805.08430 (2018)
19. Zambre, R., Grodowitz, M., Chandramowlishwaran, A., Shamis, P.: Breaking band: a breakdown of high-performance communication. In: Proceedings of the 48th International Conference on Parallel Processing, pp. 1–10 (2019)
20. Zhu, X., Chen, W., Zheng, W., Ma, X.: Gemini: a computation-centric distributed graph processing system. In: 12th {USENIX} Symposium on Operating Systems Design and Implementation ({OSDI} 2016), pp. 301–316 (2016)

Connectivity and Routing Algorithm of the Data Center Network HSDC

Hui Dong, Jianxi Fan$^{(\boxtimes)}$, Baolei Cheng, Yan Wang, and Jingya Zhou

School of Computer Science and Technology, Soochow University,
Suzhou 215006, China
jxfan@suda.edu.cn

Abstract. In order to satisfy the rapidly increasing demand for data volume, large data center networks (DCNs) have been proposed. In 2019, Zhang et al. proposed a new highly scalable DCN architecture named HSDC, which can achieve greater incremental scalability. In this paper, we give the definition of the logical graph of HSDC, named H_n, which can be treated as a compound graph of hypercube and complete graph of the same dimension. First, we prove that the connectivity and tightly super connectivity of H_n are both n. Then, we give an $O(n)$ routing algorithm to find a shortest path between any two distinct nodes in H_n, and prove the correctness of this algorithm. In fact, we also prove that the distance constructed by this algorithm is no more than $2d+1$ if $d < n$ and at most $2d$ if $d = n$, where d is the Hamming distance between the start and end nodes, and the diameter of H_n is $2n$.

Keywords: Data center network · Connectivity · Routing algorithm · Shortest path

1 Introduction

With the rapid expansion of cloud-based services, large data center networks (DCNs) have been proposed. It is necessary to design a network architecture and related protocols to interconnect thousands or even hundreds of thousands of servers in a single data center. In order to satisfy the rapidly increasing demand for data volume, the performance of DCN has been continuously improved. In many DCN architectures, there are many DCNs inspired by some special interconnected networks. For example, Fat-Tree [1] is based on the Fat-trees interconnection network [2], BCube [3] is based on the generalized hypercube [4], and BCDC [5] is based on the crossed cube. It is known that hypercube is widely used in parallel computers due to its super features. In 2019, Zhang et al. [6] proposed a new DCN architecture named HSDC based on the hypercube, whose highly scalable architecture can achieve greater incremental scalability. The HSDC architecture is constructed by employing 2-port servers and low-cost

© IFIP International Federation for Information Processing 2021
Published by Springer Nature Switzerland AG 2021
X. He et al. (Eds.): NPC 2020, LNCS 12639, pp. 407–419, 2021.
https://doi.org/10.1007/978-3-030-79478-1_35

commodity m-port switches. Zhang et al. compared the static characteristics of HSDC with other DCNs and the analysis results demonstrate that HSDC is a superior candidate for building large-scale data centers.

In this paper, we focus on the logical graph of HSDC. Our main contributions as follows.

1. We give the definition of the logical graph of HSDC, named H_n. Then, we show that the connectivity and tightly super connectivity of H_n are both n.
2. We propose an $O(n)$ node-to-node shortest routing algorithm in H_n, and prove the correctness of this algorithm. We also prove that the length of the shortest path constructed by this algorithm is no more than $2d + 1$ if $d < n$ and at most $2d$ if $d = n$, where d is the Hamming distance between two given distinct nodes, and the diameter of H_n is $2n$.

This paper is organized as follows. Section 2 provides the preliminaries used throughout this paper and gives the formal definition of H_n. The proofs about connectivity and tightly super connectivity of H_n are given in Sect. 3. In Sect. 4, a node-to-node shortest routing algorithm for H_n is described. Section 5 concludes the paper.

2   Preliminaries

2.1   Terminology and Notation

The basic topology of a data center network can be represented by a graph $G = (V(G), E(G))$, where the switches are regarded as transparent network devices [7, 8, 15] and the remaining server set is represented by the node set $V(G)$, the links between servers are represented by the edge set $E(G)$. We follow the symbol and definition of the graph proposed by Hsu and Lin [9]. For any two distinct nodes u and v, if $(u, v) \in E(G)$, then u and v are neighbors, and the neighbor set of u is denoted as $N_G(u) = \{v \mid (u, v) \in E(G)\}$. The degree of node u is expressed by $deg_G(u) = |N_G(u)|$. The minimum degree of node in G is expressed by $\delta(G)$. A path in G is a sequence of edges $P = ((a_0, a_1), (a_1, a_2), \ldots, (a_{k-1}, a_k))$ where $a_i \in V(G), 0 \le i \le k$, $a_i \ne a_j$ and $i \ne j$. And we denote the path $P - a_k = ((a_0, a_1), (a_1, a_2), \cdots, (a_{k-2}, a_{k-1}))$. The length of a path P is the number of edges in P. For any two distinct nodes a and b, we write the path from a to b by $a \sim b$ and use $a_i \to a_j$ where $i \ne j$ to denote an edge (a_i, a_j) in the path. The distance between a and b is written as $dist(a, b)$, which is the minimum value of all path lengths between a and b. The diameter of G is the maximum distance between any two distinct nodes in G, denoted as $max\{dist(a, b) \mid a, b \in V(G) \ and \ a \ne b\}$. Let G and G' be two graphs. If G is isomorphic to G', we will write $G \cong G'$.

Let F be a subgraph of G, denoted as $F \subseteq G$, if $V(F) \subseteq V(G)$ and $E(F) \subseteq E(G)$. The clique in G refers to a set of nodes such that there exists an edge between any two nodes. It can be seen that the induced subgraph of a clique is a complete subgraph of G. For any subset $F \subset G$, $G - F$ denotes deleting all nodes in F and removing the edges with at least one end-node in F. For any non-empty subset $F \subset G$, if $G - F$ is disconnected, then we called F is a *separating set* of G. The maximal connected subsets of $G - F$ are called *components*. Reliability has always been a concern in networks. Connectivity can assess the reliability of a network. In the following, we make no distinction between graphs and networks. The connectivity of G is denoted by $\kappa(G)$, which is defined as the minimum cardinality of a set of nodes, if any, whose deletion disconnects G or makes G be a trivial graph. In the case of node failure, connectivity plays a crucial role in measuring the fault tolerance of network. If $\kappa(G) \geq k$, the graph G is said to be k-connected. A k-regular k-connected graph is super k-connected if any one of its minimum separating set is a set of the neighbors of some node. In addition, if deleting the minimum separation set will cause the graph to contain two components (one of which has only one node), the graph is tightly super k-connected.

2.2   Topological Structure of H_n

By using n-port switches, the $HSDC_n(n)$ architecture is constructed based on n-dimension hypercube. The $HSDC_n(n)$ can be defined as follows.

Definition 1. *[6] In $HSDC_n(n)$, the nodes and edges are defined as follows:*

(1) The switches and servers are identified as $(x_n \cdots x_1; 0)$ and $(x_n \cdots x_1; y)$, respectively;

(2) The edges are defined as $((x_n \cdots x_1; 0), (x_n \cdots x_1; y))$ and $((x_n \cdots x_1; y), (x_n \cdot \cdots x_{y+1} \overline{x_y} x_{y-1} \cdots x_1; y))$;

where $x_i \in \{0, 1\}, n \geq 2, 1 \leq i \leq n, 1 \leq y \leq n$ and $\overline{x_y}$ is the complement of x_y.

Figure 1 shows the structure of $HSDC_4(4)$.

Definition 2. *[10] Given two regular graphs G and K, the compound graph $G(K)$ is obtained by replacing each node of G by a copy of K and replacing each link of G by a link which connects corresponding two copied of K.*

We treat the logical graph H_n of HSDC $(HSDC_n(n))$ as a compound graph $G(K)$, where G is a n-dimensional hypercube Q_n and K is the same dimensional complete graph K_n. In the following, we will introduce the definition of hypercube and complete graph.

Definition 3. *[11] The node-set V of n-dimensional hypercube Q_n consists of all binary sequence of length n on the set $\{0, 1\}$, i.e., $V = \{x_1 x_2 \cdots x_n | x_i \in \{0, 1\}, i = 1, 2, \cdots, n\}$. Two nodes $x = x_1 x_2 \cdots x_n$ and $y = y_1 y_2 \cdots y_n$ are linked by an edge if and only if x and y differ exactly in one coordinate, i.e., $\sum_{i=1}^{n} |x_i - y_i| = 1$.*

Proposition 1. *[11] The hypercube Q_n has the following properties.*

(1) Q_n is n-regular, has 2^n nodes and $n2^{n-1}$ edges;
(2) Q_n is bipartite;

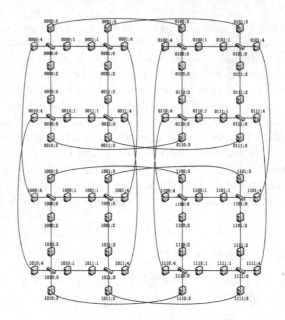

Fig. 1. The structure of $HSDC_4(4)$.

(3) Q_n is hamiltonian if $n \geq 2$; and eulerian if n is even;

(4) Q_n has the diameter $d(Q_n) = n$;

(5) Q_n has the connectivity $\kappa(Q_n) = \lambda(Q_n) = n$;

(6) Q_n is a Cayley graph $C_\Gamma(S)$ and, hence, is node-transitive, where $\Gamma = Z_2 \times \cdots \times Z_2, S = \{100 \cdots 00, 010 \cdots 00, \cdots, 00 \cdots 01\}$;

(7) Q_n is edge-transitive.

Definition 4. *[9] A complete graph is a simple graph in which every pair of distinct nodes is connected by an edge.*

According to the definition of hypercube, compound graph, and the structure of HSDC. Next, we give the formal definition of H_n.

Definition 5. *The logical graph of HSDC, named as H_n where n is an integer with $n \geq 2$. The node-set V is represented as $(x_n x_{n-1} \cdots x_1; y)$ where $x_n x_{n-1} \cdots x_1$ is the label of the node in Q_n and y is the label of the node in K_n. Two nodes $u = (x_n x_{n-1} \cdots x_1; y)$ and $v = (x'_n x'_{n-1} \cdots x'_1; y')$ are adjacent if and only if one of the following conditions is satisfied:*

(1) $x_n x_{n-1} \cdots x_1 = x'_n x'_{n-1} \cdots x'_1$ and $y \neq y'$;

(2) $y = y'$ and $x_n x_{n-1} \cdots x_1, x'_n x'_{n-1} \cdots x'_1$ differ only in the y-th bit.

We call the edge that satisfies the first condition is a clique edge, and the edge satisfies the second condition is a hypercube edge or cross edge. For each node $u \in V(H_n)$, if $(u, v) \in E(H_n)$ is a clique edge, we say v to be an inner-neighbor

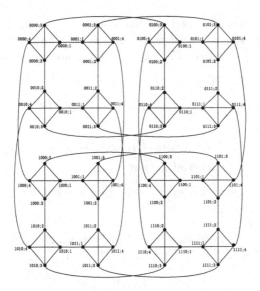

Fig. 2. The structure of H_4.

of u, and v to be an external-neighbor of u when (u, v) is a cross edge. Figure 2 shows the structure of H_4.

In this paper, we let

$$A = \{x_n x_{n-1} \cdots x_1 | x_q \in \{0, 1\}, q = 1, 2, \ldots, n\}.$$

We know that H_n consists of 2^n disjoint cliques. For any $x_n x_{n-1} \cdots x_1 \in A$, let $V' = \{(x_n x_{n-1} \cdots x_1; y)| y = 1, 2, \ldots, n\}$. Then $H_n[V'] \cong K_n$, we use i to denote $x_n x_{n-1} \cdots x_1$'s decimal value and B_i to denote $H_n[V']$. Then we denote

$$I_{2^n} = \{i | i = 0, 1, \ldots, 2^n - 1\}.$$

Proposition 2. H_n has the following properties.

(1) H_n is n-regular;

(2) H_n has $n2^n$ nodes and $n^2 2^{n-1}$ edges;

(3) Each node in H_n is associated with a clique and has only one external-neighbor.

3   Connectivity and Tightly Super Connectivity of H_n

As the number of nodes in H_n continues to increase, the failures of the node become the norm. Generally, reliable data transmission in H_n is based on the condition of any set of faulty nodes. In other words, any nodes in H_n may fail. In this case, assuming that the connectivity of H_n is κ, and the number of faulty nodes in the structure is at most $\kappa - 1$, that is, there is at least one fault-free path between any two distinct fault-free nodes, which can be used for reliable communication between the two nodes. Let F be a faulty node set of H_n, and for any integer $i \in I_{2^n}$, we set $F_i = B_i \cap F$. For convenience, we also let

$$I = \{i \in I_{2^n} \mid |F_i| \geq n-1\}, J = I_{2^n} - I,$$

$$J_0 = \{j \in J \mid |F_j| = 0\}, J_1 = J - J_0 = \{j \in J \mid 1 \leq |F_j| \leq n-2\},$$

and

$$B_J = \cup_{j \in J} B_j, F_J = \cup_{j \in J} F_j.$$

Obviously, $B_j - F_j$ is connected for any $j \in J$.

Lemma 1. *For any subset F of H_n with $|F| \leq n-1$ and $n \geq 2$, we have $|I| \leq 1$ and $B_J - F_J$ is connected.*

Proof. Since $|F| \leq n-1$, we have $|I| \leq 1$ (otherwise, $2n-2 \leq |F_I| \leq |F| \leq n-1$, a contradiction). Let $|J_1| = m$. Then $|J_0| = 2^n - |I| - m$. Note that

$$
\begin{aligned}
|J_0| &= 2^n - |I| - m \\
&\geq 2^n - |F| \\
&\geq 2^n - (n-1) \\
&\geq 3.
\end{aligned}
$$

Then we have $J_0 \neq \emptyset$. Now, we shall show that B_{J_0} is connected through induction on $|J_0|$.

(1) When $|J_0| = 3$, we have $n = 2$. It is easy to see that B_{J_0} is connected.
(2) In the induction step, assume that the statement is true for $|J_0| = k$, where $k \geq 3$.
(3) When $|J_0| = k+1$, since for any $i \in J_0$, there are at least $n-(n-1) = 1$ cross edges between B_i and $B_{J_0-\{i\}}$, where $B_{J_0-\{i\}}$ is connected by induction. Hence, B_{J_0} is connected.

For any $j \in J_1, |F_j| \leq n-2$, we know $B_j - F_j$ is still connected since $B_j \cong K_n$, and the connectivity of K_n is $n-1$. To prove that $B_J - F_J$ is connected, it is suffices to prove that $B_j - F_j$ is still connected to B_{J_0} for any $j \in J_1$. For each B_j with $j \in J_1$, there are at least $n - (m-1) - |I|$ cross edges between B_j and B_{J_0}. Since there exists at least one faulty node in B_j for any $j \in J_1$, we have

$$|F_j| = |F| - |F_I| - |F_{J_1-\{j\}}| \leq n-1 - (n-1)|I| - (m-1).$$

Thus, we have

$$
\begin{aligned}
[n-(m-1)-|I|] - |F_j| &\geq [n-(m-1)-|I|] - [n-1-(n-1)|I|-(m-1)] \\
&= n-(m-1)-|I|-n+1+(n-1)|I|+(m-1) \\
&= (n-2)|I|+1 \\
&\geq 1,
\end{aligned}
$$

which implies that there exists at least one fault-free cross edge between B_j and B_{J_0}, i.e., $B_j - F_j$ is connected to B_{J_0}. By the arbitrariness of j, $B_J - F_J$ is connected. $\square$

Theorem 1. $\kappa(H_n) = n$ for any integer n with $n \geq 2$.

Proof. By Whitney's inequality, we have

$$\kappa(H_n) \leq \lambda(H_n) \leq \delta(H_n) = n.$$

Thus, we just need to show $\kappa(H_n) \geq n$ in the following. That is, we need show that $H_n - F$ is still connected when $|F| = n - 1$. We know that $0 \leq |I| \leq 1$. Otherwise, $2n - 2 \leq |F| = n - 1$, a contradiction.

When $|I| = 0$, by Lemma 1, $H_n - F = B_J - F_J$ is connected.

When $|I| = 1$, say $I = \{i\}$, then $|F_i| = |F| = n - 1$, B_i has only one node, say v, and $J_0 = J = I_{2^n} - \{i\}$. Similarly, by Lemma 1, $B_{I_{2^n} - \{i\}}$ is connected. Note that each node in H_n has exactly one external-neighbor by Proposition 2. Then, the node v in $B_i - F_i$ is connected to some node in $B_{I_{2^n} - \{i\}}$.

Thus, $H_n - F$ is connected. □

Theorem 2. H_n is tightly super n-connected.

Proof. Let F be a minimum separating set of H_n. Then $|F| = n$ by Theorem 1.

According to the definition of tightly super connectivity, we just need to show that $H_n - F$ has exactly two components, one of them is an isolated node.

When $n = 2$, $|F| = 2$, say $F = \{u, v\}$, if there exist one node x and $N_G(x) = \{u, v\}$, then $H_n - F$ has exactly an isolated node and a connected component.

Next, we consider the case when $n \geq 3$. It is clear that $|I| \leq 1$ (otherwise, $2n - 2 \leq |F_i| \leq |F| = n$, a contradiction).

Case 1. $|I| = 0$.

When $|I| = 0$, we have $H_n - F = B_J - F_J$. First, we know that for any $j \in J_1$, $1 \leq |F_j| \leq n - 2$, then $B_j - F_j$ is connected. In the following, we just consider the case that $B_J - F_J$ is not connected. In this case, we know that for any $j \in J_1$, we have $2 \leq B_j - F_j \leq n - 1$, therefore, at least two nodes in $B_j - F_j$ are fault-free. $B_J - F_J$ is not connected, if and only if there exist two distinct fault-free nodes in $B_j - F_j$, say v_1, v_2, and their external-neighbors are both faulty. Then, we know that (v_1, v_2) is an isolated edge, a contradiction.

Case 2. $|I| = 1$.

Suppose $I = \{i\}$, we distinguish the following two cases according to the size of $|F_i|$.

Case 2.1. $|F_i| = n$.

Obviously, $V(F_i) = V(B_i)$. We have $B_i - F_i = \emptyset$ and $H_n - F$ is equivalent to remove a clique from H_n, which does not affect the connectivity of H_n. Therefore, $H_n - F$ is connected, a contradiction.

Case 2.2. $|F_i| = n - 1$.

Clearly, $|F_J| = |F - F_i| = n - (n - 1) = 1$. Let $F_J = \{u\}$. We know $|B_i - F_i| = n - (n - 1) = 1$. Thus, $B_i - F_i$ is a node, say v. Since v has only one external-neighbor, say v'. Then $B_i - F_i$ is connected to $B_J - F_J$ if $v' \neq u$. We have that $H_n - F$ is connected, a contradiction.

Now we consider that $B_i - F_i$ is not connected to $B_J - F_J$. This situation is only when $v' = u$, then v becomes an isolated node in $H_n - F$. Next, we need show that $B_J - F_J$ is connected. We know that $B_J = B_{J_0} \cup B_{J_1}$ and $F_J = \{u\}$, thus, we know $u \in B_j$ where $j \in J_1$. Since $|V(B_j - \{u\})| = n - 1$, $B_j - \{u\}$ is connected. As a result, any nodes in $B_j - \{u\}$ has one external-neighbor in B_{J_0}, which implies $B_j - \{u\}$ is connected to B_{J_0} and $B_J - F_J$ is connected. Thus, v is an isolated node in $H_n - F$ and $H_n - F - \{v\}$ is connected.

Combining the two cases above completes the proof. $\qquad\square$

4 Shortest Routing Algorithm

In this section, we will propose an efficient node-to-node routing algorithm in H_n, called HRouting, to get a shortest path between any two distinct nodes of H_n. Routing is a basic feature to ensure that the network can communicate. A good routing algorithm can reduce the node-to-node transmission delay in the network, and reduce the packet loss rate. As a compound graph of hypercube and complete graph, the shortest path between any two distinct nodes in H_n is inspired by the method of hypercube Q_n. The method of hypercube is as follows. Let $x = x_1 x_2 \cdots x_n$ and $y = y_1 y_2 \cdots y_n$ be any two distinct nodes of Q_n, the shortest path between x and y can obtained by this way: start at x and end at y by continuously changing the different bits from left to right. For example, let $x = 0101011$, $y = 1010010$, then

$$x = 0101011, \mathbf{1}101011, \mathbf{1}0\mathbf{0}1011, 101\mathbf{1}011, 1010\mathbf{0}11, 101001\mathbf{0} = y$$

is a shortest path between x and y, where the boldface bits are obtained by each change. Therefore, the distance between x and y is determined by the number of coordinates of different bits in the two nodes. This number becomes the Hamming distance, denoted by $H(Q_n; x, y)$. We designed a node-to-node shortest routing algorithm suitable for H_n by using the method of continuously changing bits. The algorithm is as follows:

HRouting
Input: an n-dimensional HSDC, H_n, and two distinct nodes $a, b \in H_n$
       where $a = (x_n x_{n-1} \cdots x_1; y)$, $b = (u_n u_{n-1} \cdots u_1; z)$;
Output: a shortest path from node a to node b in H_n;
1: function HRouting(H_n, a, b)
2:     $a_1 \leftarrow (x_n x_{n-1} \cdots x_1)$, $b_1 \leftarrow (u_n u_{n-1} \cdots u_1)$, $d \leftarrow H(Q_n; a_1, b_1)$,
       $Q \leftarrow \text{DIF}(a_1, b_1)$, $P \leftarrow (a)$
3:     function Find-Path(a, b, d)
4:         if $d = 0$ then
5:             $P \leftarrow (P, b)$
6:         else if $d = 1$ then

```
7:              if y = z and x_y ≠ u_z then
8:                  P ← (P, b)
9:              else if y ≠ z and Q[0] = y or z then
10:                 if Q[0] = y then
11:                     P ← (P, (b_1; Q[0]), b)
12:                 else
13:                     P ← (P, (a_1; Q[0]), b)
14:                 end if
15:             else
16:                 P ← (P, (a_1; Q[0]), (b_1; Q[0]), b)
17:             end if
18:         else if 2 ≤ d ≤ n − 1 then
19:             if y ∈ Q then
20:                 c = (x_n ⋯ x̄_y ⋯ x_1; y)
21:             else if y ≠ z and Q[0] = z then
22:                 c = (x_n ⋯ x̄_{Q[1]} ⋯ x_1; Q[1])
23:             else
24:                 c = (x_n ⋯ x̄_{Q[0]} ⋯ x_1; Q[0])
25:             end if
26:             P ← (Find-Path(a, c, 1) − c, Find-Path(c, b, d − 1))
27:         else if d = n then
28:             c = (x_n ⋯ x̄_y ⋯ x_1; y)
29:             P ← (P, Find-Path(c, b, d − 1))
30:         end if
31:     end function
32:     return P
33: end function
34: function DIF(a_1, b_1)
35:     Q ← ()
36:     for i = n to 1 do in parallel
37:         if x_i ≠ u_i then
38:             Q ← Q ∪ {i}
39:         end if
40:     end for
41:     return Q
42: end function
```

Apparently, the length of the path constructed by algorithm HRouting is dependent only on the coordinate representation of the source and destination nodes. The core of the algorithm is a sub-algorithm Find-Path, we find that the most time is taken in lines $27 - 29$, which can be looped at most n times and the time complexity can be computed in $O(n)$ time. The lines 34–42 construct a list to store the addresses of a_1 and b_1 with different coordinates, which takes $O(n)$ time. The $H(Q_n; a_1, b_1)$ also takes $O(n)$ time. Therefore, the time complexity of algorithm HRouting is $O(n)$.

Next, we will prove the correctness of the algorithm by Hamming distance . Let

$$a = (x_n x_{n-1} \cdots x_1; y), b = (u_n u_{n-1} \cdots u_1; z), a_1 = (x_n x_{n-1} \cdots x_1), b_1 = (u_n u_{n-1} \cdots u_1),$$

$$d = H(Q_n; a_1, b_1), Q = \text{DIF}(a_1, b_1) = \{i | 1 \leq i \leq n, x_i \neq u_i\}.$$

When $d = 0$, which means node a and node b are in the same clique, and the shortest path is (a, b); When $d = 1$, if $y = z$ and $x_y \neq u_z$, which indicates that (a, b) is a cross edge of H_n, and the shortest path is (a, b). Both cases above are $(a, b) \in E(H_n)$. Next, we will consider the case $(a, b) \notin E(H_n)$.

Case 1. $d = 1$.

We use the following method to find a shortest path from a to b.

$$a \sim a^{(0)} \sim b, a^{(0)} = (x_n x_{n-1} \cdots \overline{x_{Q[0]}} \cdots x_1; Q[0]).$$

When $y \neq z$ and $Q[0] = y$, the shortest path is $a \to (b_1; y) \to b$;
When $y \neq z$ and $Q[0] = z$, the shortest path is $a \to (a_1; z) \to b$.
In the remaining cases, the shortest path is $a \to (a_1; Q[0]) \to (b_1; Q[0]) \to b$.

Case 2. $2 \leq d \leq n$.

We find an intermediate node c by reducing the Hamming distance by 1 each time, then the problem is transformed into finding a shortest path between node c and node b. We must ensure that the node c found every time is optimal. We regard the sub-algorithm Find-Path as a cyclic invariant of this algorithm. Next, we need to prove that the cyclic invariant holds at each loop. At the beginning of the algorithm, we first compute the Hamming distance of the two nodes, then input the two nodes and Hamming distance into the sub-algorithm Find-Path. In the sub-algorithm, we give a specific method to determine the intermediate node c to ensure that the cyclic invariant holds. The path from a to b is construct by this way:

$$a \sim a^{(0)} \sim a^{(1)} \sim \cdots \sim a^{(d-1)} \sim b,$$

among them,

$$a^{(0)} = (x_n x_{n-1} \cdots \overline{x_{Q[0]}} \cdots x_1; Q[0]), a^{(1)} = (x_n x_{n-1} \cdots \overline{x_{Q[1]}} \cdots \overline{x_{Q[0]}} \cdots x_1; Q[1])$$

where $\overline{x_{Q[1]}}$ and $\overline{x_{Q[0]}}$ appear in an undefined order, and so on.

We use the distance from node a to node $a^{(0)}$ as an example to analyze the distance from node $a^{(i)}$ to node $a^{(i+1)}$ in the above steps, and the distance between the remaining two nodes is consistent with it. Through the Case 1, we know that the length from node a to node $a^{(0)}$ has the following cases:

(1) $y = z$ and $x_y \neq u_z$, the length is 1;
(2) $y \neq z$ and $Q[0] = y$ or $Q[0] = z$, the length is 2;
(3) otherwise, the length is 3.

It can be seen from the above three cases that we must perform an accurate conversion to ensure that the obtained node c is optimal. For example, when $y \in Q$, we put $a \sim a^{(y)}$ in the first step, and the length of path $a \to (x_n x_{n-1} ... \overline{x_y} ... x_1; y)$ is 1, which is smaller than the other cases. In each conversion, the above analysis is required. Therefore, it can be ensured that the resulting path is the shortest.

Lemma 2. *Let* $a = (x_n x_{n-1} \cdots x_1; y)$, $b = (u_n u_{n-1} \cdots u_1; z)$ *be any two distinct nodes in* H_n. *And* $a_1 = (x_n x_{n-1} \cdots x_1)$, $b_1 = (u_n u_{n-1} \cdots u_1)$, $d = H(Q_n; a_1, b_1)$, $Q = DIF(a_1, b_1) = \{i | 1 \le i \le n, x_i \ne u_i\}$. *The distance between* a *and* b *is:*

$$dist(a,b) \begin{cases} = 2d + 1 & \text{if } y \notin Q \text{ and } z \notin Q; \\ = 2d - 1 & \text{if } y \ne z \text{ and } y, z \in Q; \\ = 2d & \text{if } y = z \text{ and } y, z \in Q \text{ or only one of } y, z \in Q. \end{cases}$$

And the length of the shortest path constructed by this algorithm is no more than $2d + 1$ *if* $d < n$ *and at most* $2d$ *if* $d = n$.

Proof. According to the algorithm HRouting, constructing a path from a to b has the following three cases. Next, we will discuss the length of the path in these cases.

Case 1. $y, z \notin Q$.

We let $a^{(0)} = (x_n x_{n-1} \cdots x_1)$, $a^{(1)} = (x_n x_{n-1} \cdots x_{Q[0]} \cdots x_1)$ and so on. Thus, the shortest path from a to b is as follows:

$$a = (a^{(0)}; y) \to (a^{(0)}; Q[0]) \to (a^{(1)}; Q[0]) \to \cdots$$
$$\to (a^{(i)}; Q[i-1]) \to (a^{(i)}; Q[i]) \to (a^{(i+1)}; Q[i]) \to \cdots$$
$$\to (a^{(d-1)}; Q[d-2]) \to (a^{(d-1)}; Q[d-1]) \to (a^{(d)}; Q[d-1]) \to b.$$

We know that the length of the path $(a^{(0)}; y) \to (a^{(0)}; Q[0]) \to (a^{(1)}; Q[0])$ is 2 and the length from $(a^{(i)}; Q[i-1])$ to $(a^{(i+1)}; Q[i])$ is 2 where $i \in \{1, 2, \dots, d-1\}$, and such conversion has been carried out $d - 1$ times, adding the path from $(a^{(d)}; Q[d-1])$ to b, the distance from a to b is $2d + 1$.

Case 2. $y \ne z$ and $y, z \in Q$.

Let $y = Q[0]$, $z = Q[d-1]$, which means $(a^{(0)}; y) = (a^{(0)}; Q[0])$ and $(a^{(d)}; Q[d-1]) = b$. After the analysis of Case 1, we can conclude that the distance from a to b is $2d + 1 - 1 - 1 = 2d - 1$.

Case 3. $y = z$ and $y, z \in Q$ or only one of $y, z \in Q$.

Let $y \in Q$, and the case $y = z \in Q$ is equal to only one of $y, z \in Q$. Through the analysis of Case 2, the distance from a to b is $2d + 1 - 1 = 2d$.

After the analysis of the above three cases, we know that when $d = n$, only the latter two cases may occur. Therefore, the length of the shortest path constructed by this algorithm is no more than $2d + 1$ if $d < n$ and at most $2d$ if $d = n$. □

Theorem 3. *The diameter of* H_n *is* $2n$.

418   H. Dong et al.

Proof. According to the Lemma 2, we know that the distance between any two distinct nodes is no more than $2d + 1$ if $d < n$ and at most $2d$ if $d = n$. Thus, the diameter of H_n is $2n$. □

5 Conclusions

The connectivity $\kappa(G)$ is an important factor determining the reliability of a network. In this paper, we give the connectivity and tightly super connectivity of H_n, which is the logical graph of the data center network HSDC, and construct a shortest node-to-node routing algorithm HRouting. Finally, we summarize the length of the shortest path between any two distinct nodes and prove that the diameter of H_n is $2n$. In the next work, we will study the restricted connectivity of H_n [12,16,17]. Furthermore, we consider that there are some hypercube variants, such as crossed cubes [13], spined cubes [14], etc., whose diameters are smaller than that of the hypercube. They can be used to design DCNs by the method in [6], which is worthy of our further study.

Acknowledgment. This work was supported by the Joint Fund of the National Natural Science Foundation of China (No. U1905211), the National Natural Science Foundation of China (No. 61972272) and the Project Funded by the Priority Academic Program Development of Jiangsu Higher Education Institutions.

References

1. Al-Fares, M., Loukissas, A., Vahdat, A., Scalable, A.: Commodity data center network architecture. ACM SIGCOMM Comput. Commun. Rev. **38**(4), 63–74 (2009)
2. Leiserson, C.E.: Fat-trees: universal networks for hardware-efficient supercomputing. IEEE Trans. Comput. **34**(10), 892–901 (2012)
3. Guo, C., et al.: BCube: a high performance, server-centric network architecture for modular data centers. In: ACM SIGCOMM Conference on Data Communication (2009)
4. Bhuyan, L., Agrawal, D.: Generalized hypercube and hyperbus structures for a computer network. IEEE Trans. Comput. **33**(4), 323–333 (2006)
5. Wang, X., Fan, J., Lin, C.-K., Zhou, J., Liu, Z.: BCDC: a high-performance, server-centric data center network. J. Comput. Sci. Technol. **33**(2), 400–416 (2018)
6. Zhang, Z., Deng, Y., Min, G., Xie, J., Yang, L., Zhou, Y.: HSDC: a highly scalable data center network architecture for greater incremental scalability. IEEE Trans. Parallel Distrib. Syst. **30**(5), 1105–1119 (2019)
7. Guo, C., Wu, H., Tan, K., Shi, L., Zhang, Y., Lu, S.: DCell: a scalable and fault-tolerant network structure for data centers. ACM SIGCOMM Comput. Commun. Rev. **38**(4), 75–86 (2008)
8. Wang, X., Fan, J., Lin, C.-K., Jia, X.: Vertex-disjoint paths in DCell networks. J. Parallel Distrib. Comput. **96**, 38–44 (2016)
9. Hsu, L.-H., Lin, C.-K.: Graph Theory and Interconnection Networks. CRC Press, Boca Raton (2009)
10. Guo, D., et al.: KCube: a novel architecture for interconnection networks. Inf. Process. Lett. **110**(18–19), 821–825 (2010)

11. Xu, J.: Combinatorial Theory in Networks. Science Press (2001)
12. Wang, X., Fan, J., Zhou, J., Lin, C.-K.: The restricted h-connectivity of the data center network DCell. Discret. Appl. Math. **203**, 144–157 (2016)
13. Efe, K.: A variation on the hypercube with lower diameter. IEEE Trans. Comput. **40**(11), 1312–1316 (1991)
14. Zhou, W., Fan, J., Jia, X., Zhang, S.: The spined cube: a new hypercube variant with smaller diameter. Inf. Process. Lett. **111**(12), 561–567 (2011)
15. Wang, X., Erickson, A., Fan, J., Jia, X.: Hamiltonian properties of DCell. Networks Comput. J. **58**(11), 2944–2955 (2015)
16. Li, X., Zhou, S., Guo, X., Ma, T.: The h-restricted connectivity of the generalized hypercubes. Theor. Comput. Sci. **850**, 135–147 (2021)
17. Fan, J., Jia, X., Cheng, B., Yu, J.: An efficient fault-tolerant routing algorithm in bijective connection networks with restricted faulty edges. Theor. Comput. Sci. **412**(29), 3440–3450 (2011)

CCRP: Converging Credit-Based and Reactive Protocols in Datacenters

Yang Bai, Dinghuang Hu, Dezun Dong$^{(\boxtimes)}$, Shan Huang, and Xiangke Liao

College of Computer, National University of Defense Technology,
Changsha 410073, China
{baiyang14,hudinghuang19,dong,huangshang12,xkliao}@nudt.edu.cn

Abstract. As the link speed has grown steadily from 10 Gbps to 100 Gbps, high-speed data center networks (DCNs) require more efficient congestion management. Therefore, proactive transports, especially credit-based congestion control, nowadays have drawn much attention because of fast convergence, near-zero queueing and low latency. However, in real deployment scenarios, it is hard to guarantee one protocol to be deployed in every host at one time. Thus, when the credit-based protocols are deployed into DCNs incrementally, the network will convert to multi-protocol state and face the following fundamental challenges: (i) unfairness, (ii) non-convergence, and (iii) high buffer occupancy. In this paper, we propose a new protocol, called CCRP, aiming for converging credit-based and reactive protocols in data centers. Targeting the mostly deployed protocol, i.e. DCQCN based on explicit congestion notification (ECN), in DCNs, CCRP leverages the forward ECN to detect the network congestion in data queue and optimizes feedback control of the credit-based transports. Our experiment results show that this design can address the unfair link allocation and converge with reactive protocols rapidly. Furthermore, CCRP achieves high utilization and low buffer occupancy at the same time.

Keywords: Data center · Credit-based and ECN-based protocol · Multi-protocol converging

1 Introduction

The data center networks (DCNs) are growing rapidly in size and link speed in recent years. A large data center uses a Clos network of shallow buffered switches to connect more than 100,000 computers. In the past decade, the link speed has steadily increased from 10 Gbps to 100 Gbps [2]. These evolutions have enabled low-latency and high-bandwidth communications in data centers. At the same time, it presents a series of challenges to congestion control [1].

Many reactive congestion control protocols [3–8] have been proposed to solve these challenges. Reactive protocols use congestion signals (e.g., packet loss, explicit congestion notification (ECN) and network delay) to make accurate

© IFIP International Federation for Information Processing 2021
Published by Springer Nature Switzerland AG 2021
X. He et al. (Eds.): NPC 2020, LNCS 12639, pp. 420–434, 2021.
https://doi.org/10.1007/978-3-030-79478-1_36

responses after congestion occurs, which can maintain good average performance under long traffic conditions. However, due to the slow detection of network congestion, it is difficult for reactive protocols to achieve the "correct" rate in each round, which is deciding for small flows and tail performance.

Therefore, the current line of work introduces a new method called proactive congestion control [9–13], which has received much attention in recent years. Among these technologies, one of the most promising deployments in future data centers is ExpressPass [11]—a credit-based proactive congestion algorithm, which can provide zero data loss, fast convergence, low buffer occupancy, and high utilization.

Due to their attractive advantages, credit-based transports, especially ExpressPass, are highly recognized by academia [20,21]. However, current DCNs, such as Google and Amazon, still mainly deploy ECN-based reactive protocols like DCTCP [6] and DCQCN [5]. Thus, the gradual deployment of ExpressPass into DCNs is a visible task in the future. Nonetheless, deploying credit-based protocols [14,15] like ExpressPass in DCNs will bring many challenges to the fairness of bandwidth allocation, especially in multi-tenant DCNs [25,26]. We show in Sect. 2 that simply mixing ExpressPass with reactive protocols deployed in real DCNs will cause serious trouble.

Therefore, we will face severe challenges when incrementally deploying ExpressPass with existing reactive transports in the current DCNs. The root cause is due to the different ways of detecting network congestion. Reactive protocols detect network congestion based on those indirect and passive congestion signals used in the data queue, such as packet loss [22,23], ECN [5,6,24] and network delay [7,17]. Taking DCQCN as an example, when the queue length exceeds the ECN threshold in switch, the data packets will be marked with congestion experienced (CE) codepoint. Then, DCQCN can detect congestion by simply identifying whether the packets are ECN-marked at the end hosts. However, ExpressPass acquires congestion information from the credit queue. As shown in Fig. 1, a clear physical isolation exists between data queue and credit queue under Expresspass. ExpressPass uses the credit loss rate as the congestion indicator. When congestion is detected, ExpressPass reduces the credit sending rate at the receiver.

Thus, if we mix Expresspass with DCQCN traffic in the network, Expresspass can not detect the network congestion in the data queue and will transmit packets at a full speed, even the queue length exceeds the buffer size in switch. In contrast, DCQCN will reduce its sending rate continually until its bandwidth occupancy approaches zero, since a great quantity of packets may be marked with the CE codepoint in the data queue. We conducted several multi-protocol experiments to prove the aggressiveness of ExpressPass when coexisting with other three different types of reactive algorithms: DCQCN (FECN-based), CUBIC [29] (drop-based) and Timely (delay-based). The result indicates that ExpressPass is too aggressive for all of them, thus, the unfairness caused by the physical isolation must be eliminated.

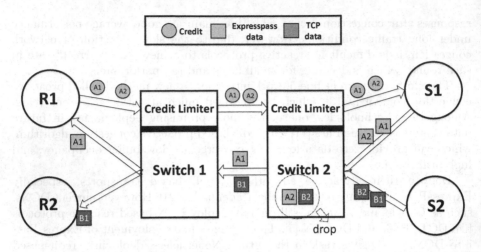

Fig. 1. The Dilemma of Deploying ExpressPass in DCN: ExpressPass gets network congestion information only in credit queue. Thus, when there is other traffic (ep. TCP flows) in the network and congestion occurs in the data queue, Expresspass will preempt the bandwidth, resulting in a large number of queues, even packet loss.

The core problem of conflicting with reactive protocols is that the credit-based transports like Expresspass only detect network congestion through the credit queue, so a natural idea is to optimize the congestion detection mechanism for ExpressPass so that it can also detect congestion in the data queue. Therefore, we propose a new scheme called CCRP, which aims to achieve the symbiosis between credit-based protocols and reactive protocols. The key points of CCRP are as follows.

- CCRP breaks the isolation between the credit queue of credit-based protocols and the data queue by adding the ECN marking mechanism.
- We make a trade-off between the throughput and latency of the multi-protocol network by adjusting the threshold of the random early detection (RED) ECN marking scheme in the switch data queue.
- We replace the old feedback control of the credit-based protocols by a new ECN-based control algorithm, so that CCRP can also detect and deal with the network congestion occurs in the data queue.

Our new ECN-based feedback control in CCRP can detect and respond to network congestion in a few RTTs without affecting the performance of the reactive protocol stack. CCRP ensures fairness between different protocols with cross-protocol convergence time reaching milliseconds. The average buffer occupancy is also reduced to less than 170 KB under CCRP. Moreover, when CCRP coexists with few traffic under other congestion algorithms in the network, the transmission can be completed at high convergence speed without introducing additional overhead. Simulating the current DCN common partitioning/aggregation mode shows that CCRP can greatly reduces the tail delay and also ensure that the average flow completion time (FCT) in a multi-protocol network will not be affected.

2   Background and Motivation

2.1   DCN Needs the Credit-Based Protocols

In the past decade, reactive protocols have played an important role, because they achieve high throughput and low buffer occupancy rate in DCNs. So far, many data centers are still deploying reactive protocols, such as DCQCN and DCTCP, to prevent the network from collapsing under heavy and sudden traffic.

However, due to the increased link speeds and shallow buffered commercial switches, the buffer size for per Gbps link speed is decreasing. For example, DCQCN result in unfairness due to the slow response time, which puts DCQCN in straits. In addition, the simulation result shows that when coexisting with a large number of concurrent flows, the instantaneous queue length is much larger than the maximum queue capacity under DCQCN, leading to low QOS for DCN.

Therefore, in recent years, credit-based proactive algorithms have attracted widespread attention. Unlike reactive protocols, credit-based proactive protocols like ExpressPass are characterized by the merits of high throughput, fast convergence and bounded-queue. ExpressPass is a hop-by-hop proactive congestion control algorithm. Before sending data packets, sender sends a credit request to the receiver. After receiving the request, receiver sends the credits to the sender on a per-flow basis in an end-to-end manner. The Switches then rate-limit the credits and decide the available bandwidth for packets which will flow in the reverse direction. As shown in Fig. 1, credit packets throttled to 5% bandwidth ensure that traffic is transmitted within the link capacity. ExpressPass can achieve lossless transmission at only 5% bandwidth cost by using credits. However, Expresspass hasn't been deployed in DCNs. To deploy incrementally in data centers, ExpressPass must be optimized to coexist with the already widely deployed reactive protocols, such as DCQCN and DCTCP.

2.2   The Challenges of Deploying Credit-Based Protocols in DCNs

Credit-based transports must coexist with other traditional protocols in DCNs, however, whether two kind of traffic can converge fairly is a main problem. In Fig. 2, we assume that flow 1 to N are scheduled by two different protocols—ExpressPass and DCQCN. Then the question arises, if all the senders send data to the receivers simultaneously in these topologies, can the bottleneck link resource be allocated in a fair manner?

Figure 1 shows the dilemma of deploying ExpressPass in DCNs. The credit queue for Expresspass is isolated from the data queue for other protocols. Thus, when coexisting with other traffic in the network, the transmission rate of the ExpressPass traffic will not be reduced, since Expresspass detect network congestion only through the credit queue. In contrast, other "reactive" flow will

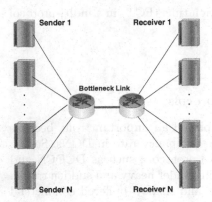

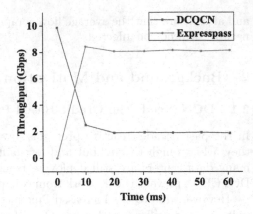

Fig. 2. Dumbbell topology: can the bottleneck resource be allocated in a fair way?

Fig. 3. The Problem of Multi-protocol in DCNs. Most bandwidth are occupied by Expresspass once it is injected into network.

be restricted because they can detect the network congestion in the data queue by using different congestion signals (ECN, RTT or packet loss). Consequently, ExpressPass preempts all resources of the bottleneck link aggressively, while the "reactive" flow can only wait.

To verify our analysis, we design an experiment based on the topology shown in Fig. 2 by using OMNeT++ simulator. We let DCQCN run first, and then insert ExpressPass traffic into the network after 10ms. We use long flows so that they can be transmitted continuously. In addition, we set the link speed to 10Gbps and the propagation delay to 5 μs. The result is shown in Fig. 3, as Expresspass inserted into network, it preempts all resources of the bottleneck link. ExpressPass can always occupies the bandwidth quickly, while the other "reactive" flows could only be restricted and wait. Therefore, ExpressPass must be improved to coexist with reactive protocols, which is a quite a challenging job.

3 CCRP Design

3.1 Basic Idea

As we describe in Sect. 2, the main problem is that Expresspass can not receive any congestion information from the data queue due to the isolation between the credit queue and the data queue. Thus, we propose a new protocol called CCRP, which has achieved great success by using appropriate congestion signals for the credit-based proactive protocols, developing a new feedback control schemes, and determining reasonable network configurations. The key idea of CCRP is to optimize the feedback control and congestion detect scheme of the credit-based protocols, so that it can break the isolation between the data queue and the credit limiter to achieve great convergence when coexisting with other traffic.

Algorithm 1: ECN-based Feedback Control on Receiver
1: $ECN\_\alpha \leftarrow 1$, $\omega \leftarrow 0$, $cur\_rate \leftarrow initial\_rate$, $DCQCN\_Timer \leftarrow FALSE$
2: **repeat**
3:     $credit\_Loss = \#\_dropped\_credit/\#\_sum\_credit$;
4:     $ECN\_ratio = \#\_ECN\_packet/\#\_sum\_packet$;
5:     **if** $ECN\_ratio \geqslant target\_ECN\_ratio$ **then**
6:         $ECN\_\alpha = (1-g)*ECN\_\alpha + g*ECN\_ratio$;
7:         $tmp\_rate = cur\_rate*(1-(target\_ECN\_ratio + ECN\_\alpha)/2)$;
8:         **if** $DCQCN\_Timer = TRUE$ **then**
9:             Use ECN-based feedback control of DCQCN;
10:         **end if**
11:     **end if**
12:     **if** $credit\_Loss \leqslant target\_loss$ **then**
13:         ▷ (increasing phase)
14:         $\omega = (\omega + \omega_{max})/2$;
15:         $cur\_rate = (1-\omega)*tmp\_rate + \omega*max\_rate$;
16:     **else**
17:         ▷ (decreasing phase)
18:         $cur\_rate = tmp\_rate*(1-credit\_loss\_rate)$;
19:         $\omega = max(\omega_{min}, \omega/2)$;
20:     **end if**
21: **until** End of flow

In CCRP, we choose FECN to deliver congestion information of data queue as it can be provided by commodity switches in DCN.

Specifically, when the network is converted to a congested state, low mode stage of DCQCN feedback control starts; when the network is not crowded, ExpressPass's credit feedback control algorithm will be fully effective. For ECN-based feedback control, once we deploy a reasonable ECN threshold on the switch, CCRP will automatically reduce the sending rate immediately after receiving ECN-marked packet, because only when there is some other non-ExpressPass traffic in the network, the queue length in switch will exceeds the ECN threshold. In addition, when ECN-marked packet is no longer received in multiple RTTs, CCRP will send credits more excessively.

3.2   ECN-Based Feedback Control

As an effective technique to detect network congestion, using ECN is not a rare occurrence in reactive protocols. However, applying ECN to credit-based proactive protocols is a novel work. Our ECN-based feedback control focuses on two issues: (i) How to react appropriately to the different types of congestion information from credit queue and data queue. (ii) How to detect congestion more effectively.

First, we need to keep the good performance of the credit-based transports. When there is little "reactive" traffic in the network environment, credits can be sent excessively to achieve high convergence. To this end, in the initial few

RTTs, CCRP enables traffic tend to send packets at the link capacity. After multiple RTTs, if not getting any packet marked with CE codepoint, we set the *DCQCN Timer* as true and assume that there is no other "reactive" traffic in the network and take a more aggressive approach.

Here, we must make a trade-off between convergence and packet loss. Before the network environment is determined, it's easy to cause packet loss when the sender sends credits at high speed in the manner of Algorithm 1. We can design the phase to send packets by using slow start scheme, which will harm the convergence of Expresspass. There are the reasons for sending credit at high rate in CCRP:

- As the link speed has grown steadily from 10 Gbps to 100 Gbps, the transmission of data flow will be completed in much shorter time. Under 100Gbps network, the AvgFCT of 0-100KB small flows would be around 2 RTTs [16], which indicates that even one RTT is quite important for these small flows. Thus, If CCRP starts at a low speed, it may waste the bandwidth.
- Starting at high rate can help CCRP quickly detect whether there is other "reactive" flows in DCNs.
- When there is few other "reactive" flows in the network, the characteristic of high of convergence can be guaranteed for credit-based protocols.

In addition, we use ECN to detect the network congestion of data queue. When Expresspass coexist with other "reactive" traffic in the network, some packets will be marked with CE codepoint and the low mode of DCQCN feedback control will be triggered. After serval increasing and decreasing stages, the ECN ratio will converge to the target_ECN_ratio recursively.

Finally, in CCRP, we also design a variant version of the credit-based increase and decrease phase to make full use of the link capacity information provided by the credit queue. The variable ω that we added to these phases floats between ω_{min} and ω_{max}, and can achieve slow self-increase and rapid decrease. Based on this, we have designed the ECN-based feedback control algorithm, which is shown in Algorithm 1. With this algorithm, when coexisting with other "reactive" traffic in the network, CCRP can allocate the bottleneck link bandwidth in a fair manner instead of disrupting other traffic aggressively. Also, CCRP can keep the advantages of bounded queue and high convergence of credit-based protocols through the acceleration algorithm of DCQCN. Our experiments show that the new version of credit-based feedback control is strongly suitable for multi-protocol networks.

3.3   Parameter Choice

Target_Loss: Since the credit-based protocols like Expresspass can disrupt other traffic roughly, we need to set a lower target_loss in the variant version of credit-based control phase to reduce the aggressiveness in the early stages of deploying CCRP. Thus, we set 0 for the target_loss to adapt to the current multi-protocol network environment.

Target_ECN_Ratio: In the current shallow-buffer switch environment, target_ECN_ratio should be set as 0, which will ensure that the average queue length in switch is around the ECN threshold K. We also provide an interface by defining the target_ECN_ratio to improve feedforward compatibility of DCN, so that we can control the switch buffer usage by modifying the parameters at the host instead of modifying the threshold at the switch.

ω_{max}: The aggression factor ω is particularly significant in CCRP feedback control algorithm. Based on our experiments, we find in most cases, the credit_loss is less than the target_loss since CCRP does not always utilize all the bandwidth. Thus, ω is tend to get closer to ω_{max} in multi-protocol network. In order to reduce the aggressiveness of CCRP, we choose a smaller ω_{max}. To choose an appropriate value for ω_{max}, we did a parallel experiments between CCRP and DCQCN and finally found that 0.04-0.07 is suitable for ω_{max} to ensure fairness. In our experiments, ω_{max} is set to 0.06 and the evaluation of the range of ω_{max} is shown in Sect. 4.

3.4 Endhost and Switch Mechanism

Marking at CP: Based on the random early detection scheme, we use instantaneous queue length to detect network congestion. DCTCP recommends to set Kmin and Kmax to the same value K, so that congestion can be detected and handled quickly. DCQCN advocates to use three parameters, Kmin, Kmax, and Pmax to mark packets. However, it's not efficient because in most cases, there is no ingress/egress traffic and queue occupancy is close to zero. Therefore, we set Kmin as 5KB and Kmax as 200KB in CCRP.

Controller at RP: Different from other protocols, the ECN-based feedback control algorithm of CCRP is on the receiving side. The controller of the receiver can provide great convenience, since we can detect congestion accurately by checking whether the data packet is marked with CE codepoint. Compared with traditional method of using ACK to notify the sender to cut the congestion window, CCRP can also reduce the load of the link by reducing the credit sending rate at the receiver.

Bandwidth Allocation of Credit/Packet Channel: CCRP doesn't change the design of the credit packet size and the separate queue on the switch. An 84B size Ethernet frame credit can trigger the sender to send a 1538B size Ethernet frame packet. Therefore, 5% of the link capacity is used for credit transmit, while the remaining 95% of the link capacity is allocated for data packets. Even if the credit channel is not fully utilized in multi-protocol networks, the design remains unchanged since the traffic of DCNs is changing rapidly.

4   Evaluation

In this section, we measure the performance of CCRP from five perspectives: (i) utilization of the bandwidth (ii) fairness (iii) convergence speed (iv) flow comple-

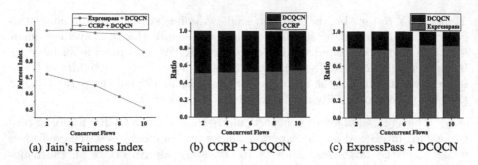

(a) Jain's Fairness Index   (b) CCRP + DCQCN   (c) ExpressPass + DCQCN

Fig. 4. Fairness measurement. CCRP can achieve fairness greatly due to the ECN-based congestion control, while ExpressPass cannot guarantee fairness.

tion time (v) queue length. All the experiments are completed with OMNeT++ simulator [27,28,30] and the ratio of CCRP/ExpressPass to DCQCN is 1:1.

Utilization of the Bandwidth: Firstly, we measure utilization since one of the benefits of using ECN is high utilization. As we described in Sect. 2, Expresspass must provide 5% of the link bandwidth to transmit credits, so that the utilization of CCRP and Expresspass is near to 95%. We compare the performance of CCRP, Expresspass and DCQCN in the same multi-protocol network environment, and the results show that all the three protocols can make full use of network bandwidth. The utilization rate of the network in which the credit-based protocol and the ECN-based protocol coexist is 95%, while the utilization of only ECN-based protocol is close to 100%.

Fairness: CCRP aims to optimize the feedback control algorithm and reduce the aggressiveness of credit-based proactive protocols so that they can coexist with other tradition "reactive" traffic in the network. Thus, fairness is the most significant metric in our evaluation. We mainly did two experiments to measure the fairness of CCRP in multi-protocol networks. We calculate the average bandwidth of each flow in a 100 millisecond interval by using the Jain's fairness index and the result is shown in Fig. 4a. Due to the aggressiveness of credit-based protocols, fairness between Expresspass and DCQCN is poor. Besides, as more concurrent traffic being injected into network, Expresspass will suffer from packet loss and fairness will deteriorate further. On the contrary, as shown in Fig. 4a, CCRP performs much better than Expresspass. We attribute this improvement to the ECN-based feedback control in CCRP. As shown in Fig. 4b and 4c, the fairness between the two types of traffic is evaluated by the ratio of CCRP/Expresspass to DCQCN. This measurement only focuses on the unfairness between different traffic and ignores the internal unfairness caused by packet loss. The result also shows that CCRP can ensure fairness when coexising with other "reactive" traffic.

Convergence: Convergence is also a highlight of our work. We did a series of experiments to simulate the convergence of CCRP/ExpressPass and DCQCN when they coexist in the network. Specifically, there are four types of hosts

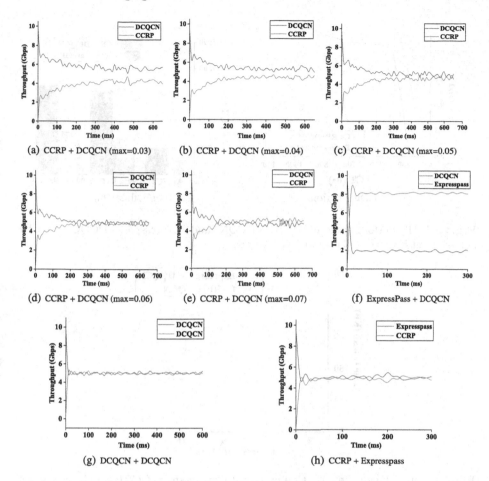

Fig. 5. Convergence measurement. When ω_{max} ranges from 0.04-0.07, CCRP can converge to fairness with DCQCN, while ExpressPass cannot converge to fairness.

(A to D). Type A machine (running ExpressPass or CCRP, sender) connect type C machine (running ExpressPass or CCRP feedback control, receiver) and type B machine (running DCQCN, sender) connect to type D machine (running DCQCN, receiver) with 10 Gbps links via ECN-enable switch. A to C and B to D are through the same path. The switch creates two connections to simultaneously fetch two large flows from sender A and D. Since ω_{max} is one of the most important variable of ECN-based feedback control algorithm in CCRP, in our experiments, we range ω_{max} from 0.03-0.07.

As seen from Fig. 5b, 5c, 5d, 5e, when ω_{max} ranges from 0.04 to 0.07, CCRP can greatly reduce the aggressiveness of Expresspass and converge with DCQCN perfectly. When the aggression factor is set to 0.07 as shown in Fig. 5e, the convergence speed is only 100 ms slower than that of DCQCN as shown in Fig. 5g. In contrast, Fig. 5f shows that ExpressPass with DCQCN cannot achieve

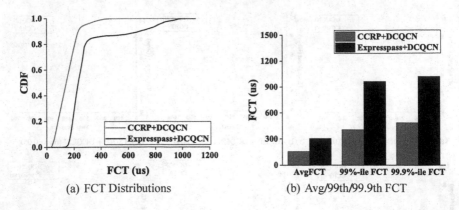

(a) FCT Distributions   (b) Avg/99th/99.9th FCT

Fig. 6. FCT Performance of CCRP+DCQN and Expresspass+DCQCN. CCRP achieves much better FCT than Expresspass.

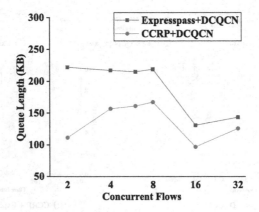

Fig. 7. Average Queue Length. Compared with Expresspass, CCRP avoids bursty traffic and reduces the buffer occupancy.

convergence in the multi-protocol network. However, when ω_{max} is too small (ω_{max}=0.03), as shown in Fig. 5a, although CCRP can also help DCQCN seize the bandwidth, the result of convergence is not ideal. Finally, Fig. 5h shows that both CCRP and Expresspass have the same performance with high convergence.

Flow Completion Time: Since the FCT is one of the most important performance metrics of network congestion protocols, we also use FCT as a comparison metric. We plot the FCT distributions in Fig. 6 and the Avg/99th/99.9th FCT in Fig. 7. All the simulation results show that, CCRP achieves much better FCT than Expresspass. We believe that our new ECN-based feedback control breaks the isolation between the data queue and credit queue, helping CCRP deal with the network congestion in data queue and improve the FCT performance. However, Expresspass cannot detect the network congestion in the data queue and send packets aggressively, causing severe packet loss and the increase of FCT.

Queue Length: The last major indicator is the buffer occupancy. Due to the shallow buffered switches, low buffer occupancy is also the performance that we pursue in our work. Thus, we measured the average queue length of the switch, which characterizes the queue under general circumstances. As shown in Fig. 7, compared with Expresspass, CCRP can achieve much smaller queue length when coexist with DCQCN in the network.

Summary: After the detailed measurement and analysis, we conclude that CCRP can greatly narrow the competitiveness difference between credit-based proactive protocols like ExpressPass and traditional reactive protocols like DCQCN. Compared with Expresspass, CCRP can converge with DCQCN perfectly and achieve high Utilization, fairness, small FCT and low buffer occupancy at the same time.

5 Related Work

RTT-based Protocols: For those congestion control algorithms (Timely [7] and DX [17]) which are based on delay, RTT is a very important congestion signal. They do not require any information feedback from the switches. Only the continuous record of delay of packets at the host can determine whether congestion happens. Timely belongs to a different class of algorithms that use delay measurements to detect congestion. Unlike TCP Vegas [17], which is window-based and maintain a queue close to the minimum RTT, Timely is a rate-based algorithm that employs a gradient approach and does not rely on measuring the minimum RTT. It works well with NIC support, despite infrequent RTT signals. Compared to DCTCP, Timely can significantly reduce queuing delay. Reducing CPU utilization of end hosts is not a goal for Timely. Different from Timely, DX implements accurate latency measurements using a DPDK driver for the NIC and the congestion control algorithm is within the Linux TCP stack, which is similar to the conventional window-based proposals.

Credit-Based Feedback Control: Credit-based congestion control in data centers is inspired by credit-based flow control [19] for other interconnected systems. ExpressPass uses a similar idea like TVA [31] that performs rate-limit requests at the router and CCRP inherit that method. Furthermore, in high-performance networks, proactive congestion control uses grants for congestion control. Unlike CCRP, those schemes use speculative packets on a grant-based basis to avoid wasting preparing the data transmission. Although they are difficult to implement and have extra preprocessing time overhead, and those trade-offs are hard to balance, they provide an idea for the credit-based protocols in the DCNs. We look forward to finding a reasonable compatibility solution for other credit-based transports. Moreover, compared with CCRP, end-to-end credit-scheduled congestion control focus on incast problems based on the receiver. Those transmission control algorithms add an extra control layer to make sure senders only transmit according to some quota assigned to them.

6   Conclusion

In this paper, we propose a new protocol called CCRP, aiming for incrementally deploying the credit-based congestion control in current data centers. CCRP breaks the isolation between the data queue and the credit rate limiter by using ECN as the congestion signal. The new efficient ECN-based feedback control algorithm that we use to control the credit sending rate can guarantee high performance of CCRP without interfering with other traffic in the network. The evaluation results show that CCRP can greatly narrow the competitiveness difference between credit-based proactive protocols like ExpressPass and traditional reactive protocols like DCQCN. Compared with Expresspass, CCRP can converge with DCQCN perfectly and achieve high Utilization, fairness, small FCT and low buffer occupancy at the same time. Therefore, CCRP has high applicability in the incremental deployment of credit-based congestion control in data centers.

Acknowledgment. We would like to thank the anonymous reviewers for their insightful comments. We gratefully acknowledge members of Tianhe interconnect group at NUDT for many inspiring conversations. The work was supported by the National Key R&D Program of China under Grant No. 2018YFB0204300.

References

1. Singh, A., et al.: Jupiter rising: a decade of clos topologies and centralized control in Google's datacenter network. Commun. ACM **45**, 188–197 (2016). https://doi.org/10.1145/2785956.2787508
2. Jose, L., et al.: High speed networks need proactive congestion control. In: Proceedings of HotNets, pp. 1–7 (2015). https://doi.org/10.1145/2834050.2834096
3. Wilson, C., et al.: Better never than late: meeting deadlines in datacenter networks. In: Proceedings of SIGCOMM, pp. 50–61 (2011). https://doi.org/10.1145/2018436.2018443
4. Wu, H., et al.: ICTCP: incast congestion control for TCP in data-center networks. In: Proceedings of CoNEXT, pp. 1–12 (2010). https://doi.org/10.1145/1921168.1921186
5. Eran, H., et al.: Congestion control for large-scale RDMA deployments. In: Proceedings of SIGCOMM, pp. 523–536 (2015). https://doi.org/10.1145/2785956.2787484
6. Alizadeh, M., et al.: Data center TCP (DCTCP). In: Proceedings of SIGCOMM, pp. 63–74 (2010). https://doi.org/10.1145/1851182.1851192
7. Mittal, R., et al.: Timely: RTT-based congestion control for the datacenter. In: Proceedings of SIGCOMM, pp. 537–550 (2015). https://doi.org/10.1145/2785956.2787510
8. Hong, C., et al.: Finishing flows quickly with preemptive scheduling. In: Proceedings of SIGCOMM, pp. 127–138 (2012). https://doi.org/10.1145/2377677.2377710
9. Gao, P., et al.: pHost: distributed near-optimal datacenter transport over commodity network fabric. In: Proceedings of CoNEXT, pp. 1–12 (2015). https://doi.org/10.1145/2716281.2836086

10. Perry, J., et al.: Fastpass: a centralized "zero-queue" datacenter network. In: Proceedings of SIGCOMM, pp. 307–318 (2014). https://doi.org/10.1145/2619239. 2626309
11. Cho, I., et al.: Credit-scheduled delay-bounded congestion control for datacenters. In: Proceedings of SIGCOMM, pp. 239–252 (2017). https://doi.org/10.1145/3098822.3098840
12. Jiang, N., et al.: Network congestion avoidance through speculative reservation. In: Proceedings of HPCA, pp. 1–12 (2012). https://doi.org/10.1109/HPCA.2012.6169047
13. Montazeri, B., et al.: Homa: a receiver-driven low-latency transport protocol using network priorities. In: Proceedings of SIGCOMM, pp. 221–235 (2018). https://doi.org/10.1145/3230543.3230564
14. Michelogiannakis, G., et al.: Channel reservation protocol for over-subscribed channels and destinations. In: Proceedings of HPCA, pp. 52:1–52:12 (2013). https://doi.org/10.1145/2503210.2503213
15. Nan, J., et al.: Network endpoint congestion control for fine-grained communication. In: Proceedings of SC, pp. 35:1–35:12 (2015). https://doi.org/10.1145/2807591.2807600
16. Hu, S., et al.: Augmenting proactive congestion control with aeolus. In: Proceedings of APNet, pp. 22–28 (2018). https://doi.org/10.1145/3232565.3232567
17. Lee, C., et al.: Accurate latency-based congestion feedback for datacenters. In: Proceedings of USENIX ATC, pp. 403–415 (2015). https://doi.org/10.1109/TNET.2016.2587286
18. Brakmo, L., et al.: TCP Vegas: new techniques for congestion detection and avoidance. In: Proceedings of SIGCOMM, pp. 24–35 (1994). https://doi.org/10.1145/190314.190317
19. Kung, H., et al.: Credit-based flow control for ATM networks: credit update protocol, adaptive credit allocation, and statistical multiplexing. In: Proceedings of SIGCOMM, pp. 101–114 (1994). https://doi.org/10.1145/190314.190324
20. Zhang, Y., et al.: BDS: a centralized near-optimal overlay network for inter-datacenter data replication. In: Proceedings of EuroSys, pp. 1–14 (2018). https://doi.org/10.1145/3190508.3190519
21. Mittal, R., et al.: Revisiting network support for RDMA. In: Proceedings of SIGCOMM, pp. 313–326 (2018). https://doi.org/10.1145/3230543.3230557
22. Alizadeh, M., et al.: pFabric: minimal near-optimal datacenter transport. In: Proceedings of SIGCOMM, pp. 435–446 (2013). https://doi.org/10.1145/2486001.2486031
23. Fall, K., et al.: Simulation-based comparisons of (Tahoe, Reno and SACK TCP). In: Proceedings of SIGCOMM, pp. 5–21 (1996). https://doi.org/10.1145/235160.235162
24. Zats, D., et al.: DeTail: reducing the flow completion time tail in datacenter networks. In: Proceedings of SIGCOMM, pp. 139–150 (2012). https://doi.org/10.1145/2377677.2377711
25. Judd, G., et al.: Attaining the promise and avoiding the pitfalls of TCP in the datacenter. In: Proceedings of NSDI, pp. 145–157 (2015). https://doi.org/10.5555/2789770.2789781
26. He, K., et al.: AC/DC TCP: virtual congestion control enforcement for datacenter networks. In: Proceedings of SIGCOMM, pp. 244–257 (2016). https://doi.org/10.1145/2934872.2934903
27. http://omnetpp.org/

28. https://inet.omnetpp.org/
29. Ha, S., et al.: CUBIC: a new TCP-friendly high-speed TCP variant. ACM SIGOPS
    Oper. Syst. Rev. **42**, 64–74 (2008). https://doi.org/10.1145/1400097.1400105
30. Varga, A., et al.: An overview of the OMNeT++ simulation environment. In: Pro-
    ceedings of SIMUTools, pp. 1–10 (2008). https://doi.org/10.1145/1416222.1416290
31. Yang, X., et al.: A DoS-limiting network architecture. In: Proceedings of SIG-
    COMM, pp. 241–252 (2005). https://doi.org/10.1145/1080091.1080120

Storage

CompressedCache: Enabling Storage Compression on Neuromorphic Processor for Liquid State Machine

Zhijie Yang, Rui Gong, Lianhua Qu, Ziyang Kang, Li Luo, Lei Wang[(⊠)], and Weixia Xu

College of Computer Science and Technology, National University of Defense Technology, Changsha, Hunan, People's Republic of China
{yangzhijie,Leiwang}@nudt.edu.cn

Abstract. Spiking Neural Network (SNN) based neuromorphic processors have gained momentum due to their high energy efficiency. As a kind of SNN, Liquid State Machine (LSM) shows potential in domains such as image recognition and speech recognition, and it is simpler to train than other SNNs. In neuromorphic processors, weights and synapses are stored on-chip to reduce the energy cost of data movement. However, the storage of them is redundant if the deployed network on the neuromorphic processor is LSM which is a sparse SNN. By exploiting the sparsity of LSM, adopting storage compression can reduce the power consumption of the processor or enable a single chip to deal with more complex tasks with more logic neurons. In this work, we propose a lossy storage compression method, Compressed Sparse Set Associative Cache (CSSAC) which makes use of the sparsity and the robustness of LSM. We apply CSSAC on an LSM-oriented neuromorphic processor to demonstrate how the hardware design supports CSSAC to enable storage compression and complete LSM computation. CSSAC does not introduce much metadata overhead to ensure the compression effect, nor does it decrease the accuracy of LSM or the performance of the processor. Experimental results show that in our implementation, CSSAC can, at best, result in 14%–55% reduction in on-chip storage and 5%–46% reduction in power consumption of the processor under different weight data widths on MNIST, NMNIST, DVS128 Gesture datasets.

Keywords: Spiking neural network · Neuromorphic processor · Liquid state machine · Storage compression

1 Introduction

SNNs [1–3] and neuromorphic processors [4–6] have attracted much attention and developed rapidly due to the characteristics of modeling the behavior of

© IFIP International Federation for Information Processing 2021
Published by Springer Nature Switzerland AG 2021
X. He et al. (Eds.): NPC 2020, LNCS 12639, pp. 437–451, 2021.
https://doi.org/10.1007/978-3-030-79478-1_37

neurons in the brain and high energy efficiency. As a kind of SNN, LSM [1] has shown great potential in the fields of image recognition and speech recognition [7]. Because it is natural to use LSM to recognize the spike trains produced by various new sensors, such as Dynamic Vision Sensor (DVS) [8] and Dynamic Audio Sensor (DAS). Besides, compared with other SNNs, the training of LSM is simpler because only the readout layer of it, which is generally a single-layer fully connected layer, needs to be trained. Moreover, different readout layers can share the same versatile reservoir layer which is responsible for data pre-processing, to deal with multiple tasks.

In neuromorphic processors like TrueNorth [4] and Loihi [5], all synapses and weights are reserved on-chip storage to support the deployment of different kinds of SNNs with dense or sparse connectivities. However, the storage reserved for weights and synapses is redundant if the deployed network on the neuromorphic processor is LSM which is sparse. It limits the number of logic neurons of LSM that a single chip with the fixed area can support, which influences the processing ability and the best accuracy of LSM. Besides, in the neuromorphic processor such as TrueNorth, the power consumption used for storage is several times that of computing and communication. Thus, compressing the storage of weights and synapses can reduce power consumption or increase the number of logic neurons on a single chip without adding more storage, which is vital to enabling a single chip to handle more complex tasks and the construction of multi-core neuromorphic processor to simulate larger-scale biological neural networks in the next generation.

In this work, we propose CSSAC, a lossy storage compression method for LSM-oriented neuromorphic processor. It makes use of the sparsity and the robustness of LSM to enable storage compression without incurring accuracy loss of LSM. To demonstrate how the hardware design supports CSSAC to enable storage compression and LSM computation, we design a hardware neuron for LSM-oriented neuromorphic processor using CSSAC storage organization. Thus, CSSAC can be used in hardware neurons of similar neuromorphic processors deployed sparse SNNs like LSM. To sum up, our main contributions are as follows:

- We design a lossy storage compression method, CSSAC, for LSM-oriented neuromorphic processor. It makes use of the sparsity and the robustness of LSM to enable storage compression on weights and synapses of LSM and does not incur LSM accuracy loss, large metadata overhead nor processor performance degradation.
- We design a hardware neuron for LSM-oriented neuromorphic processor using CSSAC storage organization, demonstrating how the hardware design supports CSSAC to reduce the storage and power consumption and to complete LSM computation.

The experimental results show that, in our implementation, CSSAC can, at best, result in 14%–55%, reduction in storage and 5%–46%, reduction in power consumption under different weight data widths on MNIST, NMNIST [9],

DVS128 Gesture [10] datasets when compared with the uncompressed implementation.

2 Background and Motivation

In this section, we will introduce the basic structure of LSM and compressed sparse storage methods. Then we will introduce our motivation, the sparsity of LSM and the robustness of LSM.

2.1 Liquid State Machine

As shown in Fig. 1, LSM consists of the following three components. The input layer, which is a feed-forward neural network for receiving external spike trains produced by new sensors such as DVS and DAS. The reservoir layer, which is a spiking recurrent neural network composed of multiple neurons for data pre-processing. The readout layer, which can be many kinds of structures such as Support Vector Machines (SVM), fully connected neural networks, and linear regression models, etc. with plastic weights for classification.

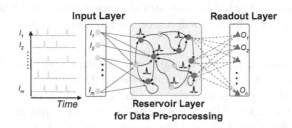

Fig. 1. The typical structure of LSM. The reservoir layer is a spiking recurrent neural network for data pre-processing with implastic weights. The weights in the readout layer are plastic.

As the core of LSM, the reservoir layer is the most time-consuming and has the most complex structure, among the three layers of LSM. As shown in Fig. 1, there are two different types of neurons in the reservoir layer. Ones are the excitatory neurons (the dark green ones) and others are the inhibitory neurons (the light green ones). So there are four kinds of synapses in the reservoir layer according to the difference between the starting and ending neurons. They are excitatory-to-excitatory synapse, excitatory-to-inhibitory synapse, inhibitory-to-excitatory synapse, and inhibitory-to-inhibitory synapse.

The topology of the reservoir layer is generated according to different connection probabilities of the four connections in network initialization. The weights of the reservoir layer will remain unchanged during both inference and training after the initialization. While only the weights of the readout layer are plastic and can be trained to do classifications of different tasks. This feature makes LSM training simpler and less time-consuming than other SNNs.

2.2 Compressed Sparse Storage Formats

Compressed sparse storage formats are used to exploit the sparsity of neural networks to enable storage compression. The main idea of it is that only the non-zero entries will be stored, together with their indices which uniquely identify each entry. The existing sparse storage formats includes Compressed Sparse Row (CSR) [11], Compressed Sparse Fiber (CSF) [12], co-ordinate [13] and their variants [14]. In these formats, the non-zero entries are stored contiguously in the memory along with their indices. For example, each entry in CSR is $(dw + iw)$ long, where dw and iw are the bit widths of the non-zero elements and their indices, respectively. The bit width of the index is determined by the number of entries before compression. Therefore, when the network sparsity is high enough, using these compressed sparse storage methods can bring benefits. However, when the network sparsity is not high enough, the metadata overhead brought by them will make the effect worse or even counterproductive.

2.3 Motivation

In this section, we will introduce the sparsity and robustness of LSM which provides us a chance to enable lossy storage compression on LSM-oriented neuromorphic processor. Then we will introduce our motivation.

The Sparsity of LSM. Lsm is spare both in space and time. The sparsity in space of LSM is the key to storage compression. During the initialization of the reservoir layer, the four types of synapses are randomly generated with different connecting probabilities. Through a large number of experiments, we find the optimal connection probabilities that can make the LSM network reach the highest accuracy under different datasets. With the optimal connection probabilities, averagely, the total connection probability is about 34.7%. In other words, 65.3% of all weights are zero. Thus these weights can be compressed and their storage can be saved by using the compressed sparse storage method.

The Robustness of LSM. We observe that if we randomly replace a certain proportion of the non-zero weights with a non-zero value in the reservoir layer, the LSM accuracy will not decrease after the replacement. So LSM has a certain degree of robustness.

We conduct an experiment to further quantify the robustness of LSM. First, we generate and initialize an LSM network. Then we train the weights of its readout layer until the accuracy of the network is converged. After that, we keep the weight of the readout layer unchanged, randomly replace a certain percentage of the non-zero weights with a non-zero value in the reservoir layer. We define this kind of operation as the random disturbance. After the disturbance, we observe the relationship between the random disturbance ratio and accuracy loss. As shown in Fig. 2, when the random disturbance ratio is less than or equal to 5%

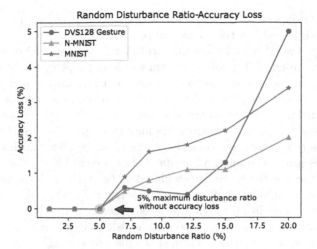

Fig. 2. Relationship between random disturbance ratio on non-zero weights and accuracy loss under different datasets.

on the MNIST, NMNIST, and DVS128 Gesture datasets, the LSM accuracy will not lose.

In summary, the static sparsity of LSM provides us a chance to enable storage compression on LSM-oriented neuromorphic processor. The robustness of LSM allows us to change a small part of non-zero weights without incurring the accuracy loss of LSM. These two features of LSM create the foundation for the lossy sparse compression method on LSM-oriented neuromorphic processor to reduce the power consumption or increase supported logic neurons with the fixed chip area.

3   Compressed Sparse Set Associative Cache

In this section, we will present the details of CSSAC and analyzes the metadata overhead it brings. The discussion about the sensitivity of the parameters is in Sect. 6.

The main idea of the CSSAC approach is to compress the storage by storing only the non-zero weights on the chip and organizing the weight memory as a read-only set-associative cache. During the processor initialization, All non-zero weights are transferred to the on-chip weight memory to be stored. Weights that have nowhere to be stored due to the storage limit will be discarded. But their synapses information is preserved on the chip. Thus discarded weights can be replaced by other weights stored on chip when needed.

3.1   Details of the Method

In the CSSAC method, we first group all weights including zero ones and non-zero ones of a neuron into equal groups. Then we generate tags based on higher bits of their addresses for them. With the tag, a weight can be distinguished from other weights within the same group.

All non-zero weights and their tags will then be transferred to the belonging set in memory on-chip. But some of them will have no place to store because we reduce entries in each set in on-chip memory by the same amount. The number of reduced entries in each set is determined by the compression ratio under the random disturbance ratio without accuracy loss. Thus, these weights will be discarded. Note that some storage units may be empty. The on-chip memory is organized as a read-only set-associative cache after the above initialization. Each stored entry is $(dw + tw)$ long, where dw and tw are the bit widths of the weights and their tags respectively. tw is calculated as $tw = \lceil log2(N) \rceil$, where N is the number of entries in a set before the compression. Besides, all of the synapses information is stored in an on-chip adjacent vector in which each bit indicates whether a synapse exists or not, to distinguish weights that are discarded in compression from zero weights. Thus, if the discarded weights are needed, their existence can be known through synapses information and they can be replaced by the weights stored in the same set to be used.

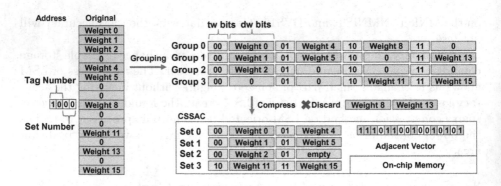

Fig. 3. Compressed sparse set-associative cache.

During the process of computation, a request for weight will lead to simultaneous accesses to both the weight memory and the adjacent vector. By the modulus operation between the requested weight index and the number of sets, the corresponding set number is generated. All tags in the target set are read out and compared with the tag of request weight. If the tag of the requested weight hits one of the tags in the set, the corresponding weight is read out to be used. If not and the bit corresponding to the requested weight in the adjacent vector is "1", the first item in the same set is read out to replace the requested one.

As shown in Fig. 3, we give an example of the CSSAC. Assume that a neuron has 16 synapses and weights. Only 9 of synapses are existent, i.e. the weights of them are non-zero, due to the static sparsity. Firstly, weights are grouped into 4 groups equally based on the modulo operation of their indexes. Each set has four entries. So the bit width of the tag is 2. The entries of each set are reduced to 2 in on-chip memory. During the process of transferring all non-zero weights and their tags to on-chip memory, *weight* 8 and *weight* 13 are discarded because of the limitation of storage space. Besides, the adjacent vector is also set to store all synapses information without compressing.

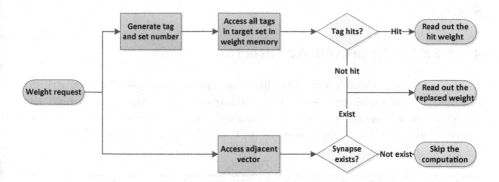

Fig. 4. The process of accessing a request weight in CSSAC.

The process of accessing a request weight is executed as the sequence in Fig. 4 and the storage of CSSAC is organized as on-chip storage shown in Fig. 3. For instance, if *weight* 3 is requested, the computation will be skipped. Because the synapse of *weight* 3 is found as "0" in the adjacent vector. If *weight* 8 is requested, its tag will not be found in weight memory. But in the adjacent vector, the synapse of *weight* 8 will be found as "1". Thus, the first entry in the same set, *weight* 0, is read out to replace it.

3.2   Metadata Overhead

Given all weights entries of in-degree synapses of a neuron is a if it supports fully connect with other neurons. These entries are divided equally into s sets. We reduce r entries per set to compress the storage for there are not that many synapses needed to be stored due to the static sparsity of LSM. Thus the total metadata overhead M is computed as follows, which consists of tag and synapse information stored in the adjacent vector.

$$M = [(\lceil log2(\frac{a}{s})\rceil) \times (a - s \times r)] + (1 \times a) \qquad (1)$$

where $1 \leq s \leq a$ and $1 \leq r \leq \frac{a}{s}$. The compression ratio C is calculated as follows:

$$C = \frac{s \times r}{a} \times 100\% \qquad (2)$$

The storage reduction rate R considered metadata overhead is calculated as follows:

$$R = [1 - \frac{M + (1 - C) \times a \times dw}{a \times dw}] \times 100\% \qquad (3)$$

where dw is the quantization bit widths of the weights. The discussion about the sensitivity of storage reduction under different quantization bit widths is in Sect. 6.

Compared with the conventional compressed sparse storage method, CSSAC has a better effect on the medium sparse network such as LSM. Because it introduces less metadata overhead than conventional methods which are discussed in Sect. 6.

4   CSSAC-Improved Architecture

In this section, we will briefly introduce the working process of a typical LSM-oriented neuromorphic processor. Then we introduce the hardware neuron design in detail to demonstrate how the hardware neuron supports CSSAC storage organization to reduce weight storage and completes LSM computation.

Algorithm 1: Workflow of typical LSM-oriented neuromorphic processor

---

Input: external input $spike_{it}$, $i \leq I$, $t \leq T$ // I is the number of input neurons
Output: Classification result R
for $t = 1; t \leq T$; // T is the number of time steps in one sample picture **do**
    for $i = 1; i \leq N$; **do**
        for $j = 1; j \leq I + N$; // N is the number of hardware neurons **do**
            if $spike_{jt} == 1 \&\& synapse_{ij} == 1$ **then**
                | $voltage_i = voltage_i + weight_{ij}$;
            end
        end
        if $voltage_i \geq threshold$ **then**
            $spike_{i+I,t+1} = 1$; //Generate internal spikes as input for the next time step.
            $voltage_i = 0$;
            $state_i = state_i + 1$;
        end
    end
end
R = Readout(state); //Readout is the function of readout layer of LSM.

Typical LSM-oriented neuromorphic processor works by timestep as Algorithm 1. In each time step, the external input spike train and their indices are sent to the hardware neuron by shift registers cycle by cycle. Each neuron receives the spike and index in each clock cycle and the weight is accessed according to the received index to perform membrane voltage accumulation. When all the external input spikes in a time step are processed, each neuron compares its membrane voltage with the pre-stored threshold. And each neuron will generate an output spike if the voltage is larger than the threshold for the use in the next time step as an internal input spike. Then, the computation of the next time step can be started. After all the time steps of a sample picture are performed, the acquired liquid states are used to get the classification result.

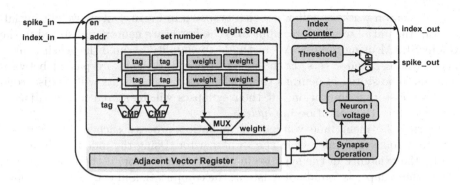

Fig. 5. Block diagram of the hardware neuron.

4.1 Hardware Neuron

The function of the hardware neuron is receiving the input spike, performing the accumulation of membrane voltage of neurons, and generating the output spike. As shown in Fig. 5, the structure of a neuron consists of the following components. A weight SRAM and a tag SRAM are used to store the weights of all logic neurons in a hardware neuron using CSSAC organization with parallel comparators and a multiplexer. An adjacent vector register that stores the uncompressed synapses information. Registers that stores the threshold and all membrane voltages of logic neurons. A synapse operation module is used to perform the accumulation of membrane voltage. A comparator used to compare the threshold with membrane voltage and to decide whether to generate an output spike or not. An index counter which indicates the index of the logic neuron being used.

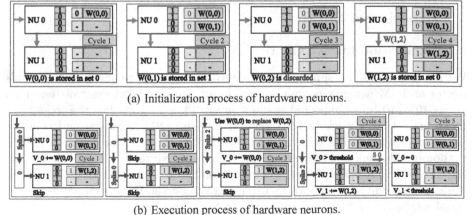

(a) Initialization process of hardware neurons.

(b) Execution process of hardware neurons.

Fig. 6. Working process of hardware neurons organized using CSSAC.

The neuron works as follows, which is shown in Fig. 6. During weight initialization, the initial weights are input into the hardware neuron and stored in the weight SRAM using the CSSAC method. To simplify, assume that each neuron has 4 synapses and 2 sets. Each set has 1 entry. Weights are passed between neurons to be stored in neurons they belong to. Some weights will be discarded due to the storage limitation but their synapses will be stored in the adjacent vector such as the condition in *Cycle* 3.

During the membrane voltage accumulation process, each neuron receives the input spike and index from the shift register. Using the index, each neuron checks the existence of the synapse in the adjacent vector. If the input spike is "0" or the synapse is found not existent, the computation in this cycle is skipped as *NU* 1 dose in *Cycle* 1, 2, and 3. If the input spike is "1" and the synapse exists, set number and tag are generated according to the input index. Then all the tags of the target set are accessed to be compared with the generated tag. If the generated tag does not match any tags in the set, the weight in the first place of the set is directly fetched to perform the accumulation computation of membrane voltage as *NU* 0 does in *Cycle* 3 of the execution process. The computational model of the neuron is performed as the leak-integration-firing (LIF) neuron model [7].

After processing all the input spikes, neurons will enter the phase of output spike generation. The calculated membrane voltage is compared with the pre-stored threshold. If the membrane voltage is greater than the threshold, an output spike is generated and the membrane voltage is reset as *NU* 0 does in *Cycle* 4 and 5 of the execution process. Otherwise, there is no output spike and the membrane voltage of the logic neuron is directly written back to the corresponding register. And the membrane voltage of the next logical neuron to be processed is taken out for computation during the same time step. Until voltage updating computations of all logic neurons are finished, computation of the next time step will be started then.

5   Experiment Setup

5.1   Simulation Infrastructure

We use Brain 2 [15], a spiking neural network simulator, to generate the topology of an LSM network containing 256 input neurons, 1024 reservoir neurons, and a 1024*10 fully-connected readout layer. Then we initialize the weights in LSM, train the network to convergence, test the LSM accuracy, and conduct the random disturbance experiment of weights in the reservoir layer. We use a python-based simulator to simulate the stored procedure of CSSAC and acquire the discard ratios under different compression ratios. Note that the effect of the discard ratio and the random disturbance ratio on the LSM accuracy is nearly equal.

5.2 Hardware Implementation

We implement the hardware architecture using RTL-level code and evaluate in 32 nm ASIC technology to get experiment data of hardware. We first implement an uncompressed version of the neuromorphic processor using 1024 uncompressed hardware liquid neurons. It uses shift registers for spike transmission and contains the necessary buffers for data exchange. We then use CSSAC-improved hardware neuron implementation to replace the neurons in the uncompressed version of the neuromorphic processor. Then we get a compressed version of the neuromorphic processor implementation.

5.3 Datasets

For image recognition, we use a subset of the MNIST and N-MNIST, each including 10k images for training and 10k samples for testing. For the DVS dataset, we use the DVS128 Gesture dataset [10] which contains 11 hand gestures from 29 subjects under 3 illumination conditions.The highest accuracies the LSM we use can achieve in MNIST, N-MNIST, DVS128 Gesture datasets are 87.1%,93.1%, and 85.6%, respectively while they are 99%, 99%, and 94% [10] in state of the art work [16] using DNN.

5.4 Measurements

First, we measure the sensitivity of the discard ratio under the different number of sets to find the optimal parameter configuration of CSSAC. Second, we measure the compression effect under different weight data widths compared with CSR compressed sparse format. Then we measure the power consumption reduction of the processor brought by CSSAC. The baseline is the implementation without storage compression.

6 Evaluation

6.1 Discard Ratio Sensitivity Analysis on Number of Sets

To study the impact of the number of sets on the discard ratio in CSSAC stored procedure, we examine the storage compression under different numbers of set. In infrastructure, each reservoir neuron has 1280 synapses (256 from input neurons and 1024 from internal reservoir neurons). Figure 7 (a) shows different configurations of CSSAC. First, we determine the number of sets. Then we compress the storage by reducing the number of entries in each set, i.e. ways. The configuration points under the blue dotted line plane will not bring accuracy loss. Each CSSAC configuration point corresponds to a storage reduction rate. As shown in Fig. 7 (b), the fewer sets there are, the more tolerant the discard ratio is to the storage reduction rate. Because the memory is becoming more similar to the fully associative cache when the number of sets gets smaller. But the hardware overhead of the memory increases when the number of sets gets smaller for that it needs more parallel comparators to compare the tags in the same set. So the number of sets can not set to be too small.

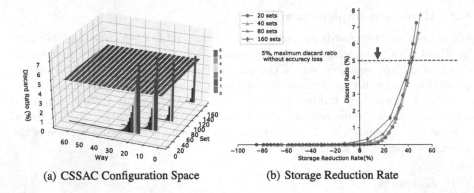

(a) CSSAC Configuration Space   (b) Storage Reduction Rate

Fig. 7. The relationship between the storage compression and the weight discard ratio under different sets and ways numbers configuration when the data width of weight is 8-bit.

6.2 Compression Effect Sensitivity Analysis on Weight Data Width

To compare the compression effect of the CSSAC, hash addressing, and CSR [11], we conduct storage compression using these three methods under different weight data widths. Figure 8(a) shows the maximum storage reduction that can be achieved by the three methods under different weight data widths. Although the CSR method only stores non-zero weights and the storage utilization is 100%, its compression effect is worse than CSSAC due to its high metadata overhead. Another reason for the poor performance of CSR applied to LSM is that the sparsity of LSM is not particularly high, thus limiting the effect of CSR. So stored in CSR, the total storage with metadata overhead is even larger than the storage before compression.

As for hash addressing, we use a simple hash function to recode addresses for non-zero weights. The non-zero weights whose addresses are collided will be discarded. We use this method as a lossy sparse compression method to compare with CSSAC. Because this approach has less metadata overhead, it works better when the weight data width is lower. However, due to the high collision rate (more than 6%) brought by this method, the accuracy of LSM will be reduced, so we do not adopt this method.

6.3 Power Consumption Evaluation

Compressing storage with CSSAC brings power consumption reduction of the processor. We synthesize the uncompressed implementation and the compressed implementation with CSSAC of the neuromorphic processor to show the relationship between the power consumption reduction and the compression ratio. As shown in Fig. 8(b), CSSAC brings 5%–46% reduction in power consumption under different weight data widths.

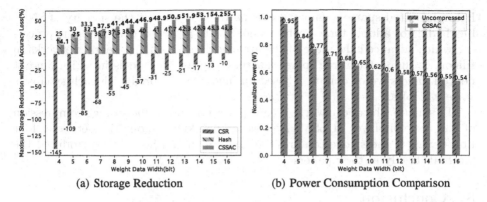

(a) Storage Reduction   (b) Power Consumption Comparison

Fig. 8. The compressing effect and power consumption sensitivity under different weight quantization.

6.4 Performance Evaluation

Before storage compression using LSM sparsity, memory access in the neuromorphic processor is accomplished by direct addressing. Therefore, only one clock cycle is required when accessing the weight. In the case of using CSSAC, access to the synaptic information in the adjacent vector is also done by direct addressing and thus requires one clock cycle. But access a weight requires two clock cycles for this process contains two steps, tag comparing and weight selecting out which need two clock cycles in total. However, only if the input spike is "1" and the synapse is existing will the two-cycle weight access process be performed in full. Due to the sparsity of LSM in time and space, the actual probability fully-executed weight access is about 0.1% averagely in the LSM we use under the mentioned three data sets. Thus, using the CSSAC results in less than 0.2% reduction in the performance of the neuromorphic processor approximately.

7   Related Work

Wang et al. [7] presented a general-purpose LSM-oriented neuromorphic learning processor with integrated training and recognition for real-world pattern recognition problems. They did not take advantage of the sparsity in LSM for storage compression. Jin et al. [17] proposed a novel sparse and self-organizing LSM architecture with a spike-timing-dependent plasticity mechanism for efficient on-chip training. In their work, they exploited the sparsity of the readout layer and realized up to 29.2% synapse reduction. But they didn't pay attention to the sparsity of unchanged weights and synapses in the reservoir layer of LSM, which took up more storage than the readout layer. Because in their work, the number of reservoir layer neurons was only 135, the storage of weights in the reservoir layer might not be a big deal. TrueNorth [4] was a neuromorphic processor which was composed of 4096 neurosynaptic cores tiled in a 2D array.

It implemented sparse memory access patterns to exploit the sparsity of SNNs but it did not adopt storage compression. Loihi [5] was a neuromorphic processor which advanced the state-of-the-art modeling of spiking neural networks in silicon. It supported three sparse matrix compression models in which fan-out neuron indices were computed based on index state stored with each synapse's state variables.

To sum up, the above works do not pay attention to the storage compression of the reservoir layer in LSM. And we do not know about the details of how Loihi support the sparse compression because the authors only introduced the methods briefly in their papers.

8   Conclusion

In neuromorphic processors, the storage of weights and synapses is redundant if the deployed network is sparse, such as LSM. In this work, we design a lossy storage compression method, CSSAC which makes use of the sparsity and the robustness of LSM. CSSAC does not introduce much metadata overhead nor does it decrease the accuracy of LSM or the performance of the processor. We apply CSSAC on an LSM-oriented neuromorphic processor. Experimental results show that in our implementation, CSSAC can bring much reduction in storage and power consumption of the neuromorphic processor, which is meaningful to enabling a single chip to handle more complex tasks and the construction of multi-core neuromorphic processors to simulate larger-scale biological neural networks in the next generation.

Acknowledgement. This work is founded by National Key R&D Program of China [grant numbers 2018YFB2202603], HGJ of China (under Grant 2017ZX01028-103-002) and in part by the National Natural Science Foundation of China [grant numbers 61802427] and [grant numbers 61832018]. And thanks to the reviewers for their efforts.

References

1. Maass, W., Natschlager, T., Markram, H.: Real-time computing without stable states: a new framework for neural computation based on perturbations. Neural Comput. **14**(11), 2531–2560 (2002)
2. Diehl, P.U., et al.: Conversion of artificial recurrent neural networks to spiking neural networks for low-power neuromorphic hardware. In: 2016 IEEE International Conference on Rebooting Computing, pp. 1–8 (2016)
3. Krizhevsky, A., Sutskever, I., Hinton, G.E.: ImageNet classification with deep convolutional neural networks. Commun. ACM **60**(6), 84–90 (2017)
4. Akopyan, F., et al.: Truenorth: design and tool flow of a 65 mW 1 million neuron programmable neurosynaptic chip. IEEE Trans. Comput.-aided Des. Integr. Circuits Syst. **34**(10), 1537–1557 (2015)
5. Davies, M., et al.: Loihi: a neuromorphic manycore processor with on-chip learning. IEEE Micro **38**(1), 82–99 (2018)
6. Benjamin, B.V., et al.: Neurogrid: a mixed-analog-digital multichip system for large-scale neural simulations. Proc. IEEE **102**(5), 699–716 (2014)

7. Wang, Q., Jin, Y., Li, P.: General-purpose LSM learning processor architecture and theoretically guided design space exploration. Biomed. Circ. Syst. Conf. 1–4 (2015)

8. Berner, R., et al.: Dynamic vision sensor for low power applications. Int. Symp. Consum. Electr., 1–2 (2014)

9. Orchard, G., et al.: Converting static image datasets to spiking neuromorphic datasets using saccades. Front. Neurosci. 437(2015)

10. Amir, A., et al.: A low power, fully event-based gesture recognition system. Comput. Vision pattern Recognit. 7388–7397 (2017)

11. Buluc, A., et al.: Parallel sparse matrix-vector and matrix-transpose-vector multiplication using compressed sparse blocks. ACM Symp. Parallel Algorithms Archit. 233–244 (2009)

12. Smith, S., et al. SPLATT: efficient and parallel sparse tensor-matrix multiplication. Int. Parallel Distrib. Proc. Symp. 61–70 (2015)

13. Zhang, S., et al.: Cambricon-x: an accelerator for sparse neural networks. Int. Symp. Microarchitecture, 1–12 (2016)

14. Pal, S., et al. OuterSPACE: an outer product based sparse matrix multiplication accelerator. High-performance Comput. Archit. 724–736 (2018)

15. Stimberg, M., Romain, B., Goodman, D.F.M.: Brian 2, an intuitive and efficient neural simulator. eLife (2019)

16. He, W., et al.: Comparing SNNs and RNNs on neuromorphic vision datasets: similarities and differences. arXiv (2020)

17. Jin, Y., Liu, Y., Li, P.: SSO-LSM: a sparse and self-organizing architecture for liquid state machine based neural processors. Int. Symp. Nanoscale Archit. 55–60 (2016)

ODCP: Optimizing Data Caching and Placement in Distributed File System Using Erasure Coding

Shuhan Wu[1], Yunchun Li[1], Hailong Yang[1,3(✉)], Zerong Luan[2], and Wei Li[1]

[1] School of Computer Science and Engineering, Beihang University,
Beijing 100191, China
`hailong.yang@buaa.edu.cn`
[2] College of Life Sciences and Bioengineering, Beijing University of Technology,
Beijing 100083, China
[3] State Key Laboratory of Mathematical Engineering and Advanced Computing,
Wuxi 214125, China

Abstract. Many current distributed file systems use erasure-coding based data redundancy techniques to improve the reliability of data storage. Such techniques can significantly improve the effective storage utilization. However, there are several drawbacks to the above techniques. Firstly, they introduce non-negligible computation overhead for decoding. Secondly, traditional data caching and placement strategies become less effective in such cases. To solve the above drawbacks, this paper proposes a new data cache allocation mechanism based on simulated annealing and a new data placement strategy based on convex optimization, which effectively reduces data block transmission delay and decoding delay. We have implemented the proposed data placement strategy in the real-world distributed file system *Alluxio*, and evaluated the performance of our strategy. Experiment results show that our strategy can significantly reduce the file read delay compared to traditional data placement strategies.

Keywords: Distributed file system · Erasure coding · Decoding latency · Data placement strategy · Cache allocation strategy

1 Introduction

The distributed file system provides an excellent solution for storing and processing large scale data. However, the unbalanced accesses for hot data in distributed file system often cause severe performance degradation. For instance, studies [11] have shown that in a Facebook cluster, for more than 50% of the time, the frequency of visits to the most popular links exceeds 4.5× than the average visits of ordinary links. Such a phenomenon of extremely unbalanced data accesses often leads to overwhelmed load on storage nodes and causes the slowdown of the entire

X. He et al. (Eds.): NPC 2020, LNCS 12639, pp. 452–464, 2021.
https://doi.org/10.1007/978-3-030-79478-1_38

distributed file system [8,15]. The widely adopted method to address the load unbalance problem is to cache data and optimize data placement. Particularly, erasure-coding based techniques have been proposed to reduce the storage cost of keeping multiple data copies in the distributed file system for reliability [6,11], such as Ceph [2] and HDFS [12]. However, erasure-coding based techniques have their own drawbacks [6,9]. Firstly, the decoding process introduces extra computation overhead and thus leads to longer data access delay. Secondly, the decoding overhead cannot be addressed by traditional data caching and placement strategies, because the overhead highly depends on the data block to be decoded. Therefore, a new approach needs to be designed to optimize the data caching and data placement targeting the distributed file system with erasure-coding.

To solve the above challenge, we propose a data cache allocation mechanism based on simulated annealing and a data placement strategy based on convex optimization. Evaluate results on real-world distributed file system *Alluxio* with erasure coding shows that our approach can significantly reduce file access delay.

Specifically, the main contributions of this paper are as follows:

- We propose a new data placement strategy that decomposes data placement problem into two stages of sub-optimization problems, and solves them using simulated annealing algorithm and convex optimization method, which dramatically reduces the complexity for computing the optimization results.
- We propose a new data cache allocation mechanism based on simulated annealing algorithm, which identifies the most profitable file blocks and allocates them in the data cache to achieve low read latency.
- We build a file read delay model that incorporates the decoding delay model and data transmission delay model. This model can effectively guide the design of data placement strategy for optimizing the file read latency.
- We implement the proposed approaches in real-world distributed file system *Alluxio*, and demonstrate the effectiveness of our approaches for reducing file read latency by comparing with traditional data placement approaches.

The rest of this paper is organized as follows. Section 2 introduces the background of data caching and data placement as well as the motivation of this paper. We present the design and implementation of our *ODCP* in Sect. 3. We evaluate the effectiveness of *ODCP* in Sect. 4. Section 5 presents the related work on the data caching and placement, and we conclude this paper in Sect. 6.

2 Background and Motivation

2.1 Erasure Coding

The most commonly used Erasure Code is RS code, which divides the original file into k file blocks, and then generate r redundant blocks through the encoding matrix. k plus r equals n, which is denoted as (n, k) coding. It is an MDS code [5] (maximum distance separable code), which means that for (n, k) encoding, any subset with k blocks is obtained from the set of n blocks, the original file can be recovered.

2.2   Data Cache Allocation

In the erasure-coded scenario, due to the MDS code's characteristics, the read delay of the entire file is determined by the k-th arriving file block. Therefore, when the current k-1 block contains a cached block, the traditional backup cache mechanism can not accelerate file access. To solve this problem, Aggarwal V et al. proposed a functional caching mechanism in [1]. In this caching mechanism, the cache area stores the re-encoded blocks that still satisfy the MDS code's characteristics. With this caching mechanism, the cache block can always speed up file access. Therefore, based on functional caching, this paper proposes a new caching strategy for decoding delay optimization.

2.3   File Read Probability

Unlike traditional file access, for erasure-encoded files, the read request is uncertain, because of the characteristics of its MDS code, not every block must respond to the read request [10]. Therefore, we set a probability value for each block to represent its response probability when the read-write agent sends requests for a file. If the sum of all block probabilities is k, then there are k file block responses per access on average. The file access frequency and file block read probability are directly related to the storage node load. Therefore, this paper takes the read probability distribution as the optimization variables and converts it into a file placement strategy.

2.4   Motivation

In the distributed file system, due to the uneven frequency of data access, there are often severe data hot spots. For erasure-encoded files, because of its MDS code character and decoding overhead, traditional optimization techniques are not sufficient [3]. Secondly, many optimizations for erasure codes tend to pay more attention to the transmission delay, while the decoding delay is less studied or ignored. However, Fig. 1(a) shows that the decoding delay is significant compared to the transmission delay. And the results in Fig. 1(b) show a strong linear relationship between the decoding delay and the number of redundant blocks, which indicates there is room for optimization of the decoding delay. In order to maintain data consistency and high performance, many current distributed file systems such as HDFS use write-once design, in which the read operations are much more popular than write. Therefore, our work mainly focuses on the read operations.

3   Design and Implementation

3.1   Data Cache Allocation Using Simulated Annealing

There are two problems with the functional cache [1]: first, the re-encode process increases the encoding workload and write delay. Second, it does not have any

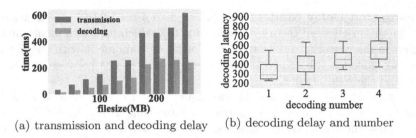

(a) transmission and decoding delay   (b) decoding delay and number

Fig. 1. Early experiment results

optimization in terms of decoding delay. Placing the re-encoded block in the cache area increases the probability that it participates in decoding greatly. Therefore, we limit the file blocks stored in the cache area to the original blocks. For the allocation of the cache area, we define the selection matrix mtx, which indicates which file blocks are selected to enter the cache area, where the elements can only take 0 or 1. The elements with value of 1 represent the file block where file i can be placed on node j. To search for the optimal selection matrix mtx, we continuously reducing the cost C as shown in Eq. 1, where α is scale factor, P is the read probability distribution, indicating the probability of sending a file block read request for file i on node j, λ is the read frequency of each file.

$$C = \alpha \cdot mean(\sum_{i=1}^{m} p_{ij} \cdot mtx_{ij} \cdot \lambda_i) + (1 - \alpha) \cdot std(\sum_{i=1}^{m} p_{ij} \cdot mtx_{ij} \cdot \lambda_i) \quad (1)$$

Then we use the search algorithm based on simulated annealing to find a near-optimal cache allocation scheme. The algorithm has a chance to accept a worse solution than the current optimal solution, which can prevent it from falling into the local optimal. Simultaneously, the algorithm's random factors will gradually decrease with the increase of the number of iterations to ensure the final convergence of the algorithm.

3.2 Building File Read Delay Model

When accessing erasure-coded files, the read-write agent reads a file in two steps: transmission and decoding. The decoding process starts only after the transmission of the k-th block is completed. Therefore, this paper will model the two processes and combine them as the read delay model.

The upper limit O of the weighted average read delay of all files is as shown in Eq. 2, where $\bar{U}_i$ and $\bar{T}_i$ represent transmission delay and decoding delay.

$$O = \sum_{i=1}^{m} \frac{\lambda_i}{\sum_{i=1}^{m} \lambda_i} (\bar{U}_i + \bar{T}_i) \quad (2)$$

Transmission Delay Model. This paper cites a read latency estimation formula based on queuing theory proposed in [13], which has been mentioned and verified in many works [1,13,14]. But in order to combine it with the decoding delay, we added a subscript k to represent the difference between the original block and the redundant block.

First the statistics required in the model need to be calculated as follows. the average value of each node's transmission time $E[X_j]$ in Eq. 3, variance σ_i^2 in Eq. 4, the total request amount of node j Λ_j in Eq. 5, the second-order origin moment Γ_j^2 in Eq. 7, the third-order origin moment Γ_j^3 in Eq. 8. And μ_j represents the service rate of node j. ρ_j in Eq. 6 representing the request strength.

$$E[X_j] = \frac{1}{\mu_j} \tag{3}$$

$$\sigma_i^2 = E[X_j^2] - E[X_j]^2 \tag{4}$$

$$\Lambda_j = \sum_{i=1}^{m}(P_{ij1} + P_{ij2})\lambda_i \tag{5}$$

$$\rho_j = \Lambda_j \mu_j \tag{6}$$

$$\Gamma_j^2 = E[X_j^2] \tag{7}$$

$$\Gamma_j^3 = E[X_j^3] \tag{8}$$

where X_j is the transmission delay of a single file block, λ_i is the file access rate. The optimization variable P_{ijk} represents the probability of sending a read request to file i on node j, where k represents the block type ($k = 1$ represents the original block, and $k = 2$ represents redundant block). m represents the total number of files, and n represents the total number of nodes. The transmission delay $\bar{U}_i$ is as shown in Eq. 9:

$$\bar{U}_i = z_i + \sum_{j=1}^{n}\frac{P_{ij1} + P_{ij2}}{2}(E[Q_j] - z_i) + \sum_{j=1}^{n}\frac{P_{ij1} + P_{ij2}}{2}\sqrt{(E[Q_j] - z_i)^2 + Var[Q_j]} \tag{9}$$

where z_i is an auxiliary variable. Besides, Q_j represents the total transmission delay of reading file blocks on node j. The form of $E[Q_j]$ and $Var[Q_j]$ is as defined in Eq. 10 and 11:

$$E[Q_j] = \frac{1}{\mu_j} + \frac{\Lambda_j \Gamma_j^2}{2(1 - \rho_j)} \tag{10}$$

$$Var[Q_j] = \sigma_j^2 + \frac{\Lambda_j \Gamma_j^3}{3(1 - \rho_j)} + \frac{\Lambda_j^2(\Gamma_j^2)^2}{4(1 - \rho_j)^2} \tag{11}$$

Decoding Delay Model. The encoding and decoding process of the erasure code is essentially matrix multiplication operation. The *coding matrix* is composed of an *identity matrix* and a *redundant matrix*. After multiplying with the *data matrix*, the *original blocks* and the *redundant blocks* are obtained. Pick any k blocks from them, and then take the corresponding rows from the *coding matrix* to form a *residual matrix*, and inverse it to get the *recovery matrix*. Use the *recovery matrix* to recover the original *data matrix*. However, the *original blocks* do not need to be calculated during the recovery process, and other lost blocks need to be calculated. So there is a linear relationship between the number of *redundant blocks* and the decoding delay. A mathematical model is established to estimate the decoding delay $\bar{T}_i$ and its form is as defined in Eq. 12:

$$\bar{T}_i = \eta \frac{S_i}{k_i + r_i} \sum_{i=1}^{m} \lambda_i (1 \cdot r_{i,Cached} + \sum_{j=1}^{n} P_{ij2}) \tag{12}$$

The decoding time is positively correlated with the load of the agent, the file block size, the number of redundant blocks participating in decoding. For file i, the redundant blocks in cache will certainly participate in decoding, other redundant blocks of this file will participate in decoding according to probability. Where η is the scale factor, S is the file size, k_i and r_i are the original and redundant blocks of file i. To minimize decoding delay, let $r_{i,Cached} = 0$. Then the form of $\bar{T}_i$ turns into Eq. 13.

$$\bar{T}_i = \eta \frac{S_i}{k_i + r_i} \sum_{i=1}^{m} \lambda_i (\sum_{j=1}^{n} P_{ij2}) \tag{13}$$

3.3 Formulating the Optimization Problem

In order to find the probability distribution under which the lowest average read delay can be achieved, a convex optimization problem needs to be formulated. We use Eq. 2 as the objective function. Read probability distribution P and the auxiliary variable z are used as optimization variables. And constraints are added as follows.

$$P_{ij1} \cdot P_{ij2} = 0 \tag{14}$$

$$\sum_{i=1}^{m} d_i \leq C \tag{15}$$

$$\sum_{j=1}^{n} P_{ij1} \cdot P_{ij2} = k_i - d_i + 1 \tag{16}$$

$$ceil(P_{..1} + P_{..2}) = \neg mtx \tag{17}$$

To minimize the read delay and reduce the complexity of the transmission delay model, we use Eq. 14 to ensure that a node can only store one block of a file at most. Inequality 15 ensures the sum of the number of blocks of all files in the cache cannot be greater than the capacity of the cache area, where d_i is the number of blocks of file i in the cache, and C is the capacity of the cache. Equation 16 ensures the sum of the read probability of each file on all nodes plus the number of blocks already in the cache minus redundant request equals to k. Add an additional redundant read request is to reduce the influence of straggler. Equation 17 ensures that the read probability distribution obtained must meet the premise of the previous cache allocation. The convex optimization problem is defined as 18.

$$min \sum_{i=1}^{m} \frac{\lambda_i}{\sum_{i=1}^{m} \lambda_i}(\bar{U}_i + \bar{T}_i)$$

$$s.t. \ 14, 15, 16, 17$$

$$var. \ P_{ijk}, z_i$$

(18)

3.4 Solving the Convex Optimization Problem

This subsection introduces the challenges of this optimization problem and the solutions we proposed. First of all, the constraints of the real number range and the integer constraint d_i coexist in the constraint conditions, which belong to the mixed-integer constraint problem. Usually, it is difficult to find the optimal solution for this type of problem directly. Secondly, the optimization problem has two sets of variables, reading probability distribution P and auxiliary variable z. It is difficult to optimize both at the same time.

Our solution to the integer mixed constraint problem is to decompose the originally unified problem into two stages: cache allocation and storage node data placement. When the cache allocation strategy is determined, the variable d_i becomes a constant, Eq. 15 will be satisfied, and Eq. 16 becomes a real range constraint. Therefore, there is no integer constraint.

And inspired by other work [1,13,14], this paper uses a method called *alternate optimization* to solve the two sets of variable problem. It alternately optimizes two sets of variables until the objective function converges.

Then the mapping relationship between the optimal solution and the data placement strategy must be established. First, according to the variable d_i, the corresponding number of blocks of each file are put into the cache area. The original blocks are placed preferentially. Secondly, if the block probability of requesting a file to a node is not 0, the corresponding block must be prepared. In sum, our approach optimizes reading delay by placing data according to the data placement strategy and initiating file requests based on the solution of Eq. 18.

4   Evaluation

4.1   Experimental Setup

We evaluate the distributed file system *Alluxio* with our proposed approaches on a cluster of 10 nodes. The cluster contains one *Master node*, one *Client node* (as a read-write agent), and eight *Slave nodes*. There are 3 types of configuration of the *slave nodes*, including one model1 (Intel Xeon Phi 7210, 200 GB Memory, 12TB HDD), four model2 (Intel Xeon E5-2620 V4, 12 GB Memory, 100 GB HDD), and three model3 (Intel Xeon E5-2620 V2, 8 GB Memory, 200 GB HDD). The network bandwidth is $1gbps$ between all nodes.

4.2   File Read Latency Optimization

We test and analyze the overall file access latency and the latency of the two stages it contains. We test and compare common random strategies, round-robin strategies, the optimization strategy *sprout* proposed in [1], and our optimization strategy. They are written down as *random, round, sprout, opt,* respectively. According to our cluster size, we set the standard parameters of erasure coding in the experiment to $(k, n) = (4, 8)$. The reading probability λ of each file are taken as 0.009, 0.011, 0.01, 0.012, 0.014, 0.013. The capacity of the cache area is 8 file blocks. The file sizes are randomly selected between 25 MB and 250 MB. For smaller files, they are usually merged into bigger files in distributed file systems to achieve better performance.

Average Block Transmission Delay. Accessing a file requires obtaining a sufficient number of file blocks before entering the next stage of the decoding process. Therefore, the read delay of a file block dramatically affects the entire file's overall access delay. As shown in Fig. 2(a), we evaluate the file block access delay under different data access patterns.

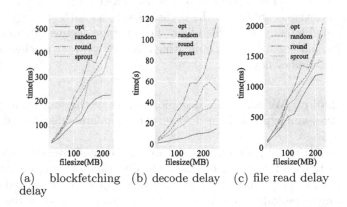

(a)   blockfetching   (b) decode delay   (c) file read delay
delay

Fig. 2. Different types of delays under four different data access patterns.

The results show that the round-robin strategy has the longest block read delay among all strategies. This is because under the round-robin strategy, the density of access requests received by a single slave node fluctuates periodically. Therefore, when the slave node is busy, it will slow down the transmission process of a series of file blocks. The random strategy alleviates this periodicity, so the block read delay decreases.

The opt strategy reaches the best of all strategies. The reasons are as follows. In the sprout strategy, cache allocation and transmission delay optimization problems are simultaneously modeled in an optimization problem. But in this article, these two problems are divided into two steps. This method significantly reduces the complex constraints in the optimization problem and the difficulty of solving. And a more reasonable cache allocation scheme makes the file block read delay have a better optimization effect. Compared with the other three strategies, the opt strategy reduces the average block read latency by 36.9%, 45.6%, and 27.9%, respectively.

We also evaluate and analyze the change in the average read latency of file blocks for each strategy with different cache sizes, as is shown in Fig. 3.

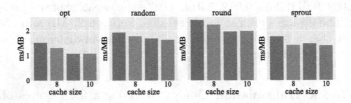

Fig. 3. Impact of data cache capacity on block read delay.

We use *ms/MB* to express the average block read delay to eliminate the impact of the delay change caused by the file block size. It can be seen that, overall, the increased capacity of the cache area under each strategy will reduce the average read latency of the file block. The average decline rate of each strategy are 10.3%, 5.5%, 6.5%, 6.9%, indicating that opt strategy reaches the highest cache utilization efficiency.

Decoding Delay. We count the decoding delays of the four strategies under various file sizes and express them through the cumulative decoding delay of the entire test process.

As shown in Fig. 2(b), decoding delay of random and round-robin strategies increase rapidly with the size of the files. The decoding delay of the round-robin strategy is the longest, and the frequency of occurrence of redundant blocks during reading is periodic. When the read-write agent is busy at decoding, the decoding process of each file is slowed down; when it is idle, the decoding capability is wasted. Therefore, the total decoding delay is greatly increased. The random strategy eases this periodicity. The optimization of the request queue by the sprout strategy further eases the periodicity mentioned above. At the same time, because we place redundant blocks on nodes with lower IO bandwidth, the optimization process reduces the probability of requests on low IO bandwidth nodes, which indirectly reduces the number of redundant blocks, which also reduces decoding delay. But because there is no specialized optimization for decoding delay, there is still optimization space. Opt strategy has been specifically optimized for decoding delay. While ensuring the request queue's optimization effect, it also greatly reduces the number of redundant blocks. So opt strategy achieves the lowest decoding delay among the four strategies. Compared with the other three strategies, opt strategy reduces the decoding delay by 36.1%, 46.3%, and 30.9%, respectively.

Average File Read Delay. The average file reading delay is a comprehensive reflection of the strategy optimization effect. It is the composite result of the previous average block read delay and decoding delay.

As shown in Fig. 2(c), due to the disadvantages of the previous average block read delay and decoding delay, the round-robin strategy has the longest file access delay among all four strategies. The random strategy is slightly lower than the round-robin strategy. The sprout strategy optimizes the request queue to reduce the average file read delay significantly. Finally, due to the more detailed optimization of opt strategy, including cache allocation, file block transmission delay optimization, and decoding delay optimization, we obtain the lowest file read delay among all strategies. After standardizing the file read latency according to file size, opt strategy reduces the file read latency on average of 29.8%, 32.6%, and 19.9% compared to the other three strategies.

4.3   Parameter Sensitivity Analysis

Redundancy. Higher redundancy has better reliability, but it is usually inferior in decoding delay and file size. During the experiment, we found that redundancy is an important factor that affects the decoding delay optimization effect. We use the form of decoding delay at different k values in Fig. 4 to show the effect of varying redundancy on the optimization effect of decoding delay. The redundancy is 5/8, 4/8, 3/8. As the redundancy reducing, the gap between various strategies is decreasing. That is because as the proportion of redundant blocks decreases, the optimization for redundant blocks in the optimization strategy gradually disappears. Finally, the decoding delay approaches the unoptimized strategy.

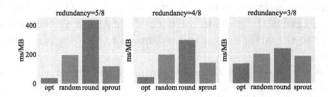

Fig. 4. Decoding delay under different settings of parameter k.

Straggler. The straggler is a widespread problem in distributed file systems and distributed computing frameworks. Once a straggler appears in the system, the entire task is often slowed down due to the *bucket effect*. Opt optimization strategy uses redundant read requests to reduce the impact of a straggler.We artificially restrict *slave2*. Its network bandwidth was limited to *100mbps* to simulate the situation of a straggler.

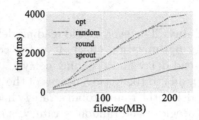

Fig. 5. File read delay when encountering straggler.

As shown in Fig. 5, in the case of a straggler, the file read delay of each strategy increases. But opt strategy initializes a redundant read request before the end of the transmission process. Before the last file block arrives, it can enter the decoding stage, greatly reducing the straggler impact. Therefore, in this particular case, compared to the other three strategies, opt strategy decreases the file read delay by 67.5%, 66.9%, 48.0%.

5   Related Work

Liao *et al.* proposed a data layout strategy for distributed file systems based on data access frequency in [7]. This method first analyzes the history information of block access sequence of a specific application, and then uses the *k partition algorithm* to divide the files into multiple groups according to the frequency of data access. Afterward, the data is distributed in groups. In short, this newly proposed data placement strategy makes the data evenly distributed, and the data block access rate tends to be balanced.

Vaneet Aggarwal *et al.* proposed a functional caching method to minimize service delay in erasure code storage clusters in [1]. This paper optimizes the caching mechanism in the erasure code storage system. Making the cache blocks in the cache and the data blocks in the cluster constitute a decoding combination that conforms to the MDS code. And optimizing the data placement according to the file access delay.

HE and others investigated the redundancy setting of the Hadoop cluster in [4]. The default number of backups used in HDFS is 3. That is, each file block must be stored three times. A higher number of backups means higher storage resource consumption, but it also brings higher data availability and data locality. Therefore, a backup method is proposed in the article to backup more frequently accessed files to improve the performance of data access.

6   Conclusion

To address the long file read delay in distributed file system using erasure-coding based redundancy policy, we propose a new data cache allocation mechanism and data placement strategy using simulated annealing and convex optimization, respectively. In addition, we implement our approach in real-world distributed file system *Alluxio*. The experiment results show that our approach can effectively reduce the file read delay by an average of 29.8%, 32.6%, and 19.9%, compared to traditional *random*, *round* and *sprout* data placement strategies.

Acknowledgements. This work is supported by National Key Research and Development Program of China (Grant No. 2020YFB1506703), National Natural Science Foundation of China (Grant No. 62072018), and the Open Project Program of the State Key Laboratory of Mathematical Engineering and Advanced Computing (Grant No. 2019A12).

References

1. Aggarwal, V., Chen, Y.F.R., Lan, T., Xiang, Y.: Sprout: a functional caching approach to minimize service latency in erasure-coded storage. IEEE/ACM Trans. Networking **25**(6), 3683–3694 (2017)
2. Aghayev, A., Weil, S., Kuchnik, M., Nelson, M., Ganger, G.R., Amvrosiadis, G.: File systems unfit as distributed storage backends: lessons from 10 years of ceph evolution. In: Proceedings of the 27th ACM Symposium on Operating Systems Principles, pp. 353–369 (2019)
3. Bao, H., Wang, Y., Xu, F.: An adaptive erasure code for jointcloud storage of internet of things big data. IEEE Internet Things J. **7**(3), 1613–1624 (2019)
4. Ciritoglu, H.E., et al.: Investigation of replication factor for performance enhancement in the hadoop distributed file system. In: Companion of the 2018 ACM/SPEC International Conference on Performance Engineering, pp. 135–140 (2018)
5. Ding, C., Tang, C.: Infinite families of near mds codes holding t-designs. IEEE Trans. Inf. Theor. (2020)
6. Li, Z., Lv, M., Xu, Y., Li, Y., Xu, L.: D3: deterministic data distribution for efficient data reconstruction in erasure-coded distributed storage systems. In: 2019 IEEE International Parallel and Distributed Processing Symposium (IPDPS), pp. 545–556. IEEE (2019)
7. Liao, J., Cai, Z., Trahay, F., Peng, X.: Block placement in distributed file systems based on block access frequency. IEEE Access **6**, 38411–38420 (2018)
8. Mazumdar, S., Seybold, D., Kritikos, K., Verginadis, Y.: A survey on data storage and placement methodologies for cloud-big data ecosystem. J. Big Data **6**(1), 15 (2019). https://doi.org/10.1186/s40537-019-0178-3
9. Mohan, L.J., Rajawat, K., Parampalli, U., Harwood, A.: Optimal placement for repair-efficient erasure codes in geo-diverse storage centres. J. Parallel Distrib. Comput. **135**, 101–113 (2020)
10. Nicolaou, N., Cadambe, V., Prakash, N., Konwar, K., Medard, M., Lynch, N.: Ares: adaptive, reconfigurable, erasure coded, atomic storage. In: 2019 IEEE 39th International Conference on Distributed Computing Systems (ICDCS), pp. 2195–2205. IEEE (2019)

11. Rashmi, K., Chowdhury, M., Kosaian, J., Stoica, I., Ramchandran, K.: Ec-cache: load-balanced, low-latency cluster caching with online erasure coding. In: 12th {USENIX} Symposium on Operating Systems Design and Implementation ({OSDI} 16), pp. 401–417 (2016)
12. Veeraiah, D., Rao, J.N.: An efficient data duplication system based on hadoop distributed file system. In: 2020 International Conference on Inventive Computation Technologies (ICICT), pp. 197–200. IEEE (2020)
13. Xiang, Y., Lan, T., Aggarwal, V., Chen, Y.F.R.: Joint latency and cost optimization for erasure-coded data center storage. IEEE/ACM Trans. Networking 24(4), 2443–2457 (2015)
14. Yu, Y., Huang, R., Wang, W., Zhang, J., Letaief, K.B.: Sp-cache: load-balanced, redundancy-free cluster caching with selective partition. In: SC18: International Conference for High Performance Computing, Networking, Storage and Analysis, pp. 1–13. IEEE (2018)
15. Zhang, X., Cai, Y., Liu, Y., Xu, Z., Dong, X.: Nade: nodes performance awareness and accurate distance evaluation for degraded read in heterogeneous distributed erasure code-based storage. J. Supercomputing, pp. 1–30 (2019)

Towards Optimizing Deduplication on Persistent Memory

Yichen Li, Kewen He, Gang Wang$^{(\boxtimes)}$, and Xiaoguang Liu$^{(\boxtimes)}$

College of Computer Science, Nankai University, Tianjin, China
{liyc,hekw,wgzwp,liuxg}@nbjl.nankai.edu.cn

Abstract. Data deduplication is an effective method to reduce data storage requirements. In data deduplication process, fingerprint identification may cause frequent on-disk fingerprint lookups which hurt performance seriously. Some locality-aware approaches were proposed to tackle this issue. Recently, the Persistent Memory (PM) brings low latency and high bandwidth, and has become a hotspot in data storage. Deduplication systems with fingerprints stored on PM will provide extremely fast on-disk fingerprint lookup, and therefore traditional locality-aware approaches designed for slow devices are likely no longer valid.

In this paper, we model the traditional locality-aware approaches and analyze their performance on PM. Inspired by the analysis, we propose an optimized PM-based fingerprint identification scheme in which the fingerprint cache is replaced with a simple, low-cost read buffer, and the order of the Bloom filter and the read buffer is swapped. The experimental results on real PM devices show that, compared with the traditional locality-aware approaches, the proposed scheme improves the fingerprint identification throughput by 1.2–2.3 times.

Keywords: Data deduplication · Persistent memory · Fingerprint identification · Bloom filter · Cache

1 Introduction

Data deduplication is a popular method for data reduction, which can greatly save storage space and network bandwidth by eliminating duplicate data. Typically, data deduplication consists of four steps: data chunking, fingerprinting, fingerprint identification, and data storing. Specifically, a deduplicated system firstly divides the data stream into data chunks (normally 4 KB–128 KB), and calculates their unique fingerprints using a cryptographically secure hash signature (e.g. MD5, SHA-1, SHA-256), and then identifies redundant chunks by comparing their fingerprints and finally, unique data will be stored.

This work is partially supported by National Science Foundation of China (U1833114, 61872201, 61702521); Science and Technology Development Plan of Tianjin (18ZXZNGX00140, 18ZXZNGX00200).

Fingerprint identification is a key step in deduplication and is also an I/O intensive step. In general, DRAM is not large enough to hold all the fingerprints, and hence we must store them on disk. Therefore, on-disk lookup for fingerprints will become a serious bottleneck of the entire system. Locality-aware approaches such as DDFS [1] were proposed to reduce the accesses to low-speed disk by using Bloom filter and cache, which can achieve a very high cache hit rate due to good temporal and/or spatial locality in data streams. This kind of approach has been widely used in deduplication systems to improve fingerprint identification performance in which fingerprints are stored on HDD or SSD.

Recently, the development of persistent memory (PM) has attracted a lot of attention. The latency of PM is several orders magnitude lower than those of SSD and HDD. Therefore, if we build deduplication systems by storing fingerprints on PM rather than SSD and HDD, looking up fingerprints will take much less time. Traditional locality-aware approaches designed for slow devices like HDD and SSD aiming to reduce on-disk lookup may be not effective for deduplication systems based on PM. In such systems, the performance bottleneck may be transferred from disk I/O to other parts.

In this paper, we model the traditional locality-aware approach and analyze its performance on PM. Inspired by the analysis, we propose two optimization strategies for deduplication with PM. The contributions of this paper are as follows.

- We model the typical locality-aware fingerprint identification approach and analyze the impact of PM on its performance.
- We find out that the overhead of fingerprint cache is two heavy for deduplication with PM and propose to replace it with a simple and low-cost read buffer to exploit the spatial locality in data streams more effectively.
- We find out that Bloom filter becomes a significant performance bottleneck of fingerprint lookup and propose to adjust the order of Bloom filter and read buffer for highly duplication data to overcome this problem.
- We conduct experiments on real-world datasets and show that the proposed optimizations improves the throughput by 1.2–2.3 times.

The remainder of this paper is organized as follows. Section 2 surveys the related work and Sect. 3 presents our motivation. Section 4 models the fingerprint identification and analyze the performance on PM. Section 6 presents the experimental results of different fingerprint identification algorithms. Section 7 concludes the paper.

2   Background and Related Work

2.1   Data Deduplication

Since data deduplication is generally applied to where a huge amount of data is involved, we have to store all fingerprints on disk rather than in DRAM. Therefore, fingerprint identification may cause frequent accesses to low-speed disks, which becomes a severe bottleneck of data deduplication. There are many researches focusing on this problem [1–6], in which a number of locality-aware approaches are proposed. It is found that redundant data tend to reappear as similar sequences in real-world workload, which is called the spatial locality. Data Domain Deduplication File System (DDFS) [1] is one of the earliest deduplication systems exploiting the spatial locality in workload. DDFS uses Bloom filters and Locality Preserved Caching (LPC) to reduce disk I/O. Since traditional cache algorithms do not work well for caching fingerprints, LPC is designed to exploit the spatial locality in workload to eliminate the disk I/O bottleneck in deduplication. By combining Bloom filter and LPC, DDFS reduces 99% of disk accesses in fingerprint identification.

Lazy Exact Deduplication [6] is another locality-aware approach. Deduplication systems such as DDFS look up fingerprints on disk whenever a cache miss occurs, so they are called "eager" deduplication in [6]. The lazy deduplication, however, buffers the incoming fingerprints and then searches for them on disk in batch. The basic idea is to combine multiple fingerprint lookup into one singer on-disk lookup. The lazy strategy can significantly reduce the number of on-disk lookups but increases the overhead of in-memory cache operations. In general, because most data streams to be deduplicated have excellent locality, locality-aware approaches are widely used in deduplication [1,6,8].

2.2 Persistent Memory

Persistent Memory (PM) provides low latency, high bandwidth, persistence and byte-addressability, and thus has attracted a lot of attention to exploring its performance. In recent years, there have been a lot of studies on programming models [9], file systems [10], data structures [11], and key-value store [12] on PM. Table 1 shows the performance of PM devices. Recent search [8] shows that real PM device, Intel Optane DC Persistent Memory Module [13], exhibits 100~300 ns random or sequential read latency which is 2~4× longer than DRAM's. Considering the limited write endurance and capacity of persistent memory, data deduplication may become an important part of PM in the future.

Table 1. Storage device latency and bandwidth

Device	Latency	Bandwidth
DRAM	60 ns	64 GB/s
PM	300 ns–1 μs	5–10 GB/s
SSD	50 μs–80 μs	250 MB/s
HDD	10 ms	2.6 MB/s

NV-dedup [14] implements an in-line deduplication system based on the Persistent Memory File System (PMFS). It proposes a fine-grained metadata table and lightweight consistency strategy for metadata store in persistent memory.

Regardless of the DRAM capacity, NV-dedup indexing all fingerprints in DRAM, and therefore the spatial locality in data streams is not considered in this work. However, with the help of the traditional locality-aware approaches, we can improve the performance of fingerprint identification on a huge amount of data.

3   Motivation

For deduplication systems storing fingerprints on PM, due to extremely low access latency, the traditional locality-aware approaches designed for slow devices may be no longer suitable now. To better understand the effect of the traditional approaches on PM, we conducted experiments on Intel's Optane PMM, as the details are shown in Sect. 6. We have the following observations.

Fingerprint lookup on PM is very fast. Compared with HDD, the overall fingerprint identification time is reduced by more than 90% with PM. Moreover, it is very fast to look up fingerprints on PM, which is only 3% of the total time. Even if we directly look up fingerprints on PM without any filtering and caching, the performance is much better than that on HDD

Traditional locality-aware approaches become less effective. With the traditional locality-aware approaches, the fingerprint identification time is reduced at most by 40% on PM. However, for HDD, it can improve performance by hundreds of times [1]. In other words, the traditional locality-aware approaches still work with PM, but far less effective than with HDD.

Bloom filter and cache become the main bottlenecks. The Bloom filter and cache can avoid 99% on-disk lookup, which is very important for deduplication systems using HDD. However, they take over 90% of the overall time when storing fingerprints on PM, which become the new bottlenecks in deduplication.

4   Modeling and Analysis

In this section, we focus on locality-aware approaches for deduplication, which adopts Bloom filter and locality-preserved cache. Specifically, those kinds of approaches first check whether the fingerprint is duplicate by using a Bloom filter. A negative answer means that the fingerprint is *definitely* not in the fingerprint set, and a positive answer indicates that it is *very likely* in the set so that a cache lookup needs to be performed next. However, false positives exist, which will cause unnecessary cache misses and disk accesses, just to find that the fingerprints are unique. Cache missing will cause a fingerprint lookup on disk. If the fingerprint exists, some of its neighbor fingerprints will be prefetched to the cache together to increase the cache hit rate. According to the results of Bloom filter lookup, fingerprint identification can be divided into three cases.

a) Negative: A negative answer given by the Bloom filter means that the data chunk is unique and no further search in cache and on disk is needed. Therefore we have Eq. (1) that shows the negative search time T_n. N_n is the number of negative answers and L_B is the latency of a single lookup in Bloom filter. Bloom filter can greatly reduce access to fingerprints index on disk by identifying most unique data chunks.

$$T_n = N_n \times L_B. \tag{1}$$

b) True positive: True positives indicate that the data chunks are actually duplicate. The time T_{tp} of this case is shown in Eq. (2). $N_{tp}(= N_d)$ is both the number of false positive answers and the number of duplicate fingerprints. L_C and L_D are the latency of a single lookup in cache and on disk respectively. R_{miss} refers to the cache miss rate. Therefore, the last two terms of Eq. (2) denote the time taken by looking up fingerprints further in cache and on disk respectively. We will analyze the impact of cache on performance later in this section.

$$T_{tp} = N_{tp} \times L_B + N_d \times L_C + N_d \times R_{miss} \times L_D. \tag{2}$$

c) False positive: Here, the data blocks are unique but judged to be duplicate. Therefore, we still need to search their fingerprints further in cache and on disk although it is impossible to find them. False positives waste a lot of time and hence should be reduced by increasing the size of Bloom filter. The lookup time T_{fp} of false positives is given by,

$$T_{fp} = N_{fp} \times (L_B + L_C + L_D) = N_u \times R_{fp} \times (L_B + L_C + L_D), \tag{3}$$

where $N_{fp} (= N_u \times R_{fp})$ refers to the false positive rate of Bloom filter, N_u is the number of unqiue fingerprints. Therefore, if the total fingerprints is N $(= N_u + N_d)$, the total time for fingerprint identification is,

$$\begin{aligned} T &= T_n + T_{tp} + T_{fp} \\ &= N \times L_B + (N_u \times R_{fp} + N_d) \times L_C + (N_u \times R_{fp} + N_d \times R_{miss}) \times L_D. \end{aligned} \tag{4}$$

We can see from Eq. (4) that the main effect of Bloom filter on the fingerprint identification time is the lookup latency L_B and the false positive rate R_{fp}. The larger the two factors are, the longer the identification time is. L_B is determined by the hash computation used in the Bloom filter, and R_{fp} mainly depends on the relative size of the Bloom filter to the data. For the systems storing fingerprints on HDD and SSD, since L_B and L_C is much lower than the disk access latency L_D, so previous work concerning fingerprint identification optimization mainly focused on decreasing R_{fp}, that is, decreasing the number of disk accesses. However, we can't infinitely increase the size of the Bloom filter to decrease R_{fp}.

When we store fingerprints on PM, L_D becomes very close to L_B and L_C, and thus Eq. (4) is no longer dominated by the third term. To optimize fingerprint identification, we need to find a good trade-off between the time taken by the Bloom filter itself (the first term) and the time saved by its low false positive rate (the last two terms). A big and complex Bloom filter will decrease the false positive rate effectively and then reduce in-cache and on-disk lookup time, but the improvement may be offset by its own cost. According to our experimental results in Sect. 6, as the size of Bloom filter grows, the fingerprint identification

Y. Li et al.

time doesn't change appreciably. This indicates that a smaller Bloom filter is enough for deduplication with PM.

Similarly, the cache algorithms also take time themselves, especially the complicated ones. When HDD/SSD is used to store fingerprints, the on-disk lookup time saved by cache is much higher than that spent in cache lookup, and therefore a cache is necessary for fingerprint identification. However, when PM is introduced, we must carefully trade off between the two parts of time (the second and the third terms in Eq. (4)). An effective but high-cost cache algorithm may not suitable for deduplication with PM. For example, in [6], a highly effective cache algorithm is proposed. However, our experimental results show that, compared with another simpler but faster cache algorithm, it causes performance degradation in PM-based systems because of its high overhead. We found that even a simple cache algorithm like LRU is too heavy for fingerprint identification with PM. This inspires us to turn to a lightweight approach to exploit spatial locality in data streams, which may slightly increase the third term in Eq. (4) but significantly decrease the second term.

5 Design Choices

According to previous analyses, we can draw the following conclusions helpful to design an optimized fingerprint identification method with PM.

- Lookup in Bloom filter takes much time, and thus reducing the amount of work performed on Bloom filter may improve the overall performance.
- Cache lookup and cache prefetching latency are important now. Cache algorithms such as the one used in lazy exact deduplication are too heavy for deduplication with PM.

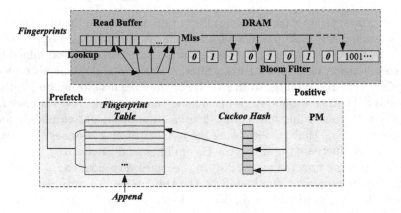

Fig. 1. Design with PM

Inspired by these conclusions, we proposed a fingerprints identification framework as Fig. 1 shows, in which we adopt the following design choices.

a) Read buffer: We replace the relatively heavy fingerprint cache with a simple, low-cost read buffer to exploit the spatial locality in workload. We use a simple hash table to implement the read buffer. When we find a duplicate fingerprint on PM, we load its subsequent fingerprints together to DRAM (in our experiments, 50 neighbor fingerprints are prefetched). If the buffer is full, the oldest fingerprints in the buffer will be replaced without using any cache eviction algorithm. So a prefetching is quite light, only involves one *memcpy* from PM to DRAM. No other operations and data structures are involved to increase the hit rate. A buffer lookup needs only a simple hash table search. In general, traditional cache algorithms such as LRU are designed under the consideration of the temporal locality, which needs dedicated data structures and operations to record the least recently used information to determine which old item should be replaced. But a simple read buffer doesn't have these overhead. Despite sacrificing a certain hit rate, it still improves performance by saving the above costs. Our experimental results show that read buffer can still obtain a hit rate of about 90% which indicates effective exploitation of the spatial locality in data streams. Moreover, its own cost is much lower than the traditional cache, and then the overall performance is improved.

b) Log-structured fingerprints table: To preserve the spatial locality of the data layout, we use a log-structured fingerprints store on PM. A cuckoo hash table indexed by fingerprints is also deployed on PM. A newly arrived fingerprint is appended to the fingerprints store. Therefore, for adjacent data chunks in the data stream, their fingerprints are also neighbors in the log-structured store. We can just prefetch consecutive fingerprints from PM to DRAM to exploit the spatial locality, and only a single *memcpy* operation needs to be performed, which is very fast. The cuckoo hash provides fast fingerprint lookups.

c) Adjusting the order of operations: After replacing the heavy cache with a lightweight read buffer, we found that the time spent in this part becomes much shorter than that taken by Bloom filter. This observation inspires us to swap the order of the read buffer and the Bloom filter. Although this brings more lookups in the read buffer, the additional time contributes little to the overall time. Meanwhile, the work on Bloom filter is cut down drastically, which may reduce the overall time,

$$T' = N \times L_C + (N_u + N_d \times R_{miss}) \times L_B + (N_u \times R_{fp} + N_d \times R_{miss}) \times L_D, \quad (5)$$

where we ignore the difference between the miss rates of the two procedures here for simplicity. Compared with Eq. (4), we can see that the performance is improved, that is $T' < T$, if and only if the following inequality holds,

$$N \times L_C + (N_u + N_d \times R_{miss}) \times L_B < N \times L_B + (N_u \times R_{fp} + N_d) \times L_C, \quad (6)$$

that is,

$$\frac{L_C}{L_B} < \frac{N_d \times (1 - R_{miss})}{N_u \times (1 - R_{fp})} \approx \frac{N_d \times (1 - R_{miss})}{N_u} \approx \frac{R_d \times (1 - R_{miss})}{1 - R_d}, \quad (7)$$

where R_d ($\approx \frac{N_d}{N}$) is the duplication rate of the dataset. So, if the duplication rate R_d meets:

$$R_d > \frac{L_C}{L_B \times (1 - R_{miss}) + L_C},\tag{8}$$

adjusting the order of the read buffer and Bloom filter can effectively improve the performance. The larger R_d is, the more effective the new order is.

6   Experimental Results

6.1   Experiment Settings

We conducted our experiments on a machine equipped with two 18-core Intel Xeon Gold 5220 processors run at 2.2 GHz. The machine has 4 Intel Optane DC persistent memory (128 GB each) installed in socket 0. The ext4-DAX file system is mounted on the PM devices. A Seagate 4TB HDD is also used for comparison. All the code is compiled using GCC 4.8.5. We use PMDK to map files into virtual address space and use `clflush` and `mfence` to persist fingerprints to PM.

We used two datasets to evaluate our deduplication methods. *Src* refers to the source code of CentOS, Fedora, Ubuntu, etc., which is collected from a server at Nankai University[1]. The total size is 272.12 GB and the duplication rate is 53.12%. *FSL* refers to the snapshots of students' home directories published by the File system and Storage Lab (FSL) at Stony Brook University [15]. We randomly select a part of data within 7-day intervals from the year 2011 and 2014[2]. The total size is 101.037 GB and the duplication rate is 20.69%.

We implemented the traditional lazy and eager methods for comparison. We implemented our new design for PM based on the eager method but replace the fingerprint cache with a simple read buffer and swap the order of the Bloom filter and the read buffer. We call it the buffer method. We only measure and compare the fingerprint identification time.

6.2   Overall Performance

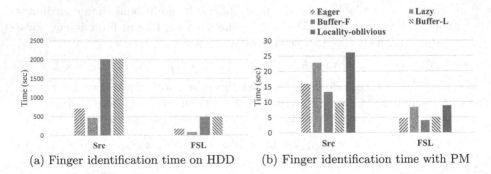

(a) Finger identification time on HDD   (b) Finger identification time with PM

Fig. 2. Fingerprint identification time

---
[1]   http://ftp.nankai.edu.cn/.
[2]   http://tracer.filesystems.org/.

We first evaluate the fingerprint identification time on HHD and PM. To ensure a very low false positive rate, the Bloom filter uses 6 hash functions and has a size of 1 GB. Figure 2 shows the results. *Locality-oblivious* refers to the method that searches the fingerprints directly on PM. *Buffer-F* refers to the method that adopts a lightweight read buffer. *Buffer-L* is based on Buffer-F and further swaps the order of the read buffer and Bloom filter.

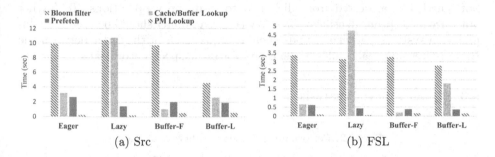

(a) Src   (b) FSL

Fig. 3. Breakdown of fingerprint identification time with PM

From Fig. 2(a) we can see that, when fingerprints are stored on HDD, both locality-aware methods perform better than the buffer method because of a much higher cache hit rate and the lazy method performs the best because it significantly reduces disk I/O through batch lookup. The buffer method is 3–4 times slower than the locality-aware methods. When we store fingerprints PM, the overall fingerprint identification time is reduced by up to 97.23%, which mainly due to the extremely low latency of PM. The locality-aware method still works with PM and reduces at most 32% of time compared with *Locality-oblivious*. However, the gap is much narrower than that with HDD. For both datasets on PM, the buffer method performs best and the lazy method performs worst (excluding Local-oblivious), which is consistent with our analysis. For dataset *Src* with a higher duplication rate, *Buffer-L* performs best and is 1.7–2.3 times faster than the locality-aware methods and 2.7 faster than Local-oblivious. However, for *FSL* dataset with a low duplication rate, *Buffer-L* is not so effective and even slower than the eager method. *Buffer-F* performs best, which is 1.2–2.1 times faster than the locality-aware methods. It is worth noting that the lazy method takes nearly the same time as *Locality-oblivious*, which is mainly due to the high cost of the cache algorithm.

Figure 3 shows the breakdown of fingerprint identification time. Different from fingerprint identification on HDD, lookup on PM only accounts for 2% of the overall time. Lookup in Bloom filter and cache takes up 52.8% and 44.8% of the total time respectively in *Eager*. With a read buffer, lookup on PM takes a little more time but the time spent in cache is effectively reduced. Although a certain hit rate is sacrificed, the low latency of the read buffer significantly reduces the overall time. For dataset *Src*, adjusting the order of the Bloom filter and read buffer can effectively reduce the time cost in the Bloom filter but increases a small amount of in-cache lookup time. As a result, the overall time is effectively reduced. However, for the dataset *FSL*, adjusting the order may cause performance degradation. For data with a low duplication rate, the Bloom filter is much more important than the read buffer. Adjusting the order reduces few lookups in the Bloom filter but increases much more lookups in read buffer.

To summarize, with fast PM, the fingerprint identification process takes much less time. Traditional locality-aware approaches still work but the performance bottleneck is transferred from disk I/O to in-memory operations. To further optimize fingerprint identification, a low-cost read buffer should be used in dedu-plication systems. Other methods such as adjustment of the order between the Bloom filter and read buffer are effective for some specific workloads.

6.3   Quantitative Analysis

Table 2. Performance details of different methods

Dataset	Src		FSL	
Method	Eager	Buffer	Eager	Buffer
R_{fp}	1.5%		1.1%	
R_{hit}	98.65%	94.89%	99.17%	95.16%
L_B	0.1531 µs	0.1517 µs	0.139 µs	0.141 µs
L_C	0.14241 µs	0.0366 µs	0.13457 µs	0.0378 µs
L_D	0.38901 µs (PM)			

We tested the values of the parameters involved in our analytical model described in Sect. 4 with two datasets on our experimental platform. Table 2 shows the results. For convenience, we rewrite Eq. (4) as,

$$T = N \times L_B + N_d \times L_C + N_u \times R_{fp} \times (L_C + L_D) + N_d \times R_{miss} \times L_D. \quad (9)$$

With fixed L_D, the first and second terms respectively refer to the contri-bution of the lookup latency in the Bloom filter and cache on the overall time. The third and fourth terms refer to the effect of the cache hit rate and false positive rate respectively. We substitute the parameter values of the buffer and eager methods with dataset *src* into Eq. (9), and we obtain,

$$T_{PM}^{Eager} = 0.15 \times N + 0.14 \times N_d + 0.0079 \times N_u + 0.00525 \times N_d, \quad (10)$$

$$T_{PM}^{Buffer} = 0.15 \times N + 0.03 \times N_d + 0.00615 \times N_u + 0.019 \times N_d. \quad (11)$$

The coefficients of the third and fourth terms in Eq. (10) is much smaller than those of the first and second terms, which means that the lookup latency in the Bloom filter and Cache becomes the main factor affecting the overall fingerprint identification time. In contrast, in Eq. (11), although a certain amount of extra

PM accesses is introduced (that is, the fourth term is increased), the lookup time in cache/buffer is greatly reduced (that is, the second term is effectively reduced). As a result, identification for duplicate fingerprints takes much less time. This conclusion is also true for the dataset *FSL*, what's more, for datasets with a higher duplication rate, the read buffer is more effective.

It worth noting that reordering the Bloom filter of read buffer is effective for dataset *Src* but less effective for dataset *FSL*, we substitute the values of L_B, L_C and R_{hit} into Eq. (8),

$$\frac{L_C}{L_B \times (1 - R_{miss}) + L_C} = \frac{0.0378}{0.141 \times 0.9516 + 0.0378} = 21.9\%. \qquad (12)$$

which means that the reordering strategy improves the performance only when the duplicate rate of the dataset is higher than 21.9%. However, the duplicate rate of *FSL* is smaller than 21.9%, therefore reordering does not work here. Since the hit rate and lookup latency may change with different datasets, swapping the order between the Bloom filter and read buffer is more suitable for datasets with high duplication rate.

6.4   Bloom Filter Size

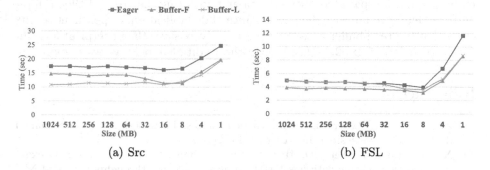

(a) Src   (b) FSL

Fig. 4. Impact on Bloom filter size

As we analyzed in Sect. 4, the Bloom filter can effectively filter out the unique data chunks. However, a low false positive rate may not be essential for deduplication systems with PM. We explore how the size of the Bloom filter impacts the performance. We can see from Fig. 4 that *Buffer-L* performs best on *Src* and *Buffer-F* performs best on *FSL* at all Bloom filter sizes. When the Bloom filter is large enough (32 MB–1024 MB), the false-positive rate is low. Therefore the performance gap between different methods is narrow, and the main factor that affects the overall performance is the read buffer or cache.

However, when the Bloom filter is between 32 MB and 8 MB, the overall fingerprint identification time *Eager* and *Buffer-F* is reduced as the size of the Bloom filter becomes smaller. We found that the Bloom filter smaller than 32 MB achieves a lower lookup latency, it may benefit from CPU L3 Cache. That is, a smaller Bloom filter leads to less CPU cache misses. Although on-PM lookup time increases, due to a large number of lookup on the Bloom filter becomes faster, the overall performance gets much improvement. As a result, With a size of 8 MB, *Buffer-F* and *Buffer-L* perform the same with an extremely low lookup latency in Bloom filter. When the Bloom filter is much smaller (8 MB-1 MB), due to the extremely high false positive rate, it needs much more PM accesses to identifies the fingerprints, resulting in severe performance degradation.

In summary, the fingerprint identification with PM is not sensitive to the size of the Bloom filter, which is consistent with our modeling. A small and fast bloom filter may perform better in deduplication systems.

7   Conclusion

In this paper, we model the typical locality-aware fingerprint identification approach to better understand the performance of the deduplication system with PM. With PM, the identification time becomes extremely low, the hit rate of cache and the positive rate of the Bloom filter is less important for deduplication. We propose a simple and low-cost read buffer which obtains better performance by exploiting the spatial locality of data and adjusting the order of Bloom filter and read buffer to improve the performance of deduplication. Experiment results show that the read buffer based method effectively saves the fingerprint identification time. It is 1.2×–2.3× faster than the traditional locality-aware approach.

References

1. Zhu, B., Li, K., Patterson, R.H.: Avoiding the disk bottleneck in the data domain deduplication file system. In Fast **8**, 1–14 (2008)
2. Xia, W., Jiang, H., Feng, D., Hua, Y.: SiLo: a similarity-locality based near-exact deduplication scheme with low RAM overhead and high throughput. In USENIX ATC, pp. 26–30 (2011)
3. Bhagwat, D., Eshghi, K., Long, D.D., Lillibridge, M.: Extreme binning: Scalable, parallel deduplication for chunk-based file backup. In: Proceedings of the MASCOTS 2009, pp. 1–9. IEEE (2009)
4. Debnath, B.K., Sengupta, S., Li, J.: ChunkStash: speeding up inline storage deduplication using flash memory. In: USENIX ATC, pp. 1–16 (2010)
5. Lillibridge, M., Eshghi, K., Bhagwat, D., Deolalikar, V., Trezis, G., Camble, P.: Sparse indexing: large scale, inline deduplication using sampling and locality. In Fast **9**, 111–123 (2009)
6. Ma, J., Stones, R.J., Ma, Y., Wang, J., Ren, J., Wang, G., Liu, X.: Lazy exact deduplication. ACM Trans. Storage (TOS) **13**(2), 1–26 (2017)
7. Meister, D., Kaiser, J., Brinkmann, A.: Block locality caching for data deduplication. In: Proceedings of the Fast., pp. 1–12 (2013)
8. Yang, J., et al.: An empirical guide to the behavior and use of scalable persistent memory. In Proceedings of the FAST (2020)

 9. Rudoff, A.: Persistent memory programming. Login: Usenix Mag. **42**(2), 34–40 (2017)
10. Xu, J., Swanson, S.: NOVA: a log-structured file system for hybrid volatile/non-volatile main memories. In: 14th USENIX Conference on File and Storage Technologies (FAST 2016), pp. 323–338 (2016)
11. Nam, M., Cha, H., Choi, Y. R., Noh, S. H., Nam, B.: Write-optimized dynamic hashing for persistent memory. In: 17th USENIX Conference on File and Storage Technologies (FAST 2019), pp. 31–44 (2019)
12. Lepers, B., Balmau, O., Gupta, K., Zwaenepoel, W.: KVell: the design and implementation of a fast persistent key-value store. In: Proceedings of the 27th ACM SOSP, pp. 447–461 (2019)
13. Beeler, B.: Intel optane dc persistent memory module (pmm) (2019)
14. Wang, C., et al.: Nv-dedup: high-performance inline deduplication for non-volatile memory. IEEE Trans. Comput. **67**(5), 658–671 (2017)
15. Tarasov, V., Mudrankit, A., Buik, W., Shilane, P., Kuenning, G., Zadok, E.: Generating realistic datasets for deduplication analysis. In: USENIX ATC, pp. 261–272 (2012)

Author Index

Printed in the United States
by Baker & Taylor Publisher Services

Printed in the United States
by Baker & Taylor Publisher Services